Electronic Media
Then, Now, and Later

Norman J. Medoff

Northern Arizona University

Barbara K. Kaye

The University of Tennessee

PEARSON

Boston • New York • San Francisco

Mexico City • Montreal • Toronto • London • Madrid • Munich • Paris

Hong Kong • Singapore • Tokyo • Cape Town • Sydney

Executive Editor: Karon Bowers
Series Editor: Molly Taylor
Development Editor: Jennifer Wall
Editorial Assistant: Michael Kish
Senior Marketing Manager: Mandee Eckersley
Senior Production Administrator: Donna Simons
Composition and Prepress Buyer: Linda Cox
Manufacturing Buyer: JoAnne Sweeney
Cover Administrator: Kristina Mose-Libon
Editorial–Production Service: Communicáto, Ltd.
Interior Designer: Denise Hoffman
Cover Designer: Susan Paradise
Photo Researcher: Katharine S. Cook
Illustrations: Denise Hoffman
Electronic Composition: Denise Hoffman

For related titles and support materials, visit our online catalog at www.ablongman.com.

Between the time website information is gathered and then published, it is not unusual for some sites to have closed. Also, the transcription of URLs can result in unintended typographical errors. The publisher would appreciate notification where these errors occur so that they may be corrected in subsequent editions.

Many of the designations used by manufacturers and sellers to distinguish their products are claimed as trademarks. Where those designations appear in this book and Allyn & Bacon was aware of a trademark claim, the designations have been printed in caps or initial caps.

Library of Congress Cataloging-in-Publication Data

Medoff, Norman J.
  Electronic media : then, now, and later / Norman J. Medoff, Barbara K. Kaye.
    p. cm.
  Includes bibliographical references and index.
  ISBN 0-205-34530-1
  1. Multimedia systems.   2. Digital media.   3. Digital communications.
  I. Kaye, Barbara K.   II. Title.

  QA76.575.M44 2005
  006.7—dc22

                                                                    2004059474

Photo and permissions credits appear on page 358, which constitutes a continuation of the copyright page.

Printed in the United States of America
10 9 8 7 6 5 4 3 2 1   *VHP*   09 08 07 06 05 04

With warm memories and love

Joan B. McOmber
1931–2003

Thaddeus R. Kowalewski
1919–2004

Contents

Preface   xix

Chapter 1
Tuning In to Electronic Media   1

SEE IT THEN   2

- **Origins of Electronic Media**   2
- **Characteristics of Traditional Mass Media**   6

SEE IT NOW   8

- **Characteristics of the World Wide Web**   8
    - What Is the Internet?   8
    - Technology   8
    - Content   9
    - Why Digital?   10
- **Trends and Terminology**   10
    - Convergence   10
    - Consolidation   12
    - Commercialism   12

SEE IT LATER   13

- **Current and Future Influences**   13
    - Desktop Production   13
    - E-Mail/Instant Messaging   13
    - Cell Phones   14
    - Online Journals and Blogging   14
    - Downloading Music and Movies   14
- **Top Ten Reasons for Studying Electronic Media**   15
- **Summary**   16

Chapter 2
Radio   17

SEE IT THEN   18

- **Early Inventors and Inventions**   18
  Electrical Telegraphy   18
  Electrical Telephony   19
  Point-to-Point Electrical Communication   19
  Wireless Transmission   20
  A Tragic Lesson   21

- **Radio Becomes a Mass Medium**   23
  Broadcasting   24
  World War I   25
  The Radio Corporation of America   25
  The 1920s   25

- **The Beginnings of Commercial Radio**   27
  Technical Problems   28
  Chain Broadcasting   28
  Copyright Issues   28
  Radio Receivers   29
  The Network System   29

- **Government Involvement**   30
  A Few Important Words   30
  Competition for NBC   30

- **Influences of Early Radio**   31
- **World War II**   33
- **AM Radio**   34
- **FM Radio**   35

SEE IT NOW   36

- **The Telecommunications Act of 1996**   37
- **Other Delivery Systems**   37

SEE IT LATER   37

- **Radio Goes Digital**   38
- **The Role of Government**   39
- **Summary**   39

Chapter 3
Television   41

SEE IT THEN   42

- **The Experimental Years   42**
  - Early Innovations   42
  - World War II   43
  - Off to a Slow Start   43
- **The Big Freeze   44**
  - The Birth of Cable   45
  - VHF and UHF   45
  - Color Television   46
  - Domination of the Networks   47
  - Relationships with Affiliates   47
- **The Golden Age   48**
  - Going Live   48
  - Theatrical Influences   49
  - Blacklisting and Broadcasting   49
- **Upheaval and Education   50**
  - The "Vast Wasteland"   50
  - The Tumultuous 1960s   50
  - Educational Television Goes Public   51
- **Increased Choice and Competition   52**
  - Government Regulation   52
  - Social Awareness Programming   53
  - The Networks Lose Ground   54
  - Deregulation Revisited   54
  - Electronic News Gathering   54
  - The Networks Regroup   55

SEE IT NOW   55

- **More Network Challenges   55**
  - CNN   55
  - Angry Affiliates   55
  - New Networks   56
  - Satellite Television   56
  - New Regulations   56
- **Digital Television   56**

SEE IT LATER   57

- **Industry Structure   57**
- **Technological Challenges   58**
- **Summary   59**

Chapter 4
Cable, Satellite, and Other Delivery Systems   61

SEE IT THEN   62

- **Cable Delivery   62**
  Regulatory Problems Lead to Reception Problems   62
  The FCC's Dilemma   62
  Community Antennas   63
  Cable Develops as a Delivery System   64
- **Satellite Delivery   68**
  Satellite Television   68
  Satellite Radio   68
- **Point-to-Point or One-to-One Communication   70**

SEE IT NOW   70

- **Cable Delivery   70**
  Cable Subscription Rates   71
  Signal Carriage versus Retransmission Consent   71
  Technology   71
  Consolidation and Integration   72
- **Satellite Delivery   73**
  Satellite Master Antenna Television   73
  Satellite Television   73
  Satellite Radio   74
- **Microwave Delivery   75**
- **Point-to-Point or One-to-One Communication   76**
  Cell Phones   76
  Data Services   77

SEE IT LATER   78

- **The Changeover to Digital   78**
- **Cable Delivery   78**
- **Satellite Delivery   79**

- Point-to-Point or One-to-One Communication   79
- Internet Delivery   80
- Summary   81

Chapter 5
The Internet   83

SEE IT THEN   84

- History of the Internet and the World Wide Web   84
- Internet Resources: What They Are and How They Got Here   84
    - Electronic Mail   84
    - Electronic Mailing Lists   85
    - Newsgroups   85
    - Chat Rooms   85
    - Instant Messaging   86
    - World Wide Web   86
    - Weblogs   86
- The Rise of Internet Radio   87
- Television's Migration to the Web   88

SEE IT NOW   88

- How the Internet Works   88
- Internet Users   90
- Navigating the World Wide Web   91
- The World Wide Web and the Mass Media   91
    - Online Radio Today   93
    - From Over the Air to Over the Internet   94
    - Downloading Music from the Internet (Don't Try This at Home)   95
- The Internet and Television   97
    - Audience Fragmentation   97
    - Using Television, Using the Web   98
    - Selecting Television Programs and Websites   98
    - Channel and Website Repertoire   98
    - The Web and Television News   99
    - Is the Web Stealing Television's Viewers?   100

SEE IT LATER   102

•   Weblogs   102

Look Out Big Media, Big Politics   102
Instant Messaging   104
Local Internet Radio   105
Secret Messages Online   105

•   Summary   105

Chapter 6
Programming   107

SEE IT THEN: Radio   108

•   Types of Programs   108

Music   108
Dramas   108
Comedies   109
Back to Music   109

SEE IT NOW: Radio   111

•   Types of Programs   111

Music   111
News and Information   111
Noncommercial   113

•   Where Radio Programs Come From   113

Local Programs   113
Network/Syndicated Programs   114

•   Who Pays for Programs   114

•   How Programs Are Scheduled   114

•   Who Schedules Programs   114

SEE IT THEN: Television   115

•   Types of Programs   115

Anthologies   116
Variety Shows   116
Game and Quiz Shows   117
Comedies   118
News   118
Children's Shows   119
Sports   119
Movies and Miniseries   120

SEE IT NOW: Television   121

- **Types of Programs**   121

  Narrative Programs   121

  Nonnarrative Programs   122

  Noncommercial Television   128

- **Where Television Programs Come From**   129

- **Who Produces Programs**   129

  Production Companies   129

  Networks   129

  Syndicators   131

- **Who Pays for Programs**   132

  Producers   132

  Networks   132

  Affiliates   132

  Syndicators   132

- **What Types of Channels Carry What Types
  of Programs**   133

  Broadcast Networks   133

  Cable Networks   135

  Premium and Pay-per-View Channels   135

  Local Origination and Local Access Channels   135

- **How Programs Are Scheduled**   136

SEE IT LATER: Radio and Television   137

- **Marketing Syndicated Programs**   137

- **On the Horizon**   138

- **Summary**   139

Chapter 7
Advertising   141

SEE IT THEN   141

- **Advertising: 3000 B.C.E. to 1990**   142

- **Early Radio Advertising**   143

  Sponsored Radio   145

- **Early Television Advertising**   146

  Sponsorship   146

  Spot Advertising   147

  A New Look   149

Creative Strategies   149
Target Advertising   150
Cable Advertising   150

SEE IT NOW   151

• **Advertising: 1990 to Present**   151
From a Business Perspective   151
From a Consumer Perspective   152
Electronic Media   152
Radio Advertising   152
Television Advertising   154
Cable Advertising   157
Internet Advertising   159
Advertising Agencies   164
Advertising Campaigns   165

SEE IT LATER   167

• **Criticisms of Advertising**   167
• **Summary**   169

Chapter 8
Audience Measurement and Sales   171

SEE IT THEN   172

• **Early Ratings Systems**   172

SEE IT NOW   173

• **Gathering Audience Numbers**   173
Radio and Television   173
The Internet   178
• **Calculating and Reporting Radio and Television Audience Numbers**   179
Means of Calculating   179
Means of Reporting   182
• **When Audience Numbers Aren't Enough**   184
Music Research   186
Television Program Testing   186
Television Quotient Data   187
Online Consumer Profiling   187
• **Translating Audience Information to Sales**   187

- **Buying and Selling   188**
    - Radio and Television   188
    - Cable Television   191
    - The Internet   192

SEE IT LATER   194

- **The Never-Ending Quest for Ratings   194**
    - New Technology   194
    - Separating Cable and Satellite Ratings   195
    - Program Strategies   195
- **Summary   196**

Chapter 9
Business and Ownership   197

SEE IT THEN   198

- **Finding a Business Plan That Worked   198**
- **Business Models   198**
    - The Broadcast Star Model   200
- **Ownership by Broadcast Networks   202**
    - *The Report on Chain Broadcasting*   202
    - Network Ownership Since 1945   202

SEE IT NOW   204

- **Ownership of Broadcast Stations   204**
    - Owner Qualifications   204
    - Competing for a License   205
    - Construction Permits   205
    - Keeping the License   205
    - Finances   206
    - Renewing the License   207
    - Owning versus Operating   207
- **Ownership of Broadcast Networks   207**
    - Reverse Compensation   208
    - Group Ownership   209
- **Ownership of Other Delivery Systems   210**
    - Cable Television   210
    - The Internet   211
    - Web Radio   211
- **Cross-Ownership   212**

SEE IT LATER   213

- **Broadcast Stations**   213
  Radio   213
  Television   214
- **Cable and Satellite Providers**   214
- **Multichannel Multipoint Distribution Services**   215
- **The Internet**   215
- **Summary**   215

Chapter 10
Operating, Producing, and Distributing   217

SEE IT THEN   218

- **Radio**   218
  Operation   218
  Programming and Production   219
- **Television**   221
  Operation   221
  Production   221
- **Cable**   223
  Operation   224

SEE IT NOW   226

- **Radio**   226
  Structure of a Typical Station   226
- **Television**   232
  Structure of a Typical Station   232
  Studio versus Field Production   236
- **Cable and Satellite Systems**   238

SEE IT LATER   239

- **Production and Distribution**   239
- **Broadcast Media**   241
- **Cable Television**   242
- **Satellite Delivery**   242
- **Summary**   243

Chapter 11
Corporate, Educational, and Institutional Media   245

SEE IT NOW   246

- **Corporate Media   246**
  Corporate Media's Business Model   247
  Functions of Corporate Media   249

- **Users of Corporate Media   250**
  Business and Industry   250
  Education   250
  Government   251
  Medical and Health Care   251
  Organizations and Professional Associations   251

- **Applications of Corporate Media   251**
  Education and Training   251
  Production Demonstrations and Sales   252
  Motivation   252
  Internal Communication   252
  External Communication   252
  Program Types and Styles   253

- **Production of Corporate Media   253**
  Preproduction   254
  Production   255
  Postproduction   256

- **Program Distribution   256**

- **Program Evaluation   257**

SEE IT LATER   258
- **Summary   259**

Chapter 12
Regulation, Legal Issues, and Ethics   261

SEE IT THEN   262

- **The Beginnings of Regulation   262**
- **The Basis for Regulatory Power   263**

• **Overview of Regulation**   **263**
  The Early 1900s   263
  World War I: 1917–1918   264
  The Radio Act of 1927   264
  The Communications Act of 1934   265
  Advertising   266
  Chain Broadcasting   266
  Ownership   266
  Political Programming   267
  The Freeze: 1948–1952   268

• **Other Legal Concerns**   **269**
  Defamation   269
  Editorializing   269
  The Fairness Doctrine   270
  Industry Scandals   270
  Deregulation   271
  The Public Broadcasting Act of 1967   271

SEE IT NOW   272

• **The Telecommunications Act of 1996**   **272**
• **The FCC Today**   **273**
  Licensing   273
  Rule Making and Enforcement   273
• **Other Regulatory Influences**   **275**
• **The FCC and Indecency, Obscenity, and Violence**   **276**
  Indecency   276
  Inappropriate Programming Content   276
  Obscenity and Violence   277
• **The FTC and Advertising**   **277**
  Deceptive Advertising   277
  Infomercials   278
  Controversial Products   278
  Spam   278

SEE IT LATER   279

• **FCC Concerns**   **279**
  Digital Conversion   279
  Ownership   280
  Cable Delivery   280
  The First Amendment   281

- **Other Legal Issues   281**
  - Free Speech   281
  - Privacy   282
  - Libel and Slander   283
  - Copyright   283
  - Taxation   285
- **Ethical Issues   285**
  - Ethical Guidelines   286
  - Ethical Dilemmas   286
- **Summary   289**

Chapter 13
Influences and Effects of the Mass Media   291

SEE IT THEN   292

- **Strong Effects   292**
  - Magic Bullet Theory   293
  - Propaganda and Persuasion Theories   293
- **Limited Effects   294**
- **Moderate Effects   296**
- **Powerful Effects   297**

SEE IT NOW   298

- **Research on the Mass Media   298**
  - Survey Research   299
  - Content Analysis   299
  - Laboratory Experiments   299
  - Field Experiments   299
- **Effects of Mediated Violence   300**
  - Behavioral Effects   301
  - Affective and Emotional Effects   302
  - Cognitive Effects   303
  - Effects on Children   304
- **Effects of Offensive Song Lyrics   304**
- **Effects of Video Games   306**
- **Effects of the Internet   307**
- **Agenda Setting   307**
- **Uses of and Gratifications from the Mass Media   308**

SEE IT LATER   309

- Media Violence   309

- New Communication Technologies   311

- Children's Nutrition   312

- Summary   313

Chapter 14
New Technologies, New Lifestyles   315

SEE IT NOW AND SEE IT LATER   316

- Messaging Systems   316
  - Cell Phones   316
  - Personal Digital Assistants   317
  - Multifunctional Devices   318
  - Telephones and the Internet   319
- Computers   320
  - Wearable Computers   320
- Music   320
  - Private Audio   320
  - File Sharing   321
- Television   321
  - Digital Video Discs   322
  - Digital Video Recorders   322
  - New Ways to Watch Television   324
- Cameras   325
  - Webcams   325
  - Digital Cameras   326
- Home Networking   327
- A Wireless World   328
- Summary   329

References   331

Index   347

Preface

Until perhaps ten years ago, teaching an introductory course on electronic media meant teaching the history, structure, economics, content, and regulation of *broadcasting*. Broadcasting and broadcasters were at the epicenter of all that was electronic media. In fact, the concept of a world of electronic media that didn't revolve around broadcasting and that wasn't based on the traditional mass communication model seemed far away and abstract.

Much has changed in the last ten years, however. Today, students live in a nonlinear, digital world in which traditional broadcasting plays a much diminished role. For example, they no longer need to wait for over-the-air radio to hear new music or even their favorite tunes. The Internet provides multiple streams of music, much of which can be shared and downloaded for future playback on computers or portable devices. Many college dorm rooms now provide high-speed Internet connections, which facilitates music and movie file sharing. Furthermore, college students are beginning to pass up the multicomponent stereo systems and small-screen television sets that have been popular since the 1960s. Instead, they're designing their own entertainment and information systems by selecting from among a variety of compact, portable, high-quality music playback devices, digital televisions, computers, and high-speed Internet connections. Students have also become more adept than ever before at handling, editing, and storing media content for their personal use. Finally, they're also becoming online content providers, with live journals and blogs.

So, given all these developments, does this mean that the traditional electronic media are not worth discussing? Should teaching about electronic media begin with the birth of the World Wide Web? Is the predigital world irrelevant or obsolete? Obviously, we don't think so.

Electronic Media: Then, Now, and Later is rooted in the notion that studying the past not only facilitates understanding the present but also helps in predicting the future. Just as we can show how broadcast television spawned the cable industry, we can trace how the cable industry led to the satellite industry and how both have led to a digital world—one in which convergence has blurred the lines separating media functions and in which old-style broadcasters have expanded, consolidated, and adapted what they do to embrace new forms of electronic media.

The study of electronic media should address more than just the delivery systems used to reach mass audiences. Personal electronic devices that deliver information and entertainment selected by individual consumers should be covered as well. Devices such as digital phones and personal digital assistants (PDAs)—which are capable of surfing the Internet, recording and sending video images, playing music, and allowing interpersonal communication with voice or text—have changed the modern lifestyle to the point that they must be included in any discussion of the digital electronic media revolution. Digital video recorders, such as TiVo, may change how audiences schedule their time with television, giving a different meaning to the network concept of appointment viewing.

This book provides a link between the traditional world of broadcasting and the contemporary universe of digital electronic media, which offers individuals increasingly greater control over listening, viewing, and electronic interaction. As both emerging electronic media professionals and discriminating electronic media consumers, today's students must know about these changes and understand how they will affect the future of the industry.

Organization of the Text

With the knowledge that what comes next is based on what came before, we would like to acknowledge Edward R. Murrow and his programs *Hear It Now* (1950–1951) and *See It Now* (1951–1958) for suggesting the structure of this text. Each chapter of the book is organized chronologically into these sections:

- *See It Then* begins with the invention or inception of the topic (e.g., television) and traces its development up to the 1990s and the Telecommunications Act of 1996.
- *See It Now* discusses activities and developments from the 1990s to the present.
- *See It Later* starts with the present and makes general predictions about what will happen in the digital world of tomorrow.

Underlying this organization is the idea that change in electronic media rarely occurs without past events providing the opportunity or demand for change.

Chapter 1 summarizes the history of electronic media, introduces industry terms, and discusses current media trends. Chapters 2 through 5 give overviews of the various delivery systems: radio; television; cable, satellite, and microwave; and the Internet, respectively. In these chapters, topics include the history and characteristics of each medium, its place in today's world of electronic media, and what place it will likely have in the future.

Chapters 6 through 8 look behind the scenes of electronic media. Chapter 6 considers how programming is developed for the various delivery systems. We watch television to see a program, we listen to the radio to hear music, and we use the Internet to connect us to information. Clearly, content is essential to the existence of electronic media. Chapter 7 is about advertising. The electronic media industry couldn't survive if it provided its content for free, so it sells its viewers, listeners, and users to advertisers, who pay the content providers for the opportunity to advertise their goods and services to the media audience. Chapter 8 looks at audience measurement and sales, considering the complex relationship among the numbers of viewers, listeners, and users; the popularity of programming; and the cost of advertising to reach desired consumers.

Chapters 9 through 12 cover the business and regulatory sides of the electronic media industry. Chapters 9 and 10 investigate ownership and operation of the various types of delivery systems. Chapter 11 focuses specifically on corporate media, an area in which many students will likely find careers. Chapter 12 covers regulation of the electronic media industry along with the legal and ethical issues faced by its professionals.

The last two chapters of the book consider electronic media from a consumer standpoint. Much has been written in academic journals and the popular press about the social and cultural effects of mass media. Chapter 13 condenses available research and presents several theoretical perspectives, tying them to contemporary issues and concerns. Moving away from theory to application, Chapter 14 is a guide to consumer use of new electronic media devices. It discusses new technologies, how they are used or will be used, and how they are changing people's lifestyles today and perhaps tomorrow.

Features

Special features are sprinkled throughout the text to enrich students' learning experience and keep them informed and interested:

- Each chapter opens with a graphic *outline* of the See It Then, See It Now, and See It Later sections, which offers students an overview of the chapter's content and organization. That outline is followed by a set of *learning objectives,* which focuses students on the key points to be discussed.

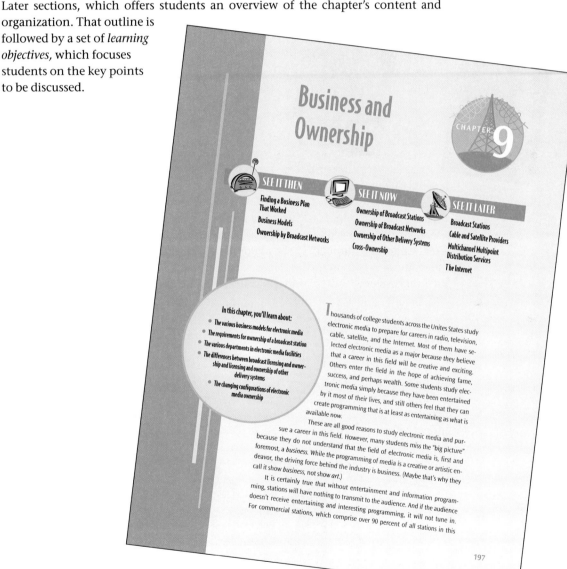

- *Zoom-Ins* provide Web links to lead students to further exploration, along with exercises and activities that students can enjoy in the classroom and on their own.
- *FYI* boxes supplement the text discussion with interesting facts and in-depth information about such topics as how to create HTML (Chapter 5), media coverage of 1960s violence and civil unrest (Chapter 13), and how advertisers plan to combat ad skipping on digital video recorders (Chapter 14).

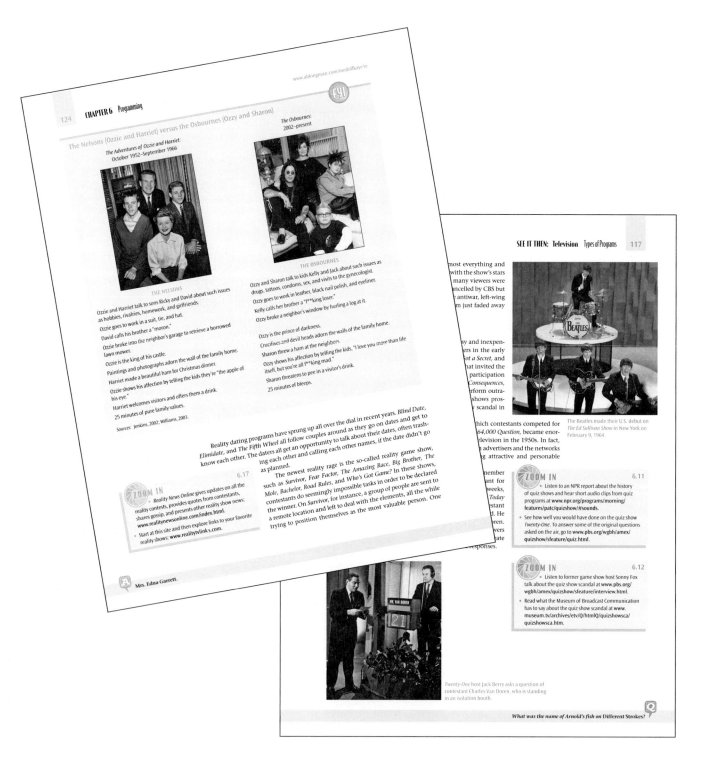

- *Career Tracks* introduce experts in electronic media, who share the experiences that led them to their current jobs and give tips for getting started in this challenging industry.
- The *factoid quiz* that runs along the bottoms of the pages will prompt students to test their knowledge and learn interesting and relevant information pertaining to the chapter.

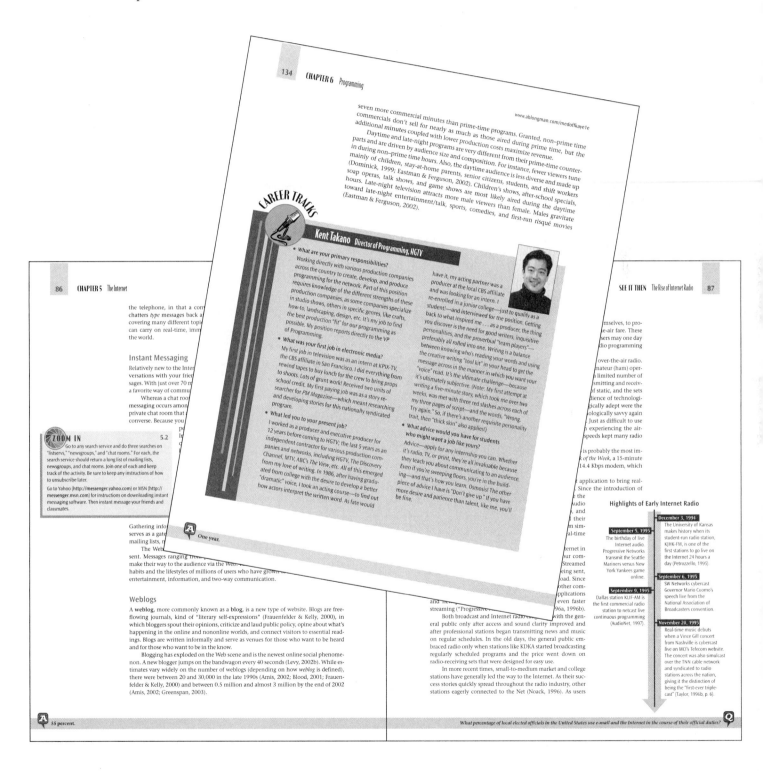

- A rich array of *photographs, drawings, and tables* explain and expand on topics presented in the text. The many historic photographs, in particular, support the chronological development of the book and bring historic events to life.

22   CHAPTER 2   Radio

Late at night on April 15, the *Titanic* collided with a huge iceberg in the North Atlantic Ocean, ripping open the hull and causing the ship to rapidly take on water. Supposedly, the ship's radio operator had received warnings about icebergs being dangerously close to the ship's path, but he had somehow refused to heed them. Instead, the operator had requested that other ship radio operators clear the airwaves to allow the *Titanic* to send personal messages from the ship's famous passengers to Europe and the United States (Hilliard & Keith, 2001, p. 13).

After the *Titanic* collided with the iceberg and began to sink, the radio operator on board began sending out SOS signals. Unfortunately, the collision occurred late at night and most of the wireless operators on other ships in the area had already gone off duty. Only the operator on one ship, the *Carpathia*, heard the signal and responded to the call. Although the *Carpathia* was able to rescue some 700 passengers from the *Titanic*, about 1,500 perished when the ship went down.

One of the many legends that emerged from the *Titanic* tragedy involved a young wireless operator named David Sarnoff. Stationed at a wireless operation inside Wanamaker's Department Store in New York City, he heard the signal from the *Titanic* and the response from the *Carpathia*. As the legend goes, Sarnoff stayed at his wireless station for the next 72 hours and received important information about survivors from the signals sent out by the *Carpathia*. The government had ordered that the airwaves be cleared of other operators during the days that the tragedy unfolded. As a result, Sarnoff was able to pass along exclusive information about survivors to the *New York American* daily newspaper.

A young David Sarnoff at his wireless station in Wanamaker's Department Store.

The New York Times.

TITANIC SINKS FOUR HOURS AFTER HITTING ICEBERG;
866 RESCUED BY CARPATHIA, PROBABLY 1250 PERISH;
ISMAY SAFE, MRS. ASTOR MAYBE, NOTED NAMES MISSING

The news reported about the sinking of the *Titanic* in April 1912 came from wireless radio transmissions.

TITANIC DISASTER GREAT LOSS OF LIFE EVENING NEWS

A 97 percent.

SEE IT NOW Point-to-Point or One-to-One Communication   77

Dr. Martin Cooper (above left) is considered the inventor of the portable phone and made the first call on one in 1973. The Canyon MK 900 (above right) is a mobile briefcase phone that dates back to around 1980. The complete setup for this phone cost around $2,000, so not many people had one. Today's cell phones (left) not only can make calls but also have features like digital picture taking and sending, Internet access, music storage and replay, text messaging, and game playing.

---

the Mass Media   95

ons that were

occurs when
mber is elec-
unt appears
where you
ted to the
y contacts
processing
ormation
edit card
ays the

always
nd and
many
s the
ss or
read
vari-
for-
ack

99 Cents per Download

So where does your 99 cents go when you pay to download a song from a legal music site? Here's an example from Apple Computer's iTunes:

- Apple Computer (34¢)
- Artist (10¢)
- Publisher/songwriter (8¢)
- Record label (47¢)

Source: Spors, 2003.

ter on a cen-
enters the name of
on their computers. With the
o the user's computer (Cohen, 2000).
our music files from your PC to a portable player are
music with you anywhere and that you can download and organ-
r music you want to hear. Whether your portable music device plays MP3
tes, cassette tapes, or CDs, it lets you escape into another world. Taking a bus ride or long flight, grocery shopping, exercising, and other mundane activities are all easier to endure with your favorite music. Time seems to go by faster when music breaks the monotony and the silence. In fact, the use of portable music players is sometimes criticized for making it too easy to avoid the world at hand and to shut out other people.

Although it's legal for music owners to record their personal, store-bought CDs in another format or to a portable player, sharing copies with others who haven't paid for the music is considered piracy and copyright infringement. At first, music file-sharing sites seemed like a good idea, but they quickly ran into all kinds of copyright problems and found themselves knee deep in lawsuits. After building a clientele of about 80

households had cable television?   Q

Free Music/Fee Music

The Web is almost impossible to regulate. Music industry regulators have the difficult task of chasing down illegal sites. But as illegal sites are shut down, others are opened up. On any given day, about 800 million files are available for copying on illegal services like KaZaa, WinMX, and Grokster ("Kiplinger Monitor," 2003). Here's what's involved in using the legal services available:

LEGAL SERVICE	MONTHLY SUBSCRIPTION?	DOWNLOAD ALBUMS?	PRICE PER DOWNLOAD
MusicNet (AOL)	Yes	No	Monthly fee plus $.79*
Real One Rhapsody	Yes	No	Included in monthly fee
iTunes	No	Yes	$.99 single ($10 album)*
musicmatch	No	Yes	$.99 single ($9.99 album)*
Napster	No	Yes	$.99 single (30-sec. clips free) ($9.95 album)*

*2003 prices
Sources: Croal, 2003; Roberts, 2003.

How much of the decrease in CD sales in 2001 was attributed to Internet downloading services?   Q

- Finally, each chapter ends with a *summary* of content, which students will find useful in both their initial reading and later review of the text.

Supplements to the Text

Student Resources

COMPANION WEBSITE: WWW.ABLONGMAN.COM/ MEDOFFKAYE1E   The Companion Website contains chapter learning objectives, summaries, flashcards, and Web links and features crossword activities and practice tests. In addition, it uses flash animation to show how various communication technologies work, such as AM/FM waves, cable television, cellular phones, and the Internet.

Instructor Resources

INSTRUCTOR'S MANUAL AND TEST BANK   The Instructor's Manual contains chapter-at-a-glance grids, chapter summaries, learning objectives, lecture outlines, and key terms with definitions. It also provides ideas to activate class discussion and exercises to illustrate the concepts, principles, and skills of mass communication. The Test Bank contains multiple-choice, true/false, short-answer, and essay questions.

---

cover the entire contiguous 48 states. Unlike cable and its ability to provide two-way communication through an infrastructure already in place, satellites are restricted in the two-way arena: that is, consumers cannot send or uplink from their homes or offices.

Although satellite may become the mass distribution system of choice in the future, it may not be able to provide what consumers want most: a one-stop telecommunications provider. Satellite delivery will most likely continue to operate as it has for the past 10 years, as a multichannel provider of entertainment and information that competes directly with cable for subscribers.

Summary

Beginning in the 1920s, radio was a dominant force, grabbing the attention of millions of Americans. Radio developed the business model of a medium that's supported by advertising dollars. Programming was mostly live and involved music performances. The radio industry also spawned the national networks, which rose to power in the late 1920s and have maintained that power ever since.

Television inherited the business model and network structure developed by radio and soon took its prime-time audience and programming, as well. By the early 1950s, television dominated electronic media, and radio, primarily AM, had to look for another programming formula. The networks had to adjust to the complicated task of producing television; as studios became larger, rehearsal time increased, expensive and bulky equipment was purchased, and additional personnel were hired and trained. The demand for television signals in rural areas gave birth to the cable television industry.

Radio responded to the decrease in audience listenership by moving away from live programs to programs featuring recorded music. Records were played on the air by disc jockeys, who spoke directly to the audience in an informal, conversational way. Radio changed from a medium of programs to a medium of formats.

Radio and television production have not changed much over the years. Program formats are similar, and production techniques have changed gradually with technology. The signal flow in both audio production and television production is much the same today as it has been for the past 50 years. The most significant change in production has occurred with the introduction of digital equipment. Compared to its analog counterpart, digital equipment produces a better-quality product and gives production personnel more flexibility to experiment.

Distribution patterns have changed over the past 50 years. Although radio transmission is much the same as it was in the 1920s, television distribution has changed greatly. Instead of receiving their programs directly over the air from broadcasters, about 80 percent of all the television audience receives television programs from either a cable system or a satellite television provider.

Satellite radio has also begun to sign up subscribers. Satellite radio is a subscription service that provides many channels of radio, some of which are commercial free. This service takes the format concept that radio adopted in the early 1950s and provides many variations of programming through one service.

The Telecommunications Act of 1996 has accelerated the consolidation of electronic media since its passage. Increasingly, more stations and media properties are owned by a smaller number of owners. Convergence in both technology and business is an ongoing phenomenon. Cross-ownership of media encourages the owners of one medium to use both its technology and content in another medium. Vertical integration within large media companies allows them to provide their own programming,

Excluding the Super Bowls, Olympic coverage, and episodes of the epic miniseries Roots, what was the most-watched television show?

TESTGEN COMPUTERIZED TESTING   This user-friendly interface enables instructors to view, edit, and add questions, transfer questions, and print tests in a variety of fonts. "Search" and "Sort" features allow instructors to locate questions quickly and arrange them in a preferred order.

POWERPOINT PRESENTATION PACKAGE   This text-specific package is a collection of lecture outlines and graphic images keyed to every chapter in the text. Hot links in the slides direct lecturers to the Companion Website, which provides animated illustrations of technical processes and ideas. (This package is available at http://suppscentral. ablongman.com.)

Acknowledgments

We would like to thank the following individuals for their contributions to this project: Amy Smith, Amanda Souers, Brenna Sapper, Steve Campagna, Brahm Resnik, Moira Tokatyan, Donna Castillo, Jeff Marmorstein, Price Hicks, Steve Paskay, Chris Wooley, and Dan Houck.

Thanks, as well, to the folks at Allyn & Bacon:

- Molly Taylor, Series Editor: Thanks for initiating the book and for cracking the whip and keeping us moving with the project.
- Mandee Eckersley, Senior Marketing Manager: We're counting on you to let the world know about the book.

- Michael Kish, Editorial Assistant, and Jennifer Wall, Development Editor: Thanks for your direction and for the endless e-mails telling us what more we still had left to do.
- Donna Simons, Senior Production Administrator, and freelancers Susan Freese and Denise Hoffman: Thanks for putting together all of the pieces and turning our manuscript into a book.

We would also like to thank those individuals who reviewed an early draft of this book for Allyn & Bacon and provided useful comments and suggestions: Stephen Adams, Cameron University; William Jenson Adams, Kansas State University; Stewart Blakley, Brenan University; Mark J. Braun, Gustavus Adolphus College; Craig A. Breit, Cerritos College; John Chapin, Penn State University; Andrew M. Clark, University of Texas at Arlington; Diane M. Dusick, San Bernardino Valley College; David J. Fabilli, Point Park College; Rodney Freed, University of Tennessee at Martin; G. Richard Gainey, Ohio Northern University; C. Benjamin Hale, Texas Wesleyan University; Scott Healy, Sullivan County Community College; Tim Moreland, Catawba College; Steve Muntz, Marshalltown Community College; Michael D. O'Brien, Northwestern College; John M. Odell, City College of San Francisco; Jerry R. Renaud, University of Nebraska–Lincoln; Bennett Strange, Louisiana College; Douglas L. Sudhoff, Northwest Missouri State University; Randall Vogt, Shaw University; Justin P. West, Holyoke Community College; and Norman Youngblood, Texas Tech University.

A number of individuals were willing to provide personal information for the Career Tracks features. Our thanks go to Jennifer Burgess, John Dille, Doug Drew, Trey Fabacher, Jason Moore Greenke, John Montuori, Reggie Murphy, Norm Pattiz, Jay Renfroe, Kent Takano, Mavel Vidrio, and Chris Wooley. We appreciate the special help of these individuals as well:

- John Dille for his patient reading and suggestions for the business chapters
- Steve Dick of Southern Illinois University for creating a terrific Companion Website and for saving us from having to learn flash animation
- Glenn Reynolds, Instapundit blogger extraordinaire, who over several lunches taught us everything we know about blogging and vlogging
- Jim McOmber, for taking time away from his legal studies at Vanderbilt University to begin the test bank questions, and John Dillon of Murray State University, for successfully completing those questions, many of which are sure to have students groaning
- Lynn Medoff, whose editing help came at just the right time
- Stephen Perry of Illinois State University for writing a fabulous Instructor's Manual that is sure to liven up classroom discussion
- Stephen Perry and Arnold Wolfe of Illinois State University for creating the PowerPoint materials

Finally, to our families:

- My special thanks and love to my wonderfully patient family—Lynn, Sarah, and Natalie Medoff—who gave me sympathy and tolerated my unavailability until the book was finished.
- A big thank-you hug and lots of love to my husband, Jim McOmber, for listening and nodding politely whenever I groused about the book. Jim, I promise I'll make up for all those lost weekends we could have spent on the golf course.
- Hugs and kisses to our mothers, Esther Medoff and Janina Kowalewski.

Norman J. Medoff
Barbara K. Kaye

Tuning In to Electronic Media

 SEE IT THEN

Origins of Electronic Media

Characteristics of Traditional Mass Media

 SEE IT NOW

Characteristics of the World Wide Web

Trends and Terminology

 SEE IT LATER

Current and Future Influences

Top Ten Reasons for Studying Electronic Media

In this chapter, you'll learn about:

- The origins of communication, mass communication, and electronic media
- The characteristics of the mass media and the effects the media can have
- The characteristics of the World Wide Web
- Current trends in mass media and electronic media
- How technology is changing the way we use media
- Reasons to study electronic media

Can you think of a day in the recent past that you didn't use some form of electronic media? It would have had to be a day when you were not at home, not in your car, not on campus, not in a hotel, and not in a fitness club, grocery store, or shopping mall.

Chances are, you can't come up with a day. It is almost impossible to totally escape electronic media in today's world. Even if you don't see it or hear it, it is there—signals from broadcast stations, satellites, and wireless Internet connections are pervasive. Even when you are backpacking in a remote area, some signals are there. Your only means of escape would be to ignore electronic media by not using a television, radio, stereo system, or computer.

Would you want to go without electronic media? Not likely. We tune in to find out about our world and to know about the things that affect our everyday lives: the weather, the traffic report, the stock market, the horrors of 9-11, or the local news. We also tune in simply to be entertained by the Super Bowl, *ER, The Bachelorette, Everybody Loves Raymond, The Simpsons,* the latest popular music songs on a Top 40 radio countdown show, or our favorite disc jockey or a music-downloading site on the Web. The electronic media provide us with messages that influence us in many ways.

This book will "tune in" to many aspects of the electronic media that are not readily apparent, despite its prevalence. We will investigate the history, structure, delivery systems, economics, content, operations, regulation, and ethics of electronic media from the perspectives of what happened in the past (*See It Then*), what is happening now (*See It Now*), and what might happen in the future (*See It Later*).

SEE IT THEN

Origins of Electronic Media

The desire to communicate is a part of being human. We humans have always needed to express ourselves and to share those expressions with others, but it took a long time before we could do so successfully. About 100,000 years ago, humankind developed the capacity to communicate using speech. Through the ages, humans have used various systems to send messages. They used various visual systems, like smoke signals, semaphores (flags), pigeons, and human messengers, each of which had its own advantages and disadvantages. Each system worked when the conditions were just right but was limited at least some of the time. For instance, smoke signals and semaphore systems did not work at night because they depended on sunlight for the receiver to see the signal. Pigeons could carry very small messages but were susceptible to natural predators and severe weather. Human messengers were slow and could be captured during times of conflict or war. About 40,000 years ago, humans drew pictures on the walls of their caves to show one another about their lives.

A 40,000-year-old cave painting recently discovered in India.

As humans became more verbal and communicative and as each person's sphere of contacts expanded, efforts to communicate became more sophisticated. This did not happen quickly, however; it took many years for written language to develop. In fact, writing came into use about 5,000 to 6,000 years ago. With written language, humans no longer had to rely solely on what they could remember or on how far the human voice could carry.

Humans wrote on clay tablets as early as 4000 B.C.E. to make portable but durable records of transactions and observations. One thousand years later, the Egyptians used the fibrous plant papyrus as a convenient and somewhat durable way to store information, transactions, and other human expressions. At the time, a form of picture writing called **hieroglyphics** evolved. About 2000 B.C.E.,

Hieroglyphics from inside a tomb in Egypt.

Native American pictographs from a rock wall in Arizona.

Human Desire to Communicate with Aliens

SETI, which stands for *search for extraterrestrial intelligence,* took over this function for the National Aeronautics and Space Administration (NASA) when a budget crisis caused NASA support to be withdrawn. SETI is a nonprofit organization that monitors the radio spectrum for signals from other star systems in the hopes that it will hear a radio signal from intelligent life on another planet. It uses a huge receiving station located in Arrecibo, Puerto Rico, to monitor millions of radio channels simultaneously, mostly by computer.

SETI hasn't found anything yet. Perhaps extraterrestrial beings don't use radio waves to send signals. Maybe they prefer cable or some other technology that cannot be detected with the equipment used at the SETI site. The point here is that humans have a strong desire to communicate with others (humans or extraterrestrials), and they are willing and able to spend the time and money to make that contact.

To learn more about SETI, go to **www.seti.org.**

the Egyptians developed an alphabet of 24 characters and began to store information in libraries (Medoff, Tanquary, & Helford, 1994; Schramm, 1988, p. 28). In the western United States, early Native Americans carved **pictographs** in rocks to show others what they saw and how they lived their lives.

In the middle of the fifteenth century, Johannes Gutenberg, a metal worker in Europe, experimented with a system to print multiple copies of an original page using a system of movable type. Using a modified wine press, Gutenberg printed pages for books by putting together individual letters. The letters were then coated with ink and pressed onto paper using the press. The result was a printed page that could be duplicated many times with high quality and low cost. For the first time, *one* individual with a printing press could reach *many* people with high-quality copies of a book or newspaper.

In 1844, Samuel F. B. Morse developed a system of communication using electricity that allowed people to send messages over long distances almost instantaneously. The invention, the **telegraph**, could send messages from one source point to other points using a system of dots and dashes—short on/offs and long on/offs to spell out words one letter at a time. The telegraph worked well as long as the distant point had the equipment and a skilled operator to receive and translate the coded message into words. Some 20 years later, in 1876, Alexander Graham Bell invented the **telephone**, a device that then as now only required a person to speak into the mouthpiece. Both of these inventions were designed to facilitate *person-to-person* (or *one-to-one*) communication over distances.

As books and newspapers became popular, the practice of communicating to many people at once became common. This *one-to-many model* of communicating was not a balanced two-way model, however. The audience (the *many*) could possibly communicate back to the sender, but this communication, known as **feedback,** was limited. As such, this process became known as **mass communication.** The **mass media** comprise the channel that uses a mechanical (e.g., a printing press) or electronic (e.g., broadcast transmitter) device to deliver messages to a mass audience.

Although the concept of mass communication using media technology was born in the 1400s with Gutenberg's printing press, it was not until 1833 that mass communication became a reality in the United States. That year, Benjamin Day began publishing a newspaper that was designed to reach a mass audience. He set the price of his paper, the *New York Sun,* at one penny. By reaching out to a large urban audience and providing a readable and entertaining

Johannes Gutenberg and the first printing press.

Communication Models

SHANNON AND WEAVER MATHEMATICAL MODEL

Models are created to help us understand processes and concepts. In 1949, Shannon and Weaver (1949) developed a model based on message transmission that helps explain the process of communicating. That model, also known as a *linear model,* works well to explain telephone communication.

The elements of that model are the *information source,* the *transmitter,* the *channel,* the *receiver,* and the *destination.* The information source (a person) uses a transmitter (a telephone) to send a signal through a channel (telephone wires) that is received by a receiver (another telephone) and then heard at the destination (a person). In mass communication, the information source (say, a weathercaster at a television station) uses a broadcast television transmitter to send a signal using broadcast waves through the air (channel) that is received by a television receiver and then seen and heard by the viewer (destination). Additional concepts, such as noise that can interfere with the process, were added to the model to make it more generalizable.

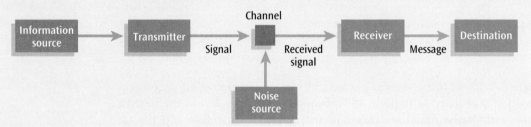

Source: Based on Shannon & Weaver, 1949.

SCHRAMM-OSGOOD COMMUNICATION MODEL

Schramm and Osgood (Schramm, 1954) used a simplified model to explain communication. Using only three basic elements—a *message,* an *encoder,* and a *decoder*—this model demonstrates the reciprocal nature of communication between two people or entities. It shows how communication is a two-way process, in which the participants act as both senders and receivers of messages.

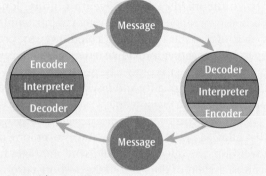

Source: Schramm, 1954.

SCHRAMM MASS COMMUNICATION MODEL

In an attempt to create a model to explain mass communication, Schramm (1954) used one source to represent an *organization* that sends out *many identical messages* to the *audience* comprised of many individual receivers, who are connected to groups of others and pass along information about the messages from the initial receiver. The dotted lines in the model represent *feedback* from the receivers, which is delayed and not explicit. The organization must then infer the meaning of the feedback (such as ratings for a program) and act accordingly.

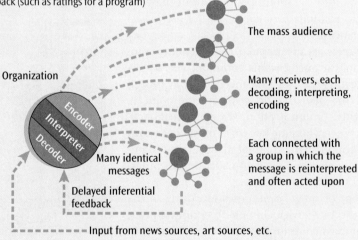

Source: Schramm, 1954.

paper, Day created this country's first mass medium. Thus, the newspaper became the first mass medium designed to inform and entertain. It was structured on a **commercial model:** that is, advertisers provided most of the money needed to print and distribute the paper and keep it profitable.

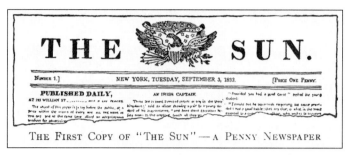

THE FIRST COPY OF "THE SUN" — A PENNY NEWSPAPER

The *New York Sun* was the first of the so-called penny press newspapers.

Once the concepts of mass communication, mass media, and commercial support were in place, the stage was set for the next big innovation: **electronic media.** As the focus of this book, electronic media are viewed as a subset of media, not just a subset of mass media. In other words, topics that involve electronic *mass* media are not the only topics to be addressed. The term *electronic media,* as discussed in this book, refers to both electronic mass media (e.g., broadcasting) and electronic personal media (e.g., cell phones). We will discuss models for both the one-to-many and one-to-one styles of communication achieved by using electronic devices. Doing so will allow for a broad view of electronic media, one that includes the traditional mass media and devices such as cell phones, computers, and digital media that blur the distinction between mass and personal media.

In addition to reaching the audience with print, the media looked to technology to reach the audience with sound. With the invention of the telephone to communicate the spoken word, people looked for easier and wireless ways to communicate the written word. In the early twentieth century, Guglielmo Marconi developed **radio telegraphy,** which could send a signal from point to point. This technology was similar to Morse's telegraph but without the wires. Soon after this wireless technology became viable, other inventors produced a system for transmitting the human voice and other sounds, such as music, from one source to many people. This invention signaled the beginning of broadcasting and eventually the start of commercial electronic media. Newspapers, magazines, clubs, and even schools discussed radio and stimulated interest in the new national medium (Sterling & Kittross, 2002). In the late 1920s, Americans were fascinated with **radio.**

Radio enjoyed its place as the only instantaneous and electronic medium for over 30 years. During this time, it developed most of the formats for broadcast shows (later used for television), enjoyed financial success, and was a mainstay in American culture. That changed after World War II, when **television** broadcasting started to become popular. Many of the popular shows on network radio shifted over to television, providing the new medium with an audience already familiar with the programs' formats, in general, and the programs' stars, in particular.

Since the early 1950s, television has been a media powerhouse, dominating the national audience. Television has enjoyed being in great demand by advertisers, who often have to wait in line to buy time on desirable network shows. Beginning in 1946 and lasting into the 1980s, the three major networks—ABC, CBS, and NBC—claimed almost 90 percent of the national prime-time viewing audience (Walker & Ferguson, 1998). Since then, the viewing audience has been fragmented by cable, satellite, and the Internet. Even so, the broadcast television industry remains a dominant force in the national media, which we will look at later in this book.

Television, in its many forms—broadcast, cable, satellite, video cassette, and DVD—has been the center point of the American media for over 50 years. It is the medium that people turn to for news and has been considered the "primary and most credible source of news . . . as well as a source of information on social issues" (Roper Starch, 1997). While this is true today, it may change in the near future as Internet applications continue to become more accessible to the masses.

The **Internet,** a network of networks that connect computers to each other, allows users to find information, entertainment, and personal communication and to do so easily for a low cost. Although still in its infancy, the Internet is a *paradigm breaker*—a medium that defies previous models of electronic media. It has grown more rapidly than any other medium in history. We will discuss the Internet later in this chapter and also in Chapter 5.

Characteristics of Traditional Mass Media

Each mass medium has specific benefits and is best suited for specific types of communication: for example, television for broadcasting messages to a large, geographically and demographically diverse audience; radio for airing local information to a local audience and delivering specialized programming to specialized audiences; and so on. Each medium can be differentiated from the others by considering the following characteristics: audience, time, display and distribution, distance, and storage (Bonchek, 1997; Pavlik, 1996).

AUDIENCE   Traditional media differ in the audiences they reach. Radio and television are single-source media that reach large audiences simultaneously, while other media, such as the telephone, reach only one person at a time.

TIME   Media also differ in terms of whether they transmit and receive information in an asynchronous or synchronous manner. With **asynchronous** media, there is a delay between when the message is sent and when it is finally received. Newspapers, books, and magazines, which are printed well in advance of delivery, are all asynchronous media, as are video tapes, CDs, and films. With **synchronous** media, there is no perceptible delay between the time the message goes out and the time it is received. Synchronous messages from television, radio, and telephone are received almost instantaneously after transmission.

Just because a medium is synchronous doesn't mean it's interactive, however. Radio and television broadcasts are synchronous but not considered interactive per se. Listeners can call radio request lines, and viewers can call in to vote for their favorite on *American Idol*. But this is *feedback* (an audience message sent back to the source of the communication), rather than true interactivity.

DISPLAY AND DISTRIBUTION   Media also differ in how they display and distribute information. **Display** refers to the technological means (e.g., video, audio, text) used to present information to audiences or individual receivers. **Distribution** refers to the method used to carry information to receivers. Television's audio and visual images are distributed by broadcasting, cable, microwave, or direct broadcast satellite. Radio is generally transmitted by broadcasting, although direct broadcast satellites now send radio signals to subscribers across the country.

DISTANCE   Mediated messages are transmitted over both short and long distances. Some media are better suited for long-distance delivery and others for short or local transmission. Print media need to be physically delivered to their destinations, which can be cumbersome and expensive over long distances. Electronic media deliver messages through the airwaves, telephone lines, cable wires, satellites, and fiber optics, giving them a time and cost advantage over print.

STORAGE   Message **storage** is limited to media that have the means of housing large amounts of information. For instance, CD-ROMs and computer hard drives have the capacity to store millions of bits of data, whereas newspaper publishing offices typically have limited space for storing back issues. Until recently, television stations had to rely on small video tape libraries, but most are in the process of changing to digital storage of all programs.

LISTENING AND VIEWING BEHAVIOR   Electronic media have affected the lives of Americans for the past one hundred years. The effects are many and can be categorized in three general areas:

- *Cognitive effects:* Electronic media bring a flood of information to us. We learn about the weather, the stock market, our favorite sports team, world news, health, science, nature, and just about anything we can think about. As a result of using electronic media, we are more knowledgeable about the world and gain insights into topics that we would never experience on our own. We know what the inside of a prison looks like, we can vicariously experience the thrill of skydiving, and we can even observe the horrors of war.
- *Emotional effects:* Electronic media give us information that may make us form attitudes toward things and ideas. For instance, watching a show about how the local animal shelter is underfunded and forced to euthanize increasingly more animals might make the audience more sensitive to the idea of spaying or neutering their pets. Even hearing a sentimental or raucous song on the radio might cause our mood to change. The electronic media can make us feel.
- *Behavioral effects:* The electronic media can persuade us to change our behavior. After watching a show about people who lost their homes to a wild forest fire, audience members might donate money to help provide emergency food and shelter. Hearing the pledge drive on a local National Public Radio station might prompt listeners to phone in their pledges for money. In addition to behavioral effects from a viewing or listening experience, the electronic media have also changed how people use their time. We spend a large portion of each day with electronic media.

How we experience the electronic media also influences how we live our lives. Starting in the late 1920s, people gathered around the living room radio in the evening to listen to popular network programs. This habit of relying on radio for home entertainment at night set the stage for the popularity of television. Americans were already in their living rooms each night, ready to be entertained. When television finally became a reality after World War II, people sat around their TV sets watching Milton Berle, Arthur Godfrey, Lawrence Welk, and Lucille Ball, along with baseball games and boxing matches. Gone were the days of sitting out on the porch, taking a stroll in the neighborhood, and sitting around the parlor singing and playing the piano.

With the introduction of television, radio narrowed its focus to attract specialized audiences—for instance, rock 'n' roll music programming to attract teenagers. Stations that did not program rock 'n' roll attempted to reach an adult or family audience by using a different type of music and less repetition. Radio listening became a popular activity outside the home with the advent of the transistor radio in the 1950s. It was small and light and could be carried anywhere. At the time, being properly equipped for the beach meant bringing along a portable transistor radio. The notion of personal electronic media was born.

Transistors found their way into the design of television sets, as well. Audiences moved away from the living room and the large console TV set and began viewing small TVs in other rooms of the home, especially the bedrooms. Although these sets were not truly portable because they required standard AC electrical power, television viewing became more of an individual activity. The electronic media had become personalized.

Media Use Statistics **FYI**

Research that looks at how much time is spent with media shows a surprising finding: Adults (18 years and over) spend about 3,400 hours per year using media, or about 9.3 hours per day. When combined, media time spent with television, radio, recorded music, newspapers, magazines, books, movies, and online activity accounts for more of our activity per day than anything else, even sleeping or working. Television viewing occupies almost 70 percent of the total time spent. What's not surprising is that since the early 1990s, the amount of time spent online has been increasing and the amount of time spent with newspapers has been decreasing (Dizard, 2000).

SEE IT NOW

Characteristics of the World Wide Web

Although popular use of the **Internet** is only about 10 years old, it has become an incredibly important part of our daily media behavior, mostly because of that portion of the Internet that allows the use of graphics, sound, and video known as the **World Wide Web.** This is especially true of teenagers, who now spend more time with digital media (the Internet, computers, and video games) than with television. The numerical difference in use is not that great—3.5 hours each day for digital media and 3.1 hours for television—but it may signal what will happen in the future (Corporation for Public Broadcasting, 2003).

What Is the Internet?

Simply stated, the Internet is a worldwide network of computers. Millions of people around the globe **download** information from the Internet every day. The Internet also provides an opportunity for people to **upload** material. An individual can create a website that will be viewed by thousands.

Before any medium can be considered a *mass medium,* it needs to be adopted by a critical mass of users, which is generally about 50 million users (Markus, 1987; Neufeld, 1997; "Why Internet Advertising?" 1997). The Internet has emerged as a new mass medium at an unprecedented speed. Radio broadcasting (which began in an era with a smaller population base) took 38 years of operation to reach the magic 50 million mark, and television took 13 years (Shane, 1999). The Internet surpassed 50 million regular U.S. users sometime in late 1997 or early 1998, only about 5 years after emergence of the World Wide Web ("How Many Online?" 2001; Neufeld, 1997; "Why Internet Advertising?" 1997).

So far, the Internet has been discussed as a combination of various mass media. This combination can be thought of as the product of **convergence,** which one researcher has defined as the "coming together of all forms of mediated communication in an electronic, digital form, driven by computers" (Pavlik, 1996, p. 132). Another researcher has defined *convergence* as the "merging of communications and information capabilities over an integrated electronic network" (Dizard, 2000, p. 14). The Internet is a convergence of many of the characteristics of traditional media (text, graphics, moving pictures, and sound) into one unique medium.

Technology

The World Wide Web is a technologically separate and unique medium, yet it shares many properties with traditional media. Both its similarities and differences have made it a formidable competitor for the traditional mass media audience.

When comparing the traditional media, each can be distinguished by unique strengths and weaknesses. Radio is convenient and portable and can be listened to even while the audience is engaged in other activities. Television is aural and visual and captivating, while print (magazines, newspapers, and books) is portable and can be read anytime, anyplace. The Web has some of these same advantages. For example, people can listen to online audio while attending to other activities, they can read archived information anytime they please, and they can sit back and be entertained and captivated by graphics and video displays. The Internet also offers benefits that aren't found in traditional media: two-way communication through e-mail, bulletin boards, and chat rooms and interactivity at websites. In addition, the Internet provides online versions of print media, which can be read electronically or even printed to provide a portable version—for instance, the *New York Times* at www.nytimes.com; *Rolling Stone* at

The cell phone.

www.rollingstone.com; *Elle Magazine* at www.elle.com; and *Spin Magazine* at www. spinmagazine.com.

While the Internet's proponents highly tout this medium, it falls short of traditional media in some ways. A computer is required to access online material, and unless you're lucky enough to have a laptop, you're limited to going online wherever your computer is connected. Even if you do have a laptop, you can only go online at a few select places that offer connections. Wireless Internet and hand-held computers, or personal digital assistants (PDAs), may oneday allow connecting anytime, anywhere, but these opportunities are limited and just now being tested in some areas. For the most part, the Internet is still not very portable.

Furthermore, the Internet is not yet able to deliver popular television programs because of technical limitations, and with few exceptions, regular television programs are not available online. Similarly, online radio stations may have technical problems and low-quality audio signals if their connection to the Internet is not fast enough. Also, online material often takes longer to download than it takes to turn on a television or radio or open a book or magazine.

Content

What makes the Web unique is that it can display information in ways similar to television, radio, and print media. Radio delivers audio, television delivers audio and video, and print delivers text and graphics. The Web delivers content in all of these media, thus blurring the distinction among them.

The Web's big advantage over traditional media is its lack of constraints in terms of space and time. Radio and television content are both limited by available airtime, and print is constrained by the available number of lines, columns, or pages. These limitations disappear online. Cybernews and entertainment are not confined to seconds of time or column inches of space but are free flowing, with the amount of content being determined by writers or webpage designers.

Although the amount of content is unlimited, the speed of online delivery is limited by **bandwidth**, which is the amount of data that can be sent all at once through a communication path. Think of bandwidth as a water faucet or a pipe. The width of the faucet or pipe determines the amount of water that can flow through it and the speed at which it flows. Similarly, bandwidth limits the speed of information flow and thus affects content. Web designers may reduce content to increase speed, for example. Bandwidth is becoming less of a concern, however, with the trend toward broadband connections with increased data speeds.

A more real concern for webcasters is the punitive licensing fees that have been imposed by the organizations and companies that represent older media. The **Recording Industry Association of America** (**RIAA**) has imposed music-licensing fees on webcasters that are costly enough to force many stations to terminate their audio streams.

The unique nature of the Internet has traditional media looking over their shoulder, as this new medium could supplant them. Ted Turner, the media magnate who started the WTBS Superstation and the Cable News Network (CNN), and Michael Crichton, author of *Jurassic Park* and other best-sellers, have both proclaimed that old-style media, especially newspapers, are dinosaurs on their way to extinction in this age of new communication technology (Pavlik, 1996). However, traditional media may not have as much to fear from the Internet and convergence as they think. Looking back, a new medium has never brought about the demise of an old medium. Radio did not erase print media from the face of the earth, and television did not eliminate radio. Newer media have, however, eroded the audiences of existing older media and thus may have affected their ability to generate advertising dollars.

Traditional media must adapt to a new competitive environment if they want to survive. Many media outlets have done so by delivering their content online, by

What movie starring Jodie Foster as a scientist who "listened to the stars" showed humans making first contact with extraterrestrial beings?

extending their existing services and adding new ones, and by repackaging their content. The Internet, in many instances, is supplementing existing media rather than replacing them (Kaye & Johnson, 2003).

Why Digital?

Occurring in all mass media and most notably in electronic mass media is the process of **digitization**, in which **analog** signals (continuous waves) are transformed into binary or discontinuous signals, which can be **compressed** (reduced) and thus more easily stored and sent. In binary format, large amounts of information can be archived on the Internet and retrieved for later use, so users don't have to search through torn pages or garbled video and audio tapes to find the information they are seeking.

In later chapters of this book, you will read about how the government agency that regulates electronic media, the **Federal Communications Commission (FCC)**, has mandated that all television stations broadcast digital signals by the year 2006. With this changeover, all of the current frequencies used for analog television broadcasting will be given back to the FCC for use by other services or devices, such as cell phones. Many questions have come up about this transition, particularly the question as to whether an analog TV set will work with a digital signal. The answer is no, not directly, but set-top boxes will be available that can translate a digital signal into an analog signal for older television sets. Digital and digital-ready sets will be able to both receive and exhibit digital television signals, whether they are from broadcast signals, cable, or satellite.

Satellite direct digital radio service began in 2002 with satellite services XM Satellite Radio and Sirius Satellite Radio. These services require a special satellite radio receiver and a paid subscription. Digital terrestrial radio may not be far off for broadcasters, however. A digital radio broadcast system called **IBOC (in band, on channel)** has been developed that will allow analog radio receivers to get the traditional analog-type signal and digital radio receivers to get a high-quality digital broadcast radio on the same frequencies as in the past.

Trends and Terminology

The electronic media industry has changed dramatically over the past 10 years, most notably since 1996, when the Telecommunications Act was signed into law. As the technology and rules regarding ownership change, it will be important to understand a number of issues in the field of electronic media.

Convergence

One of the dominant trends in electronic media in the past 10 years is convergence. In addition to the definitions of convergence provided earlier in this chapter, *convergence* also refers to the blurring of the boundaries between the different types of electronic communication media. This trend is in sharp contrast to how these media services have been over the past 50 years. The media and other telecommunication services, like voice telephony and online services, have traditionally been distinct, using different methods of connecting with their audiences or users as well as different *platforms,* such as television sets, telephones, and computers. Moreover, these services have been regulated with separate laws and even separate legislators.

With new digital technology, both older and newer services can be conducted over the same network and devices can be integrated for computing, telephony, and other media. In other words, when you are connected to the Internet via a broadband (Ethernet) connection in your dorm room, you can receive radio webcast radio stations, retrieve your e-mail, listen to music, download a book, or use instant messaging to have a real-time conversation (including both audio and video) with people located

Convergence

The term *convergence* has been a buzzword in the study of media for some time now. When the term first came into common use, many people thought that traditional media would be replaced and converged or that digital media would take over or supplant the old media. But in fact, the old and new media are co-existing. Much of the content in any given *USA Today* newspaper can be obtained by going to the *USA Today* website. The same is true for the *New York Times,* which even has a service that will send stories from the day's paper to your e-mail. Instead of paying 50 cents for a paper copy of the newspaper, wouldn't you rather go directly to the Web? The problem, obviously, is that you must have a computer with you when you want to read the paper. Laptop computers are still expensive and somewhat heavy, and they don't fold as easily as newspapers.

So people are still buying newspapers because it still fulfills their needs and fits their lifestyle. When that changes, then the hard-copy circulation of newspapers may change. In other words, just because a medium can be duplicated and made available digitally, it doesn't mean that its analog form will no longer be viable.

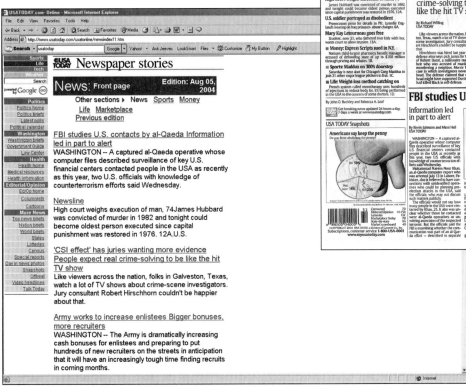

anywhere in the world (Bangemann & Oreja, 1997). Some cell phones and PDAs have the capability (although limited) to receive calls, download material from the Web, take and send digital pictures, store and play MP3 music files, and even surf the Web.

So, are books still considered print media if you can download them on your computer? If a broadcast radio station simulcasts its signal on a website, does that mean the station is a digital medium? Obviously, convergence has blurred the lines that distinguish one medium from another, such that the traditional definitions of these media need to be reevaluated.

Consolidation

Media companies are quite aware of how convergence has changed the electronic media business. Companies like News Corporation, owner of the FOX network, have reconfigured themselves to include new media outlets (they bought a satellite television company) and are also buying more of what they already own (they bought more television stations to strengthen their network).

This trend, known as **consolidation**, has been facilitated by the Telecommunications Act of 1996, which relaxed most of the limits on ownership. Since 1996, ownership trends have changed dramatically, especially in radio. The total number of radio stations that can be owned by any one company is no longer limited, although the number of stations one company can own in any one market is somewhat restricted. One company, Clear Channel Communication, owns more than 1,200 radio stations nationwide.

Cross-ownership refers to the ownership of both a broadcast station and a newspaper in the same market. Cross-media ownership has mostly been discouraged by the government because it reduces the diversity and number of media "voices" in a given market. (Read more about this in Chapter 12, Regulation, Legal Issues, and Ethics.) The cross-media ownerships formed in the 1920s still exist in some cities because of a process was known **grandfathering**.[1] Mergers between large media companies can also result in a single company owning both broadcast properties and newspaper properties in the same market. When this happens, the FCC generally allows a grace period during which the company will correct the situation by selling off one of its properties. The industry expects that the FCC will relax cross-ownership rules soon; however, many believe that the rules should remain strict.

Commercialism

The trend toward **commercialism** can be explained by this statement: Stations are on the air to make money. This is the reality that corporate America has brought to electronic media. Some people have mistakenly believed that the goal of commercial electronic media is to create and distribute high-quality entertainment and information programming to the audience (Chester & Larson, 2002). This may have been somewhat true throughout the early 1990s, when broadcasting stations were owned by small, privately held businesses, which took pride in having a dedicated audience and only had to please themselves when it came to programming content and advertising sales. Back then, profit margins were good (10 percent to 25 percent was common), allowing small business owners to thrive.

With the trend of consolidation, more and more stations are owned by fewer and fewer owners. Plus, these owners are more corporate in nature and often publicly held. A publicly held company has stockholders, whom the officers of the company must try to please. Most often, the stockholders are not happy unless the company is making a profit and the value of the shares of stock they hold are increasing in value. When the stockholders are unhappy with the company's performance, the officers of the company may lose their jobs. Some of the workers at stations that have been taken over by giant group owners have complained of the huge profit expectations (i.e., 40 percent to 50 percent) demanded by corporate headquarters.

In addition, the strong seller's market for broadcast stations has led to extremely high prices. When a company incurs a huge debt to acquire a station, it takes a lot of revenue to pay off that debt. Sometimes, a group will buy a station and then have to sell off much of the station's assets just to be able to pay the mortgage or business loan. For example, suppose a company that owns two stations in a market buys a third station. Instead of using the newly acquired station's studios and separate antenna tower, it may use the existing studios and antenna towers and sell the property and equipment from the new station. The company will then use the proceeds from the sale to pay off part of the debt incurred by buying the station.

SEE IT LATER

As mentioned earlier, this book focuses on electronic media, which have traditionally been defined as mass media delivered electronically. The book also presents an expanded view of electronic media to include personal media. Innovations in personal media (e.g., the ability to download music from a file-sharing source) have prompted noticeable changes in the way young people listen to and learn about music. Specifically, they are moving away from broadcast radio and toward the World Wide Web. This has caused a shakeup in the music industry, which is losing money due to decreased CD sales (Pruitt, 2002). The topics discussed in the following section are all relevant to what is happening now in electronic media and are certain to influence media and media use in the future.

Current and Future Influences

Desktop Production

Another trend in electronic media can be found in the production process itself—the process of actually making programs. In the last 10 years, more and more of that process of making programs has been accomplished using computers. Although there are still some quality differences, small computers can now perform many of the production tasks that had to be performed by expensive, stand-alone equipment in the past. People can even edit video or audio and thus produce television or radio programming in their own homes.

How this change will influence the electronic media industry is unknown. Perhaps having the ability to produce programs with desktop computers will lead to greater **media literacy**, in which the audience has knowledge and understanding not only of the meaning of the content of the media but also of the power of the media, the intent of the media, and the influence of the media (Potter, 1998; Silverblatt, 1995).

E-Mail/Instant Messaging

The Internet has changed our electronic media behavior by introducing a new form of electronic person-to-person communication. Consider that the Internet was seen as "an obscure technical toy" until the development of user-friendly browsers in 1992 (Dizard, 2000). And even though e-mail was available before 1992 through online services like Prodigy, America Online, and Compuserv, it was not widely used. Since then, e-mail has become a vitally important way to communicate with others. We conduct business and keep in touch with family and friends quickly, easily, and for almost no cost (Kaye & Medoff, 2001). Although e-mail is generally asynchronous, we constantly check it for recent messages.

Some recent innovations, such as **instant messaging** and **chat rooms**, allow us to talk to others who are connected in real time. Instant messaging, or IM, provides a one-to-one electronic conversation channel. We can type real-time messages to people who are on our "buddies" lists. With a microphone and webcam, we can see others connected to the IM service as we speak to them. Compared to the days when the only means of long-distance communication was writing a letter or making an expensive phone call, the Internet provides an inexpensive, quick, and efficient means for keeping in close (and sometimes constant) communication with others.

Cell Phones

Just a few years ago, it was unusual to find a college student with his or her own cell phone. Having a cell phone was expensive and considered a luxury for almost everyone except the heavy business traveler. Now, it is unusual to find a college student without one. Students talk to each other between classes and most other times when they aren't in their dorm rooms or apartments, where their so-called landline phones are located. As a result, people with cell phones stay closer to friends and family. Since cell phone calling plans now commonly include free long-distance calls and no roaming charges, keeping in contact with friends at other universities and relatives in other states has become even easier and less expensive.

In addition to making voice calls, a popular feature of cell phone plans is **text messaging.** The user can tap in a short message using the keypad of the phone and send it as easily as making a call. Students use text messaging when they can't talk, such as during classes, in movies, and at work. Thus, staying in nearly constant contact with friends and relatives is the result of this technology.

Online Journals and Blogging

Yet another new communication behavior has evolved from use of the Internet: **online journaling.** This recent practice has been embraced by many young people, and especially college students, who have broadband connections. An online journal (also called a *live journal*) is similar to a print diary. The user creates a site by using a free on-line journal service like LiveJournal, which provides space on its server for webpages created by individuals. These webpages have information about the personal lives of the people who created them. Some parts of online journals are public and anybody can go to the site and read or view it. Other parts can be kept private, allowing access only to people who are on a list of friends made by the author of the live journal.

Similar to live journals are **weblogs,** also known as **blogs.** They are webpages posted by individuals (**bloggers**) who want to express themselves on a variety of topics. Commonly, bloggers deal with political issues, citing sources like newspaper articles and other bloggers and giving their own commentary and opinion.

All of these services allow one-to-one and one-to-many communication, such that people from all over the world can find out about the lives and opinions of online journal users and bloggers. As with many of the services provided by the Web, these types of electronic publishing simply did not exist before the mid 1990s. Yet the use of online journals and blogging is a fast-growing trend that is certain to influence how we get and respond to information in the future. These innovations all encourage the audience to interact with the media, something that was uncommon in the days of traditional media. Clearly, technology is changing how we receive and respond to the electronic media, and the changes are occurring more rapidly than ever before.

Downloading Music and Movies

The use of personal electronic media has also changed mass media habits. For example, the use of broadband connections and CD burners by Internet-savvy young people has changed the way many of them obtain music for personal use. They can download songs from a variety of file-sharing sites and burn them to inexpensive blank CDs. Although this practice raises serious copyright and ethical questions, the practice of downloading music through file sharing has become widespread. It extends to Hollywood movies, as well. Somehow, digital versions of new movies have made it to the Web, from which they can be downloaded and burned to CDs or DVDs. These practices, if they continue, will certainly change the way the music and feature film industries conduct business and distribute their products.

The electronic media comprise a large, dynamic, and high-profile industry in the United States, and what goes on within it is interesting to us: We follow the stories and the stars, and we depend on it for information about the world. We continue to use electronic media in the traditional way, as passive consumers of content. However, through e-mail, online journals, and blogging, we are taking on the role of media creator, and this trend is perhaps at its very beginning.

Using electronic media.

Top Ten Reasons for Studying Electronic Media

Electronic media is a dynamic and powerful field that merits closer study, for many reasons:

1. *We spend so much time with it.* Few things command as much time and attention in our lives as our interactions with electronic media. In each household that has a television set, it is on for an average of 7 hours and 44 minutes per day, which is more than the time spent working, going to school, shopping, or exercising. Sleep is the only activity that is more time consuming (Nielsen Media Research, 2003; Straubhaar & LaRose, 2004).

2. *Electronic media present us with the icons of pop culture.* How many people have not heard of Madonna, Michael Jackson, Marilyn Monroe, Elvis Presley, David Letterman, Jay Leno, Michael Jordan, The Beatles, Britney Spears, Jennifer Lopez, Bart Simpson, Justin Timberlake, and Carson Daly? These people, so familiar in our everyday lives, became prominent with the help of electronic media.

3. *We share experiences from electronic media, and they become currency for socializing.* We talk about things we see on television and hear on the radio: the Super Bowl, *American Idol, Survivor, Friends, Wheel of Fortune, Star Trek,* military activities, and the weather forecast. We talk about movies that we have seen on DVDs and their soundtracks on CDs.

4. *The electronic media is an ambassador of our culture.* American electronic media is pervasive in many parts of the world. That means that the perceptions that people in other countries have formed about us are based on what they have seen in the movies and on television.

5. *What happens in electronic media is interesting.* This industry gets quite a bit of news coverage. Some shows are dedicated to news about the electronic media and movie personalities, such as *Entertainment Tonight* and *Access Hollywood.*

6. *Career opportunities are available in electronic media, but it is a highly competitive field.* The more you know about electronic media, the easier it will be to get a job in the industry.

7. *The electronic media influence all areas of our lives:*
   - Speech—We learn new phrases and meanings for words and slang.
   - Customs and traditions—The portrayal of holiday festivities, like the dropping of the "apple" on New Year's Eve, shapes how we observe these holidays.
   - Styles of clothing, cars, and technology—We see and hear about these products through electronic media, and we are tempted to try them out.
   - Sense of ethics and justice—We view many stories of good and evil and even experience real courtroom dramas by viewing one of the many courtroom shows on television.
   - Perceptions of others in our society and distant countries—For example, National Geographic programs show us how people in South America live.
   - Lifestyles—We learn about other people's lives and our own by watching talk shows, self-help shows, and advice shows.

8. *We need to understand the effects that the electronic media have on us.* By the time we finish high school, we have been subjected to many thousands of hours of electronic media. What effect does that have on us? Are we different than our parents or grandparents because we have used so much electronic media? Do electronic media have a quick and direct effect on us or a slow, subtle, cumulative effect?

9. *Studying electronic media and becoming media literate will helps us to be discriminating consumers who can make good media choices.*

10. *The electronic media are always changing, and as they change, so do we.* For college students interested in a career in electronic media, knowing about these changes will present appropriate strategies for job seeking.

What did the early Egyptians use papyrus for?

Summary

Humans have been communicating for thousands of years, fulfilling an innate desire to reach out to others. But until recently, the number of people we could communicate with was limited to those we could see face to face or contact by letter. Since the mid nineteenth century, electricity has enhanced various forms of communication and allowed us to communicate over long distances and to many people at once. Through the use of electronic media—radio, television, and the Internet—we now can communicate with a huge number of people in a very short period of time.

Traditional mass media share characteristics such as audience, time, display, distribution, distance, and storage. Electronic media are not constrained by time and distance. Electronic media can have cognitive, emotional, and behavioral effects on the audience, influencing and changing people's lives.

The Internet has emerged as a new mass medium at an unprecedented speed. It was adopted rapidly and represents a combination or convergence of various mass media. With the Internet, we can communicate with a large audience for low cost and short turnaround time. The process of digitization simplifies the formats through which information is transmitted.

Numerous trends are changing the media industry and how we relate to and use electronic media. Convergence is the combining of media and thus the blurring of the distinctiveness among them. Consolidation involves fewer companies owning more electronic media stations and businesses. Some trends have resulted directly from changes in technology. For example, desktop production has been fueled by digital technology and faster computers, which allow individuals to create content for electronic media on a single computer.

Technology has also provided new ways of communicating with others. E-mail and instant messaging facilitate our communication with others across distances in either a synchronous or asynchronous timeframe. Cell phones make personal communication easy and inexpensive and encourage us to keep in touch with others on a more regular basis; they are also capable of text messaging and allow surfing the Internet. Young people are creating online journals to share their personal experiences and observations. Bloggers create personal webpages that tend to focus on political issues.

The study of electronic media is important not only as a field of intellectual pursuit but also as a means of preparing oneself for a successful career. Our use of electronic media takes up a lot of time in our daily lives. Thus, we need to be critical consumers. American electronic media provide a window for the rest of the world to view our culture. Finally, we should recognize that electronic media is a dynamic force in our society that is constantly changing. We need to study the changes and understand that they affect us deeply.

Note

1. In the 1920s, some newspapers were encouraged to start radio stations in their communities, since they had mass media experience and the resources to experiment with the new medium of broadcasting. Some of these historic cross-ownerships still exist today; for example, the owners of the *Pittsburgh Post-Gazette* also own television station KDKA in Pittsburgh.

Radio

  SEE IT THEN

Early Inventors and Inventions
Radio Becomes a Mass Medium
The Beginnings of Commercial Radio
Government Involvement
Influences of Early Radio
World War II
AM Radio
FM Radio

 SEE IT NOW

The Telecommunications
Act of 1996
Other Delivery Systems

SEE IT LATER

Radio Goes Digital
The Role of Government

In this chapter, you'll learn about:

- The technological antecedents of radio
- The people who began radio
- The growth of commercial radio and radio networks
- How radio evolved as a result of technological changes and business changes

Until the mid 1800s, communicating over distances involved long periods of time between transmission and reception. Signal systems such as the semaphore used by the Romans and the French and smoke signals used by Native Americans were rapid, but the amount of information that could be transmitted quickly and effectively was limited.

The electrical telegraph in the early 1880s was the first invention to improve on distance and time in long-distance communication. However, the wires required by this method of communication were vulnerable to attack or accident and therefore not always reliable. A system was needed that would allow communication to travel over long distances, carry meaningful messages, and do so without wires. That system was radio.

This chapter will discuss how radio waves were discovered, the major inventors behind the development of radio, how radio became a mass medium, and what delivery systems are available now and will be in the future.

SEE IT THEN

Early Inventors and Inventions

The nineteenth century was a time of tremendous technological growth around the world. The Industrial Revolution, which began in England in the early part of that century, took off in the United States just after the Civil War and continued into the early 1900s. A variety of communication technologies were invented along the way, in this country and abroad, all leading to the development of radio.

Electrical Telegraphy

In an attempt to increase communication distance, speed, and quantity, inventors tried a number of different methods. Samuel F. B. Morse, an American who was at the time well known as an artist, became interested in the use of electromagnets for the purpose of signaling. In 1835, he created the **electrical telegraph,** an instrument that used pulses of current to deflect an electromagnet, which moved a marker to produce a written code on a strip of paper. The next year, he changed the system so that it embossed paper with a system of dots and dashes, which later became known as **Morse code.** This simple code allowed telegraph operators to send messages quickly over long distances (once the wires were in place) and could be interpreted universally by all telegraph operators.

Morse patented the system in 1840, and the U.S. government provided funds for a demonstration of this new technology. A line was set up between Washington, DC, and Baltimore. After dealing with some technological problems (some of which were remedied by Ezra Cornell, for whom Cornell University is named), the first official message, "What hath God wrought," was transmitted and received on May 24, 1844. The government allowed private businesses to develop the electrical communication industry, a policy that would be repeated in later years with other communication technologies. By 1861, a transcontinental line was in place, allowing messages to be sent and received across the United States (Sterling & Kittross, 2002).

An advertisement for the first telegraph.

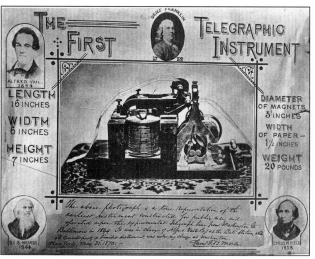

Even though the electrical telegraph conquered the problems of distance and speed, it still presented some challenges. First, it required building a costly system of wires between senders and receivers. Second, it only worked as long as the wires were in place. This meant, for example, that outlaws could cut the wires between two points and prevent news about a train robbery from being sent to law enforcement officials. Third, the system required that messages be sent by a trained telegraph operator who knew how to send and receive in Morse code.

Once a message was decoded, delivering it to the appropriate receiver also proved problematic. The local address of the receiver had to be found, and a courier had to physically travel from the telegraph office to the receiver's home or place of business. Ironically, physically delivering the message to the receiver often took a great deal more time than sending the message across the country. In addition, since people were charged by the letter or word, messages were often short and somewhat cryptic. Thus, they often lacked specific meaning or emotion. Finally, the telegraph was a restricted system. Western Union was the dominant company in the business, and it controlled all messages and allowed only company-trained operators to use the system. In sum, the electrical telegraph was not a user-friendly system for most purposes.

Electrical Telephony

Demand grew for a communication system that would provide two-way communication and that could be used by individuals without special training. That system appeared in 1876, when Alexander Graham Bell invented the electrical telephone. On March 10 of that year, Bell called out to his assistant, "Mr. Watson, come here; I want to see you" through his experimental system. One year later, a regular telephone line was constructed between Boston and Somerville, Massachusetts.

Electrical telephony provided a means for individuals to communicate in real time, using regular language with no deciphering needed and allowing two-way conversation. Of course, the costs and logistics of building the wired system prevented many people from using this invention quickly or easily. As in the case of the telegraph, signals only went to places that had been wired to receive and transmit them. Even areas that had been wired sometimes had problems, as when bad weather caused telephone lines to break and created lapses in service. Despite these drawbacks, however, the growth of distance communication was assured.

Point-to-Point Electrical Communication

Both electrical telegraphy and electrical telephony were designed and used as systems to facilitate **point-to-point communication.** Using either of these systems, one person could send a message to another person at a distant location. The speed at which the signal traveled through the wires was the same as the speed of light (186,000 miles per second), which meant the message reached its destination within seconds of transmission. Obviously, the rapid speed and ability to send understandable messages made the telegraph and the telephone superior to previous message delivery systems, such as smoke signals, drum beats, the semaphore system, and even the various ways of delivering mail.

Electrical point-to-point communication proved its value in many situations, including uses like the announcement of the arrival of incoming trains and trucks. By the late 1800s, manufacturers and merchants could get updates via telegraph messages or phone calls that would tell them when their materials or products would be arriving. Similarly, information about the weather could also be relayed to persons about an incoming storm or drastic change in temperature. These systems worked fairly well when the lines remained intact, but of course, they failed if the lines were damaged.

Since the arrival times of ships and the people and goods they were bringing were important pieces of information, there was some demand to be able to reach ships at sea. But neither the telegraph nor the telephone allowed sending or receiving information to or from ships when they were not in port. This problem generated strong interest in the idea of sending electrical messages *without wires.* Given the importance of the shipping business and the potential for profit, possible solutions were sought from scientists, innovators, and inventors.

A system had to be developed that would allow signals to travel over long distances, to carry meaningful messages, and to do so without wires. Interestingly, even before the use of wired telephone transmission, scientists around the world were experimenting with wireless transmission.

What is the dividing line that determines whether a station's call letters will begin with a K or a W?

Wireless Transmission

JAMES CLERK MAXWELL   As early as 1864, a Scottish physicist named James Clerk Maxwell predicted that signals containing information similar to that of the telegraph could be carried through space without the use of wires. In 1873, he published a paper that described radiant waves that were invisible. These waves, which later became known as **radio waves**, were part of a theory that suggested that signals could travel over distances and carry information. That theory, which became known as **electromagnetic theory**, used mathematical equations to demonstrate that electricity and light are very similar and both radiate at a constant speed across space.

HEINRICH HERTZ   Most people who study the advent of radio accept that numerous contributions were made by scientists around the world. Heinrich Hertz, a physicist from Germany, used Maxwell's theory to build a crude detector of radiated waves in 1886. Hertz set up a device that generated high-voltage sparks between two metal balls. A short distance away, he placed two smaller electrodes. When the large electric spark jumped across the gap between the two large balls, Hertz could see that a smaller spark appeared at the second set of metal balls. It was proof that electromagnetic energy had traveled through the air, causing the second spark. Hertz never pursued the idea of using the waves to transmit information, but his work is looked on as being crucial to the use of electromagnetic waves for communicating. In fact, the basic unit of electromagnetic frequency, the **Hertz**, was named after him.

In the late 1890s, an English physicist named Sir Oliver Lodge devised a way to tune both a transmitter and a receiver to the same frequency to vastly improve signal strength and reception. Another scientist noted for contributing improvements in the wave detector and antenna is Alexander Popoff, a Russian who experimented in the 1890s. Interestingly, Popoff's work was dedicated to finding a better way to detect and predict thunderstorms.

GUGLIELMO MARCONI   An Italian inventor, Guglielmo Marconi, is generally credited with the first practical demonstration of the wireless transmission of signals. After reading about Hertz's experiments, Marconi tried to use electromagnetic waves to transmit information. Not only was he able to improve on Hertz's invention, but he also noted that having an antenna above ground improved signal transmission and added a telegraph key to encode signals.

When Marconi approached the government of his native Italy for a patent and financial support, they expressed no interest. Fortunately for Marconi, his mother was a citizen of Great Britain, which was at the time a strong maritime power and thus very interested in developing a system to contact ships at sea. Through his mother's contacts, Marconi found the head of the telegraph office of the British Post Office, William Preece, who had also done some wireless experimentation. Britain provided Marconi with a patent and the financial support he needed to further develop his wireless system.

In 1899, Marconi showed that radio waves could be sent and received over long distances by sending a signal across the English Channel. Just two years later, he sent a signal (the letter *S* in Morse code) from Great Britain to North America, convincing many that wireless communication across great distances was becoming a reality. However, around 1901, the system was designed to carry dots and dashes, or Morse code, and not the human voice. Since the telephone had been invented over 25 years earlier, people

Guglielmo Marconi at work with his wireless radio.

The Mississippi River. West is K and east is W.

had already been exposed to voice communication over long distances and so expected that radio should be able to carry voice messages, as well.

Some historians credit American inventor Nathan Stubblefield as the first person to successfully transmit the human voice using radio waves, although he used ground conduction rather than transmitting through the air. Regardless, in 1892, Stubblefield supposedly communicated the words "Hello Rainey" to his assistant during an experiment conducted near Murray, Kentucky (Hilliard & Keith, 2001, p. 6).

REGINALD FESSENDEN   A Canadian electrical engineer constructed a high-speed alternator (a device that generates radio energy) to carry voice signals. On Christmas Eve, 1906, Reginald Fessenden transmitted a voice signal from his home at Brant Rock, Massachusetts, to ships at sea along the East Coast of the United States. He sent out music played on a violin, readings from the Bible, and season's greetings to all that could hear the signal. Many people consider this transmission the first public radio broadcast with sound, instead of Morse code.

LEE DE FOREST   In 1899, American inventor Lee De Forest earned a Ph.D. from Yale University with a dissertation that investigated wireless transmissions, and in 1900, he developed a wireless system to compete with Marconi's. In addition, De Forest constructed a device that would amplify weak radio signals. His invention was an improvement of one constructed by John Fleming, an engineer from England. Fleming had developed a radio wave detector in a sealed glass tube that came to be known as the **Fleming valve** or **diode tube.** This device, which looked like a household lightbulb, was able to detect radio signals that contained the human voice, but it didn't amplify the signal. De Forest added a third element to the diode tube to make a *triode tube,* later known as the **audion.** This device amplified the voice signal enough to allow voice transmission using radio waves. De Forest filed for a patent for his invention in 1906.

Lee De Forest with his audion tube.

De Forest was very good at generating publicity with events like the broadcast of a phonograph record from the Eiffel Tower in Paris, which was received 500 miles away. But he was not a skillful businessman. He spent much of his time trying to create a viable business in the radio industry, despite many financial setbacks. He also had numerous legal problems with patents. One of the most difficult involved the 1914 invention of a regenerative or feedback circuit, which was also discovered at about the same time by Edwin H. Armstrong, another radio inventor. De Forest won the legal battle, even though he couldn't explain it in court. Regardless, historians often give Armstrong credit for this invention, which made receiving radio signals much easier (Lewis, 1991).

A Tragic Lesson

In the early 1900s, radio was somewhat of an oddity. Although many hobbyists were experimenting with radio transmissions and radio demonstrations were used for publicity purposes at fairs and department stores, only two companies were making parts for radio receivers. Government officials had a better overall view of the usefulness of radio for health and safety. By 1910, many nations had established regulations to guide the use of radio, particularly in terms of maritime uses. And just two years later, a tragedy occurred that heightened awareness of the power of radio forever.

In mid April 1912, an "unsinkable" luxury liner named the *Titanic* set out on its maiden voyage from England, bound for the United States. Its passengers, mostly wealthy and well-known people, expected a luxurious trip across the Atlantic Ocean on the newest and most sophisticated ocean liner ever built. The *Titanic* was equipped with the most modern technology available at the time, including a wireless radio and people trained to operate it.

Late at night on April 15, the *Titanic* collided with a huge iceberg in the North Atlantic Ocean, ripping open the hull and causing the ship to rapidly take on water. Supposedly, the ship's radio operator had received warnings about icebergs being dangerously close to the ship's path, but he had somehow refused to heed them. Instead, the operator had requested that other ship radio operators clear the airwaves to allow the *Titanic* to send personal messages from the ship's famous passengers to Europe and the United States (Hilliard & Keith, 2001, p. 13).

After the *Titanic* collided with the iceberg and began to sink, the radio operator on board began sending out SOS signals. Unfortunately, the collision occurred late at night and most of the wireless operators on other ships in the area had already gone off duty. Only the operator on one ship, the *Carpathia,* heard the signal and responded to the call. Although the *Carpathia* was able to rescue some 700 passengers from the *Titanic,* about 1,500 perished when the ship went down.

One of the many legends that emerged from the *Titanic* tragedy involved a young wireless operator named David Sarnoff. Stationed at a wireless operation inside Wanamaker's Department Store in New York City, he heard the signal from the *Titanic* and the response from the *Carpathia.* As the legend goes, Sarnoff stayed at his wireless station for the next 72 hours and received important information about survivors from the signals sent out by the *Carpathia.* The government had ordered that the airwaves be cleared of other operators during the days that the tragedy unfolded. As a result, Sarnoff was able to pass along exclusive information about survivors to the *New York American* daily newspaper.

A young David Sarnoff at his wireless station in Wanamaker's Department Store.

The news reported about the sinking of the *Titanic* in April 1912 came from wireless radio transmissions.

Some historians dispute this legend about David Sarnoff (the source of which was Sarnoff, after he became president of RCA). Whatever the case, the story marks an interesting and important milestone in the development of the wireless (Lewis, 1991, pp. 105–107). Namely, it proved to the world that the wireless radio could be indispensable for safety. Obviously, ships at sea needed to have immediate contact with the rest of the world. In addition, this story demonstrates the power of radio to disseminate information to many people at a time. The information that Sarnoff received was relayed to one newspaper and then many more, which printed stories about the *Titanic,* its passengers, and the *Carpathia's* efforts to save lives.

The publicity surrounding this tragic event led to government scrutiny of the role of the wireless radio. Governments worldwide sought to increase wireless conformity and compatibility. The U.S. Congress passed the Wireless Ship Act of 1910, which required a ship with more than 50 passengers to carry a radio that could reach another radio 100 miles away. The ship also had to have aboard a person capable of operating the radio. Two years later, Congress passed the Radio Act of 1912, a forerunner of subsequent legislation to regulate radio transmissions. This act required the licensing of radio operations used for the purpose of interstate commerce. It also required licensed operators to be citizens of the United States and stated that licenses must be obtained from the U.S. Secretary of Commerce and Labor, who had jurisdiction over commercial radio use in this country. (For more about this act, see Chapter 12 on regulation.)

Radio Becomes a Mass Medium

Both Fessenden and De Forest did some early promotional voice transmissions to heighten awareness and demand for their inventions, but neither set up a regular schedule of programs for the general audience. The reasons for this were many, but perhaps the most important one was that very few people had radio sets at the time. Moreover, those people who did have radios and a working knowledge of the technology were mostly hobbyists and amateur radio operators who communicated primarily with each other. Their communication was person to person and conducted in Morse code.

In 1909, Charles D. "Doc" Herrold, who operated a technical college in San Jose, California, began to send transmissions using voice on a regular schedule. According to former students of the school, the station that Herrold began transmitted popular music of the time along with some speeches and other "talk." In some ways, this station might be considered the first real broadcast station, since it was scheduled, provided voice transmissions, and was sent out to the general public (although few people had radio receivers). In a sense, it was also the first college radio station. Herrold's operation was one of the first to be licensed after the Radio Act of 1912, and it continued operation until World War I. It came back on the air in early 1922 with the call letters KQW. The station was later sold and then moved to San Francisco, where it became KCBS, a station that still broadcasts today.

In 1916, a Westinghouse engineer named Dr. Frank Conrad began to send both voice and music programs from his home in Pittsburgh to the Westinghouse plant located about five miles away. Eventually, he also began to play music by placing a microphone next to a phonograph. This became so popular that he scheduled music programs for Wednesday and Sunday evenings, rather than try to fulfill all of the requests he received from people who knew about his transmissions. Some consider Conrad the first **disc jockey**, or **DJ**. Conrad's station, then known as 8XK, was licensed to Westinghouse in 1920 as KDKA. It was one of the first commercial broadcast stations in the United States.

Another station that claims to be the first licensed station on the air is 8MK-WWJ in Detroit. It started out as 8MK, an amateur station that first went on the air from a

What percentage of people use radio as their first source of news?

"radio phone room" in the *Detroit News* building. The license for this station was eventually issued to the *Detroit News* for station WWJ on March 3, 1922 (Sterling & Kittross, 2002, p. 66).

Broadcasting

When early experimenters such as De Forest, Herrold, and Conrad sent entertainment over the airwaves to gain some publicity and please friends, they were clearly attempting to reach a small segment of the population, which is often referred to as **narrowcasting.** The term **broadcasting,** which would be used to describe mass transmission to the general public, actually comes from agriculture. Seeds could be planted in rows, or broadcast, by a person walking and casting them in all directions by using a circular motion (Lewis, 1991).

Before 1916, radio experimenters felt that radio would be most useful for sending information to sites that could not be wired for telephone or telegraph. Likely uses included ship-to-shore or ship-to-ship communication and communication that had to travel over terrain that presented problems for wiring, such as harsh weather, high altitude, and large bodies of water. The idea of using radio signals to send messages to a large, general audience simply had not yet surfaced. But a conscientious radio telegraph operator named David Sarnoff was giving quite a bit of thought to the potential uses of radio.

Sarnoff had stayed with radio as a career after his experience with relaying news of the *Titanic* disaster. By 1916, he had become commercial manager of American Marconi and continued to look for ways to make money using radio. Although historians dispute its authenticity (e.g., Benjamin, 1993), a memo was found in 1920 that was supposedly written earlier by Sarnoff and addressed to the manager of the firm. In it, Sarnoff outlined an idea that contains the essence of what radio broadcasting would become. Namely, he suggested

> a plan of development which would make radio a "household utility" in the same sense as the piano or phonograph. The idea is to bring music into the house by wireless. . . . The problem of transmitting music has already been solved in principle and therefore all the receivers attuned to the transmitting wavelength should be capable of receiving such music. The receiver can be designed in the form of a simple "Radio Music Box" and arranged for several different wavelengths, which should be changeable with the throwing of a single switch or pressing of a single button. . . . The box can be placed on a table in the parlor or living room, the switch set accordingly and the transmitted music received. There should be no difficulty in receiving music perfectly when transmitted within a radius of 25 to 50 miles. . . . The same principle can be extended to numerous other fields as, for example, receiving of lectures at home which can be made perfectly audible; also events of national importance can be simultaneously announced and received. (Gross, 2003, pp. 14–15)

In addition, Sarnoff's memo stated how money could be made from the enterprise. Rather than suggest some sort of subscription fee or advertising, Sarnoff suggested that large profits could be gained from the sale of radio receivers to the general public.

In retrospect, it seems as if this idea should have been grasped immediately. But in fact, it was ignored by American Marconi and other companies in the radio business at the time. The idea of Sarnoff's "Radio Music Box" simply did not catch on, for many reasons, including the need for the audience to wear earphones to hear the signal, the fact that much of the radio equipment at the time was complicated and unreliable, and the lack of public interest in this service. Also, the people who held the power in the radio industry were engineers and businesspeople, who were not particularly interested in entertaining the masses (Sterling & Kittross, 2002, p. 43).

48 percent.

World War I

When the United States entered World War I in 1917, the federal government decided that it wanted to use radio to help communication within its armed forces and among the armed forces of its allies. In addition, the government felt that for security reasons, it must prevent foreign radio operators from operating in the United States. Therefore, the federal government took over the operation of all high-power stations in the country. In fact, in 1917, it even closed down the amateur and experimental stations for the same reason.

This government action led to two developments in radio: First, operating a station during the war required government training for many people, and second, helping the war effort stimulated the technological development of radio. In turn, these developments helped stimulate the growth of the radio industry after the end of the war in late 1918.

The Radio Corporation of America

After World War I, the British-owned Marconi company sought to strengthen its position as the leader in long-distance radio communication. It tried to buy a large number of the powerful Alexanderson alternators produced by General Electric (GE) for its American subsidiary, American Marconi, which essentially would have given Marconi a near monopoly in transatlantic radio. Since the U.S. government had just taken steps to avoid foreign control of radio in the country, it was opposed to the sale of equipment to British-owned Marconi. The government considered the idea of continued control of the radio industry but lacked the skilled operators needed to do so. Moreover, opposition from American Telephone and Telegraph (AT&T), the Marconi company, and amateur radio operators was strong enough to convince the government to back off, allowing the radio industry to be in the hands of private enterprise. Owen Young, an officer of GE, persuaded the company to buy enough of American Marconi to control it. And so British Marconi was allowed to buy alternators for its foreign radio transmitters (Sterling & Kittross, 2002, p. 57).

Soon after taking control of American Marconi, GE decided that its strength and expertise were in manufacturing, not radio communication. It formed the Radio Corporation of America (RCA) in October 1919 to conduct its radio business, generated by the former American Marconi stations. In the next few years, much legal wrangling occurred over which company controlled which patents on broadcast equipment. In 1920, GE, RCA, and AT&T signed an agreement to pool their patents. Westinghouse, their only big competitor, decided to join the group in 1921, leading to a consortium of companies that would move broadcasting to the next level. By 1922, GE, Westinghouse, AT&T, and United Fruit (a small company that held desirable patents) had become the corporate owners of RCA. With this development, approximately 2,000 patents were pooled and an effective manufacturing and marketing plan was enacted, in which radio receivers would be manufactured by GE and Westinghouse and sold exclusively by RCA.

The 1920s

Broadcasting as we know it began during the 1920s. After World War I, the technology was greatly improved, and people who gained radio skills and experience during the war became interested in experimenting with radio. But the business sector lagged behind, showing very little interest in the technology, since up to that time, radio had been a point-to-point business.

As noted earlier, some of the groundwork for commercial broadcast radio was laid as early as 1909 with Doc Herrold's experimental broadcasts. It was Dr. Frank Conrad's broadcasts on station 8XK in 1916, which became KDKA in 1920, that really began

1920 Presidential Election

Until 1920, the sounds of presidential campaigns had been heard only by phonograph record. That changed on election night, November 2, 1920, when returns from the presidential election were broadcast. With this, radio became a force in the political process, bringing the live events and real sounds of political campaigns directly to the audience.

Another innovation also was made in the 1920 presidential election: Election returns within a radius of 300 miles of Pittsburgh were received and transmitted by wireless telephone. This process was created by the Westinghouse Electric & Manufacturing Company and its subsidiary, the International Radio Telegraph Company. The returns were received directly from an authoritative source and sent by a wireless telephone stationed at East Pittsburgh. Receiving stations of almost any size or type could catch the messages within the radius by using a crystal detector, a tuning coil, a pair of telephone receivers, and a small aerial. Using a two-stage amplifier, the operator would attach the receivers to a phonograph, so that messages could be heard anywhere in a medium-sized room.

Source: Electrical Review, 1920. For more about this broadcast, go to www.kdkaradio.com/kdka.asp?contentGUID ={1B08F8DC-1CD1-4801-ADF5-05306593FA17}&groupName=KDKA%20History.

the broadcast era. After the war, Conrad was allowed to resume broadcasting. His broadcasts were meant for a general audience and were informational and entertaining. After covering the 1920 presidential election, Conrad continued his programming with regularly scheduled shows, and local people bought radios to listen to these broadcasts. The programs were mostly music, much of which came from live bands that performed in a tent on the roof of the building that housed the station. After high winds destroyed the tent, a bona fide studio was built that allowed the bands to play indoors and have a good sound. Although the station started in Conrad's garage, it was later moved to a more suitable building and gained the support of the Westinghouse Company.

The sale of amateur wireless sets caught the attention of Westinghouse in 1920. The company decided to promote and broadcast a program each evening in the hope that people would get into the habit of listening nightly. The real goal was to sell receivers and promote the name of the Westinghouse Company. During this time, a department store in Pittsburgh ran an ad in the *Pittsburgh Press* for amateur wireless sets selling for $10 (Hilliard & Keith, 2001, p. 22).

The number of stations that went on the air immediately after KDKA's early broadcasts was not overwhelming. In fact, only 30 stations had been granted licenses to broadcast by January 1, 1922. That number grew to 218 by May 1 of that year, and by March 1923, there were 556 licensed stations. During 1923, over 500,000 radio receivers were produced by American manufacturers.

Department stores and hotels set up radio stations on their properties to draw customers. These businesses were especially active in radio because they often owned tall buildings that provided good locations for antennas. Live music was the most popular form of radio entertainment, although some sporting events, like heavyweight prize fights and World Series baseball games, drew huge audiences, consisting of as many as half a million people. Other people were drawn to radio for political programming, like President Warren G. Harding's Veterans Day speech from Arlington Cemetery near Washington, DC.

Factory-built receivers became common in American homes in 1921. A sophisticated receiver cost $60 and a simple one only $10. Since the daily pay for the average worker at that time was about $1, few Americans could afford a sophisticated receiver, but

Radio Stations on the Air: 1921–1925

The increase in radio stations on the air began in 1921 and exploded in 1922–1923, when the number went from 30 to over 550. A slight decrease occurred after that boom, followed by another increase in 1924–1925.

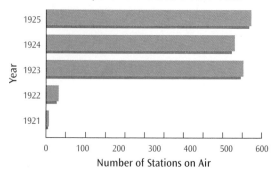

Source: Sterling & Kittross, 2002, p. 827.

many bought the less expensive model. Westinghouse promoted sales of the sets by owning radio stations in the towns where it had manufacturing plants.

In 1922, there was a huge amount of radio station activity. Over 600 licensed stations began broadcasting that year, although many also went off the air after only a short time. Westinghouse seemed to be having great success with broadcasting, perhaps due at least in part to the fact that it also sold radio receivers. Other broadcasters simply didn't have a way to pay for the expenses incurred in the continuous operation of a radio station. Most of the owners of one or more stations were radio receiver manufacturers and dealers and businesses involved with electrical device repair. In almost all cases, the radio station was put on the air as a sideline to the main business of the company that held the license.

Also in 1922, another technological innovation was demonstrated: the **superheterodyne receiver**, invented by Edwin Armstrong (who later developed FM radio). This device greatly improved the ability of radio to be received at great distances from the transmitting station. Later that same year, a broadcast originating from London was received at station WOR in New York.

In 1923, the federal government adopted the four-letter **call sign rule**, such that stations west of the Mississippi River were assigned K as the first letter and stations east of the Mississippi were assigned W as the first letter. Note that KDKA in Pittsburgh was licensed shortly before this rule went into effect and is an exception. Many colleges and universities put stations on the air during 1923 in the hope that doing so would help supplement the education of their students.

A Radio in Every Home, the Internet in Every Hut

The rapid technological advancement of early radio led H. P. Davis, a Westinghouse vice-president, to state, "A receiving set in every home, in every hotel room, in every schoolroom, in every hospital room. . . . It is not so much a question of possibility, it is rather a question of how soon" (Hilliard & Keith, 2001, p. 33).

Interestingly, President Bill Clinton made a similar statement regarding access to the so-called Information Superhighway, as presented by the Internet. In October 1996, Clinton stated, "Let us reach a goal in the twenty-first century of every home connected to the Internet and let us be brought closer together as a community through that connection" ("Clinton Unveils Plan," 1996). He also stated later, "Our big goal should be to make connection to the Internet as common as the connection to telephone today" ("Internet in Every Hut," 2000).

The Beginnings of Commercial Radio

In the early 1920s, radio stations were often started for the purpose of supporting or promoting a product or service offered by the station owner. This formula generally didn't work, however. Even though the demand for radio receivers exceeded the supply, having a large audience didn't guarantee success. The radio industry had yet to come up with a way to make radio pay for itself, let alone make a profit. (Interestingly, owners of Internet websites faced the same dilemma in the late 1990s, when they began to look for ways to make their sites bring in enough money to pay their expenses and justify keeping them online.)

In 1922, WEAF, the AT&T-owned station in New York, provided broadcasters with a novel way to make money from their stations. Using part of the economic model for making money from the telephone system, WEAF acted as a common carrier and sold time to advertisers. This procedure, known as **toll broadcasting**, was similar to that used when a long-distance call was made and charges were presented to the caller. Like the caller, the advertiser would pay a toll for the time used on the air. This concept was a critical part of the new economic model for supporting radio. It provided funds to the broadcaster to pay expenses, helped the advertiser reach an audience to sell a product or service, and kept broadcast programming free to the audience (Banning, 1946). (For more about WEAF's early advertising, see Chapter 7, Advertising.)

Again, in retrospect, it would seem that toll broadcasting should have been an instant sensation among broadcasters, but it did not catch on immediately. At a radio conference in 1922, U.S. Secretary of State Herbert Hoover disparaged the idea of toll broadcasting, stating that a service with as much promise as radio should not "be drowned in advertising chatter" (Hilliard & Keith, 2001, p. 30).

Technical Problems

The proliferation of radio stations in the early 1920s led to some technical problems. Due to a lack of foresight on the part of the government, all of the stations licensed to operate were assigned the same wavelength: 360 meters. Essentially, all of the stations intending to reach a general audience were operating on the same frequency. When a radio receiver receives more than one signal on the same frequency, the result is often interference and noise, rather than radio programming.

To solve this problem, the government initially encouraged stations in the same geographical area to take turns broadcasting. For instance, Station A would broadcast from 6:00 to 8:00 P.M. and Station B would broadcast from 8:00 to 10:00 P.M. Some stations voluntarily went off the air at night to allow larger stations with more sophisticated programming to be heard by the audience. This type of cooperation didn't last long, especially after stations found ways to bring in money through advertising.

Chain Broadcasting

In 1923, another piece of the broadcast puzzle was added by WEAF. Just after the beginning of the year, WEAF sent a musical performance over the telephone lines (owned by AT&T, its parent company) to a station in Boston, and the program was broadcast simultaneously by both stations. This interconnection was called **chain broadcasting**, and while this term is not commonly heard today, it still appears in legal documents. The more common term used now is **network**. Both terms refer to stations that are interconnected for the purpose of broadcasting identical programs.

Other forms of programming also started at this time. Information programming was common, offering lectures, news, political information, weather announcements, and religious items. Sports broadcasting also attracted a large audience.

Politicians seized the opportunity to reach many constituents through the medium of radio. Before radio, they had to rely on newspapers to communicate their messages accurately. This was sometimes a problem, however, because then as now, newspaper reporters, columnists, and editors wrote the articles, not the politicians themselves. Politicians preferred that voters heard their messages directly, not as interpreted (or edited) by newspaper writers. Radio allowed the politician's words to be heard as they were spoken and also connected a voice with the politician's name. This gave politicians and other public officials the ability to reach many people at once with an immediacy never before achieved. Radio also gave power to politicians by airing their speeches and interviews and making their voices familiar to large audiences. This was true not only for local politicians but also for state and federal politicians, who could reach constituents across the state or even across the country with a single speech or message.

Copyright Issues

As programming included more and more music, musicians began to complain that radio stations could use their work without permission (and, more importantly, without the artists receiving any compensation). The stations felt, however, that using copyrighted phonograph music actually benefited the artists by promoting their work.

Out of this conflict emerged the **American Society of Composers, Authors, and Publishers (ASCAP)**, which negotiated a fee with WEAF in 1923 to use copyrighted material. Specifically, WEAF agreed to pay $500 for the year. After a court case upheld ASCAP's right to negotiate these fees, the organization made usage agreements with other stations. The broadcasters responded by forming the **National Association of Broadcasters (NAB)**, a trade group that, among other things, negotiates with ASCAP.

In their cars.

Radio Receivers

As discussed earlier, the number of radio receivers in the United States grew dramatically during the 1920s. In just one year, from 1923 to 1924, the number of sets went from 0.5 million to over 1.25 million. This phenomenal growth was due in part to the fact that manufacturers had begun marketing inexpensive sets, which were affordable to most people. At this point, it had truly become a mass medium.

Interestingly, in 1924, Congress passed a bill that stated that the airwaves belonged to the people, not to stations or networks (Hilliard & Keith, 2001, p. 43; Settel, 1960, p. 44). This concept is an important one. It would be seen again in later legislation that formed the long-lasting rules and regulations for broadcasting for the remainder of the twentieth century.

The Network System

In 1926, the elements were in place to construct a true network system of broadcasting, and RCA, GE, and Westinghouse combined to form the **National Broadcasting Company (NBC).** NBC bought AT&T-owned WEAF, which essentially took AT&T out of broadcasting and practically eliminated the competition. NBC initially had 19 stations, which were interconnected for the purpose of simultaneously broadcasting programs. NBC's opening special, a gala event with live music from popular orchestras and singers, was carried by 25 stations and reached millions of listeners. By the end of 1926, NBC's success with one network, the Red network, led to its formation of a second network, the Blue network. [1]

Magazine advertisements for radio: 1930s.

Government Involvment

In early 1927, Congress passed the Radio Act of 1927, which formed a federal regulatory body for radio, the **Federal Radio Commission (FRC).** The role of this commission was to organize and administrate radio in the United States; specific responsibilities included issuing licenses, assigning frequency bands to the various types of stations and specific frequencies to individual stations, and designating station power levels.

To be licensed, a station had to be able to prove that it could provide enough funding to operate and to be able to control its programming. The FRC had the power to deny licenses to stations that were attempting to form a monopoly. In addition, a license could be denied to a station owned by a telephone company trying to control a radio station or by a radio station trying to control a telephone company. The FRC also had the power to develop regulations for stations and networks of stations. According to the 1927 act, the U.S. Secretary of Commerce was authorized to inspect radio stations, license operators of stations, and assign call letters.

A Few Important Words

At first, both listeners and broadcasters welcomed the Radio Act of 1927, thinking it would clear up all of the interference problems and make radio easier to listen to and radio stations easier to operate. But the act also set down a requirement that stations must operate in the **"public interest, convenience, and necessity."** These somewhat nebulous words have often been a point of contention between broadcasters and regulators. The FRC and later (after 1934) the **Federal Communications Commission (FCC)** used these words to explain why the commission was interested in regulating programming and content (Goodman & Gring, 2003; "Public Interest," 1929).

Another feature of the 1927 act was that all existing radio licenses became null and void 60 days after its passage. This forced all stations operating at the time to reapply for licenses, which allowed the FRC to assign frequencies to stations with the intent of minimizing interference and bringing some order to the chaos of the radio band. The result was that the powerful stations were treated well and given desirable frequencies, while the less powerful stations were given less desirable frequencies. Other stations, such as college stations, which had little power in a business or political sense, were simply forced off the air or bought out by commercial stations.

Competition for NBC

The financial success of NBC caused others to consider competing with the powerhouse networks. In 1927, one such group, the United Independent Broadcasters (UIB), met with limited network success, primarily because it was not well funded. In fact, AT&T would not lease interconnecting lines to UIB because of the fear of nonpayment.

Oddly enough, UIB was rescued by an unlikely corporate player, the Columbia Phonograph Company. Columbia had been in direct competition with another phonograph company, the Victor Phonograph Company, and the two ultimately played important roles in the development of the radio broadcast networks. Victor was about to merge with RCA (the parent company of NBC), a move that worried Columbia because of RCA's huge name recognition and business power. Also, Columbia feared that Victor might gain a tremendous edge by its association and use in the broadcasting business. Columbia decided to get into the broadcasting business by merging with UIB to form the Columbia Phonograph Broadcasting System (CPBS).

A cigar company executive, William S. Paley, was impressed with the results from advertising on the new network. And so in 1928, when CPBS encountered financial

Todd Storz and Gordon McLendon.

difficulties, Paley bought a controlling share of the network and became its president. Eventually, this company and its network became known as the **Columbia Broadcast System**, or **CBS.** Paley controlled CBS until 1983, becoming one of the most well known electronic media moguls in the United States.

In 1928, the nation had three nationally operating radio networks: NBC Red, NBC Blue, and CBS. Radio receivers continued to be highly desirable, and set sales continued to climb rapidly. Approximately 15 million American homes had radio receivers. Another important aspect of broadcasting also began in 1927. It was not a network innovation or a new form of programming. In fact, it was a manufacturing idea: putting a radio receiver in the dashboard of a car. Since many of the radio sets sold at this time were battery powered, putting receivers into automobiles (all cars had batteries) was a logical idea. This innovation began a love affair between car drivers and broadcast radio that exists to this day. The automobile provided the portability needed to help make radio an indispensable medium for the past 75 years.

Joining NBC and CBS, another network entered the picture in 1934, the Mutual Broadcasting System (MBS). It was a cooperative programming network but did not own any stations. Getting a later start than the big-two competitors, MBS never had a comparable audience size or advertising desirability.

A young William S. Paley, who would become a network media mogul.

Influences of Early Radio

The excitement generated by broadcasting lured many people to experiment with radio, both transmitting and receiving. Many hobbyists built their own radio receivers, and a number of them also dabbled in radio transmitting. Those who wanted to transmit messages did so with point-to-point communication on the frequencies set aside for amateur, or "ham," radio operators. The print media also embraced radio to a certain extent. For example, many newspapers added a section that dealt with radio schedules, discussions of programs, and even technical tips for better reception.

With radio, Americans were also exposed, for the first time, to the concept of free entertainment and information programming (once the initial price for the receiver was paid). Although newspapers were very inexpensive, radio appeared to be free and could be enjoyed in unlimited amounts by the audience. Moreover, it did not require literacy. Radio also encouraged people to stay home and listen to free programs, rather than go to vaudeville shows at their local theaters. "Talking" motion pictures, a product of the late 1920s, drew large audiences but did not seem to slow down radio's growth. The phonograph record industry was forced to cope with people who now could receive free music on the radio, rather than pay for expensive records that often were of low quality.

Another interesting influence of radio was its ability to allow people all over the country to actually hear the voices of politicians, celebrities, sports heroes, and even common people. Regional dialects softened somewhat, as the audience heard professional announcers read scripts over the air. These announcers usually gave correct pronunciations and eschewed regional dialects. Although this influence on language is difficult to measure, it is obvious that the early radio audience had a steady stream of sophisticated role models who could speak their language very well.

It is interesting to note that about this time (the 1920s), the number of daily newspapers in the United States began to decline. Although many factors likely brought about this change, one factor might have been the availability of broadcast news and other delivery systems. Regardless, the number of daily newspapers in the United States had been rising steadily for many years up until 1920 but then started a decline that continues today.

Which of the men who helped to create the radio industry insisted that he be addressed as General rather than Mister?

ATWATER KENT
RADIO

Calming down

Advertisement for Atwater Kent
Radio: 1927.

As the audience depended more and more on radio for entertainment and information, the stations and networks started to use news as an audience attention getter. Radio newscasts had begun in the 1920s, but NBC started a regular network nightly newscast with Lowell Thomas, a known reporter, on its Blue network in 1930. This signaled the beginning of a serious news effort by the radio industry and the networks.

This development was not lost on the newspapers, who had long been wary of radio as competition for news. This concern was translated into action in 1933, when the newspaper industry decided to force the radio stations and networks to limit their newscasts. Namely, the newspaper industry pressured the wire services to refuse radio station business. This incident was the first formal action taken by newspapers in what became known as the **newspaper/radio war.** The newspapers also started to refuse to print radio program schedules without charge. The radio industry retaliated by hiring freelance reporters to gather news.

Radio and newspapers settled the war by signing the **Biltmore agreement** (named after the hotel in New York where the agreement was signed). This agreement limited network radio to the following news programming:

1. two newscasts per day: one before 9:30 A.M. and one after 9:00 P.M. (to protect the morning and evening editions of newspapers)
2. commentary and so-called soft news, rather than hard news reporting
3. use of the Press-Radio Bureau, which would supply the networks and stations with news through subscriptions
4. no radio news-gathering operations
5. no sponsorship of news shows

Disney v. Sony

The type of action that the newspaper industry took against the radio industry in the 1930s has been seen periodically since then, as in the case of *Disney v. Sony* in 1976. At the time, Disney Studios was trying to prevent the copying of Disney movies and other products by individuals with home video cassette recorders, the earliest of which were made by Sony. Disney was unsuccessful in this action. As in the case of the Biltmore agreement, actions that have tried to stop new media technologies from developing have been mostly unsuccessful.

The Biltmore agreement didn't last long. Since the agreement was between the radio networks and the newspapers, independent and local stations, especially those in big cities, felt that they could continue gathering and reporting news. Moreover, newscasters, who had previously read the news in a direct way, became *commentators* and read the news in the context of commentary. Not even the wire associations upheld the restrictions of the agreement. Soon after it was signed, two wire associations (International News Service and United Press) decided to accept radio station business and tailored their news feeds for broadcast. Even though the Biltmore agreement was short lived and difficult to enforce, it is a classic example of efforts by an existing medium to slow the growth and competition of a newer medium.

After the failure of the Biltmore agreement, the radio industry became more active and more sophisticated in its news broadcasting. That sophistication was personified by newscasters like Edward R. Murrow, who, in the late 1930s and early 1940s, broadcast a live half-hour report for CBS on events occurring in Europe. Murrow began a tradition of high-quality news reporting on radio that lasted not only through World War II but continued on with reporters like Walter Cronkite and Dan Rather, who started in radio but became famous on television.

World War II

During the late 1930s, Americans, with the help of radio, were paying attention to the hostilities taking place in other parts of the world. To many, it seemed as if the world was gearing up for a huge and possibly cataclysmic war. The public's strong reaction to Orson Welles's *War of the Worlds* broadcast in 1938 underscored the facts that radio was a powerful disseminator of information and that people were on edge about security and the likelihood of war. (For more about this historic broadcast, see Chapter 13.)

After the Japanese attack on Pearl Harbor, on December 7, 1941, the networks interrupted their regular programming with an announcement about it. And the next day, President Franklin D. Roosevelt gave a speech to a huge national audience, reported to be 62 million people (Hilliard & Keith, 2001, p. 92). He described the attack as "a day that will live in infamy" in this, one of the most commonly heard speeches from that era.

> **ZOOM IN**   2.1
> Go to this website to hear a clip of this famous speech by President Roosevelt: **www.northwinds.net/bchris/home.html**. Go to the "War Years" link and click on "FDR."

Upon entering World War II, the U.S. government immediately took steps to support the overall war effort. Amateur radio transmitters were shut down in fear of information being sent to the enemy, and regular broadcasting at some West Coast stations was curtailed to prevent enemy aircraft from using the broadcast signal to locate American cities. All short-wave stations capable of sending a signal overseas were brought under government control, and manufacturers of radio parts and equipment were required to convert to manufacturing equipment that would directly aid the war effort.

During the war, the building of new radio stations stopped. Materials that had been used to construct stations were deemed as scare resources by the government and used directly to support the war effort. A small number of new stations did get on the air between 1942 and 1945, but the government curtailed most of the growth of the industry.

Despite the difficulty faced by Americans during these years, radio continued to be popular. It was something that people could enjoy without direct cost, and it also kept them aware of what was happening in the world. In addition, people needed the entertainment, and radio was there to provide it, drawing large and often devoted audiences.

It was this ability to draw a large audience, along with a tax break, that helped radio cash in during the war years. Fearing that some companies would gain huge profits from government contracts during World War II, lawmakers imposed a 90 percent excess-profit tax on American industry (Sterling & Kittross, 2002, p. 232). Basically, this meant that for every dollar of profit a company made, it had to give back 90 cents in the form of taxes. But there was a loophole in the tax law that allowed companies to get a bit more for their money. That is, they could use their profits to pay for advertising and be taxed at the rate that existed before the war, or about 10 percent. This became a huge incentive for companies to keep advertising, even during the hard times of the war. And of course, some of this advertising was done on the radio. Even when companies did not have products to sell, they kept advertising for the purpose of keeping their company name or product name in front of the audience.

Another factor also helped radio advertising sales. Even though advertisers often preferred to use the newspaper, at times, they could not. Again, because of the war effort, the paper used to make newspapers (newsprint) was needed by the government and the amount available for other purposes was restricted. This shortage caused newspapers to limit the size of each edition, regardless of the demand for advertising. As a result, newspapers reluctantly turned away advertisers, who then bought radio advertising instead.

Which of the original inventors of radio had trouble explaining how his inventions worked when testifying in court?

AM Radio

The domination of radio by the networks continued into the early 1950s, with the networks continuing to provide programs in the same style as they had since the 1930s. This all changed with the rise of television, and network radio programming had to adapt dramatically. Stations experimented with different styles of radio programming to stay economically viable. Entertainment programs gave way to news programs.

Some shows were actually broadcast on both radio and television at the same time, a practice known as **simulcasting**. When most of the American audience had easy access to a television set, however, this practice was terminated. If the show was good enough to hear, it was probably good enough to be seen, as well. Audiences eventually preferred the television versions, which made the radio versions unprofitable.

By 1960, radio network programming had become much like what it is today: a news service provided by a national news provider. The network presence at local stations was primarily news on the hour or half-hour. Late-breaking important stories were aired in headline form and then followed with more coverage in the scheduled newscast.

Most of what had made radio popular had changed. It was no longer the daytime companion and nighttime focus of people's attention. Radio was forced to figure out a way to keep an audience and pay its bills. It couldn't afford to spend money to hire writers and actors to create drama or comedy, especially since the networks were now doing that with television.

Radio stations began to have individual announcers take **air shifts** in blocks—for example, from 6:00 to 10:00 A.M. each morning—and play music, announce song titles and artists, and read weather or brief news reports. These announcers became known as **disk jockeys**, or **DJs**, because most of the time they were playing phonograph records, or *disks,* on the air.

Many stations, trying to differentiate themselves in a competitive market, selected a specific style of music and played it most of the time. The result was that stations specialized in, for example, country and western music, black-influenced music (known as rhythm and blues), classical music, popular music, and so on. With this, radio stations began to depend on the music industry for popular music. Information about record sales was distributed by trade publications, and radio programmers readily accepted the process of playing "what's hot" on their stations, knowing that at least part of the audience was not only familiar with the music but also liked it and would spend money to buy the record. This trend gave birth to the **Top 40** radio format, which used a small **playlist** of familiar and popular songs (see Chapter 6, Programming).

The relationship among stations, disc jockeys, and record companies was also significant in making music popular. If a disc jockey in a large market heard and liked a song that might be popular with the audience, it got played. The more plays it got on the radio, the more records were sold. The record companies noticed this close relationship between disc jockeys and hit songs, and it eventually led to problems. In 1959, the FCC began investigating charges that disc jockeys across the country were taking bribes in exchange for giving records airplay. Some disc jockeys were indeed guilty of selling their influence with the audience, which became known as the **payola** scandal.

A slightly related form of influence buying and selling also was exposed at about this time. Many radio performers (not just disc jockeys) were accused of selling their influence by giving on-air *plugs,* or free promotion or advertising for products or services. This practice became known as **plugola** and resulted in both congressional and FCC actions to prevent it from recurring.

In 1960, a few big shifts in network programming signaled the changes that would affect radio in the years to come. For instance, former radio network stations lost all of their network entertainment programming, which had brought audiences to them in the first place. Stations like KFAX in San Francisco adopted an all-news format, and KABC, an ABC-owned station in Los Angeles, adopted an all-talk format. Other interesting changes followed. WABC, an ABC-owned station in New York, was struggling and had very low ratings. It tried the Top 40 format that was becoming popular across the country, and within a year, ratings rose dramatically.

FM Radio

Up to this point, all of our discussion about radio has really referred to **AM radio,** or signals in the band from 535 KHz to 1,600 KHz. All stations that broadcast in this band use **amplitude modulation** (hence AM) in order to carry voice communication. This is a method of combining audio information with the basic carrier wave that is sent from the broadcast antenna to a receiving antenna. Amplitude modulation combines the audio with the carrier wave by varying the size or height of the wave (its amplitude).

This system was developed in the very early days of radio and had its problems. One was that AM was susceptible to the static caused by thunderstorms and electrical equipment, which created noise distortion on the receiving end. Another was that the fidelity (or sound reproduction) was limited, such that AM could not reproduce very high frequency sounds (such as the high notes from a violin or piccolo) or very low frequency sounds (such as the low notes from a bass drum or bass violin).

Edwin H. Armstrong, discussed earlier as the inventor of the superheterodyne radio receiver, sought to improve radio by eliminating the static and improving the fidelity. After experimenting for many years and applying for patents in 1930 (which

The Armstrong/Sarnoff Conflict

Edwin H. Armstrong's FM radio invention seemed like a natural for the radio networks: less static, better sound, and a receiver that picked the strongest signal on the frequency without interference. Despite those technological advancements, David Sarnoff, the head of RCA and a friend of Armstrong's, decided against supporting FM. Rather, he wanted to spend more time and energy on the development of television and to avoid having to pay Armstrong for his invention. Later, Sarnoff testified in court that "RCA and NBC have done more to develop FM than anybody in this country, including Armstrong" (Lewis, 1991, p. 317). Armstrong fought Sarnoff and his company for patent infringement, vowing to continue "until I'm dead or broke" (Lewis, 1991, p. 327).

This conflict began with a lawsuit by Armstrong against RCA and NBC in 1948 and continued through 1953. By then, Armstrong had run out of money to pay his lawyers, and the prospect of receiving damages from RCA in the near future (lawyers estimated it would take until 1961) seemed remote. On January 31, 1954, despondent over a dispute with his wife and the continuing battle with Sarnoff and RCA, Armstrong jumped to his death from his tenth-story bedroom window, "the last defiant act of the lone inventor and a lonely man" (Lewis, 1991, p. 327).

Edwin H. Armstrong, with a portable radio he designed.

were granted in 1933), Armstrong gave a public demonstration of his system, called **FM** or **frequency modulation**, in 1935 (Lessing, 1956). He explained how the frequency of each wave was modulated by the sound transmitted and then demonstrated the superior audio quality of the system.

Despite its providing better sound and no static, FM broadcasting started out slowly, faltered, and then got a new life beginning in the 1960s. One important discovery that Armstrong made was that frequency modulation required more bandwidth. Instead of the 10 KHz channel used by AM broadcasting, FM required 20 times more space for each channel, or 200 KHz. The government set aside the 42 to 50 MHz band for FM radio beginning January 1, 1941. By the end of 1941, there were about 40 FM stations on the air, but the service was barely commercial, as many of the stations were not fully powered and some were experimental. About 400,000 receivers were used by audiences at this time.

ZOOM IN   2.2

Go to the Companion Website for this text to learn about AM, FM, carrier waves, and radio bands: www.ablongman.com/medoffkaye1e.

During World War II, interest in FM waned and only a few new stations went on the air. The government decided that the original band reserved for FM radio (which later became the space for channel 1 in the VHF television band) was needed for government services. The FM band was therefore reassigned to 88 to 108 MHz in 1945, and FM radio broadcasting in the 42 to 50 MHz band ceased in 1948. As a result, many listeners owned FM radios that would no longer receive FM signals.

FM stations did not operate profitably for some time, and total FM revenues did not pass $1 million until 1948 (Sterling & Kitross, 2002, p. 295). In the 1950s, FM stations actually started going off the air for lack of financial support. This trend began to change in 1961, when the FCC authorized FM *stereo broadcasting*. When American youths started to notice the superior sound quality of FM and inexpensive receivers from Germany and Japan became readily available, the FM audience grew. At that same time, the FCC turned down a proposal for AM stereo, signalling the long, slow decline of AM and the rise of FM (Hilliard & Keith, 2001, p. 171).

FM grew steadily in the late 1960s and throughout the 1970s. High-fidelity stereo systems also became popular. The quality of FM stereo broadcasting, coupled with a programming change toward more popular music and the availability of FM radios in cars, helped FM make tremendous growth in audience popularity. That popularity didn't immediately translate into profitability for FM stations, however. Although revenues climbed from the early 1960s into the mid 1970s—from $10 million in 1962 to $308.6 million in 1975—more FM stations were losing money than making money (Sterling & Kittross, 2002, p. 428).

It took until the late 1970s/early 1980s before FM radio gained an equal footing with AM radio. In 1978, the FM audience surpassed the AM audience for the first time. By the late 1980s, the FM audience was larger than the AM audience, commanding almost 75 percent of the total national radio audience (Sterling & Kittross, 2002, p. 501). Almost all car and portable radios now had an easily tunable FM band, which made FM as easy to find and listen to as AM. In addition, the audience was now well aware of the superior sound quality of FM.

SEE IT NOW

In the 1990s, the radio industry continued to program to very specific audiences. This was especially true in large markets, where 30 or more stations vied for an audience. FM stations had mainly music formats, and AM stations migrated toward news, talk, and religion.

The Telecommunications Act of 1996

A big change in the radio industry came with the Telecommunications Act of 1996, which virtually lifted ownership restrictions in radio. A group could own as many stations as it wanted, as long as it didn't own too many in any one market.

Since 1996, stations have been bought and sold at a dizzying pace, with many small owners succumbing to the tremendous pressure and big money offered by large owners. For instance, in 2004, Clear Channel Communications owned 1,216 stations in 190 markets and Infinity Broadcasting owned 185 stations in 40 markets. As a result of this legislation, the radio industry has become more formulaic and more similar from market to market. Groups that own similar-format stations in different markets often use similar (and sometimes identical) music play lists and even DJs.

Technology has enhanced the similarity trend, as automation allows many tasks to be done on a small desktop PC. **Voice tracking**, which is the prerecording of DJ talk and announcements for use later at one or many stations, can be accomplished at the DJ's home with a personal computer. Some DJs have never even visited the markets in which their voices are broadcast on the radio. Thus, radio has lost some of its localism.

Other Delivery Systems

Although television has received a government mandate to change from analog broadcasting to digital broadcasting within the next few years, radio has been left as is to operate in the analog realm. Despite this somewhat benign governmental neglect, however, radio has begun to get pressure to upgrade to digital from several competing services.

Cable companies began to offer audio services in the late 1990s, grabbing the attention of many radio listeners. A satellite-distributed service, such as DMX from Liberty Media, offers up to 100 channels of continuous music 24 hour a day, 7 days a week, with no commercials and no DJs. This service is similar to other premium cable services—that is, subscribers pay about $10 per month extra for the service, which requires a special decoder. In some cases, the decoder's remote control has an LED that displays information not available from a radio station: the name of the song, the artist, the album, and the composer of the song. These services also offer several variations of particular kinds of music, such as a contemporary country channel and a classic country channel. Satellite television providers include similar music service channels for their subscribers.

By 2002, two companies—XM Satellite Radio and Sirius Satellite Radio—had begun delivering satellite digital radio directly to subscribers. Similar to cable service, satellite radio requires a special receiver and a subscription that costs $10 to $13 per month for about 100 channels. These services started out slowly but have grown rapidly as automobile manufacturers have offered receivers capable of satellite radio in new cars.

The Internet also provides numerous music service sites that use a programming concept first put forth by the cable and satellite services. As such, many channels are available at a single service site, representing just about every music format possible.

SEE IT LATER

In sum, competing services now supply much of what radio has supplied for the last 80 years. For instance, satellite radio continues to sign up subscribers. Music also can be heard over the Internet 24 hours a day, 7 days a week, with no annoying DJ chatter or commercial clutter. Nonlicensed radio stations on the Internet can mimic licensed radio stations without the technical and content restrictions imposed on broadcast stations by the FCC.

Many people argue that online radio cannot compete with broadcast radio because people expect radio to be portable. The issue of portability may be fading away, however, as wireless Internet connections are becoming more common in places like universities, hotels, restaurants, and some cities. Consider that a small computer with a wireless connection is very similar to a small portable radio but, of course, capable of doing a lot more than just delivering radio. Audience members can multitask; in addition to listening to a radio station or audio service on the Internet, they can also do e-mail, word process a paper or report, check on their stock performance, and read their favorite news service. Even the automobile, once the exclusive domain of broadcast radio, now offers other services with wireless capability.

Legislation has also had an ongoing effect on broadcast radio. As noted earlier, the consolidation of ownership has encouraged stations to save money by using voice tracking, which allows a few DJs to be heard on group-owned stations in many markets. Radio syndication has also contributed to radio's sameness across markets. The music playlists in many stations in different markets are identical. Local radio has become formulaic. With all these changes, radio has lost some of what has made it so popular over the years—its localism. A DJ heard in Kansas City might be the same one heard in San Diego, and the music might be identical, as well.

In the past few years, the FCC has been granting licenses to **low-power FM (LPFM)** stations in cities across the United States. These stations offer nonprofit organizations the opportunity to reach local audiences with just 100 watts of power; this is enough to reach listeners within a few miles of the station. Localism might be rejuvenated, at least somewhat, through stations like these.

Perhaps broadcast radio is going through the same situation that it did in the 1950s, when television took over its prime-time evening audience. Radio once again may have to reinvent itself to ensure its viability. The industry is taking a step toward the future by embarking upon digital broadcasting.

Radio Goes Digital

While broadcast television stations have been ordered to change over to digital, radio stations have been initiating that change on their own. Their goal is to switch to digital while keeping all existing radios from becoming obsolete (which is what happened when the FCC moved the FM band in 1945). With a system called **IBOC (in band, on channel)**, broadcasters can use their existing frequencies to broadcast in digital and analog at the same time. The digital signal will be of high quality, even on the AM band. In addition, audience members who are happy with analog can stay with analog.

ZOOM IN   2.3
Go to **www.ibiquity.com** to sample digital radio and learn about its technology and implementation. Ibiquity Digital is a company that's backed by radio industry leaders to develop digital broadcast radio.

IBOC also holds the promise of providing an additional revenue stream for local broadcasters. Because of the size of the bandwidth available to licensed broadcasters and the ability of digital broadcasting to make very efficient use of the band, additional signals may be available. In other words, a classic rock station on IBOC might be able to offer a classic 1970s station, a 1980s station, and a 1990s station, all within the same channel that now provides only one analog signal. The IBOC receiver will be capable of receiving and separating these signals so they will be easily tunable by the digital radio audience. There are other ancillary services being discussed and tested. For instance, breaking news, sports, weather, and traffic information can be delivered separately from the main audio program. The main audio program will also provide the ability to pause, store, fast forward, index, and replay audio programming.

Some international broadcasters, such as British Broadcasting and Voice of America, began digital radio broadcasting in 2003. However, they use a different standard than the one adopted by the United States ("Broadcasters Start Digital Radio Service," 2003).

The Role of Government

The FCC has long been interested in preserving localism in electronic media. Over the years, this has been reflected in its attitude toward local broadcast stations, which have been encouraged to serve their communities. Local broadcast television and radio stations enjoy a competitive advantage over satellite services because they provide the programming, news, and talk that people want to see and hear about their community.

So far, satellite television and radio have been national, although satellite television services have been required to provide local stations (at an extra cost to the subscriber). The FCC may decide to allow satellite services to provide local programming, commercials, and even news. If it does, it could change the revenue stream for all electronic media and have serious implications for local broadcasters. Namely, local broadcasters would be forced to compete for local advertising dollars with national satellite services and some siphoning off of local dollars would certainly occur. Thus, local broadcasters would have to fight even harder to keep their revenues from shrinking.

Summary

Communication modes have changed over the years in response to the human desire to go beyond face-to-face contact. Since the beginning of the twentieth century, humankind has developed the technology to reach people over long distances in a matter of seconds. First using the wired telegraph and telephone and then using radio telegraphy and telephony, people have been able to communicate both one to one and one to many. The ability to communicate one to many using radio signaled the beginning of electronic mass media.

Entrepreneurs and inventors like Guglielmo Marconi, Lee De Forest, Edwin H. Armstrong, Frank Conrad, and David Sarnoff propelled radio from an experimental system to an industry and storehouse of American culture. From its modest audience size in 1920 to its peak in 1950, radio was the mass medium of the people.

The U.S. government has played a role in the development of the radio industry by ensuring that control stayed in the hands of American companies, as evidenced by its seizure of all powerful radio transmitters during World War I. Rather than keep control after the war, the government released control, and since that time, the radio industry has been a commercial enterprise, guided by market factors more so than government intervention. At first, radio stations experienced numerous problems with technology, some of which stemmed from them all using the same frequency for broadcasting. The government corrected that problem by establishing separate frequencies for stations in the same market and region. The government also established the philosophy that the airwaves belong to the people and that broadcast stations must operate in the "public interest, convenience, and necessity."

Networks NBC Blue and Red and CBS controlled radio from the late 1920s through the 1940s. However, NBC was forced to sell off one of its networks, which eventually became ABC. These networks' programming innovations set the stage for many years of

Which of the inventors of radio climbed to the tops of tall buildings to have fun and to impress friends?

audience loyalty and appreciation. In fact, many of the program types developed during these years made the transition to television and continue to the present. Radio strongly influenced American society by providing free entertainment and information and by letting people hear the actual voices of celebrities and government officials. Radio also siphoned some of the interest away from other media, like newspapers and feature films.

AM radio lost its network entertainment programming and prominence in the minds of the audience when television was introduced after World War II. But AM radio reinvented itself by developing music formats hosted by disc jockeys. FM radio, which rebounded from a serious setback when the FCC changed its band location, gained dominance in musical programming after the introduction of stereo broadcasting in the 1960s. By the 1980s, the FM audience was larger than the AM audience. Once again, AM had to reinvent itself, which it did by concentrating programming more on talk, news, and religion instead of music.

The Telecommunications Act of 1996 triggered a dramatic increase in consolidation because it relaxed ownership rules, and this consolidation has led some industry watchers to criticize radio for losing its localism. New services like cable, satellite, and Internet audio have begun to challenge the radio industry. These services de-emphasize disc jockeys and play more music, but they cannot compete with traditional radio when it comes to providing local news and information using a technology that is portable and without direct cost to the audience.

Note

1. NBC networks Blue and Red—along with their lone network competitor, CBS—dominated broadcasting for the next 15 years, until the government ruled that one company could not own two networks. This rule eventually became known as the *duopoly rule*. NBC was forced to sell off the Blue network, which later became ABC. The buyer was Life Savers candy magnate Edwin J. Noble.

Edwin H. Armstrong.

Television

 SEE IT THEN

The Experimental Years
The Big Freeze
The Golden Age
Upheaval and Education
Increased Choice and Competition

 SEE IT NOW

More Network Challenges
Digital Television

SEE IT LATER

Industry Structure
Technological Changes

In this chapter, you'll learn about:

- The inventors and inventions that led to the development of broadcast television
- How television became the medium that took over for radio
- Technological innovations that are changing the industry
- Some of the forces that have changed both television programming and the television audience

While some experimenters and inventors worked with radio waves and the ability to send sounds across distances, others were more interested in transmitting live pictures. Experiments in television began in the 1880s, but commercial television broadcasting was not ready to begin business until the early 1940s. Then, U.S. involvement in World War II put any further development on hold, as resources were deemed essential for the war effort.

Television got off to a slow start again after the war, but the opportunities it offered were seen by many, including veterans returning from the war and AM broadcasters wishing to expand their businesses. The Federal Communications Commission (FCC) was flooded with requests for licenses and ordered a freeze on accepting applications for stations. Decisions made during the freeze led to the emergence of cable, UHF/VHF, and color television and to the solidification of the networks.

Television shaped U.S. history with its presentation of the Vietnam War and social unrest in the 1960s as well as the social awareness of the 1970s. In the 1980s, viewership splintered with the appearance of cable networks such as CNN, MTV, and HBO, creating a less homogeneous television landscape. While conglomeration may bring back some of that homogeneity, technology looms on the horizon that may put individual viewers in charge of what they watch and when.

SEE IT THEN

The Experimental Years

Early Innovations

Early thinking about how to send pictures using electricity was divided into two camps: the mechanical scanning camp and the electronic scanning camp. **Mechanical scanning** was a method that employed a spinning disc system that used one disc to record the visual image for sending and another one for viewing. Paul Nipkow developed a mechanical scanning system in 1884 in Germany. Other experimenters followed, including John Logie Baird from England. In 1926, Baird developed a workable system to send live television images. The British Broadcasting Corporation (BBC) adopted his system and began sending television broadcasts in 1936. By today's standards, the system then was primitive, using only 30 horizontal lines of information (i.e., 525 lines are now used for analog television).

Electrical scanning was developed by Westinghouse researcher Vladimir K. Zworykin. In 1923, he developed a working **electronic television** scanning system that did not require the mechanical spinning disks of previous systems and produced a better picture. His camera tube, the **iconoscope**, was a photo-sensitive device that converted light into electrical energy. Zworykin is also credited with developing a TV receiver using a similar device called a **kinescope**,[1] which was a **cathode ray tube** similar to the large glass picture tubes that can still be found in television sets today. When the Radio Corporation of America (RCA) took over the research activities of General Electric (GE) and Westinghouse, Zworykin's boss was David Sarnoff, who was interested in electronic television and building a television network.

In 1930, the leaders in television technology—RCA, GE, and Westinghouse—decided to join forces to develop electronic television. Zworykin worked with engineers from RCA and GE, and by 1936, an experimental television station, W2XF in New York, began transmitting television pictures. By 1939, a 441-line picture had been developed and the station was transmitting on a regular schedule.

In 1922, inventor Philo T. Farnsworth designed a system for electronic television, and in the early 1930s, he accumulated a number of television system patents that made improvements to the system developed by the RCA group. Although RCA almost always bought the companies that held patents in order to acquire their technology, Farnsworth managed to convince RCA to *license* his patents. This gave him control over his inventions and substantial earnings in royalties from RCA (Ritchie, 1994; Schatzkin, 2003; Schwartz, 2000).

Vladimir K. Zworykin with the television cathode ray tube he invented.

Philo T. Farnsworth with an early television receiver.

An early television set from the 1930s.

Development of the electronic television continued throughout the 1930s, and television made its debut at the New York World's Fair in 1939, accompanied by a speech by President Franklin D. Roosevelt. In 1941, the FCC, advised by the **National Television System Committee** (known as the **NTSC**), adopted a standard for operation. Namely, on July 1, 1941, commercial television broadcasting began by FCC approval. Compared to radio, television required much more space (i.e., bandwidth) on the electromagnetic spectrum. For instance, while AM radio requires 10 KHz and FM requires 200 KHz, television requires 6 MHz, or 30 times as much space as FM and 600 times as much as AM. At this point, the television picture had 525 horizontal lines of information, up from the 441-line picture first put forward by RCA.

ZOOM IN   3.1

• For animation and illustrations about over-the-air television signals, television scanning lines, and streamed video, go to the Companion Website for this book: www.ablongman.com/medoffkaye1e.

• To learn more about the origins of television, go to www.farnovision.com/media/origins.html.

World War II

Commercial television broadcasting was ready to begin business in 1941, but U.S. involvement in World War II essentially halted the development of the new technology. In early 1942, the federal government decided that manufacturing television stations and receivers used materials and equipment that were needed for the war effort, and so television broadcasting almost stopped entirely.

As World War II drew to a close, limitations on resources began to change and restrictions were gradually removed. Radio stations were again being built, and materials once deemed scarce were again available to industry. Television, which had been talked about by many but seen by few, was about to get a real test in the marketplace. Yet even after the war ended, it was almost two years before materials were available to resume television station construction and set manufacturing (Smith, Wright, & Ostroff, 1998).

This image of Felix the Cat was the result of early electrical scanning experiments.

Off to a Slow Start

The effort to bring television to homes across the country began again after the war. In 1945, there were only 6 television stations on the air, and three years later, on January 1, 1948, there were only 16 (Sterling & Kitross, 2002, p. 827). Many reasons explain the slow growth of television, but perhaps the most important was that building a television station required more technological knowledge than building a radio station. Television added pictures to the sounds, making the construction of a broadcast facility much more complicated. And with additional technological complications came additional expenses. Television required more space, more equipment, and more personnel. Also, investors were concerned that not many people owned television sets. The public support that television has enjoyed for the past 50 years simply did not exist until the end of the 1940s, when the U.S. economy began to boom. At the same time, television set prices began to decrease and television programming options began to increase, setting the stage for massive growth in the television industry.

By late 1948, there were still only 34 stations on the air, but numerous applications were being submitted to the FCC for new licenses. Many of these applications came from AM broadcasters who wanted to start television stations. Interestingly, newspaper companies were encouraged to join in the television industry by the FCC and government, for two reasons: Newspaper companies had experience in mass media, and they could afford to build new television stations. Several newspaper companies built powerful stations that are still on the air today. For instance, WGN (whose call letters are also an acronym for the World's Greatest Newspaper) in Chicago was built by the Tribune company, owner of the *Chicago Tribune* and other papers, and WTMJ was built by the owner of the *Milwaukee Journal*.

Similar to what happened in the early days of the feature film industry, the new television industry offered opportunities for many people. Veterans returning from the war, who had radar experience, often became television engineers. Others moved from camera operation to director to producer in a matter of months. The race was on to provide a lot of television programs, and the talent pool of people qualified to work in television was still quite small.

The Big Freeze

The increased number of new applications for television licenses after World War II hit the FCC quite hard. Although it was familiar with AM radio applications and had a set procedure for allocating stations to markets,

Advertisements for early television sets.

the FCC simply was not prepared to deal with licensing television stations. And so in 1948, the FCC essentially threw up its hands and yelled "Freeze!"

The FCC had an overall plan—specifically, to provide local television service to as many markets as possible, to give maximum television coverage nationwide, and to prevent interference. However, it was not prepared to enact the specifics of the plan. The freeze was meant to halt new station applications for a limited duration (say, six months), which would give the engineers at the FCC time to figure out the specifics of how to allocate frequencies and achieve the agency's goals. Instead, the plan took almost four years to develop to a point at which the FCC felt it could lift the freeze and accept new applications for stations.

The Birth of Cable

Since the freeze came at a time when many stations had been planned but not yet licensed, many cities didn't get television stations built before the order began. People in many markets expected television stations to go on air during this time, but they were simply left out. Interestingly but not surprisingly, this situation led to the birth of **community antenna television (CATV)**, the precursor to modern-day cable television.

In communities that did not have local stations, enterprising individuals found a way to provide television. (These were often appliance store owners, who wanted to sell television sets, and telephone line engineers.) They built systems that included a large, sensitive antenna that brought in television signals from distant stations. They accomplished this by placing the antenna on the top of a nearby hill or a location just outside town that could receive television signals and then running an antenna cable to a central location in town. From there, they ran a wire that carried the television signals to each individual home that was willing to pay a fee for the television reception. (See Chapter 4 on cable and other delivery systems.)

VHF and UHF

The freeze on licensing new television stations ended in April 1952, when the FCC issued *The Sixth Report and Order;* it had a master plan for the allotment of stations to channels and markets. Included was the opening of the **ultra-high frequency band**, or **UHF**, which allotted channels 14 through 83 to television stations across the United States. This seemed like a great idea, except for the fact that none of the television sets manufactured up to that time actually could receive those channels without using a converter. Until 1952, all stations were licensed to the **very-high frequency band**, or **VHF** channels 2 through 13.

Stations were licensed to the UHF band in many cities, but they often didn't have large audiences because existing sets couldn't receive the signal. Also, the nature of the ultra-high frequency of the channels above 13 made both transmission and reception more difficult. UHF signals do not travel as far as VHF signals; therefore, a UHF station requires quite a bit more power than a VHF station just to reach the same geographical area. Sets without UHF tuners required set-top converter boxes, but they were not as easy to operate as VHF tuners, which clicked into place on each channel. As a result, the set-top boxes required more adjusting. Also, in order to receive UHF signals, a different style of television antenna was required. Combination antennas were sold that received both VHF and UHF signals, but many households had more than one antenna. Sometimes, each antenna had to be aimed in a different direction to receive the various signals available in the market.

In 1962, Congress passed the All-Channel Receiver Act, amending the Communications Act of 1934. The 1962 act authorized the FCC to mandate that all television sets

The first color television was made by RCA in 1954 and sold for around $1,000—or about $6,000 in today's money.

manufactured in 1964 and beyond must be able to easily tune both VHF and UHF stations. Despite this legislation, the inequality between stations on the two bands remained. Until cable television became widespread and provided good-quality signals for all stations on the system, VHF signals dominated. In fact, a common saying about stations in the first decades of television broadcasting was that getting a VHF license was like getting a "license to print money." Although it was never quite that easy, VHF stations with network affiliations dominated the market and commanded the majority of television advertising dollars.

Color Television

In the 1950s, the public was just beginning to get used to the idea of black-and-white television, but the networks were experimenting with systems to bring full color to television broadcasting. In fact, one of the issues dealt with during the freeze was the changeover from black-and-white television broadcasting to color. This became an issue of concern for the FCC because it was looking carefully into the allotments of spectrum space for television, and at that time, color television appeared to require more channel space than black-and-white television.

Two competing systems emerged that both fit into the existing 6 MHz of channel space allotted for each television station. The CBS system used a mechanical color wheel that transmitted a color signal. This system was not compatible with existing black-and-white sets at the time; plus, it was somewhat difficult to maintain and also produced noise. RCA promoted a competing system that accomplished color television broadcasting electronically, rather than mechanically. After much wrangling and debate, the FCC supported the CBS color system in October 1950.

The public was not quite ready to buy the sets, had CBS or its manufacturing partners even produced them in the months following the decision. Very few programs had been prepared for color broadcasting, and very few audience members could have afforded color television sets. As the United States turned its attention to the Korean War in 1951, the issue of color television faded in importance.

At the end of 1953, the FCC reversed itself and selected the electronic color system developed by RCA. This was decided in part because CBS lacked the conviction to continue its push for color and the NTSC accepted the RCA version. No doubt, David Sarnoff, head of RCA, also campaigned for acceptance of his company's system. The RCA system was improved from the original and is still used by broadcasters in the United States today.

Although other better-performing systems have been adopted worldwide, the NTSC (RCA) system has remained intact in the United States and will continue until it is replaced in 2006 by digital television. The 525-line system has been criticized repeatedly over the years, not only for its lower resolution as compared to other systems but also because engineers have often found it unreliable. The NTSC acronym has sometimes been explained to stand for "Never Twice the Same Color."

Despite adoption of the RCA color system, there was not a mad rush either to manufacture color sets or to broadcast color programs. Since almost all television cameras produced at the time were black and white, very few programs were produced for broadcasting in color. Also, people were just beginning to buy black-and-white sets, which

ZOOM IN   3.2
Go to the Companion Website for this text, www.ablongman.com/medoffkaye1e, for information and animation of black-and-white versus color and analog versus digital signals.

were very expensive at the time. In sum, the situation was similar to the one now, with the proposed switch from analog to digital television broadcasting. Digital TV sets are selling slowly because they are expensive and few digital programs are available.

Domination of the Networks

As had been the case in radio during the 1930s and 1940s—radio's Golden Age—the networks dominated television from its inception. Interestingly enough, the financial power that the networks had accumulated from radio was used to bankroll the new medium of television. Stations with network affiliations did well, while independent stations often struggled for audiences, programming, and money.

The freeze helped solidify the networks. During the four freeze years, stations scrambled to affiliate with the two powerful networks, CBS and NBC. Thus, two years after the freeze ended, CBS and NBC had more than three-quarters of all stations that were affiliates (Sterling & Kittross, 2002, p. 636). ABC, which was formed after NBC divested its Blue network in 1943, was always a distant third in number of stations and audience size. ABC was so financially strapped that in 1951, it chose to merge with United Paramount Theaters to receive a cash infusion and stay in business. A fourth network, the Du Mont network, had many affiliates in medium- and smaller-sized markets, but it experienced problems similar to ABC with audience size and ceased operation in 1955.

Relationships with Affiliates

Beginning in the early days of radio, the networks exerted quite a bit of control over the affiliates. The reason behind this was simple: The networks provided the high-quality entertainment that made the local stations both popular and sophisticated. Big-name stars from Hollywood and New York could be heard on local stations in small towns across the country. Without the big-name stars and high-quality programs, a local station was nothing special—often a so-called Mom and Pop operation owned by a group of small businesspeople. The networks' ability to bring stars and desirable programs to the affiliates continued into the television era.

Television programming has always been expensive to produce. In the early days, the networks, using the money they had banked during the Golden Age of radio, was able to produce enough programming to allow local stations to provide some news, public affairs, children's programs, and sports. Drama, situation-comedy, and even variety shows were too expensive for most local stations, however. Given their experience with producing these types of programs, the networks continued doing so into the television era that began after World War II.

Independent stations were forced either to produce shows on their own or to seek programming material from independent producers or syndicators. In the early 1950s, not much quality programming was available from these sources. This made affiliation with a television network very attractive, both financially and operationally. It was easier to get programs from the network than to produce them at the station or to get them from other sources. More important, network programs were usually better than locally produced or independently produced programs.

These harsh facts of life in the television industry meant that network affiliation was highly valued. The networks had their pick of stations in a given market and were in a very strong bargaining position with their affiliates. In other words, the networks could often dictate financial terms and the availability of airtime to the local stations. Another result was that most television markets that had three stations or less had no independent stations. The top three stations in a market affiliated with CBS, NBC, and ABC. In most cases, the independent stations were newcomers to a market or broadcast on a less desirable UHF channel.

In what year did Saturday morning children's television programming begin?

The networks also had quite a bit of freedom from regulation. While local stations were regulated directly by the FCC, the networks were only regulated through the stations they owned. Very little legislation and regulation hampered the networks directly.

The affiliations between local stations and networks were renewable every year. However, from the post–World War II years until recently, an affiliation with a network usually lasted for many years. Often, the relationship between a network and an affiliate began in the very early days of the station's existence and remained unchanged. That relationship had several components. The local station provided its airtime (known as **clearance**) and its audiences to the network, and the network provided a dependable schedule of high-quality shows to the local affiliate. In addition, the affiliate was paid for its airtime. This practice, known as **station compensation**, was based on the size and the demographic makeup of the audience delivered by the station to the network and its advertisers.

In the early days of television, NBC and CBS both had money, strong VHF affiliates, and an inventory of radio programs that were set to make the transition from radio to television. Besides the shows themselves, the networks also enjoyed the relationship between the shows and their advertisers. The shows that made the change from radio to television often brought their sponsors along. And for an established show with a loyal following, this created an instant audience of loyal television viewers. Getting high-quality programs was especially important to local affiliated stations because independent stations had to produce their own programs. Not only was production expensive, but it was also technologically challenging and often resulted in a product that was lower in quality and appeal than the networks' offerings.

If there was a problem with network programming in the early days of television, it was that television was really radio with pictures. Many of the same programs, with the same stars, switched from radio to television. And while this transition was comfortable for the audience, it didn't encourage much experimentation or the development of new program types and styles. Despite this, the years after World War II were the Golden Age of television, when audiences and advertisers flocked to the tube.

The Golden Age

In the 1950s, television was severely restricted by technological factors. Cameras were large and heavy, and strong lighting (which generated quite a bit of heat as well as light) was required to get a good video image. Portable video cameras did not exist and neither did video tape (until after 1956). Although about one-quarter of the prime-time programs were recorded on film, most shows had to be produced live.

Going Live

Most programs at that time were produced in a studio. For instance, news shows were mostly just a newscaster reading the news, with an occasional piece of film accompanying the story. Programs like talk shows, game shows, and music and variety shows were also relatively easy to produce. The look of television then was simple and straightforward. There were no fancy special effects.

Even so, live shows often had an edge to them. Viewers became accustomed to the ever-present possibility that things could go wrong. Actors forgot their lines, doors would not open, lights would not work, and a host of other things that could go wrong sometimes did. Video tape was not invented until 1956, and even then, it was very expensive, prohibiting all but the largest stations and networks from using it.

Kinescopes (fyi)

The method used to preserve live television shows and show them in different time zones was referred to as *kinescope recording*. Developed by Du Mont, NBC, and Kodak, this was a primitive method of storing visual images by aiming a film camera at a television monitor showing the program to be recorded. Kinescopes (as they have been referred to over the years) were not good quality and required time for developing and shipping to stations. After video tape became available in 1956, kinescopes ceased to be a viable medium for storing video programs. Now they are considered rare and are collector's items.

ZOOM IN   3.3

For more about kinescopes, go to **www.museum.tv/archives/etv/K/htmlK/kinescope/kinescope.htm** and **www.ablongman.com/medoffkaye1e**, the Companion Website for this text.

Theatrical Influences

From 1948 to 1957, the networks began looking for ways to get people to buy their first television sets. Most programming came from New York City, the location of the networks' headquarters and television studios. Programming was thus influenced by Broadway.

Some of the programming during this period was created by people who worked in the theater and had an interest in the new television medium. Original television plays (called *anthologies*) were aired, often written by big-name theatrical writers and sometimes performed by big-name actors. Programs like *Kraft Theater* and *Studio One* featured live, high-quality dramas that attracted educated viewers who were likely to buy expensive TV sets.

Interest in this first-rate work was high at first, but it diminished after the composition of the audience changed from highly educated to less educated people. Also, audience taste began to favor programs that were shot on location and had more action and adventure than plays. In addition, advertisers didn't care for the some of the serious dramatic topics shown on the anthologies.

Blacklisting and Broadcasting

After World War II, the U.S. government and society in general became very aware of the growing power and nuclear capabilites of the Soviet Union. In addition, Americans feared that communism was spreading in other parts of the world.

The general attitude toward communism was not just that it was different than the American system but that it was a political ideology that would be used to take over the world. Politicians seized on these fears and used them for political gain. In the early 1950s, a small group of former Federal Bureau of Investigation (FBI) agents published a newsletter called *Counterattack*. Its purpose was to encourage Americans to identify and even shun people who demonstrated sympathy or ideological agreement with communism. Another publication, *Red Channels: The Report of Communist Influence in Radio and Television,* described the communist influence in broadcasting and named 151 people in the industry who supposedly had communist ties. The names of these people were put on a **blacklist**, and they were essentially no longer permitted to work in broadcasting or related industries. *Red Channels* was published just as North Korea, a communist country, invaded South Korea. The Unites States got involved in the conflict, and hence the nation's role in stopping communism began, as American troops were sent to fight in a foreign land.

The Korean War, which lasted until 1953, reinforced many Americans' feelings that communism had to be stopped, and the idea that communism had infiltrated broadcasting triggered activities to stop it. While no individual's association with communist activities was ever proven, the mere listing of a person's name in *Red Channels* prevented him or her from continuing a career in

Advertisement for 1958 Philco Predicta.

broadcasting. The networks and advertising agencies even employed individuals to check the backgrounds of people working in the industry. If a person's name showed up in any list of communist sympathizers, he or she could not be hired to work for the network, the advertising agency, or any project or program produced by either. New employees were expected to take a loyalty oath before working. People who were suspected of communist activities were expected to confess and name their communist associates.

The most prominent of the politicians who used Americans' fear of communism to strengthen his own political power was a U.S. Senator from Wisconsin, Joseph McCarthy. He used televised congressional hearings about communism in the U.S. Army to further his notoriety. Eventually, McCarthy's tactics caught up with him. He was challenged by Edward R. Murrow on the *See It Now* show that aired on March 9, 1954. In the show, excerpts of speeches given by McCarthy were replayed to uncover his inconsistencies. In the end, McCarthy was shown to be a bully who ignored fact and used innuendo to level accusations.

> ### ZOOM IN   3.4
> • Learn more about blacklisting by going to www.museum.tv/archives/etv/B/htmlB/blacklisting/blacklisting.htm.
> • The paranoia about blacklisting even led the FBI to investigate school teachers and college professors. To learn more about this, go to www.lexisnexis.com/academic/2upa/Afbi/McCarthyBlacklisting.asp.

The *Red scare,* as it was known, created a very bad atmosphere for broadcasting and its employees. The cloud of blacklisting continued until 1962, when radio comedian John Henry Faulk, who had been blacklisted in 1956, won a multimillion-dollar lawsuit against AWARE, a group that had named him as a communist sympathizer. The effect of the lawsuit was that the blacklisting practices went from upfront and public to secretive and private. The *blacklist* became a *graylist,* which was used in broadcasting to identify people who might have subversive ideas, especially those who embraced communism. The practice of graylisting lasted into the 1960s (Faulk, 1964; Foley, 1979; Vaughn, 1972).

Upheaval and Education

The "Vast Wasteland"

In 1961, recently appointed FCC Chairman Newton Minow stated at the National Association of Broadcasters convention that television programming was a "vast wasteland." Critics have latched onto that remark as accurately depicting the quality of the programming offered by most television stations—at that time and even since that time.

While few would argue that television has traditionally offered many hours of intellectually light programs, it has and still does serve a function beyond pure entertainment. For example, television allowed Americans to witness history during the tumultuous decade of the 1960s. This journalistic function both solidified the importance of television in American society and gave it real credibility as a provider of valuable information.

The Tumultuous 1960s

Some of the events covered by television during the 1960s included the presidential debates between candidates John F. Kennedy and Richard M. Nixon; the 1962 Cuban missile crisis; the 1963 assassination of President John F. Kennedy and the subsequent killing of his accused assassin, Lee Harvey Oswald; the 1968 assassinations of Martin Luther King, Jr., and Robert Kennedy; and man's first walk on the moon in 1969. In addition, continuing coverage of the escalating war in Vietnam, domestic unrest regarding racial issues, and violent demonstrations during the 1968 Democratic convention in Chicago allowed the public to view historical events in an upclose and personal way never before possible.

The coverage of these events and the debate surrounding them led American society into a difficult time, one in which people responded to what they saw. Americans were deeply affected by the events and issues presented on television—for example, realistic footage of rioting in the streets and the horrors of war. In addition, the proliferation of violent action shows on television led many to wonder if the media were somehow encouraging people to behave in violent ways.

The U.S. government responded to the violence on television and in society in 1968 by creating a research commission, the Commission on the Causes and Effects of Violence. In 1969, the Senate asked the U.S. Surgeon General to investigate the relationship between television and violent behavior. The results, published in early 1972, stated that violence on television can lead some individuals to violent behavior. Although the findings fell short of pointing to television as the *cause* of increased violence in society, it fueled the efforts of action groups like the **Action for Children's Television (ACT)**, which sought to focus congressional attention on the content of television and its effect on children.

Educational Television Goes Public

During the television freeze that followed World War II, the FCC was lobbied both by commercial broadcasters and the **Joint Committee on Educational Television (JCET)** regarding noncommercial television stations. The commercial broadcasters tried to prevent the FCC from reserving television channels for noncommercial television stations, while the JCET lobbied for noncommercial television use. The result was that the FCC reserved 242 channels (80 VHF and 162 UHF) for noncommercial use at the end of the freeze. Since then, the FCC has increased the number of channels dedicated for this use across the country to a total of 600.

In 1959, noncommercial television producers formed a network called **National Educational Television (NET)** to operate as a cooperative, sharing venture among stations by sending prerecorded programs by mail. After one station aired a program, it sent it to the next station, and so on. This inexpensive and low-tech network, which became known as a "bicycle network," didn't allow stations in different locations to air the same program at the same time.

In 1967, the **Carnegie Commission on Educational Television (CET)**—a group comprised of leaders in politics, corporations, the arts, and education—published a report about noncommercial television that recommended that the government establish a *corporation for public television*. Until that point, noncommercial television had been strongly associated with educational television, such as lecture programs. The CET wanted to change the direction of noncommercial television so as to provide a broader cultural view.

The eventual result of the report and discussion that followed was the Public Broadcasting Act of 1967. The term *broadcasting* was used instead of *television* because Congress decided to include radio as well as television in the legislation. The act provided that a corporation would be set up, with the board of directors appointed by the President of the United States, and that support would come from Congress. Having a corporation oversee public television was intended to provide some distance between the government and the noncommercial network.

The corporation that was formed in 1968, the **Corporation for Public Broadcasting (CPB)**, was meant to support both the producers who created programs and the stations that aired them. However, CPB was not allowed to own or operate any stations. Rather, the **Public Broadcasting Service (PBS)**, the television network arm of CPB, would operate the network that connected the participating stations. PBS went on the air in 1969 and began distributing programming to member stations five nights a week, including a children's show called *Sesame Street*.

How many TV sets were in American homes in 1931?

PBS, like CPB, is a private, nonprofit corporation whose members are public television stations. Its mission has been direct involvement in program acquisition, distribution, and promotion for its stations. Although PBS doesn't produce programs, it does support programs produced by PBS stations and helps acquire programs from independent producers around the world. PBS has also been involved in developing engineering and technology and in marketing video products (e.g., video tapes of programs) to the public. In addition, PBS administers the PBS Adult Learning Service, which provides televised college courses for credit to almost 500,000 students each year.

PBS is unlike the commercial networks because it doesn't sell advertising. Instead, PBS gets its funding from a variety of national, regional, and local sources. Audience members provide almost 25 percent of the funding through direct donations. State governments provide about 18 percent, and CPB (along with federal grants and contracts) adds about 16 percent. Businesses add another 16 percent, state universities and colleges add over 6 percent, and foundations provide an additional 5 percent. Because it does not get 100 percent of its funding from ratings-conscious advertisers, like the commercial networks do, the programming philosophy of PBS is more oriented to providing programs of cultural and educational interest.

Because the president appoints the leaders of CPB, it sometimes gets caught up in politics. When Richard Nixon was president, he vetoed a funding bill for CPB because he didn't like the fact that it allowed PBS to air information programs that showed his administration in an unfavorable light. Nixon's action resulted in the resignation of some CPB officials, who were replaced by people who favored Nixon's view of the role of CPB and PBS. Although this event was unusual in the history of CPB, it shows that public television is influenced by the presidential administration in power (Sterling & Kitross, 2002, p. 426).

Increased Choice and Competition

The television broadcast industry was affected by huge changes that began in the 1970s. Video cassette recorders (VCRs) began to be used in industry and in homes. Audiences learned to have more control over television through **time shifting**, or recording a program and viewing it later.[3]

Satellite distribution of television programming was tried by new services like **Home Box Office (HBO)** with great success. In fact, HBO ushered in a new era—that of the distribution of programming via satellite—which led to the growth of the cable industry and the concept of audiences paying for television programming from sources other than broadcast stations and networks. (See more about HBO in Chapter 4, Cable, Satellite, and Other Distribution Systems.) National cable channels began to appear that resembled broadcast networks but did not require licensing by the FCC. The big-three networks were beginning to see some real competition for audience time, but their audience sizes and revenues continued to climb.

Government Regulation

The FCC enacted some new rules in the 1970s that encouraged competition in the television business. The first was the **prime-time access rule (PTAR)**, which prevented network affiliates in the top 50 markets from programming more than three hours of network shows in prime time (i.e., 7:00 P.M. to 11:00 P.M. Eastern and Pacific; 6:00 P.M. to 10:00 P.M. Central and Mountain). The FCC's goal was to encourage more local programming at television stations. Unfortunately, most of the stations affected by the rule resorted to finding inexpensive programming, rather than producing their own. The result was more game shows and other syndicated fare.

Another FCC rule prevented the networks from acquiring financial interest and control or syndication rights over independently produced programs that aired on the networks. Known as the **fin/syn rule**, it allowed both independent producers and syndicators to reap bigger financial rewards from successful television programs.

A third rule, the **duopoly rule**, prohibited a company that owned a television station or AM or FM radio station in a market from acquiring another station in that market. In other words, the owners of a TV station could not buy another TV station in the same market. The FCC obviously feared that multiple-station ownership in a given market could lead to a broadcast monopoly.

A fourth rule was an attempt put forward by the NAB to reduce the amount of sex and violence on television that would be seen by children. Known as the **family hour**, it attempted to restrict sex and violence on television before 9:00 P.M. (8:00 P.M. Central). The rule was strongly opposed by many creative people in the industry, who felt that it restricted creativity and the right of free speech. In other words, many people didn't like the NAB's attempt to dictate program content to the industry. Others were opposed to the idea because they suspected that the NAB was bowing to pressure from the FCC.

These four restrictions on television remained in place for some time, but all ultimately were abolished. The FCC's willingness to deregulate, which began in the late 1970s, overcame its need to restrict broadcast television—at least in the areas just mentioned.

Social Awareness Programming

The 1970s also saw a new type of situation-comedy program, or sitcom, that included a social consciousness. Shows like *All in the Family, Maude,* and *The Jeffersons* encouraged the audience to think about social issues such as the Vietnam War, abortion, and racism by examining them within a humorous context. The critical and financial success of these shows kept these issues in front of the public and encouraged other producers to include socially relevant topics in entertainment television programs. In addition, audiences and social pressure groups took action to persuade electronic media to stop stereotyping minorities and to include more of these individuals in the media workforce, management, and ownership structure.

In the 1970s, cities all over the country were being wired for cable television. Satellite-to-home television also was a reality, although it was most popular in sparsely populated areas, where cable wasn't available and homeowners had the space and money for a large receiving dish. Yet despite these developments, the major networks did very little to change what they presented to the audience. Network schedules revealed little innovation. Program formats that had been successful for many years in both radio and then television remained in place during the 1970s. After all, broadcast television provided free entertainment to anyone who could afford a television set.

Unlike the early days of television—when television sets were expensive and purchased only by upscale, educated people—television sets became very affordable in the 1970s. Low-priced television sets were a result of manufacturers enjoying the economy of scale: The more sets that were produced, the cheaper it was to manufacture each set. Another factor was that foreign companies, especially those from Japan (Sony, Panasonic, and Toshiba), were producing low-cost, high-quality color television sets and selling them in the United States.

Regardless, the size of the audience grew, and despite losing its strong share dominance of the audience, the audience for the television networks grew. As a result, network advertising revenues grew, as well.

The Networks Lose Ground

The networks maintained a powerful position in their dealings with affiliates from the early days of television up to the 1980s. The three major networks enjoyed 90 percent of the viewing audience at the beginning of the 1980s, but during later years, the viewing audience had a shift in behavior. Instead of relying on the broadcast networks for the television-viewing fare, the audience began to spend more and more time with *cable* channels. National cable channels like CNN, MTV, and ESPN and pay channels like HBO and Showtime gained larger shares of the audience, as most of the country's big cities became wired for cable television. The introduction of the FOX network gave viewers yet another broadcast choice. Rentals of VCR videos further eroded the network-viewing audience.

As viewers' options proliferated, they spent less and less time with the big-three broadcast networks. During the 1980s, the networks combined share of the prime-time audience shrank by about one-third, going from almost 90 percent to 60 percent (Bellamy & Walker, 1996).

Deregulation Revisited

The broadcast deregulation trend that began in the late 1970s continued through-out the 1980s. Some have even said that the *de*-regulation of the 1970s became the *un*-regulation of the 1980s. The results were less public service programs, no limit on the number of commercials per hour, a much easier license renewal process, no trafficking restrictions (i.e., an owner had to hold a broadcast station at least three years before it could be sold), and less recordkeeping. In 1984, the FCC upped ownership limits from the *rule of sevens* (which allowed owning only 7 stations in any service, AM, FM, or TV) to 12 stations in either radio service and up to 25 percent of the total television house-holds nationwide. In 1992, the limits were raised again, allowing up to 40 radio stations per owner and some relaxation of the duopoly rules.

Electronic News Gathering

Another technological development of the 1980s was the miniaturization of the components needed to produce broadcast-quality video. As portable video cameras became common at networks and television stations across the United States, news gathering and reporting changed.

In earlier days, news was shot on film and then developed and edited, preventing stories from being ready for the 6:00 P.M. newscast. Anchors would report a breaking story and then give the "Film at eleven" promise. Beginning in the late 1970s and becoming widespread in the 1980s, battery-powered portable video cameras, easy video-editing procedures, and lower-priced editing systems made the production of a news story shot in the field easily available for earlier broadcasts. On a late-breaking story, the anchor could now say, "We will have that video for you later in this program."

Gathering news video in the field became known as **ENG**, for **electronic news gathering**, which noted the difference between shooting film for news and shooting video. With ENG, broadcast news changed in several ways; namely, video was cheaper and easier to produce. The Cable News Network (CNN) started operation and competed directly with the broadcast networks for the news audience because news stories could be easily and quickly produced. In addition, the use of satellites for news gathering was initiated, which allowed a news crew in a satellite news truck with uplink capability to shoot video from just about anywhere and transmit it to the station via satellite.

The Networks Regroup

Broadcasting revenues, which had for decades been on the rise, started to level off toward the end of the 1980s. One of the results of this decline in revenues was a change in ownership at the network level. In 1985, GE bought RCA, the parent company of NBC, and Capital Cities Communications, a broadcast group, bought ABC. And in 1986, for the first time since the demise of the Du Mont network in 1955, television had a fourth commercial network, the FOX television network. FOX was started by Rupert Murdoch, who owned News Corporation, and it was named after the film studio Twentieth Century Fox, also owned by Murdoch's company. The network slowly built a prime-time schedule, despite losing large sums of money in the early years. In 1988, FOX lost $80 million (Sterling & Kittross, 2002, p. 475). It took another five years until FOX began scheduling prime-time programming seven nights per week.

Since broadcast network revenues were declining and despite the competition from cable, satellite, and even a new network (FOX), many executives of the big-three networks decided that their strategies were working fine and didn't require overhauling. New ideas clashed with old, and the direction of the television industry became a source of tension. Generally, the big-three networks managed to change very little with the times, leading some industry critics to refer to them as the "three blind mice" (Auletta, 1991).

SEE IT NOW

The 1990s brought many changes to television. During this decade, the *Internet* became a household word and promised to bring dramatic changes to the media landscape. Moreover, new networks appeared, cable channels proliferated, and direct broadcast satellite became economically viable.

More Network Challenges

CNN

The 1991 Gulf War gave TV news operations the opportunity to use satellite technology to deliver quality news reporting from half a world away. The big winner with audiences was CNN, with its 24-hours-per-day coverage. The broadcast networks could not afford this extensive coverage because they could not **preempt** their advertiser-supported entertainment programs (i.e., show their own programs instead). Also, the networks didn't have the infrastructure of news bureaus and reporters in the field. CNN did have that structure, and as a result, it became an important source for breaking international news. CNN's reputation as a premier source for news was solidified.

Angry Affiliates

As a result of having smaller audiences, the networks had less power over the advertising market and their own affiliates. Angered over having less advertising slots available in prime time, the affiliates continued to preempt network programs and instead aired programs they produced or obtained. Some stations believed that the network compensation they were receiving for their airtime was not enough. Other stations didn't want to sign long-term agreements with the networks, preferring to keep the network affiliation option flexible.

New Networks

By the time FOX finally had filled its prime-time schedule, two other groups had also started new networks. The **WB Television Network** (owned by Warner Brothers, a film studio) and the **United Paramount Network**, or **UPN** (owned by the United Paramount film studio) began their prime-time television programming in 1995. These networks took on affiliates that had formerly been independent stations and were usually smaller stations with smaller audiences.

Neither of these two networks had a noticeable influence on the big-three networks' viewership. The WB and UPN programmed fewer hours per week and had significantly smaller audiences than ABC, CBS, and NBC. Yet despite the weak performance of the two new entries, a third new network was started by television group owner Bud Paxson. **PAX** attempted to counterprogram to its competition by offering family-friendly programming and avoiding shows heavy in violence. Although the network still exists, it offers little direct competition to the other six networks.

In some cases, local stations changed network affiliations. Ownership changes among stations in groups triggered some big switches in network affiliations in the early 1990s. As a result of a television group changing hands, some stations in the group switched affiliations from CBS to FOX. (See Chapter 9, Business and Ownership.)

Satellite Television

In the mid 1990s, **direct broadcast satellites (DBS)** brought another television delivery system to consumers. Using a small dish, rather than the large one used since the 1970s, consumers could enjoy many high-quality channels for about the same price as cable. Two companies now compete for subscribers nationally: the DISH Network and DirecTV. (See Chapter 4 for more about satellite delivery.)

New Regulations

Broadcasting changed significantly with the passage of the Telecommunications Act of 1996. Namely, the policy on owning television stations went from a 25 percent limit on the size of the national audience that one television group could reach to a 35 percent limit of the national audience. After the act was passed, large television groups became even larger by buying more stations.[4]

Digital Television

Digital television, or DTV, allows transmission of television programs in a wide-screen, high-resolution format known as **high-definition television (HDTV)**. It also allows transmission in **standard definition (SDTV)**, similar to an existing television picture, but with better color reproduction and less interference. HDTV is one type of SDTV. While the current analog picture has 480 lines of resolution, the HDTV picture can have up to 1,080 lines, or more than twice as much picture information. In addition, the HDTV picture has a wider *aspect ratio* (i.e., the relationship between screen width and height), yielding a 16:9 picture (16 units wide, 9 units high) that more closely resembles a wide-screen movie picture and more closely reproduces how our eyes see than the 4:3 picture of analog television.

The FCC has decreed that all television stations will broadcast in digital using the ATSC A/53 standard by the year 2006 (FCC, 1998). Not only has this FCC-mandated technological change signaled the end of one era and the beginning of another, but it has also forced many stations to make large investments in new digital equipment. This switch to digital has not offered immediate rewards, as stations don't have an immediate way to generate any more income than they did with analog-only broadcasting.

Audiences have not embraced the new digital broadcast technology, either. A digital set costs many times more than an analog set, and the digital signal, delivered by broadcast only, must be received with some type of broadcast-receiving antenna. Since over three-quarters of the audience use either cable or satellite to deliver television programs, knowledge of and interest in these antennas has been low. The rush to purchase expensive digital television sets is *not* on.

Regardless of the mandate, television stations will have the capability of transmitting multiple programs in SDTV or, in some cases, two HDTV programs. Audio quality for both HDTV and SDTV will be similar to the quality of a CD and will include up to five channels of sound, an improvement over analog transmission. Digital data services can also be transmitted via digital transmission, allowing stations to send news, program schedules, and product information to the audience at the same time as the television program.

Analog versus Digital

Duplicating an analog signal is like pouring water from one jar to another. After you finish pouring, the new jar will be almost full and a few drops will be left in the old jar. When you duplicate in analog, the entire signal is not duplicated. Some gets lost in transit.

Duplicating a digital signal is like pouring marbles from one jar to another. In this case, the new jar will be full of marbles and the other jar will be completely empty. Digital transfer allows the entire sampled signal to be duplicated, and the copies are identical to the original. Although some say that the process of digital sampling misses some of the original (like the content represented by the spaces between the marbles), the process is very accurate.

ZOOM IN   3.5

- The Advanced Television Systems Committee (ATSC) is an international, nonprofit organization that helps to develop voluntary standards for digital television. More information about this group is available at **www.atsc.org**.

- For more information about digital television, go to the Companion Website for this text: **www.ablongman.com/medoffkaye1e**. In particular, see the animation that explains digital television transmission, resolution, pixels, and aspect ratio.

- Other sources include the FCC site (**www.fcc.gov/dtv**) and the PBS site (**www.pbs.org/opb/crashcourse**).

Analog television sets will not be able to receive digital signals. Instead, these older sets will have to have converter boxes that can receive digital signals and translate them into analog signals. Digital sets will be able to receive analog signals, however.

SEE IT LATER

Industry Structure

Since the Telecommunications Act of 1996 was signed into law, the electronic media landscape has changed noticeably. Fewer and fewer owners are controlling more and more broadcast stations. Ownership rules are being relaxed, allowing media companies to buy more properties in a category (i.e., radio stations or television stations) and to cross traditional lines. For example, some companies now own a television station and a daily newspaper in the same market. The issues related to cross-ownership have not been settled, however.

It is difficult to predict how changes in ownership will ultimately change television. The FCC rules on ownership are still evolving but have a strong predisposition toward relaxation of rules and deregulation. That means that fewer companies will program more stations. Consolidation in radio has led to more formulaic and less local programming. This same trend is likely for television, as well.

FYI

The Gannett Company

Media giants like Gannett can own many newspapers and television stations, some even in the same city. That's the case in Phoenix, Arizona, where Gannett owns the *Arizona Republic*, a daily newspaper, and KPNX-TV, the NBC affiliate. In some cases, cross-ownership began in the early days of broadcasting, before rules were in place to prohibit it. In Gannett's case, cross-ownership occurred because the company owned the television station first and then acquired the newspaper. The problem for Gannett will occur when its television station applies for license renewal. If the cross-ownership rules have not been changed to allow this combination in one market, Gannett may face nonrenewal of its television license and be forced to sell off either the station or the newspaper.

Technological Challenges

Once television broadcasting converts to digital, television sets will be much more similar to computers than they have been in the past. Computers with CD drives, DVD drives, and high-quality speaker systems will serve as centers for home entertainment, as they will be able to play any digitally recorded medium and receive any online radio or audio service. The missing link has been the ability to receive network, cable, and satellite television on a computer monitor without special hardware or extreme effort. Digital broadcasting (and digital cable and satellite delivery) will blur the lines of distinction between using television sets for entertainment only and using television monitors for computer work.

This blurring of distinction has encouraged some of the big names in the computer industry—Apple, Microsoft, Dell, and Gateway—to get into selling equipment to the audience for both computing and entertainment needs. Not only does this change the competitive environment in home entertainment, but it also changes how audiences will use their computers and where they will place them in their homes.

TV-on-DVD also has become a factor in television viewing. The sales of television programs on DVD generated $1.5 billion in 2003. Young viewers are willing to buy a whole season of a TV series on DVD to avoid annoying commercials, to get a better-quality picture, and to set their own viewing times (Maynard, 2004).

Digital video recorders, such as TiVo, may have an enormous impact on television advertising because they can eliminate commercials from the playback of TV shows. These devices are being made easily available through cable and satellite providers. Some analysts predict that 36 to 79 million consumers will acquire them in the next several years (Higgins, 2004).

Some cable channels and the networks are considering DVD and video game use when attempting to reach young audiences. Moreover, they are considering putting prime-time shows on later at night or perhaps repeating them at a later time to reach those that use other entertainment options during prime time. In addition to integrating some shows with the Internet, the networks are considering connections between TV shows and cell phones. For example, FOX TV's *American Idol* encouraged voters to send text messages to vote for their favorites (Romano, 2004).

The broadcast network audience share will continue to decrease in the years to come because the audience will have more choices. The networks may find that their profitability depends increasingly on being able to deliver programs that other services cannot provide or that they, the networks, can best provide. For example, the networks can deliver live programs, like news and sports, and can operate profitably by offering reality shows that do not require large payments to stars, writers, and independent producers. The networks will continue to be challenged by technological changes and other delivery systems. As a result, they will continue to vertically integrate by buying program-producing and program-syndication companies, which allows them to gain control over programming sources and outlets. They will also utilize new programming services on other delivery systems (e.g., cable, satellite, and the Internet) and even new technologies to keep their audience share large enough to attract advertisers.

Television broadcasters are looking for ways to have a place in the digital future. Some are discussing the economic and technological feasibility of a subscription-supported, multichannel broadcasting service. Viewers would subscribe to the service

A: About 25,000 hours.

and get a set-top box that would receive (and descramble) 20 to 30 signals of digital television, including HDTV. It would be an over-the-air service, allowing any set in the household with a set-top box to receive the signals without having to construct a system of wires in the home. The process is still evolving and will require broadcasters to pool their signals and cooperate to create the service, which may be a difficult goal to achieve (Jessell, 2002).

Although it is does not now pose a threat to large television producers, the ability of individuals to create television programs looms on the horizon. Digital tools for the production of high-quality television, once the exclusive domain of "big media," are now becoming available to many. Personal technology of this type may change the future production of television programs (Gillmor, 2004).

Summary

Early experimenters in television tried two methods to obtain pictures: a mechanical scanning system and an electronic scanning system. The electronic system was eventually adopted as the standard. Although many inventors were involved in the development of electronic television, two of the most important were Vladimir K. Zworykin and Philo T. Farnsworth.

The FCC authorized commercial television broadcasting in 1941, but the industry didn't grow until after World War II, when the materials needed for television equipment manufacturing became available. After the war, television grew so rapidly that the FCC could not keep up with license applications or technical issues. In 1948, the FCC put a freeze on all television license applications that lasted until 1952. During the freeze, the FCC considered the allocation of spectrum space to stations, the issues of VHF and UHF stations in the same markets, color television, and educational channels.

As they had done during the previous 20 years in radio, the broadcast networks dominated television. Stations with network affiliations did well because of network programming. Independent stations had to resort to older programs from syndication as well as sports and locally produced programs.

At first, television was a live medium. In the 1950s, many high-quality, dramatic programs were written live to attract educated audience members who could afford the cost of a television set. Program production changed when video tape became available and programs were no long produced live in the studio. The television audience changed when the price of a TV set dropped and programs were adapted to appeal to a less educated audience. The early days of television had some challenges, including creation of a blacklist of people working in the industry who supposedly had communist sympathies.

The importance of television became more evident in the 1960s when events such as the assassinations of John F. Kennedy, Martin Luther King, Jr., and Robert Kennedy were covered extensively by the networks. That decade also saw coverage of the Vietnam War, violence in the streets, racial tension, and the first man on the moon. In 1967, Congress signed the Public Broadcasting Act, signaling the birth of a network dedicated to noncommercial broadcasting.

In the 1970s, cable television attracted audiences with its premium channels (like HBO) and excellent reception. VCRs gave the audience the ability to rent movies and record programs off the air. In the 1980s, these alternate delivery systems became stronger, with more programming available. The number of channels grew considerably with the addition of cable networks like CNN, MTV, and ESPN. Broadcast deregulation was a guiding principle for the FCC, and many rules were modified or removed entirely. Television technology improved and electronic news gathering using portable video equipment became common in stations across the country. During this decade, a new commercial network, FOX, began operating. Overall, the audience size grew, but the networks' share of the audience declined because viewers had more choices.

The 1990s began with extensive coverage of the Gulf War, giving television an opportunity to show live video from the other side of the world. A new technology, direct broadcast satellite, began service to audiences, providing many high-quality channels and direct competition to cable. The passage of the Telecommunications Act of 1996 changed many of the rules reagrding ownership of electronic media stations and allowed television group owners to acquire as many stations as they wanted, up to a cap of 35 percent of the national audience. This relaxation of ownership rules resulted in fewer groups owning more stations and thus consolidating the television station business. In the 1990s, three new television networks emerged: the WB, UPN, and PAX. In the last half of the 1990s, the Internet became popular. People began to spend more time online and less time in front of their television sets.

Consolidation of station ownership is almost certain to continue in the future and to raise issues about diversity and localism. The role of the networks continues to change from one of a delivery system for independently produced programs to one that delivers network-owned and -produced programs. The convergence of computers and television will continue drawing corporations like Apple, Microsoft, Dell, and Gateway into the television business. Digital broadcasting is mandated to replace analog broadcasting by 2006, but considerable questions remain as to whether the audience will be willing and able to receive it.

Notes

1. The term *kinescope,* first used as the name of Zworykin's picture tube, was also used later to describe the films that recorded live television shows before video tape came into use.

2. Video cassette recorders (VCRs) were popular but still expensive in the late 1970s. Because of their high price, significant saturation (i.e., 50 percent of all households) was not reached until 1988. VCR prices dropped in the 1990s, and by the end of that decade, saturation had reached 85 percent (*Home Video Index,* 2004).

3. In June 2003, the FCC decided to raise the television ownership cap from 35 percent to 45 percent, but this rule change was blocked by a court in Philadelphia (Labaton, 2003). In November 2003, a compromise was reached that allowed television groups to increase their national audience reach to 39 percent. As of late 2004, the court favored promoting diversity over increasing the audience cap.

Cable, Satellite, and Other Delivery Systems

CHAPTER 4

 SEE IT THEN

Cable Delivery

Satellite Delivery

Point-to-Point or One-to-One Communication

 SEE IT NOW

Cable Delivery

Satellite Delivery

Microwave Delivery

Point-to-Point or One-to-One Communication

 SEE IT LATER

The Changeover to Digital

Cable Delivery

Satellite Delivery

Point-to-Point or One-to-One Communication

Internet Delivery

In this chapter, you'll learn about:

- How regulation of television led to a new delivery system
- The differences between broadcast delivery and other types of delivery systems in both mass media and person-to-person communication
- The business, technology, and programming of cable, satellite, and other delivery systems
- What changes can be expected in the future for electronic media delivery

Numerous changes have occurred in electronic media since 1895, when Marconi first sent out Morse code messages via radio waves. The industry changed from point-to-point communication to point-to-multipoint communication when commercial radio began in the early 1920s. That model stayed in place as broadcast television dominated electronic media beginning in the late 1940s. But since that time, a combination of technological, economic, and political factors have brought about changes in how the audience receives electronic messages.

This chapter looks at how the delivery of programming has grown and changed from an industry dominated by broadcasting to one that includes cable delivery, satellite delivery, and microwave delivery. Cable receives more attention in this discussion because it is the delivery system of choice for more than two-thirds of the viewing audience. In addition to the discussion about the delivery of programming to mass audiences, point-to-point communication using electronic devices will be discussed, as well.

SEE IT THEN

Cable Delivery

From the early days of television experimentation until the late 1970s, most people, especially those in big cities, received television directly from the broadcast stations. Their television sets were attached to antennas that received the broadcast signal directly from the local television stations. People in rural areas and other smaller markets outside major metropolitan markets received a signal from one or more major market stations with the help of small transmitters located nearby. These transmitters received the television signal from the station and then retransmitted it to homes in the rural area. This retransmitting device, known as a **translator**, would send the signal out on a special frequency to avoid interfering with the signal of the originating station.

Translators were not used in the very early days of television, however, and many of the people who lived in areas far from big cities or where the television signal was blocked by hills or mountains couldn't receive television signals. In other words, broadcasting could not deliver the programs to the audience that wanted them, which led to the birth of a related delivery system: cable television.

Regulatory Problems
Lead to Reception Problems

The circumstances surrounding the birth of cable can be best understood by going back to the late 1940s, when the television industry was just beginning. Television found an eager audience for its programs, which took many shows directly from radio and added pictures. The audience wanted to *see* their favorite radio stars and *watch* the new shows, such as the *Texaco Star Theatre,* starring Milton Berle, and *Your Show of Shows,* with Sid Caesar and Carl Reiner.

After the public heard all about television and viewed some programs in their neighbors' homes, appliance stores, or bars, they were eager to buy sets and begin watching. The problem was that television stations were located primarily in large cities like New York, Philadelphia, and Chicago. Each of these markets had several stations and brought big-name talent to the audience. People were rushing to buy television sets, and companies were rushing to get licenses for television stations to deliver the programs. The stage was set for television to begin a huge growth phase. But there was a problem: The Federal Communications Commission (FCC) was inundated with applications for new stations.

The FCC's Dilemma

The FCC had a great deal of difficulty assigning stations to frequencies or channels. In the late 1940s, the FCC felt that it had to take time to study the issue of channel assignment to stations before it could deal with the vast number of applications that had accumulated. The result was the *freeze.* As noted in Chapter 3, the FCC put a freeze on all applications for television station licenses. Although it was initially meant to be temporary and last only six months, the freeze lasted four years, from 1948 to 1952. During this time, television became very popular, but if you didn't live in or near a major market, you were essentially shut out of the television boom.

Community Antennas

As the saying goes, "Need is the mother of invention," and so the situation led to some innovation. Appliance store owners found that people in smaller markets wouldn't buy television sets because they couldn't get a local television signal. These store owners needed to find a way to bring a television signal to their town.

There are competing stories about who came up with a specific solution to the problem of reception of distant television signals, but they all involve innovators who were either appliance store owners, like John Walson, or people who had some knowledge about signal transportation over wires, like L. E. Parsons. Essentially, some innovators realized that a television antenna placed on top of a hill or mountain could possibly bring in distant signals. In states with hills and mountains, like Pennsylvania and Oregon, and a combination of a few big cities and many small towns, people began experimenting not only with signal reception but also with a business plan. The so-called *Music Box memo* was a plan to sell radios by providing attractive programming on the radio. This was similar to the appliance store idea: Figure out a way for people to get the desired entertainment, and sell the appliances (television sets) to meet the need. In rural Pennsylvania, John Walson placed an antenna on top of a nearby mountain to receive television signals. He then brought customers up the mountain to demonstrate the television sets he placed there (Massey & Baran, 2001).

The flaw in Walson's business plan was that there just were not enough stations on the air to satisfy demand. Many small and medium markets didn't have television stations, and markets in rural and mountainous areas couldn't get television reception in the city, only on top of the mountain or in another location away from the city. What was missing was the ability to distribute signals to places that couldn't ordinarily receive them.

The idea of sharing or distributing signals after reception first started in New York City. Apartment dwellers there could get television signals but had to place an antenna on the roof of the building to do so. Landlords soon became wary of granting permission for rooftop placement because of potential disputes over the best locations, problems over maintaining the antennas and their masts, and the basic ugliness of the proliferating metal antennas. These problems were solved with the concept of a **shared antenna system.** One good antenna was used to receive the television signal and to distribute it to the apartments through a system of wires ("Television Antennas for Apartments," 1947). This system, also known as a **master antenna system,** was the forerunner of the small cable system that grew throughout the United States.

These two concepts—placing an antenna in a location that could get good reception and distributing and sharing the signal after reception—combined to form the basis of what became known as **community antenna television,** or **CATV.**

L. E. Parsons of Astoria, Oregon, is credited with starting the first commercial cable system. In 1948, he placed an antenna on top of a hotel in Astoria to receive the signal of a Seattle station and then connected a long line from the antenna to his apartment. Local interest grew considerably when word got out that Parsons had the only television within 100 miles that could receive a signal. He also placed a line from the antenna to the television set in the lobby of the hotel (Phillips, 1972).

Eventually, Parsons obtained limited permission to run wire through the underground conduits to businesses in downtown Astoria. Consumer demand led to Parsons wiring many homes, although he didn't initially have permission to string

These rooftops in New York City have both receiving antennas for broadcast signals and microwave antennas for multichannel multipoint delivery systems (MMDSs). The building in the background is the Empire State Building, which has housed signal transmitters for many years.

his wires on utility poles. The result was a somewhat primitive delivery system that nonetheless became a viable business, the Radio and Electronics Company of Astoria. Parsons also began consulting with others who wanted to set up similar systems elsewhere (Parsons & Frieden, 1998).

ZOOM IN   4.1
Go to the Companion Website for this text, www. ablongman.com/medoffkaye1e, to see a diagram that explains the basics of CATV.

Bob Tarlton was an appliance dealer in Lansford, Pennsylvania, whose business was connected to an antenna on top of a nearby hill. He was interested in manufacturing equipment that would amplify and distribute the television signals. Milton Shapp, owner of Jerrold Electronics (and future governor of Pennsylvania), joined forces with Tarlton, and eventually, Jerrold Electronics became the leader in manufacturing equipment for the community antenna television industry.

Thus, the birth of the cable industry was not a result of an earth-shaking technological breakthrough. Rather, it was a business that grew out of strong demand for television from an audience hungry for entertainment. In fact, few patents were issued during the beginnings of cable television because the technology it used was based on the simple distribution of existing broadcast signals.

Cable Develops as a Delivery System

Cable delivery began as a service that helped broadcasters reach their intended audiences. Viewers were willing to pay for television reception and improved signals. The introduction of translators caused cable owners to rethink their model. In many cases, cable systems had begun using microwave transmission to import television signals from distant large markets, rather than just the closest large market. Bringing in distant signals gave the audience a reason to subscribe beyond reception of nearby television stations. Also, some cable systems began offering their own channels with local programs. Cable companies became **multichannel video program distributors (MVPDs).**

Beginning in 1965, cable systems were required to carry signals from all "significantly viewed" stations in their market, a rule that became known as the **must-carry rule.** In other words, cable systems had to carry local stations. Rulings by the FCC in 1972, authorizing domestic satellite relays of television signals, helped cable develop its business plan. These rulings allowed the satellite distribution of signals to cable systems in any part of the country (FCC, 1972). Cable systems were required to carry signals from the big-three networks (ABC, CBS, and NBC) and to obtain them from the market closest to the system. (This was known as the **anti-leapfrogging rule.**) Importing signals from independent stations was similarly limited.

This 1972 legislation also set down the **nonduplication** (or **syndicated exclusivity) rules,** which prevented cable systems from showing a syndicated program from a distant station if a local station in the market was showing the same program. In addition, the FCC ruled that new systems had to have at least 20 channels and two-way capacity (FCC, 1972). The added technical requirements made building cable systems more expensive, and this slowed down the growth of cable systems in all but the largest markets.

The tide turned in 1977, when the federal government started to be influenced by deregulation sentiment. Until that time, cable had been handed down numerous restrictions that hampered its development. Congress relented and dropped most **carriage rules** (i.e., what signals the systems carried) for small systems, allowed unrestricted importation of foreign language and religious programs, and rescinded the minimum capacity rule. Perhaps most important, it dropped the anti-leapfrogging rule (FCC, 1976).

This last change created a new category of broadcast stations. Some stations, like Ted Turner's WCTG (later WTBS) in Atlanta, were now free to begin satellite distribution of their signals to cable systems across the country. These stations (including WGN from Chicago and WWOR from New Jersey, near New York City) provided programming like major league sports and popular sitcoms off the networks. They became known as **super-stations** because they were shown on cable systems nationwide and broadcast locally.

When satellite distribution of signals became a reality, the cable industry looked closely at the idea of distributing programming from sources other than the broadcast networks. The popularity of the superstations was unmistakable. And so the cable industry began to think of other ways of attracting customers and adding new revenue streams.

CABLE ADDS PAY CABLE   As a result of the 1972 and 1976 FCC rulings, cable systems were able to import signals for retransmission to their customers. The limitations on what signals could be imported revolved around which *broadcast* signal could be brought into a market, rather than which signal from any source could be brought in. Cable-only channels were not restricted.

In the early 1970s, Sterling Manhattan Cable in New York City, which was owned by Time, Inc., decided to put together an entertainment channel featuring live sports and movies. The result was a new company called **Home Box Office,** or **HBO.** At first, HBO experienced limited success by selling its programming to other cable companies in the Northeast. Growth was limited by technological factors, as HBO used a system of microwave transmitters and receivers to distribute its signal.

Gerald Levin, then president of HBO, looked to satellite distribution of the program signal. Some legal wrangling (*HBO v. FCC,* 1977) resulted in relaxed rules regarding what programs companies like HBO could present and the size (and therefore the cost) of the receiving equipment needed for cable systems to add satellite-distributed programs. Once these rules were relaxed, the door was open for **pay cable,** in which subscribers paid extra for the premium channels. HBO was the first company to deliver programming via satellite. Basically, HBO programs were uplinked to a satellite, picked up by a cable company's satellite dish, and then delivered via cable to the homes of subscribers. As such, satellite delivery changed the use and purpose of cable television. Rather than just deliver network programming via cable, new cable networks supplied subscribers with original programming.

Viewers' desire for new and varied programming choices led to a huge increase in cable television subscriptions. In 1978, another pay cable service, Showtime, emerged. Growth exploded soon thereafter, with the number of cable systems capable of receiving satellite signals growing from 829 in 1978 to over 2,500 in 1980 (Parsons & Frieden, 1998, p. 54).

The cable industry also embraced the idea of providing channels that were advertiser supported. These stations made money following a model similar to that of broadcast television; they were not subscription channels. In some cases, the cable company had to pay per subscriber for these channels, but it often passed the cost on to the audience. This time marked the beginning of many of the cable channels that have become as familiar as the broadcast networks, such as the USA Network, the Christian Broadcasting Network, C-SPAN, ESPN, CNN, MTV, and BET.

Cable systems also provided channels with local programming. These **local origination channels** included all kinds of programs obtained by the cable system as well as **public access programs** produced by subscribers using equipment and facilities provided by the cable system.

COPYRIGHT ISSUES RESURFACE   Imagine being able to take a product made by several companies and being able to resell it without paying those companies for the use of their product. That is essentially what the cable companies did from the late 1940s until the late 1970s. Although broadcast stations benefited indirectly from cable because the cable service sent those stations' signals to audience members who couldn't otherwise

ZOOM IN   4.2

The idea of using satellites for communication purposes was first publicized in a 1945 article appearing in *Wireless World,* which was written by novelist and scientist Arthur C. Clarke. He theorized that three satellites in geostationary orbit (22,300 miles above the equator) could be used to relay information to the entire globe (Clarke, 1945). For a graphic of geostationary satellites and distribution of signals to cable companies, including superstations, go to the Companion Website for this text: www.ablongman.com/medoffkaye1e.

get them, the broadcast stations were providing their product to the cable companies free of charge.

There were numerous problems with this way of doing business, especially for the broadcasters, who were paying high fees for programming. After years of complaints and some failed legal actions, the broadcast stations finally persuaded Congress to consider this issue of cable using broadcast programming for free. Congress decided to readdress the entire issue through the Copyright Act of 1976. This act established the Copyright Royalty Tribunal to enforce the fees charged to cable companies for the use of imported television signals. Although this seemed like a fair and equitable way of paying copyright holders, the tribunal found that none of the participants were happy with either the collection of fees or the payments made. In 1993, Congress ended the Copyright Royalty Tribunal and gave its responsibilities to the Library of Congress.

To be sure, the tribunal had continual problems. Nonetheless, the fact that it was established and temporarily settled the question of copyright liability was one of several reasons that cable grew so rapidly in the late 1970s and early 1980s. Several other factors contributed to this growth, as well, including the fact that national satellites were available for communication. In addition, some of the restrictions on pay cable were eliminated and the federal government moved toward a free-market attitude. Namely, the government allowed the marketplace to decide how a new delivery system, like satellite-delivered cable television (and pay cable), would serve the needs of the market. Cable growth was also encouraged in July 1980, when the FCC (FCC, 1980) rescinded its rules regarding syndicated exclusivity and distant signal importation, which had protected local television stations. (For more about these rules, see Chapter 12.)

FRANCHISING By the early 1980s, cable had become a service that the audience subscribed to not only to get good signal reception but also to get a much wider variety of signals than was available through broadcast delivery alone. Demand for cable delivery became strong and was prevalent across the United States. Growth was hampered in many cases, however, because of the franchising process that cable companies had to follow in order to begin serving an individual market.

Franchising was the means by which a community gave permission to a company to begin to serve its residents with cable television. The city council (or a committee appointed by the city) would publish a **request for proposals (RFP)**, weigh the merits of the proposals submitted, and then vote for the best proposal. The winning cable company would then be awarded the franchise, giving it permission to construct a cable system.

Although almost every city and town of any size has already completed the franchise process by the late 1970s and early 1980s, cable companies were furiously competing for the right to establish service across the country. The battles for large markets were particularly intense and at times somewhat questionable from an ethical perspective. Since a cable franchise was practically an exclusive right to build a system in a market, it was very valuable. And once built, a system could depend on long-term customers who paid their bills every month; this was like owning a utility, such as an electricity or telephone service. For many companies and investors, these elements provided a formula for long-term stability and profitability. The cable companies needed this type of guarantee of long-term income because laying cable throughout the market and building the **head end** (i.e., where the incoming television signals were processed and then sent out to subscribers) required large sums of money.

The process of franchising was both political and financial. It was financial in terms of the community trying to get the best deal for itself and its residents. It was political in terms of all of the public relations and persuasion involved to convince the city council or committee to accept the proposal written by the cable company. The competition for the franchise was often a race to win the hearts and minds of the city council or committee members who were voting. After a time, the focus shifted a bit from the cable companies trying to write the best cable franchise proposal to other methods of persuading council or committee members to vote for their companies. This led to some less than ethical techniques of persuasion.

In some cities, council or committee members were allowed to invest in the companies that submitted proposals. These stock deals were often made more attractive by low-cost loans from the competing cable companies. From a business standpoint, the practice made no sense, except that the person who became an investor also might have had a critical vote to cast during the franchise decision process. This practice became known as the *rent-a-citizen* part of franchising, and it cast a dubious light on the ethical behavior of both the cable companies and the citizens involved in the process.

Another part of the franchising process was the actual proposal of service for the city. The proposal consisted of a description of what kind of system would be built, including the number of channels available to customers through "basic" and "pay" subscriptions, the monthly charge for service, the identification of access channels, and the equipment needed for access and local origination studios. The proposal also spelled out service to the schools, local government, fire stations, and police department; technical capabilities, such as two-way video and audio; the data services to be provided; the fees paid to local government; and the timetable for construction of the system.

Clearly, the number of issues that cable companies had to address before being granted the franchise was often quite lengthy. And the detail that was required of these proposals would seem to indicate that both parties knew what they were getting. That was not always the case, however.

After a franchise was awarded, it was sometimes discovered that what had been promised was not actually affordable. In the rush to put forward the very best proposal, companies sometimes promised more than they could afford or deliver, given what was technologically feasible at the time. In short, "The attitude of the most aggressive [cable system] operators was to promise anything to win the franchise and worry about fulfilling the promises later" (Parsons & Frieden, 1998, pp. 56–57). A long-time cable executive described the cable company tactics at the time by saying, "All of us in the business oversold. . . . The game was promise the world, get the franchise, and then go in for franchise renegotiations" (Yutkin, 2000).

These promises were made with the **"Blue Sky"** period of cable development ahead. That was a period in the 1970s and early 1980s, when cable was perceived by many as a panacea for the delivery of television programs and improved health care, safety, and education. It was also expected (and this eventually did occur) that the iron grip of the big-three networks would be relaxed as cable provided a more open marketplace for the delivery of programming and other services.

Although many of the predictions about delivery of programming materialized, most of the predictions for other services did not. Many of these shortcomings can be explained by the fact that the financial model—which included building the infrastructure of channels for health care, fire and safety monitoring, and banking—just did not work. Providing these community services via cable rarely made it to the testing stage.

After getting the franchise award and putting its basic system in place, the cable company often went back to the city council to discuss the reality of the financial situation. With a partially built system in place, it was not likely that another cable company would be willing to come into town. Also, the technology for providing the promised services would be just as expensive for another company. All of the options that the city had at this point seemed to involve legal fees and perhaps long legal battles.

In the end, the city typically renegotiated to get the cable system installed and running, abandoning some of the technological dreams promised during the "Blue Sky" era. The cable company got its monopolistic franchise, and the city got a scaled down but economically viable cable system.

"Renting a Citizen" for Cable

Some cable companies tried to influence city officials with attractive stock deals. For instance, in 1982, a Denver councilwoman received a terrific stock deal from one of the franchise applicants and observed that the only person she knew who didn't own cable stock was the coach of her son's little league football team. (She later discovered that he didn't live in the city of Denver.) And in Milwaukee in 1982, an applicant for the cable franchise retained two local political consulting firms: one to help pitch its case and the other to prevent the first firm from helping any of the competitors (Hazlett, 1989).

THE CABLE ACT OF 1984   During the 1970s and early 1980s, the FCC continued to back away from regulating the cable industry. And as it did, local governments enacted rules to keep the cable industry in check while the cities and towns benefited. Somewhat beleaguered with demands from local policymakers, the cable industry lobbied the FCC to help provide a balance between what local governments could demand and what cable companies could provide.

The result of the lobbying effort was the Cable Communications Policy Act of 1984, an amendment to the Communications Act of 1934. This new act provided a number of guidelines for the relationship between cable companies and the communities that they served. It included specific rules regarding the municipality's control over rates and programming, the cable companies' ability to retain their franchises, and the theft of cable services by audience members. In addition, the FCC reasserted the cities' power to require access channels as part of the franchise agreement, the anti-cross-ownership philosophy that prevented broadcast and cable ownership in the same market, and the protection of subscriber privacy by requiring disclosure of the use of subscriber information. With these rules in place, the cable companies could continue wiring the major markets and thus established cable as a financially stable major player in electronic media.

Satellite Delivery

As discussed earlier in this chapter, satellite technology was instrumental in the development of cable. When satellite distribution of video programs to cable companies became both technically and economically feasible, the cable industry grew rapidly. It is somewhat ironic that satellite now poses a threat to the cable industry it helped launch.

Satellite Television

The same technology that allows point-to-multipoint video communication for the purpose of program distribution from program providers to cable systems also allows program distribution directly to audience homes. This technology was first available to consumers in the mid 1970s, when HBO began sending its signal to cable companies throughout the United States.

Early technology required a large receiving dish, 8 to 15 feet across, to receive the satellite signals. As a result, the price of the equipment was high and a large space was needed to install it. The receiving dish was large because its size was directly related to the frequency at which the signal was sent. The C Band—the space in the electromagnetic spectrum used by these communication satellites—required a large dish to best receive the signals. During the early years of satellite television, or the late 1970s to the early 1990s, satellite owners were those who could not get cable. Many lived in rural areas or other places where cable companies could not feasibly provide service or had not been forced to by a franchise agreement.

A satellite-receiving dish in the yard of a rural house.

Satellite Radio

Satellites also have been used to distribute radio programming. Since the early 1980s, when radio became a medium of *formats* rather than *programs*, consultants and programming services have been providing stations with preprogrammed content in two categories: individual syndicated programs and features and all-day format services.

Well before satellites were used to distribute programming, radio stations received a variety of **electronic transcriptions,** or recordings that provided programming to stations. They came from companies like Drake-Chenault, who would provide recordings for a week or month of

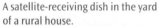

Westwood One

Westwood One, a radio syndication company started by Norm Pattiz, acquired the Mutual Broadcast System in 1980 and sought a distribution system to provide programming to member stations. Until that time, syndicated radio programs had usually been supplied on tape or LP (i.e., vinyl records). Radio networks were still considered wired and supplied programming via phone line. The networks began to consider delivery via satellite after observing the success of HBO and superstations. And so Westwood One began to distribute programs to its Mutual Broadcast System affiliates via satellite. Even though not all of its member radio stations had satellite-receiving equipment at that time, Westwood One was able to find a satellite-receiving station somewhere in the market that could supply the radio station with the programming.

Westwood One now provides over 150 news, sports, music, talk, entertainment, feature, live event, and 24/7 formats. Moreover, through its subsidiaries, Metro Networks/Shadow Broadcast Services, Westwood One provides local content to the radio and television industries, including news, sports, weather, traffic, video news services, and other information. Westwood One includes CBS Radio News, CNN Radio News, NBC Radio News, and MTV, VH1, CMT, and BET radio.

For more about this syndicator, go to **www.westwoodone.com**.

programming. The station would play the recordings and add local station identification messages, commercials, weather, and so on to ensure that the listeners felt that the station was still local and not just a recording.

At first, the transcriptions came through the mail in the form of records or tapes. The program content was mostly music of a particular format, such as country and western or Top 40. Many individual programs, like syndicated talk or music countdown shows (e.g., *American Top 40*), were also syndicated. Some services allowed a local announcer to act as a disc jockey, but in fact, he or she had no control over the programming content.

Later, these services switched to satellites for distribution of their programming. Doing so allowed one programming (or syndication) center to simultaneously supply many stations with programming content.

CAREER TRACKS

Norm Pattiz   Chairman, Board of Directors, Westwood One

- **What is your job? What do you do?**
  I am Chairman of the Board and Executive Producer of Entertainment Programming for Westwood One.

- **How long have you been doing this job?**
  Since I founded the company in 1976.

- **What was your first job in electronic media?**
  I was a sales rep and eventually sales manager of KCOP-TV in Los Angeles.

- **What led you to the job?**
  I was working at an advertising agency that placed a high volume of television and radio advertising. The station reps wore the best suits, drove the nicest cars, had expense accounts to go to the best restaurants, and worked in a very exciting industry.

- **What advice do you have for students who might want a job like yours?**
  Take every opportunity you can to become familiar with the media that you wish to become a part of. Get inside the door. Internships, volunteer work, campus stations, entry-level positions—anything to become part of the enterprise. And one more thing: Read the "trades." Industry trade papers are an excellent way to find out what's going on, who the players are, what trends exist, and where the opportunities are within the industry.

How many American households subscribe to a multichannel delivery system that is not cable?

Point-to-Point or One-to-One Communication

With the invention of the telephone in 1876, the electronic delivery of personal media became part of Americans' lives. Since that time, we have become more and more dependent on electronic point-to-point or one-to-one communication in our everyday lives. Almost everyone in the United States has access to at least one telephone line.

By the 1980s, our use of the telephone had grown beyond real-time, point-to-point communication. We were also sending **faxes** via telephone lines and even attaching **answering machines** to them to record the voice messages of people trying to contact us. Answering machines became message centers and freed us from the confines of home. We no longer had to wait around for an important call; the caller could simply leave a message. Sometimes, we even preferred to leave a message, rather than talk to someone. We also discovered that we could screen calls so as to know who was calling or hear his or her message without having to answer. We could also conduct business by providing an informative outgoing message: "If you're calling about the red Toyota, sorry, it's already been sold." Or we could be funny: "If your call is about good news or money, leave a message. If not, send me a letter."

This flexible use of telephone delivery for more than just real-time talking opened the door to other types of phones and even other uses. By the mid 1990s, cell phones were gaining in popularity. Most people know what cell phones are, but not everyone knows how they were developed or how they work. As with many new communication devices, we tend to think of the cell phone as a recent invention. But interestingly, one of the first prototypes was developed in 1947 as a way to communicate from cars. This innovation was limited, however, because the FCC only allowed 23 simultaneous conversations in the same area.

Initially, the cost of making cell phones was too high to allow them to be available to the masses. And because of the FCC's apathy in relegating airwave usage for wireless communication, the introduction of wireless phones to the public was further delayed. Then in 1978, AT&T and Bell Labs introduced a cellular system and held general consumer trials in Chicago. Within a few years, other companies were also testing cellular systems and pressured the FCC to authorize commercial cellular services.

The first portable telephone units, called *transportables* or *luggables,* were big and heavy but appropriate for some applications. Cell phones were commercially available in 1984. There were 5.3 million cell phone subscribers by 1990 (Sidener, 2002).

 **SEE IT NOW**

Cable Delivery

At the beginning of the 1990s, **cable penetration** (i.e., the percentage of households that subscribe compared to those that could subscribe) reached 56.4 percent. By the end of the 1990s, that figure had reached over 67 percent. As of 2004, the percentage of television households that could be wired by cable was 95 percent and cable penetration was 71.3 percent. In addition, of the more than 73 million cable subscribers, two-thirds received at least one pay cable channel (NCTA, 2004).

Today, most towns and cities of any size have been wired for cable, and many of the systems have switched over from analog cable to digital cable. Digital cable allows *signal compression,* which means the system can provide more channels and services to the audience without changing the basic distribution.

Cable Subscription Rates

During the 1990s, after years of consumer complaints about rates and service, Congress got involved in the cable business by dabbling in rate control. In the Cable Television Consumer Protection Act of 1992, Congress mandated that the FCC had the power and the need to control rates for basic cable subscriptions. The FCC did just that in 1993 and 1994 by controlling subscriber fees. This action not only limited the amount that cable companies could charge their subscribers, but in some systems, it also required cable companies to reduce their rates and make refunds to some subscribers.

This desire to regulate cable rates had faded by the second half of the 1990s. In 1996, Congress decided to terminate its rate control over the cable industry, and in 1999, it ended rate regulation. As a result, since 1996, cable television rates have increased 45 percent, nearly three times the rate of inflation (Consumers Union, 2002).

Signal Carriage versus Retransmission Consent

The Cable Television Consumer Protection Act of 1992 also set down what broadcast signals cable systems could or should carry. Cable systems with more than 12 channels had to reserve channels for all local broadcast stations. In addition, the broadcast stations were given the right to negotiate for the use of their signals.

While true negotiating for payment never really happened, the result of this legislation was interesting. The big cable companies, or **multiple system operators (MSOs)**, declared that they would not negotiate with broadcasters for signal use but instead would offer them a dedicated channel to use for an additional service. In other words, instead of giving the broadcast stations money for the right to carry them on the system, the cable companies offered to give the broadcasters an additional channel. This resulted in some new cable channels, as the networks used the allotted channel space to start new cable channels that were owned by broadcasters. Cable channels MSNBC (from NBC), ESPN-2 (from ABC), and fX (from FOX) all had their beginnings from these negotiations.

Technology

About 12,000 cable systems are now in operation across the United States, and many of these are now capable of digital signal transmission. The advantage of the digital signal in cable is that it can be compressed, allowing more than one signal to be sent out in the space previously required for one analog television signal. This process is called **multiplexing.**

Although digital cable has not yet been totally accepted by subscribers, the new technology will eventually take over all analog cable systems. Because the majority of televisions in use cannot receive digital signals directly, the use of a set-top box will be required. Digital-cable-ready televisions are still the exception, rather than the rule.

Cable Subscriptions

Nielsen Media Research–NTI releases these data about cable subscriptions in January of each year:

YEAR	"BASIC" CABLE CUSTOMERS	"BASIC" CABLE/ TELEVISION HOUSEHOLDS
2003	73,365,880	67.7%
2002	73,525,150	68.9%
2001	72,958,180	69.2%
2000	69,297,290	67.8%
1999	68,537,980	68.0%
1998	67,011,180	67.4%
1997	65,929,420	67.3%
1996	64,654,160	66.7%
1995	62,956,470	65.7%
1994	60,495,090	63.4%
1993	58,834,440	62.5%
1992	57,211,600	61.5%
1991	55,786,390	60.6%
1990	54,871,330	59.0%
1989	52,564,470	57.1%
1988	48,636,520	53.8%
1987	44,970,880	50.5%
1986	42,237,140	48.1%
1985	39,872,520	46.2%
1984	37,290,870	43.7%
1983	34,113,790	40.5%
1982	29,340,570	35.0%
1981	23,219,200	28.3%
1980	17,671,490	22.6%

Source: Nielsen Media Research.

ZOOM IN 4.3

You can view a typical digital cable lineup from 2004 at the Companion Website for this text: www.ablongman.com/medoffkaye1e. Or visit either of these sites:

- www.twckc.com/services/lineups/schednet.asp
- www.southriding.net/html/committees/ showFaq.php3?id=53

What percentage of cable customers subscribe to digital cable?

Typical Channel Lineup

In 1984, Group W Cable (Westinghouse's cable division) offered the following channels to its Eugene/Springfield, Oregon, subscribers:

CHANNEL	SERVICE
2	TNN (The Nashville Channel)
3	CNN
4	KOZY (Local origination)
5	ESPN
6	KMTR (NBC affiliate)
7	KOAC (PBS affiliate)
8	KVAL (CBS affiliate)
9	Time and public service announcements
10	KEZI (ABC affiliate)
11	C-SPAN/Local access
12	KPTV (Independent brought in from Portland)
13	Classified ads

At the time, some 20 years ago, this was a typical cable channel lineup. Some premium channels were also available, requiring a set-top converter. Group W's basic service cost less than $7 per month in early 1984, but was raised to over $10 during the year.

Besides adding more channels to the system, another advantage of digital cable is that it provides interactive cable, with which the subscriber can send signals back to the cable head end. This two-way communication opens possibilities for **video on demand (VOD)**, a service that allows the subscriber to order any program, at any time and to have it sent directly to him or her.

An even newer service that is becoming common is **near video on demand (NVOD)**. With NVOD, movies can be aired at staggered starting times or on several channels, giving viewers a choice of the most convenient time for viewing. Many digital cable systems offer a wide selection of NVOD offerings, but few currently offer VOD.

Consolidation and Integration

As of early 2004, two companies—Comcast Cable Communications and Time Warner Cable—controlled about 44 percent of all subscribers, and the top four MSOs—Comcast, Time Warner, Charter Communications, and Cox Communications—controlled almost two-thirds of the business. Clearly, the cable industry has become an **oligopoly:** a market environment controlled by a small number of companies, with the majority of the business in the hands of a few companies.

The owners of cable companies don't just own cable companies. In addition, they often own companies that own other mass media providers and even nonmedia properties. For example, Time Warner owns many different companies, including the country's largest Internet service provider, America Online (AOL). In addition to properties like *Time, Fortune,* and *People* magazines, AOL owns Warner Bros. film studio, New Line Cinema (a film-producing company), HBO, Turner Broadcasting (Superstation WTBS, CNN, TBS), and Time Warner, its cable ownership division.

Companies that own cable systems, broadcast stations, cable channels, production companies, and film companies are able to provide their own content for their electronic media outlets. This controlling of production and distribution is known as **vertical integration,** and it presents both an opportunity and a cause for concern. A company can provide its own programs for a cable channel on its own systems. And by having guaranteed space on a cable system, the company can be assured that the programs will air and that it will at least recover some of its initial investment through advertising. Independent program providers, on the other hand, have no such guarantee and are therefore less likely to take creative chances with their programs. What's more, a large company may produce a hit program and restrict its distribution by deciding that only its own systems will carry the program.

ZOOM IN   4.4

MSOs have become gigantic, multibusiness companies with holdings in media and other businesses.

- To learn more about the cable giant Comcast, go to **www.comcast.com.**

- To get an idea about how diversified Time Warner is and how broad its influence can be, go to **www.timewarner.com** and click on "Companies." This company is not only concerned with the delivery of entertainment and information but also with its creation and production.

The large MSOs have responded to this criticism of vertical integration by stating that because some airings and income are guaranteed for their new programs and services, they are more likely to take chances and produce programs for smaller audiences, as is the case with channels like BET (Black Entertainment Television) and Discovery. This response has been met with skepticism, however. Many believe that the large MSOs are relying on what has worked in the past, rather than taking creative risks. Generally, the smaller, independent media companies take the risks in order to be noticed and generate business.

Despite this justification from the MSOs, the FCC is keeping an eye on vertical integration, to some extent. For example, its trying to keep the unethical use of the power of vertical integration in check by preventing a cable system from having more than 40 percent of its first 75 channels occupied by cable channels and other services that are owned (at least in part) by the cable system or its parent company.

About 30 percent, as of 2004.

Another concern in the cable industry has been heard in broadcasting and other media for many years. Namely, when only a few companies own almost all of the outlets of a particular medium, only a few voices will be heard. In other words, there will be no diversity of opinion, and the information that goes out to the public will come from a limited number of sources and therefore present a limited number of viewpoints. The cable companies have responded by saying that because of the economics of scale, larger companies can afford to provide better services in many ways, while also providing the financial security that media outlets need to stay in business. Regardless of the viewpoint held by either the public or the FCC, it seems likely that consolidation in the industry will continue until just a few giant companies are left in the cable business.

Satellite Delivery

Three different types of satellites are now being used for communication purposes:

1. **Geosynchronous satellites** are parked in an orbit 22,300 miles above the earth's equator. These stationary satellites provide services to cable companies and television stations along with direct broadcast satellite video and audio to homes.
2. **Middle-earth orbiters** are satellites that travel in a lower orbit—beneath 22,300 miles but over 1,000 miles above the earth. These nonstationary satellites are used for voice and data transmission and also for the global positioning system (GPS) devices, which have become common in recent years.
3. **Low-orbit satellites** are nonstationary and travel from 100 to 1,000 miles above the earth. They are used for personal communication services, such as mobile phones, Internet access, and video conferencing.

Satellite Master Antenna Television

SMATV is an acronym for **satellite master antenna television**, which is also known as *private cable*. Essentially, an SMATV system is similar to a very small cable system. Rather than have a whole community be served by the system, SMATV will serve one or several adjacent buildings. The SMATV head end, located on the premises of the buildings being served, will receive the satellite signals. This type of system doesn't require a franchise authorization because it is self-contained and on private property, thus avoiding the right of way approval necessary for a citywide system (*Chicago v. FCC*).

> **ZOOM IN**   4.5
> Go to this text's Companion Website, www.ablongman.com/medoffkaye1e, for a diagram of an SMATV system.

The most common locations for SMATV systems are urban apartment buildings and suburban apartment complexes. Approximately 1 million households are served by SMATV, although this number varies as apartment buildings are built or convert to city cable systems. In addition to providing video programming, some systems also offer Internet access and other telecommunication services.

Satellite Television

Large satellite television dishes became increasingly uncommon in the 1980s and practically disappeared in the early 1990s. Beyond that, early satellite systems simply could not compete with the simple access to programs provided by cable and multichannel multipoint distribution systems (MMDSs). New companies dedicated to providing a **direct broadcast satellite (DBS)** system to subscribers had been working to create the technology needed to do this and at the same time be competitive with cable.

Growth of DBS

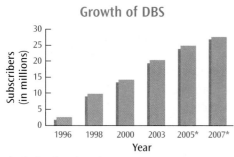

*Projections from the Yankee Group.

For more informatiom about satellite television, go to the Satellite Broadcasters Association's website: **www.sbca.com**.

Success came in 1994 with a company called DirecTV, a subsidiary of General Motors–owned Hughes Electronics. A competitor, the DISH Network, was launched in 1996. Although the cost of these services to consumers was slightly higher than that of cable, they offered about 150 channels of high-quality television—often, more than twice what cable offered. DBS also offered channels that were not offered by cable. Moreover, the signal was excellent, in part because it was transmitted digitally to a small 18-inch dish and then converted to analog for analog television sets. To deal with the complex installation of the satellite system, the cost was often included in the fee required to start the service.

One disadvantage of DBS was that until 1999, it was not allowed to carry local broadcast stations on its feed to homes. This forced subscribers who really wanted local programming either to continue subscribing to cable or to begin using some type of antenna that would bring in local stations over the air. For many consumers, this was not acceptable. Paying for both cable and DBS was expensive and involved paying for quite a bit of duplication. Also, very few people wanted to switch to an antenna while viewing just to see the local news or other programs. This problem was rectified in 1999, when the Satellite Home Viewers Act (SHVA) mandated that local broadcast signals could be carried on DBS.

To date, there have been two major players in the DBS business: DirecTV and the EchoStar/DISH Network (owned in part by the same company that owns the FOX network, News Corportation). These two companies have been fighting for subscribers against each other and against cable. In March 2002, DirecTV and EchoStar/DISH Network proposed to the FCC that they merge and create one national provider of DBS service. The government rejected the merger idea, however, preferring to maintain two providers that could compete with each other and give the audience a choice.

According to J. D. Power, a consumer marketing survey company, video customers are generally happier with DirecTV and EchoStar/DISH Network than they are with cable companies (Higgins, 2003). The Yankee Group, a technology research firm, has predicted that the number of DBS subscribers will grow to 25 million by the end of 2005.

XM 's Hugh Panero (top) and Sirius's Joseph Clayton (bottom) are the executives who run satellite radio in the United States.

Satellite Radio

In 2001, XM Satellite Radio successfully began a radio service that sends a satellite signal to cars and homes equipped with special satellite receivers. It was formed with the help of investors from automobile manufacturing, broadcast radio, and satellite broadcasting: namely, General Motors, American Honda, Clear Channel (the nation's largest radio group), and DirecTV. The antenna required for XM service is quite small, and signal reception is nationwide. XM provides 100 channels of audio programming, offering music, news, sports, and children's programming directly to homes and cars. A subscription is required even if you own a receiver for XM. In addition to satellites, XM

has small terrestrial transmitters called *repeaters* that augment the satellite signal to ensure listeners in big cities can get the signal when the satellite signal is blocked by large buildings.

XM's competition comes from Sirius Satellite Radio, which began its service shortly after XM did. Sirius uses three satellites, whereas XM uses two. Sirius also provides 100 channels of audio service, including 60 channels of commercial-free music and 40 channels of news, sports, talk, and children's programming.

Although these companies tout satellite radio as the service that will change radio the way satellite-distributed cable services changed television, satellite radio got off to a slow start. Auto manufacturers didn't begin to install satellite radio capable receivers in new cars until 2003. All other cars must be retrofitted with a new receiver or adaptor of some sort to receive the signal. Also, listeners must subscribe to the service before they can receive it.

One drawback to satellite radio is that, like DBS satellite television, for the first five years, local stations will not be offered in its lineup of channels. This raises the question about why people listen to radio at all—just for the programs or for some local information, as well. It will take some years for the satellite radio industry to mature and find its audience. And only then will it be clear whether the audience is large enough to support two services. If not, will the satellite radio companies merge into one national provider?

> **ZOOM IN** 4.6
> • For a diagram showing satellite radio (including repeaters), go to the Companion Website, www.ablongman.com/medoffkaye1e.
> • For more about the two satellite radio companies, XM and Sirius, go to www.xmsatelliteradio.com and www.siriussatelliteradio.com.

Microwave Delivery

Multichannel multipoint distribution systems (MMDSs), mentioned earlier, are systems that can deliver television programming without wires. In some ways, this type of system is similar to broadcast delivery because the signal is transmitted through the air and received directly by a receiving antenna at a home or business. MMDS differs from broadcast because it delivers a multichannel signal of up to 33 channels and uses a much higher frequency. This delivery system is similar to a cable system. In fact, MMDS is also referred to as *wireless cable*.

MMDS features a head end similar to that of a cable system, which receives signals from over the air, satellite, and microwave-distributed television. All of the signals received at the head end are converted to a frequency in the microwave portion of the electromagnetic spectrum. The signals are then sent to a microwave transmitter and antenna, which sends them out to customers who subscribe to the service. The signals are low in power compared to those of a television station, as MMDS transmitters usually transmit a power of less than 100 watts.

This antenna receives television signals from an MMDS provider.

Because of its high frequency, MMDS relies on line-of-sight transmitting. In some cases, the signal is sent to a location where a repeater is used to redirect the signal to areas that have reception difficulties. Given this, MMDS has enjoyed limited success in metropolitan areas that were slow to adopt cable or where the terrain made cable wiring difficult. One community in which MMDS has worked fairly well is Tucson, Arizona, where the terrain allowed for an MMDS transmitting antenna to be located in an elevated location that served a large part of the metropolitan area. At the customer's home, the signal is received either by a **parabolic antenna** (which can concentrate a weak signal to make it a strong one) or another small rooftop antenna and sent to a frequency converter, which converts the signals to standard television channels.

> **ZOOM IN** 4.7
> Go to www.ablongman.com/medoffkaye1e, the Companion Website for this text, for a diagram of an MMDS.

MMDS may seem superior to cable because it doesn't require stringing cable throughout the town in order to reach customers. But MMDS has had only limited success. One difficulty is that it requires a microwave antenna to be mounted on the property of the customer and aimed properly to receive the signal. Another problem for MMDS is that the spectrum allocation for the service is limited to 200 MHz (from 2.5 GHz to 2.7 GHz). Since each television sig-nal requires 6 MHz in bandwidth, this means only 33 channels can be sent by any MMDS. Compared to the number of channels offered by cable systems and satellite services, MMDS is obviously limited, making it uncompetitive and therefore not nearly as desirable.

Point-to-Point or One-to-One Communication

Not all electronic communication follows the one-to-many model. The use of electronic point-to-point or one-to-one communication for both pleasure and business has skyrocketed. People expect to be able to communicate with others easily, quickly, and from any location.

Pagers provided a one-way version with some alphanumeric messaging. But when digital **cell phones** became relatively cheap, versatile, and dependable in the late 1990s, pagers dropped from popularity. Since that time, cell phones have taken over. Another form of electronic point-to-point communication is **data transfer,** which is a common daily occurrence for anyone who uses a credit card to make a purchase.

Cell Phones

In May 2002, more than 135 million Americans were cell phone customers—18 times the number of users 10 years ago (Hahn & Dudley, 2002). American teens comprised 32 million of the 135 million consumers, spending $172 billion on cell phones and accessories in 2001 (Creno, 2002). The number of users is projected to grow to 200 million by the year 2005.

ZOOM IN   4.8

Go to the Companion Website for this text, www.ablongman.com/medoffkaye1e, for a description of how cell phones work.

In July 2002, the Bush administration allotted more radio spectrum for the use of wireless communication services. The U.S. Commerce Department's National Telecommunications and Information Administration will work closely with the FCC and industry to make more spectrum space available by the end of 2010 in order to continue to meet American consumers' wireless voice and data communication needs.

The term *mobile telephone* has given way to the more familiar *cellular* or *cell phone*. *Mobile* describes how it's used, and *cellular* describes how it works. A cell phone is really a type of two-way radio. Basically, a city or county is divided into smaller areas called *cells,* usually a few miles in radius. Each cell contains a low-powered radio transmitting/receiving tower that covers the cell area. Collectively, the cell towers provide coverage to the entire larger area, be it a city or county or some other region. The size of each cell varies according to geographic terrain, number of cell phone users, demand, and other criteria.

When you make a call, it's picked up by the cell tower and transmitted over an assigned radio frequency. When you move out of the cell while still talking, a switching mechanism transfers your call from that cell to a new cell area and to the corresponding radio frequency. Most of the time, you won't notice the switch, but sometimes, as you travel from one cell area to another, your call may be dropped because of spotty (or "hit and miss") coverage.

Finding it too expensive to keep both landline and cellular service, between 3 and 5 percent of cell phone users have cancelled their landline phones. Furthermore, according to the International Telecommunication Union—an international organization within the United Nations in which governments and the private sector coordinate global telecom networks and services—the number of U.S. landline phones has dropped by 5 million, or nearly 3 percent, since 2000 (Carroll, 2003). This trend should be watched closely because widespread dropping of landline telephones will shift many dollars toward the cell phone service providers and away from the regional Bell operating companies (RBOCs), which do not have a big role in cell phone service.

Cell Phone Subscribers

The number of cell phone subscribers in the United States varies considerably from source to source for a number of reasons, including the date in the year of measurement. This graph shows estimated cell phone subscribers by year.

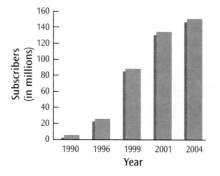

Dr. Martin Cooper (above left) is considered the inventor of the portable phone and made the first call on one in 1973. The Canyon MK 900 (above right) is a mobile briefcase phone that dates back to around 1980. The complete setup for this phone cost around $2,000, so not many people had one. Today's cell phones (left) not only can make calls but also have features like digital picture taking and sending, Internet access, music storage and replay, text messaging, and game playing.

Data Services

Another use of electronic media involves the corporate world. Transactions that were previously done by telephone are now conducted using data networks.

A prime example of this application of electronic communication occurs when you use a credit card. When you swipe your credit card, your account number is electronically sent to the credit card-issuing company's data bank. If your account appears to be OK, the company will send a signal to the store (i.e., the terminal where you swiped your card), authorizing the purchase. The transaction is then routed to the credit card company's merchant services. The credit card issuing company contacts VISA, MasterCard, American Express, or whomever through an electronic processing network. The credit card company then contacts the card issuer, and the information about the transaction is posted or recorded on your credit card account. The credit card company (VISA, etc.) then pays the card issuer, and the card issuer then pays the merchant for the transaction.

Although this may seem complicated, it all happens quickly and almost always without problems. What makes it happen is the capability of data services to send and receive information quickly and accurately. This credit card example is just one of many uses that businesses make of electronic communication. Another example is the service-oriented function of being able to track a package sent by Federal Express or UPS. Information about a package can be followed online because each package is read through a bar code attached to it, which essentially states where the package is at various stages of the sending process. At each station, the package is recorded and the information is transferred through data service lines to a central point. Consumers can track packages by going to a website that shows the current information.

SEE IT LATER

The Changeover to Digital

Americans today understand the digital revolution and the advantages that digital transmission of media present, yet they don't often feel compelled to make changes in their personal lives to accommodate these technological changes.[1] In particular, they don't necessarily want to pay more to get digital, regardless of the better quality and more channels it offers (i.e., through digital broadcast television, digital cable, satellite television, and satellite radio).

The delivery systems industry is therefore at a crossroads. Technological innovations and business realities are driving changes in this industry, and the delivery systems that succeed will be those that have business plans that work. In order to get to that point, the companies involved must understand what the audience wants and how much it is willing to pay for it.

Between now and 2006, television broadcasters will be switching to digital broadcasting. This is not an option; it has been mandated by the FCC. By 2006, all television signals are supposed to be digital, whether they are broadcast, cable, or satellite. In reality, however, there is a provision in the requirement that will allow broadcasters to push that deadline to a later time. Until the digital set penetration is 85 percent of television households in the country, the changeover from analog to digital will not be finalized.

ZOOM IN   **4.9**
For an up-to-date view of the future of television and its various delivery systems, go to **www.ablongman. com/medoffkaye1e**, the Companion Website for this text.

The FCC is working to help the transition. In 2003, it passed a ruling that approved the technical and labeling standards, which seek to allow digital cable signals to flow seamlessly into TV sets without the need for a set-top box. The goal is to make receiving digital signals from a variety of delivery systems easier ("Throw Away," 2003).

Cable Delivery

Cable systems have the advantage of already being wired throughout the United States. Of the households that are wired for cable (about 97 percent of all homes), more than two-thirds already subscribe. Moreover, two-thirds of all basic cable subscribers also get additional cable services. This means that someone in each of the 73 million cable households in this country pays a cable bill every month. In about 40 million of those households, that monthly bill includes not only basic but some expanded level of pay-cable service (NCTA, 2003).

These numbers seem to indicate an entrenchment in cable television that won't easily go away. Although there is some "churn" in cable (i.e., turnover among subscribers), the figures have been fairly steady, despite competition from satellite television. Obviously, cable television is keeping its audience happy—or at least happy enough to keep subscribing.

Cable companies are now upgrading their systems from analog to digital. Digital systems allow more channel capacity; therefore, cable systems will continue to entice subscribers with more basic channels, more premium channels and packages, and more pay-per-view. In the effort to find more revenue, cable companies are heavily promoting Internet access through cable modems. By offering another service through the same cable wire, the cable companies are broadening their relationship with subscribers. This added service will cut down on customer turnover, as subscribers who also use cable for their Internet connection will be less likely to switch to satellite TV. Subscribing to Internet access through a cable modem usually creates a package deal that requires subscribing to regular cable services, as well. Companies that are able to upgrade their systems to digital and provide additional services, like video on demand (VOD) and Internet access, should be able to keep their market share, while those that are slow to upgrade will continue to lose subscribers (Somayaji, 2003).

Satellite Delivery

DBS companies DirecTV and EchoStar/DISH Network continue to attract customers by offering more than 100 television channels for about the same monthly fee as basic cable service, which offers around 70 channels. The pricing and quality of DBS has helped these companies increase the number of subscribers, many of whom have switched from cable or are just starting their own households. The satellite television companies will continue to do best in areas where consumers cannot get high-speed Internet access or new video services from the local cable company.

Industry analysts Veronis, Suhler, and Stevenson (2003) predict that the number of hours each person spends with cable and satellite television channels will increase over the next few years, from about 950 hours per year in 2003 to about 1,026 hours per year in 2007. The hours spent with broadcast stations is expected to decline.

A recent feature offered by satellite services is a digital video recorder that can automatically record favorite shows, pause a show while it's being watched, and provide other services that allow the audience to have more control over their viewing experience. (See Chapter 14 for more about digital video recorders.) In addition, satellite delivery companies plan to combine services with other telecommunication companies to offer telephone service, creating a telephone/television package. Doing so will attract consumers who want the simplicity of a combination electronic mass media and electronic personal communication service.

Satellite radio is still in its infancy and bears the burden of proving itself to the electronic media audience. Although most households are willing to pay for a subscription to cable or satellite television, this isn't true for satellite radio. Part of the problem lies in the dedicated receiver required by the services. To date, the receiver is located in the car or the home, forcing a tough choice by the audience. XM and Sirius both have transportable versions of the receiver, which can be used in a car, boat, or home.

By expanding the variety of places the audience can receive the service, the subscription base for satellite radio should increase. Neither of the existing satellite services has yet reached a break-even point, and neither likely will in the near future. Generally, satellite radio is expected to grow by taking market share from advertiser-supported media (Veronis, Suhler, & Stevenson, 2003).

Point-to-Point or One-to-One Communication

Technological innovation is occurring rapidly in the cell phone arena. The next generation of cell phones will let users more easily take digital pictures, surf the Web, perform instant messaging, play games, access e-mail, and download images, programs, and ring tones from the Internet. These phones also will have high-quality color screens and better voice-activated dialing. In addition, cell phones will continue to merge with personal digital assistants (PDAs) to provide an all-in-one portable communication and computing device.

Cell phones will continue to show strong growth as their versatility, ease of use, and competitive prices encourage more customers to go wireless. Yet despite the popularity of cell phones in this country, the United States lags behind some countries in Asia and Europe, which have penetration rates as high as 85 percent ("Greenville, SC, Tops," 2002).

In 1980, what percentage of television households had cable television?

The new capabilities of cell phones may bring some legal and ethical problems, as well. The managers of athletic clubs and other facilities with locker rooms worry about lawsuits stemming from cell phone picture taking. Also, some cell phone users take advantage of this picture-taking feature to take snapshots of pages from magazines and books so they don't have to buy them. But cell phones may also provide individuals with more security. In Japan, a young female store clerk used a cell phone to take a digital picture of a man who had fondled her on a commuter train. She then called the police and sent them the picture, leading to the prompt arrest of the perpetrator (Kageyama, 2003).

An FCC ruling in late 2003 allowed cell phone users to keep their current numbers when switching cell phone providers. It also allowed customers with landlines to drop that service but keep the number should they switch to a cell phone. This has allowed people to go wireless without worrying about missing the calls made by people who know their published landline phone numbers. Moreover, this change has made cell phone numbers more permanently associated with their users, a relationship previously enjoyed only by landline phones (Browning, 2003).

A current trend that will continue into the future is the convergence of various data and voice networks. Worldwide telephone, cable TV, wireless communication, and computer data networks are becoming less stand-alone systems. That is, they are converging into a powerful unified network based on the Internet protocol packet-switching system, which is versatile and can transmit any kind of information quickly and at low cost.

What this means is that rather than having people make calls to verify transactions, place orders, or move money from businesses to banks and so on, computers are doing it over high-speed broadband wires. And as the amount of information transferred continues to grow, the need for more bandwidth will grow, as well. This need will lead companies in this industry, such as AT&T and Sprint, to seek better ways of moving information from point to point. One method of accomplishing this will be by building and utilizing a **fiber optic network**. Fiber optic wires are capable of transferring more information than either telephone wires or cable.

As is the case for other delivery systems, telecommunications companies will continue to consolidate. Recent and proposed mergers, such as that between Cingular and AT&T in 2004, will form huge companies, leading this part of the industry to an oligopoly similar to those in the cable and satellite industries.

Internet Delivery

The delivery of radio and audio services via the Internet will continue to grow, supported by faster connections, improved compression (to keep sound quality good), but less bandwidth. The possibilities for television program delivery via the Internet are quite real, but the technology is simply not good enough to compete with existing delivery systems. The bandwidth required for full-motion, full-screen television is currently greater than the bandwidth capacity for data transfer. Compression programs are being developed, which will reduce the amount of bandwidth needed for this use, but real-time television program delivery via the Internet is still years away.

In the last few years, some companies have offered video on demand over the Internet. The movie *Shrek,* one of the first popular movies shown, was offered by a company called Intertainer.[2] The movie drew a large audience and had a $3.95 per viewing cost. Intertainer had made some distribution deals with Dreamworks, MGM, and Warner Bros. film studios (Graham, 2002). It is estimated that by 2006, there will be 7.6 million video on demand users over Internet-delivered networks ("Number of VOD Users," 2002).

Another likely development in the future will be the change from wired to wireless transmission of information. In the United States, many large firms, including banks, are making a commitment to **WiFi** (a standard for wireless Internet connections), or wireless information transfer. Since this new technology changeover will require cooperation among network providers, application and software developers, information technology vendors, device manufacturers, content providers, and industries, it will not happen quickly. The next five years is a reasonable timeframe.

Consumer use of WiFi is growing daily. Restaurants, coffee shops, hotels, and universities are just some of the places that are providing wireless Internet service for their customers and students. Data transfer speeds are increasing and connecting is easy. Laptops and PDAs are used to connect to the Internet without the annoyance of wires. When WiFi or similar wireless technology can provide an Internet connection to a car as it is moving, a new era of radio program delivery will begin. One company is working on a satellite-delivered wireless Internet service that will provide both audio streaming and video ("Internet Radio Coming," 2003).

Looming on the horizon is the business of using the Internet and WiFi to make phone calls. The quality of transmission of phone calls using the Internet is improving, and momentum is building for **VOIP (voice over Internet protocol)**. This system might allow consumers to avoid the large telephone companies and use the Internet instead, something that is already done in other countries (Kanellos, 2003). (For more about VOIP, see Chapter 5.)

Summary

Audience members don't pay much attention to delivery systems except when selecting a service or paying the monthly bill. For most of the audience, television is television whether it comes from broadcast, cable, or satellite.

Electronic media delivery systems deliver both entertainment and information to mass audiences. These systems are broadcasting, cable, satellite, multichannel multipoint distribution systems (MMDSs), and satellite master antenna systems (SMATVs). Other systems, like cell phones and data services, deliver content to individuals using a one-to-one model and usually do not deliver entertainment. The Internet delivers information and some entertainment, but thus far, it has not been able to deliver television content similar to that of the other mass delivery systems.

Cable television started out in the late 1940s as a small-time system to help reach the audience that could not be reached by regular terrestrial broadcasting. Strong growth began in the mid 1970s, when cable systems began to use communication satellites to receive programming from all over the country and also began to develop their own programming through national cable channels, pay channels, local origination, and pay-per-view. The cable industry is now switching over from analog to digital signal transmission. Digital cable has a larger channel capacity than analog and doesn't involve stringing additional wires to homes. The industry has consolidated and is now an oligopoly, such that a very few multiple system operators (MSOs) have large numbers of subscribers.

The satellite television industry started with much the same mission as early cable: to reach the audience that could not be reached by other systems. In the mid 1990s, two companies, DirectTV and EchoStar/DISH Network, began to market satellite services that provide a digital signal that can be received by a small dish. These services provide many signals for about the price of standard cable service. From the late 1990s until now, satellite-delivered television has grown steadily.

An important trend in delivery systems is vertical integration. Large media companies now own networks, television stations, newspapers, magazines, cable channels, book publishing companies, movie studios, syndication companies, and television program producing companies. This trend has caused concern among smaller companies that do not own many different media-related entities. One large media company can dominate many aspects of the delivery industry just by supplying its own programs and selling them only to company-owned media outlets and affiliates.

Satellite radio was in the works for about 10 years but didn't begin selling subscriptions until 2001. Two companies, XM Satellite Radio and Sirius Satellite Radio, each provide about 100 channels of digital audio to subscribers for about $10 to $13 per month. Many of the channels are commercial free and provide music and information in a wide variety of styles and formats. A special radio receiver is required to receive the signals, and only paying subscribers can receive them.

Cell phones have become common both in the United States and abroad. Cell phone use has been beneficial to society by providing a means for emergency communication and for friends, family, and acquaintances to stay in touch. The picture-taking ability of new cell phones can create ethical and legal problems regarding privacy. Cell phone use will continue to increase, and cell phones themselves will continue to evolve into multifaceted communication devices.

Data services allow companies to use computers to transmit financial and other business information from point to point, as in credit card purchases for goods and services. The information is transmitted digitally to a central location, where approval for the transaction is made and then relayed back to the store or place of business.

In the future, more delivery systems will become digitized. As broadcast television transmission becomes digital over the next few years, so will the cable systems and satellite systems. The audience will have to upgrade their receiving equipment to keep pace with these delivery systems.

Digitization, convergence, and consolidation of media will also continue. While media consumers will benefit from the technological advances that will occur, individuals, consumer groups, and the government are concerned about a small number of companies controlling too much of the industry. In the future, the audience will have more electronic media choices, with better technical quality and more portability, but it will also have to struggle with having a smaller number of competitors in the industry and the possible negative consequences that creates.

Notes

1. Although people in the United States take electronic media for granted and many are knowledgeable about digital media, much of the world's population, especially people in less-developed countries, cannot afford digital media and have very little, if any, experience with it.
2. Intertainer (www.intertainer.com) filed a $1.6 billion law suit against Sony, Time Warner, Universal Studios, and Movielink, a video on demand (VOD) company set up by these studios. Intertainer claimed that the studios hampered its ability to be successful by cutting off its supply of films and hiring away some of its talent to work for Movielink.

The Internet

 SEE IT THEN

 SEE IT NOW

 SEE IT LATER

SEE IT THEN

History of the Internet and the World Wide Web

Internet Resources: What They Are and How They Got Here

The Rise of Internet Radio

Television's Migration to the Web

SEE IT NOW

How the Internet Works

Internet Users

Navigating the World Wide Web

The World Wide Web and the Mass Media

The Internet and Television

SEE IT LATER

Weblogs

In this chapter, you'll learn about:

- The origins of the Internet and its various functions and resources
- How the Internet works and how it is used by individuals and electronic media professionals
- How young people are using the Internet for music, video, and films and other sources of entertainment and news
- How traditional media outlets are using the Internet to promote their nononline fare
- How the future use of the Internet will impact individuals and the media business

Although many people believe that the Internet is a 1990s invention, this electronically networked system was actually envisioned in the early 1960s. And in just 40 years, technology has developed from being able to send one letter from one computer to another to being able to send almost 10 billion messages around the world every day.

In this chapter, you'll learn about Internet resources, how the Internet works, and the benefits and challenges of online television and radio. You will also read about weblogs, which increase participation in world events, and instant messaging, which keeps us in touch with friends and family, perhaps better than an occasional letter or an expensive long-distance phone call. The Internet has brought improvements to some people's lives and caused problems in others' lives. With every new technology, only by understanding where it came from can we help guide where it is going.

SEE IT THEN

History of the Internet and the World Wide Web

Vinton Cerf, "father of the Internet."

Tim Berners-Lee, "father of the World Wide Web."

In the early 1960s, scientists approached the U.S. government with a formal proposal for creating a decentralized communications network that would be used in the event of a nuclear attack. By 1970, **ARPAnet** (Advanced Research Projects Agency) was created to advance computer interconnections ("Internet History," 1996, Krol; 1995; Pavlik, 1996).

The network established by ARPAnet soon caught the attention of other U.S. agencies, who saw the promise of using an electronic network for sharing information among research facilities and schools. While disco music was hitting the airwaves, Vinton Cerf, later known as "the father of the Internet," and researchers at Stanford University and UCLA were developing packet-switching technologies and transmission protocols that allow the Internet to function. In the 1980s, the National Science Foundation took on the task of designing a network that became the basis for the Internet as it's known today. At the same time, a group of scientists in the European Laboratory of Particle Physics (CERN), headed by Tim Berners-Lee, "the father of the World Wide Web," was developing a system for worldwide interconnectivity that was later dubbed the **World Wide Web** ("Internet History," 1996; Krol, 1995; Pavlik, 1996).

Prior to creation of the Web, information stored on the Internet could be retrieved only through a series of complicated steps and commands. The process was difficult, time consuming, and required an in-depth knowledge of Internet protocols. As such, the Internet was of limited use. In fact, it was largely unnoticed by the public until undergraduate Mark Andreessen and a team of other University of Illinois students developed Mosaic, the first Web browser. Mosaic allowed users to access and share Web-based information through clickable hyperlinks instead of difficult commands and interfaces. Mosaic caught the attention of Jim Clark, founder of Silicon Graphics, who lured Andreessen to California's Silicon Valley to enhance and improve the browser. With Clark's financial backing and Andreessen's know-how, Netscape Navigator was born. This enhanced version of Mosaic made Andreessen one of the first new-technology, under-30-year-old millionaires ("Marc Andreessen," 1997). Since Mosaic and Netscape Navigator, several other browsers—most notably, Internet Explorer—have hit the market.

ZOOM IN   5.1
To see webpages from the good old days, go to www.archive.org and access the WayBack Machine, a service that brings up websites as they were in the past. The archives go as far back as 1996.

Internet Resources: What They Are and How They Got Here

The **Internet** is a vast network of computers from all over the world with no central office or headquarters. People often think of the Internet as one entity, but it is actually comprised of several resources or components that function differently and are used for different reasons.

Electronic Mail

Electronic mail, or **e-mail,** is one of the earliest Internet resources and is currently one of the most widely used applications. The first known e-mail was sent from UCLA to Stanford University in 1969, when researchers attempted to send the word *login*. They managed to send the letter *L* and then waited for confirmation that it had made it to Stanford. They then sent the letter *O* and waited and waited until it arrived. Then they sent the letter *G,* but due to a computer malfunction, it never arrived. Just as the letter *S* was the first successful transatlantic radio signal, the letters *L* and *O* made up the first successful e-mail message (Segailer, 1999).

E-mail has come a long way since that first attempt. Today, e-mail is the most widely used Internet resource, with 9.8 billion messages flying through cyberspace every day. By 2005, four times as many messages will be zapped through the network. In 2000, there were about 505 million e-mail mailboxes, and that number is expected to increase to 1.2 billion by 2005 (Hafner, 2001; "36 Billion E-Mails," 2001).

E-mail has taken on even greater importance since the anthrax-tainted postal mailings in 2001. Hesitancy to handle mail sent through the U.S. Postal Service had businesses scrambling for ways to reduce the number of incoming packages and envelopes. The creation of online marketing and billing, business-to-business e-mail, and new systems for collecting and verifying online signatures has reduced reliance on traditional types of mailing (Callaghan & Gibson, 2001).

Electronic Mailing Lists

Electronic mailing lists are similar to e-mail in that messages are sent to electronic mailboxes for later retrieval. The difference is that e-mail messages are addressed to individual recipients, whereas electronic mailing list messages are addressed to an electronic mailing list's address and then forwarded only to the electronic mailboxes of the list's subscribers.

Electronic mailing lists connect people with similar interests. Most such lists are *topic specific,* which means subscribers trade information about specific subjects, like college football, gardening, computers, dog breeding, and television shows. Many clubs, organizations, special interest groups, classes, and media use electronic mailing lists as a means of communicating among their members. Newsletters, class handouts, club meeting dates, and so on are sent out through the list, rather than as photocopies or other paper materials that are sent through the U.S. Postal Service. Most electronic mailing lists are open to anyone; others are available only on a subscribe-by-permission basis.

Electronic mailing lists are often referred to generically as *listservs;* however, LISTSERV is the brand name of an automatic mailing list server that was first developed in 1986. There are other list servers, such as Majordomo, that also automatically manage and distribute messages posted by their subscribers (Listserv, 2003).

Newsgroups

Similar to electronic mailing lists, **newsgroups** bring together people with similar interests. Newsgroups are discussion and information exchange forums on specific topics, but unlike electronic mailing lists, participants are not required to subscribe and messages are not delivered to individual electronic mailboxes. Instead, newsgroups work by archiving messages for users to find and access at their convenience. Think of a newsgroup as a bulletin board on which flyers are posted and left hanging for people to come by, sift through, and read. On the other hand, using an electronic mailing list is similar to walking around the neighborhood and putting flyers in people's mailboxes.

Chat Rooms

A **chat room** is another type of two-way, online communication. What makes a chat room different is that participants exchange live, real-time messages. It's almost like talking on

Tom Toles, Buffalo (N.Y.) News

What percentage of computer users send e-mail more often than they make long-distance telephone calls?

the telephone, in that a conversation is going on, but instead of *talking,* so-called chatters *type* messages back and forth. There are many different types of chat rooms covering many different topics. The most exciting thing about chat rooms is that you can carry on real-time, immediate-response conversations with people from around the world.

Instant Messaging

Relatively new to the Internet, **instant messaging (IM)** lets you carry on real-time conversations with your friends. But of course, instead of talking, you type in your messages. With just over 70 million users in the United States today, IM has quickly become a favorite way of communicating (Emling, 2002b).

Whereas a chat room conversation occurs among anonymous individuals, instant messaging occurs among people who know each other. Instant messaging is basically a private chat room that alerts you when friends and family are online, waiting for you to converse. Because you are synchronously linked to someone you know, IM has a more personal feel than a chat room and is more immediate than e-mail. Instead of sending messages for anytime retrieval, you're actually conversing with friends and family in real time. Newer IM software boasts video capabilities, so you and your online buddies will feel like you're in the same room.

ZOOM IN   5.2

Go to any search service and do three searches on "listservs," "newsgroups," and "chat rooms." For each, the search service should return a long list of mailing lists, newsgroups, and chat rooms. Join one of each and keep track of the activity. Be sure to keep any instructions of how to unsubscribe later.

Go to Yahoo (**http://messenger.yahoo.com**) or MSN (**http://messenger.msn.com**) for instructions on downloading instant messaging software. Then instant message your friends and classmates.

World Wide Web

The World Wide Web consists of millions of websites, each containing many pages of information. The Web presents information in text, graphic, audio, and video formats, making it unique from other Internet resources. Point-and-click browsers, first developed in the early 1990s, make it easy to travel from website to website. Gathering information is as easy as clicking on your mouse. In some cases, the Web serves as a gateway to other Internet resources. You can often access e-mail, electronic mailing lists, newsgroups, and chat rooms from websites.

The Web is changing the way information and entertainment are received and sent. Messages ranging from personal news to national and international headlines make their way to the audience via the Web. The Web is also altering existing media use habits and the lifestyles of millions of users who have grown to rely on it as a source of entertainment, information, and two-way communication.

Weblogs

A **weblog**, more commonly known as a **blog**, is a new type of website. Blogs are free-flowing journals, kind of "literary self-expressions" (Frauenfelder & Kelly, 2000), in which bloggers spout their opinions, criticize and laud public policy, opine about what's happening in the online and nononline worlds, and connect visitors to essential readings. Blogs are written informally and serve as venues for those who want to be heard and for those who want to be in the know.

Blogging has exploded on the Web scene and is the newest online social phenomenon. A new blogger jumps on the bandwagon every 40 seconds (Levy, 2002b). While estimates vary widely on the number of weblogs (depending on how *weblog* is defined), there were between 20 and 30,000 in the late 1990s (Amis, 2002; Blood, 2001; Frauenfelder & Kelly, 2000) and between 0.5 million and almost 3 million by the end of 2002 (Amis, 2002; Greenspan, 2003).

The Rise of Internet Radio

Almost all local radio stations have established websites to promote themselves, to provide both news and information, and sometimes to cybercast over-the-air fare. These websites lend credence to the media industry's concern that Internet users may one day discover that they no longer need radios. Instead, they'll just access radio programming over the Internet.

The rise of Internet radio somewhat mirrors the development of over-the-air radio. In the early days of wireless radio, the airwaves were dominated by amateur (ham) operators using specialized crystal sets whose signals were picked up by a limited number of listeners who had receiving sets (usually other ham operators). Transmitting and receiving sets were difficult to operate, the reception was poor and full of static, and the sets themselves were large and cumbersome, leaving only a small audience of technologically advanced listeners. In the early days of radio, the technologically adept were the first to gravitate toward the new medium. In the 1990s, the technologically savvy again took the lead, but this time, they paved the way for *cybercasting*. Just as difficult to use radios with poor reception once kept the general public from experiencing the airwaves, bandwidth limitations and slow computer and modem speeds kept many radio fans from listening via the Internet.

All that has changed in recent years. In fact, Internet radio is probably the most improved online technology. In the old days of the Internet, *Geek of the Week,* a 15-minute online program, took almost two hours to download using a 14.4 Kbps modem, which was considered very fast at the time (Quittner, 1995).

RealAudio, now known as RealNetworks, was the first application to bring real-time audio on demand over the Internet (Berniker, 1995). Since the introduction of RealAudio in 1994, thousands of radio stations have made the leap from broadcast to online audiocast. By using RealAudio technology, AM and FM commercial radio, public radio, and college stations can enjoy larger audiences and expand their broadcast fare. This new technology has moved them from simply providing prerecorded audio clips to transmitting real-time audio in continuous streams.

Streaming technology pushes data through the Internet in a continuous flow, so information is displayed on your computer before the entire file has finished downloading. Streamed audio and video selections can be played as they're being sent, so you don't have to wait for the entire file to download. Since RealAudio's introduction some 10 years ago, several other companies have developed similar audio-on-demand applications and new protocols for increasing bandwidth for even faster streaming ("Progressive Networks," 1996; Rafter, 1996a, 1996b).

Both broadcast and Internet radio caught on with the general public only after access and sound clarity improved and after professional stations began transmitting news and music on regular schedules. In the old days, the general public embraced radio only when stations like KDKA started broadcasting regularly scheduled programs and the price went down on radio-receiving sets that were designed for easy use.

In more recent times, small-to-medium market and college stations have generally led the way to the Internet. As their success stories quickly spread throughout the radio industry, other stations eagerly connected to the Net (Noack, 1996). As users

Highlights of Early Internet Radio

December 3, 1994
The University of Kansas makes history when its student-run radio station, KJHK-FM, is one of the first stations to go live on the Internet 24 hours a day (Petrozzello, 1995).

September 5, 1995
The birthday of live Internet audio. Progressive Networks transmit the Seattle Mariners versus New York Yankees game online.

September 6, 1995
SW Networks cybercast Governor Mario Cuomo's speech live from the National Association of Broadcasters convention.

September 9, 1995
Dallas station KLIF-AM is the first commercial radio station to netcast live continuous programming (AudioNet, 1997).

November 20, 1995
Real-time music debuts when a Vince Gill concert from Nashville is cybercast live on MCI's Telecom website. The concert was also simulcast over the TNN cable network and syndicated to radio stations across the nation, giving it the distinction of being the "first-ever triple-cast" (Taylor, 1996b, p. 6).

Highlights of Early Internet Television

September 1994
CBS connects to Prodigy, a proprietary online service.

February 1995
The Weather Channel debuts on CompuServe; a forum provides an outlet for discussing the weather and the channel's coverage.

March 1996
WRNN-TV, a New York–based cable regional news network, launches a website with live online video reports.

March 1996
Lifetime is one of the first cable networks to launch a website.

September 1996
NFL games are shown live online. Highlights from previous games, player profiles, and other background information is accessible while watching live game action in an onscreen show.

October 1996
American Cybercast launches the first TV-type network online and the first online soap opera, *The Spot*.

November 1998
CNN, ABC News, MSNBC, and Fox offer real-time election night coverage, providing up-to-the-minute results for voters.

become more familiar with the Web in general and learn where to find the radio programming of their choice and as computer and Internet technology become less expensive, are easier to use, and deliver better sound quality, online radio may become just as popular as its over-the-air counterpart.

Television's Migration to the Web

The World Wide Web is still in the early stages of development, similar to television in the 1950s (Bimber, 1996). Early television programs were largely adapted to the new medium from radio. Programs such as *Amos 'n' Andy, Life of Riley, The Guiding Light, You Bet Your Life,* and *The Lone Ranger* all originated as radio programs, as did many other shows televised in the 1950s. Given the ability of television to bring so much more life to a program than radio ever could, producers began creating new, exciting, dynamic shows.

Many ardent fans have long hailed television as the ultimate form of entertainment. You can watch television anytime, anywhere, and you get to choose what to watch by the push of a button or the flick of a switch. Yet despite the popularity of watching television, the viewing public is always looking for new ways to boost their viewing pleasure.

Over-the-air television was once the primary means of receiving programming. Although cable was established early in the life of television, it didn't take hold with viewers until the 1970s. More recent technologies, especially satellite, gave rise to newer means of program delivery, and the Web itself was hailed as the "television of the future." The Web was sometimes likened to an advanced form of old interactive television, in which interactivity is the core attraction.

Internet technologies didn't catch up with television. Thus, the 1990s closed with some full-motion video, but the Internet did not evolve into a substitute for television. Internet users with high-end computers could watch short video clips, at most. Users crossed into the twenty-first century with the hope that their desktop machines would soon be capable of receiving both the Internet and television.

 **SEE IT NOW**

How the Internet Works

The Internet operates as a packet-switched network. It takes bundles of data and breaks them up into small packets or chunks that travel through the network independently. Smaller bundles of data move more quickly and efficiently through the network than larger bundles. It's kind of like when you move and dismantle your stereo system. You might put the tuner and CD player in the car but the speakers in the back of the truck. The stereo is still a complete unit, but when transporting, it's more convenient to move each part separately and then reassemble all of the components when you get them to your new place. Briefly, that's how the Internet works, except it disassembles data rather than a stereo system and reassembles the whole unit at its destination point.

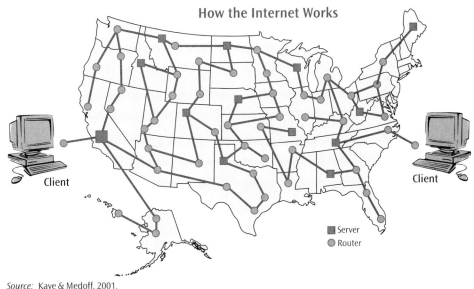

How the Internet Works

Client   Client

■ Server
● Router

Source: Kaye & Medoff, 2001.

On a larger level, an e-mail message, webpage information, image, or other online data flows through interconnected computers from its point of origin to its destination. For example, your computer is the origination point, known as the **client.** The message you send to a friend leaves your client computer and then goes to a server. From there, it travels to one or several routers, then to a server, and finally to your friend's computer, which is also called a *client.*

Servers are basically powerful computers that provide continuous access to the Internet. A server sends message packets to a **router,** a computer that links networks on the Internet. A router sorts each packet of data until the entire message is reassembled, and then it transmits the electronic packets either to other routers or directly to the addressee's server. The server holds the entire message until an individual directs his or her client computer to pick it up (Krol, 1995).

Servers and routers know where to deliver online messages through a system called **transmission control protocols/Internet protocols (TCP/IP),** which define how computers electronically transfer information to each other on the Internet. **TCP** is the set of rules that governs how smaller packets are reassembled into an IP file until all of the data bits are together. Routers follow **IP** rules for reassembling data packets and data addressing so information gets to its final destination. Each computer has its own numerical IP address (which the user usually does not see), to which routers send the information. An IP address usually consists of between 8 and 12 numbers and may look something like *166.233.2.44.*

Because IP addresses are rather cumbersome and difficult to remember, an alternate addressing system was devised. **Domain name system (DNS)** basically assigns a text-based name to a numerical IP address using the following structure: *username@host.subdomain* (Eager, 1994). For example, in *MaryC@anyUniv.edu,* the user name, *MaryC,* identifies the person who was issued Internet access. The @ literally means "at," and *host.subdomain* is the user's location. In this example, *anyUniv* represents a fictitious university. The **top-level domain (TLD),** which is always the last element of an address, indicates the host's type of organization. In this example, *edu* shows that *anyUniv* is an educational institution.

FYI

Top-Level Domains (2002)

.aero	Air transportation industry	.int	International
.arpa	Internet infrastructure	.mil	Military
.biz	Business	.museum	Museum sites
.com	Commercial	.name	Individuals
.coop	Cooperative organization	.net	Network support company
.edu	Education, university	.org	Nonprofit/nongovern-
.gov	Government		mental agency
.info	General use	.pro	Professional

Sources: Foust, 2002; Stellin, 2001.

Internet Use by Demographic Group

AGE

18–27	79%
28–39	79%
40–49	71%
50–58	61%
59–68	43%
69+	18%

RACE/ETHNICITY

White	62%
Black	43%
Hispanic	62%

HOUSEHOLD INCOME

<$30,000	40%
$30,000–$49,000	69%
$50,000–$74,000	83%
$75,000+	89%

Source: "Internet Penetration Demographics," 2004.

Internet Users

The Internet has gone from a largely unknown medium to one now used by over 165 million Americans, or about 58.5 percent of the population ("How Many Online?" 2002). An estimated 72 million go online on an average day ("Daily Internet Activities," 2003). Estimates on the number of *hours* users spend online vary widely, but most research indicates that individuals spend between 9.5 and 15 hours per week online ("Almost Three-Quarters in U.S. Online," 2001; "GVU's Tenth WWW User Survey," 1998; Kaye & Johnson, 2002, 2003; "What's Your Daily Dose?" 1997). Almost one-third of users access their e-mail every day ("Internet News Audience," 1999).

Although male users originally dominated the Web, women's share of use has increased to the point that they now surpass male users: 50.6 percent of American adults with Internet access are women and 49.4 percent are men ("Changing Online Population," 2000). Women users tend to be slightly younger (31.9 years) than their male counterparts (33.4 years). Generally, online users tend to be highly educated and more affluent than the U.S. population at large, and users tend to live in urban and suburban areas ("Shifting Internet Population," 2003). About 40 percent of Internet users are college graduates, compared to just 22 percent of all Americans ("GVU's Tenth WWW User Survey," 1998; "Internet and American Life," 2000; "Internet News Audience," 1999).

College students are the most avid of computer and Internet users.

College Students and the Internet

- 86 percent use the Internet.
- 85 percent own a computer.
- 73 percent use the Internet more than the library.
- 72 percent check e-mail everyday.
- 71 percent go online more than once a day.
- 66 percent use at least two e-mail addresses.
- 65 percent report absences to professors via e-mail.
- 61 percent spend one to four hours online per day.
- 60 percent have downloaded music.
- 26 percent use instant messaging.
- 20 percent began using the Internet between the ages of 5 and 8.

Sources: "Half of All College Students," 1999; Irvine, 2002; "Majority of U.S. College Students," 2002.

How Many Online?

This table shows the number of Internet users by continent for the year 2002 with projected growth each year through 2006. An *Internet* user is defined as an individual who consistently uses the Internet with access from work, school, home, or multiple locations.

CONTINENT	YEAR				
	2002	2003	2004	2005	2006
North America	212,625,000	222,882,250	234,422,143	244,682,327	256,154,022
Central/South America	25,603,581	32,653,405	43,793,278	59,450,160	80,780,979
Europe	163,532,970	195,513,220	224,840,203	240,579,018	257,419,549
Middle East/Africa	9,235,050	10,707,998	11,571,220	12,535,406	13,616,264
Asia/Pacific	151,284,715	203,625,480	238,007,338	273,034,857	313,433,527
Total Worldwide	562,281,316	665,382,353	752,634,182	830,281,767	921,404,341

Source: Waite, 2002.

About 20 percent.

Navigating the World Wide Web

Web browsers, such as Netscape Navigator and Internet Explorer, are the tools that allow access to online content. Browsers interpret hypertext markup language, or HTML (which is Web programming language), and reconstruct text and graphics. **Hypertext** is "non-linear text, or text that does not flow sequentially from start to finish" (Pavlik, 1996, p. 134). The beauty of hypertext is that it allows **nonlinear** or **nonsequential** movement among and within documents. Hypertext is what lets you skip all around a website, in any order you please, and to jump from the beginning of a page to the end and then to the middle, simply by pointing and clicking on hot buttons, links, and icons.

As noted earlier, Mosaic was followed by many other Web browsers. Although all Web browsers operate similarly, each has its own unique features. Netscape Navigator (commonly referred to as Netscape) and Microsoft's Internet Explorer (IE), the two most popular and widely used, fiercely compete for audience share. In the mid 1990s, Netscape led the U.S. market, but IE now dominates with about a 90 percent share of users. Netscape holds only about a 7 percent share, and Mozilla and other browsers fight for the remaining small share of the market. The situation could change dramatically, however, as America Online (AOL) goes through with its proposal to switch its browser from IE to Netscape (Hicks, 2004; Millard, 2003).

Online services, such as AOL and Prodigy, are proprietary companies that provide information to their subscribers. These proprietary services provide customers with access to e-mail and the World Wide Web as well as other online databases, and they provide server space for subscribers to post personal homepages (Berkman, 1994).

Rather than go through a proprietary service, many users connect to the Internet through an **Internet service provider (ISP)**, which provides telephone dial-up service, or through cable modem service, which is provided by a local cable company. Cable modems transmit data at speeds much faster than telephone lines, but monthly access fees are generally higher for cable than for telephone service.

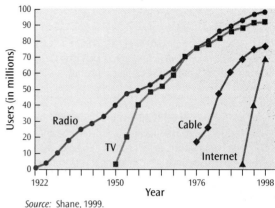

Media Adoption Rates

Source: Shane, 1999.

ZOOM IN 5.3

Go to the following websites to find out more about who goes online:

- NUA Surveys   www.nua.com/surveys/how_many_online/index.html
- GVU Surveys   www.cc.gatech.edu/gvu/user_surveys/
- The Pew Research Center Survey   http://people-press.org

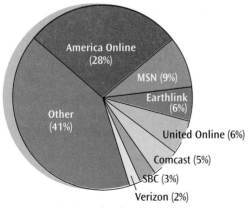

Internet Access by Provider

America Online (28%)
MSN (9%)
Earthlink (6%)
Other (41%)
United Online (6%)
Comcast (5%)
SBC (3%)
Verizon (2%)

Source: "By the Numbers," 2004.

The World Wide Web and the Mass Media

Many Internet users are abandoning radio and television for the Internet, figuring that it's better to access static-free, online audio than to listen to an over-the-air broadcast and that it's more convenient to read about current events and watch video clips online than to wait for a televised newscast.

One of the main concerns about online content doesn't regard delivery but the nature of the content itself. Decentralized

Hypertext Mark-Up Language (HTML)

HTML is the World Wide Web programming language that basically guides an entire document or site. For instance, it tells browsers how to display online text and graphics, how to link pages, and how to link within a page. HTML also designates font style, size, and color.

Specialized commands or tags determine a document's layout and style. For example, to center a document's title—say, *How to Plant Roses*—and display it as a large headline in italics, the tags *<center><H1><I>* are inserted before and after the title, respectively, like this:

<center><H1><I>HOW TO PLANT ROSES...</i></h1></center><P><UL><B>

The first set of commands within the brackets tells the browser to display the text centered and in italics. The set of bracketed commands containing a slash tells the browser to stop displaying the text in the designated style.

The HTML source code for most webpages can be viewed by clicking on the "View" pull-down box in the Netscape tool bar and then clicking on the "Document Source" option. Note in the screen showing the source code that the *<img src=hangl.gif align=left>* command places the image of the hanging flowers next to the headline.

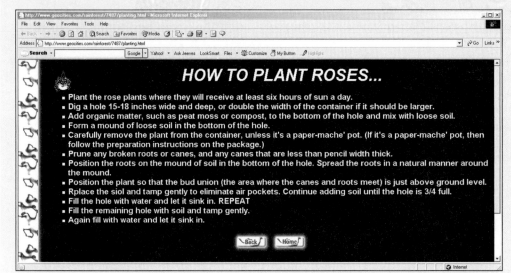

Simple text-based website.

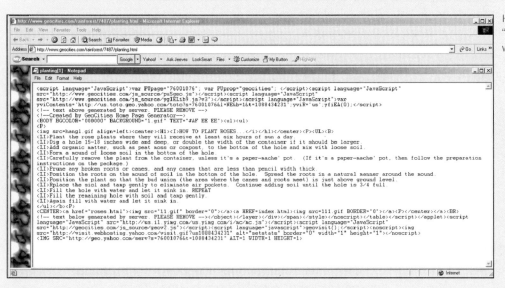

HTML source code for "How to Plant Roses" webpage.

information dissemination means that online materials are often not subjected to traditional methods of source checking and editing. Thus, they may be inaccurate and not very credible.

When listeners tune to radio news or viewers watch television news, they are generally aware of the information source. They know, for instance, that they're listening to news provided by National Public Radio (NPR) or watching the ABC network. In addition, broadcast material is generally written and produced by a network or an independent producer or credentialed journalist. In general, audiences rely on these sources and believe them to be trustworthy, accurate, and objective.

However, Internet users, especially novices, cannot be sure that what they read and see online is credible and accurate, especially if it is posted by an unfamiliar source. Many websites are posted by reliable and known sources, such as CNN and NBC. However, anyone can produce a webpage or post a message on a bulletin board or chat room, bringing into question source credibility. Internet users must grapple with the amount of credence to give to what they see and read online. Thus, it's a good idea to sift through cyber information very carefully. Users should be cautious of accepting conjecture as truth and of using Web sources as substitutes for academic texts, traditional books, and other media that check their sources and facts for accuracy before publication.

Online Radio Today

Being a disc jockey (DJ) or a station manager or owner is a dream for many people. But with Internet know-how, an online connection, and the right software, that dream can come true. Getting into the business of online radio is much less expensive and a whole lot easier than buying a broadcast station or competing with other DJs for a couple of hours of over-the-air time.

Many people aren't interested in delivering radio programming, but they sure do like to listen to it. Internet radio is catching the ears of Web users and has the potential of becoming a viable alternative to over-the-air broadcasting. Online radio offers so much more to its audience than broadcast stations, which are limited by signal range and audio-only output. Internet radio can deliver audio, text, graphics, and video to satisfy a range of listener needs ("Radio Fans Tuning Online," 2001).

Currently, almost all of the nation's 13,000 radio stations have some sort of Internet presence (*Broadcasting & Cable Yearbook,* 2002–2003). While some audio sites are actually radio station websites that retransmit portions of their over-the-air programs, others produce programs solely for online use and are not affiliated with any broadcast stations. Many of these sites offer very specific types of music in an attempt to reach small target audiences. A site may feature, for example, Swedish rock, Latin jazz, or other very specific and hard-to-find music. There are hundreds of audio programs available on the Net. To hear them, you just need to go to any online search service or radio program guide to get the time and place of a live program or a long list of website addresses on which audio files reside.

Radio station websites are promotional by nature, and most also offer local news and entertainment information and have the capability of transmitting audio clips or delivering live programming. However, doing so has hit a snag. Live audio is a great way for consumers who don't have access to a radio or who live outside the signal area to listen to their favorite station. But after many complaints from record labels, artists, and others, the Library of Congress implemented royalty fees, requiring webcasters to pay 7 cents per song per listener. While labels and artists claim this fee is too low, online music providers say it's too high. They argue that they can't possibly generate enough online advertising to cover the cost and so have stopped streaming. Over-the-air radio stations already pay royalties (usually a percentage of revenue for the music they

Cost per Music Download

As these figures show, webcasters pay for their popularity:

Song played 100 times per day = $7 per day

Song played 1,000 times per day = $70 per day

Song played 10,000 times per day = $700 per day

Song played 100,000 times per day = $7,000 per day

Song played 1,000,000 times per day = $70,000 per day

play) but have been exempt from paying for each song played. The implementation of royalty fees has caused many stations to stop streaming their music. Other stations have made agreements with third-party sites that stream a station's signal but charge users a subscription fee that is used to cover per-song royalties (Bowman, 2002; Ho, 2002).

Instead of cutting cybermusic, it would seem that the music industry would be happy that it exists. Cybercasting is a great way to get exposure for little-known artists, who have a hard time getting airplay on traditional stations. Additionally, listeners can easily sample new music, and links are often provided to sites for purchasing CDs. But the industry argues that listening to music online doesn't boost sales, and if people can listen to their favorite music for free, they're unlikely to buy it (Bowman, 2002).

Online radio's woes are not limited to paying royalties. It seems that commercial actors want to be paid extra when commercials containing their voices are played online. Four of the nation's largest commercial radio companies, representing thousands of stations across the United States, bowed to pressure from the American Federation of Television and Radio Artists and stopped streaming commercials over the Internet in spring 2001 ("Radio Stations Shut Down," 2001).

Some stations have resumed streaming their content but sans commercials and are investigating software that deletes over-the-air commercials and replaces them with Internet-only ones ("Clear Channel Returning," 2001). The combination of paying per-listener royalty fees and the dispute concerning commercial actor fees has radio stations thinking about whether the fees are worth the benefits of live streaming.

From Over the Air to Over the Internet

Broadcast stations are concerned that their listening audience is leaving them behind for the Internet. While some studies claim that radio listening is decreasing among Internet users, others claim that radio is gaining favor among those who go online.

As mentioned already, early online radio was difficult to listen to and hard to access. Downloading a music file took an excruciatingly long time. Moreover, the playback was tinny and music would often fade in and out. Few Internet users had computers that could handle audio, and few stations were streaming live content (Quittner, 1995). Given these problems, several older studies found that only 5 to 13 percent of Web users reported that the amount of time they spent listening to over-the-air radio had decreased as a result of using the Web ("American Internet User Survey," 1997; Bromley & Bowles, 1995; Kaye, 1998).

More recently, a study of politically interested Internet users has reported that 27.7 percent spend less time with radio news since becoming Internet users (Kaye & Johnson, 2003). Yet other studies have discovered that those who go online are actually more likely than nonusers to listen to the radio ("Internet News Audience," 1999; Stempel, Hargrove, & Bernt, 2000). It could be that the more time users spend on the Internet, the less time they have to devote to other media use, such as radio listening. On the other hand, it could be that the Internet and radio are compatible media. Both can be used at the same time.

Rather than turn on a radio and wait for a long period of time to hear news or music, Internet users seem to have discovered that they can just as easily connect online and listen to audio-streamed news and music at their convenience. And so, Internet users may not be turning their backs on traditional radio content but rather abandoning the old over-the-air delivery for the new online delivery, which provides clearer audio at convenient times (Kaye & Johnson, 2003). One study found that about 17 percent of Internet users often or sometimes listen to Internet-based radio while they are online ("TV Watching Down," 2001). If listeners are going to go to the Internet, stations should offer streamed programming and other broadcast content so that listeners at least migrate to the stations' online counterparts.

25 percent.

Downloading Music from the Internet
(Don't Try This at Home)

In 1999, Internet use was transformed when college student Shawn Fanning created **Napster,** the first software for finding, downloading, and swapping **MP3** (Moving Picture Experts Group, Audio Layer 3) music files online. Young adults' love for music made the MP3 format and MP3 player the hottest trend since the transistor radio.

All that file sharing, both legal and illegal, spawned a new way to obtain and listen to music. Gone are the days when a song clip could take up to an hour to download and then be so garbled that it wasn't worth the effort. Now, MP3 audio often sounds better than what plays over the airwaves, and you can download tunes and take them anywhere, instead of carrying around CDs or tapes.

Downloading music has really become quite the rage. Of the 60 million Internet households in the United States, about 25.8 million (43 percent) regularly download music (Emling, 2002a). This means that an incredible amount of music is flowing between the Internet and the nation's PCs.

Most music-swapping sites neither own nor sell music. Rather, they work by looking into a user's hard drive, making note of all the MP3 songs, and listing them on a central registry. When the user wants to download music, he or she just enters the name of the artist or song and sees who else on the network has it on their computers. With the push of a button or two, the song is copied onto the user's computer (Cohen, 2000).

The advantages of moving your music files from your PC to a portable player are that you can take your music with you anywhere and that you can download and organize whatever music you want to hear. Whether your portable music device plays MP3 files, cassette tapes, or CDs, it lets you escape into another world. Taking a bus ride or long flight, grocery shopping, exercising, and other mundane activities are all easier to endure with your favorite music. Time seems to go by faster when music breaks the monotony and the silence. In fact, the use of portable music players is sometimes criticized for making it too easy to avoid the world at hand and to shut out other people.

Although it's legal for music owners to record their personal, store-bought CDs in another format or to a portable player, sharing copies with others who haven't paid for the music is considered piracy and copyright infringement. At first, music file-sharing sites seemed like a good idea, but they quickly ran into all kinds of copyright problems and found themselves knee deep in lawsuits. After building a clientele of about 80

99 Cents per Download

So where does your 99 cents go when you pay to download a song from a legal music site? Here's an example from Apple Computer's iTunes:

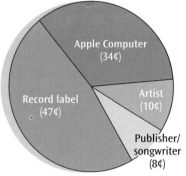

Apple Computer (34¢)
Record label (47¢)
Artist (10¢)
Publisher/ songwriter (8¢)

Source: Spors, 2003.

Free Music/Fee Music

The Web is almost impossible to regulate. Music industry regulators have the difficult task of chasing down illegal sites. But as illegal sites are shut down, others are opened up. On any given day, about 800 million files are available for copying on illegal services like KaZaa, WinMX, and Grokster ("Kiplinger Monitor," 2003). Here's what's involved in using the legal services available:

LEGAL SERVICE	MONTHLY SUBSCRIPTION?	DOWNLOAD ALBUMS?	PRICE PER DOWNLOAD
MusicNet (AOL)	Yes	No	Monthly fee plus $.79*
Real One Rhaposody	Yes	No	Included in monthly fee
iTunes	No	Yes	$.99 single ($10 album)*
musicmatch	No	Yes	$.99 single ($9.99 album)*
Napster	No	Yes	$.99 single (30-sec. clips free) ($9.95 album)*

*2003 prices
Sources: Croal, 2003; Roberts, 2003.

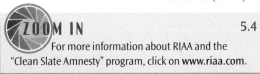

TOP 15   Most Downloaded Artists (2003)

1. Eminem	9. Ludacris
2. 50 Cent	10. Justin Timberlake
3. Nelly	11. Linkin Park
4. R. Kelly	12. 2Pac
5. Jennifer Lopez	13. Mariah Carey
6. Jay-Z	14. Ja Rule
7. Christina Aguilera	15. Sean Paul
8. Lil' Kim	

Source: Levy, 2003b.

million users but facing several years of legal wrangling, Napster went offline in July 2001 ("Judge Cues," 2002; Richtel, 2001, 2002).

Napster made its comeback in late 2003, but this time, it's legal. The service now charges users per download, with the payments going to music companies, publishers, and artists to make up for what they claim to have lost in CD sales ("Let's Make a Deal," 2001; "Napster Previews New Service," 2002). The question is whether Internet users will now pay for what they used to get for free. One study has reported that only about one-quarter of Internet users who downloaded music in the past would be willing to pay to do so in the future ("Most Net Users," 2001), and another study has claimed that only about one-third of college students would pay more than $8.50 per month to download music ("Students Would Pay," 2001). Yet another report found that people who download free music do so to sample it but then delete it because it takes up too much space on their hard drives. If they like the music, they'll go out and buy it (Husted, 2002).

The recording industry isn't finished with music pirates, however, and is now turning its attention to individual users. In fall 2003, the Recording Industry Association of America (RIAA) sued nearly 300 music lovers, targeting excessive users. The RIAA is serious about getting its message out: "Importing a free song is the same as shoplifting a disc from a record store" (Levy, 2003b, p. 39). In some cases, the RIAA is holding individuals liable for millions of dollars in lost revenue, sometimes equaling up to $150,000 per song. The RIAA is already working out settlements in the $3,000 to $5,000 range (Levy, 2003b) and has proposed a "Clean Slate Amnesty" program for those who want to avoid litigation by issuing a written promise to purge their computers of all files and never download music again (Self, 2003). Although it's recognized that the RIAA can't go after everyone, just over half of those who regularly download music claim that the recent crackdown has made them less likely to continue to pirate music (Levy, 2003b). Indeed, a new study shows that the percentage of U.S. Internet users who download music has dropped from 29 percent to 14 percent (Stone, 2004).

ZOOM IN   5.4

For more information about RIAA and the "Clean Slate Amnesty" program, click on **www.riaa.com**.

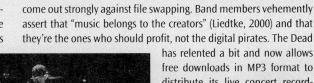

The Grateful Dead: Live Recording Swapping (Yes), Online File Swapping (No)

The Grateful Dead has long been allowing the recording of its concerts, and the band has even gone so far as setting aside areas at live shows so fans can maximize the quality of its recordings. Deadheads around the world happily swap and copy the tapes, and band members are grateful they do so, as long as fans don't profit from the tapes.

Even though the band is a pioneer in music swapping, it has

come out strongly against file swapping. Band members vehemently assert that "music belongs to the creators" (Liedtke, 2000) and that they're the ones who should profit, not the digital pirates. The Dead has relented a bit and now allows free downloads in MP3 format to distribute its live concert recordings, as long as the distribution is for noncommerical purposes only (Krigel, 1999; Liedtke, 2000).

The Internet and Television

Many claim that using the Internet is functionally similar to using television: Users face a screen displaying text and graphics, which, in some instances, also includes audio and video components. Switching from website to website is, in some ways, similar to changing television channels. When Internet users wish to switch from one website to another, they may do so by typing in a known **uniform resource locator (URL)**, by simply clicking on a hotlink, or by clicking on their browser's "Back" and "Forward" buttons, which function like the up and down arrow keys on a television remote control device. Even the lingo of Web browsing is borrowed from television. Commonly used terms such as *surfing* and *cruising,* which are used to describe traversing from one website to another, are also used to describe television channel-switching behavior (Kaye & Medoff, 2001).

Now, new combo computer monitors/televisions further integrate the utility of the Internet and television. Flat-panel displays connect into DVD players, VCRs, and cable television yet also operate in a PC mode. These displays also feature picture-in-picture capabilities that let you size the television window so you can watch your favorite program while using your computer (Miller, 2002).

While full-blown television programs are not yet available over the Internet, **RealNetworks** is setting itself up as a cable provider for the Internet. RealNetworks' RealOne SuperPass subscription service brings television to the screen. Subscribers with Real-Player Plus select among CNN, ABC News, The Weather Channel, CNN Money, and FOX Sports for online, full-motion video of network programming. Subscribers are also treated to Major League Baseball and NASCAR video highlights along with several audio programs. Down the road, RealNetworks sees itself as a pay-per-view, on-demand, online television provider (Keefe, 2002).

The Web is slowly evolving from a static text and graphic medium to one capable of delivering full-motion video. Even so, it still isn't possible to deliver program-length content online. Even when such delivery becomes technologically possible, the television industry will need to determine whether it is economically feasible to do so. Until then, Internet users will have to be content with short video clips.

Audience Fragmentation

The traditional broadcast television model expected programs to appeal to millions of viewers. Then cable television came along and altered the model by introducing **narrowcasting**, in which topic-specific shows are expected to appeal to smaller but more interested and loyal audiences. The Internet has taken narrowcasting a step further by targeting information to smaller groups and individuals and cybercasting it straight to home computers and even to pagers and cell phones. The Web is thus becoming a "personal broadcast system" (Cortese, 1997, p. 96).

The television industry is worried that the Web is further fragmenting an already fragmented audience. In the early days of television, viewership was mostly shared among three major broadcast television networks, which were and still are fiercely competitive. (Even a small percentage gain in the number of viewers means millions of dollars of additional advertising revenue.) Cable television, which often offers 60-plus channels, has only further fragmented the viewing audience. Now, as viewers increasingly subscribe to cable and satellite delivery systems and turn to the Web as a new source of information and entertainment, the size of television's audience is eroding further—and with it, potential advertising revenue.

To help offset audience loss and to retain current viewers, most television networks have established websites on which they promote their programs and stars and offer visitors insights into the world of television. Many new and returning television shows are heavily promoted online with banner ads, a website, and sometimes a special chat room. As one TV executive said, "The more they talk about it, the more they watch it" (Krol, 1997, p. 40). Television program executives view the Internet as a magnet to their televised fare.

Using Television, Using the Web

In many ways, how we use the Web closely mirrors our television viewing. There are two basic ways we watch television: instrumentally and ritualistically. *Instrumental viewing* tends to be goal oriented and content based; we watch television with a certain type of program in mind. *Ritualistic viewing* is less goal oriented and more habitual in nature; we watch television for the act of watching, without regard to program content (Rubin, 1984).

Internet users also connect to the Web both instrumentally and ritualistically. Sometimes, we may go online seeking specific information; we pay attention to content and actively move from site to site with a clear goal in mind. At other times, we may get on the Web because it's a habit or just to pass time, exploring sites by randomly clicking on hotlinks.

You can't use the Web as mindlessly as you can watch television, but many pages are designed to let you kick back and become a "web potato" instead of a "couch potato." Pages are designed to be compelling and hold your attention longer on each screen, so you don't have to scroll and click as much. Longer video and audio segments are aimed at keeping you glued to the screen for longer periods of time. As video monitors become larger and resolution clearer, you'll feel like you're watching television, rather than a computer (Kaye & Medoff, 2001).

Selecting Television Programs and Websites

Wielding a television remote control device gives viewers the power to create their own patterns of television channel selection. Some viewers may quickly scan through all the available channels, while others may slowly sample a variety of favorite channels before selecting one program to watch (Heeter, D'Allessio, Greenberg, & McVoy, 1988). Television viewers tend to surf through the lowest-numbered channels on the dial (2 through 13) more often than the higher-numbered channels (Bollier, 1989). Unlike television, however, the Web doesn't have prime locations on its "dial," so one website doesn't have an inherent location advantage over another (Levy, 1995). However, sites with short and easy-to-remember domain names may be accessed more frequently than their counterparts with longer and more complicated URLs ("TCP/IP Green Thumb," 1998).

Channel and Website Repertoire

As users become adept at making their way around the Web, customized styles of browsing are emerging. Some users may only access a set of favorite sites, while others may not be loyal to any particular site. When viewers sit down to watch television, they usually grab the remote control and start pushing buttons. But instead of randomly moving from one channel to another, most viewers have developed a favorite set of channels they go through first. Most viewers' channel repertoire consists of an average of 10 to 12 channels, regardless of the number of channels offered by their cable systems (Ferguson & Perse, 1993; Heeter, 1985).

These television-viewing behaviors may be transferred to using the Web. As users become more familiar with online content, they may develop their own repertoire of favorite sites that they link to regularly. These selected sites can be easily bookmarked for instant and more frequent access (Kaye & Medoff, 2001).

Similar to how television adapted its programs from radio, many websites reproduce materials that have already appeared in traditional media. For instance, many news sites and other media-oriented sites are made up largely of text taken directly from the pages of newspapers, magazines, brochures, radio and television scripts, and other sources. In some cases, however, materials are adapted more specifically to the Web. The text is edited and rewritten for visual presentation and screen size, and short, summary versions may be linked to longer, detailed ones. Bold graphic illustrations, audio and video components, and interactive elements also enliven webpages and give them a television-like appearance (Kaye & Medoff, 2001).

Television-oriented sites are still typically used to promote televised fare and are among the most popular websites, excluding search services. Each of the big-three television networks (ABC, NBC, and CBS) and dozens of cable networks tried out the Web for the first time in 1994 (Mandese, 1995), and all now have their own websites. You can go online to find out the week's guest line-up on *The Late Show with David Letterman,* to find out what happened on your favorite soap opera, to chat with other fans about your favorite show or star, and to find out about upcoming episodes.

Multitasking takes on new meaning when it involves using the Web and watching television at the same time.

The Web and Television News

The Web is an ideal venue for reporting the news in that it eliminates the constraints of time and space. Most news organizations gather more information than they have the time to air or the space to print. But on the Web, an unlimited amount of news can be presented. Stories don't have to be written to fill a small number of seconds or inches in a column. Online news is sometimes written as a summary with a link to an in-depth version as well as related stories. Hyperlinked stories give site visitors greater control over the news they receive by allowing them to select those reports they find most interesting.

The Web also has other advantages in reporting news. Late-breaking news can be added almost instantaneously, and stories can be updated and amended as needed. Moreover, online archives of yesterday's news are available to news junkies, who no longer have to worry about missing a television newscast. Additionally, Web news is richly presented in audio, text, video, and graphic formats. Whereas radio is bound to audio, television to audio and video, and newspapers to text and graphics, the Web has limitless options for presentation. Radio news on the Web is presented visually, television news with text, and newspaper stories with audio. The characteristics that distinguish radio and television news presentation from one another fade on the Web (Kaye & Medoff, 2001).

The Web has becoming increasingly important to both television networks and affiliate stations as an alternative means of distributing around-the-clock information about the latest events. Television stations often work with Internet companies to help develop and maintain their online news presence. For example, Internet Broadcasting Systems (IBS) develops, operates, and sells advertising on television station websites. IBS brings the latest news to station websites by placing online journalists in station newsrooms and through its partnerships with CNN Newsource and the Associated Press.

Online media are having a difficult time distinguishing themselves from their competitors. Given this, media sites are turning to brand awareness to motivate consumers to select one site over another, such as CBS SportsLine over ESPN online. The media aim to transfer their strong brand names, such as NBC and CNN, to the online environment. Internet experts speculate that early users of the Internet were not brand sensitive but rather tried out many different sites and returned to the ones they liked the best, regardless of the site's originator. Users who are more Web tentative tend to be brand loyal and stick to known sites. In other words, a Web surfer who regularly watches CNN on television may be more likely to access CNN Interactive than another Web news site (Haring, 1997).

What two types of websites do U.S. women between the ages of 18 and 24 visit most often?

Regardless of whether news is generated by radio or television online content delivery is evolving as the Web gains recognition as a distinct medium. Traditional ways of reporting and presentation are giving way to dynamic and interactive methods that hold promise for engaging and drawing new audiences to the Web.

Is the Web Stealing Television's Viewers?

Just as radio's audience was encroached on by broadcast television and, in turn, broadcast television's viewers were drawn to cable, many fear that the Internet is slowly attracting users away from radio and television. Time spent on the Web is time that could be spent watching television, in particular.

In the mid 1990s, the Internet was touted as the up-and-coming substitute for television. The physical similarities between a television and a computer monitor, coupled with the promise that online content would soon be as plentiful and exciting as that on television, led people to believe that the Internet would soon replace television (Neufeld, 1997). The novelty of the Internet also drew many television viewers out of plain curiosity.

During this time frame, there was some movement away from television. Early reports claimed that between 18 and 37 percent of Web users were watching less television than they had before becoming users (Bromley & Bowles, 1995; "GVU's Tenth WWW User Survey," 1998; "Internet Eats into TV Time," 1996; Kaye, 1998; "Why Internet Advertising?" 1997). More recent reports have been mixed on whether people are tuning out of television and into the Internet. Some academic and industry studies claim that the Internet is cutting more deeply into the time spent watching television than with other traditional media (Cole, 2001; Nie & Ebring, 2000). Yet other studies claim that the Internet has not affected the time viewers spend with television (Cai, 2002; "Getting Serious Online," 2002; "Homes with Net Access," 1998; Kaye & Johnson, 2003; Lin, 2001), except perhaps among those individuals who watch little television in the first place ("TV v. Net," 1998).

Some of the Internet audience may have tired of waiting for television-like video and programming and so turned back to the broadcast medium. People seem to flock to a new medium because it's new, but when the novelty wears off, they gradually return to their previous media use patterns (Perse & Dunn, 1998). Recent research has shown that households with Internet access are more likely to buy pay-per-view programming and to pay $50 or more per month for cable or satellite services than homes without Internet access ("Net and TV," 2001). Internet users are apparently still finding time to watch television.

Before people start watching their computers as they now watch their televisions, online content must become as compelling and visually interesting as that on television and deliver programming rather than promotions. Quality online programming is expensive to produce, and only if networks start "charging millions for an online ad" will they be able to justify "proportional investment in content creation" (Shaw, 1998, p. 18). In the meantime, online polling is a new way of engaging television viewers and directing them to specific websites. Scrolling video at the bottom of the television screen directs viewers to these online polls. Online voters selected two new cast members for CBS's *As the World Turns,* and the network also asked viewers to cast new stars for its *Guiding Light* (Hall, 2003). The National Dog Show competition, which aired on Thanksgiving Day, 2003, asked viewers to vote online for the "Best in Show" dog (Yu, 2003), and the 2003 broadcasts of college football games urged viewers to connect to

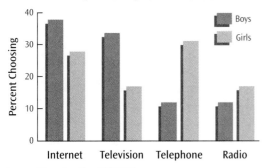

Kids' Choice

What would kids 8 to 17 years old choose
if told they could only have one medium?

Source: "More Fun Than TV?" 2002.

the Capital One site to vote for their favorite college mascot. Online voters have also helped select the winner of *American Idol,* Major League Baseball all-star players, and Super Bowl most valuable players.

Television is a bit protected from Internet pillaging for several reasons. Online technology still can't deliver the same clear video as television, and television-quality programs are not yet available on the Web. The Web is exploding with sites that complement traditional offerings but also offer content not found elsewhere. Some websites offer short episodes (*webisodes*) of online-only programming. Free of the time and space constraints that plague traditional media, Web authors and designers can expand their offerings and produce Web-only materials and Web versions of traditionally delivered fare.

Given the ongoing advances in full-motion video technology, one day, you'll be able to download a television program and watch it in its entirety (Rupley, 1996). The Web has the potential of carrying traditionally televised fare and enhanced interactive programming and competing with the television industry for the viewing audience. Someday, television viewers may abandon the medium for newer online delivery systems. There are many indications that television and the Internet will eventually unite, making it unnecessary for a household to have both a traditional television set and a separate computer with Internet access. In the meantime, the Web is primarily a promotional vehicle for the networks' broadcast programs and their limited Web-only programming fare. It is also a unique medium, on which original and adapted content live side by side.

FYI

A Sampling of Radio and Television Online

SITES THAT LINK TO THOUSANDS OF RADIO STATION WEBSITES

Radio Locator   www.radio-locator.com

Radio Tower   www.radiotower.com

BRS Radio Directory   www.radio-directory.fm

SITES THAT LINK TO TELEVISION STATION WEBSITES

Newslink   www.newslink.org/broad.html

NEWS SITES

ABC Television   www.abcnews.com

ABC Radio Network   www.abcradio.com

BBC   www.bbc.co.uk/radio

BBC Radio   www.bbc.co.uk/radio1

CBS Television   www.cbs.com

CBS SportsLine   www.cbs.sportsline.com/cbssports

CNN Interactive   www.cnn.com

ESPN SportsZone   http://msn.espn.go.com

FOXNews Online   www.fox.com

National Public Radio   www.npr.org

MSNBC   www.msnbc.msn.com

Radio Free Europe   www.rferl.org

Voice of America   www.voa.gov

TELEVISION STATION SITES

KGTV   www.thesandiegochannel.com

KLAS-TV   www.klas-tv.com

KPIX-TV   www.cbs5.com

WBIR-TV   www.wbir.com

WBOC-TV   www.wboc.com

WFLA-TV   www.wfla.com

TELEVISION BROADCAST NETWORKS ONLINE

ABC   http://abc.go.com

CBS   www.cbs.com

NBC   http://nbc.com

FOX   www.fox.com

PAX   www.paxtv.com

UPN   www.upn.com

WB   www2.warnerbros.com/web/main/television/ television.jsp

PBS   www.pbs.org

TELEVISION CABLE NETWORKS ONLINE

Comedy Central   www.comcentral.com

Discovery Channel   www.discovery.com

Dominion (Sci-Fi Channel)   www.scifi.com

E! Online   www.eonline.com

ESPN   http://espn.go.com

HBO   www.hbo.com

The Learning Channel   http://tlc.discovery.com

Lifetime   www.lifetimetv.com

MTV Online   www.mtv.com

Nick-at-Nite   www.tvland.com/nickatnite

ONLINE TELEVISION LISTINGS

TV Guide Online   www.tvguide.com

SEE IT LATER

Weblogs

Although weblogs (also known as *blogs*) have been part of the Internet landscape since the late 1990s, they became widely popular shortly after September 11, 2001. These diary-type sites were an ideal venue for the outpouring of grief and anger that followed the terrorist attacks on the United States (Jesdanun, 2001; "Weblogs Offer Forum," 2001). The subsequent war on Iraq served as the catalyst for hundreds of so-called warblogs, thus establishing weblogging as an activity that's here to stay (Levy, 2003a).

There are several types of weblogs. The basic or general-topic weblog is the most popular type. It is produced by a single writer who contributes short items on various topics and posts comments sent in by blog readers. The basic weblog is an open forum, in which anyone can read and participate in the discussion. Other types of weblogs are generally more topic specific or closed in nature. Gaining in popularity are the personal journal types of weblogs that individuals use to communicate with family and friends. Many college students have weblogs, on which they post photos, daily diaries, and other personal information to share with others (Foley, 2003; Hamilton, 2003; Outing, 2002).

While personal diary-style weblogs are important to a small set of friends and families, general-topic weblogs attract a broader sphere of attention and can cause much controversy. A weblog is hosted by a *blogger*. He or she may be a journalist, someone with expertise in a specific area such as law or politics, or any everyday person who enjoys an exchange of opinions. *Blog readers* (those who access a blog) send their comments about a current event, issue, political candidate, or whatever they want to the blogger. These comments are often accompanied by links to more information and analysis and to related items. The blogger posts the blog readers' comments and links and adds his or her own opinions and links to more information. Blog readers are attracted to the free-wheeling conversation of weblogs and to the diverse points of view posted by the blogger and other blog readers (Palser, 2002; Wolcott, 2002).

Look Out Big Media, Big Politics

Perhaps what is most attractive about weblogs is that they're hosted by individuals, rather than by big media. Liberals turn to weblogs to escape what they perceive as the conservative media, while conservatives go online to escape from what they perceive as the liberal media (Kaye & Johnson, 2004). There's a weblog out there for everyone, of every political persuasion and most every interest, so blog readers can comfort themselves knowing they're communicating with like-minded people.

Today's *blogosphere* (or collective world of weblogs) is dominated by white, highly educated, high-income conservative and libertarian males (Levy, 2002a; "Reader Demographics," 2002; Seipp, 2002). But as more people discover this online world, it will likely attract a more diverse audience. By 2007, Internet users are expected to get more of their news from blogs than from the *New York Times* (Levy, 2002c).

Blogs are the places where online intellectuals, the digital and politically elite, and everyday people meet to exchange ideas and discuss the latest developments about war and peace and a myriad of other topics without the interference of traditional media. As such, bloggers are part of a new, tech-savvy crowd who often scoop the media giants and provide more insight into current events than can be found in the traditional media. Although some media executives are fearful that the blogosphere will steal their audience, other media corporations and journalists have set up their own blogospheres. FOXNews.com and MSNBC.com contain blogging areas, but because their content is edited, blogger purists don't consider them true weblogs. Many journalists use their weblogs as extensions of their traditional radio, television, or print commentary, which is limited by time and space.

The media once considered themselves the watchdogs of the government, but now, the bloggers have taken over as the watchdogs of both the government and the media (Kurtz, 2002). Like vultures, bloggers circle around media websites, often criticizing and commenting on news stories and correcting errors even before the printed versions have hit the newsstands or the electronic versions have zipped through the airwaves. Bloggers immediately swoop into action when they read or hear of a controversial report or a story they deem as biased or factually incorrect. As one blogger commented, "This is the Internet and we can fact check your ass" (c.f. Reynolds, 2002). Bloggers are an "endless parade of experts . . . with Internet-style megaphones ready to pounce on errors," thus keeping the traditional media and the government honest (Rosenberg, 2002). Yet journalists claim that the so-called experts are really just "wannabe amateurs badly in need of some skills and some editors" (Rosenberg, 2002).

As blogging has gained in popularity and more online users have tiptoed into the blogosphere, the media's power has been "redistributed into the hands of many" (Reynolds, 2002). Bloggers often outscoop the traditional media and bring stories into the limelight that those media may otherwise have buried. For example, Trent Lott's infamous glorification of Senator Strom Thurmond's 1948 desegregationist campaign was printed on page 6 of the *Washington Post* and missed entirely by the *New York Times*. Only when well-respected bloggers homed in on the remark did the mainstream press run with the story (Freese, 2002). Similarly, when Rush Limbaugh remarked on ESPN that the media had overrated Philadelphia Eagles quarterback Donovan McNabb because they wanted a black quarterback to do well, bloggers were all over the remark in a matter of minutes, way before the traditional media could get their stories out. The search engine Google directed the first mention of the story to the weblog *rushlimbaughtomy.blogspot.com,* which posted a picture of Rush with an American flag taped to his mouth (Silence, 2003).

Many mainstream journalists have started accessing weblogs to look for tips and stories, which they then take to the traditional press. When the publisher of the weblog *ScrappleFace* penned a parody news story, in which Donald Rumsfeld apologized for calling Germany and France the "Axis of Weasels" for their opposition to the U.S. plan to invade Iraq, the phrase caught on and was soon picked by the *Wall Street Journal* and the *Economist* (Yousefzadeh, 2003).

These stories are just a few examples of how bloggers are increasingly influencing and shaping news coverage. As bloggers continue to outscoop the traditional media, to provide access to in-depth commentary and diverse viewpoints, and to point out media errors, they will become even more influential in shaping political and cultural ideology.

---

fyi

My Life as a Blogger
by Glenn Reynolds, InstaPundit

I teach Internet law, which means that I'm always looking for something interesting to do on the Web. Back in August 2001, I decided to start a weblog. I hoped to draw a couple of hundred readers, mostly fellow academics and lawyers. On September 10, 2001, I had 1,600. The next day, I had nearly triple that number, and it's continued to climb. (Yesterday [10/8/03], I had 150,000.) To me, this has demonstrated the tremendous power of the Web, in which "viral marketing" is not just a buzzphrase but the only thing that really works.

What's interesting to me about blogging is the intensely personal nature of most blogs, even those that don't deal with personal topics. When I've met other bloggers, I've found them to always be just about exactly what I expected from reading their blogs. In an age of increasingly bland and homogenized Big Media, I think that's one of the things that makes blogs so appealing. And I think that appeal has made weblogs a useful check on the biases of Big Media organizations. Bloggers can be biased, too, but you don't have to guess at their biases: A blog *is* a disclosure of the blogger's biases.

My Life as a Live Journal Keeper
by Michelle, College Student

How do you start a live journal?

There are a couple different ways to start a live journal. You can go to the website (e.g., www.livejournal.com) that hosts them and get a regular free account. Until recently, you had to get a code from a person that already had a live journal, but the website changed its policy and now anyone can start one. A paid account is also available, which allows the user more features than a free account.

What do you use a live journal for?

I write random tidbits about my day, just whatever I feel like saying. I also use the journal to post pictures, keep up with what my friends are doing, and have my own personal webspace. My friends can leave comments on the site about the things I have written. I also use the "communities," which are just like regular live journals, but when you join a community, you can post in it for everyone else in the community to read and make additional comments. Some examples of communities are madradhair, add_students, and stencil_art.

Why do you have a live journal?

Because I am better at keeping up with a live journal than writing letters. I also like reading what my friends have to say about their lives. It's a good way to pass time and document my life. I also like looking back at past entries. I can choose who has access to my journal (publicity) of my entries; they can either be public, friends only, or for my eyes only. I do enjoy personalizing my journal using html.

How many of your friends have live journals?

I currently have about 30 people on my "friends" list, most of whom I know personally, although there are at least two people on the list that I have never met. The list keeps on growing as I get to know more people at college.

How often do you visit other people's live journals?

I visit other people's journals nearly every day. From my journal, I can go to my friends' journals by just clicking on "my friends page list," which shows who made new entries. I check this page quite often to see which friends have updated their journals.

While blogs provide a free and open marketplace of ideas, they are not subject to the strict editorial standards and source and fact checking that characterize the traditional media. A good deal of the information found on blogs is, in fact, not carefully scrutinized and may often be in error. Many critics contend that online information is not as credible as that from the traditional media. Yet others contend that weblogs are credible because the online world scrutinizes the information found there. Indeed, weblogs are perceived by some as being more credible than other online information and traditional media sources (Johnson & Kaye, in press).

ZOOM IN 5.5
See demo vlogs at www.screenblast.com/buzzmachine.

ZOOM IN 5.6
Explore a weblog by reading the comments and following the links to other information. Try http://globeofblogs.com, or www.bloghop.com, or www.lights.com/weblogs/directories.html.

Moving beyond weblogs, Internet technology has created *videologs,* also known as *vlogs.* Relatively new to the scene, vlogs are kind of mini-video documentaries. Commentaries, rants, and raves are all presented as full-motion video. Anyone equipped with a digital video camera and special software (which will set you back less than $200) can produce his or her own vlog. What role vlogs will take in the world of news and politics remains to be seen, but they have the potential to tackle television journalism.

Instant Messaging

Instant messaging is a less expensive and more convenient way of connecting to friends and family than picking up the telephone. America Online is the leader in instant messaging, with over 42 million at-home users and 9 million at-work users ("IM Users Increasing in U.S.," 2001). Although IM is a big hit with millions of Internet users, it lacks service-to-service interconnection capabilities. In other words, AOL's instant messenger (AIM) blocks out users of other systems, such as MSN's Messenger. This lack of compatibility is like having your AT&T long-distance call being blocked by your friend's Sprint long-distance service, allowing you to connect only if you both signed up with the same long-distance company.

New services, most notably Trillian, let users hook up with friends who subscribe to other instant messaging systems. Even though market analysts forecast that IM systems that allow interconnection will fare better than those that do not, AOL implemented a block that prevents Trillian from accessing its system. Trillian responded by blocking AOL's block, AOL responded with yet more blocking, and so the fight continues. AOL claims that it's not against interoperability as such but just against Trillian, which AOL claims is soliciting its members' names and passwords.

Regardless, system interoperability is the key to IM's long-term success. While small steps are being taken, such as providing compatibility between AIM and Apple's iChat, more needs to be done before IM becomes an everyday form of communication (Emling, 2002b).

Local Internet Radio

Local Internet radio sounds like an oxymoron: How is it possible for the Internet to be local? Using new air-to-web technology, radio stations may soon stream content solely to listeners in their local broadcast markets. Air-to-web technology works by finding a local listener's street address and then generating a list of broadcast stations that can be picked up by an antenna. When the listener connects to a local station's website, the air-to-web software pinpoints his or her home address and e-mails a special access code that is used to connect to the radio station's audio stream.

Air-to-web radio may be a good solution for limiting the total outlay of royalty fees. Rather than stream to a global audience and pay 7 cents per song per listener (many of whom are out of the local broadcast and market area), stations only pay for local online listeners. Air-to-web radio offers webcasters a system that's not open to the world but that may better serve their local market needs (Kreschbaumer, 2002).

Secret Messages Online

The attention being paid to terrorism and the ways in which terrorists may communicate with each other online has resurrected concerns about an old form of passing veiled messages. *Steganography,* which is Greek for "hidden writing," is one of the oldest methods of passing secret messages. The ancient Greeks wrote messages on wooden tablets and then covered the messages with wax; the recipients merely scraped off the wax to read the messages. Steganography was such a big concern during World War II that even crossword puzzles and notes accompanying flower deliveries were viewed with suspicion.

In today's world, there's fear that terrorists and other criminals are using steganographic techniques to hide messages within digital photographs, music files, and other digital postings (Kolata, 2001). Stealth messages can be inserted in digital files and images such that the alterations are not visible to the human eye or ear without special decoding software. The result is that secret messages can be sent over the Internet without directly communicating with the receiver. There are no e-mails, no remote log-ins, no bulletin board postings, no subscriptions, no instant messaging, or no other ways to trace the recipient or the sender. There's only a digital file that anyone can download but only those with encryption software can interpret (Kolata, 2001).

Summary

The history of the Internet is longer than most people think. It dates back to the 1960s, when scientists were experimenting with a new way to share information and keep connected in times of crisis. In its early days, the Internet was largely limited to communicating military, academic, and scientific research and was accessed by using complicated commands. In 1993, the first Web browser, Mosaic, came on the scene and the Internet quickly caught the public's attention. Since then, it has become the most quickly adopted new medium in history (Markus, 1990).

Without a doubt, the Internet has changed our lives tremendously. Perhaps the Internet has most influenced us politically in terms of how we access news and information. We no longer have to passively sit and absorb whatever news and information the traditional media want to send our way. Nor do we have to rely on them for political news and candidate information. Online technologies have sprouted new ways of gaining news and information and having an individual voice. Despite these unique qualities, the Internet also has many of the same properties as the traditional print and broadcast media. It delivers audio, video, text, and graphics in one package.

Not only has the Internet changed the way we receive and provide information, but it is also altering our traditional media use behaviors. Millions of people around the world log onto the Internet on a regular basis. For some, the Internet will always be a supplement to radio and television, but for others, the Internet may become the medium they turn to first for news, information, and entertainment.

Online radio delivery has attracted many users who prefer clicking a button to hear their favorite audio over tuning in to an over-the-air station. For audio providers, online radio is relatively easy to set up and inexpensive to maintain. Given all this, cyberradio is the ideal medium for those who want to reach a global audience.

People have been enamored with television and the act of watching television since the 1940s, which means it will be hard, if not impossible to tear them away from this medium. For people to abandon television for the Internet, it will have to resemble television in how it's used, in program quality, and in content delivery.

Clearly, the Internet is quickly catching up with radio and television when it comes to news delivery. In many ways, the Internet has surpassed radio and television when it comes to providing in-depth news. The Web is not constrained by time and space, as are the traditional media. News can be posted immediately and updated continuously, as the situation warrants. Moreover, weblogs and vlogs redistribute news and information delivery from established media into in the hands of everyday people.

Broadcast radio and television networks and stations are competing among and between themselves and with the Internet, often with their own online counterparts. Television and radio must compete with the Web for a fragmented audience and precious advertising dollars. The traditional media are concentrating their efforts on designing websites that will draw viewers away from their online competitors. But at the same time, they have to be sure that they don't lure viewers to the Web at the expense of their over-the-air fare. Even though research differs on whether the Internet is taking time away from radio and television, even a short amount of time spent online is time taken away from the "old-line media" (Dizard, 2000).

The Internet is still a relatively new medium, and so no one knows for sure what form it will end up taking as it keeps changing and adapting to technological innovations and diverse social and cultural needs. But what we do know is that it's had an enormous impact on the radio and television industries. If the prognosticators are right, the Web will eventually merge with radio and television, offering both conventional radio and television fare and Web-based content through a single device.

Programming

CHAPTER 6

SEE IT THEN: Radio

Types of Programs

SEE IT NOW: Radio

Types of Programs

Where Radio Programs Come From

Who Pays for Programs

How Programs Are Scheduled

Who Schedules Programs

SEE IT THEN: Television

Types of Programs

SEE IT NOW: Television

Types of Programs

Where Television Programs Come From

Who Produces Programs

Who Pays for Programs

What Types of Channels Carry What Types of Programs

How Programs Are Scheduled

SEE IT LATER: Radio and Television

Marketing Syndicated Programs

On the Horizon

In this chapter, you'll learn about:

- The origins and development of broadcast programs and formats
- Where programs come from, who pays for them, and how they are scheduled
- The different types of programs and how they are used today
- New developments in programming and how technology will impact programming in the future

In the very early days of radio, amateur operators just put something on the air—often, at the spur of the moment. Maybe someone would drop by the station to sing or play an instrument or to espouse some point of view to whomever was listening. Some years later, radio station licensing criteria required the transmission of *scheduled* programming. Sports, news, music, church services, and dramas were among the types of programs that listeners crowded around their radios to hear. By today's standards, the level of static and generally poor audio quality that characterized these programs would make them unlistenable, but to yesterday's audience, radio was magic.

In this chapter, you'll learn about the development of radio programming. You'll read about types of station formatting, how stations get music, how your favorite songs get on the air, and who decides how often they're played. The chapter then moves on to television programming. You'll learn about the different types of television programs and find out how program ideas are developed, how programs finally make it to the air, and how program-scheduling strategies are used keep you tuned to a channel.

SEE IT THEN: Radio

Types of Programs

Music

In one of the first live radio performances, opera singer Enrico Caruso sang "O Solo Mio" live from the Metropolitan Opera in New York in 1910. Lee De Forest, the disputed inventor of the audion tube, masterminded the performance to promote radio.

ZOOM IN   6.1
Hear Caruso as he sang live from the Met almost 100 years ago at www.old-time.com/golden_age/osolemio.ram.

By the late 1920s, music was the main source of radio programming. In 1927 and 1928, about three-quarters of the programming aired by New York City stations and stations affiliated with NBC Blue and NBC Red networks was devoted to music (Ahmed, 2001; Sterling & Kittross, 2002, p. 73). Most of the music was created live for broadcasting, since the quality of phonograph records broadcast over the air was very poor. Musicians performed in small studios that were set up to look like miniature concert halls or ballrooms; they were often decorated with potted plants, such as palm trees. The phrase *potted palm music* refers to the style of radio programming of that era.

By the end of the 1920s, radio programming had reached a form that set the standard for the next 20 years. Stations experimented with the types of programs they could easily broadcast and what the audience wanted to hear. In those days, radio-transmitting equipment was bulky, heavy, and hard to move around, so live remotes (as we know them today) were virtually impossible. In 1921, KDKA covered the Dempsey-Carpentier prize fight with a temporary transmitter set up in New Jersey. It was fortunate for KDKA that Carpentier was knocked out in the fourth round, because shortly after the fight ended, the station's transmitter melted into one big heap of metal (Head, Sterling, & Schofield, 1994).

As new types of radio programs were developed and became popular with the listening audience, the amount of time set aside for musical programming declined, and by the late 1940s, only about 40 percent of the programming was music oriented (Ahmed, 2001). Comedies, soap operas, dramas, quiz shows, and children's programs filled the airwaves from the 1930s to the 1950s and were broadcast during regularly scheduled times, much like television programs are today. Most newspapers printed radio program guides, just like they do for television today, so listeners knew when it was time to run inside to hear their favorite shows, such as *The Green Hornet, Jack Benny,* and *The Lone Ranger.*

Dramas

Radio network programming relied heavily on **serial dramas**, which were coined *soap operas* because they were often sponsored by laundry soap manufacturers. However, they could have just as easily been called *cereal operas* because the first serial drama,

Betty and Bob, was actually sponsored by General Mills (Massey & Baran, 1996). These 15-minute dramas appealed largely to the female audience and dominated the daytime airwaves. In the evening, listeners tuned in to episodic dramas, which revolved around the same characters for each show but resolved the story within a single episode.

Comedies

Comedians such as Jack Benny, George Burns, and Bob Hope all got their start in 1930s radio programs and later made a successful transition to television. Variety shows were popular and featured a combination of stand-up comedy, music, and entertaining vignettes.

Amos 'n' Andy made its radio debut in 1928 and was the first nationwide hit on American radio. Avid fans would stop what they were doing to crowd around the radio to hear the latest antics of their two favorite characters. In addition to being popular, *Amos 'n' Andy* was also one of the most controversial programs on the air. The title characters were "derived largely from the stereotypic caricatures of African-Americans" and played by white actors who "mimicked so-called Negro dialect" (*Amos 'n' Andy Show,* 2003). Freeman Gosden and Charles Correll, the white creators and voices of the program, "chose black characters because blackface comics could tell funnier stories than whiteface comics," rather than for racist purposes. Even so, the program quickly came under fire from the black community and the National Association for the Advancement of Colored People (NAACP) (Mershan, 2003). As the show progressed, the characters grew beyond being caricatures and became beloved by the radio audience. In fact, NBC claimed the program was just a popular among black listeners as among white listeners (Campbell, 2000). The program moved to CBS television in 1951 but only remained on the air for two more years.

Back to Music

Radio thrived throughout the 1930s and 1940s and became Americans' primary source of entertainment. People couldn't imagine anything better than having entertainment delivered right to their living rooms. But then came television—a new-fangled device that combined sound with images. Television quickly won the hearts and eyes of the public, who pushed their radio sets into some dark corner and proudly displayed their shiny new televisions. In 1946, only about 8,000 U.S. households had a television set, but just five years later, some 10 million households were enjoying the small screen (Grant & Meadows, 2002).

As television gained in popularity, popular radio shows gradually moved over to this new medium. As radio soaps, comedies, quiz shows, dramas, and the like became television shows, radio found itself scrambling to replace these programs or face empty airtime. Consider that the loss of network radio programs also meant the loss of advertising revenue. Radio executives knew they had to do whatever they could to save radio from dying off all together.

The easiest way to fill airtime was with recorded music. After all, radio is an audio-only medium, so audio-only programming is the perfect fit. From the late 1940s to the mid 1950s or so, radio gave itself a makeover. It emerged as a stronger medium and found its place alongside television.

ZOOM IN   6.2

Every Sunday from 1930 to 1954, the Mutual network aired one of the most popular radio programs ever, *The Shadow.* The program enthralled listeners with its famous opening line, "Who knows what evil lurks in the hearts of men; The Shadow knows," which was followed by a sinister laugh ("Famous Weekly Shows," 1994–2002). Listen to audio clips of *The Shadow* at www.old-time.com/sights/shadow.html.

ZOOM IN   6.3

Learn more about *Amos 'n' Andy* and hear sound clips at either of these sites:

- www.otr.com/amosandy.html
- www.museum.tv/archives/etv/A/htmlA/ amosnandy/amosnandy.htm

ZOOM IN   6.4

To listen to clips of popular old radio programs such as *Amos 'n' Andy, Bob Hope, Fibber McGee and Molly, The Red Skelton Show, Abbott and Costello,* and *The Adventures of Ozzie and Harriet,* go to www.old-time.com/golden_age/index.html.

Charles J. Correll and Freeman F. Gosden wore blackface as characters Amos and Andy.

Radio's portability, as well as its ability to provide soothing background noise, lends it to listening while doing other things.

Several technological innovations helped radio make the transition to a music-dominated medium. For instance, the invention of the transistor made radios smaller and more portable, and automobile manufacturers started adding radios to cars. Through these smaller, more portable radios, listeners discovered that musical programs made for a soothing background. They could work, relax, and even drive while listening to music. The radio didn't demand their full attention, as did television.

Eventually, radio executives discovered that their medium was a powerful tool in filling the needs of the local public, and they began offering music programming that appealed to the local community. Radio stations discovered that they couldn't be all things to all people, so they addressed smaller niche audiences with specialized musical tastes through station **formatting.** The various stations began playing particular types of music throughout the day. Maybe one station played only classical, another blues and jazz, another big band, and so on. Each station developed its own identity and attracted a certain audience through its musical format.

Realizing that music fans were spending a great deal of money on records, enterprising radio programmers looked at the artists whose records were selling well. The radio industry soon got into the habit of checking record sales to predict what songs and what performers would go over well on the radio. This link between the music industry and radio stations started in the early 1950s continues as strong as ever today.

ROCK 'N' ROLL   In the mid 1950s, radio stations were still suffering from having lost part of their audience to television. And then, rock 'n' roll saved the day. Young people went crazy over this new sound, and parents went crazy trying to keep their teens away from this wild new music. The more kids were told they couldn't listen, the more they wanted to listen.

The term *rock 'n' roll* was originally a slang term that meant "sex." The new sound combined the black rhythm-and-blues sound of Memphis with the country beat of Nashville and thus became the first "integrationist music" (Campbell, 2000, p. 72). Rock 'n' roll was embraced by many different types of people and thus provided a way to break away from the "racial, sexual, regional, and class taboos" of the 1950s (Campbell, 2000, p. 76). The music united blacks and whites, men and women, northerners and southerners, and the rich and the poor. What's more, rock 'n' roll became the music that defined the baby-boom generation.

Rock 'n' roll caught on quickly with teens in the 1950s.

About the same time that rock 'n' roll steamrolled its way onto the music scene, radio stations were experimenting with **disc jockeys (DJs):** announcers who played the tunes and established a rapport with the station's listeners. Alan Freed was probably the most influential DJ of all time. He is credited with coining the term *rock 'n' roll,* for being the first DJ to play rhythm-and-blues and black versions of early rock to his mostly white audience in Cleveland, and for being instrumental in introducing teenagers to this exciting new sound (Campbell, 2000).

Rock 'n' roll fans closely identified with the stations that played their type of music, while anti–rock 'n' rollers sided with the stations that refused to broadcast the controversial sound. The publicity that resulted from this conflict sparked a renewed interest in radio and elevated its popularity and ratings. Capitalizing on the popularity of rock 'n' roll, radio programmers

Fats Domino, Little Richard, and Chuck Berry (left to right) were among the black performers who helped usher in rock 'n' roll.

Todd Storz and Bill Stewart created the first **Top 40 format** for a station in Omaha, Nebraska (Hilliard & Keith, 2001, p. 152). This format featured a mixture of up-and-coming hit songs, current hit songs, and songs that had been hit songs; they were all mixed, so that a song from each category was played during each hour. The number of different hit songs was about 40—hence, the name *Top 40*. The Top 40 format caught on in many cities across the country and appealed especially to young people, who identified with the music and enjoyed the accompanying chatter from the disc jockeys.

Rock 'n' roll was initially thought of as a flash-in-the-pan musical style that would be popular only with a small number of young teenagers. However, it proved to be the magic formula that rekindled interest in radio.

SEE IT NOW: Radio

Types of Programs

Music

By the end of the 1950s, radio programs had pretty much focused on recorded music and most stations had established an identity with their format. Then and now, program formats are usually based on budget, local audience characteristics and size, and potential advertising revenue. Program formats change as new stations enter a local market, as the economy fluctuates, as market characteristics change, and as music changes.

News and Information

About two-thirds of all-news and news/talk stations in the United States are on the AM dial (*Broadcasting & Cable Yearbook, 2002–2005*). In the early 1960s, the Federal Communications Commission (FCC) opened up spectrum space for FM, which has a sound quality superior

> **ZOOM IN** 6.5
> Learn more about different types of music and station formats at these websites:
> - New York Radio Guide www.nyradioguide.com/formats.htm
> - Arbitron www.arbitron.com/national_radio/arlt.htm
> - News Generation www.newsgeneration.com/radio_resources/formats.htm

to AM. FM was slow to catch on with listeners, due mainly to availability. (Most radios didn't even have an FM dial.) But once radios were manufactured with an FM dial and FM radios were available in cars, new and hip stations began popping up on the dial.

By the early 1970s, only about 30 percent of listeners tuned exclusively to FM stations, but 20 years later, three-quarters of radio listeners preferred FM (Campbell, 2000). Music-oriented AM stations couldn't come close to the quality of sound emanating from their FM competitors. And so they either migrated to the FM band or stayed on the AM band but changed their format to news and information or another format in which audio quality wasn't so important.

The **news/information format** falls into three basic categories:

1. **All-news stations** air primarily national, regional, and local news about weather, traffic, and special interest feature stories. The reports are usually repeated on a schedule throughout the day. The news cycle may occasionally be interrupted for a special in-depth report or talk show or another program that's not part of the usual schedule.
2. The **news/talk format** consists of a combination of call-in talk shows and short newscasts that may break in once an hour and between other shows. Most talk programs air during regularly scheduled times; they are usually aired in one- to four-hour segments to keep listeners tuned in for long periods of time.
3. The **sports/talk format** is similar to the news/talk format but focuses mainly on sporting topics and regularly scheduled live sporting events. Sports talk usually includes call-in programs and may emphasize local sports, especially if a professional or big-name college team is located within the broadcast area.

Note that these categories are not mutually exclusive. Often, an all-news station will air a talk or sports program as well (Eastman & Ferguson, 2002).

ZOOM IN 6.6
Surf your FM radio dial and listen to some stations you're unfamiliar with. How long does it take you to identify each station's format and target audience? What cues tipped you off to the format? Do some stations play up their format identity more than others?

Alan Berg
Popular radio talk show host Alan Berg was gunned down in his Denver driveway in 1984 by members of The Order, a white-supremacist group. The group had been taunting Berg with hostile on-air calls before the killing. The liberal Berg was a champion of free speech, even for those who murdered him.

Liberal and Conservative Talk Radio

The news/talk format is often a mixture of news and entertainment. The hosts set the tone with their own opinions, humor, off-the-cuff remarks, wild accusations, cynical remarks, light-hearted conversation, and other interjections that keep the audience entertained and amused yet informed about current events and politics. Listeners enter the fray by calling in and venting on the air.

Ever since Rush Limbaugh led the way with his acerbic, conservative talk show, the format has come under fire for its politically right-wing bias and lack of balance and fairness. The National Association of Broadcasters estimated in 1998 that 75 to 80 percent of radio talk show hosts were politically conservative (Campbell, 2000; Eastman & Ferguson, 2002).

Some local radio stations pick up a few moderate and liberal syndicated shows, and some air their own local programs. But in fact, there are no big-name national hosts to spread the left (or liberal) philosophy. To counteract conservative talk radio, a new progressive radio network, Air America, began broadcasting in early spring 2004. Listeners with more progressive viewpoints are happy to have a forum in which they can express their views without "being called dopes, morons, traitors, Feminazis, evildoers and communists" by conservative hosts (Atkins, 2003).

To listen to Air America, go to **www.airamerica.com**.

Sean Hannity, conservative radio talk show host.

Al Franken, liberal radio talk show host.

Noncommercial

Noncommercial (or **educational**) **stations** are usually owned and operated by colleges and universities, religious institutions, and towns and are usually found at the lower end of the FM dial, between 88 and 92 megahertz. In general, noncommercial stations first emerged in the 1920s. However, some stations, such as the University of Wisconsin's WHA, existed as *wireless telegraphy* (telegraphic code instead of voice) stations in the early 1900s (Head, Sterling, & Schofield, 1994).

Because these stations are noncommercial, they don't bring in revenue from advertising dollars. Instead, they rely on other forms of revenue, such as monetary donations, government grants, and **underwriting**, which is a monetary donation in exchange for an on-air announcement or program sponsorship. Unlike the advertisements that run on commercial stations, underwriting donations must abide by FCC regulations that limit promotional content.

Most noncommercial programming comes from the station's own library of donated materials and station-produced community affairs and news shows. Currently, about 1,700 nonprofit stations broadcast in the United States. Many are housed on college campuses (Campbell, 2000).

Community and college stations are usually not as rigidly formatted as commercial stations. Listeners are often treated to a variety of music, all within the same day—from classical to jazz to alternative rock to blues and so on. Additionally, news, talk, and sports programs may be thrown into the mix. The eclectic nature of noncommercial stations draws listeners who are tired of listening to the same old rotated music offered by most commercial stations. College stations are especially known for introducing new artists. Well-known bands such as Nirvana, Pearl Jam, and R.E.M. owe much of their success to college radio.

TOP 20 Formats of U.S. Radio Stations: 2002–2003

1. Country
2. Adult Contemporary
3. Oldies
4. News/Talk
5. Religious
6. Christian
7. Sports
8. News
9. Talk
10. Gospel
11. Contemporary Hits/Top 40
12. Classic Rock
13. Rock/Album-Oriented Rock
14. Spanish
15. Classical
16. Jazz
17. Urban Contemporary
18. Diversified
19. Educational
20. Middle of the Road

Source: Broadcasting & Cable Yearbook, 2002–2003.

NATIONAL PUBLIC RADIO PROGRAMMING   After Congress established the Corporation for Public Broadcasting in 1968, the corporation, in turn, set up the National Public Radio (NPR) network in 1970. NPR's mission "is to work in partnership with its member stations to create a more informed public—one challenged and invigorated by a deeper understanding and appreciation of events, ideas and cultures" ("How NPR Works," 2003).

National Public Radio distributes both NPR and independently produced programs to its member stations. In 2003, 770 NPR member stations aired network programs to about 22 million listeners each week ("NPR's Growth," 2003). NPR has won many programming awards and delivers such favorites as *Morning Edition, All Things Considered, Car Talk,* and *The Motley Fool Radio Show.*

ZOOM IN 6.7

- Learn more about National Public Radio (NPR) at www.npr.org.

- Tune in to your local NPR member station. Listen to at least one news program, one music program, and one other program of your choosing. How do NPR programs differ from those on commercial radio stations?

- Listen to your college radio station. How is it different from the commercial stations in your area?

Where Radio Programs Come From

Local Programs

Most music-format local radio stations rely on their own libraries for music. They often build these libraries from free promotional CDs supplied by record companies, who, in turn, rely on the stations to play their titles.

Local stations may produce their own newscasts, weather and traffic reports, and sports shows featuring university and high school coaches, local sporting events, and other type of community programs. News, talk, and sports programs are generally very expensive to produce, however, so only big-market stations can usually afford to create their own programs.

Name the two main families on Soap.

Network/Syndicated Programs

Given the cost of producing enough programming to fill airtime 24/7, radio stations may rely on network and syndicated programs for news/talk/information shows. **Network programs** tend to include music, news, commercials, on-air talent, and other program elements. The local station doesn't have to provide any programming; instead, it buys it all in one package. **Syndicated programs,** on the other hand, are individual shows that a station airs in between its own programs. For instance, a local station may broadcast its own music until noon, air a syndicated talk show until 3 P.M., and then return to its own programming for the rest of the day.

Network and syndicated programs are commonly delivered via satellite from radio networks and syndicators. Stations either broadcast the live satellite feed or tape it for later airing. Infinity syndicates Howard Stern's talk show. The programs of G. Gordon Liddy, Don Imus, Dr. Laura Schlessinger, Rush Limbaugh, Dr. Dean Edell, Rick Dees, and Casey Kasem are among the most popular programs syndicated by Premiere Radio Networks, who provides more than 60 programs to 7,800 radio affiliates ("Premiere Radio Networks," 2002).

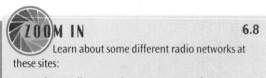

ZOOM IN   6.8
Learn about some different radio networks at these sites:

- Premiere Radio Networks   www.premrad.com
- ABC Radio   www.abcradio.com
- Westwood One   www.westwoodone.com
- Jones Radio Network   www.jonesradio.com
- Tribune Radio Network   www.tribuneradio.com

Who Pays for Programs

Radio stations foot the bill for their own local programming. They pay for the talent, production equipment, physical space, and copyright fees (which go to music licensing agencies), but most of the music itself is provided free of charge by recording companies. It's very common for recording companies to send demo discs of their new releases to stations across the country. However, stations that specialize in classic rock and other types of music, such as classical, have a harder time obtaining free CDs and often have to purchase their own music libraries. (Record companies don't bother sending out free CDs of 200-year-old classical pieces, which will draw small audiences, or 20-year-old hits, which listeners aren't going to rush out to buy.)

Stations may pay cash and/or negotiate for commercial time in exchange for syndicated programs. Stations that are affiliated with a radio network, such as Westwood One, trade commercial time for network programs. In other words, the network provides the programming free of charge but reaps revenue by selling commercial time to national advertisers; the stations save themselves the cost of talent and other operating costs.

How Programs Are Scheduled

Airtime is a valuable commodity, and so every *second* needs to be scheduled. Station management sets up program clocks (also known as *hot clocks* and *program wheels*), which are basically minute-by-minute schedules of music, news, weather, commercials, and other on-air offerings for each hour of the day. For example, the first five minutes of the noon to 1:00 P.M. hour may be programmed with news, followed by two minutes of commercials, followed by a 15-second station promotion, followed by a 10-minute music sweep (music that's uninterrupted by commercials). Each hour may vary, depending on audience needs and time of day. For instance, morning drive-time music sweeps may be cut by 30 seconds for traffic updates, and the 6:00 P.M. hour may include five extra minutes of news.

Who Schedules Programs

In the early days of music formatting, which songs made it to the airwaves and how often they were played was largely left to the DJ's discretion. After the payola scandal in the late 1950s, when DJs were caught taking money from record companies to play and

Illustration of Program Clocks

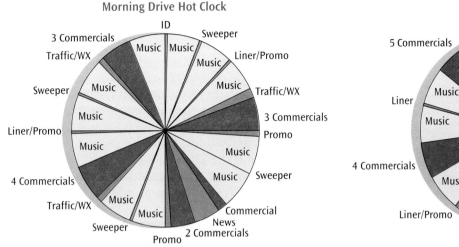

Source: Eastman & Ferguson, 2002.

promote their new releases, station management shifted the programming function from the DJs and formed a new position: **program director.**

Once upper management has settled on a station's format, the program director is responsible for everything that goes out over the air. He or she selects the songs, or type of music, and comes up with a **playlist**, which is basically a roster of songs and artists that will be featured by the station. The playlist reflects the station's format and is usually determined by audience demand and CD sales.

The playlist determines the **rotation**, or the frequency with which and times of day the songs are played. Favorite songs and current hits are usually played most frequently, while older and less popular numbers may have a so-called lighter rotation. Most stations use some form of computerized rotation to prevent the playing of different songs by the same artist too closely together or the playing of too many slow-tempo selections in a row.

Program directors also schedule nonmusic programs. For instance, a station may air two family- and relationship-oriented/advice call-in programs consecutively in the early afternoon to keep the 25- to 50-year-old females listening but then switch to a political talk program during drive time to attract commuters and males.

> **ZOOM IN** 6.9
> See if you can get a radio station's playlist or rotation from the station or its website.

SEE IT THEN: Television

Types of Programs

In the early days of television, executives were faced with the challenge of what to put on the air. After all, people weren't going to buy TV sets if there was nothing to watch. In pondering what kinds of programs to create, the executives decided to take existing radio programs and put them on television. Instead of just having sound stages, where radio actors spoke into microphones, sets were built and scenes were acted out in front of a camera. Many radio programs soon had televised counterparts, and eventually, as more and more people bought televisions, radio programs were phased out in favor of their televised versions.

Anthologies

In the early days of television, New York City was the center of the industry, and thus programs were influenced by Broadway plays. Live productions of serious Broadway dramas, known as **anthologies**, became common fare on television in the late 1940s and early 1950s.

Anthologies were hard-hitting plays and other works of literature, many of which were adapted for presentation on television. They were often cast with young talent from radio and local theater, some of whom went on to become major theatrical and television stars. Robert Redford, Joanne Woodward, Angela Lansbury, Chuck Connors, Paul Newman, and Vincent Price all got their starts acting in televised anthologies. In its 11-year run on television, *Kraft Television Theater* produced 650 plays, featuring almost 4,000 actors and actresses (Brooks & Marsh, 1979).

Anthologies were enormously popular into the late 1950s but lost their appeal when expanded production capabilities led to the use of on-location sets. This brought a new look to television programs and an increased demand for sophisticated, action-oriented productions.

ZOOM IN   6.10

Read more about anthologies on the Museum of Broadcast Communications website: www.museum.tv/archives/etv/A/htmlA/anthologydra/anthologydra.htm.

Variety Shows

Variety shows, once a mainstay on radio, transferred quickly to television in the early years. They were common for several reasons: namely, they were entertaining and relatively easy to produce. Programs such as *The Ed Sullivan Show* (1948–1971), *The Jackie Gleason Show* (1952–1971), *The Carol Burnett Show* (1967–1978), and *The Red Skelton Show* (1951–1971) featured singing and dancing, stand-up comedy and comedy skits, along with other light-hearted entertainment.

Many entertainers launched their careers on variety shows. The Beatles, Dinah Shore, and Bob Hope all made their American television debuts on *The Ed Sullivan Show.* For audience members, variety shows often provided the first exposure to new talent. Elvis Presley's 1956 appearance on *Ed Sullivan* made headlines when the show's producers refused to show his gyrating hips and shot him only from the waist up.

Although many variety shows were quite successful and enjoyed long runs, others could not produce the big ratings to justify their production expenses. During its 23 years, *The Ed Sullivan Show* continued to draw a large but mostly older audience; even so, it was taken off the air by CBS in an effort to provide more modern, hip programming. *The Smothers Brothers' Comedy Hour* (1967–1975) was probably the most contemporary variety show of its time—and also the most controversial. It was wildly popular among young adults, who loved how it poked fun at

Actors Paul Muni and Joan Wetmore rehearse (above) and then shoot (right) a scene from an anthology production on *The Philco Playhouse.*

politics, government, church, family, and almost everything and everyone. Network censors often butted heads with the show's stars over the irreverent nature of the material, and many viewers were outraged at the program. The show was soon cancelled by CBS but later taken up by ABC and still later by NBC. The antiwar, left-wing gags ultimately ran their course, and the program just faded away (Brooks & Marsh, 1979).

Game and Quiz Shows

Studio-based game and quiz shows, which were easy and inexpensive to produce, were also very popular with viewers in the early days of television. Shows like *What's My Line, I've Got a Secret*, and *To Tell the Truth* were all variations on simple ideas that invited the audience to get involved and play along. Audience participation increased with shows like *Beat the Clock* and *Truth or Consequences*, which often had members of the studio audience perform outrageous stunts for money and prizes. Quiz and game shows prospered and increased in popularity until the quiz show scandal in the late 1950s.

At first, quiz shows were small-time contests, in which contestants competed for small prizes. Then big-money quiz shows, such as *The $64,000 Question*, became enormously popular after their introduction to prime-time television in the 1950s. In fact, there was continual pressure on quiz show producers from advertisers and the networks to keep the ratings up. Producers responded by finding attractive and personable contestants who would keep the drama level high.

Charles Van Doren, a young, handsome, witty faculty member at Columbia University, was selected as an ideal contestant for NBC's *Twenty-One*. Van Doren's winning streak lasted for 15 weeks, and he became a media celebrity, even earning a job on the *Today* show. All was well in Van Doren's life until defeated contestant Herb Stemple came forward and said that the show was rigged. He claimed that he had been forced to deliberatley lose to Van Doren. Stemple divulged that the program's producers gave the answers to the favored contestants and coached them on how to create suspense by acting nervous and uncertain about their responses.

The Beatles made their U.S. debut on *The Ed Sullivan Show* in New York on February 9, 1964.

ZOOM IN 6.11
- Listen to an NPR report about the history of quiz shows and hear short audio clips from quiz programs at www.npr.org/programs/morning/features/patc/quizshow/#sounds.
- See how well you would have done on the quiz show *Twenty-One*. To answer some of the original questions asked on the air, go to www.pbs.org/wgbh/amex/quizshow/sfeature/quiz.html.

ZOOM IN 6.12
- Listen to former game show host Sonny Fox talk about the quiz show scandal at www.pbs.org/wgbh/amex/quizshow/sfeature/interview.html.
- Read what the Museum of Broadcast Communication has to say about the quiz show scandal at www.museum.tv/archives/etv/Q/htmlQ/quizshowsca/quizshowsca.htm.

Twenty-One host Jack Berry asks a question of contestant Charles Van Doren, who is standing in an isolation booth.

What was the name of Arnold's fish on **Different Strokes?**

The cast of *I Love Lucy* (from left to right): Lucille Ball, Vivian Vance, William Frawley, and Desi Arnaz.

ZOOM IN   6.13

- To learn more about *I Love Lucy*, go to www. museum.tv/archives/etv/I/htmlI/ilovelucy/ilovelucy.htm.
- Listen to the *I Love Lucy* theme song, take a virtual tour of the set, and read about the program's origin at www. tvland.com/shows/lucy.

ZOOM IN   6.14

Learn more about Edward R. Murrow and hear audio clips of his news reports:

- http://statelibrary.dcr.state.nc.us/nc/bio/literary/ murrow.htm
- www.otr.com/murrow.html
- www.museum.tv/archives/etv/M/htmlM/murrowedwar/ murrowedwar.htm

As it turned out, *Twenty-One* was not the only quiz show that was rigged; cheating occurred on many programs. Van Doren and other contestants, producers, writers, and people who worked behind the scenes were indicted by a federal grand jury for complicity in the scandal but received suspended sentences. Van Doren, who was probably the most beloved and well-known contestant, suffered greatly from the scandal. He lost his teaching position at Columbia, as well as his job on the *Today* show, and lived in relative obscurity from then on.[1]

After the scandal, quiz shows all but disappeared from prime-time television until *Who Wants to Be a Millionaire?* debuted in 1999, some 40 years later.

Comedies

Situation comedies were perfect for television because they could be shot in a typical three-sided stage that was decorated to look like a simple apartment or home. Most early comedies were family oriented, and the comic aspect was noted in the dialogue between the characters, rather than in visual gags. However, Lucille Ball excelled at physical comedy and changed the face of television by insisting on using three cameras to film *I Love Lucy* (1951–1957). If a physical gag or antic failed, the scene could be reshot or edited for maximum effect. Multiple camera filming paved the way for other comedies that featured more physical comedy than comic dialogue.

News

After the press-radio wars, radio news was limited largely to special report bulletins and information programs, such as President Franklin D. Roosevelt's Depression-era "fireside chats," which kept Americans abreast of the country's economic situation. But with the United States' entry into World War II, there was renewed interest in and growth of radio news.

Edward R. Murrow was perhaps the most well-known journalist of that era. He broadcast dramatic, vivid, live accounts from London as it was being bombed. After the war, Murrow hosted *Hear It Now*, a weekly news digest program, which led to *See It Now*, the first nationwide televised news show. *See It Now* was also the first investigative journalism program, a style that has since been imitated by contemporary programs such as *60 Minutes* and *Dateline NBC* (Campbell, 2000). Murrow focused not only on the major events of the day but also specifically on the everyday people involved in those events. Many Americans hailed Murrow for his heroic role in bringing an end to Senator Joseph McCarthy's rampage on people he accused of being communists, which culminated in the early 1950s. At a time when both legislators and the media were too timid to challenge McCarthy, Murrow stood up for the people who were being persecuted and claimed that McCarthy had gone too far.

Daily news programs as we know them today were slow to arrive on television. NBC and CBS didn't expanded their 15-minute newscasts to 30 minutes until 1963, and ABC followed in 1967. In 1969, the networks aired newscasts six days per week and finally every day of the week by 1970.

The cast of *The Howdy Doody Show* (from left to right): "Buffalo Bob" Smith, puppet Howdy Doody and his puppet friend, and Clarabell the Clown, played by Bob Keeshan (who later starred as Captain Kangaroo).

Children's Shows

Most of the early television shows produced for children were variety-type programs with clowns, puppets, and animals. *Kukla, Fran, and Ollie* (1948–1957) featured Fran and her puppet friends. Like many shows of its time, *Kukla, Fran, and Ollie* was aired live, but unlike other shows, the dialogue was unscripted. *The Howdy-Doody Show* (1947–1960), hosted by Buffalo Bob Smith, featured Howdy Doody, an all-American boy puppet with 48 freckles (one for every state in the union). Programs such as *Zorro* (1957–1959) and *The Lone Ranger* (1949–1957) also were very popular with children, as were science fiction/adventure shows like *Captain Video and His Video Rangers* (1949–1950).

Captain Kangaroo (1955–1984), one of the longest-running children's programs of its time, prided itself on being slow paced and calming. Captain Kangaroo and his sidekick, Mr. Green Jeans, taught children about friendship, sharing, getting along with others, and being kind to animals. Segments of the program were interspersed with the cartoon adventures of Tom Terrific and Mighty Manfred the Wonder Dog.

Sports

Televising live sporting events presented several challenges in technology. Stations had to figure out how to get the cameras and other equipment to the site of the event; then, once there, they had to figure out how to position the cameras to capture all the action, which was often difficult. Boxing, wrestling, bowling, and roller-derby matches were easy to cover because they were played in relatively small arenas and didn't require much camera movement. The match-up on May 17, 1939, between collegiate rivals Columbia and Princeton was the first televised baseball game. The action was covered by one camera positioned on the third baseline (Massey & Baran, 1996).

History of Children's Shows

1947
Howdy Doody–The first superstars of children's television.

1949
Crusader Rabbit–The first made-for-television animated show.

1949
Bozo the Clown–One of the longest-running television shows ever.

1953
Winky Dink and You–Instructed children to put a special acetate sheet on the television screen to write on with crayons to help Winky Dink solve problems.

1955
Captain Kangraoo–Taught children how to behave and offered lessons in morality.

1955
The Mickey Mouse Club–Children loved the Mouseketeers.

1961
The Rocky and Bullwinkle Show–Its sharp satire was a hit with kids and adults.

1963
Mr. Rogers–Children loved having him in the neighborhood; on the air until 2000.

1969
Sesame Street–Perhaps one of the most influential children's television shows.

1971
The Electric Company–A mature *Sesame Street*.

1981
The Smurfs–Popular but controversial 1980s cartoon.

1987
Teenage Mutant Ninja Turtles–Action-oriented but non-violent characters.

1992
Barney–Most-loved character by children under age 5.

1993
Mighty Morphin Power Rangers–Included the first girl superhero.

1996
Blues Clues–An adorable puppy detective.

2002
Rolie Polie Olie–A boy robot.

Source: McGinn, 2002.

ZOOM IN 6.15
Find out more about *Howdy Doody* at www.howdydoodytime.com/index.html.

ZOOM IN 6.16
Find out more about old television shows at these sites:
- TVLand   www.tvland.com
- Nick-at-Nite   www.tvland.com/nickatnite

Who was Mallory Keaton's fiancé on **Family Ties?**

The first television broadcast of a baseball game, which was between Columbia University and Princeton University at New York's Baker Field on May 17, 1939.

As production capabilities increased and cameras became more portable, television moved to covering more action-packed sports. Multiple cameras could easily follow basketball and football games. Even sports such as golf, which are played in large areas, could be televised.

Movies and Miniseries

Television viewers have enjoyed theatrical movies from their living rooms since the 1940s, when British movie companies rented films to television stations. Not to be outdone by their overseas counterparts, American movie studios delivered to television stations mostly low-budget fare, such as westerns.

Televised movies became so popular that in 1954, millionaire Howard Hughes, owner of RKO studios, sold older RKO films to General Tire & Rubber Company, who showed the films on *Million Dollar Movie,* which aired on its independent television station in New York. NBC's *Saturday Night at the Movies* debuted in 1961 and was quickly followed by ABC's *Sunday Night at the Movies.* By the mid 1960s, the television schedule boasted many programs that showcased theatrical films, many of which drew very large audiences. When Alfred Hitchcock's movie *The Birds* hit the television airwaves in 1968, five years after its theatrical release, it reaped a 40 share of the audience. Another movie classic, *Gone With the Wind,* captured half of all viewers for two nights in 1976 (Gomery, 2003).

In the 1970s, the overabundance of theatrical movies being presented on the air led to **made-for-television movies.** Different from theatrical releases, which are produced for showing in movie theaters, made-for-television movies were produced for the television audience and made to accommodate commercial breaks (Eastman & Ferguson, 2002; Gomery, 2003). Movies such as *Brian's Song* (1971), *Women in Chains* (1972), and *The Waltons' Thanksgiving Story* (1973) frequently drew larger television audiences than did hit theatrical films (Gomery, 2003).

The Reagans and CBS

When CBS caved to pressure and threats of boycotts and decided to pull its miniseries *The Reagans* two weeks before it was scheduled to air during the November 2003 sweeps period, it unleashed a controversy larger than the movie itself. Based on pre-airing reports, the $9 million production was lambasted by the Republican National Committee and other conservatives for being an unbalanced portrayal of the former president (Ryan, 2003).

Proponents of pulling the program claimed the network had the responsibility of presenting the story in a fair and accurate manner. The producers of the show claimed the events depicted in the movie had been well documented. After CBS dropped the miniseries, it was picked up and aired by Showtime ("CBS Buckles," 2003; Lafayette, 2003). Showtime claimed that the movie was a docudrama, not a documentary, and that all docudramas "take some dramatic license" (Lafayette, 2003, p. 10).

Television industry executives and others were critical of CBS for succumbing to pressure and giving up the right to free speech. An editorial in *TelevisionWeek,* a trade magazine, speculated that "at a time when the government is firmly under GOP control, it is not realistic to think that CBS or any major broadcaster would be unaware that the attacks [on the miniseries] were linked directly to the highest levels of the Republican Party and the ever-more-powerful conservative movement. Our concern is that this kind of fear-driven decision-making may become increasingly common as media corporations become larger, more cautious and more bottom-line oriented" ("CBS Buckles," 2003, p. 10).

Nick Moore.

The made-for-television movie spawned the **television miniseries,** which is a multipart, made-for-television movie that airs in several installments, rather than a two- or three-hour segment (Eastman & Ferguson, 2002). Miniseries often tackled controversial issues that were not appropriate for regularly scheduled programs. Successful miniseries from the 1970s and 1980s included *Lonesome Dove, Holocaust, Shogun, The Winds of War,* and most notably, the 12-hour *Roots* (1977), which won nine Emmy's and one Golden Globe award. Just over half of U.S. viewers (51.1 rating, 71 share) tuned in for the final episode of *Roots,* and 85 percent watched at least part of the program (Bird, 2003; Gomery, 2003).

LeVar Burton in a scene from the television miniseries *Roots.*

SEE IT NOW: Television

Types of Programs

There are many different **genres** (or types) of television programs, each of which is distinguished by its structure and content. Television programs can be categorized as either narrative or nonnarrative. **Narrative programs** weave a story around the lives of fictional characters played by actors. Dramatic programs and situation comedies such as *ER, NYPD Blue,* and *Everybody Loves Raymond* present fictional stories that are scripted and acted out. **Nonnarrative programs** present real situations and feature real people, not actors (such as game show contestants and hosts, news anchors, sports stars, and so on). Even though it can be argued that every television program tells a story, nonnarrative programs tell stories that are real and don't come from fictional scripts. Game shows, talk shows, reality shows, and sports and news shows are all types of non-narrative programs (Butler, 2001).

Narrative Programs

Types of narrative programs include dramas, serials, and situation comedies.

DRAMAS   A dramatic series presents viewers with a narrative that is usually resolved at the end of each episode; in other words, the story does not continue from one episode to the next. A drama typically features a recurring set of primary characters that find themselves involved in some sort of situation, often facing a dilemma, that gets worked out as the action peaks and the episode comes to a climax and resolution.

ER star Maura Tierney as a nurse tending to patient James Belushi.

Dramas are often subcategorized by the subject matter. For example, police and courtroom dramas are popular today, as shown by such programs as *NYPD Blue, Law & Order,* and *The Practice.* These shows give us a look into the lives of cops on the streets and lawyers in the courtroom. Medical dramas fade in and out of popularity. Nonetheless, NBC's *ER* has consistently ranked number-one in the Nielsen weekly ratings and has succeeded in maintaining a steady audience since its 1994 debut.

SERIALS   More commonly known as *soap operas,* these programs have an ongoing narrative from one episode to the next. Serials are different from other types of dramas in several ways. There's little physical action; instead, the action takes place within the dialogue. Also, there are many primary characters. Serials typically have many

Who wrote the 1977 TV miniseries Roots?

storylines going on at the same time, such that characters are involved in several plots simultaneously that may not be resolved for years, if at all. When it finally seems like a resolution is at hand (say, a marriage and a happy life), a twist in the story leads to more uncertainty (did she unknowingly marry her long-lost brother?) and to a new, continuing storyline. *The Guiding Light* (which started on radio in 1937), *All My Children,* and *One Life to Live* (winner of the 2002 Emmy for outstanding daytime drama) are the more popular soap operas of today.

Although most soap operas air during the daytime hours and are thought to be intended largely for women, prime time has seen its share of soaps. (However, to attract male viewers, the networks are careful not to call them *soaps.*) These programs were particularly popular on prime time in the 1980s, when viewers were treated to a peek into the fictional lives of the rich on such programs as *Dallas* (1978–1991), *Dynasty* (1981–1989), and *Falcon Crest* (1981–1990).

The cast of *Everybody Loves Raymond* (from left to right): Brad Garrett, Peter Boyle, Doris Roberts, Ray Romano, and Patricia Heaton.

SITUATION COMEDIES   Situation comedies are usually half-hour programs that present a humorous narrative that's resolved at the end of each episode. *Sitcoms,* as they are often called, feature a cast of recurring characters who find themselves caught up in some situation. Sometimes, the situation itself is not funny, but it's handled in a humorous fashion. For example, on *Friends,* at first glance, it did not seem very funny when Ross had to tell Mona that Rachel had moved in with him, but the plot took a humorous twist when Mona unexpectedly showed up on his doorstep. At other times, the situation itself creates the humor, like in *Frasier,* when class-conscious Roz found the perfect boyfriend but then discovered he was a garbageman. The television sitcom has been a prime-time staple that has kept viewers laughing for decades.

Nonnarrative Programs

As stated earlier, nonnarrative programs run the gamut from game shows and talk shows to news and public affairs programs.

GAME SHOWS   Television viewers love the competitive nature of game shows. It's fun to watch contestants compete for prizes and money, and it's also fun to play along. Many game shows are formatted so the television audience can participate. Most viewers have "bought a vowel" while watching *Wheel of Fortune* or guessed the cost of a refrigerator on *The Price Is Right.* Of course, we can't forget about *Who Wants to Be a Millionaire?* How far could you go without using a lifeline?

The characters in *The Simpsons* (back row): Homer and Marge; (front row, left to right) Maggie, Lisa, and Bart.

Television viewers often root for their favorite contestants and develop a feeling of kinship with them, especially if they're on for more than one show, like a returning *Jeopardy!* champ. Before the quiz show scandal broke in the late 1950s, the viewing audience idolized winning contestants, who often appeared on magazine covers and at civic ceremonies.

Although it took years for the public to regain its trust in game shows, the power of a good contest eventually overcame the skepticism. Game shows today are immensely popular, as demonstrated by *Wheel of Fortune,* which is the "highest rated syndicated show in television history" (Gross, 2000, p. 247).

The set of *Jeopardy!* which is hosted by Alex Trebek.

REALITY SHOWS *Candid Camera,* the first reality-type program, premiered in 1948 under its original radio title, *Candid Microphone.* The show featured hidden camera footage of unsuspecting people who were unwittingly involved in some sort of hoax or funny situation that was contrived as part of the program. After catching people's reactions to outlandish and bizarre situations, host Allen Funt would jump out and yell, "Smile, you're on *Candid Camera!"*

In newer reality shows, the camera literally follows people around. Nothing is scripted, and the actors are just ordinary people. The first such program was *An American Family,* which aired on PBS in 1973. It followed a year in the real life of Mr. and Mrs. Loud and their five teenagers from Santa Barbara, California. The program documented the parents' marital problems (which later led to divorce), and the audience watched as son Lance came out of the closet and became the first openly gay person to appear on television. *An American Family* reflected the changing lifestyles of the times and stood in stark contrast to unrealistic, idealized, fictional family programs, such as *The Brady Bunch* ("An American Family," 2002).

Following in *An American Family's* footsteps is MTV's *The Osbournes,* which portrays the everyday family life (sans oldest daughter Aimee) of Ozzy Osbourne, former member of heavy metal group Black Sabbath. The cameras were even there when Ozzy's wife, Sharon, underwent treatment for colon cancer (Gundersen, 2002). Attracting an average of 6 million viewers per week, *The Osbournes* is the biggest show ever on MTV. Just watching the bumbling Ozzy taking out the garbage or heating up a burrito is funny. Whether they're throwing a baked ham at the noisy neighbors, potty training their dogs, or turning on sprinklers to repel nosy fans, the Osbournes have created a whole new program genre: the reality sitcom (Peyser, 2002).

COPs (1989) is one of the longest-running reality programs. The basic premise of the show is simple: A camera crew follows around police on their beats and tapes their confrontations with suspects. Other early reality programs, such as *Rescue 911* (1989–1996) and *America's Most Wanted* (1988), also depicted real-life rescue and crime situations but were scripted and played by actors representing the people involved in the real-life situations. *America's Funniest Home Videos* (1990) also breaks the typical reality format. Instead of professional camera operators taping antics, ordinary people tape each other doing silly things and send in their tapes with the hopes of having them shown on television and winning a cash prize.

The Nelsons (Ozzie and Harriet) versus the Osbournes (Ozzy and Sharon)

The Adventures of Ozzie and Harriet:
October 1952–September 1966

The Osbournes:
2002–present

THE NELSONS

THE OSBOURNES

Ozzie and Harriet talk to sons Ricky and David about such issues as hobbies, rivalries, homework, and girlfriends.	Ozzy and Sharon talk to kids Kelly and Jack about such issues as drugs, tattoos, condoms, sex, and visits to the gynecologist.
Ozzie goes to work in a suit, tie, and hat.	Ozzy goes to work in leather, black nail polish, and eyeliner.
David calls his brother a "moron."	Kelly calls her brother a "f**king loser."
Ozzie broke into the neighbor's garage to retrieve a borrowed lawn mower.	Ozzy broke a neighbor's window by hurling a log at it.
Ozzie is the king of his castle.	Ozzy is the prince of darkness.
Paintings and photographs adorn the wall of the family home.	Crucifixes and devil heads adorn the walls of the family home.
Harriet made a beautiful ham for Christmas dinner.	Sharon threw a ham at the neighbors.
Ozzie shows his affection by telling the kids they're "the apple of his eye."	Ozzy shows his affection by telling the kids, "I love you more than life itself, but you're all f**king mad."
Harriet welcomes visitors and offers them a drink.	Sharon threatens to pee in a visitor's drink.
25 minutes of pure family values.	25 minutes of bleeps.

Sources: Jenkins, 2002; Williams, 2003.

Reality dating programs have sprung up all over the dial in recent years. *Blind Date, Elimidate,* and *The Fifth Wheel* all follow couples around as they go on dates and get to know each other. The daters all get an opportunity to talk about their dates, often trashing each other and calling each other names, if the date didn't go as planned.

ZOOM IN   6.17
• *Reality News Online* gives updates on all the reality contests, provides quotes from contestants, shares gossip, and presents other reality show news: www.realitynewsonline.com/index.html.
• Start at this site and then explore links to your favorite reality shows: www.realitytvlinks.com.

The newest reality rage is the so-called reality game show, such as *Survivor, Fear Factor, The Amazing Race, Big Brother, The Mole, Bachelor, Road Rules,* and *Who's Got Game?* In these shows, contestants do seemingly impossible tasks in order to be declared the winner. On *Survivor,* for instance, a group of people are sent to a remote location and left to deal with the elements, all the while trying to position themselves as the most valuable person. One

fyi

Surviving an Avalanche:
How *America's Funniest Home Videos* Are Selected

"When *America's Funniest Home Videos* premiered in 1990, it hit with a bang. Within two weeks we were receiving about 5,000 tapes a week so we quickly had to develop a system to handle that avalanche. After each VHS cassette was assigned a unique number, and logged it into a database, it then went to the screeners. To find the 60 or more clips needed for each half-hour episode the 10 screeners had to sift through at least 4,000 per week. Their selections were then scored on a scale of 1 to 10 with all 5 and above passing up to me for my review. The screeners had a very high "kill ratio" but I usually watched at least 80 tapes a day, picking and packaging the best and tossing the rest. I then worked with the voiceover writers and sound effects editors to ensure that each clip got the best possible comedy icing on the cake.

"After the show's Executive Producer, Vin Di Bona, approved the playback reel of clips we took them into the studio and taped the show before a live audience. Each playback reel had at least 15 more clips than needed for each show. That way we could watch the reaction of the studio audience and toss out the tapes that weren't working before editing the final version of the show for air. This basic system, plus talent, dedication and a unique sense of comedy has made AFHV an international mega-hit for over 14 years."

Source: Steve Paskay, Co-Executive Producer, *America's Funniest Home Videos* (1990–1995).

person is voted off the show each week by his or her fellow castaways until a winner is chosen at the end. *American Idol* is a kind of updated *Gong Show* from 1976 but with an interactive twist, in that viewers vote for the winners. In one of the biggest shows of 2002–2003, viewers voted more than 230 million times. This reality talent show also features a panel of judges who make often cutting cracks at the contestants after they have sung their hearts out and tried their best to win (Peyser & Smith, 2003).

Other new reality formats include *Trading Spaces,* in which neighbors redecorate each other's homes, and *Queer Eye for the Straight Guy,* in which five gay men give a straight guy advice on home decorating, clothing, grooming, food, and culture. The Fab Five's endearingly funny and helpful advice has drawn new attention to the Bravo network. The program saw a 62 percent spike in ratings at the end of July 2003 (it's fourth week on the air) and went on to draw about 2.8 million viewers each week (Gordon & Sigesmund, 2003).

TALK SHOWS   While early talk shows may have been news oriented and serious in nature (and some still are), many today are exploitive and sensationalized. Some viewers claim they watch talk shows for the information, but others claim the programs are purely entertaining. Even when the talk show topic is totally crazy, there's usually something to learn or reflect upon (even if it's just being glad that you're not in the same situation as the guests).

On many current talk shows, the studio audience hoots and hollers and otherwise expresses their approval or disapproval of the guests, who willingly air their dirty laundry to millions of viewers. Serious subjects such as AIDS, alcoholism, and incest become nothing more than fodder for a rambunctious audience that's encouraged by the shows' producers to yell at the guests. The viewing audience really can't be blamed for criticizing talk shows, considering the bizarre nature of some of the topics: "I was abducted by space aliens" and "My mother is my teenage boyfriend's lover." In this sense, talk shows can be considered modern freak shows, whose viewers watch just to laugh at the freaks.

Yet in another sense, talk shows serve a very important function by informing and educating the viewing audience. In past years, talk show hosts such as Phil Donahue and Dick Cavett promoted intellectual discourse about controversial and important matters. Today, hosts such as Oprah Winfrey and Dr. Phil McGraw present both sides of a controversy and discuss contemporary and pressing issues. Viewers learn about many

Talk show hosts Dr. Phil McGraw and Oprah Winfrey.

ZOOM IN   6.18
Learn more about talk shows at the website of the
Museum of Broadcast Communication: www.museum.tv/
archives/etv/T/htmlT/talkshows/talkshows.htm.

interesting and valuable topics, such as the latest developments in medicine, how to recognize signs of mental illness, how to lose weight, how to get fit, the difference between organic and non-organic vegetables, and what distinguishes different religions and cultural lifestyles.

PUBLIC AFFAIRS SHOWS   Making its debut in 1947, *Meet the Press* was the first television interview show and is still the longest-running network program. Program guests discuss politics and current events and treat subjects in a serious manner ("About *Meet the Press*," 2003; Massey & Baran, 1996). *Meet the Press* was the precursor to public affairs programs such as PBS's *Washington Week* and *The NewsHour with Jim Lehrer*.

NEWS   In 1980, when Ted Turner started Cable News Network (CNN), his critics dubbed it the "Chicken Noodle Network" and mocked, "It'll never work. No one wants 24 hours of news." But Turner proved them all wrong. There was an appetite for 24/7 news, and it has continued to grow.

The increase in television news viewership has coincided with a decrease in newspaper readership, especially among younger people. In the 1990s, only about one-third of Americans under age 35 read the newspaper on a regular basis, and only half of 18- to 24-year-olds read the paper at all (Dominick, 1999). Another readership study found that 69 percent of senior citizens had read the paper the day before, compared to 28 percent of younger respondents (Dizard, 2000).

Newspapers are not the only news medium shunned by young people. Despite the availability of around-the-clock television news, about 4 out of 10 Americans age 18 to 30 are nonusers of any type of news media. In fact, they know less and care less about news and public affairs than any other generation in the past 50 years (Dizard, 2000). This disinterest among young people brings on new challenges to the television news industry to lure this group of viewers to the screen.

When we watch television news, we're watching a local newscast, a broadcast network newscast, or a cable network newscast:

Peter Jennings, anchor of ABC's *World News Tonight*.

Connie Chung, host of CNN's *Connie Chung Tonight*.

- A **local newscast** is produced by a local television station, usually a network affiliate, and serves primarily the local community. Community news and events are the main focus of a local newscast. Depending on the size of the market and the community, most local stations have a small staff of reporters (who sometimes double as anchors) who gather the news and write the stories. It's not economically feasible for each station to send reporters all over the world, so local stations also get news stories from the **wire services**, such as the Associated Press (AP) and Reuters, and from their networks, which transmit written copy and video footage via satellite to local stations.

- **Broadcast network news** specializes in national and international rather than local news. Peter Jennings (ABC), Tom Brokaw (NBC), and Dan Rather (CBS) are likely the most well known network news anchors. Networks also produce morning and prime-time news programs. The *Today* show (NBC), *Good Morning America* (ABC), and *The Early Show* (CBS) wake up viewers with light-hearted information and entertainment fare, sprinkled with a few minutes of hard news. The networks turn to more serious and concentrated reporting of important issues in their prime-time news programs. Shows such as *20/20* (ABC), *PrimeTime* (ABC), *Dateline* (NBC), *48 Hours* (CBS), and *60 Minutes* (CBS) bring in-depth coverage of current issues and events.

Alien Life Form.

- CNN's success as a 24-hour **cable news network** demonstrated the need for an all-day newscast. Viewers were no longer content to wait for the 6 or 11 o'clock newscast to learn about an event that happened hours earlier. They wanted to see the action when it happened—"All the news, all the time." Cable networks were perfect for filling that need. Today, CNN continues to be one of the most widely watched and relied upon news sources around the world, even though other all-news cable networks have been created. Following in CNN's footsteps, FOXNews, CNBC, MSNBC (a Microsoft and NBC partnership), and ESPN (sports news) all specialize in international and national news, in-depth analysis, and special news programs.

Television news—whether local, broadcast network, or cable network—is certainly not without its critics. Even with 24-hour news shows, there's way too much going on in the world than can be shown on a television newscast. So it's up to the news producers to be the **gatekeepers** and decide what news should go on the air and how it should be presented. Viewers' complaints cover a lot of ground: that too much attention is given to stories that are of little importance but have flashy video, that the news is often sensationalized, that stories are too superficial, that not all stories are believable, that the news is politically biased, and that news organizations won't air reports that show certain politicians or companies in an unfavorable light.

Many viewers are concerned about the bias and low credibility of news accounts, especially when news sources such as FOXNews air stories that clearly reflect their political points of view. In such a heavily competitive environment, news networks are always trying to distinguish themselves. FOX's answer is "Wave the flag, give 'em an attitude, and make it lively" (Johnson, 2002, p. 1A). They have positioned themselves as an opinion page, sharing views to the right of center. As competition remains strong, the fear is that other networks may, too, be tempted to "claim political niches the way FOX has" (Johnson, 2002, p. 1A).

Indeed, the viewing public casts a critical eye toward television news. For example, one study showed that about three-quarters of the public view the three major news networks and CNN as credible. Yet believability ratings are 10 points lower than in the 1990s, and only about one-third of viewers are "very satisfied" with television news, down from 43 percent in 1994 (Pew Research Center, 2000). Many viewers are turning to the Internet for their news. Several studies have found that the Internet is cutting deeply into television-viewing time ("GVU's Tenth WWW User Survey," 1998; Klein, 2000; SIQSS, 2000), and just over one-third of politically interested Internet users claim they spend less time with television news since first going online (Kaye & Johnson, 2003).

MOVIES AND MINISERIES   Theatrical movies, made-for-TV-movies, and miniseries still abound on television, and with the advent of cable channels and **pay-per-view** (cable companies that charge viewers a fee to watch a particular movie), there are even more choices available. Plus, if viewers don't like what's on the air, they can always rent a video or DVD of a movie of their choice.

Theatrical films have adjusted to television by updating their release cycles. A theatrical film is first released to the movie theaters. When the box office receipts get low, the film is pulled from the theaters and sometimes held for a second release. Within about six months of the final theatrical release, the movie is usually distributed on video cassette or DVD rental and then later made available for sale. After it's no longer shown at the theater, the movie may be on pay-per-view and later licensed to pay-cable networks, such as HBO and The Movie Channel. After it has made the rounds on the cable channels, the movie is released for network airing, and after a couple of years, it will be inexpensive enough for broadcast by an affiliate or independent station (Eastman & Ferguson, 2002).

On what show did the Simpsons first appear?

Made-for-TV movies, which are often specifically produced for broadcast cable network audiences, can be very profitable. Cable networks such as Lifetime and HBO produce made-for-TV movies that will appeal to their viewers and fit into their schedules. Made-for-TV movies also enjoy later profits from video cassette and DVD sales and rentals (Eastman & Ferguson, 2002).

Contemporary miniseries are usually scheduled to air on consecutive nights or over successive weeks. As such, they are known as short-form and long-form productions, respectively. After the riveting 30-hour *War and Remembrance* (1988–1989), which cost more than $100 million to produce, ratings for such long-form miniseries plummeted. The networks turned instead to shorter four- to six-hour miniseries, such as *Million Dollar Babies* and *The Burden of Proof* (Eastman & Ferguson, 2002).

Noncommercial Television

In addition to establishing NPR, the Corporation for Public Broadcasting also created the Public Broadcasting Service (PBS) in 1969. PBS is devoted to airing "television's best children's, cultural, educational, history, nature, news, public affairs, science and skills programs" ("Public Broadcasting Service," 2002).

PBS is known for airing quality programs that are often both educational and entertaining. Children's programs such as *Mr. Rogers' Neighborhood* (which first aired on WQED, Pittsburgh, in 1967), *Sesame Street* (1969), *Barney and Friends* (1992), and *Teletubbies* (1997) are must-watches for millions of kids. Other PBS program milestones include *Masterpiece Theater* (1971), *NOVA* (1974), *Great Performances* (1974), *American Playhouse* (1982), and *Civil War* (1990), a Ken Burns epic documentary ("Masterpieces and Milestones," 1999).

Some contemporary PBS programs include *American Family,* about the everyday life of a Hispanic family living in East Los Angeles; *Antiques Roadshow,* a traveling show that

ZOOM IN   6.19
• Learn more about the Public Broadcasting System (PBS) at **www.pbs.org.**
• Watch a PBS program and consider how it differs from a broadcast or cable program of the same genre.

Cast members in the early days of *Sesame Street* (1969).

The Tracy Ullman Show.

offers appraisals of antiques and collectibles; *Frontline,* an investigative documentary program that delves into the issues of today; *The World of National Geographic,* which provides a look at the world in which we live; *NOVA,* about science and technology; and *Keeping Up Appearances,* one of several British comedies.

As of mid 2002, PBS had 349 member stations that aired programs watched by almost 100 million viewers every week. PBS is watched about eight hours per month by about 73.2 percent of all U.S. television-owning families ("Public Television Audience," 2002).

Where Television Programs Come From

Every television program starts with an idea, and anyone can come up with an idea. Nonetheless, the ideas from established writers and producers usually get the most serious consideration.

The process of getting a program on the air usually starts with a **treatment,** a description of the program and its characters. Next, the writer or producer **pitches** the idea to a network or production company. The pitch is basically a detailed description of the program and the characters as well as outlines of some episodes. If network executives think the project is worthwhile, they'll go forward with a **pilot,** a sample episode that introduces the program and characters to viewers. Pilots are often spectacular productions that draw in viewers. Unfortunately, when some programs make it to the schedule, their subsequent episodes aren't nearly as grand as the pilot, and disappointed viewers may stop watching the show.

About 2,000 to 4,000 program proposals are submitted each year to networks and production companies. Of those, maybe 100 will be filmed as pilots, between 10 and 20 will actually make it to the air, and about 5 will run for more than one season.

Who Produces Programs

A television program can be produced by any of several sources, including major and independent production companies and broadcast and cable networks.

Production Companies

Most major production companies—such as Columbia TriStar, Warner Bros., and Twentieth Century Fox—started as movie production houses and have been around for years. Some of the major production companies own or have financial interest in some of the television networks and may produce programs for those networks. Major production houses have brought us such programs as *Friends* (Warner Bros. Television) and *Frasier* (Paramount Network Television), for instance.

In contrast to the huge conglomerates with ties to the networks, independent production houses are small companies. For example, *NYPD Blue, Philly,* and *Hill Street Blues* were originated by Bochco Productions. Independent producers sell broadcast rights to the networks but retain program ownership.

Networks

In 1970, the FCC enacted **financial interest and syndication rules (fin/syn),** which stated that a network could only produce three-and-a-half hours' worth of its weekly prime-time programs; the rest had to come from outside production companies. In

The Reverend Jerry Falwell with Teletubby character Tinky Winky.

What was the name of the principal on **Saved by the Bell?**

mandating fin/syn, the FCC hoped that independent producers would bring more diversity to prime-time programming and break what it considered the networks' monopoly over the production and distribution of television programs. Because FOX did not exceed 15 hours of prime-time programming, it was exempt from fin/syn. This exemption helped FOX produce its own programs and eventually develop into a full-fledged network (Walker & Ferguson, 1998).

As new competition from cable networks and satellite-delivered programs eroded network audiences, the FCC relaxed and then rescinded fin/syn in 1995. As a result, the competition between the networks and independent producers has heated up, with the producers charging that the networks are biased toward airing their own programs, rather than those owned by outside producers. Also, since the networks stand to make quite a bit of money down the road from syndication, they're likely to keep their own poorly rated programs on the air at the expense of independently produced programs that may have higher ratings. The networks contend, however, that this ongoing competition has led to higher-quality programming. Moreover, they counter charges of keeping low-rated programs on the air with examples of networks canceling their own programs, as when ABC canceled *Ellen*.

Even though PBS is a network, it's noncommercial and nonprofit. Thus, it isn't financially feasible for PBS itself to produce programs. Instead, PBS obtains programs from independent producers, from some PBS stations that do produce shows, and from other sources around the globe. PBS acts only as a distributor in that it transmits programs to its member stations via satellite.

CAREER TRACKS

Jay Renfroe   Television Production Co-Owner, Writer, and Producer

• **What is your job? What do you do?**

I own an LA-based television production company. I create and produce reality and scripted television shows for the networks, syndication, and cable. Currently, we produce *Blind Date* and *Fifth Wheel* for first-run syndication and have several series at the networks, including the surreal *Life* for the WB. We are currently entering the scripted one-hour drama and one-half comedy arenas as well as feature films. In the reality world, I am an executive producer, and in the scripted world, I both executive produce and write.

• **How long have you been doing this job?**

Been in the business for 20 years. I've been a partner in Renegade Entertainment for 8 years now.

• **What was your first job in electronic media?**

I wrote/directed commercials and industrials in Atlanta.

• **What led you to the job?**

Studied TV/film production in college, did some sports production, had a comedy troupe in Atlanta, produced stand-up comedy for HBO/Showtime, wrote a play in Los Angeles, which led to writing the screenplay for Tri-Star based on the play, which led to creating and writing a sitcom for CBS, which led to forming my own company with an old college friend from Florida State University. We're still partners.

• **What advice would you have for students who might want a job like yours?**

Do everything. I was a camera operator, editor, lighting director, theatrical director, writer. Learn every job, and you'll be a better producer. The more material you can create and produce, the more confidence you'll have in yourself as a leader. Learn your own voice and how to communicate your vision to everybody involved in the production. Execution is everything.

The Oprah Winfrey Show

When Oprah Winfrey first announced that she would take her show off the air after the 2005–2006 season, stations scrambled to find a replacement for her time slot. In most markets, *The Oprah Winfrey Show* airs during the 4:00 to 5:00 P.M. time slot as a lead-in to the station's early evening news program. Because the lead-in show is so important in delivering an audience to the news program, stations are willing to pay syndicators top dollar for a high-profile show. Since many stations decided to move *Dr. Phil* from the 3:00 P.M. time slot into the *Oprah* time slot in 2005, they paid huge license fees to King World Syndication.

Then, Oprah had a change of heart and decided to keep her show on the air at least through the 2007–2008 season. Since *Oprah* consistently beats out *Dr. Phil* in the ratings, it gets to stay on in the more desirable 4:00 P.M. time slot, leaving *Dr. Phil* at 3:00 P.M.

Stations that have already paid King World license fees for *Dr. Phil* are concerned about making their money back, now that *The*

Oprah Winfrey Show is staying on the air. With such formidable competition, it's unlikely that *Dr. Phil* will become the number-one-rated talk show. With lower ratings and a 3:00 P.M. time slot, stations can't charge their advertisers as much as they could if *Dr. Phil* was on at 4:00 P.M. Confounding the problem is a contractual agreement between Oprah's production company, Harpo, and *Dr. Phil*. When Harpo helped launch *Dr. Phil*, it forbade it from going head-to-head against *The Oprah Winfrey Show* in any market. That means stations can't simply move *Dr. Phil* to 4:00 P.M. and charge more for commercial time in an attempt to recoup their license fees.

Many station executives are furious. They were willing to over-pay for *Dr. Phil* for the years leading up to the 2005–2006 season when they believed they would make up the expense after *Oprah* went off the air. But that opportunity is no longer available. They will have to find some other way to make back what they paid out.

Source: Albiniak, 2003.

Syndicators

Television syndicators are companies that sell television programs to local television stations, cable television networks, and other media outlets. Local television affiliates and independents both depend on syndicated material to fill out their broadcast schedules. There are two basic types of syndicated programs: off-network and first-run.

Off-network syndicated programs are those that once ran or still run as regularly scheduled programs on one of the broadcast networks. For example, even though new episodes of *Seinfeld* are no longer being produced, you can probably see old episodes daily on a local broadcast station or cable network.

Classic programs like *I Love Lucy* are also commonly syndicated. *Lucy* was the first program to be shot on film in front of a live audience. This means that, unlike other live shows that were either not recorded at all or recorded on poor-quality kinescopes, old episodes have retained their quality for more than half a century (Campbell, 2000). The program's production quality was so high that it could easily be rerun and syndicated today and enjoyed by the audience just as much as the first time it was shown.

Prime-time network programs usually run once a week, but once they have been syndicated to a local station, they often run five days a week (also known as *stripping*). In order to have enough episodes for syndication, prime-time programs need to stay on the air for at least 65 episodes. (That way, they can be shown Monday through Friday for 13 weeks.) However, most stations won't pick up a syndicated program unless there are at least 100 to 150 episodes, with 130 being the ideal number. (That means 26 weeks of Monday through Friday airings.) Popular programs sometimes go into syndication even though they're still on during prime time. For example, in 2001, *Everybody Loves Raymond* went into the off-net syndication market and was distributed to local stations by King World Productions, even though it remained one of the most highly rated network programs.

TOP 10	Syndicated Programs: April 21–27, 2003	
PROGRAM		**RATING**
Wheel of Fortune (first-run)		8.8
Jeopardy! (first-run)		7.0
Friends (off-net)		6.6
Everybody Loves Raymond (off-net)		6.4
Seinfeld (off-net)		6.3
Seinfeld (weekend) (off-net)		6.0
Oprah Winfrey (first-run)		5.9
Entertainment Tonight (first-run)		5.5
Wheel of Fortune (weekend) (first-run)		5.1
Judge Judy (first-run)		4.8

Source: "Top 25 Shows," 2003.

First-run syndicated programs are produced for television stations but not intended for prime-time network airing. Examples of first-run syndicated programs include *Jeopardy! Wheel of Fortune,* and *The Oprah Winfrey Show* (all syndicated by King World Productions) as well as *Elimidate* (Telepictures Distribution) and *The Fifth Wheel* (Universal Worldwide TV).

Who Pays for Programs

Producers

When a network or production company produces a television program, it pays the production costs. Producing just one episode can cost millions of dollars, but rarely is an episode sold for more than the cost of production. Producers therefore create programs with an eye toward first-run syndication and network airings. They hope their programs are on the air long enough to make it to the off-network syndication market. The producers will see a profit after a program has been shown on a network and is then sold to a syndicator for future airings. At this point, a successful program commands a high price that will more than cover the original production cost.

Networks

Television networks pay independent producers for their programs. Specifically, the network actually buys the rights to the program, but the producer maintains ownership. In some cases, a network will cover the costs of producing its own programs. The network also pays its affiliates (through a contractual relationship) to air the programs. In turn, the network makes money by selling commercial time to advertisers.

Affiliates

An affiliate is paid by a network to air each of the network's programs. The amount of compensation depends on the network, the popularity of the program, and the size of the viewing audience. For example, to air a program during prime time, the network could pay the affiliate from several hundred dollars to several thousand dollars per hour.

In the 1990s, the networks tried to reduce these payments, claiming that affiliate stations could make up for lost compensation through the sales of commercial time that the networks provide in each program. The affiliates were up in arms over the proposed reduced compensation. Faced with growing competition from FOX, the potential for new broadcast networks, and the availability of syndicated programs as alternatives to network shows, the networks backed down (Walker & Ferguson, 1998).

Affiliate stations do, however, pay for syndicated first-run and off-network shows, either as cash or as part of a barter agreement with the syndicator. With a *cash purchase,* the station simply pays the syndicator for the right to air the program and, in turn, the station sells commercial time. In a *straight barter agreement,* the station gets a program for free but the syndicator gets to sell a portion of the available commercial time, leaving only a small amount of time for the station to sell. A *cash-plus-barter arrangement* works almost the same way as a straight barter, but the station pays a small amount of cash in exchange for more commercial time.

Syndicators

Syndicators pay the costs of producing their own first-run syndicated shows. For example, King World Productions is responsible for the cost of producing *Jeopardy!* King World turns a profit, however, by selling the program to television stations. Syndicators also pay the costs of off-network programs, which they then sell to television stations through various cash, straight barter, and cash-plus-barter arrangements.

PBS PRODUCTIONS   As noted earlier, PBS obtains programs from independent producers and their member stations. Thus, the PBS network/member station programming relationship is opposite the relationship between the commercial networks and affiliates. That is, PBS member stations pay the network for programs and generate revenue through membership drives and from federal, state, and local government funding.

CABLE OPERATORS   Cable operators/providers, such as Comcast, pay cable networks monthly distribution fees based on their numbers of subscribers. Cable operators, in turn, generate revenue by collecting monthly subscription fees from consumers and by selling commercial time. Some cable programs come from the networks with presold commercial time. In other cases, cable systems barter with cable networks for more commercial time, which they sell locally. Premium cable networks, such as HBO, require a fee-splitting financial relationship. In exchange for carrying a premium cable network, a local cable operator agrees to give the network about half of the fees it collects from its customers, who subscribe to the premium network.

What Types of Channels Carry What Types of Programs

Broadcast Networks

The broadcast television networks vie for the largest possible audience. Up until about 1980, the big-three networks (ABC, CBS, NBC) shared approximately 90 percent of the television-viewing audience. By the late 1990s, as cable television gained favor among viewers and as new broadcast networks (FOX, PAX, WB, UPN) hit the screen, ABC, CBS, NBC, and FOX found themselves sharing between about 47 percent and 66 percent of the audience (Dizard, 2000; "TV First," 2003; Walker & Ferguson, 1998).

Despite the fact that their collective audience has shrunk, individually, ABC, CBS, NBC, and FOX still attract more viewers than any other new broadcast or cable network.

PRIME TIME   Airing programs that appeal to a large audience is the key to success for the broadcast networks. With popular programming, the networks can supply large audiences to their advertisers. Even though the broadcast networks' share of the prime-time audience has decreased, they are still the mainstay of the television industry.

Most prime-time programs are designed to appeal to people across the demographic spectrum—that is, of all ages and education levels. That means you don't have to be an attorney to understand *Law & Order* or be a doctor to like *ER*. Situation comedies and dramas are the most common forms of prime-time entertainment. Prime time also includes theatrical and made-for-TV movies, one-time specials (such as the Emmy, Oscar, and Grammy award shows), and made-for-TV miniseries (serial programs with three to six episodes).

NON–PRIME TIME   Although the networks concentrate their efforts on prime-time programs, these programs are actually less profitable than non–prime time programs. Both daytime and late-night programs are less expensive to produce and contain five to seven more commercial minutes than prime-time programs. Granted, non–prime time commercials don't sell for nearly as much as those aired during prime time, but the additional minutes coupled with lower production costs maximize revenue.

Daytime and late-night programs are very different from their prime-time counterparts and are driven by audience size and composition. For instance, fewer viewers tune in during non–prime time hours. Also, the daytime audience is less diverse and made up mainly of children, stay-at-home parents, senior citizens, students, and shift workers (Dominick, 1999; Eastman & Ferguson, 2002). Children's shows, after-school specials, soap operas, talk shows, and game shows are most likely aired during the daytime hours. Late-night television attracts more male viewers than female. Males gravitate toward late-night entertainment/talk, sports, comedies, and first-run risqué movies (Eastman & Ferguson, 2002).

CAREER TRACKS

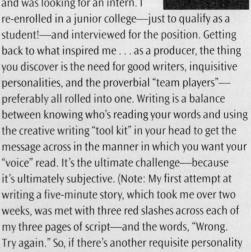

Kent Takano   Director of Programming, HGTV

● **What are your primary responsibilities?**

Working directly with various production companies across the country to create, develop, and produce programming for the network. Part of this position requires knowledge of the different strengths of these production companies, as some companies specialize in studio shows, others in specific genres, like crafts, how-to, landscaping, design, etc. It's my job to find the best production "fit" for our programming as possible. My position reports directly to the VP of Programming.

● **What was your first job in electronic media?**

My first job in television was as an intern at KPIX-TV, the CBS affiliate in San Francisco. I did everything from rewind tapes to buy lunch for the crew to bring props to shoots. Lots of grunt work! Received two units of school credit. My first paying job was as a story researcher for *PM Magazine*—which meant researching and developing stories for this nationally syndicated program.

● **What led you to your present job?**

I worked as a producer and executive producer for 12 years before coming to HGTV; the last 5 years as an independent contractor for various production companies and networks, including HGTV, The Discovery Channel, MTV, ABC's *The View*, etc. All of this emerged from my love of writing. In 1986, after having graduated from college with the desire to develop a better "dramatic" voice, I took an acting course—to find out how actors interpret the written word. As fate would

have it, my acting partner was a producer at the local CBS affiliate and was looking for an intern. I re-enrolled in a junior college—just to qualify as a student!—and interviewed for the position. Getting back to what inspired me . . . as a producer, the thing you discover is the need for good writers, inquisitive personalities, and the proverbial "team players"— preferably all rolled into one. Writing is a balance between knowing who's reading your words and using the creative writing "tool kit" in your head to get the message across in the manner in which you want your "voice" read. It's the ultimate challenge—because it's ultimately subjective. (Note: My first attempt at writing a five-minute story, which took me over two weeks, was met with three red slashes across each of my three pages of script—and the words, "Wrong. Try again." So, if there's another requisite personality trait, then "thick skin" also applies!)

● **What advice would you have for students who might want a job like yours?**

Advice—apply for any internship you can. Whether it's radio, TV, or print, they're all invaluable because they teach you about communicating to an audience. Even if you're sweeping floors, you're in the building—and that's how you learn. Osmosis! The other piece of advice I have is "Don't give up." If you have more desire and patience than talent, like me, you'll be fine.

Cable Networks

Many cable programs specialize in particular subjects, such as golfing, home and garden, or history. In contrast to the broadcast networks, which target a large, mass audience, the cable networks target smaller niche or specialty audiences. Thus, a cable network such as the Food Network is expected to appeal to people interested in cooking and so will have a much smaller audience than an ABC sitcom, which might appeal to millions of viewers. Other cable networks, such as USA, air mostly old programs from the broadcast networks, which appeal to a much larger audience.

There are hundreds of cable networks that focus on specific topics, such as sports (ESPN), music (VH-1), golfing (The Golf Channel), weather (The Weather Channel), movies (AMC, Bravo, Turner Classic Movies), news (CNN, MSNBC), science and nature (Discovery), history (The History Channel), animals (Animal Planet, My Pet TV), travel (The Travel Channel), and ethnic culture (BET, Univision), just to name a few.

TOP 10	**Cable Networks by Number of Subscribers: February 2003**

1. TBS Superstation   87,700,000
2. ESPN   86,700,000
3. C-SPAN   86,600,000
4. Discovery Channel   86,500,000
5. USA   86,300,000
6. CNN (Cable News Network)   86,200,000
6. TNT (Turner Network Television)   86,200,000
8. Nickelodeon/Nick-at-Nite   86,000,000
8. Lifetime Television (LIFE)   86,000,000
10. A&E Network   85,900,000

Source: "Top 20 Cable Networks," 2003.

Premium and Pay-per-View Channels

Premium channels like HBO, Cinemax, and Encore, along with pay-per-view and near-video-on-demand, offer programs such as movies, sports, and special events for a monthly or per-viewing charge. Cable companies offer subscribers a variety of premium channels for an extra monthly charge, whether for each channel or a package of channels. Whereas broadcast stations sometimes run old movies, HBO and the other premium channels offer viewers more recent films. HBO now even produces its own programs, expanding its offerings beyond theatrical movies.

Local Origination and Local Access Channels

Cable systems are often required to provide local origination and local access channels as part of their franchise agreements with cities and local communities. **Local origination channels**, which are operated by the local cable systems, often provide local news,

Mike Myers and Dana Carvey, stars of *Wayne's World.*

coverage of high school and local college sports, and real estate listings. **Local access channels** are public/education/government (PEG) channels that are provided free of charge to the local community. The individuals, organizations, schools, and government agencies involved are responsible for creating their own programs. As such, local access programs often serve as an electronic soapbox for ordinary citizens to speak their minds. The 1992 film comedy *Wayne's World*, starring Mike Myers and Dana Carvey, was about two loser guys with a public access show that make it to big time.

How Programs Are Scheduled

To recap, the networks are in heavy competition with each other for the largest number of viewers. In the pre–cable network, pre–remote control days of television, the big-three networks created various programming strategies that attracted viewers to their channels and then kept them there for hours. The networks' goal was to control **audience flow,** or the progression of viewership from one program to another.

Obviously, the networks *still* want to make sure that viewers go from one program to the next without changing channels. To do so, the networks use a variety of strategies in scheduling their programs. These strategies may have been more effective when there were only three networks and viewers actually had to get up and walk to their TV sets to change the channel. Nonetheless, they're still used today with much success:

• **Tentpoling:** A popular and highly rated program is scheduled between two new or poorly rated programs. The theory here is that viewers may tune to the channel early in anticipation of watching the highly rated program and thus see at least part of the less popular preceding show. Similarly, they will hopefully stay tuned after the conclusion of the popular program and catch the beginning of the next not-so-popular show.
• **Hammocking:** A new or poorly rated show is scheduled between two successful shows. After watching one favorite program, viewers will stay tuned to the channel and watch the new or poorly rated show while waiting for their next favorite program.
• **Leading in:** The idea is to grab viewers' attention with a very strong program, anticipating that they will watch that popular show and then stay tuned to the next program on the same channel.
• **Leading out:** A poorly rated program is scheduled after a popular show with the hope that the audience will stay tuned.
• **Bridging:** A program is slotted to go over the starting time of a show on a competing network. For example, the season finale of a reality show could be scheduled from 8:00 to 9:30 P.M. to compete with another network's reality program that's scheduled to start at 9:00 P.M.
• **Blocking:** A network schedules a succession of similar programs over a block of time—for example, four half-hour situation comedies scheduled over two hours. The network hopes to attract sitcom lovers and then keep them watching the whole block of shows.
• **Seamless programming:** One program directly follows another, without a commercial break or beginning or ending credits. Some programs use a split-screen technique, in which program credits and closing materials blend in with the start of the following program.

- **Counterprogramming:** One type of program, such as a drama, is scheduled against another type of a program, say, a sitcom, on another network. Counterprogramming can work especially well if a strong program of one type is scheduled against a struggling show of another type.
- **Head-to-head programming:** This is the opposite of counterprogramming; that is, two popular shows of the same genre are pitted against each other. For example, one network may schedule its highly rated reality show against another network's highly rated reality show to get viewers to choose its show over the competition.
- **Stunting:** A special program, such as an important sporting event or a holiday program, is scheduled against a highly rated, regularly scheduled show on another network. Although the network may capture new viewers only for its special program, it is still drawing viewers away from the competition on the occasion.
- **Repetition:** Used mostly by cable networks, this involves scheduling a program such as a movie to air several times during the week or even during the day.
- **Stripping:** Normally used for syndicated programs, stripping occurs when a program is shown at the same time five days a week. For instance, *The Oprah Winfrey Show* is a stripped program; it airs Monday through Friday at 4:00 P.M. in most markets.

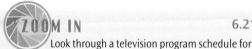

ZOOM IN 6.21

Look through a television program schedule for the current season, and find examples of each type of programming strategy. Then check out program ratings in the latest issue of *Broadcasting & Cable* magazine or another source.

After years of losing audience share to cable, broadcast network executives today are searching for new strategies to retain viewers. In addition to common programming strategies, the networks are now considering getting rid of the traditional television season, the period that runs from mid September to mid May. Instead of introducing new shows in September and as mid-season replacements, the networks plan to debut programs all year round. Additionally, instead of the typical 22-episode season, the networks will offer programs in bursts of 8-, 10-, and 13-week episodes (Carter, 2004).

SEE IT LATER: Radio and Television

Marketing Syndicated Programs

As television and radio technologies have developed, audience uses of these media have changed and thus so has the business of programming. In 1962, television programmers started their own association, the National Association of Television Program Executives (NATPE), which now claims more than 4,000 corporate members. Each year at the NATPE convention, syndicators and producers market their shows to station managers and programmers. The NATPE convention is considered the primary venue for buying and selling syndicated television programming. Syndicators and programmers set up elaborate booths inside the convention center, where they schmooze and wheel-and-deal with station executives. Syndicators and producers hawk game shows and talk shows and other first-run and off-network syndicated shows.

But as television has changed, so has NATPE. New to the convention floor are media technology companies that are demonstrating new ways to deliver programming in direct competition with traditional television stations. Additionally, with more networks producing their own shows and distributing them to their affiliates, affiliates have less need to purchase programs from syndicators. Moreover, as television station ownership rules are being relaxed, program directors are often buying syndicated shows for station groups, rather than individual stations. This makes it easier for the syndicators, who can pitch their products to fewer decision makers and cover more stations with a single transaction (Schlosser, 2002a).

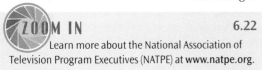

ZOOM IN   6.22
Learn more about the National Association of
Television Program Executives (NATPE) at www.natpe.org.

As a result of the changing marketplace, many syndicators have recently pulled out of the NATPE convention. They claim that with station consolidation, there are fewer program buyers and ultimately not enough to justify the cost of attending the convention. In 2002, convention attendance dropped by about one-third from the previous year (Schlosser, 2002b). However, the 2004 NAPTE convention was slightly more active than in the previous two years (Albiniak & Bednarski, 2004). Just where NATPE and the business of buying and selling programs will go remains to be seen, but as the industry changes, so must the traditional ways of doing business.

On the Horizon

Communication technologies like the VCR and the Internet have freed us from the constraints of broadcast schedules. We no longer have to tune in our radios or televisions at certain times to hear the news or watch our favorite shows. In a sense, these new technologies have made us our own programmers. What else is on the horizon?

Online audio has clear advantages over traditional radio. Online listeners don't have to depend on local stations to hear their favorite music, and they can connect to hometown news. Online listeners can select their own type of music and listen to it in the order they prefer.

Granted, the clarity of online audio may not be as good as over-the-air radio, and you can't take the Internet with you to the beach or the park. However, new portable MP3 players allow users to download music—sometimes hundreds of hours of music. Users create their own playlists according to a type of music, a tempo, or their own mood and organize it according to preference.

Satellite digital radio offers a wide range of commercial and commercial-free stations, allowing us to program our own music from the front seats of our cars. Suppose you're a jazz fan driving through rural Nebraska, and you have trouble picking up your kind of music from over-the-air local stations. With satellite radio, you can listen to jazz or any other type of music no matter where you're located. Plus, you don't have to worry about driving out of a station's broadcast range; the signal stays with you.

While the quality of **online video** still isn't close to television quality, it may one day be a formidable competitor. In the meantime, most online television sites merely serve as promotional vehicles for their broadcast and cable counterparts. However, some media sites stream live newscasts. On September 11, 2001, ABC News streamed its live television newscast of the World Trade Center tragedy. Many people were at work that day and without access to a television set, but by connecting to the Internet, they got to see exactly what was being shown on ABC.

As of now, media outlets generally do not run programs in their entirety on the Internet, but they may do so one day. Given the Internet's vast storage capabilities, viewers might eventually be able to go online and watch any program whenever they want to, without being tied to a television schedule.

You don't have to wait for the Internet to become your own programmer. Newer digital video recorders (DVRs)—also known by brand names UltimateTV, TiVo, and ReplayTV—give you control of your viewing schedule. DVRs do away with video tapes yet let you record and store about 30 hours of programming on a hard disk. You can watch saved programs whenever you want and skip recording commercials all together (Harmon, 2002).

A DVR will digitally record from satellite television and automatically store whatever television show you're watching. You can even record two shows at once, even while channel surfing back and forth. If you want to make your favorite snack but are engrossed in a live program, you can pause, go and make your snack, and then come back and pick up the program where you left off. With a DVR, you have ultimate control over your viewing patterns. You can fast forward, reverse, pause, instant replay, or slow motion and never miss a scene ("ReplayTV 4000," 2002; "What Is TiVo?" 2002; "What Is Ultimate TV?" 2002).

Now that these new technologies have put consumers in the programming driver's seat, what will happen to the media programmers' carefully laid out strategies? Radio and television stations are programmed to deliver the largest number of listeners and viewers possible to their advertisers. Radio stations are formatted to meet the needs of the local market, but how effective will their strategies be if listeners subscribe to satellite radio or create their own playlists and download music from the Internet to an MP3 player? Similarly, television-programming strategies intended to improve audience flow will no longer be valid if viewers can watch programs in whatever order and whenever they want. Counterprogramming, hammocking, tentpoling, and other such strategies have no meaning in the DVR world.

Summary

Radio started out as a home entertainment system that brought programs into listeners' homes. Early radio programs were much like what is shown on television today (but of course, without the video). Dramas, comedies, soap operas, quiz shows, and many other types of programs filled the radio airwaves.

As television gained in popularity, radio's audience diminished. Many popular radio programs made the transition from radio to the television screen when it was realized the audience would rather watch Jack Benny than listen to him on the radio. Radio needed to find a way to be compatible with television, and it did so by formatting stations rather than airing programs. Stations concentrated on playing one or two types of music, or formats, be it rock 'n' roll, classical, middle-of-the-road, easy-listening, jazz, country, or some other type. Station formatting depends on the market and the competition.

Television emerged in the late 1940s and took its place as a mass medium in 1948, when the numbers of sets, stations, and audience members all grew by 4,000 percent (Gross, 2003). Radio listeners willingly moved to the new medium, especially as old radio programs began appearing on the screen. Anthologies and dramas were popular in the 1950s, but as new production techniques and more portable cameras made outside location scenes possible, the audience's taste moved to more realistic and action-packed shows.

With the growth of cable television, the broadcast networks' share of the audience declined. They found themselves in heavy competition not only with each other but also with the new cable networks. Television programmers attempt to maintain their audience through programming strategies that control audience flow from one program to another.

As the Internet, DVR, and other new media technologies emerge, media consumers will gain increasing control of their own viewing schedules and become their own programmers. The networks' best-laid plans will be thwarted as consumers find ways to avoid being tied to programming schedules and serving as a captive audience for advertisers. As television and radio consumers, we have much to look forward to in the coming years. How we receive electronic information is changing very quickly, as is the business of programming.

Note

1. Numerous references can be found about the quiz show scandal. For instance, a movie titled *Quiz Show* debuted in 1994 (produced by Robert Redford), and many books have been written that discuss quiz shows and the scandal itself (e.g., Halberstam, 1993; Hendrik, 1987).

Advertising

 SEE IT THEN
Advertising: 3000 B.C.E. to 1990
Early Radio Advertising
Early Television Advertising

 SEE IT NOW
Advertising: 1990 to Present

SEE IT LATER
Criticisms of Advertising

In this chapter, you'll learn about:

- Advertising on electronic media: radio, television, cable, and the Internet
- How advertising agencies provide advertising for electronic media
- The advantages and disadvantages of advertising on electronic media
- Common criticisms of advertising

Advertising plays a huge role in the U.S. economy and fulfills many consumer needs, as well. It is so prevalent and accepted as part of everyday life that its importance is often overlooked. Advertising is so prolific and we have become so accustomed to seeing and hearing promotional messages that we don't always notice them. We'll watch a string of television commercials between programs, yet five minutes later, most of us won't be able to remember what products or brands the commercials were advertising. We'll flip through magazines and look at the nice full-color ads, but when asked what products we saw, there's a good chance we won't remember. The point is that advertising can have a subtle effect on us. We don't always realize that the reason we purchased a product is because we were influenced by an advertisement for it.

Most people tend to think of advertising as a modern-day phenomenon, when actually, it has been around for thousands of years. The origins of advertising can be traced back to ancient Babylon, where tradesmen inscribed their business names on clay tablets, and later to medieval England, where tavern owners distinguished their establishments with creative names and signs. Even back then, merchants recognized the need to get the word out about their product or service. Although the advertising of long ago was nothing more than written names or figures drawn on signs, these methods of promotion led the way to modern advertising. Today, advertising is a very complex business that employs principles of psychology, sociology, marketing, economics, and other sciences and fields of study for the end purpose of selling something.

Before a product or service can be sold, it must first be marketed. In other words, it must be packaged, priced, and distributed to sellers or directly to buyers. But before we can buy a product or service, we must be aware that it exists, and most of the time, we find out about a product through some type of promotion. But what is *promotion*?

Promotion can be thought of as an "umbrella" term that includes any endeavor to create awareness about a product or service. Even when you wear a T-shirt or a cap bearing a company's logo or the name of your school, you're promoting that product. Other types of promotion include word of mouth, free trials and demonstrations (demos), newspaper ads, billboards, coffee mugs imprinted with logos, and flyers left on windshields. Even though these can all be considered *promotions,* some fall under the definition of *marketing* and others under *advertising.*

In radio and television, the term *promotion* generally refers to stations and networks selling their programs and images to their audience and to their advertisers. Stations and networks use their own time and buy time on other media—including print, billboards, and the Web—to promote themselves and their fare to viewers, listeners, and advertisers. Media promotion involves specific strategies that apply to nonmedia businesses. In this chapter, however, *promotion* refers to the larger marketing function for nonmedia business.

Marketing and advertising are connected but not synonymous. Traditionally, marketing includes pricing, distribution, packaging, and promotional efforts that go beyond paid advertisements. **Marketing** has been defined as "the process of planning and executing the conception, pricing, promotion, and distribution of ideas, goods, and services to create exchanges that satisfy individual and organizational objectives" (Vanden Bergh & Katz, 1999, p. 155). **Advertising** is a subcategory of marketing and thus more narrow in scope. It has been defined as "nonpersonal communication for products, services, or ideas that is paid for by an identified sponsor for the purpose of influencing an audience" (Vanden Bergh & Katz, 1999, p. 158). More simply, advertising is any "form of nonpersonal presentation and promotion of ideas, goods, and services usually paid for by an identified sponsor" (Dominick, 1999, p. 397) or "paid, mass mediated attempt to persuade" (O'Guinn, Allen, & Semenik, 2000, p. 6).

According to these definitions of marketing and advertising, word of mouth and providing free trials and demos can be considering *marketing* functions, whereas newspaper ads, television commercials, billboards, coffee mugs imprinted with logos, and flyers left on windshields can be considered *advertising.*

Although promotion and marketing are closely tied to advertising, this chapter is specifically about advertising. It begins with an overview of the origins of advertising in 3000 B.C.E. and moves to the twentieth century, with the development of radio and television and later cable and the Internet. Advertising with electronic media is discussed in the context of the advertising industry, where advertising agencies, campaign creation, and advertising regulation are all addressed. The chapter ends with a look at the criticisms aimed at contemporary advertising.

fyi

Four Ps of Marketing

1. Product
2. Price
3. Place
4. Promotion
   4A. Advertising

ZOOM IN   7.1

Close your eyes and think about all of the promotional messages in the room where you're sitting. Now open your eyes and look around the room. How many advertising messages do you count? Be sure to include clothing, posters, coffee mugs, pens, pencils, calendars, and other everyday items imprinted with logos. How many of the advertisements did you remember before you looked? Do you tend to notice most of the advertising messages around you, or do you tend not to pay any attention?

 **SEE IT THEN**

Advertising: 3000 B.C.E. to 1990

It's hard to imagine, but advertising has actually been around since about 3000 B.C.E. Babylonian clay tablets have been found inscribed with the names of merchants. The ancient Egyptians used papyrus (much more portable than clay tablets) to advertise rewards for escaped slaves, and the ancient Greeks used town criers to advertise the arrivals of ships carrying various goods. The ancient Romans hung stone and terra cotta signs outside their shops to advertise the goods sold inside.

It was Johannes Gutenberg's invention of the printing press around 1450 that gave people the idea of distributing *printed* advertisements. Toward the end of that century, church officials were printing handbills and tacking them up around town. The first printed advertisement for a product is thought to have appeared in Germany around 1525; it promoted a book about some sort of miracle medicine.

The growing popularity of newspapers in the late 1600s and early 1700s led to the further development of print advertising. In 1704, the *Boston Newsletter* printed what is thought to have been the first newspaper ad, promising to pay rewards for runaway slaves. Benjamin Franklin, one of the first publishers of colonial newspapers, endorsed advertising and increased the visibility of ads placed in his papers by using larger type and more white space around the ads, not unlike what we see in today's newspapers. Until the mid 1800s, most newspaper ads were in the general form of what we know today as *classified ads,* or simply lines of text (Russell & Lane, 1999).

Advertising took on a new role in the 1800s with the Industrial Revolution. Countless new machines were invented, leading to huge increases in manufacturing. People moved away from their rural farms and communities into the cities to find work in factories. The cities' swelling populations and the mass production of goods gave rise to mass consumption and a mass audience. Advertising provided the link between manufacturers and consumers. People found out about new products from newspaper and magazine ads, rather than from their friends and families.

Manufacturers soon realized the importance of advertising, especially the use of newspapers and magazines to get the word out about their products. However, they didn't always do a very good of job promotion. What they needed was someone to help design ads, write copy, and sell media space to them. Volney B. Palmer was just that someone, and he filled the void by opening the first advertising agency in Boston in 1841. Volney contracted with newspapers to sell advertising space on a commission basis. About 30 years later, another promotions pioneer, Francis Ayer, worked for the advertisers. He opened the first full-service agency in Philadelphia, where he wrote, produced, and placed print ads in newspapers and magazines (Campbell, 2000).

With more agencies came new insights into consumerism and eventually new techniques of advertising. In fact, by 1860, people were looking at full-color advertisements in their favorite magazines, thanks to new cameras and linotype machines ("Emergence of Advertising," 2000).

Early Radio Advertising

A new form of advertising was born with the advent of the radio. At first, radio was slow to catch on with the public because there weren't very many programs on the air. People weren't about to buy radios if there was nothing to listen to. The 1921 heavyweight boxing championship between Jack Dempsey and Georges Carpentier was one of the first radio broadcasts. As each punch was thrown in Hoboken, New Jersey, telegraph operators tapped out the move to Pittsburgh, Pennsylvania, station KDKA, which translated the signals for vocal reporting over the airwaves. This and other such broadcasts piqued people's interest and led them to using the radio for entertainment. As more people purchased radios and the medium increased in importance, broadcasters grappled with how they were going to finance this endeavor.

In the early 1920s, stations and individuals were broadcasting for free. That is, they were airing programs but not generating any revenue for their efforts. Setting up a radio station meant buying expensive transmitters, receivers, and other equipment. Plus, broadcasters and other personnel had to be paid salaries. Given these costs, there was a collective call among broadcasters to figure out a way to generate income, because they knew this "gratuitous service cannot continue indefinitely" (White, 2001). In 1924, *Radio Broadcast* magazine announced a contest with a $500 prize for the person who could come up with the best answer to the question "Who is going to pay for broadcasting and how?" (White, 2001).

Although the idea of commercial radio was undergoing serious discussion, radio advertising was largely considered in poor taste and an invasion of privacy. Many consumers and broadcasters were resistant to over-the-air commercialism and claimed that radio shouldn't be used to sell products. Then-Secretary of Commerce Herbert Hoover,

Ad from *Radio Broadcast* Magazine: May 1924.

WHO IS TO PAY FOR BROADCASTING AND HOW?

A Contest Opened by RADIO BROADCAST in which a prize of $500 is offered

What We Want

A workable plan which shall take into account the problems in present radio broadcasting and propose a practical solution. How, for example, are the restrictions now imposed by the music copyright law to be adjusted to the peculiar conditions of broadcasting? How is the complex radio patent situation to be unsnarled so that broadcasting may develop? Should broadcasting stations be allowed to advertise?

These are some of the questions involved and subjects which must receive careful attention in an intelligent answer to the problem which is the title of this contest.

How It Is To Be Done

The plan must not be more than 1500 words long. It must be double-spaced and typewritten, and must be prefaced with a concise summary. The plan must be in the mails not later than July 20, 1924, and must be addressed, RADIO BROADCAST Who Is to Pay Contest, care American Radio Association, 50 Union Square, New York City.

The contest is open absolutely to every one, except employees of RADIO BROADCAST and officials of the American Radio Association. A contestant may submit more than one plan. If the winning plan is received from two different sources, the judges will award the prize to the contestant whose plan was mailed first.

Judges

Will be shortly announced and will be men well-known in radio and public affairs.

What Information You Need

There are several sources from which the contestant can secure information, in case he does not already know certain of the facts. Among these are the National Association of Broadcasters, 1265 Broadway, New York City; the American Radio Association, 50 Union Square, New York, the Radio Broadcaster's Society of America, care George Schubel, secretary, 154 Nassau Street, New York, the American Society of Composers and Authors, the Westinghouse Electric and Manufacturing Company, the Radio Corporation of America, the General Electric Company, and the various manufacturers, and broadcasting stations.

Prize

The independent committee of judges will award the prize of $500 to the plan which in their judgment is most workable and practical, and which follows the rules given above. No other prizes will be given.

No questions regarding the contest can be answered by RADIO BROADCAST by mail.

General Electric.

who later became president, claimed that radio programming shouldn't be interrupted with senseless advertising. Such antiadvertising sentiment even extended to some station owners.

A Long Island, New York, real estate firm was the first to take AT&T-owned radio station WEAF up on its offer of toll broadcasting. And on August 28, 1922, the firm paid $50 for 10 minutes of time to persuade people to buy property in the New York area. While this type of advertising may seem like a modern-day infomercial, AT&T didn't consider these toll messages advertising but simply courtesy announcements because the prices of the products and services were never mentioned. The toll method never really caught favor with the advertisers and so proved to be a financial bust. However, WEAF's toll idea eventually led to **sponsored programs:** radio shows that were produced by advertisers and their agencies.

In 1923, the Browning King clothing company bought weekly time on WEAF and sponsored the Browning King Orchestra. Of course, whenever the orchestra was announced, so was the company's name. But in keeping with WEAF's anticommercial sentiment, the announcers were careful not to mention that Browning King sold clothing. Other companies, and then later advertising agencies, took the lead from Browning King and assumed production of radio programs in turn for being recognized program sponsors.

Radio advertising seemed to boost product sales. The Washburn Crosby Company (now known as General Mills) saw the sales of Wheaties cereal soar after introducing the first singing commercial on network radio in December 1926. In the areas in which the Wheaties jingle was aired, the cereal became one of the most popular brands, but in the areas in which the commercial didn't air, sales were stagnant.

The increasing cost of operating a radio station eventually led to the acceptance of over-the-air advertising. By the late 1920s, the initial reluctance gave way to these financial concerns, and broadcasters, along with the pubic, endorsed the idea of advertising-supported radio, even though it was largely in the form of sponsorships.

ZOOM IN 7.2
- Learn more about WEAF's first commercial and listen to a short clip of the spot at www.old-time.com/commercials/com_hawthornect.ram.
- Listen to old-time radio commercials at *Old Time Radio:* www.old-time.com.
- Explore these fun, interesting pages within the *Old Time Radio* site:
  www.old-time.com/commercials/unusual_bizarre.html
  www.old-time.com/commercials/index.html
  www.old-time.com/weekly

ZOOM IN 7.3
Listen to the first singing commercial at www.old-time.com/commercials/com_wheaties.ram.

Sponsored Radio

At first, sponsored radio seemed like a good idea. An advertising agency, along with a sponsoring company, would produce a program, usually 15 minutes in length, which was paid for by the company. The ad agency benefited by being paid for its creative work, the company benefited by gaining brand recognition and hopefully sales, and the audience benefited by being made aware of a product but without being subjected to blatant promotional messages.

Usually at the beginning, in the middle, and at the end of a program, the announcer would tell a short narrative that tied the sponsor's name in with the program. Sometimes, the product was mentioned in the script, as in *Oxodol's Own Ma Perkins,* in which use of the company's products was woven into the storyline (Massey & Baran, 1996). The American Tobacco Company sponsored *The Lucky Strike Hit Parade,* a program that played the best-selling records. Every time the announcer said the name of the program, the audience would hear the name brand Lucky Strike. By naming the program after the cigarettes, Lucky Strike's brand recognition increased. The theory was that listeners would be so thankful that advertisers were providing free programming that they would purchase their products out of gratitude. Thus, smokers

ZOOM IN 7.4
To listen to old radio sponsorships for programs such as *Little Orphan Annie* (sponsored by Ovaltine) and *Your Hit Parade* (sponsored by Lucky Strikes), go to www.old-time.com/weekly.

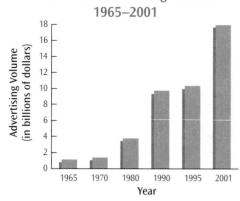

Total Radio Advertising Volume: 1965–2001

Sources: "Coen's Spending Totals," 2003; Dominick, Sherman, & Copeland, 1996.

who listened to *The Lucky Strike Hit Parade* were presumably likely to purchase Lucky Strike cigarettes.

Despite the benefits of sponsorship, radio stations began to resent that they had no control over program content. Ad agencies and advertisers were fully responsible for program content and even had complete control over performers. For example, the ultra-conservative Rexall Drugs would not let their spokesman, Jimmy Durante, appear on a four-network campaign program that was soliciting votes for Democratic President Franklin D. Roosevelt. Sponsors also bought particular time slots for their programs; thus, the radio networks had no control over when programs aired. Consequently, at hours of peak listenership, the networks were forced to air unpopular programs, when they would have preferred to air shows that would draw large audiences.

By the mid 1940s, the network owners were getting tired of ceding program control to ad agencies and advertisers, and so CBS radio network owner William S. Paley came up with a new plan for programming and advertising. He set up a CBS programming department that was charged with developing and producing new shows. In turn, the network would recoup its expenses by selling space within the programs to advertisers. Although CBS liked the plan, the ad agencies vigorously opposed it, as they wanted to keep control over programs and advertisers. Eventually, programming became the network's responsibility, but the agencies that bought network time within programs still controlled casting and scheduling. Then, as radio shows moved to television, the need for radio networks diminished and along with it, radio program sponsorships and agency control over programs.

As network radio programs gave way to individual station programming, advertising was increasingly sold not as sponsored programs but as time within and between programs. The number of these advertising spots increased substantially between 1965 and 1995, as did advertising revenue.

Early Television Advertising

Although the public got its first glimpse of television at the 1939 New York World's Fair, this new medium didn't immediately catch on. World War II interrupted television set manufacturing and program transmission, stalling television's adoption by consumers until about three years after the war. In 1948, Americans were going crazy over television, and the industry exploded with new stations, new programs, new sets, and new viewers, realizing growth of over 4,000 percent (Head, Spann & McGregor, 2001). Television quickly became a mass medium and promised to be as popular as radio. That left industry executives struggling with how to make television a lucrative medium.

Sponsorship

Television advertising was based largely on radio's sponsorship model. Advertisers and their agencies produced sponsored programs such as *Texaco Star Theater* (1948–1953) and *Kraft Television Theater* (1947–1958). However, television programs were much more expensive to produce than radio programs, and agencies and advertisers found themselves spending thousands of dollars each week. The Kudner Agency spent about $8,000 per week for *Texaco Star Theater,* an amount that quadrupled three years later, and Frigidaire spent about $100,000 for each Bob Hope special it sponsored. This was a lot of money to be spending on promotion, and the high cost of television sponsorship kept all but a few of the largest advertisers off the air. It soon became apparent that television advertising had to change.

Spot Advertising

NBC television executive Pat Weaver (father of *Alien* star Sigourney Weaver) extended William Paley's idea of selling ad time within radio programs to television and came up with what is known as the *magazine style* of television advertising. This approach later became known as **spot** or **participation advertising.** Weaver had figured out that television could make more money by selling time within and between programs to several sponsors than by relying on one sponsor to carry the entire cost. His idea was similar to the placement of magazine advertisements between articles. Instead of sponsors purchasing television program sponsorships, they would purchase advertising in one-minute units. Weaver's plan also promoted the production of programs by network and independent producers, keeping advertisers out of the business of programming.

With Weaver's plan, advertisers found it much less expensive to purchase one minute of time, rather than fifteen minutes, and they didn't have to concern themselves with program content. Affordable airtime brought many more advertisers (especially smaller, lesser known companies) to television for the first time, much to the chagrin of larger, wealthier sponsors and ad agencies, who were concerned about losing their broadcast dominance.

Bulova watch company was the first advertiser to venture to television and also the first company to purchase spot radio time (as opposed to a program sponsorship). Starting in 1926, the United States ran on Bulova time with its well-known radio commercial announcements: "At the tone, it's 8:00 P.M. B-U-L-O-V-A. Bulova watch time." Bulova later adapted its radio spot to television. On July 1, 1941, Bulova paid $9 to a New York City television station for a 20-second ad that aired during a Dodgers-Phillies baseball game. The Bulova commercial showed a watch face with the current time but without the audio announcement. Bulova later kept the close-up of the watch face but added a voice announcing the time.

Television advertising was unique. Advertisers had a new and popular mass medium that brought product and audience together. For the first time, viewers could sit in their own living rooms and see what a product looked like and how it worked. For instance, they could watch a brand of laundry soap remove stubborn stains or toothpaste whiten dentures. Advertising and television were a highly successful pairing.

Yet television advertising didn't have a very smooth beginning. In the early years, many television programs were produced live, and production techniques were crude and clumsy. Soap sponsors touting the whitening power of their products discovered that on early black-and-white televisions, viewers couldn't tell the difference between *white* and *whiter*. They had to hold up a white shirt next to a blue one and pretend it had been washed with a competing soap.

An early television commercial demonstrating how to use the Ultra-Vac jar opener.

Live product demonstrations often didn't go off as planned either, embarrassing the advertiser and the product spokesperson. Aunt Jenny, a character on the *Question Bee,* dripped beads of perspiration from the hot studio lights onto the chocolate cake she had just freshly baked with Spry. To make matters worse, she licked some cake off the knife blade and then cut more slices with the same knife. Spry wasn't happy, to say the least. Neither was *Variety* magazine, who called the whole business of television "unsanitary."

In another bungled demo, Gillette hired a hand model to demonstrate its new automatic safety razor, except, of course, it wasn't so automatic. The razor stuck and the television audience watched as the hands desperately struggled to unstick it but to no avail. (That was the last live product demonstration for Gillette. From then on, they pre-recorded their commercials.) In a Kellogg's Corn Flakes commercial, the announcer couldn't eat the cereal and endorse the product at the same time, so he figured that with the help of the camera, he would just pretend he was eating. Unfortunately, the camera-man zoomed out too far, and viewers watched in amazement as the announcer discarded spoonfuls of cereal over his shoulder. Refrigerator doors that were stuck shut, can openers that wouldn't open cans, and spokespeople holding up one brand but trumpeting another are just some of the other debacles of live television commercials (Ritchie, 1994).

Despite these bloopers, advertisers continued to promote their products on the air-waves, and so television executives cheered as they watched advertising revenues rise rapidly throughout the 1950s. Although the decade was still rife with sponsored programs, such as *The Dinah Shore–Chevy Show* (1951–1957) and *The Colgate-Palmolive Comedy Hour* (1950–1955), sponsors and agencies were gradually giving up control over production, scripts, and stars. Weaver's magazine concept slowly became the primary way to sell television advertising time.

Program sponsorship took a severe hit with the quiz show scandal that rocked the television industry in the late 1950s. At the time, television quiz shows were the most popular programs on the air. While some were produced by sponsors and their advertising agencies, others were produced by the networks themselves. The competition for viewers was enormous, as there were many quiz shows on the air and they were often on at the same time. Winning contestants were on week after week, and audience members began to follow them and cheer them on. To keep popular contestants on the air (and thus to keep viewers watching the shows), sponsors started to secretly give well-liked contestants the answers to the questions beforehand. One contestant, who had lost to a competitor who had been given the right answers, finally came forward and

Frank Sinatra, endorsing EKCO products in a commercial that aired during his show.

Betty Furness, rehearsing for a live commercial for Westinghouse.

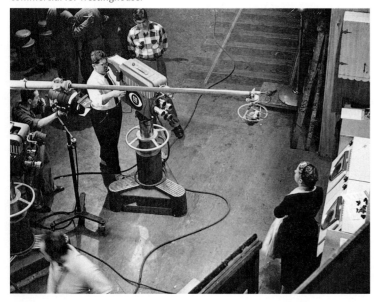

exposed the quiz shows as fraudulent. When the scandal made the headlines, the public was outraged at the deception and blamed the networks, even though it was the sponsors who had cheated. The networks figured that if they were going to be held responsible for televised content, then they should take over programming from the agencies.

The networks pushed for control not only of program content but also of what programs would appear on television and when they would be on the air. The networks had the public on their side, and later, the influential *Advertising Age,* the advertising industry's major trade publication, strongly urged advertising agencies to regain their reputations by leaving the production of television programs to the television industry. Further, the publication pushed for separating sponsors and programs by switching entirely to the magazine-style concept of advertising sales as quickly as possible.

Throughout the 1960s, most television commercials were sold in 60-second units known as **spots.** Because programs were no longer produced and sponsored by single advertisers, a number of advertisers could purchase time spots within and between programs. Thus, many different commercials were shown during the course of one program, initiating a new kind of competition. Consider that when an advertiser *sponsors* a program, that brand is the only one promoted during the entire program. But with spot advertising, a variety of products and brands are promoted during the course of a show. For many advertisers, this was the first time they had faced strong competition for the audience's attention. They had to come up with creative ways to make their product or brand stand out from the others. Slogans, jingles, and catchy phrases started to make their way into commercials.

A New Look

Television advertising took on a slightly new look in 1971 as the result of a federal government ban on tobacco commercials. Cigarette companies had been among television's biggest advertisers, until they were forced to transfer their advertising dollars from the airwaves to print, leaving broadcasters scrambling to fill unsold time. The television networks quickly discovered that many other companies simply couldn't afford to buy commercial time in 1-minute blocks, but they could buy time in less expensive 30-second units. More advertisers buying shorter commercials meant more commercial spots per hour. This arrangement proved profitable for the networks, as they could sell two 30-second spots for more money than they could one 60-second spot. The effect on an hour of television programming was that programs became infiltrated with more and shorter spots.

In 1965, about 70 percent of all commercials were 60 seconds in length. That percentage decreased throughout the late 1960s. Four years after the 1971 ban on tobacco advertising, only 11 percent of commercials were 60 seconds in length and almost 80 percent were 30-second spots. By 1985, almost 90 percent of all commercials were 30 seconds in length and only 2 percent ran for a full minute. Throughout the 1980s, the length of commercials began to vary and included 10-, 15-, 20-, and 45-second spots. The 15-second spots especially caught favor, and by 1990, they accounted for about one-third of all commercials (Orlik, 1998).

Although they are rare, sponsorships do still occur. Ford Motor Company was the sole sponsor of the movie *Schindler's List* when it made its television debut in 1997.

Creative Strategies

With more commercial spots on the air, advertisers needed to be creative to remain competitive. New strategies were therefore initiated in the 1960s. But by the 1970s and 1980s, as the number of cable channels increased, competition grew more fierce.

Faced with new creative challenges, many advertisers took on a more narrative approach in creating commercials. Rather than just show a product and recite its features, hoping to persuade people to buy it, some commercials became more like 30-second minimovies that told a story with characters and plots to mold a product or brand image. This approach, called **image advertising**, goes beyond simply promoting a product; instead, it attempts to set a perception of the product or brand in the consumer's mind. For example, most of us think of Volvo cars as being *safe* and Maytag washers and dryers as being *durable*. Advertisers have carefully crafted these and other brand images, and television's audio/visual components have reinforced them.

Clara Peller became famous in the 1980s as the "Where's the beef?" lady in a series of commercials for Wendy's.

A teenage Brooke Shields promoted Wella Balsam conditioner in the early 1980s.

Target Advertising

Throughout the 1970s and into the early 1980s, the three major television networks (ABC, CBS, and NBC) shared about 90 percent of the viewing audience and about 33 percent of all advertising dollars. Then cable television gained in popularity in the 1980s, and the networks found a new rival. Cable offered advertisers many new and specialized channels and thus niche audiences. Rather than pay a large amount of money to reach a mass audience, advertisers could easily **target** their consumers on carefully chosen cable networks. For example, Ping golf clubs can target golfers by advertising on the Golf Channel or on ESPN, instead of the more expensive networks, where only a small percentage of viewers may be interested in golf equipment. The growth of cable television's audience came at the expense of the broadcast networks, however, who watched as their share of the viewing audience diminished, along with their share of advertising revenues.

Cable Advertising

With the advent of original cable programming and then subscription channels, viewers' desire for new and varied programming led to a huge increase in cable television subscriptions in the 1980s. Early on, most cable networks were pay-cable services; in other words, subscribers either paid a fee to receive a cable network, such as HBO or Showtime, or they paid to watch a certain program, such as a boxing match. By the mid 1980s, **advertiser-supported services** were everywhere. Many of these cable networks can be identified as *basic cable:* Subscribers pay a base monthly fee for a set of cable channels. Both the cable network and the local cable service sell advertising time within these advertiser-supported programs.

As new cable channels emerged, the television-viewing audience became more fragmented, and each cable and broadcast network found itself competing for a smaller and smaller share of the audience. When there were only the big-three broadcast networks, each could be certain that about one-third of the audience was watching its programs and commercials. But with each new cable channel, all the existing channels saw their viewerships get smaller.

Both fragmented audiences and more channel choices have contributed to a decline in advertising effectiveness. With the touch of a button, a viewer can easily switch to another channel during a commercial break. That means that networks can no longer deliver a steady audience to their advertisers and that advertisers face the challenge of reaching a fickle audience. The proliferation of new cable channels has eroded the broadcast networks' share of the audience to about 60 percent while cable penetration has grown to about 68 percent of all U.S. households (Collette, 2002).

When audience share increases or decreases, so do advertising dollars, which is why the cable and broadcast industries are in such heavy competition. Even though cable television still has a long way to go before its advertising revenues catch up with those of the networks, every dollar they make is a dollar less for the broadcast networks.

ZOOM IN   7.5

Watch classic television commercials at these sites:

- Classic TV ads: www.roadode.com/classic.htm
- Living Room Candidate (collection of presidential campaign commercials: 1952–2000): www.ammi.org/livingroomcandidate
- Saturday morning commercials (1960–1970): www.tvparty.com/vaultcomsat.html
- TVLand Retromercials: www.tvland.com/retromercials

SEE IT NOW

Advertising: 1990 to Present

From a Business Perspective

Clearly, no business today could survive without using some form of promotion. Some companies, such as lawfirms and medical clinics, may rely entirely on word-of-mouth referrals. Other professional services and companies may rely on a combination of referrals, the Yellow Pages, and ballpoint pens inscribed with their company's name. Other businesses may choose to create full-blown advertising campaigns. Regardless, in order to survive, a business must rely on some type of advertising.

Advertising plays several crucial roles in an entity's marketing efforts. It identifies a target audience, differentiates products, and generates revenue. It also connects the **target audience** to a product or service. Its commercials tell the audience about a product or service. Advertising also differentiates products by creating a **brand image** for each one. There are many similar items on the market, so it's up to the advertiser to make its product stand out from the rest. To do so, it has to create a positive association between the product and the consumer. Sports drinks, in general, are very similar to one another, but there may be a big difference in consumers' minds between Gatorade and POWERade. For instance, a consumer may believe that one sports drink is more effective at rehydrating than the other, even though there may not be any evidence of that at all. Brand imaging aside, ultimately, the association

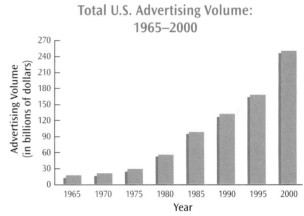

Total U.S. Advertising Volume: 1965–2000

Source: "Media Trends Track," 2003.

U.S. Advertising Volume by Medium: 2002

MEDIUM	BILLIONS OF DOLLARS	PERCENTAGE OF TOTAL SPENDING	PERCENTAGE CHANGE FROM 2001
Direct mail	$46.07	19.4	+3.0
Newspapers	44.03	18.6	−0.5
Broadcast television	42.07	17.8	+8.2
Miscellaneous	30.73	12.9	+2.8
Radio	18.88	8.0	+5.7
Cable television	16.30	6.9	+3.6
Yellow Pages	13.78	5.8	+1.4
Magazines	11.00	4.6	−0.9
Outdoor	5.18	2.2	+0.8
Internet	4.88	2.1	−13.5
Business publications	3.98	1.7	−11.0
Total	$236.88	100.0	+2.4

Source: "U.S. Ad Spending," 2004.

consumers make with a product rests solely in their own minds and changes with new experiences and information.

ZOOM IN   7.6
Think of a brand of a product that you like and one that you don't like—maybe running shoes, colas, sports cars. What's your image of each brand, and why do you prefer one instead of the other?

Advertising generates revenue by communicating messages that persuade people to purchase a product or service. Advertising's role in profit generation is much more complex than mere purchasing. Rather, it involves persuading people to buy a product in the first place and generating **brand loyalty**, or the repeated purchase of a product. These are all important contributions to revenue and profit.

From a Consumer Perspective

While people often claim that they're annoyed by commercials, they also recognize the benefits they get from them. Commercials serve educational, social, and economical purposes. Although it may seem hard to believe at times, advertising can be educational; after all, it's the way we learn about new products and services. In many instances, the first time a potential customer hears of a new offering is from a commercial.

Advertising also serves a social function in that the commercials we see on television or listen to on the radio reflect popular culture. They often include the hottest celebrities, the latest trends, and the most popular music. Products are advertised within our cultural environment. Commercials also reflect society's values and give people a sense of belonging. For instance, after the 9-11 terrorist attacks on Washington, DC, and New York City, many commercials contained shots of the American flag and other symbols of national unity.

Advertising also benefits us economically by promoting free enterprise and competition. The results of these forces are product improvements, increased product choices, and lower prices.

Electronic Media

Each electronic medium—radio, television, and the Internet—has strengths and weaknesses as a marketing tool. Smart media buyers know which products do best on which medium and in which market. They also know which creative strategies and appeals work best for the different media audiences. It's impossible to say that one medium is *always* better than the others. In some circumstances, radio may be the most effective medium; in other cases, television may be preferable; and in others, the Internet may be superior. There are many different factors to consider before deciding which medium to use and how often to use it.

Radio Advertising

Radio commercials are generally 30 or 60 seconds in length. The radio commercials you hear are a combination of **local**, **national**, and **network** spots. One of radio's strengths is the ability to reach a local audience. About 79 cents of every dollar of time is sold to local advertisers who wish to have their message reach the local community. Local restaurants,

TOP 10   U.S. Advertisers by Ad Spending: 2002

1. General Motors
2. Time Warner
3. Proctor & Gamble
4. Pfizer
5. Ford
6. Daimler Chrysler
7. Walt Disney
8. Johnson & Johnson
9. Sears, Roebuck
10. Unilever

Source: "Top 25 U.S. Advertisers," 2004.

Cindy Crawford and Christie Brinkley.

car dealerships, and stores know that by advertising on the radio, they're reaching the audience that's most likely to visit their local establishments.

National spots are those that air on many stations across the country. For example, McDonald's may buy time on selected radio stations in many different regions. If they have a special promotion going on in the South, they'll run their commercials on stations located in that market area.

A *network buy* is when a national advertiser buys time on a network of radio stations that are affiliated with the same company. Some of the larger radio networks are ABC Radio, which actually has five different networks, and Westwood, which has six different networks. Networks sometimes consist of stations that run similar programming, such as Westwood Country, or are made up of stations in a large geographic area, such as the Southwest. When advertisers buy time on a network, they're buying spots on all of the affiliated stations. The advertiser benefits from this one-stop shopping and also gets a range of stations that will reach its target audience.

> **ZOOM IN** 7.7
> • Next time you listen to the radio, see if you can identify local versus national spots.
> • Listen to newer radio commercials at http://surf.to/commercials.

ADVANTAGES OF RADIO ADVERTISING

- *Local*—Radio ads reach a local audience, the most likely purchasers of local products and services.
- *Flexible*—A radio spot sometimes can be sold, produced, and aired all in the same day. Copy can quickly be changed and updated. Advertisers don't have to run the same commercials throughout the day.
- *Targets an audience*—Advertisers target selected audiences through station buys. The various program formats found in radio make it easy for advertisers to reach their markets. For example, alternative rock stations will reach that all-important teen and college-age market.
- *Low advertising cost*—Radio is inexpensive in terms of the number of listeners reached. It has one of the lowest cost-per-thousand rates of all media.
- *High exposure*—Radio's low cost allows for high exposure. Advertisers can afford to buy many spots, so their commercials are heard many times. Through repeated exposure, listeners learn the words to jingles, memorize phone numbers, and remember special deals and other commercial content.
- *Low production costs*—Radio commercials are generally inexpensive to produce. Some are simply read live by an announcer, which doesn't require any audio production beyond copywriting.
- *High reach*—Almost everyone in the nation listens to the radio some time each week. Nearly 75 percent of all consumers tune in every day, and about 95 percent listen at least once a week (Shane, 1999).
- *Portable and ubiquitous*—Radios can be small and lightweight, making them very portable. They are everywhere: at work, at sporting events, at the beach, at the gym, on boats, on buses, on trains, in homes, in hospitals, in cars, in bars, and most everywhere else.
- *Commercials blend with content*—Radio is known and accepted as a commercial medium, and many commercials blend with content. Commercials with background music and jingles often sound similar to songs, and commercials with dialogue may sound similar to talk show conversations.

DISADVANTAGES OF RADIO ADVERTISING

- *Audio only*—Radio involves only the sense of hearing; thus, listeners can be easily distracted by what else they may be doing or seeing. The audio-only format also makes it difficult for listeners to visualize a product.

What product is "The Nighttime, Sniffling, Sneezing, Coughing, Achy, Stuffy Head, Fever So You Can Rest and Have a Good Morning Medicine"?

- *Background medium*—Radio is often listened to while people are engaged in other activities (like working, driving, reading, and eating), and so they don't always hear commercials.
- *Short message life*—Radio ads are typically 30 seconds long, which isn't much time to grab someone's attention, especially if he or she is involved in another activity. It's more difficult for radio than television to capture an audience's attention. Also, unlike print, where people can go back to an ad and write down the information, once a radio spot has aired, the information is gone. Missed messages may not be heard again.
- *Fragmented audience*—Most markets are flooded with radio stations, all competing for a piece of the audience. Listeners can be fickle, often changing stations many times throughout the day. Fragmentation forces many advertisers to expand their reach by purchasing time on several stations in one market.

ZOOM IN   **7.8**

Next time you're driving in the car or just listening to the radio with another person, make note of all the commercials that play during a commercial break. Then wait about 10 minutes and ask the person you're with how many of the commercials he or she can remember.

Television Advertising

Many people consider television the strongest advertising medium. The combination of audio and visual components captures viewers' attention more so than other venues. Plus, almost everyone watches television. Television delivers an audience of millions to advertisers, who reap the benefits of this widespread promotion.

Despite its strong points, television—especially broadcast television—is not the best advertising outlet for all advertisers. Not everyone needs to reach a large mass audience, nor do they have the budget to produce television spots. For many advertisers, cable television offers more audience for less money.

TELEVISION COMMERCIALS   As discussed earlier, most television commercials are 30 seconds in length, but they can run 15, 45, or 60 seconds. Most commercials air in clusters, or **pods**, of several commercials between and within programs. Advertisers may be guaranteed that their commercials will not air in the same pod as a competitor's commercial. In other words, a Ford commercial may not air in the same pod as a Chevrolet commercial. The commercials aired within a particular program are known as spots, or **participations**, and commercials that air before and after programs are known as **adjacencies.**

Cost of a 30-Second Spot on Prime-Time Broadcast Network Programs: Fall 2003

PROGRAM	NETWORK	COST
Friends	NBC	$473,000
Will & Grace	NBC	$414,500
ER	NBC	$404,814
Survivor	CBS	$390,367
Scrubs	NBC	$360,950
Coupling	NBC	$316,400
CSI	CBS	$310,324
The Simpsons	FOX	$296,440
24	FOX	$292,200
Monday Night Football	ABC	$272,867

Source: Linnett, 2003.

Sometimes, rather than buying commercial time, companies resort to **product placement**, where they pay to have their product used in or visible within a program scene. Having Jerry and friends drive around in a Saab on *Seinfeld* can be just as effective as airing a traditional commercial. This is not a new phenomenon. Early radio sponsorships that scripted characters mentioning or using a product were a form of product placement. But product placement is making a comeback (especially on cable networks) as a creative way to set advertisements apart from the typical 30- and 60-second spots. FOX's *The Best Damn Sports Show Ever* has experimented with product placement by turning the set into a sandwich shop to promote Quizno's and into a lemonade stand to promote a brand of lemonade. Additionally, what appeared to be spontaneous conversation between the show's hosts about Dockers pants was actually a scripted commercial message. The potential drawback of product placement is that advertisers give up

Nyquil.

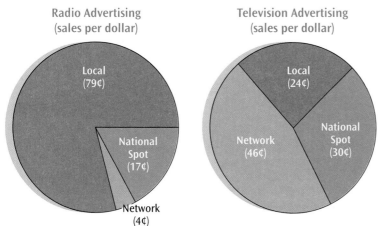

Radio versus Television Dollars

Radio Advertising (sales per dollar)
- Local (79¢)
- National Spot (17¢)
- Network (4¢)

Television Advertising (sales per dollar)
- Local (24¢)
- Network (46¢)
- National Spot (30¢)

control over how their product will be presented, perhaps risking it being shown in an unfavorable light (Fitzgerald, 2002).

Like radio commercial time, television commercial time is bought as network, national, and local spots. Advertisers who want to reach the largest audience possible may place their commercials on broadcast network programs. Automobile, shampoo, toothpaste, and fast-food commercials, for example, most often appear on network programs, which often draw millions of viewers. These spots are very expensive to purchase, so network time is usually reserved for the limited number of advertisers who can afford it.

Advertisers may buy national spots in which they place their ads on individual stations in certain markets. For example, in February, a national manufacturer of patio furniture may buy commercial spots on stations throughout Florida. By April, the company may reduce its commercial spending in the Sunshine State and instead buy spots on stations in Georgia and South Carolina, or it may just place its commercials on stations located in beach communities along the East Coast.

Local advertisers are generally hometown businesses that want to reach customers within a single market or geographic region. A restaurant with one or two locations in Knoxville, Tennessee, may buy time on one or two local television stations that reach the greater Knoxville market. Buying network time would be much too costly and serve no useful purpose, as it's unlikely that anyone from Seattle would drive to Knoxville for dinner.

Public service announcements (PSAs) and **station promos** are also types of on-air radio and television promotions. Public service announcements promote nonprofit organizations, such as the American Lung Association and the United Way, as well as social causes, such as "Friends don't let friends drive drunk" and "Click it or ticket" seatbelt advocacy. Most stations air PSAs at no charge and run them whenever they can fit them into the regular schedule. Radio and television stations also promote their own programs on their own stations. Frequently, a promo airing in the morning will promote an afternoon drive-time show or an afternoon television promo will alert viewers about a special program coming up later that evening.

TOP 10 Syndicated Programs in Ad Pricing: 2003

PROGRAM	AD PRICE
1. *Friends*	$221,567
2. *Seinfeld*	$414,500
3. *Entertainment Tonight*	$149,400
4. *Everybody Loves Raymond*	$124,379
5. *Will & Grace*	$122,784
6. *Wheel of Fortune*	$82,950
7. *The Oprah Winfrey Show*	$81,740
8. *Jeopardy!*	$77,100
9. *That '70s Show*	$75,546
10. *World Wrestling Entertainment*	$63,005

Source: "Top 25 Shows," 2004.

ZOOM IN   7.9
Watch television commercials at these sites:
- AdvertisementAve (Contemporary spots): www. advertisementave.com
- AnimalMakers (Spots featuring animals): www. animalmakers.com/index.html

What hair product commercial features the line "If you can't tell, why should we"?

ADVANTAGES OF ADVERTISING ON TELEVISION

- *Visual and audio*—Television's greatest advantage is its ability to bring life to products and services. The combination of sight and sound grabs viewers, commands their attention, and increases their commercial recall. Viewers often remember the words to commercial jingles, company slogans, and mottos, and more important, they remember information about the products themselves.
- *Mass appeal*—Television commercials reach a broad, diverse audience. So rather than just target a narrow customer base, advertisers can appeal to a large, mass audience.
- *High exposure*—Although the high cost of a television spot generally limits the number of times it can be aired, one exposure will reach many people simultaneously. It's often the case that more than one person is watching a television set at the same time.
- *High reach*—All but about 2 percent of U.S. households have at least one television set, and almost 80 percent have two or more sets (Shane, 1999). In an average U.S. household, the television is on for about 7½ hours per day. Adults spend about 4½ hours per day watching television and children and teens about 3 hours a day ("Trends in Television," 2000). Thus, television reaches millions of viewers per day. Advertisers with products that appeal to a broad audience can use television to achieve maximum reach and exposure.
- *Ubiquitous*—Television is everywhere. It's rare to go someplace that doesn't have a television. As such, television is more than a medium; it's a lifestyle. People schedule their time around their favorite programs, and they often build relationships based on common liking of certain programs.
- *Commercials blend with content*—Commercials are cleverly inserted within or between programs, so viewers have to make an effort to avoid them. Contemporary commercials are visually exciting and have interesting narratives that capture viewers' attention before they have the chance to change channels or head to the kitchen to make a snack.
- *Variety*—With so many program types, advertisers have many options for commercial placement. For instance, a diaper marketer may choose to place commercials during soap operas, whose viewers are typically women.
- *Entertaining*—Television is highly entertaining, and this entertainment value spills over into commercials. During certain times, like the Super Bowl and the Emmy's, viewers actually find the commercials more exciting than the programs themselves.
- *Persuasive*—Television is the most persuasive commercial medium. Many people automatically believe what they see on television and consider it a credible medium. Viewers may be persuaded to try new products because of television's audio and visual components, which allow product demonstrations, and because of the narrative quality of many commercials.
- *Emotional*—Television makes us laugh, makes us cry, makes us angry, makes us happy, and otherwise engages our emotions. Effective commercials tug at our heartstrings, as we witness the emotional rewards that come from purchasing the advertised product and so are inclined to purchase it ourselves.

TOP 10 Super Bowl Ads (by viewer recognition): 1992–2002

AD	YEAR	RECOGNITION FACTOR (%)
1. Subway: Jared and weight loss	2001	79.6%
2. Columbia Pictures: *A Few Good Men*	1993	66.6
3. Columbia Pictures: *Groundhog Day*	1993	60.9
4. Budweiser: Fired	1996	60.7
5. Pepsi: Coke driver sneaks a Pepsi	1996	59.5
6. Pepsi: Shaq versus boy	1994	59.3
7. Pepsi: Cindy Crawford with boys on fence	1992	58.9
8. Universal Pictures: *Dante's Peak*	1997	58.7
9. Budweiser: Sign falls and electrocutes frog	1998	58.5
10. Diet Pepsi: Ray Charles and the Singing Hearing	1992	57.8

Source: Ackman, 2003.

Suave.

- *Prestige*—Many viewers believe that if a company is wealthy enough to buy commercial time and a product is good enough to be advertised on television, then it's good enough to buy. The glamour of television tends to rub off on products.

DISADVANTAGES OF ADVERTISING ON TELEVISION

- *Zipping, zapping, and channel surfing*—Zipping, zapping, and *channel surfing* are three terms that advertisers hate to hear. Viewers **zip** when they fast-forward through a taped commercial, and they **zap** them with a VCR that automatically skips over the commercials. Viewers **channel surf** when they move all around the television dial, sampling everything that's on at the time. All too often, when a commercial comes on, the channel gets changed. Most viewers are so adept at commercial avoidance that they instinctively know how much time they have to scan other channels and get back to their original program just as the commercial break ends. VCRs and digital video recorders are other commercial avoidance culprits. Viewers merely push a button to fast-forward through the commercials, and some newer VCRs even blank out the messages. Advertisers end up paying for an audience that doesn't even see their commercials.
- *Fragmented audience*—With cable and satellite television now offering hundreds of channels, the broadcast television audience has shrunk. Moreover, viewers have so many options that the market is very fragmented. Advertisers today have many more options, too.
- *Difficult to target*—The mass appeal of television makes it difficult and expensive to reach a specific target audience. Advertisers often end up paying for wasted coverage—paying for a large audience when they really only wanted to reach a smaller subset of viewers.
- *Not portable*—Most television sets cannot be picked up and moved around. With the exception of a few battery-operated, five-inch sets, televisions are not portable.
- *High cost*—Running commercials on television is very expensive. Dollar for dollar, it's the most expensive medium, especially when considering both production costs and airtime.
- *Clutter*—Television commercials are all grouped together, either between or within programs. It's common to see three or four commercials in a row, followed by a station promotion, by a station identification, and then three or four more commercials. In 2001, all nonprogramming time (commercials, station ID, station promotion) took up an average of 16 minutes and 8 seconds in a typical prime-time hour. Early morning television had 18 minutes and 2 seconds of nonprogramming materials, and daytime television had nearly 21 minutes devoted to nonprogram fare ("Advertising Patterns," 1999; Goetzl, 2002). When so many commercials are cluttered together, viewers tend to pay little attention to any of them, thus hampering message recall.

Cable Advertising

There are several major differences between cable and broadcast television. For example, broadcast television is free over the airwaves, but viewers have to pay to watch cable programming, which is delivered through a local cable service. And while both broadcast and cable networks generate revenue through advertising, local cable providers also generate revenue through subscriber fees.

Cable television has been around for many years, but only recently has it challenged broadcast television for audience share. For one week in the summer of 1997,

What product did actor Dustin Hoffman endorse in the 1960s?

Prime-Time Television Audience: Cable versus Broadcast

(fyi)

	AVERAGE PRIME-TIME AUDIENCE	RATING*	SHARE*
Cable networks	29.7 million	28.2	47.9
Broadcast networks	29.2 million	27.7	47.0

*See Chapter 8 for an explanation of ratings and shares.
Source: "TV First," 2003.

basic cable channels edged out ABC, NBC, and CBS with 40 percent of the prime-time audience, compared to the networks' 39 percent share (Shane, 1999). According to the Cabletelevision Advertising Bureau's analysis of Nielsen viewer data, the advertising-supported cable networks drew a larger prime-time audience than the seven broadcast networks (ABC, CBS, NBC, FOX, UPN, WB, PAX) during the 2001/2002 season ("TV First," 2003).

Cable offers viewers select program options, and so it offers advertisers narrow target audiences. Just as with the broadcast networks, advertisers buy commercial time on cable networks. Because there are many more cable networks than broadcast networks, the audience for each cable network is very small. Cable networks include the Golf Channel, Home and Garden Television (HGTV), Nick-at-Nite, the Food Network, and hundreds of others. They are perfect advertising venues for marketers who want to target specific audiences. What better place to advertise gardening supplies than on HGTV? Even though advertising-supported cable networks tend to have small audiences, advertisers are attracted to these specialized and often loyal markets.

Just over two-thirds of cable buys take place at the network level, with the remainder being spent on local cable. Local cable operators sell commercial time and also team with other cable operators to sell **interconnects.** Large cities such as New York may have several cable providers, each sending out cable programming to a specific part of the city. Interconnects allow advertisers to purchase local cable time with several providers with one cable buy. In doing so, an advertiser could simultaneously run a commercial on all of New York's cable systems for a larger audience reach.

ADVANTAGES OF ADVERTISING ON CABLE TELEVISION

- *Visual and audio*—Like broadcast television, cable television's primary strength is its ability to attract viewers through sight and sound.
- *Select audience*—Cable's wide variety of programming and networks attracts small, select, target audiences. Rather than spend money on a large broadcast audience, of which only a small percentage may be interested in the product, cable delivers specific consumers to its advertisers.
- *Upscale*—The cable television audience tends to be made up of young, upscale, educated viewers with money to spend, making cable an ideal venue for specialized and luxury items.
- *Variety*—With hundreds of cable networks to choose from, it's easy for an advertiser to match its product with its target audience.
- *Low cost*—With so many cable networks competing for advertisers, they rarely sell all of their available commercial time. The fierce competitive environment also keeps costs down, making cable an attractive buy to many advertisers.
- *Seasonal advantage*—Cable networks have learned to take advantage of the broadcast networks' summer "vacation." During those hot months when broadcast television is airing stale reruns, cable is counter-programming with shows that attract larger than normal audiences and pull viewers away from old broadcast fare.
- *Local advantage*—National spot buyers and local businesses can take advantage of cable's low cost and targeting abilities to reach specialty audiences within certain geographic areas.
- *Media mix*—The low cost of cable, coupled with the selective audience it provides, makes it an ideal supplement in the media mix.

DISADVANTAGES OF ADVERTISING ON CABLE TELEVISION

- *Zipping, zapping, and channel surfing*—Again, zipping, zapping, and channel surfing are the enemies of television—both broadcast and cable. Considering cable's wide range of offerings, it surely distracts viewers away from other cable and broadcast fare.
- *Fragmented audience/low ratings*—Cable audiences are fragmented and spread across many cable networks. These small audiences translate into low ratings for cable shows when compared to the ratings of broadcast network shows.
- *Lack of penetration*—Only about 7 out of 10 U.S. households subscribe to cable television, and while this is a substantial audience, it's still far smaller than the audience that receives broadcast television.
- *Churn*—Cable audience size is affected by *churn*. This is the turnover in subscribers, or the number who disconnect their cable service and the number of new connects.

Internet Advertising

There's some debate as to what constitutes *Internet advertising,* but it's generally considered when a company pays or makes some sort of financial or trade arrangement to post its logo or product information with the intent of generating sales or brand recognition on *someone else's Internet space.* For example, when Neiman Marcus pays to place its banner on the *Washington Post* website, this is considered *Internet advertising.* However, when Neiman Marcus sells clothing and other products on its own website, it is considered *marketing.* The distinction between online advertising and online marketing is similar to Neiman Marcus buying commercial time on a local radio station as opposed to printing a catalog with ordering information. The former is an ad, and the latter is a marketing endeavor.

The most common form of online advertisement is the **banner ad.** Traditionally, a banner has been little more than an advertiser's logo with some embellishment. To increase consumer interest and to make purchasing easier, a banner is more often than not designed as an active link to the advertiser's homepage. Banners are found on all types of websites, in chat rooms, as part of newsletters, and in other Web venues. They also take many forms: Some are embedded as part of online games, and others are posted as coupons. Recently, the typical banner ad has given way to a more exciting visual presence, the **rich-media banner.** It is not a type of ad per se but describes how an ad is designed. Different from text-only banners, rich-media banners are ads that are animated, contain audio or video, or just flash, blink, or make weird sounds.

Advertisers are concerned that with so many banner ads dancing on webscreens, users might get annoyed at the distraction and choose to ignore them all. To make sure that their messages are seen, many online advertisers opt for **pop-up**

Do Banner Ads Work?

Percentage of Internet users drawn to a site:

- After seeing a banner ad for the site: 25 percent
- After seeing a television commercial for the site: 14 percent
- After hearing a radio spot for the site: 4 percent

Source: Kranhold, 1999.

TOP 10   Pop-Up Advertisers

Research has shown that 63 companies launch 80 percent of all pop-up ads. Here are the top 10 pop-up advertisers:

COMPANY	NUMBER OF ADS (IN MILLIONS)
1. X10 Wireless	1,013
2. Orbitz	687
3. Providian	679
4. Cendant	561
5. Cassava	548
6. Dell	484
7. Bonzi	337
8. Morgan Stanley	303
9. Columbia House	223
10. Advertising.com	216

Source: "E-Commerce: The Road Ahead," 2002.

What was the first website to accept banner ads?

TOP 10 Internet Advertisers (by spending): 2002

COMPANY	AMOUNT SPENT (IN MILLIONS)
1. AOL Time Warner	$292.3
2. Microsoft Corp.	$126.3
3. Qwest Communications Int'l.	$117.3
4. Bank One Corp.	$90.8
5. Netstock Investment Corp.	$75.7
6. Ameritrade Holding Co.	$75.6
7. eDiets.com	$69.4
8. Yahoo!	$67.9
9. Bertelsmann	$61.0
10. USA Interactive	$59.2

Source: "Top 10 Advertisers," 2003.

ads, also known as **interstitials** and **superstitials.** The word *interstitial* means "in between"; thus, this type of ad appears in between pages or sites. Interstitials pop up in separate browser windows, and when customers click on them, they are usually taken to the advertisers' websites. *Superstitials* are grander versions of interstitials; they dazzle the eyes with commercial-length animation, graphics, interactive transactional engines, and near television quality video. Superstitials also appear in separate browser windows that pop up between pages or sites. Once referred to as "polite" ads, because they only played when fully downloaded and initiated by the user, some video superstitials now rudely self-start while a page is loading up, and it's often impossible to turn off the ad until after the page is fully loaded.

Another type of online advertising is the **extramercial,** which is a three-inch space to the right of the screen that is usually not visible unless the user scrolls sideways or his or her monitor resolution is sized at 1,024 × 768 or higher. A **video banner ad (v-banner)** is simply a banner ad that contains a video clip. A **webmercial** has "the look and feel of a television commercial" and may last anywhere from 5 to 25 seconds in length. Ad agencies are going beyond simply taking a television spot and putting it on the Internet. Rather, they are creating original content for the Internet audience (Elkin, 2003a).

Online advertisers have also devised new ways of annoying users with pesky ads. **Pop-unders** are known as the "evil cousins of pop-ups." Rather than pop up over the browser window, pop-unders lurk behind the browser window and surprise the user when he or she closes the browser. Many pop-unders are annoyingly difficult to close. Aptly named **skyscraper** ads extend vertically along one side of the browser window. Their long downloading times paralyze users, who must wait for the ads to download before doing anything else online (Pogue, 2002; Stone, 2002).

Known as "digital-age Hydras," seemingly innocent ad windows suddenly reproduce into multiple windows when users try to close the first ad. Perhaps the most annoying online ads are those that float around the screen, challenging users to try to nab them with the mouse. Using special Flash animation, **floaters** dance inside a browser window and even turn cursors into ads, making it almost impossible to use the page. Frustrated users find themselves playing "cat and mouse" while desperately trying to sink the floater (Pogue, 2002; Stone, 2002).

More subtle (and some say unethical) types of online advertising include online product placement, advertorials/infomercials, and buzz marketing, which blur product information with sales pitches. Product placement, as described earlier, has become more common in movies and television over the last several decades, and now products are being placed on websites, too. In 1996, Honda and K Swiss were among the first companies to pay the now-defunct online soap opera *The Spot* some $15,000 to weave a month's worth of product mentions into the story (Grumann, 1996). More common types of product placement and **advertorials/infomercials** include product promotions that appear to be part of a website's editorial. For example, an online bookstore may promote a particular book with a "recommendation" that appears to be a website

Push/Pull Strategies (FYI)

Internet advertising includes *push* and *pull* strategies. A *push strategy* means that an ad is pushed, or forced, onto consumers, whereas a *pull* refers to consumers pulling, or seeking, the ad message. Internet advertising that follows a push strategy is similar to traditional media advertising, in which commercial messages are pushed onto consumers. For example, television commercials are pushed because viewers don't have control over when and which ads to view. Advertisers are taking advantage of Internet technology by pushing new product and product improvement announcements and other promotional messages through pop-up ads, banners, e-mail, electronic mailing lists, newsletters, and so on. Web marketers also use pull strategies, such as establishing websites, delivering information through subscription services, and making weblinks that simply lead consumers to product information at their own convenience.

HotWired, the online version of *Wired* magazine, on October 27, 1994.

editorial but is actually paid for by the book publisher. Similarly, a website may offer several recipes that are accompanied by recommended wines, but a user may not know that the wine recommendations are actually paid commercial messages. Product placement and advertorials/infomercials are especially designed to attract the attention of Web users who may pay little attention to banner ads.

Buzz marketing, which has been defined as "the transfer of information from someone who is in the know to someone who isn't" (c.f. Gladwell, 2003) is a contrived version of word-of-mouth endorsement. True word-of-mouth advertising is traditionally a highly trusted and very effective type of communication (Cuneo, 2002). Whereas word of mouth implies that consumers tell others the benefits of purchasing certain products and services of their own volition, in buzz marketing (also known as *viral marketing*), a company pays people to pass themselves off as ordinary consumers using a product. For example, Vespa recently hired good-looking, hip young men and women to cruise around Southern California hot spots on their scooters. As admirers asked about the scooters, the paid endorsers touted the product and even handed out the address and phone number of the nearest Vespa dealer (Gladwell, 2003, Khermouch & Green, 2001).

The Internet also comes into play when marketers hire people to find online opportunities to talk up a product or service in the guise of an everyday person. If you're in a chat room or on an electronic mailing list or bulletin board, discussing an issue or general product, and someone mentions a particular brand, that person could be a hired promoter. The information you receive will be a sales pitch disguised as helpful information, rather than an unbiased viewpoint (Dorey & MacLellan, 2003; Godes, 2002; Khermouch & Green, 2001). Unsuspecting Internet users might be duped into buying a product or service based on buzz marketing, rather than traditional word-of-mouth promotion.

Not all online endorsements are underhanded, and cyber word-of-mouth promotion is very powerful. Consider this example: When a Harvard social studies student looked into why the popularity of fringe-rock band Weezer soared even when the band was on a recording hiatus, he discovered that of the 20,000 fans who answered his survey, one-quarter of those who bought the band's 1996 album in 2002 did so because of online word-of-mouth recommendations (Begun, 2002).

SPAM   Commercial messages for Viagra, weight loss, hair loss, body part enhancement, get-rich-quick schemes, medical cures, and a host of other products and services clog millions of e-mailboxes every day. E-mail may have started as a promising method of delivering commercial messages, but it has captured the wrath of users who are up in arms at receiving these unsolicited sales pitches, also known as **spam.** According to Internet folklore, there are two origins of the word *spam*. Some say the term comes from the popular *Monty Python* saying "Spam, spam, spam," which was nothing more than a meaningless uttering (though pronounced with an English accent, of course). Others assert that e-mail spam is akin to the canned sandwich filler: a whole lot of junk but no real meat (Tedeschi, 1998).

Regardless, spam is commonly thought of as any unsolicited message or any content that requires the user to opt out (or decline in advance). Advertisers often justify sending spam by tricking customers into signing up for the

How Spam Works

1. Spammers first obtain e-mail addresses either from low-cost "spambots" (software that automatically combs the Web), bulletin boards, lists, and other resources or from businesses that sell their customers' personal information.
2. Next, by changing Internet accounts to avoid detection, spammers send out millions of pieces of spam from one or several computers.
3. The spam messages are then sent to stealth servers, which strip away the clues that could identify their origin and add fake return addresses.
4. The spam then gets sent on to unregulated blind-relay servers in Asia, which redirect the spam, making it more difficult to trace.
5. The spam finally travels back to the United States. The circuitous route fools ISPs and spam blockers into thinking spam is legitimate e-mail.

For flash animation on how spam works, go to the text's Companion Website: www.ablongman.com/medoffkaye1e.

Source: Stone & Lin, 2002.

On what part of a webpage does a banner ad get the most clicks-throughs?

Stopping Spam

ISPs constantly scramble for new ways to outfox spammers' underhanded means of circumventing spam blockers. Here are some examples:

ISPs' Strategy: Block messages from known spammers.

Spammers' Strategy: Set up new e-mail addresses.

Example: When Mary@offer4U.com is blocked, the spammer simply changes the address to Mary@goodoffer4U.com.

ISPs' Strategy: Use a spam blocker to cross-check the address and verify the sender.

Spammers' Strategy: Mask their identity in the e-mail header, making it seem as though the message is coming from someone else.

ISPs' Strategy: Use antispam software to block messages containing marketing terms.

Spammers' Strategy: Alter the spellings of words or add invisible HTML tags to confuse the spam blockers.

Example: V*I*A*G*R*A, V1AGR@, VI<B></B>AGRA

ISPs' Strategy: Use antispam software to check messages with altered text and to block mail sent to multiple addresses.

Spammers' Strategy: Send spam out from many computers through stealth servers, so origin can't be detected.

The ISPs' newest strategy involves experimenting with software that requires sender confirmation. If the software suspects spam, it requires the sender to access a website and enter a displayed number before the message will be delivered. Since there's no one around to verify computer-generated spam that's been sent to thousands of addresses, it doesn't get delivered (Stone & Weil, 2003).

How Much Spam?

This chart shows spam as a percentage of all e-mail received:

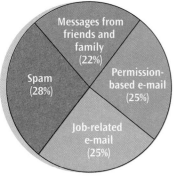

Source: Chen, 2002.

What Do Spammers Sell?

Here's a breakdown of what spammers sell by product or service:

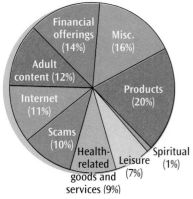

Source: Elkin, 2003b.

information. Sometimes when users are making a purchase, filling out an online poll, or just cruising through a website, they inadvertently click on or run their mouse over a link or icon that signals permission to send e-mail messages.

From a marketing standpoint, sending out promotional material via e-mail is much more efficient than waiting for potential customers to stumble upon a product's webpage or view one of the product's banner ads. Besides, it only takes a few seconds for users to recognize and delete unwanted promotional messages, so marketers figure that recipients are spared any real harm. This kind of thinking can backfire on the advertisers, however. Unsolicited e-mail can be detrimental to advertisers because customers who are spammed might harbor negative feelings and even boycott these companies' products and services (Freeman, 1999; Goles, 1998; Herlihy, 1999; Stone, 2003).

Despite spam's bad reputation, marketers are spamming full force. They sent out about 4.9 trillion unsolicited e-mails in 2003 (Elkin, 2003b).

ADVANTAGES OF ADVERTISING ON THE INTERNET

- *Worldwide marketplace*—The Internet serves as a worldwide marketplace, delivering a vast and diverse audience to advertisers. By placing advertisements on the web, companies can reach out to physically distant customers.
- *Targeting consumers*—The Internet's ability to carry messages to targeted groups is one of its most effective marketing tools. Using special services, marketers can deliver targeted advertising to customers based on their IP address or domain name, type of Web browser, and other criteria, including demographic characteristics (age, sex, income) and **psychographics**, which is the study of consumer lifestyles (interests, activities, opinions). The effectiveness of banner ads is increased when

The bottom-righthand part of the page, next to the scroll bar.

they are placed on websites with complementary content—such as a banner ad for cookware on a cooking page or a banner ad for a clothing store on a fashion page (Kranhold, 1999). The website mymeals.com sends coupons for food items based on user preferences. If a user is looking for a turkey recipe, a coupon for cranberry sauce may pop up (Bulkeley, 1999).

- *Exposure and run time*—Internet ads have longer exposure and run times than ads in traditional media. They are visible for as long as the advertisers post them, they can be accessed any time of day and as often as users wish, and they can be printed and used as paper coupons.
- *Low production costs*—Web advertisements are generally less expensive to produce than ads in traditional media, and the longer exposure and run times make them even more cost efficient. Web ads generally do not require the extensive production techniques involved in the traditional media; in fact, they can often be designed using digital imaging software. Low production cost is instrumental in attracting a wide range of businesses with small advertising budgets to the Web.
- *Updating and changing ad copy*—Updating and changing the copy and graphics of online ads can be accomplished fairly quickly. These ads can generally be designed and posted within a relatively short period of time.
- *Prestige*—The prestige of online advertising casts a positive image on both the advertisers and their products. Many Internet users expect that quality products can be purchased online.
- *Competition*—The generally lower cost of online advertising allows companies with small advertising budgets to compete with companies with more advertising resources. In this sense, the Web closes the gap between large and small enterprises and places them in the same competitive arena. Online, small businesses are not so small.
- *Quick links to purchases*—A consumer can easily make a purchase online by simply clicking on a banner ad and following the trail of links to an online order form. In many cases, newer interactive banners allow purchases to be transacted directly from the banner, without having to click through a product website.

DISADVANTAGES OF INTERNET ADVERTISING
- *Hidden persuasion*—With most traditional media, consumers are exposed to persuasive messages in an instant, often before they've even had the chance to turn away from the promotion. Although online advertisements like banner ads intrude on computer screens, the persuasive elements are often at least one click away. A consumer must be interested in the product and must click on the banner before being exposed to the sales message.
- *Creative restrictions*—Banner ads are becoming more technologically sophisticated, and many allow on-ad ordering. However, they are still somewhat restricted in creative terms. Many banners are nothing more than the equivalent of a roadside billboard. Advertisers lean toward banners that lure consumers with animation and movement, but these ads tend to slow webpage downloading to a snail's pace.
- *Fragmentation*—Despite its ability to target an audience, the Web is a highly fragmented medium. Thus, advertisers face the challenge of placing their messages on sites that will draw large enough audiences to make their investments worthwhile. With hundreds of thousands of websites and thousands of pages within each site, it is difficult to determine ideal ad placement.

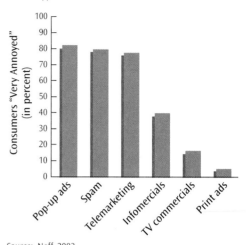

Consumers' Views on Advertising
What types of ads do consumers dislike the most?

Source: Neff, 2003.

What percentage of U.S. companies advertised on the Internet in 2000?

- *Inadequate audience measurement*— Inadequate audience measurement techniques limit an advertiser's knowledge of how many users are exposed to a message, thus hindering effective advertising buys.
- *Questionable content*—The online audience is already weary of deceptive content and the overcommercialism of the Web, and so they are not very receptive to online advertising. Many users respond unfavorably to these ads and particularly resent advertising popping up all over their screens. More troubling to many online users, especially parents, is the blurring of content and advertising aimed at children. Activists and parents are calling on sites to set limits on their advertising and to make it clear when information will be used for marketing purposes.

Advertising Agencies

Advertising agencies have long been the hub of the advertising industry. Agencies are hotbeds of creativity—the places where new ideas are born and new products come to life. Agencies are where many minds come together—account representatives, copywriters, graphic artists, video producers, media planners, advertising researchers, and others who collaborate to devise the best campaigns possible.

Advertising agencies are not all alike. There are large agencies that serve national advertisers, and there are small agencies that serve locally owned businesses. Some agencies have offices around the world, some have offices around the nation, and others have an office or two in some city or town. Some agencies have staffs of thousands, and others are one- or two-person shops. While agencies exist to serve advertisers, how they do that is not the same from agency to agency. Different types of agencies serve different functions.

FULL-SERVICE AGENCIES   Full-service agencies basically provide all of the advertising functions needed to create an advertising campaign. They plan, research, create, produce, and place commercials and advertisements in various media. They often provide other marketing services, as well, such as promotions, newsletters, and corporate videos. Some full-service agencies are very structured; each group or department focuses on its strengths, and projects are basically moved down the line in each step of the process. Other agencies are very collaborative, in that groups of people with different fields of expertise work together on a project. For instance, an account representative may collaborate with copywriters, graphic artists, researchers, planners, media buyers, and others who are assigned to his or her client.

CREATIVE BOUTIQUES   Some advertisers have an inhouse staff that plans, researches, and buys media time and space but needs help with the actual creation of a campaign. These advertisers will contract with a *creative boutique,* rather than with a full-service agency. Creative boutiques focus specifically on the actual creation of ads and campaigns and so are staffed with copywriters, graphic artists, and producers. Advertisers benefit by hiring a group of people with expertise in creative work, and they don't have to pay for the advertising services that they handle inhouse.

MEDIA-BUYING SERVICES   While some advertisers need help with creative endeavors, others have inhouse creative departments that write and produce their commercials and advertisements. Even so, they may need help with the other parts of the advertising

ZOOM IN   7.10
- For a clearer understanding of the differences among creative boutiques, media-buying services, and full-service agencies, go to each of these agency websites and read about the types of services it offers:

Creative Boutique   Little Heart: www.littleheart.com/creativeservices.html

Media-Buying Service   Marshall Advertising: www.marshalladvertising.com/

Full-Service Agency   Valentine Radford: www.valrad.com/services.asp

- For more information about advertising agencies and easy access to many agency websites, connect to the American Association of Advertising Agencies: www.aaaa.org.

Interactive Agency Success Story

Way back in 1995, Chan Suh and Kyle Shannon came together with the vision of helping companies promote themselves online, and they set up shop with their Mac computer. They called their new interactive enterprise Agency.com (www.agency.com). British Airways, one of their first clients, asked them to redesign its website. Rather than just give the site a facelift, Agency.com suggested the company rethink its online business model. As a result, British Airways ended up with an online ticketing system and a site that focused on "new ways to use interactive technology to expand market share, reduce costs, improve efficiency, and deliver great customer satisfaction" ("History," 2004).

Agency.com's success with British Airways led to new online projects with companies such as Compaq, Nike, Sprint, and Texaco. Agency.com quickly became known for its outstanding work, and

Adweek named it one of the top 10 interactive agencies for 1996. Agency.com caught the attention of Omnicom Group, a marketing communication company, and Omnicom acquired a 40 percent share in Agency.com. The interactive start-up now had the money it needed to expand its enterprise—and expand it did.

Over the next three years, Agency.com acquired or purchased stakes in 12 interactive agencies around the world. Currently, it employs over 1,000 people internationally. As the agency has grown and changed, so has its mission. It has changed from "helping businesses bring their business online to empowering people and organizations to gain competitive advantage through interactive relationships," which they do through a discipline they call *interactive relationship management* ("History," 2004).

---

process. These advertisers may contract with a *media-buying service*. Once the advertisements and commercials have been produced, they must be placed in the most effective media to maximize exposure and sales. Media-buying services are experts in media placement. They know which media are best for which products as well as which media will help their clients achieve advertising and sales goals.

INTERACTIVE/CYBER AGENCIES   Many advertisers today see the need to expand their advertising to the Internet and to CD, DVD, and other interactive platforms but discover that traditional ad agencies cannot meet this need. As an alternative, they are turning to new media/interactive agencies with expertise in Web design and interactive technology. These interactive agencies (or *cyber agencies*) often create and maintain client websites, create and place banner ads, and produce and distribute other interactive advertising materials. Interactive shops often have expertise in many areas that full-service and other types of agencies just can't provide.

Cyber agencies are criticized, however, by their full-service counterparts and others who claim that while these new media agencies are experts in interactive technology, they are not experts in advertising and marketing. Cyber agencies have recently found themselves competing with full-service shops that have created their own inhouse interactive departments. Interestingly, critics claim that these inhouse personnel may be experts in advertising and marketing but are not truly proficient with interactive technology. As a compromise, many agencies are **outsourcing** their work to interactive agencies, so advertisers get the benefit of an ad agency's advertising expertise as well as the cyber know-how of an interactive agency.

Advertising Campaigns

Airing one or two commercials here and there is not, in most cases, an effective way to sell a product or service. That's why advertising agencies specialize in planning and implementing **advertising campaigns.** A campaign may comprise a number of commercials and advertisements for radio, television, the print media, and in some case the Internet that are all tied together using the same general theme or appeal. Successful recent campaigns include those for the Volkswagen Beetle and Budweiser's "Whassup."

ZOOM IN   7.11
For a historical look at the development of Coca-Cola campaigns, go to http://memory.loc.gov/ammem/ccmphtml/colahome.html.

The Taco Bell chihuahua and the Budweiser frogs are both examples of successful advertising campaigns.

IBM's e-Commerce Campaign

Ogilvy's award-winning campaign for IBM's e-commerce division employed a media mix that included the Web. Ogilvy opened the campaign with multipage advertising in the *Wall Street Journal* that included IBM's website URL. It followed up with a flight of television commercials, targeted ads in trade publications, direct-mail packages, and banner ads—all of which directed people to IBM's website, where they received the actual selling message.

Oglivy won a gold Clio and several other prestigious advertising awards for its IBM e-commerce campaign. Additionally, its e-commerce banners won silver and gold Interactive Pencil awards for best interactive campaign and best single interactive banner (Kindel, 1999; "Winner of the Most," 1999).

ZOOM IN 7.12
Check out the Clio Award winners and learn more about this prestigious award at www.clioawards.com.

A campaign involves more than just creative strategy; it's part of the larger sales and marketing plan. It involve setting advertising and marketing objectives, analyzing a product's uses as well as its strengths and weaknesses, determining the target audience, evaluating the competitive marketplace, and understanding the media market. By using these product, audience, advertising, and marketing strategies, the creative staff has the fun task of building a series of commercials and print ads that follow the same basic theme. Copywriters, graphic artists, and video producers confer, toss around ideas, argue, change their minds, and basically put their heads together until they come up with a campaign that meets the marketing and advertising objectives. The creative staff also has to please the client and work with the media buyers in tailoring the commercials and ads to each medium's audience.

Producing a campaign is often a long, arduous, and stressful process. Clients can be difficult to please and sometimes think they know more than the advertising experts. Deadlines come up much too quickly, and the marketplace can change overnight. Moreover, the advertising business is very competitive, and agencies are always pitching advertisers for their business. Just one failed campaign can lose an ad agency a multimillion dollar account. On the positive side, being part of a successful ad campaign can be very satisfying. Agencies and their creative staffs often build client relationships that last for years. Creative staffs are recognized for their excellent work by national and international associations and by receiving Clio Awards, which are the advertising equivalents of Emmy Awards.

SEE IT LATER

Although advertising benefits us in many ways, it also contributes to what can be called *information overload*. We are bombarded with ads practically everywhere we look. Television, radio, and the Internet are all packed with ads; the nation's roadways are cluttered with billboards that urge us to pull over and eat, to buy gas, or to listen to a particular radio station; and it's almost impossible to buy a product that doesn't prominently display its name or logo. Almost everywhere we look, we're being persuaded to spend our money.

In early 2004, a federal judge ruled that horse racing jockeys could sell advertising on their riding silks. The Kentucky Horse Racing Authority had earlier prohibited this to avoid the overcommercialization that plagues other sports. Regardless, advertisers were willing to pay up to $30,000 for a jockey to wear advertising on his sleeves in the 2004 Kentucky Derby ("Jockeys Can Wear Ads," 2004).

Although public outcry against the jockeys advertising was minimal, it was loud and strong against Major Baseball League (MLB) promoting the 2004 release of the new *Spiderman* movie on its bases. As part of a marketing agreement with Columbia Pictures and Marvel Studios, MLB had planned to adorn first, second, and third bases with the red and blue Spiderman logo, but baseball fans shrieked at the idea of commercializing any part of the infield (Rovell, 2004). Although logos are commonly painted on the walls of the outfield, a baseball historian said the infield is regarded as a "magic circle" that's not to be tampered with at the risk of "offending the gods" (Maller, 2004). And so just one day after announcing the *Spiderman* promotion, MLB backed out of the infield agreement, succumbing to the thousands of calls of protest it received. MLB will promote the movies at its ballparks but not by commercializing the infield ("On Second Thought," 2004).

Although this advertising innovation didn't make it, many others have. From radio to television to clothing to bathroom stalls and now to foreheads, advertising can be found most anywhere. A London advertising agency is paying good-looking, hip college students the equivalent of $7 an hour to paste logos on their foreheads and wear them while they go about their everyday lives. Advertisers pay about $25,000 for 100 foreheads a week (Stern, 2003).

Given these developments, critics of advertising scream for relief from the overcommercialized world that it creates. And while some people try to shield themselves from advertising, others have come to accept that it is an everyday part of life. In the future, we'll likely see advertising creeping into areas that were once regarded above such peddling. Even though public protest may stem the tide, commerce will probably prevail. Advertising will probably become increasingly ubiquitous, increasingly influential, and increasingly controversial.

Criticisms of Advertising

Advertising is highly criticized, not so much for its very nature but because of its content, its negative influences on society, and the types of products it promotes.

ADVERTISING ENCOURAGES AVARICIOUSNESS AND MATERIALISM   Many people claim that advertising encourages people to buy items they don't need, often just for the sake of amassing goods. "Whoever dies with the most toys, wins" was a popular bumper-sticker slogan of the 1980s and reflects the type of thinking that encourages greed and competition between friends and neighbors based on the amount of material goods they collect. All too often, people are persuaded to spend money on goods that they can't afford and don't need because product promotions have convinced them that their self-worth depends on these purchases. College students often complain they can't afford to pay for their education, yet they purchase automobiles and computers that are way out of their price range and that they don't really need. Why? They feel these items will make them look cool, or they derive some other sort of personal benefit from having them. No one is immune from the persuasive power of advertising. It's not just college students who are buying more than they need. In 2000, the average U.S. credit card holder was carrying a little over $8,000 in credit card debt (McGinn, 2001). Many people insist that runaway debt is the direct result of advertising that promotes materialism.

ADVERTISING REINFORCES STEREOTYPES   Commercials are under fire for their unrealistic and often demeaning portrayals of women, minorities, and other individuals. Stereotypical images of women mopping floors, men being bosses, smart people being nerds, blondes being dumb, and old people being fools pervade many advertisements. Unfortunately, people's beliefs are shaped by what they see on television, and when they're repeatedly exposed to stereotypes, they come to believe what they see.

Recent pressure on advertisers has brought about some changes in how groups are depicted in commercials and other types of promotional materials. Advertisements that show people in more realistic situations, that include more minorities and women, and that depict them in a more positive light are minimizing the stereotypic portrayals of many groups.

ADVERTISING IS MISLEADING   Critics assert that commercials are often exaggerated and misleading. The Federal Trade Commission (FTC) regulates deceptive advertising, and even though many ads do not break the law, they do breach ethical standards. Many consumer groups complain about the overuse of exaggerated claims—for instance, basketball players wearing Nike shoes jumping higher than their rivals wearing other brands and Bud Light drinkers having more fun and being surrounded by more gorgeous women than other beer drinkers. Nike doesn't directly claim their shoes can make people jump higher, and Anheuser Busch doesn't state that drinking Bud Light will help men attract beautiful women. Even so, critics claim that people may associate these products with these unlikely outcomes.

Advertising defenders, on the other hand, assert that such depictions are nothing more than harmless **puffery:** exaggerated claims that a reasonable person knows are not true. Supporters claim that most people know that Nikes don't make people jump higher, no matter what an ad may suggest; thus, puffery is harmless to consumers. Critics contend otherwise and claim that puffery is unethical.

ADVERTISING EXPLOITS CHILDREN   Parents and other advocacy groups are concerned about the negative effects of advertising on children. Most children see about 20,000 commercials each year (Center for Media Education, 1997; Singer, Singer, & Zuckerman, 1997), and marketers spend about $7 billion each a year pushing products to children under the age of 12 ("FTC Action," 2000). Critics claim that children can't interpret the purpose of a commercial and judge the credibility of its claims, nor can they differentiate between program content and a sales message. Critics further contend that advertisers take advantage of children by selling them on products without their knowledge.

ADVERTISING IS INVASIVE AND PERVASIVE   "Too much advertising in too many places" is a common consumer complaint. Individuals are exposed to about 5,000 advertising messages per day, including electronic and print media, billboards, signs, banner ads, t-shirts, labels, and other advertising venues ("Love It or Hate It," 2001). Critics claim that advertisements invade our minds and our homes and overwhelm us with trivial information. Research has shown that consumers filter information; on recall tests, people remember very few of the ads they've seen or heard. Further, people tend to block out much of the advertising they're exposed to and attend to the ads that promote a product or service that they're already interested in. While many critics blast the very existence of commercials, proponents hail them as a necessary component of our free-market system.

Summary

Advertising isn't a modern-day phenomenon but has been around since the days of clay tablets. And while it has changed in many ways since its origins, its purpose has remained the same: to get the word out about a product or service.

Radio was never meant to be an advertising medium, but high costs drove entrepreneurs to come up with a way to raise money for their over-the-air ventures. Stations experimented with toll advertising and later with sponsored programs. By the time television emerged as a new medium, there wasn't any question that advertising was going to fund its existence. The only question was how best to advertise products on television. Early television experimented with radio's style of sponsored programs. This was fairly successful, until the quiz show scandal exposed the problems of sponsored programs. The television industry then borrowed the magazine concept from print and began selling commercial spots between and during programs.

Most commercials throughout the 1960s were 60 seconds in length, but they began getting shorter toward the end of the decade. The ban on tobacco advertising in 1971 left many networks and stations with unsold commercial time. They discovered that many marketers could not afford to purchase a full minute of time, so they created 30-second spots. Stations and networks were happy to find that they could sell two 30-second commercials to two different advertisers for more money than one 60-second spot to one advertiser. Throughout the 1970s, 30-second commercials began to dominate the airwaves, as they still do today.

Advertising benefits both marketers and consumers. Marketers are able to promote their products and services, and consumers get to learn about them. Advertising on each of the electronic media—radio, television, and the Internet—has its own advantages and disadvantages. Some products and services will be best served by advertising on network television, while some will reach their audiences more cost efficiently on radio or cable television. Advertisers also have a new medium on which to place their ads. Internet advertising involves more than just banner ads; there are interstitials, superstitials, extramercials, and webmercials, among others.

Effective advertising begins with an understanding of the market. Knowing which media will provide the best venues for a particular campaign is the responsibility of media market researchers. Campaign creators and management rely on advertising research to keep them on the right track. Measuring a commercial's effectiveness is a crucial part of the advertising process.

Placing a commercial here and there is usually not as effective an advertising strategy as constructing a campaign: a series of commercials and print ads with the same

What former Beverly Hills, 90210 *star made his acting debut in a Levi's commercial?*

theme. Most campaigns are created by advertising agencies. There are basically four types of advertising agencies: full-service agencies, creative boutiques, media-buying services, and interactive or cyber agencies.

For all its benefits, there are some downsides to advertising, as well. Critics claim that too much commercialism makes us greedy and materialistic. Some ads are said to promote racism and sexism through their stereotypic portrayals of minorities and women. Critics also contend that advertising exaggerates products' benefits and misleads us into buying items that we are later disappointed in or simply don't need. The effects of advertising on children is of particular concern. Most children can't tell the difference between programming and commercials and don't know if they are being given information or being sold a product. Regardless of how we may feel about advertising, without it, the media as we know them today would not exist and our world would be dramatically different.

Audience Measurement and Sales

SEE IT THEN	SEE IT NOW	SEE IT LATER
Early Ratings Systems	Gathering Audience Numbers	The Never-Ending Quest for Ratings
	Calculating and Reporting Radio and Television Audience Numbers	
	When Audience Numbers Aren't Enough	
	Translating Audience Information to Sales	
	Buying and Selling	

In this chapter, you'll learn about:

- Early and current procedures for measuring audiences
- The methods involved in collecting information about audiences
- How electronic media advertising is bought and sold
- How new technologies in electronic media create new challenges for audience measurement

Let's pretend you own a radio station. You spent all your savings to purchase the station, and to run it involves many other expenses, including your employees' salaries. How are you going to come up with the money to cover these costs? By selling airtime, of course. In selling airtime, you're really selling your listeners to your advertisers. And to do so, you must know something about your listeners: how many there are, who they are, when they listen, what music they like, and so on. Finding out this information is what prompted the development of radio audience measurement techniques, which later led to techniques for measuring television and Internet audiences, as well.

Knowledge of audience characteristics, including their use of media, is at the core of selling commercial time. This knowledge is translated into various figures, such as *ratings* and *shares,* which are then used to price commercial time and online space. Generally, the program, station, or website that draws the largest or most desirable audience can charge the most for its airtime or space.

Developing reliable and accurate ways of measuring media audiences is an ongoing process. New computer-based technologies have led to new data collection methods as well as altered older methods. Measuring the Internet audience has required adapting the methods and devices used for researching the traditional mass media audience. Audience-measuring companies are always working on more accurate and reliable ways to discover how listeners, viewers, and online users are using the media and which programs and websites they favor.

This chapter begins with an overview of early methods of obtaining audience feedback and then examines contemporary ways of monitoring radio, television, and Internet audiences. The explanations of these measuring techniques include the mathematical formulas that show how ratings, shares, and other measures are calculated and reported. The chapter then ties ratings to advertising sales by demonstrating how stations and websites use audience data to price commercial time and space.

SEE IT THEN

Early Ratings Systems

In the late 1920s, when radio advertising was just beginning to catch on, many stations were stumped as to how much to charge for commercial time. Radio stations were setting charges for time, but advertisers were hesitant to buy unless they had information about the listeners. The void was filled in 1929 when Archibald M. Crossley called on advertisers to sponsor a new way of measuring radio listenership: the **telephone recall system.** With this method, a random sample of people were called and asked what radio stations or programs they had listened to in the last 24 hours. Memory failure was the biggest drawback to Crossley's system, as listeners couldn't accurately remember what stations and programs they had tuned in to.

Crossley's fiercest competitor was C. E. Hooper, who used the **telephone coincidental method** of measuring radio listenership. Using this method, Hooper's staff telephoned a random sample of people and asked, "Are you listening to the radio just now?" The next question was something like "To what program are you listening?" followed by "Over what station is the program coming?" (Beville, 1998, p.11). Many thought Hooper's method was superior to Crossley's because it didn't rely on listeners' memory but instead surveyed exactly what they were listening to at the time of the call. Of course, the drawback to Hooper's method was that someone may have listened to a station for hours every day but just happened to have the radio turned off or tuned to another station at the time of the telephone call. Both the Crossley and Hooper methods had their flaws, but at the time, they were the best ways to measure listenership.

In the 1930s, A. C. Nielsen was also working on ways to measure the radio audience. He took a slightly different approach by using an electronic metering device, the **audimeter,** which attached to a listener's radio and monitored the stations he or she tuned to and for how long. The audimeter was the precursor to today's audience-metering devices.

In the late 1940s, Hooper supplemented telephone coincidental calling by asking listeners to keep **diaries** of their radio use. Newcomer American Research Bureau (ARB), which changed its name to Arbitron in 1973, also championed the diary method for measuring radio listenership.

The Crossley, Hooper, and Nielsen companies were the radio-ratings leaders into the late 1940s. Crossley left the ratings business in 1946, and in 1950, Nielsen bought

ZOOM IN   8.1
• Learn more about the audimeter at www.
emediaplan.com/admunch/Biographies/nielsen.asp.

• For additional information about the early days of ratings, see Module 1 at http://edtech.tennessee.edu/~dob/harmon.html.

out Hooper and thus eliminated its biggest competitor. Hooper himself, however, met a tragic death four years later, when on a duck hunting trip he slipped and fell into a rotating airplane propeller.

As television came to life in the late 1940s, the ratings services—mainly Nielsen and ARB/Arbitron—adapted their radio research methods for the new medium. And while many other ratings services emerged, none was able to overcome the market dominance of these two companies.

SEE IT NOW

Gathering Audience Numbers

Radio and Television

Media outlets need to know who's listening to their stations and who's watching their programs. A radio station manager may be interested in knowing how many listeners tune to his or her station for an average of 15 minutes per day, and a television station sales manager may want to know what percentage of television households in the market had their televisions tuned to the last game of the World Series. These types of data reflect how consumers use the media.

ARBITRON AND NIELSEN MEDIA RESEARCH   As just noted, Arbitron and Nielsen are the foremost radio and television ratings companies. Arbitron once measured both local radio and television audiences but dropped its less profitable television services in 1994, leaving television audience measurement in the hands of Nielsen Media Research.

These companies are interested primarily in how the public uses the media—what stations they tune to and what programs they listen to and watch. If a particular television program has consistently low ratings, it may be moved to another time slot or perhaps dropped. If a radio station is highly rated in the market, management knows that they have a winning format and can charge top dollar for their commercial time.

DIARIES   Having their audience keep diaries is a method used by both radio and television.

Radio Diaries   Arbitron surveys most of its markets at least once a year, although larger market areas may be surveyed more often or even on a continuous basis. Arbitron mails each participant a 7-day diary, with each day divided into 15-minute time blocks. In exchange for a small monetary reward (usually less than $5), each participant records when he or she starts and stops listening and the station (identified by call letters and/or dial position) he or she listens to during each 15-minute time block. Additionally, each participant is asked demographic information, such as age and gender, and other lifestyle information, such as hobbies and travel.

Arbitron sends diaries to a sample of listeners within Nielsen Media Research **designated market areas (DMAs).** Arbitron had developed its own market designation scheme, known as the *area of dominant influence (ADI),* but recently switched to Nielsen's DMAs. Nielsen divides the United States into 210 DMAs based on geographic location and historical television-viewing patterns. Market areas are sometimes redrawn if overall

FYI

Jenny Jones on the Chopping Block

PROGRAM RATINGS
Dr. Phil = 5.4
Oprah = 5.6
Jenny Jones = 1.5

Media executives compare program ratings to determine which programs will stay on the air. With such ratings compared to her competitors, Jenny Jones was cancelled in 2003.

Source: "Jenny Jones," 2003.

ZOOM IN   8.2
For information about Arbitron and Nielsen Media Research, visit www.arbitron.com and www.nielsenmedia.com, respectively.

THURSDAY

	Time		Station			Place			
	Start	Stop	Call letters, dial setting or station name *Don't know? Use program name.*	Mark ☒ one AM	FM	At Home	In a Car	At Work	Other Place
Early Morning (from 5 AM)	:	:							
	:	:							
	:	:							
Midday	:	:							
	:	:							
	:	:							
Late Afternoon	:	:							
	:	:							
	:	:							
Night (to 5 AM Friday)	:	:							
	:	:							
	:	:							

If you didn't hear a radio today, please mark ☒ here. ☐

A page from an Arbitron diary.

viewing behavior is altered due to changes in programming, cable penetration, satellite television subscriptions, and other factors (Webster, Phalen, & Lichty, 2000). Arbitron provides radio-listening data for the top 50 DMAs, if Arbitron's own survey areas (metro survey area and total survey area) are located within a particular DMA.

Arbitron designates 287 distinct geographic market areas as **metro survey areas (MSAs),** often referred to as *metros*. An MSA is generally comprised of a major city or several cities and their surrounding county or counties. In 2004, New York, New York, was the largest MSA and Casper, Wyoming, the smallest.

Arbitron also measures listenership in designated geographic regions known as **total survey areas (TSAs).** A TSA is made up of a major city and a larger surrounding area than a metro. For example, the population in the Casper, Wyoming, MSA is 53,700, but Casper's TSA population is 136,100 ("Market Survey Schedule," 2004). Smaller metros help low-powered stations compete in the ratings game against high-powered stations by providing smaller geographic areas of measure.

ZOOM IN   8.3

Compare DMA, TSA, and MSA maps of the Nashville, Tennessee, area in Module 3 at http://edtech.tennessee.edu/~dob/harmon.html.

FYI

TSA/MSA

Let's say Station A is a 3,000 watt station that reaches its metro area. Its ratings are low compared to those of a 50,000 watt station, Station B, just because its signal doesn't reach the entire TSA. But Station A's signal may be picked up throughout the smaller metro area, thus boosting its ratings.

TSA = 50,000 population

MSA = 25,000 population

Station A = 5,000 listeners

TSA rating = 2,500/50,000 = .05 or 5%

MSA rating = 2,500/25,000 = .10 or 10%

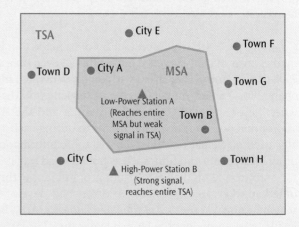

Television Diaries Nielsen Media Research also tracks television viewership through diaries. It collects viewing information from each of its 210 DMAs in the United States. In 2003, New York, New York, was the largest DMA (with 7,376,330 households) and Glendive, Montana, was the smallest (with 4,968 households).

Nielsen diaries are sent out to sample homes each November, February, May, and July, which are known as **"sweeps"** months or periods. Some larger markets may have additional sweeps during October, January, and March. Similar to the Arbitron listeners, television viewers record the programs and networks they watch in 15-minute blocks over a one-week period. They also provide demographic and sometimes lifestyle information for the diaries.

In an attempt to hike program viewership and hence ratings, television and radio station networks use sweeps periods to present special programs, season finales, and much-awaited episodes that reveal answers to long-term mysteries. But in fact, when these special programs and episodes are aired during sweeps, the ratings may be overinflated because viewers may only watch these heavily hyped episodes and not tune in during the regular season.

METERS In addition to diaries, television also uses metering devices to record viewing in 5,000 randomly selected households in the United States. The **set meter** attaches to a television and records when it's on and what broadcast, cable, and satellite programs and channels the set is tuned to. The **people meter** is a set meter with a special remote control. Each family member is assigned an identification button on the remote that

---

ZOOM IN 8.4

To find your city's DMA ranking and to see whether you live in a metered market, go to **www.nielsenmedia.com/index.html** and click on "Services."

---

fyi

Sweeps

CBS was the only winner at the halfway mark of the November 2003 sweeps.

NETWORK	TOTAL VIEWERS (MILLIONS)	PERCENTAGE CHANGE FROM SAME PERIOD LAST YEAR
CBS	14.9	+11%
NBC	11.6	−12%
ABC	10.0	−6%
FOX	7.0	−13%
WB	4.3	−11%
UPN	3.7	−14%

Source: Ryan, 2003.

Weakest Link Broken **fyi**

The Weakest Link and *The Other Half,* with February 2003 sweeps ratings of 1.8 and 1.0, respectively, were both yanked off the air. These ratings meant that only 1.8 and 1 percent of U.S. television households watched the shows. The importance of sweeps ratings can't be underestimated.

Source: "Weakest Link," 2003.

To Meter or Not to Meter **fyi**

Knoxville, Tennessee, with 478,000 television households, is the sixty-second-largest market in the United States. It converted from diary reporting to the Nielsen meter system in October 2002. Area television station executives expressed mixed feelings about the meters, especially since the $500,000 price tag for each station was about three times what they had paid for diaries. Beyond cost, some were concerned that the meters wouldn't make any difference in the stations' market positions and thus weren't worth the expense. Yet others argued that the meters would give more accurate audience data than the diaries. Knoxville, home of the University of Tennessee, has a younger than average population that is less likely to fill out diaries. This could hurt stations affiliated with the FOX or WB network, which tend to draw younger audiences. Meters, on the other hand, could more accurately reflect larger audiences for these stations.

The big advantage of being a metered market is that such a market is more likely to draw national advertisers. That means that the financial outlay for the metered ratings could be made up in increased revenue. While one station's general manager said that meters "are the best thing for the market," another sighed, "They are coming, and we are going to deal with it" (Flannagan, 2002; Morrow, 2002).

A Nielsen people meter.

What television program's final episode attracted the largest audience ever for a single episode?

Ratings and Programming Strategies

When Nielsen research indicated that males in their late teens to early twenties, who are considered the most sought after group by advertisers, watched 12 percent less prime-time television in 2003 than in the year before, broadcast network executives knew it was time to take action. But they weren't sure of what action to take. They didn't know whether the 2003 viewing behavior was an anomaly or the beginning of a trend. Using other Nielsen data, it appears that as television viewing among young males had declined, video game usage had increased 21 percent and online instant messaging and game playing had jumped 50 percent.

The networks realize their challenge is to draw young males back to television with exciting interactive programming. Otherwise, they will just have to settle "for smaller aging audiences" (Goodale, 2003).

he or she is supposed to push whenever he or she begins and then ends watching television. The people meter records both what programs are being watched and who's watching them.

CHALLENGES OF GATHERING RADIO AND TELEVISION AUDIENCE NUMBERS　Ratings are based on *estimates* of who's using radio and television and are thus not absolutes (Webster & Lichty, 1991). Each method of measurement is limited in some way. And while ratings companies do their best to ensure gathering the most accurate data possible, there are still many concerns and criticisms over how audience data are collected.

Samples　One of the most serious concerns about ratings data is the sample of viewers and listeners whose media habits are monitored. It just isn't possible to survey the entire population, so a subset, or *sample,* of listeners and viewers is selected instead. Many critics contend that sample sizes are too small—that sampling 5,000 or so television viewers from the entire U.S. population doesn't produce accurate results. Others claim that the sample size is large enough as long as it represents all of the demographic groups within a population. In other words, in a survey area in which 30 percent of the people are elderly, diaries must be sent to a group of participants that includes that percentage of elderly people. Otherwise, the diaries won't be representative of the media use in that survey area.

Ratings companies make every attempt to ensure that samples accurately reflect the survey population and often mathematically weight samples to correct over- or underrepresentation of particular groups. Even so, critics insist that too few members from ethnic and other specific demographic groups are included in most samples, yielding an inaccurate picture of media use.

Location　People watch television and listen to the radio in more places than their homes, including bars and restaurants, hospitals, at work, on the beach, in hotels, and so on. But such media use is not always recorded. The television ratings companies have argued that out-of-home use represents only a small percentage of total viewing, but most radio listening does occur outside the home at work and in cars.

The Nielsen people meter is attached to the viewer's television set.

Accuracy   Ratings companies depend on participants to fill out diaries and use people meters correctly. Yet too many listeners and viewers fail to follow diary instructions, forget to record the stations they've listened to, and write down the wrong station or channel number. All of these mistakes lead to gathering inaccurate data and thus create an incomplete picture of media use and users.

Television-metering devices are also problematic. Although the meters record what is being watched, they can't automatically record who is watching. With people meters, viewers are instructed to push their ID buttons before and after each viewing session, but many forget to do so.

ZOOM IN   8.5

For more information about the challenges of audience measurement, see Module 1 at this site: http://edtech.tennessee.edu/~dob/harmon.html.

CAREER TRACKS

John Montuori   Television Account Executive

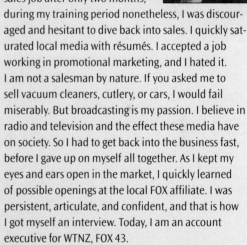

What are your primary responsibilities?

Working as an account executive for a broadcast station, my loyalty is twofold. Primarily, I was hired to sell advertising and generate revenue for my station. But in order to become a great rep, I devote myself to my clients and work to help their business grow. It is my job to create lucrative schedules and campaigns for my clients in an effort to saturate the market with a message regarding their product or service, while also meeting goals set by my station.

What was your first job in electronic media?

I was offered my first sales position before I received my diploma. I began selling for a rhythmic contemporary hits station in a very conservative market. Although the station was one of the highest rated in the city, most advertisers were afraid to attach their name to the station's edgy image. In my brief time there, I learned how to develop relationships with clients and sell them on numbers rather than format. My first step would be to sell myself as a reputable, honest, and hard-working executive. Once I gained their respect and faith, I would present them with the image of 60,000 listeners walking through their door, rather than the image the station portrayed. Unfortunately, in sales, success is not measured by how hard you work but how much money you have on the books. When the station failed to make budget for a few consecutive months, I was one of a few changes they chose to implement in an effort to preserve their format.

What led you to your present job?

After being laid off from my first sales job after only two months, during my training period nonetheless, I was discouraged and hesitant to dive back into sales. I quickly saturated local media with résumés. I accepted a job working in promotional marketing, and I hated it. I am not a salesman by nature. If you asked me to sell vacuum cleaners, cutlery, or cars, I would fail miserably. But broadcasting is my passion. I believe in radio and television and the effect these media have on society. So I had to get back into the business fast, before I gave up on myself all together. As I kept my eyes and ears open in the market, I quickly learned of possible openings at the local FOX affiliate. I was persistent, articulate, and confident, and that is how I got myself an interview. Today, I am an account executive for WTNZ, FOX 43.

What advice would you have for students who might want a job like yours?

If you feel that you belong in sales and you have the slightest doubt, you need to develop a tough skin, a poker face, and a self-confidence that radiates through the unexpected. People will beat you down in this industry. You have to expect it. Your goal is not necessarily to always fight back but to be able to stand back up when it's over, shake the dust off, and move forward. You must also be observant. You will come across a wide variety of co-workers and clients. Listen, watch, and absorb everything—good and bad. Every lesson is a lesson well learned.

The Internet

Some of the data collection methods used by the television and radio industries are also used to measure Internet audiences, and new methods have been developed specifically for the medium, as well. As with any medium, online advertisers are concerned with attracting the most eyeballs for their money. However, they face unique challenges in buying online space, figuring the number of users who saw their ads or clicked on a banner, and reaching their target audience—those people most likely to buy their products. Website operators struggle to get a clear picture of their consumers so they can convince advertisers to buy space on their sites.

ONLINE RATINGS DATA AND MEASUREMENT   A number of companies are in the business of supplying websites and advertisers with online ratings and customer profiles. Arbitron has extended its services to include Internet audience measurement, and other companies have emerged, such as Nielsen NetRatings (from a merger of Nielsen Media Research and NetRatings, a former online-only audience ratings company) and ComScore Media Metrix. Referred to as **third-party monitors**, these services employ various auditing techniques and audience-measuring methods, such as monitoring the number of times a banner ad is clicked on; providing site traffic reports by day, week, month and monitoring other website activities; and developing customer profiles. Websites use this information to sell space to advertisers, and advertisers use this information to find the best sites on which to place their banner ads.

ZOOM IN   8.6

Learn more about online ratings data by visiting these sites:

- Nielsen Net Ratings   www.netratings.com
- Arbitron   http://arbitron.com/webcast_ratings/home.htm
- ComScore Media Metrix   www.comscore.com

CHALLENGES OF GATHERING INTERNET AUDIENCE NUMBERS   The biggest challenge faced by websites and online advertisers is the lack of standardized data collection methods. Third-party monitors may use different techniques and data collection methods to

---

FYI

Measurement Differences

Back in 2001, when Jupiter Media Metrix was still in the business of measuring Web audiences, it included exposure to pop-up and pop-under ads as a website visit. However, Nielsen Media Metrix didn't count either ad type as a visit. As a consequence of such measurement differences, the number of visitors to sites that posted a large number of pop-ups would be greater if pop-ups were included than if they were excluded. In the example below, Jupiter ranked X10.com as the fourth most visited site, but Nielsen ranked it as the one-hundred-sixteenth most popular online venue.

JUNE 2001

WEBSITE VISITORS PER JUPITER MEDIA METRIX (includes pop-up ads)		WEBSITE VISITORS PER NIELSEN MEDIA METRIX (excludes pop-up ads)	
1. AOL Time Warner	72.5 mil.	1. AOL Time Warner	76.9 mil.
2. Microsoft	61.5	2. Yahoo!	68.1
3. Yahoo!	59.9	3. MSN	62.7
4. X10.com	34.2	4. Microsoft	39.4
5. Terra Lycos	33.3	5. Terra Lycos	32.5
		116. X10.com	3.8

Source: Hansell, 2001.

M*A*S*H at $450,000 per ad—$50,000 more than for a Super Bowl ad.

arrive at their figures, which can lead to contradictory and confusing reports. For example, they may use different metering techniques, select their samples differently, and have different ways of counting website visitors. Some may count duplicated visitors (for example, one person who returns to a site five times will be counted as five visitors), while others may count only the number of unduplicated visitors (for example, one person who visits a site five times will be counted as one visitor). The unit of analysis may also be defined differently from one measurement service to another. For example, an *Internet user* may be defined as "someone who has used the Internet at least 10 times" or "someone who has been online in the last six months." These variations can yield very different results.

Several associations and organizations are taking the lead in establishing Web auditing and measurement standards. The Coalition for Advertising Supported Information and Entertainment (CASIE), the Internet Advertising Bureau (IAB), and the Advertising Research Foundation (ARF), along with several third-party monitors, are at the forefront of developing new and effective means of gathering audience data and attempting to standardize definitions of terms. At the beginning of 2002, the IAB, along with eight prominent Web publishers and several advertising technology firms, issued voluntary guidelines for online advertising measurement. The IAB claims the guidelines will reduce data discrepancies, but their effectiveness will depend on whether they are followed by marketers and measurement companies (Zipern, 2002).

Going online at an Internet café is convenient and enjoyable for many people.

ZOOM IN 8.7

Learn more about gathering Internet audience data at these sites:

* CASIE   **www.casie.org**
* Internet Advertising Bureau   **www.iab.net**
* Advertising Research Foundation   **www.arfsite.org**

Calculating and Reporting Radio and Television Audience Numbers

Means of Calculating

Once ratings companies have gathered audience numbers and know how many people are watching television or listening to the radio, they conduct more meaningful analyses. For example, just knowing that 10,000 people listen to Station A doesn't have much meaning unless it's considered in the context of the total audience size. If you know that 10,000 people listen to Station A, does that mean a lot of people listen or just a few? The answer depends on the market size. If in a market of 100,000 people, 10,000 listen to Station A, then that station has captured 10 percent of the population. However, if Station A is in a market of 200,000 population, it has only drawn 5 percent of the population. Audience numbers are put in context by calculating figures such as ratings, shares, average quarter hours, and cumes.

RATINGS AND SHARES   Radio and television both use ratings and shares, and the mathematical computations for both media are identical. Calculating ratings and shares is not as difficult as you may think. Ratings and shares are simply percentages that, for the sake of simplicity, are usually expressed as whole numbers.

A **rating** is an estimate of the number of listeners or viewers who are listening to a radio station or watching a television program divided by the number of listeners or viewers in a population that have a radio or a television. Another way to think of a rating is that 1 rating point equals 1 percent of the households in the market area that have a television set. A **share** is an estimate of the number of listeners or viewers who are

Anna's Losing Weight

E! Entertainment's *Anna Nicole Smith* lost 2.5 ratings points (or 59.5 percent of its viewers) from the first- to second-season debuts. In other words, the program debuted with a 4.2 rating, but at the beginning of the second season, it only earned a 1.7 rating.

Source: Broadcasting & Cable, March 10, 2003.

listening to a radio station or watching a television program divided by the number of listeners or viewers who are listening to radio or watching television. Thus, the only difference between a rating and a share is the group that's being measured. Ratings consider everyone with a radio or television, whereas shares only consider those people who are actually listening to the radio or watching television at a given time. Consider these formulas:

$$\text{Radio ratings} = \frac{\text{Number of people listening to a station}}{\text{Number of people in a population with radios}}$$

$$\text{Radio shares} = \frac{\text{Number of people listening to a station}}{\text{Number of people in a population listening to radio}}$$

$$\text{Television ratings} = \frac{\text{Number of households watching a particular program or channel}}{\text{Number of households in a population with televisions}}$$

$$\text{Television shares} = \frac{\text{Number of households watching a particular program or channel}}{\text{Number of households in a population watching television}}$$

Now consider some specific examples:

RADIO RATINGS

Station A	$\dfrac{500 \text{ listeners}}{5{,}000 \text{ people with radios}} =$	.1 or 10%, expressed as a 10 rating (or 10 rating points)
Station B	$\dfrac{400 \text{ listeners}}{5{,}000 \text{ people with radios}} =$	.08 or 8%, expressed as an 8 rating (or 8 rating points)
Not listening to radio	$\dfrac{4{,}100 \text{ nonlisteners}}{5{,}000 \text{ people with radios}} =$	.82 or 82% of the market
Total population	5,000	

RADIO SHARES

Station A	$\dfrac{500 \text{ listeners}}{900 \text{ people listening to radio}} =$	.555 or 55.6%, expressed as a 56 rating (or 56 rating points)
Station B	$\dfrac{400 \text{ listeners}}{900 \text{ people listening to radio}} =$	.444 or 44.4%, expressed as a 44 rating (or 44 rating points)
Not listening to radio	Nonlisteners are *not* considered in the share calculation.	
Total listeners	900	
Total population	5,000	

TELEVISION RATINGS

Program A	$\dfrac{500 \text{ viewing households}}{5{,}000 \text{ households with televisions}} =$	.1 or 10%, expressed as a 10 rating (or 10 rating points)
Program B	$\dfrac{400 \text{ viewing households}}{5{,}000 \text{ households with televisions}} =$	.08 or 8%, expressed as an 8 rating (or 8 rating points)
Not watching TV	$\dfrac{4{,}100 \text{ nonviewing households}}{5{,}000 \text{ households with televisions}} =$	.82 or 82% of the market
Total population	5,000	

FOX at the Top of the Heap

For the first time in its 20 years on the air, FOX was the top-rated network in March 2003 among 18- to 49-year-old viewers:

NETWORK RATINGS

FOX = 5.6
NBC = 4.8
CBS = 4.2
ABC = 4.0

During this time frame, FOX programming (mostly due to *Joe Millionaire* and *American Idol*) was attracting more 18- to 49-year-olds than the other broadcast networks. To regain their lost audience, the other networks will have to air programs that appeal to that age group.

Source: Albiniak, 2003.

TELEVISION SHARES

Station A $$\frac{500 \text{ viewing households}}{900 \text{ households watching television}} = \begin{array}{l}.555 \text{ or } 55.6\%, \\ \text{expressed as a } 56 \\ \text{rating (or } 56 \text{ rating} \\ \text{points)}\end{array}$$

Station B $$\frac{400 \text{ viewing households}}{900 \text{ households watching television}} = \begin{array}{l}.444 \text{ or } 44.4\%, \\ \text{expressed as a } 44 \\ \text{rating (} 44 \text{ rating} \\ \text{points)}\end{array}$$

Not watching TV   Nonviewers are *not* included in the share calculation.

Total viewers   900

Total population   5,000

Notice that when ratings are calculated, all members of the population who have radios or televisions are included in the calculation, even if they're *not* listening or watching. When shares are figured, however, only members of the population who *are* listening or watching are included in the calculation. Shares, therefore, are always larger than ratings because they include a smaller segment of listeners or viewers, rather than the entire population. In the unlikely event that every person in the market watched or listened to the same show, then the rating and share would be equal.

You can see from the examples that radio and television ratings and shares are calculated in the same way but that radio measures individual listeners (**people using radio**, or **PUR**) and television measures households with televisions (**households using television**, or **HUT**). Since most households now have more than one television and household members are increasingly watching television separately, the HUT measure is giving way to **people using television (PUT)**, a measure that may be more valuable to the media industry.

Because radio runs few programs as such and because radio ratings points are so small, shares are used more heavily to measure and compare station listenership. Radio also heavily depends on average quarter hour and cume measurements, which will be discussed in the following sections.

Television relies on both ratings and shares as its primary measures of audience viewership. Ratings and shares indicate how many people are watching programs and tuning in to local stations. Comparisons are then made between programs and stations, and programming decisions are made based on ratings and shares. Television also relies on average quarter hour and cume measures but to a far lesser degree than does radio.

AVERAGE QUARTER HOUR   Radio also depends on **average quarter hour (AQH)** measurements to assess audience listenership. In almost all markets, there are more radio stations than television stations; therefore, radio station ratings are generally lower than television station ratings because there are more radio stations competing for the same listeners. To compensate for lower rating points, radio measures audience in terms of average quarter hour.

There are several AQH measures: average quarter hour *persons*, average quarter hour *rating*, and average quarter hour *share*. Arbitron defines **AQH persons** as "the average number of persons estimated to have listened to a station for a minimum of five minutes during any quarter-hour in a time period" ("Arbitron Radio Market Report,"

A Point to Remember

One ratings point represents 1,067,000 households, or 1 percent of the nation's estimated 106.7 million television homes.

Friends

How many viewers said goodbye to their *Friends* by tuning in to the final episode on May 6, 2004? And how did the viewership of the final episode of *Friends* compare to that of other popular programs?

FINAL EPISODE	VIEWERS	YEAR
M*A*S*H	105 million	1983
Cheers	80.4 million	1993
Seinfeld	76.2 million	1998
Friends	52.5 million	2004

Source: DeMoraes, 2004.

2002). AQH persons are duplicated listeners who can be counted up to four times an hour. For example, if you listen to Station A for at least 5 minutes during the 1:00 P.M. to 1:15 P.M. quarter hour, you're counted as a listener, and if you listen during the 1:15 to 1:30 quarter hour, you're counted again.

AQH rating and share are calculated as follows ("Arbitron Radio Market Report," 2002):

AQH rating = (AQH persons/Survey area population) × 100

AQH share = (AQH persons/Listeners in survey area population) × 100

CUMULATIVE PERSONS   Whereas AQH persons represents *duplicated* listeners, **cumulative persons** (or **cume**) represents *unduplicated* listeners. Arbitron defines *cume* as "the estimated number of different people who listened to a station for a minimum of five minutes in a quarter-hour within a reported daypart. No matter how long the listening occurred, each person is counted only once" ("Arbitron Radio Market Report," 2002). For example, if you listen to Station A for at least 5 minutes during the 1:00 P.M. to 1:15 P.M. quarter hour, you're counted as a listener, but if you also listen during the 1:15 to 1:30 quarter hour, you're not counted again.

Cume rating and share are calculated as follows ("Arbitron Radio Market Report," 2002):

Cume rating = (Cume persons/Survey area population) × 100

Cume share = (Cume persons/Listeners in survey area population) × 100

Although cumes are more commonly used to assess radio listenership, household television meters can also produce person cumes to measure program viewership. Since many prime-time television shows air once a week, four-week cumes are sometimes reported to assess how many people watch a program over a month-long period (Webster, Phalen, & Lichty, 2000).

ZOOM IN   8.8

- Practice doing rating, share, AQH, and radio cume calculations in Module 2 at http://edtech. tennessee.edu/~dob/harmon.html.

- The "Arbitron Radio Market Report Reference Guide" is an excellent guide to understanding and using audience measurement estimates. View it online at www.arbitron.com/downloads/purplebook.pdf.

Means of Reporting

RADIO: ARBITRON   Arbitron data are reported in a standardized ratings report; the company also tailors reports for the specialized needs of its clients. The most commonly used report is the **radio market report**, which provides radio audience estimates for each ratings period as well as market information (station and population profiles) and audience information. Rating, share, cume, and AQH numbers are broken out by age, gender, and daypart. (Dayparts are discussed later in this chapter; see pp. 188–189.) Eyeing these figures gives station management a good idea of how their station compares with other stations in the market. Whereas one station may be strongly rated among men, another may draw more women. Or a station may have strong ratings in one daypart but be weak in another. One station might outdraw the 25- to 54-year-old crowd, while another might dominate the teen listening group.

TELEVISION: NIELSEN SERVICES   Like Arbitron, Nielsen provides several standard reports and customizes others for its clients. Here is a sampling of Nielsen's reports:

- The **Nielsen television index (NTI)** provides metered audience estimates for all national broadcast television programs and national syndicated programs. Nielsen breaks out station and program rating and share figures by age and gender. When

NBC, FOX, ABC, CBS, WB, and UPN.

KNOXVILLE, TN

WK1 10/31-11/06 WK2 11/07-11/13 WK3 11/14-11/20 WK4 11/21-11/27

FRIDAY 8:00PM - 11:00PM

A page from an NSI ratings book.

you pick up a magazine or newspaper and read a report about the ratings earned by *The Simpsons*, *ER*, or *Law & Order*, the information has come from the NTI. These program ratings are used to compare and rank shows against one another. If a program is consistently rated poorly, there's a good chance it won't be on the air for very long.

- The **Nielsen station index (NSI)** provides local market television-viewing data through diaries and continuous metered overnight measurement. Metered information is processed overnight, and a report is sent to the station the next morning. Television

ZOOM IN   8.9

See how to read a ratings book and do interactive exercises in Module 2 at http://edtech.tennessee.edu/~dob/harmon.html.

What was the average price for a 30-second spot on ER during the 2002–2003 television season?

executives rely on these **overnights** for immediate feedback on how their programs and networks rate compared to their rivals. Overnights are often used to make quick programming decisions to beat out the competition. NSI provides rating and share figures for programs that air on local affiliates, such as newscasts, as well as for network shows.

CABLE RATINGS   Nielsen Media Research measures viewership of cable, pay cable, VCR, DVD, interactive television, and other new television technology through meters and diaries. Prior to the proliferation of cable networks and thus cable subscribers, ABC, NBC, and CBS vied for the largest share of the audience. Now, hundreds of cable networks compete against each other and against the big three for the audience's attention.

Nielsen reports cable ratings and shares in its **Nielsen home video index (NHI)**, which, like its other reports, breaks out figures by age, gender, daypart, and cable network. Ratings for cable programs and networks are collected like those for broadcast ratings via diaries and meters, but cable ratings are reported separately and interpreted differently from broadcast ratings.

As noted earlier, the large number of cable networks has diluted the viewing audience, and when coupled with spotty coverage (as not all cable systems carry the same cable networks), the result has been lower ratings than earned by the broadcast networks. For example, the highest-rated cable network for the week of October 22 to 28, 2001, was TNT, with a 1.9 rating. But for that same week, CBS led the pack of broadcast and cable networks with a 9.9 rating, which is nearly five times higher than TNT's rating ("Big Pipe Cable Rankings," 2001; "BroadcastWatch," 2001). The same ratings discrepancies hold true for cable network and broadcast network programs. In fairness, cable program and broadcast program ratings are interpreted differently. For example, a 3.0 rating for a cable network program is considered quite good, but it would be considered quite bad for a broadcast network program.

The newer broadcast networks—PAX-TV, UPN, and WB—face some of the same ratings challenges as the cable networks. They, too, reach a smaller audience to begin with and so can't compete with the larger, more established broadcast networks. During the week of October 22 to 28, 2001, WB's rating was 4.2, UPN's was 2.6, and PAX-TV's was 1.0. While WB and UPN received higher ratings than any of the cable networks, PAX-TV's ratings were lower than those of the top 11 cable networks for the week. Since the ratings for these three new broadcast networks were expected to be lower than those of the established networks, WB's 4.2 rating was considered quite strong under the circumstances ("BroadcastWatch," 2001).

TOP 10 Cable Network Ratings: October 27 to November 2, 2003	
NETWORK	RATING
1. Nickelodeon	1.2
2. TNT	.9
3. Lifetime	.9
4. Disney	.9
5. ESPN	.9
6. Cartoon	.8
7. HBO	.7
8. USA	.6
9. FOX News	.6
10. MTV	.5

Source: "Top 10 Cable," 2003.

ZOOM IN   8.10
Learn more about the Nielsen home video index at www.nielsenmedia.com. Click on "Services."

ZOOM IN   8.11
See the top-rated cable programs of the week at www.pazsaz.com/topcable.html.

When Audience Numbers Aren't Enough

In addition to studying media use, Arbitron, Nielsen Media Research, and other companies are also interested in studying media consumers. It's important to know both how people use the media and who those media users are. For example, snowboard advertisers want to reach young, athletic, daring individuals, and diaper manufacturers want to aim for parents. Advertisers reach their target consumers through the media and thus need to match up with a medium, a station, or program that is used by their target market.

For the radio, television, and online industries to really know their audiences, they need to look at them in ways that numbers can't provide. For example, ratings and shares may reveal which programs people watch or listen to most frequently, but they don't tell why viewers prefer one program over another, whether people prefer certain characters on a program, or why and when they like to listen to certain types of music. To find out answers to questions that numbers alone can't answer, the media industry employs specialized types of research such as music research, pilot and episode testing, television quotient data, and online consumer profiling.

CAREER TRACKS

Reggie Murphy   Marketing Research Manager, USA Today

What are your primary responsibilities?

Responsible for the day-to-day operations of the marketing research department. Manage and counsel an analytical staff in conducting research analysis and developing marketing strategies for the *USA Today* brand, utilizing both proprietary and syndicated research as well as quantitative and qualitative methodologies. Develop and manage all phases of audience research analysis and interpretation. Coordinate survey questionnaire development, conduct data analysis using multivariate statistics (with SPSS), manage focus group/ethnographic research by coordinating with research facilities, moderating/interviewing, and analyzing data. Conduct analysis of syndicated research, such as MRI, MMR, Intelliquest, and Nielsen NetRatings. Conduct proprietary research using research vendors, such as TNS, Insight Express, MORI, and BIGresearch.

Evaluate and provide resources that assist the advertising, circulation, and editorial staffs in strengthening *USA Today's* position in the competitive media environment. Develop the skills of analytical staff as they provide *USA Today's* management and sales representatives with market analysis to support them in implementing sales strategies.

What was your first job in electronic media?

My first "real" job was with a classic rock radio station in Knoxville, Tennessee—WIMZ-FM. I worked as an account salesperson.

What led you to your present job?

After working for two years in my previous job in Iowa, I wanted to move closer to the East Coast and move into a managerial position. I made several contacts in the research business and was referred to *USA Today* after an opening became available in the marketing research department.

What advice would you have for students who might want a job like yours?

1. Learn everything you can about all media (radio, television, Internet, newspaper, magazine, etc.)
2. Try to do as many internships as possible in sales, research, or marketing and promotions.
3. Go to conventions/business meetings and meet people in the media business—Network, Network, Network! Keep in touch with the people you meet. Solicit their assistance when you begin your job search.
4. Be smart, be aggressive, and do not become discouraged if the right job does not come quickly. Many positions in research require two to three years of experience, so pay your dues and the right job will come.
5. Remember that the biggest room in the world is the room for improvement. So, always continue learning and developing your skills.

Music Research

Used by radio stations, music research is used to assess radio listeners' musical likes and dislikes. As such, it is one of several tools used to determine playlists. Music research is either conducted over the telephone or in an auditorium-like setting. Researchers either call a sample of listeners or bring them together (usually hundreds) in one location to play song **hooks,** or 5 to 20 seconds each of various songs. Participants are asked to evaluate how much and why they like or dislike each song. Sometimes, smaller **focus groups** of listeners, usually less than 20, are convened to listen and discuss their preferences in depth.

Music testing is an expensive venture but often well worth the effort. It gives insight into people's music preferences, which guides station formats and play lists.

Television Program Testing

As you read in Chapter 6 on programming, television programs are subject to rigorous concept testing before they make it to the air—if they ever do make it that far. Even after programs are on the air the testing isn't over.

New programs and episodes of current programs are tested to gauge audience reactions to the plot, characters, humor, and other program elements and to the overall program itself. The test audience watches perhaps the pilot episode of a new program or the season finale of an existing show, and each person indicates his or her level of like or dislike, along with other factors, at any time during the show by turning a dial from 1 to 100 on his or her test meter: 1 if he or she hates the show and up to 100 if he or she loves the show. The meter records the viewer's reaction every time he or she changes the dial. Executives and writers rely on these screening data for content decisions. If, for example, most viewers move their dials down to 10 after hearing a joke's punch line, the program's writers may delete it.

On a broader scale, test meter information is matched up with demographic characteristics—such as age, gender, education, and income—for information about what types of viewers prefer what types of programs. For instance, the data may show that males over the age of 40 who have high incomes and are sports minded prefer action-oriented programs, that women between the ages of 18 and 34 prefer situation comedies more than police dramas, or that children prefer shows with teen characters. Given this information, the producers may add a character or a storyline that will appeal to a certain type of viewer.

FYI

Television City

The newest and perhaps one of the most visible testing centers opened in 2001 in Las Vegas. CBS's Television City Research Center is housed within the MGM Grand Hotel and attracts tens of thousands of individuals from all over the United States, who volunteer to rate programs. CBS and Viacom partnered with A. C. Nielsen Entertainment to provide the testing equipment and audience feedback reports. Basically, volunteers line up and, in groups of about 20 to 25 each, are ushered into one of six studios to watch new program pilots as well as episodes of existing shows from CBS, MTV, Nickelodeon, and other Viacom networks. Each screening lasts for about an hour (about 45 minutes to watch a commercial-free program and a 15-minute follow-up survey) ("See Point Kiosks," 2001).

Learn how you can be a member of the program test audience at www.vegas.com/attractions/on_the_strip/televisioncity.

FYI

Women Viewers Are Key to Sharon Osbourne

After two weeks on the air, Telepictures' syndicated talk program *The Sharon Osbourne Show* maintained a 1.5 household rating, mainly among women 18 to 34, a group that's very important to the success of daytime programs. If *Sharon* can hold this demographic, there's a good chance the program will stay on the air.

Source: Pursell, 2003.

TOP 5

New Broadcast Network Shows: 2003

During the first two weeks of the 2003 broadcast network season, these new shows were off to a good start. But did they sustain their ratings? As of May 2004, only *Coupling* had been cancelled, despite the fact that it was initially a highly ranked show.

PROGRAM	RATING	SHARE	RANK
1. *Coupling*	7.8	15	5
2. *Two and a Half Men*	5.9	14	14
3. *I'm with Her*	5.7	16	17
4. *Las Vegas*	5.0	13	23
5. *Hope and Faith*	4.7	15	24

Source: "Top New Shows," 2003.

Friends, at an average $455,000 per spot.

Television Quotient Data

Marketing Evaluations/TVQ, Inc., is an independent audience research company that assesses viewers' feelings about programs and performers. **Television quotient data (TVQs)** focus on viewers' perceptions of programs and stars and are often used to supplement Nielsen ratings and other data. TVQ findings are collected through mail and telephone surveys, diaries, and panel discussions that examine the familiarity and popularity of programs and actors. A low TVQ score could mean the death of a character, and a high TVQ score could shift a secondary character to a more prominent role.

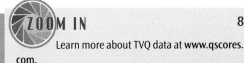

ZOOM IN   8.12

Learn more about TVQ data at **www.qscores.com**.

Online Consumer Profiling

Knowing the number of people who see a banner ad or visit a website isn't enough information to make the best advertising sale or buy. Advertisers and website managers also need to know who their customers are, what they like, how they spend their leisure time, and other personal characteristics.

The use of **cookies** is one of the most common methods of collecting online audience data. A cookie is a type of software that allows a website operator to store information about users and track their movements throughout the website. The software essentially installs itself on website visitors' hard drives, often without their knowledge or permission. The cookie creates a personal file that the company then uses to customize online information to target specific individuals (Kaye & Medoff, 2001).

The use of cookies leaves a bad taste in many people's mouths because they collect personal data that users don't always intend to give. Consumer profiling is under fire from advocacy groups, the Federal Trade Commission (FTC), legislators, and Internet users who are concerned that personal information is being collected without direct consent or knowledge. These groups are calling for sites to notify users when information is collected and to offer users a way to block the process. Profiling proponents claim consumers like cookies because they get banner ads that they're interested in and that if given the chance, hardly anyone would block the profiling function.

Some sites limit the use of cookies and rely more on voluntary surveys, in which users are asked to provide demographics and other personal data. Many users are happy to fill out these surveys, especially if they get a discounted price or some other reward for doing so.

How Consumer Profiling (Cookies) Works

A website usually hires a private company to collect and store personal data on its server. As customers travel to and within the site, the server stores their online surfing and other activities and places a cookie on each user's PC. Let's say you go to anybookstore.com and look for a book about the history of golfing. Anybookstore.com and its server company will place a cookie on your computer. So, the next time you access anybookstore.com, you may see a banner ad that pertains to golfing—perhaps for an online store where you can buy clubs. If you click on the banner and go to that golfing store, another cookie will be placed on your PC, and you may get a banner ad from anybookstore.com advertising a new book about golfing. Basically, servers remember where you've traveled, so websites know how to customize their sites and banner ads to your interests.

Translating Audience Information to Sales

Media outlets develop audience profiles based on audience numbers (such as ratings and shares), audience information (such as age, ethnicity, gender, and other personal characteristics), and lifestyle preferences (such as program and music likes and dislikes). Once an audience profile has been established and the media outlet knows who listens to its station or watches its programs, how it rates in the market, and what its most popular programs are, it can establish commercial rates for its airtime and begin selling its audience to advertisers. Again, airtime is nothing but blank seconds unless someone is listening to or watching the spot; thus, it's really the media *audience* that's being sold.

If a radio station knows that it has a strong rating among women between the ages of 25 and 49 who enjoy sports and especially golf, it has a compelling case to make to a golf or general sports store or fitness center. The station can demonstrate to the retailer that it reaches the retailer's customers.

Not only are advertisers interested in buying media that reach their target consumers, but they also want to know how they can reach the largest number of target consumers for the lowest cost. Although the price of commercial time is largely based on program and station rating points, advertisers often need more information when planning a media buy. Advertisers compare the costs of reaching their target audience using various stations and types of media. For example, perhaps area teens listen to three radio stations and also watch a television affiliate's Saturday morning line-up. Advertisers need to have some way to compare the price of airtime on each of the three radio stations and the television program. To do so, they often rely on figures such as cost per thousand, gross ratings points, and cost per point:

> **ZOOM IN**   8.13
> Try using online CPM calculators at Web Digest for Marketers: **http://wdfm.com/advertising.html**.

- **Cost per thousand (CPM)** figures are generally used to sell print and broadcast media, but Web publishers also use this traditional ad rate structure to sell online space. CPMs are one of the most widely used means of comparing the costs of advertising across different media, such as television and radio. Many people often wonder why *cost per thousand* is abbreviated *CPM* instead of *CPT*. It's because *thousand* is derived from the Latin word *mil*, which means "one-thousandth of an inch." Here's the formula:

  CPM = (Cost of a spot or schedule/Number of individuals or households) × 1,000

- **Gross rating points (GRPs)** are the total of all ratings achieved by a commercial schedule. Put more simply, it is the number of spots or commercials (*frequency*) aired in a schedule multiplied by the average rating (*reach*):

  Gross rating points = Average rating point × Number of spots

> **ZOOM IN**   8.14
> Module 3 at **http://edtech.tennessee.edu/ ~dob/harmon.html** has interactive exercises for calculating CPMs, CPPs, and GRPs.

- **Cost per point (CPP)** is the cost of reaching 1 percent (1 rating point) of a specified market. The CPP gives advertisers a way to compare the costs of rating points in various markets. The CPP can be determined using this formula:

  CPP = Cost of schedule/Gross rating points

Buying and Selling

Radio and Television

DAYPARTS   Radio is usually sold by **dayparts**, which are designated parts of a programming day. Radio breaks out the 24-hour clock into these five segments (Eastern standard time):

Morning drive	6:00 A.M. to 10:00 A.M.
Midday	10:00 A.M. to 3:00 P.M.
Afternoon drive	3:00 P.M. to 7:00 P.M.
Evening	7:00 P.M. to midnight
Overnight	Midnight to 6:00 A.M.

All in the Family, from 1972–1976.

Television is also sold by dayparts but more commonly on a specific program basis. Here are the standard television dayparts (Eastern standard time):

Early morning	6:00 A.M. to 9:00 A.M.	
Morning	9:00 A.M. to noon	⎫ Daytime*
Afternoon	Noon to 4:00 P.M.	⎭
Early fringe	4:00 P.M. to 6:00 P.M.	
Early evening	6:00 P.M. to 7:00 P.M.	
Prime access	7:00 P.M. to 8:00 P.M.	
Prime time	8:00 P.M. to 11:00 P.M.	
Late fringe	11:00 P.M. to 11:30 P.M.	
Late night	11:30 P.M. to 2:00 A.M.	
Overnight	2:00 A.M. to 6:00 A.M.	

*9:00 A.M. to 4:00 P.M. is also known as daytime.

PRICING AIRTIME   Radio and television stations set base prices for their commercial spots. Some stations, especially television, don't give out their base rates to their advertisers but rather use them as a starting point for negotiation. With the availability of new computer software, many television and radio stations have maximized their revenues through **yield management**, in which commercial prices change each week or even each day, depending on the availability of airtime. If there's high demand to advertise on a particular program, the last advertiser to commit may have to pay a higher price than the first advertiser. The station may also sell a high-demand time slot to whichever advertiser is willing to pay the highest price.

Radio prices are set up on grid-like charts that list the cost of commercial time for five various dayparts, each of which is classified by the cost of time. In order of cost, the most expensive is Class AAA, followed by Class AA, Class A, Class B, and down to Class C, the lowest priced. Since most advertisers don't want to buy what they perceive is second-rate time, some stations don't even designate a Class B or Class C time; some stations even prefer to classify their rates by daypart instead of by class.

Television relies on dayparts and program ratings to determine commercial costs. For example, a commercial spot aired during daytime will cost less than the same spot aired during prime time. Further, the cost of commercial time during a daypart may vary with the popularity of the program. The cost of running a 30-second spot during a top-rated prime-time program will cost more than airing the same spot during a lower-rated prime-time show.

FIXED BUYS   Radio and television stations charge higher rates for **fixed buys**, in which advertisers specify what time they want their commercials to run. Perhaps a fast-food restaurant wants to dominate the 11:00 A.M. to 1:00 P.M. period and thus wants its commercials broadcast every 15 minutes starting at noon. Most stations, especially radio stations, can accommodate these specific needs, but they charge a premium price for doing so.

Careful planning and buying doesn't guarantee that commercials will run during agreed-upon times or that the audience will be as large as promised. Suppose a radio station inadvertently runs a spot at the wrong time or a television network

---

overestimates the number of viewers it anticipated would watch a particular program, but the station has already charged the advertiser for the commercial time. In these and other situations in which the terms of advertising agreements are not met, stations and networks offer **make-goods** as compensation, which usually consist of free commercial time or future discounts. In some cases, the network or station will simply return payment.

RUN OF SCHEDULE   One of the most common discounted buys is called **run of schedule (ROS)**. In this type of buy, the advertiser and the salesperson agree on the number of times a commercial is going to air, but the station decides when to broadcast the commercial, depending on available time. For example, on radio, instead of purchasing 5 spots in Class AAA time, 10 in Class AA time, and 10 in Class B time, the advertiser is offered a discounted rate for the package of 25 spots, and the station will air them during whatever time classes are available. In many cases, ROS benefits the advertiser, who may end up getting more spots on the air during prime dayparts than it actually paid for or otherwise could afford. Television ROS works similarly to radio, except that spots are rotated by daypart, rather than by time classification.

FREQUENCY DISCOUNTS   Radio and television stations are willing to offer **frequency discounts** when advertisers agree to air their commercials many times during a given period, such as one month. Advertisers who buy a large number of spots reduce their cost per commercial, and the more commercial time they buy, the bigger the discount per spot. For example, suppose an advertiser could buy 10 30-second spots at $200 each for a total cost of $2,000. But if the advertiser agrees to run the ad 20 times instead of 10

CAREER TRACKS

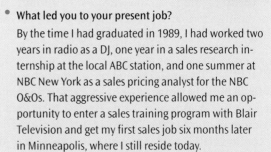

Trey Fabacher   Television Station Manager

What are your primary responsibilities?
I am currently the station manager for Viacom/CBS-owned WCCO-TV in Minneapolis, Minnesota. I oversee the sales, programming, and research operations and also participate in the direction of the entire TV station.

What was your first job in electronic media?
In my 14 years since graduation from the University of Tennessee, I have taken a progressive sales track from account executive to national sales manager, local sales manager, general sales manager, and now station manager, always focusing on servicing our clients and the overall sales performance. My first job in broadcasting was as an overnight radio DJ in Lafayette, Los Angeles, so I can really say that I started my career in the graveyard. I was able to create spec spots for salespeople, which gave me my first taste of sales. From that point, I knew I wanted to sell media, and the Broadcasting Department at the University of Tennessee exposed me to the connections to make that happen. Through various scholarships and intern

programs, I was able to make the proper connections to get a foot in the door and demonstrate my abilities.

What led you to your present job?
By the time I had graduated in 1989, I had worked two years in radio as a DJ, one year in a sales research internship at the local ABC station, and one summer at NBC New York as a sales pricing analyst for the NBC O&Os. That aggressive experience allowed me an opportunity to enter a sales training program with Blair Television and get my first sales job six months later in Minneapolis, where I still reside today.

What advice would you have for students who might want a job like yours?
This business is awesome, and real-world experience is very important in getting started. But more important is a dedicated work ethic to learning and growing. You have to be focused on success, and once you get a taste of broadcasting, there will be no looking back.

times, the station may lower the cost per spot from $200 to $125 for a total of $2,500. So, for an extra $500, the advertiser has doubled the number of commercial spots. Other frequency discounts might include six-month or yearly deals or other longer-term advertising agreements.

BARTERING   Some radio and television commercial time is **bartered,** rather than sold. Also known as *trade* or *trade-out,* bartering basically involves trading airtime in exchange for goods or services. For example, instead of charging a promoter to advertise an upcoming concert, a station may exchange the airtime for tickets of equal value. Or a station in need of office furniture may air a local office furniture store's spots in exchange for desks and chairs.

COOPERATIVE ADVERTISING   Radio and television **cooperative (co-op) advertising** is a special arrangement between a product manufacturer and a retailer; namely, a manufacturer will reimburse a retailer for a portion of the cost of advertising the manufacturer's product. For example, Sony may reimburse a local retailer for promoting Sony televisions during the retailer's commercials. Co-op agreements vary, depending on the manufacturer, time of year, new product rollouts, previous year sales, and other factors. For example, Sony may have a 3 percent of sales co-op agreement with a retailer. If the local retailer sells $100,000 worth of Sony television sets, then Sony will reimburse the retailer $3,000 of its advertising expenditure that was spent promoting Sony televisions.

Co-op agreements are often very specific and require close attention to detail in order to get sufficiently reimbursed. Many stations hire a co-op coordinator, whose primary responsibility is to help the station's advertisers track co-op opportunities. The more reimbursement advertisers receive from manufacturers, the more commercial time they can afford to purchase.

LOCAL DISCOUNTS   Radio and television stations often offer discounts to local businesses. National chains, for example, benefit from reaching a station's entire market area. McDonald's may have 20 or more restaurants in a market, any of which might be visited by the station's listeners. In contrast, a local business, such as a produce market with one store on one side of town, will probably only draw shoppers who live in close proximity and thus doesn't want to pay to broadcast to the opposite side of town. Because a large part of the station's audience may be useless to the produce market, the station may offer the market discounted airtime.

Cable Television

Selling commercial time on cable television follows a slightly different process from selling network or affiliate time. Cable network programming is transmitted through a local cable company, such as Comcast.

There are hundreds of cable program networks, and most cable companies provide subscribers with at least 50 to 60 cable networks plus the major broadcast networks. Because there are so many more cable networks than broadcast networks, the audience for each cable network is much smaller; thus, the price for commercial time is lower on cable than on broadcast networks.

INTERCONNECT   Local cable companies sell advertising spots within and between cable network programs, similar to the way broadcast affiliates sell time. Where broadcast and cable differ, however, is with multiple cable system buys. Large markets are often served by several different cable companies, each of which may serve a specific geographic region. For example, one cable company might serve the east side of a city, another the west side, another the north side, and yet a fourth the south side. If a local advertiser has stores located all over the city, then it will want to reach the entire market.

The advertiser can do so through an **interconnect buy**, in which it buys time on all the area cable companies through a one-buy cooperative pricing agreement. In some cases, arrangements are made for commercials to appear at the same time across the city.

The Internet

COUNTING ONLINE AD EXPOSURES   The Internet's struggles with audience measurement have resulted in imprecise ratings and inconsistent pricing schemes. It's often difficult to measure how many people see an online ad and thus how much it should cost. Most websites and auditors rely on the number of hits, number of click-throughs, and other means of counting their visitors:

- **Hits.** In the Web's early years, the number of website visitors was largely determined by the number of hits received on a page. A *hit* is typically defined as the number of times users access a page. This is a very poor measure of the number of site visitors, however. Fifteen hits on one site could mean 15 visitors, 1 user visiting 15 times, or a small number of users visiting several times. It's virtually impossible to say that the number of hits equals the numbers of visitors.

    Caching presents another challenge in determining the number of visitors to a site. Computers often store a copy of a visited webpage as a *cache file* (or temporary storage area) on the hard drive, rather than on the server, so when a user returns to a webpage he or she previously visited during the same Internet session, the browser retrieves the information from the cache file, rather than the server. Consequently, the site doesn't record the second hit, even though it's a repeat visit or second exposure.

    Adding to the confusion are newer *push technologies,* which rely on automated searches (also called *robots* and *spiders*) that comb the Web looking for information. Each time an automated agent scans a webpage, it is counted as a page view, although a human never saw any of the content. Even if automated searches account for only a small percentage of all website traffic, a small overestimation of visitors could cause an advertiser to spend millions of dollars more than warranted for a banner ad. Conversely, deflating the number of human page views could cost website publishers millions of dollars in lower ad rates.

- **Click-throughs.** Rather than count people (or hits) who visit a site and may not even notice a particular banner ad, many sites and advertisers rely on click-through counts, which identify the percentage of visitors who actually click through a banner ad.

    Banner ad *click-through rates (CTRs)* or pay-per-view rates are based on the percentage of website visitors who click-through a banner ad. Advertisers are charged only for the people who actually expressed an interest in the ad, not for all the others who landed on the site but didn't click on the banner.

    Advertisers hoping to reach the click-happy consumer are often disappointed with numbers that show few click-throughs. Anything over a 3 percent click-through is unusual. A banner is no longer thought of as a curiosity, so users don't click on banners as often as they used to. In 1994, when the Internet was still new, about 10 percent of users clicked on banners, but more recently, only about 2 percent of users click on ads ("Improving Their Swing," 1998; Kaye & Medoff, 2001; Vonder Haar, 1999).

    A click-through rate is calculated by dividing the number of users who click on a banner by the number of users who land on a site. For example, if 500 users visit a website but only 5 of them actually click on a banner ad, the ad has a click-through rate of 1 percent. Here is the formula:

5 visitors who click-through /500 website visitors = .01 × 100 = 1.0%

- **Cost per thousand**. Dollar for dollar, Web advertising can be more expensive than television advertising, although recently, online CPMs seem to be trending downward. But in fact, lower CPMs may actually translate into higher costs, when advertisers pay for viewers that aren't within their target audience (Boyce, 1998).

- **Time spent online**. People who spend longer periods of time reading a page and traveling within a site are more valuable to advertisers than those who just land on a page for a few seconds and then move on to another site. The longer a user spends on a page, the more likely he or she is to click on a banner; thus, some online pricing schemes are based on how long the ad stays on the screen and how long the average user stays on the page.

- **Size-based pricing**. Borrowing from the conventional newspaper advertising pricing structure, the cost of a banner ad is sometimes based on the amount of screen space it occupies. The charge for a newspaper ad is assessed according to a specific dollar amount per standard column inch area, whereas the rate for a banner ad is measured by pixel area. *Pixels* are tiny dots of color that form images on the screen (72 pixels = 1 inch). Size-based pricing is calculated by multiplying an ad's width by its height in pixels. A fee is assessed per pixel or by the total area.

- **Cost per transaction (CPT)**. An online advertiser who is charged by cost per transaction pays only for the number of users who respond to an ad. Websites and advertisers negotiate a fee or a percentage of the advertiser's net or gross sales based on the number of inquiries that can be directly attributed to a banner ad. Online advertisers are assessed a minimal charge or, in some cases, no charge at all for ad placement, but they are charged for the number of people who ask for more information or buy the product as a result of seeing the banner. CPT is a good pricing system for online merchants who are weary of investing advertising dollars that don't lead directly to sales and for high-traffic websites that are eager to earn a commission on top of a small fee for delivering an audience.

DISCOUNT ONLINE ADVERTISING SALES AND BUYS   Online advertising can be a risky venture, especially for smaller businesses with thin wallets, who are hesitant to spend their advertising dollars on a new and unproven medium. But there are several online buying strategies that advertisers can employ without risking their finances. Advertising exchanges, co-op deals, discounts, and auctions all offer discounted rates for unsold spots. Advertisers benefit from low fees, and Web space providers benefit by filling spots that would otherwise go unsold:

- **Ad auctions.** More websites mean that more ad space is available, and more ad space being available means that more advertisements are needed to fill the slots. Websites often find themselves with unsold banner spaces, which they put up for auction at reduced rates through specialized third-party sites. The thinking behind this arrangement is that getting discounted rates for unsold space is better than not getting any money at all. Plus, advertisers are more willing to take their chances on less popular sites if they are paying a discounted price for them. Just like the name implies, ad auctioneers put the space up for bid and the advertiser with the highest bid buys the space, often at less than half price (Walmsley, 1999).

- **Advertising exchanges.** Although many small businesses have terrific websites, they typically can't afford aggressive online campaigns. One way to get the word out is through an advertising exchange, in which advertisers place banners on

---

ZOOM IN   8.15

Browse through the following media kits to get an idea of how much it costs to run an ad on these sites. You'll see CPMs, guaranteed impressions, maximum run times, and other information on audience demographics, website traffic, production specifications, and sales contracts.

- New York Times on the Web Online Media kit: www.nytimes.com/adinfo/rate_banners.html or www.nytimes.com. Click on "Online media kit" in the far-left frame.
- USA Today's Online Media Kit: www.usatoday.com/a/adindex/omk/index.htm
- FieldTrip.com advertising rates: www.fieldtrip.com/advert/ad-ratecard.htm

---

each other's websites for free. For example, a company selling beauty products could place its banner on a site that sells women's shoes, and in turn, the shoe company could put a banner on the beauty product site. Neither company charges the other.

Advertising exchanges are gaining in popularity, especially among marketers who do not have much money and who don't have a large sales team. By trading space, advertisers can use sites that they many not otherwise be able to afford and thus find new outlets that reach their target audiences.

ZOOM IN   8.16

- To see how an ad auction works, go to www. ezineadauction.com.
- Read about how ad exchanges work at **www.banner-ex. com**.

- **Cooperative advertising.** In cooperative advertising, a marketer promotes, usually in the form of a review or endorsement, a product on a website and shares sales profits with the hosting site. For example, Amazon.com and other booksellers charge book publishers to promote their titles on their sites. The publisher writes a promotional review of its own book, and Amazon places the review next to an image of the book for either a set fee or for a percentage of sales made from the site.

ZOOM IN   8.17

Read about Amazon's co-op program at www.amazon.com/exec/obidos/subst/misc/co-op/co-op-main.html.

This type of co-op advertising, also known as *product placement,* has been sharply criticized for failing to make it clear to customers that the reviews are promotional pieces, not unbiased editorials written by Amazon's staff. Amazon now posts a page that explains its publisher-supported placement policy and lets users knows which ads are part of the co-op program.

- **Discounts.** Some websites offer discounted rates if banners come *online ready,* or fully coded in HTML and complete with all graphic, audio, and video files. In addition, sliding fees can be formulated based on how much formatting the website manager has to do to an ad before posting it online. Frequency discounts are also available on many websites.

SEE IT LATER

The Never-Ending Quest for Ratings

The radio, television, and Internet industries all continue the quest for accurate and reliable ways to measure their audiences. Their biggest help may come from technologies and new ways of reporting data. There are several new ways to measure the audience and to interpret numbers collected by tried-and-true methods.

New Technology

An Arbitron personal people meter.

THE PORTABLE PEOPLE METER   Hailed as a revolutionary audience-metering device, the **portable people meter (PPM)** is capable of capturing radio listening data through wireless signals. Still in the testing stage, the PPM is a small, pager-sized device that's carried by a listener and picks up and decodes inaudible signals that radio broadcasters embed in their programs. An individual attaches the PPM to his or her clothing or purse, like a pager or cell phone, and the PPM decodes the unique signal emitted by each radio station the individual hears, whether he or she is at home, in a shopping mall, in a car, or anywhere else. The PPM is the first electronic metering device that monitors in- and out-of-the-home exposure to over-the-air radio. The PPM stores each station's signals, and at the end of each day, survey participants place the device in an at-home base station that sends the codes to Arbitron for tabulation.

A *Star Trek.*

The PPM may one day be capable of monitoring broadcast and cable television viewership. Nielsen Media Research is providing Arbitron with the financial backing and research expertise needed for continued development and trials ("What's New," 2001).

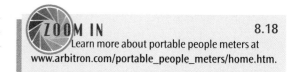

ZOOM IN   8.18
Learn more about portable people meters at
www.arbitron.com/portable_people_meters/home.htm.

GLOBAL POSITIONING SATELLITE   New Arbitron and Nielsen ventures in the testing phase utilize **global positioning satellite (GPS)** technology to track consumers' exposure to billboard advertising. With the Nielsen system, motorists and pedestrians wear small battery-operated meters that track their movements in 20-second intervals. The GPS data, along with travel diaries, are then matched up to a map of billboard sites to determine the "opportunity to see" an outdoor advertisement. The GPS system may someday be adapted for electronic media, as well (DiPasquale, 2002; "Nielsen to Test," 2002).

DIGITAL TELEVISION   Since television transmission is gradually moving from analog to digital, Nielsen is trying out new meters that are capable of measuring digital television viewing. The digital meters rely on new audio and video coding technologies to capture digital viewership patterns.

Separating Cable and Satellite Ratings

As discussed earlier, the broadcast and cable networks duke it out for ratings. And while broadcast network program ratings and shares are still far ahead of those for cable, cable is making serious inroads. For example, during the week of March 3 to 9, 2003, 24 advertiser-supported cable networks combined surpassed the 7 broadcast networks during prime time by 4.5 ratings points. Moreover, while the broadcast networks' combined share dropped by 11.1 percent, the cable networks' combined share increased by 6.4 percent from a year earlier ("Ad-Supported Cable," 2003). It's been well documented that the broadcast networks are steadily losing viewers to their cable competitors. Yet even though cable networks are collectively threatening the broadcast networks, individually, they're still behind in the ratings game.

When cable ratings are calculated, they include the number of viewers who also watch satellite-delivered programs. This increases the cable networks' ratings by making it seem as though they are drawing larger audiences. Nielsen has proposed to report cable- and satellite-delivered program ratings separately. Currently, nonbroadcast networks, such as Nick-at-Nite and ESPN, are delivered via cable and direct broadcast satellite (DBS), but they only carry local commercials when delivered via cable. Included in cable network audience estimates are those viewers who see the network via cable and thus receive the commercials *plus* those who view the network via satellite but don't receive the commercials. Thus, cable ratings may be inflated to the detriment of broadcast networks and cable advertisers, who pay for larger audiences than are being exposed to their commercials. Broadcast and cable networks and advertisers are sitting tight to see how the new system will affect advertising sales.

Program Strategies

In an attempt to keep viewers' attention through a program's last commercial break, ABC is experimenting with program structure. It has asked producers to design the dramatic narrative around five commercial breaks, instead of the usual four. Currently, the last commercial break is usually followed by fast-rolling closing credits and a preview of the next episode, followed by a cluster of commercials preceding the next program. With the new five-commercial format, the story would conclude after the last commercial break. The network is banking on boosting ratings for the final minutes of a program block and thus increasing the "value of commercial time without adding more commercials." If the strategy is successful, half-hour programs may soon wrap up after the last commercial break, as well (Greppi, 2003).

Summary

Researchers started measuring radio audiences in 1929 to give stations a base on which to price time for commercial spots and to give advertisers a way to compare stations on number of listeners and demographic characteristics. Many of the techniques used for measuring radio audiences were later used to measure audience numbers for broadcast stations and cable and broadcast networks. Today, audience ratings figure prominently in the media world and often determine the success of a program or a station.

Arbitron and Nielsen Media Research are the two primary audience measurement companies. To get a sense of the number of listeners and viewers, both companies rely on media use diaries; Nielsen also measures audiences with metering devices. Although Arbitron is mainly concerned with radio audiences and Nielsen with television viewers, they may collaborate in the development of the new personal people meter (PPM). Both companies have also ventured into the Internet and are experimenting with ways to measure the online audience.

The Internet is a new medium that poses new challenges to traditional audience measurement techniques. Metering computer use is more complex than metering television or radio use, and the definition of an *Internet user* has not been standardized. Researchers are grappling with how users should be counted, such as by number of hits or number of click-throughs. While several companies monitor traffic at websites, there are many discrepancies regarding how the audience is measured.

Audience numbers are not the only way to evaluate a media audience. Stations often employ research techniques that delve into viewers likes and dislikes as well as their motivations for watching television or listening to the radio and choosing particular stations and programs. Online marketers take advantage of customer profiling techniques, which record users' Internet travels and then deliver banner ads promoting products similar to those on other sites users have visited.

It's essential for media outlets to understand their audiences, because after all, the media are in the business of selling audiences to their advertisers. Audience numbers and profiles, along with commercial time availability, help stations establish commercial prices.

Radio and television stations use cost per thousand, cost per point, gross rating points, average quarter hour, and cume figures as tools in setting ad costs. Advertisers use these figures when making media buys to compare costs among stations and programs.

Radio and television stations offer a variety of pricing structures, depending on availability, daypart, program, and other factors. Most stations offer fixed buys, run of schedule, frequency discounts, and barter arrangements. Online advertising pricing structures also include CPM and discount buys. Unique to the medium, banners are charged by click-through rates, size-based pricing, cost per transaction, and hybrid deals.

Audience measurement tools yield, at best, gross estimates of audience characteristics and media uses, but they're only as accurate as the technology allows. Technological innovations may one day produce audience numbers that are far more accurate and reliable than what is currently available.

Between $1.3 and $1.4 million.

Business and Ownership

CHAPTER **9**

 SEE IT THEN

Finding a Business Plan That Worked

Business Models

Ownership by Broadcast Networks

 SEE IT NOW

Ownership of Broadcast Stations

Ownership of Broadcast Networks

Ownership of Other Delivery Systems

Cross-Ownership

 **SEE IT LATER**

Broadcast Stations

Cable and Satellite Providers

Multichannel Multipoint Distribution Services

The Internet

In this chapter, you'll learn about:

- The various business models for electronic media
- The requirements for ownership of a broadcast station
- The various departments in electronic media facilities
- The differences between broadcast licensing and ownership and licensing and ownership of other delivery systems
- The changing configurations of electronic media ownership

Thousands of college students across the Unites States study electronic media to prepare for careers in radio, television, cable, satellite, and the Internet. Most of them have selected electronic media as a major because they believe that a career in this field will be creative and exciting. Others enter the field in the hope of achieving fame, success, and perhaps wealth. Some students study electronic media simply because they have been entertained by it most of their lives, and still others feel that they can create programming that is at least as entertaining as what is available now.

These are all good reasons to study electronic media and pursue a career in this field. However, many students miss the "big picture" because they do not understand that the field of electronic media is, first and foremost, a *business*. While the programming of media is a creative or artistic endeavor, the driving force behind the industry is business. (Maybe that's why they call it show *business*, not show *art*.)

It is certainly true that without entertainment and information programming, stations will have nothing to transmit to the audience. And if the audience doesn't receive entertaining and interesting programming, it will not tune in. For commercial stations, which comprise over 90 percent of all stations in this country, no audience means no advertising sales. On the other hand, even if a commercial station does have entertaining programming that attracts an audience, it must be able to sell advertising and manage its expenses well enough to stay in business. Thus, a program can be considered a critical success but not last beyond a few airings. This happens most often when the audience is not large enough or the composition of the audience is not attractive enough to advertisers. Some examples of highly acclaimed but short-lived shows include *Square Pegs, My So-Called Life, American Gothic, Murder One,* and *Freaks and Geeks.*

What is needed to stay in business varies by market size. In a large market, the station's viability depends on its being able to generate enough revenue to cover expenses. In a small market, where the opportunities to generate revenue are limited, controlling expenses is an important predictor of a station's ability to stay on the air.

Claire Danes starred in *My So-Called Life.*

The bottom line here is truly the *bottom line.* Broadcasting and other forms of electronic media are businesses. They require a solid system of funding to cover expenses, pay employees, and show a profit. To do so, they rely on calculated guesswork, science (to measure audiences), good decision making (as in scheduling against the competition), and some creativity. Art alone does not pay the bills.

It is commonly thought that *broadcasting* sells *entertainment.* Actually, this isn't quite correct. The product that broadcasting sells is *you*, the audience. Broadcasters are in the business of delivering audiences to advertisers. The bigger the program's audience or the more desirable its demographics, the more attractive the program is to advertisers. The logic here is simple: Advertisers want to reach large audiences that contain the target market for their product.

SEE IT THEN

Finding a Business Plan That Worked

In the early part of the twentieth century, wireless radio was used to send information from one point to another. Ships at sea, for example, used radio to communicate with each other, as did people on land for business and safety purposes. At that time, there was no need for a financial model to make wireless radio pay for itself. The economics of the industry revolved around manufacturing the equipment and licensing the patents used to build the equipment. Early experimenters and broadcasters used wireless radio for noncommercial purposes. They had no expectations of making money but enjoyed sending messages and entertainment via wireless to other experimenters and friends.

This situation changed when early broadcasters incurred expenses purchasing equipment, building studios, and hiring people to run those stations. In the early 1920s, broadcasters looked for a way not only to repay themselves for their expenses but also to provide enough income to sustain a business.

Business Models

The owners and operators of radio stations considered a number of financial models in the 1920s to help them pay for expenses and perhaps even make a profit. In fact, other forms of electronic media offered models for making radio pay for itself, as discussed in the following sections.

THE TELEGRAPH MODEL   In this model, companies bought their own equipment and network (telegraph lines). Users of the system paid by the word for each message sent, which meant messages were often short and sometimes even cryptic. This model could possibly have been used when radio was a point-to-point communication medium. Because the sender and receiver were both identified, they could be charged for the cost of the message. This model doesn't work for broadcasting because it is essentially a one-way service and the receivers cannot be identified. What's more, the senders are not individuals or companies but rather broadcasters.

THE TELEPHONE MODEL   The telephone had its beginnings in 1876, when Alexander Graham Bell received a patent for the device he invented. The telephone system was a closed system because a telephone was installed only when a person or household was willing to subscribe to the service. Also, the equipment was owned by the telephone company (AT&T in the early days), even though the phones were in individual homes. This system didn't require professional senders and receivers, since regular voice was the means of transmission. The method of payment in this model was and still is either a flat fee per month for calls or a combination of a flat fee for local calls and a per-use (or per-minute) charge for long-distance calls.

THE PER-SET TAX MODEL   This model is a user-supported system, in which buyers pay a one-time tax added to the price of each radio purchased. Such a tax was proposed in the early 1920s by David Sarnoff as a 2 percent tax per radio. The money collected was to be sent to broadcasters to pay for programming.

THE VOLUNTARY AUDIENCE CONTRIBUTION MODEL   This model suggests that broadcasters should appeal to their audiences for contributions to pay for programming. In 1922, a station in New York attempted to make money in this way but collected only $1,000, instead of the $20,000 that it wanted to obtain; the station ended up returning the collected money. This model did not totally disappear over the years. Public broadcast stations regularly conduct on-air pledge drives to appeal for donations from their audiences, and noncommercial stations routinely raise money by selling printed program schedules and other promotional items.

THE GOVERNMENT SUBSIDY OR OWNERSHIP MODEL   In some countries, broadcasting is owned and operated by the government. This model is an extension of the policy once considered to keep the telephone and telegraph industries as part of the postal system. Just after World War I, the U.S. government debated whether to keep control of the broadcast operations that the navy had taken over for security reasons. The government observed the fierce competition between competing electronic media (i.e., telegraph and telephone) companies and preferred to avoid that situation among broadcast companies. Despite some strong lobbying to maintain control, the idea of government control over electronic media and the entertainment it produced was not acceptable to the industry and the idea was therefore dropped.

THE TOLL BROADCASTING MODEL   **Toll broadcasting** started in 1922 at WEAF, the AT&T station in New York, and it laid the groundwork for the present commercial broadcast model. Namely, it treats making a broadcast similarly to making a long-distance telephone call in that the user pays for the airtime. This model also includes the concept of *network buying*. Since WEAF was part of a 13-station group owned by AT&T, toll advertising was sold to all stations at one purchase price, which was cheaper than buying time on each station individually.

How many advertisements does the average American see every day?

This model hasn't completely disappeared from electronic media. The concept of an advertiser buying program-length time from a media outlet is alive and well today in the form of the **infomercial.** The station airing the program does not produce it but simply schedules and airs it in exchange for a fee.

THE SPONSORSHIP MODEL   In the early 1920s, advertisers were discouraged from including direct sales pitches in their messages. Instead, they were encouraged to sponsor programs and performers by paying for the costs involved. Often, this practice led to naming the program (*The Kraft Music Hall*) or the performer (The Astor Coffee Dance Orchestra) after the sponsor. Mixing advertising with entertainment programming was not initially acceptable to many people, but by 1928, advertising **sponsorship** had established itself as the primary model for providing financial support to the broadcasting industry.

THE SPOT ADVERTISING MODEL   In the late 1950s, the networks started moving away from single advertiser sponsorship of a program, for several reasons. The main reason was that sponsors wanted too much control over programs, which resulted in many problems for the networks, including the quiz show scandal of the late 1950s. In short, pressure from sponsors to gain huge audiences created ethical dilemmas for the networks.

Another reason for the move away from sponsorship was that the networks found that advertisers were willing to pass up 60-second spots in favor of less expensive 30-second spots. Not only did this give smaller advertisers the opportunity to get involved in network broadcasting, but it also gave the networks the opportunity to generate more revenue for selling the same amount of airtime. The **spot advertising model** has become the most successful model for network and local broadcasting over the past 40 years. With few exceptions, broadcast advertising no longer features program sponsorship.

THE SUBSCRIPTION MODEL   The **subscription model** for electronic media borrows from the print media, which have used selling subscriptions as a revenue stream for years. In this model, the audience pays regularly (usually, monthly or yearly) to receive the medium. Magazines and newspapers both receive substantial amounts of income from audience subscriptions. And since the vast majority of newspapers and magazines that sell subscriptions also receive advertising revenue, subscription income is usually a supplement to the overall revenue picture. This model has worked very well for the cable and satellite industries. It is also the model used by the newer services that provide direct broadcast satellite to audiences.

All of the electronic media in the United States rely on a financial model that's based on one or more of the models just described. For example, the cable industry gets the majority of its revenue from individual audience member (household) subscriptions; however, it also makes money by selling advertisements (commercials) on the channels that are supported by commercial advertising and that allow local cable sales, such as MTV, Lifetime, and CNN. In addition to the revenue gained from monthly subscriptions and advertising sales, cable companies also get revenue from pay-per-view programs.

The Broadcast Star Model

Broadcasting first tried the toll broadcasting model, then changed to the sponsorship model, and finally adopted the spot advertising model. Spot advertising has been used by both radio and television networks and stations since the late 1950s and is still the dominant model today.

Recording Industry Business Plan: A Model in Transition

The music-recording industry is going through a time when the existing model is not working well. Consumers today are angry at paying up to $19 for an audio CD. Part of the problem is that DVDs—which come complete with a movie, its accompanying soundtrack, and various features—cost little, if anything, more. Another part of the problem is that millions of people are downloading music files at file-sharing sites for free. Finally, some websites are selling 99-cent (iTunes from Apple) and even 88-cent (WalMart) legal song downloads.

About 400 to 600 ads per day.

In order for a local station to be financially successful, other components of the industry must be involved. Using a network-affiliated television station as an example, we can see how other businesses function to make the broadcast television system work. Together, these elements form the shape of a star, with the television station at the center. If we replace the center of this **star model** with a network-affiliated radio station, it could also be used to represent the radio industry as it was from the late 1920s until the mid 1950s.

At the center of the star model are television stations, comprised of three different types: **network owned and operated (O & Os)**, **network affiliates**, and **independent stations.** These types of stations differ by their relationship to the network. A network O & O is owned and operated by a network. A network affiliate has a long-term agreement with a network to run its programs and commercials. An independent station has no long-term agreement with a network and thus must find other sources for programs.

Producers create programs for networks and stations, and networks distribute those programs to their affiliates for airing at local stations. For instance, the program *Friends* wasn't created by NBC but rather by an independent television producer, Warner Bros. A producer will "shop" his or her program to any or all of the networks until he or she makes a deal for it to be aired. Sometimes, a producer will sell his or her program directly to local stations.

Syndicators rent groups of previously produced network programs—for example, sitcoms like *Seinfeld* and *Cheers*—to individual stations or groups of stations. Syndicators may also assemble Hollywood movies into packages and rent them to a station or group of stations.

Networks are companies that provide programming to stations. They do not broadcast signals to the audience; local television stations do that. Rather, the networks assemble programming and distribute it to affiliated or owned stations. The networks also pay local stations for airing their programs. This payment, called **network compensation,** acknowledges that the local station helps the network reach the audience,

Broadcast Industry Star Model

Network, Syndication, and Off-Net Programs

In the past, network programs were produced by independent producers with some support from the networks; regardless, the producer maintained control of the program. After a program accumulated a few years of episodes, the producer would go to a syndicator, who would sell the program directly to stations (or groups of stations) at a strong price—whatever the market would bear. The program would then air new episodes on the network and in syndication with reruns (often airing five days per week) on individual stations. The program would continue to air on the network until no new episodes were made. At that point, the program would be considered off-net.

Now that a network can own a controlling portion of the shows it airs, the life cycle of a TV program has changed. When a network owns a controlling interest in a program, it can decide where the program will be shown after (or even during) its network run. Since the networks have cable "sister channels" (e.g., FOX's fX), they often make deals for these sister channels to air the program, sometimes at a price lower than what the producer would get for the program on the syndication market.

For instance, *The X-Files* ran on the FOX network for a number of years. Instead of putting the show into syndication, FOX made a deal with fX, its cable channel, to run the show five days per week. The producer and the star of the show (Chris Carter and David Duchovny, respectively) sued FOX, claiming that the show will have a reduced value when it does go into syndication because of the many airings it will get on fX. Clearly, a reduction in the value of the show results in a reduction of royalties paid to the producer and the star.

thereby satisfying the advertisers' needs. The **audience** gives the television station its time and attention by watching the programs and commercials that the station airs. The **advertisers** support both the station and the network directly by paying for and supplying commercials to be aired.

The **Federal Communications Commission (FCC)** grants licenses to those businesses that apply for them and that it considers qualified to receive them. In addition, the FCC regulates broadcasting by enforcing the rules set down by Congress (e.g., the Telecommunications Act of 1996) and by creating rules of its own (e.g., limits on cross-ownership of media).

ZOOM IN　　　　　9.1
Go to the Companion Website for this book, www.ablongman.com/medoffkaye1e, for examples of television stations that are independent, network affiliates, and network owned and operated.

The star model shows the interdependence that exists between the entities and the broadcast television stations. Essentially, all of the entities depend on the television stations to stay in business. In the illustration of the model (see p. 201), each line connecting two entities represents a two-way relationship. For example, the network supplies its affiliate station with programs, and the station provides the network with an audience for its programs. These relationships have proven good for all involved, as the model has endured in television for over 50 years.

Some entities play an important role in the television industry and are not shown in the star model, including the delivery systems that provide the majority of the American audience with television programs. Cable television, satellite delivery services, and other television multichannel delivery systems are used by about 88 percent of the households in this country (NCTA, 2003).

Ownership by Broadcast Networks

The Report on Chain Broadcasting

While the networks were becoming stronger and more profitable, the affiliates were losing control over their programming. For instance, network affiliation contracts required local stations to broadcast network programming even if they had to cancel local programming. Given this and other issues, in 1938, the FCC decided that the power of the networks over the affiliates needed to be studied carefully.

That study took almost three years and resulted in *The Report on Chain Broadcasting,* presented in 1941. The report found that NBC and CBS controlled the vast majority of prime-time radio programming across the country, and the FCC deemed this monopolistic and counter to the idea of localism. The report also mandated that affiliation contracts be limited to three years, that affiliates could reject network programs, that networks could own only one affiliate per market, and that networks had the right to offer rejected programs to nonaffiliate stations.

Candy magnate Edward J. Noble bought the NBC Blue network to form the American Broadcasting Company (ABC).

The networks were not happy with the FCC's new rules and began a legal battle that went all the way to the U.S. Supreme Court (*NBC v. United States,* 1943). The FCC won the battle, which meant the networks had to change the way they conducted business with their affiliates. The most notable result of the ruling was that in 1943, NBC was forced to sell the weaker of its two networks, the Blue network, to LifeSavers candy mogul Edward J. Noble. In 1945, the new network was named the *American Broadcasting Company (ABC).* And so, the three major broadcast networks were in place, ready to dominate broadcasting for the next 50 years.

Network Ownership Since 1945

At the end of World War II, NBC, CBS, and ABC were still all radio networks. That changed rapidly, however, as television stations began to broadcast regular schedules and sign agreements with the networks to be network affiliates. As noted earlier, affiliate

NBC aired a 10-second Bulova watch commercial in 1941.

stations committed to airing the TV networks' programs in exchange for network compensation, or money paid to them for their airtime. In return, the networks gained a large national audience and were able to sell national advertising. This deal helped the networks and the affiliates prosper and grow.

In addition to prospering from advertising sales, the networks began to broadcast from stations that they actually owned and operated. Each of the networks had stations in the very largest markets and profited from the large audiences gained through network programming. The only exception to ownership was the Mutual Broadcasting System (MBS), which was more of a cooperative and did not own stations.

In the early 1950s, another television network emerged, when Allen Du Mont, the owner of a television manufacturing business, decided to start his own network. The Du Mont network was not built on a long-standing reputation in radio, as were the big-three networks. And because the stronger television stations were already affiliated with the top three established networks, the Du Mont network was never able to be better than a weak fourth in any given market. In fact, many markets only had three television stations, so Du Mont was often left out. The Du Mont network stopped its distribution of programs in 1955 (Walker & Ferguson, 1998, p. 22).

Allen Du Mont and his television sets.

NETWORK OWNERSHIP CHANGES   ABC, born from the divested NBC Blue network, never had the power of either NBC or CBS. It affiliated with the leftover stations that didn't affiliate with the two bigger networks, and because of the lower status of its affiliate stations, it couldn't generate enough revenue to stay profitable. By 1951, ABC began negotiating with companies that could serve as potential partners, and in 1953, it merged with United Paramount Theaters. While the merger brought ABC the cash it needed to continue network operations, it remained the weakest of the three networks for more than 20 years.

The big-three networks continued operations relatively unchanged from 1953 until 1985. Then, a television group owner, Capital Cities Communications, took control of ABC. Known for its ability to control expenses and show a profit, Capital Cities brought some stability to the network.

Just one year later, in 1986, RCA, the parent company of NBC, was sold to General Electric (GE), the company that had helped start RCA almost 60 years earlier. Many changes occurred as a result of this ownership change, the most significant of which was that GE decided to sell NBC's radio network to a radio program syndicator, Westwood One.

A NEW TELEVISION NETWORK EMERGES   At the same time things were happening at NBC, a new commercial television network was being put together by media company owner Rupert Murdoch. In 1986, the FOX television network, named after the film studio Twentieth Century Fox, also owned by Murdoch, came on the air. At first, FOX lost large sums of money—$80 million dollars in 1988 alone (Sterling & Kittross, 2002, p. 475). It took another five years for FOX to begin scheduling prime-time programming seven nights per week. Part of FOX's slow start was attributable to its weak affiliates and small audience, compared to the big-three networks. FOX became successful with programs like *The Simpsons* and *The X-Files,* which were targeted at young audiences.

Affiliation Switching

When the FOX network helped New World Communications buy a group of television stations in 1994, it did so because it had a plan to get its own strong affiliates in major markets. Namely, the deal specified that all stations in the New World purchase would become FOX affiliates.

This touched off a mad scramble for network affiliations among stations in some major markets. The stations in Phoenix, Arizona, underwent these interesting changes:

- KTSP (channel 10), the CBS affiliate, became KSAZ, a new FOX affiliate.
- KNXV (channel 15), the FOX affiliate, became the ABC affiliate.
- KTVK (channel 3), the ABC affiliate, became an independent station.
- KPHO (channel 5), an independent station, became the CBS affiliate.

FOX wanted to have a VHF affiliate in the Phoenix market and achieved this goal when KTSP was purchased and switched its affiliation from CBS to FOX.

FOX attempted to shift the balance among the powerful affiliates with a complicated deal in 1994. It invested $500 million in New World Communications, after which New World changed the affiliation of all of its television stations, 10 of which were in the top 50 markets, to the FOX network. The big-three lost affiliates in major markets, triggering many other affiliation changes (Albarran, 2002, p. 74).

SEE IT NOW

Ownership of Broadcast Stations

Owner Qualifications

As already mentioned, broadcast station ownership requires licensing by the FCC. The prospective owner must apply for a license and qualify in these four key areas.

CITIZENSHIP   Owners of broadcast stations in this country must be citizens of the United States, a requirement that has roots in the past. Just before World War I, foreign-owned companies like Marconi had taken an aggressive interest in radio. However, the U.S. government was disinclined to let foreigners or foreign companies control the powerful new medium, feeling that radio transmitter ownership should be in the hands of citizens. Further, the U.S. government took control of all radio transmitters in the country for the duration of World War I. Since then, the government's policy has been that owners of broadcast radio stations must be United States citizens.

CHARACTER   Although this is a very broad criterion, the law expects station owners to be people of good character. While this is difficult to show in an application, one obvious rule is that convicted felons are not allowed to own broadcast stations. Also, the FCC likes to see owners who will be directly involved in the day-to-day operation of a station.

FINANCIAL   Knowing that a new station may not be able to generate large advertising sales right from the start, the FCC expects station owners to have more money than what is required to build and start the station. In addition, new station owners should be able to operate the station for three months without depending on large advertising support.

PROGRAMMING   The FCC has maintained the policy that broadcasters can program to the public in whatever way suits the marketplace. Even so, each applicant must submit a programming plan with his or her application. The aspects of the programming plan that are subject to FCC scrutiny are public interest, convenience, and necessity. Considering these elements obviously involves a subjective judgment by the FCC, and it has made some attempts to be more specific, including publication of the 1939 *Blue Book* (as mentioned in Chapter 12).

Since the FCC can't participate in censorship, an applicant can be granted a license despite having a programming plan that the FCC doesn't like. For instance, the FCC cannot withhold a license to an otherwise qualified owner because he or she intends to program country music in a small market that already has three other country music stations. However, the FCC can withhold a license from a potential owner that intends to conduct faith healing all day long because it would not be in the public interest.

Competing for a License

In the past, the FCC screened all applicants who applied for a broadcast frequency to determine which one would be the best future broadcast station owner. This procedure was often very slow and agonizing, though, for both the applicants and the FCC. In recent years, the FCC has adopted two new procedures designed to streamline the process. The first procedure is the channel or frequency **lottery**, in which all applicants' names are put in a group and the FCC selects one at random. Once a winner has been selected, that applicant is thoroughly screened to make sure that he or she is fully qualified and that the application is complete.

The lottery procedure is being used less often since the FCC has realized that another procedure, the **auction**, can bring money to the government for the awarding of the license. Once a frequency has been deemed appropriate for a broadcast station license by the FCC, it may conduct an auction for use of the frequency. As in any auction, bidders compete by submitting their offers for the license. Once the highest bidder has been identified, then the FCC closely scrutinizes that applicant to ensure that he or she meets the criteria for ownership. If the applicant does, then he or she is granted the license.

Construction Permits

Once an applicant has been selected, reviewed, and approved, he or she receives a **construction permit (CP)**, which gives him or her authorization to build and test a broadcast station. The CP is in fact a temporary authorization that gives a new television station 2 years and a new radio station 1½ years to be ready to provide full-service broadcasting.

During this period, the station is physically constructed and the equipment is purchased and put in place. After that, the station begins testing the equipment to make sure that it works properly and that the signal is in compliance with all FCC technical regulations. If the FCC determines that the testing is successful, the station is granted a full-service license to begin broadcasting a regular schedule of programming.

Keeping the License

Once a station obtains a license, it rarely loses it. To do that, a station would have to blatantly disobey FCC rules. It's hard to lose a license in part because of the large number of broadcast stations on the air; the FCC simply can't keep a close watch on all of them. Moreover, the FCC has a graduated schedule of notifications and warnings that are sent to troublesome stations to get the attention of their owners. A station would have to ignore the so-called raised eyebrow letter (stating that the FCC is aware of a possible violation of rules), the cease-and-desist order, the forfeitures (i.e., fines), and the threats of short-term or conditional renewal before its license would be in danger of being revoked.

One area of operation that the FCC *does* monitor closely is employment practices. For the last 30 years, the FCC has been monitoring broadcast station and multichannel program providers' employment practices, believing that they are not hiring enough women and minorities. Every station must now file a yearly report of its hiring activities with the FCC. Failure to comply with hiring guidelines and other FCC rules will result in fines.

In 1998, the FCC's **Employee Equal Opportunity (EEO)** hiring practice rules were found to be unconstitutional (Naftalin, 2001). The court ruled that the FCC could not show that these rules were in the public interest. New rules were put in place in early 2000 to guide broadcasters in using the methods of recruitment expected from the FCC. Namely, the new rules require wide dissemination of job listings to ensure that women and minorities hear about them. Also, a station with more than five full-time employees must place a detailed description of its hiring efforts in its public file every year, and every two years, the station must give evidence that it is complying with the FCC's employment rules. A radio station with 10 or more full-time employees and each television station is required to submit a retirement and hiring report to the FCC at the halfway point before license renewal and at renewal time. Other companies that provide multichannel services have similar employment requirements.

A second area of FCC scrutiny is the station's **public file.** Every station is required to keep a file of important documents that can be inspected by the public—for instance, permits and license renewal applications, change requests, the FCC pamphlet *The Public and Broadcasting—A Procedural Manual*, employment information, letters from the public, information about requests for political advertising time, station programming that addresses community needs, time brokerage agreements, and information about children's programming and advertising. A public file is required for all stations regardless of their commercial or noncommercial status. A radio station must keep these documents for seven years and a television station for five. A cable company need only keep those documents relating to employment practices. This file must be kept at the station or at some accessible place to allow the public to inspect it during regular business hours.

ZOOM IN   9.2
To see the full text of this manual, go to http://ftp.fcc.gov/Bureau/Mass_Media/Factsheets/pubbroad.pdf.

Finances

Just because a station can keep its license, that doesn't mean that it can stay in business. In order to keep the signal on the air and prevent the station from **going "dark,"** the station must generate enough money to pay its bills. Keeping accurate records allows the station's general management to assess its financial health and to make good decisions about how it can pay its bills and possibly invest money in programming, personnel, equipment, and other assets, like land and buildings.

The business department of the station keeps track of all money coming into and out of the station using a bookkeeping procedure that categorizes all monetary activities. The figures generated from this procedure are then placed in a statement that accounts for all **revenue** (i.e., money received) and all **expenses** (i.e., money spent) during a given time period. That statement is known as a **profit and loss statement,** or **P & L.** The actual bottom line of this statement is the amount of money that the station has made or lost during that period of time. Another important statement from the business department is the **balance statement,** which shows the station's **assets** (i.e., what it owns) and **liabilities** (i.e., what it owes) at any given point in time.

ZOOM IN   9.3
Go to the Companion Website for this text, www.ablongman.com/medoffkay1e, to see actual profit-and-loss and balance statements for a radio station.

A When CBS had to divest some of its assets that owned cable TV and program syndication businesses.

Renewing the License

The vast majority of stations applying for license renewal are renewed with little or no trouble from the FCC. In some cases, an individual or group will challenge the right of an existing station to keep its license, which complicates the renewal process, by filing a **petition to deny renewal.** If the FCC feels that an existing station may not be serving the public, it can schedule a hearing about the renewal. Serious challenges aren't very common, but they can be both time consuming and expensive.

In recent years, the process of license renewal has become streamlined and relatively easy. The station must give information about its operation, its programming, and its owners, but it no longer has to conduct an ascertainment survey about issues in the community. The renewal form itself has even been shortened to an almost postcard size. (The form is actually eight pages long, but it has been greatly simplified.) Generally speaking, if a station follows the rules and serves the public, its license will be renewed for eight years.

License Renewal

The form used for station license renewal is FCC 303-S. Used for both radio and television stations, it asks for information and certification of the following:

- The station has been and continues to be on the air.
- The station has maintained its public file and it is current.
- The owners have filed the required ownership reports.
- Television stations must show that they have complied with the children's programming requirement of three hours per week.
- The owners of the station have not committed any felonies.

To view the form, go to **www.fcc.gov/Forms/Form303-S/**.

Owning versus Operating

Some stations are owned by one company but, for a variety of reasons, operated by another in a relationship generally known as an **LMA:** a **local marketing agreement** or a **lease management agreement.** For example, an owner who does not live near a station may pay another company or another station to run the station because doing so makes economic sense. Thus, a group that's headquartered in Ohio may not want to stretch its personnel thin by supervising the day-to-day operation of a station it acquired (perhaps through the purchase of another group) in Wyoming. Instead, the group will hire another station in Wyoming to operate the station in exchange for a percentage of the revenue.

A **joint sales agreement,** or **JSA,** is similar to an LMA but limited to sales. That is, the sales representatives for one station also sell time for another station in exchange for a percentage of the revenue.

Ownership of Broadcast Networks

As discussed earlier, some significant changes had occurred in the television networks by 1990. Namely, audience shares had declined because of increased competition from cable channels and the startup of a new network, FOX, in 1988.

In addition to the reduction in audience share caused by increased competition, CBS suffered an additional reduction when some of its strongest affiliates were sold to a company that changed their affiliation from CBS to FOX. The weakened CBS was acquired in 1995 by Westinghouse, a pioneer in broadcasting that had helped start RCA and NBC in the early 1920s.

Also in 1995, two new television networks entered the scene. The WB Television Network (owned by Warner Bros., a film studio) and the United Paramount Network, or UPN (owned by United Paramount film studio), both began prime-time programming that year. Another television network, PAX, owned by Paxson Communications, debuted a few years later. The WB, UPN, and PAX, the so-called little three, are considered minor networks compared to the big three, ABC, CBS, and NBC—or with FOX included, the big four.

In 1996, Walt Disney Company purchased ABC for $18.5 billion, at the time, the second-highest price ever paid for a U.S. company (Smith, Wright, & Ostreff, 1998). And in yet another sale with an ironic twist, CBS was sold again in 1999. The new buyer

A Media Giant: Viacom

Large media companies, such as Viacom, have acquired other media businesses, giving them a foothold in the digital environment. In addition to the television network powerhouse CBS, Viacom also owns businesses in the following related media areas:

- *Motion pictures*—Viacom owns Paramount Pictures, one of the original major motion picture studios, which has been a leading producer and distributor of feature films since 1912. In addition, Viacom owns Paramount Home Entertainment, a global leader in the distribution of prerecorded entertainment on video cassette and DVD.
- *Broadcast television*—Viacom owns the CBS television network; the UPN (United Paramount Network), a television network; Paramount Television, a television program producer; and King World Productions, which sells first-run programming, such as *Jeopardy! Wheel of Fortune*, *The Oprah Winfrey Show*, and *Dr. Phil*.
- *Cable television*—Viacom owns MTV, Nickelodeon, BET (Black Entertainment Television), CMT (Country Music Television),VH1, Showtime, The Movie Channel and Flix, Spike TV, TVLand, and Comedy Central.

- *Radio*—Through Infinity, its subsidiary, Viacom owns more than 185 radio stations across the country, including 6 of the nation's top 10 stations.
- *Outdoor advertising (billboards)*—Viacom Outdoor owns over 100,000 billboards in this country and over 800,000 billboards and other outdoor advertising displays worldwide.
- *Retail and recreation*—The company owns Blockbuster video rental stores, Paramount Parks, theme amusement parks, and about 1,700 movie theaters.
- *Publishing*—Viacom owns Simon & Schuster, a large book-publishing company.
- *Online media*—The company owns 8 businesses involved in online activity, including a financial news and information source (MarketWatch), a company that sells movie tickets online (MovieTickets.com), and TiVo, the company that has marketed a video digital recorder
- *Music publishing*—Viacom's subsidiary Famous Music has a catalog of over 125,000 song titles available for licensing.

For the latest about Viacom, go to **www.viacom.com**.

Stars from the series *Buffy the Vampire Slayer*.

was Viacom, a cable company that had once been owned by CBS. CBS had had to divest Viacom because owning it violated the FCC rule that a television network could not own a cable company. After the selloff, Viacom grew in program syndication and other media areas, finally becoming financially strong enough to buy its former parent company.

What caused all of these changes after so many years of network stability? Not any one factor but several can be identified. First, the network audience share got smaller as a result of the popularity of cable television. When cable became common, the television audience had many more viewing options. This meant that the network audience share was no longer split between just three viewing choices (Romano, 2002).

Also, the addition of new television networks added new popular programs and stars that attracted young audiences, in particular. New technologies, like video cassette recorders and satellite distribution, also reduced the big three's audience share. With the reduction in audience share, the cost of advertising on the big-three networks became more competitive, reducing the profitability of the networks. This often made shareholders nervous and eager to consider selling the networks.

Reverse Compensation

The network compensation model of the networks paying their affiliates for airtime continues to be complicated, depending on which network, which market, and which station are being considered as well as the economic situation at the time. Let's consider an example.

When the FOX network attempted to persuade the National Football League (NFL) to award its lucrative National Football Conference games contract to FOX, a problem emerged. FOX felt that it could not afford the steep price tag associated with carrying the games. In an attempt to get the contract and to get their affiliates into the deal, FOX proposed that the affiliates help pay part of the costs. The affiliates agreed and helped FOX get the NFL contract, taking it away from CBS. Essentially, the affiliates were paying the network for the programming. Regardless, getting the contract helped establish FOX as a viable fourth network. FOX's affiliates benefited not only from carrying the games but also from the higher ratings that resulted from audience flow before and after the games. In this case, the affiliates made a wise investment in their network's programming.

Another instance of reverse compensation occurred in the San Francisco market. Granite Broadcasting's station KNTV was independent but desired a network affiliation. In a unique proposition, Granite offered NBC a payment of $36 million dollars per year for the privilege of being an NBC affiliate. This ground-breaking deal further obscured the already murky picture of the relationship between television networks and their affiliates (Greppi, 2001).

Group Ownership

The broadcast industry has been undergoing consolidation since deregulation started in the late 1970s. Before 1984, one person or company could own seven AM or FM radio stations and seven TV stations. This rule of sevens then became the rule of twelves, and in 1992, a 20-station per service limit was set. These rule changes caused progressively more station selling and an increase in consolidation. Consolidation increased dramatically after the passage of the Telecommunications Act of 1996.

Consolidation decreased the number of entities that owned stations, which led to a market that was increasingly oligopolistic. Some very large companies owned many television stations, including the Paramount/CBS group, owned by Viacom (21 stations), FOX Television Stations (34 stations), Tribune Broadcasting (23 stations), and Sinclair Broadcasting Group (54 stations). The number of stations owned by these large groups changes rapidly, as deals are constantly being made to strengthen overall market position. These large **owner groups**, sometimes referred to as **supergroups**, also own many other properties, both in broadcasting and related industries. (Note that networks are group owners but group owners are not necessarily networks, even though the stations in a group may share programs.)

While owners claim that group ownership becomes more efficient and thus profitable as the number of stations in a group increases, many in the FCC and in the general

CAREER TRACKS

John Dille   CEO, Federated Media

- **What is your job? What do you do?**
  I manage a group of 14 radio stations and a daily newspaper. I manage the managers.

- **How long have you been doing this job?**
  Twenty-five years.

- **What was your first job in electronic media?**
  I was the manager of a newspaper, and I was assigned a reorganization task in a radio station by the ownership, which was nonradio.

- **What led you to the job?**
  Even though I began in newspapers, I have always loved radio. I was a distant signal listener as a kid.

- **What advice would you have for students who might want a job like yours?**
  Hook up any way you can with a station and just dig in. It isn't about the money; it's about a passion for the business.

In 1993, Paramount and Chris-Craft Industries announced plans to launch what new media venture?

Ten Largest Radio Group Owners

GROUP	ANNUAL REVENUE	NUMBER OF STATIONS
Clear Channel Communications	$3,423,450,000	1,216
Infinity Broadcasting	$2,186,675,000	185
Cox Radio	$466,850,000	78
Entercom	$455,100,000	104
ABC Radio	$424,625,000	74
Citadel Broadcasting	$366,125,000	216
Radio One	$338,100,000	66
Emmis Communication	$296,775,000	27
Cumulus Media	$292,975,000	270
Univision Communications*	$290,900,000	57

* Deal pending to acquire Hispanic Broadcasting.

Note: Groups are ranked by revenue, not number of stations.

Source: Broadcasting & Cable, September 9, 2003.

population fear that this trend will decrease diversity in both programming choices and opinions ("Ownership Limits," 1998).

Others point to these advantages and disadvantages of consolidation in electronic media:

ADVANTAGES

- More resources are available for program production and creation.
- There is a guaranteed distribution of programs to other owned stations.
- Programming can be repurposed easily from one media to another.
- Advertising packages can be sold for more than one station or for a combination of radio, television, and so on.
- Radio stations can offer a wide variety of program formats.
- Economies of scale and efficiency are enjoyed.
- The career opportunities available to employees can be favorable.

DISADVANTAGES

- Fewer "voices" are heard and therefore there is less diversity of opinion.
- Formulaic programming is often used.
- Large groups can undercut the advertising prices of smaller groups and thus eliminate competition.
- Career opportunities are reduced because the stations can function with fewer people actually running them; this also creates an overall reduction in the number of jobs available to media professionals.
- There is less local programming, especially in news.
- In some companies, there are anti-union sentiment, lower wages, and less job security.

Ownership of Other Delivery Systems

Cable Television

The cable industry has also experienced considerable consolidation. In 1970, about 20 percent of U.S. households in the top five markets were served by a **multiple system operator (MSO)**, and in the top fifty markets, 63.5 percent were served by MSOs. By 1999, almost 60 percent of households in the top five markets were served by MSOs,

The UPN television network.

Ten Largest Television Group Owners

GROUP (OWNER)	ANNUAL REVENUE	NUMBER OF STATIONS
FOX TV Stations (News Corp.)	$2,276,600,000	35
Viacom TV Stations Group	$1,814,800,000	35
NBC TV Stations (GE)	$1,744,050,000	14
Tribune Broadcasting	$1,194,350,000	26
ABC (Disney)	$1,164,250,000	10
Gannett Broadcasting	$879,800,000	21
Hearst-Argyle Television	$782,600,000	27
Sinclair Broadcast Group	$756,250,000	62
Belo Television Group	$699,775,000	19
Cox TV Stations	$633,050,000	15

Note: Groups are ranked by revenue, not number of stations.

Source: Broadcasting & Cable, January 19, 2004.

while almost 92 percent of households in the top fifty markets were served by MSOs (Sterling & Kittross, 2002, p. 873). These most recent percentages will probably not change much in the future, but some systems will likely change hands among MSOs.

The Internet

The barriers to entry into broadcasting are many. As mentioned earlier, just obtaining a broadcast license can be a difficult, time-consuming, expensive endeavor, as applicants are scrutinized closely by the FCC. By contrast, the Internet offers an opportunity for individuals of modest means and limited technical knowledge to send out programming material to a potentially large audience.

Since its inception, the World Wide Web has provided a means for individuals to publish without involving a publishing company. Almost anyone with basic computer skills can publish a website. Since 1995, World Wide Web users have also been able to create their own Web radio stations by providing either streamed or archived audio at their websites. Video can be provided, as well, but it's limited in quality because of the bandwidth it requires. Because of its First Amendment protection, the Internet offers users the capability to publish without having to qualify for a license (Kaye & Medoff, 2001).

Web Radio

Putting a Web radio station on the air is easy. All you need is a computer to function as a server; program material, such as music, that has been digitized into a file format like MP3; software that will encode the information, so it can be streamed from the server on demand; and listeners who have a decoding program and a computer that can change the digital information into sound. Given the low cost and relative ease of setting up a Web radio station, music abounds on the World Wide Web.

BROADCASTERS AND WEB RADIO   Some radio broadcasters were quick to adopt Web radio as a way to extend their signal beyond the reach of their broadcast signal. Since 1995, the Web has been able to provide audio programming to computer users by streaming audio information. Once on the Web, a radio station can be heard anywhere in the world that has Internet service.

ZOOM IN   9.4
Go to the Companion Website, www.ablongman.
com/medoffkaye1e, and link to a list of broadcast radio
stations on the Web and Internet-only stations on the
Web, including www.web-radio.com and others.

Office workers in or by tall buildings in the downtown areas of big cities can go to the website of a broadcast station and click on the "Listen Live" or similar button to receive a streamed audio signal. The signal will not be interrupted or distorted by weather, as AM signals are, allowing listeners to hear their favorite stations while working at their computer. Most radio stations now have websites to promote their "brands" and to keep up with the technology, although not all stations stream their signals. Some stations have archived programs available for downloading.

LEGAL ISSUES IN WEB RADIO   Licensed broadcasters have embraced Web radio technology, and many stations today simulcast their over-the-air signals online. Music-licensing organizations—that is, the American Society of Composers, Authors, and Publishers (ASCAP) and Broadcast Music, Inc. (BMI)—receive license payments from Web stations for the use of music whose artists they represent. Beginning in the late 1990s, the Recording Industry Association of America (RIAA) demanded and eventually received an agreement with webcasters, both licensed and nonlicensed, to receive payment for the webcasting of music performed by members of RIAA.

Other legal issues have also embroiled performers and webcasters. For example, radio program syndicators decided that broadcasters who simulcast syndicated programs on the Web were essentially doing so without permission and, more important, without paying the syndicators. The threat of having to pay high royalty fees and legal fees stopped many stations from simulcasting and diminished the attractiveness of webcasting.

Another issue has involved advertising. The American Federation of Television and Radio Artists (AFTRA) believed advertisers should pay more for talent used in advertising that was produced for terrestrial radio but also sent out over the Internet. This problem caused a number of radio stations to stop streaming (Thorsberg, 2001), until the issue was resolved in 2002. Advertisers did agree to pay talent more for their work on commercials that would be streamed.

Cross-Ownership

Cross-ownership refers to an individual or company owning a newspaper and a broadcast station in the same market. As mentioned earlier, the federal government generally wants to maintain diversity in broadcasting and to keep as many voices and viewpoints on the air as possible; thus, cross-ownership is continually scrutinized by the FCC and Congress.

The cross-ownership investigations began in 1941, when Congress noted that newspaper companies owned many of the early broadcast stations. This was of particular concern when the newspaper and the broadcast station were located in the same market. (Interestingly, newspaper ownership of broadcast stations first came as a result of government encouragement; see Chapter 3.) The cross-ownership rules were formalized in 1970 (Sterling & Kittross, 2002, p. 576). Until a rule change in 1992, the FCC would not allow one company to own more than one AM and FM station or more than one television station in the same market. In June 2003, the FCC attempted to further relax cross-ownership rules, but the change was blocked, at least temporarily, by the courts.[1]

A broadcaster can own a cable system if he or she does not own a broadcast station in the same town. Telephone companies, long prohibited from owning cable systems, have been allowed to own them since the Telecommunications Act of 1996.

Viacom (which did not own CBS at the time).

SEE IT LATER

In a speech given in May 2003, FCC Chairman Michael Powell stated that technology will soon drive communications public policy more so than politics and lobbyists (Trick, 2003). It would also be fair to say that technology may also drive ownership changes and mergers. The delivery of information and entertainment has been moving from the traditional phone line, coaxial cable, and airwaves to wireless phone, broadband, satellite, and the Internet.

These changes have motivated communications businesses to seek inroads into the new delivery systems so as to maintain their market share and strength. As of 2004, all of the major broadcast television networks were owned by companies that also own some or all of the other types of media outlets. Since changes in technology are difficult to predict, so will be the resulting changes in ownership.

Broadcast Stations

Radio

The radio industry will continue to consolidate, creating an oligopolistic industry in which the major markets are dominated by a few gigantic group owners. The furious pace of station buying and selling since 1996 has increased the cost of buying a station, to the point that buyers without "deep pockets" can't enter into the marketplace. Future buying and selling will occur in small- and medium-size markets, since stations in the larger markets have already been purchased by large group owners (Albarran, 2002).

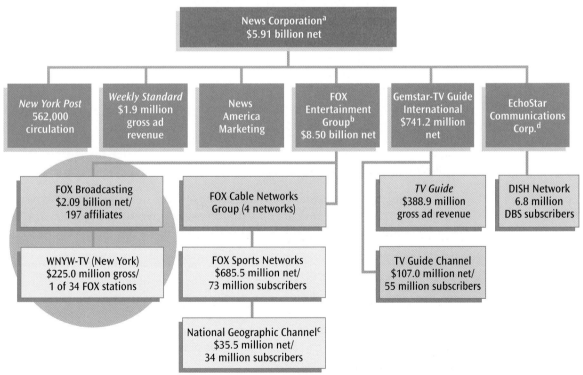

Television Network Ownership of Other Media Outlets

[a]Liberty Media Group owns 18 percent of News Corporation.
[b]News Corporation owns 85 percent of FOX Entertainment Group.
[c]FOX Cable owns 66.7 percent of the National Geographic Channel.
[d]News Corporation owns 2.2 percent of EchoStar.

In 1995, what company bought CBS?

Radio listening is projected to increase from an average of 994 hours per person per year in 2002 to 1,098 hours per person per year in 2007, not including time spent listening to broadcast stations on the Internet (Veronis, Suhler, & Stevenson, 2003). More listening time per person may translate into higher ratings and more income for radio stations.

Television

The finances of many television stations will be strained in years to come because the equipment and engineering needed for digital conversion may run into the millions of dollars. These costs will be partly offset by growth in advertising revenue. Stations will continue to change hands, as well, especially if the national television household cap is raised for television group ownership. Erosion of the television network audience by cable, satellite, and the Internet presents a serious threat to the more than half century old style of television delivery.

Recent projections show the number of hours spent watching broadcast television will decrease. In 2002, viewers each spent 786 hours per year watching broadcast television, and that number is projected to decrease to 759 hours per person per year by 2007 (Veronis, Suhler, & Stevenson, 2003). Broadcast television is moving toward *narrow-casting,* with a smaller share of the audience being available to the networks.

Networks own the vast majority of their programming, and the flow of programming is changing. Programs that once went from the networks to syndication are now going from the networks to other network-owned outlets. What's more, some programs that originate on cable go on to become prime-time network shows. For instance, in 2004, the hit show *Monk* originated on the USA channel but repeats were shown on ABC.

Continued diversification, including both new technologies and program resources, are also expected to continue. Video on demand (VOD) is expected to become more common, as the electronic media move toward digital delivery. Young people, who are growing up in a nonlinear world, will not likely want to continue being the complacent audience of linear prime-time program schedules.

Television stations will take a close look at the possibility of sending out more than one program over their digital signal, perhaps adding a pay-per-view or subscription service to their regular free over-the-air broadcasts. There has been some talk among broadcasters about a consortium of local broadcasters pooling their signals to provide an over-the-air subscription service, with multiple channels provided by each licensee (Kerschbaumer & Higgins, 2004). In some markets, such a service could provide 30 or more channels.

Cable and Satellite Providers

The cable and satellite industries both have strong revenue streams that tend to be predictable and stable because they are subscription based. A recent attempted merger between two companies in the satellite TV industry was unsuccessful, leaving room for competition between them.

The cable industry is expected to experience more consolidation in the future, resulting in even stronger MSOs (Albarran, 2002). After years of borrowing money to upgrade their systems so as to keep pace with the technology and the competition, the major MSOs are reaching the point where less capital outlay will be needed and income will start to cover the bills. In the next two years, the top six major MSOs are expected to show a profit. And with extra cash in hand, the large MSOs will likely be looking for more systems to buy (Higgins, 2004).

Consumer spending for cable and satellite service is projected to increase from $222 in 2002 to $283 in 2007 per person per year (Veronis, Suhler, & Stevenson, 2003). More people will sign up, and current subscribers may spend more for premium services. The number of hours spent with these delivery systems is expected to grow from 914 in 2002 to 1,026 hours per person per year in 2007.

Multichannel Multipoint Distribution Services

In March 1999, Sprint and WorldCom (parent company of MCI) began acquiring multichannel multipoint distribution service (MMDS) licenses. Their intention was to use the MMDS spectrum space to provide wireless broadband Internet service. This application is still in a test mode, but it may become a very important service in the future.

The Internet

Perhaps more so than the *content* of the Internet, *access* to the Internet is where change will continue. Dial-up connections are being abandoned in favor of broadband connections via DSL and cable modems. On college campuses and at corporate offices, hotels, and even commercial enterprises like coffee shops and restaurants, wired broadband is being replaced with wireless access.

The future may also hold surprises in the area of connections. While wireless access is found in more and more places, the standard of 802.11b and g (known as *WiFi*) may be replaced by ultrawideband, or UWB. UWB, which is found in the area of the electromagnetic spectrum used by garage door openers and portable telephones, has a very high speed capability: 40 to 60 megabits per second, nearly 10 times the speed of WiFi. It can also go through walls and requires less power than previous wireless systems. In the future, UWB may be used to stream video to television sets (Kuchinskas, 2003). This would open the door for Internet delivery of television, a change that would greatly affect the cable, satellite, and broadcast network businesses.

The number of U.S. households connected to broadband also will continue to climb. Jupiter Research predicts that wireless broadband households will outnumber wired (dial-up) households by the year 2004 and that the number of broadband households will reach over 31 million by 2008 (Greenspan, 2003). An important use of broadband among surveyed households was listening to music, indicating that the use of broadband computers for audio and visual entertainment may encourage shifts away from both cable subscriptions and satellite subscriptions. Consumer use is expected to increase from 154 hours per person per year in 2002 to 216 hours in 2007 (Veronis, Suhler, & Stevenson, 2003). Internet use for commerce will also expand and attract more investors but not with the intensity that led to the first Internet boom and bust (Jessell, 2004).

In July 2004, the FCC watched a demonstration of Internet delivery via powerlines, after which chairman Michael Powell stated, "Powerline technology holds the great promise to bring high-speed Internet access to every power outlet in America" ("Future Is Bright," 2004). This new technology may change the way many people access the Internet and thus affect the business of all other Internet delivery systems.

Summary

An undeniable fact about broadcasting and other electronic media is that they are businesses. They exist because they can generate enough revenue to cover their expenses and perhaps bring a profit to their owners.

Finding a business plan that would ensure success was the task of the early broadcasters. A number of business models were considered. The one that worked best for broadcasting was first based on toll broadcasting and then spot advertising, or the practice of charging advertisers for using airtime to reach potential customers. In other words, the broadcasters provided free programming to the audience, and the advertisers paid the broadcasters to reach that audience.

The federal government has traditionally encouraged diversity of opinion and ownership and discouraged the formation of monopolies. Since the late 1970s, the government has been relaxing electronic media regulation, thus permitting the marketplace to decide how electronic media should function in U.S. society.

A license must be obtained from the FCC in order to own a broadcast station. The FCC expects the prospective owner to be a citizen of this country, a person of good character, someone with enough money to build and operate the station, and someone who will program the station with an eye toward public interest, convenience, and necessity. When a new frequency becomes available, it is now commonly auctioned to the highest bidder, who must then apply and meet the requirements for licensing. In order to keep a license, the owner must continue to operate with the local market in mind and maintain a public file, containing documentation of employment information, letters from the public, information about requests for political advertising, and other information about the station's advertising and programming for children.

The three major networks—ABC, CBS, and NBC—dominated broadcasting for many years. Their ownership remained stable until the mid 1980s, when ABC and NBC were both sold and a new television network, FOX, began. In the mid 1990s, three new networks were formed by Warner Bros. (the WB), United Paramount (UPN), and Paxson Communications (PAX).

The cable industry has also undergone considerable consolidation. Small systems have been bought by MSOs, which can afford the technology, forming even larger companies.

The Internet presents many possibilities for audio and video program delivery—generally for relatively little cost and readily available technology. Radio stations can simulcast their signals on the Internet using streaming technology. Web radio has encountered some legal problems regarding copyright and advertising.

Cross-ownership occurs when one company or individual owns a broadcast station and a newspaper in the same market. The FCC has traditionally forbid these combinations but attempted to drop this restriction in 2003. This rule change has been delayed by the courts and is still a subject of much debate.

Technological changes will continue to influence ownership patterns. Traditional media owners will keep buying companies that can provide new delivery systems. Radio industry consolidation will continue but at a slower pace. Likewise, radio listening is expected to increase. Television ownership will see further consolidation, but the audience cap will most likely remain where it is, preventing the largest owners from getting much larger. Broadcast viewing hours are expected to drop, while other delivery systems will enjoy increased viewing hours. Broadcasters are considering other ways of packaging and distributing the multiple programs they will provide digitally. The satellite television industry will not consolidate but cable will, leading to bigger MSOs. The number of hours and dollars spent on satellite and cable will increase.

Methods of accessing the Internet will change as slower methods of connecting are replaced by broadband. Broadband delivery by DSL, cable modem, and WiFi may be challenged by ultrawideband or powerline delivery. Consumer use of broadband will continue to increase.

Note

1. In June 2003, this rule change was blocked by a court in Philadelphia. This issue has generated quite a bit of controversy from citizens' groups that oppose the idea of big media becoming even bigger.

Operating, Producing, and Distributing

 SEE IT THEN

Radio

Television

Cable

 SEE IT NOW

Radio

Television

Cable and Satellite Systems

 SEE IT LATER

Production and Distribution

Broadcast Media

Cable Television

Satellite Delivery

In this chapter, you'll learn about:

- How radio and television stations have operated since the 1920s
- How other delivery systems operate
- How operations have changed since the introduction of the Telecommunications Act of 1996
- The production and distribution of programming for electronic media

Beginning in the 1920s, radio was a dominant force in American society, commanding the attention of millions of people on a regular basis. Programming was live, for the most part, and included mainly musical performances. The radio industry developed the network system, which is still dominant today. In addition, radio developed the business model of selling advertising time in order to support its operation.

Television inherited both the network system and the advertising business model, and then it proceeded to take over radio's programming and audience. By the early 1950s, television dominated radio, leaving it to look for another programming formula and another audience, which it found by using disc jockeys to play recorded music. Meanwhile, the television industry had to face the unique challenges of producing television, including larger studios, more rehearsal time, expensive and bulky equipment, and additional personnel. The demand for television signals in rural areas led to the development of cable television.

In fact, the production of radio and television have not changed that much over the years. Program formats are still similar, and production techniques have changed only gradually with the technology. The distribution of these media has changed, however—particularly that of television. Moreover, new electronic media have entered the picture, and the development of digital technology has brought about significant changes. The trends toward consolidation and convergence, which have been encouraged by the government, have also had a strong influence on electronic media and will likely continue to do so in the future.

This chapter looks at the operation, production, and distribution of electronic media: namely, radio, television, cable, and satellite.

SEE IT THEN

Radio

Operation

From its origin in the early 1920s, commercial broadcast radio has had to take care of a number of functions, or **operations**, in order to send out programming over the airwaves and to make enough money to stay in business. Those functions have included general management, engineering, programming, and sales.

The operations and business functions were carried out in much the same way in all stations: Programming was sent from the network to its owned-and-operated stations or to its affiliates and then broadcast to the audience. Stations without a network affiliation originated their own programming and broadcast it directly to the audience. The organization and number of personnel at the station varied with the size of the market and the size of the station.

GENERAL MANAGEMENT   The **general management** of a radio station has traditionally been responsible for hiring and firing, payroll and accounting, purchasing, contract administration and fulfillment, and the maintenance of offices, studios, and workplaces. In addition, general management has provided leadership, made decisions, communicated with station employees, and handled organization and general planning of programming.

TECHNICAL FUNCTIONS   In the early years, the technical functions of the station included the construction, maintenance, and supervision of the station's broadcast equipment for creating programming and sending out a broadcast signal. The **chief engineer**—who maintained the transmitter and antenna operations and installed and maintained all broadcast equipment—oversaw the engineering department of the station.

The chief engineer was guided by two authorities: first, the station ownership and management and second, the federal government's regulatory agency. From 1927 to 1934, that agency was the Federal Radio Commission; after 1934, it was the Federal Communications Commission (FCC). In order to keep ownership and management happy, the chief engineer provided a strong and clear signal to the audience. In order to keep the government happy, the chief engineer made sure that the broadcast transmitter and antenna complied with all technical rules. Those rules focused mainly on transmission: the power of the station, the frequency of the transmission, the antenna location and height, and the hours of operation.

Programming and Production

The **programming** functions of early radio included securing programming from the network, if the station was both owned and operated by the network or a network affiliate, and creating enough programming to fill the broadcast transmission schedule. The programming department, led by the **program director**, was responsible for two kinds of work: planning ahead and implementing (or executing) the programming plan. Programming personnel selected and scheduled programming based on the decisions and guidelines set by general management. Often, programming decisions were made in concert with the sales department. In fact, program decisions were strongly influenced by what the sales department felt it could sell.

In addition to network programs, local stations produced programs that originated from locations other than their own studios. For example, a program would feature a big band playing music to a live audience at a hotel or dance hall. The program would originate at the band's location and be sent via telephone wires to the radio station studio; the signal would then be sent to the station transmitter.

The term **live remote** was coined to describe these types of programs, and it is still in use today. A remote was easy to do, once set up. Namely, after the microphones were put in place and the telephone lines from the hotel to the radio studio were connected, the programming could be accessed by a station engineer each day at the same time by merely flipping a switch at the studio. Live remotes were often sponsored by the hotel at which the band was playing or an advertiser that wanted to affix its name to the band for the purposes of promotion. Stations like WBT in Charlotte, North Carolina, depended heavily on live remotes. In the 1920s, the station did a remote of live music from the Charlotte Hotel every day from 12:30 to 2:00 P.M.

Some stations had musicians on the payroll to provide both musical programs and background music. It was not unusual for some radio stations to have 10 or more musicians on the full-time staff. The musicians performed live at the station in a sound studio that contained microphones to pick up the music from the instruments. The microphones were connected to an audio console that controlled the sound level for each microphone. Since the band was generally the same from day to day, the microphone setup was minimal.

Programming and production were more difficult in later years. Before World War II, programs that were produced could not be stored easliy for later use because audio magnetic tape had not yet been invented. This meant that most programming was broadcast live, which presented problems for local broadcasters. For example, if a performer was caught in a traffic jam, suddenly got sick, or otherwise didn't get to the station at the correct time, no tape was available to fill time until a substitute performer could be found. When these kinds of problems came up, the station often relied on staff musicians to perform on short notice.

> **ZOOM IN**   10.1
> Take a look at how radio remotes were done in the 1920s and how musicians provided programming from the studio. Go to the WBT site, which gives the history of this radio station: www.wbt.com/history/history.cfm.

In the early days of radio, live remotes featured performers playing to live audiences at area hotels and dance halls.

RECORDED PROGRAMS   Beginning in the 1920s, audio programs were sometimes recorded on phonograph records, referred to as *electrical transcriptions (ETs),* using the 78-rpm (revolutions per minute) speed for music or the slower 33⅓-rpm speed for voice or archives. The equipment needed for recording was large and heavy, and the resulting sound quality was poor. By the late 1930s, developments had led to recording equipment that used steel tape or wire. But in fact, these systems were also heavy, the sound quality was not very good, and the steel tape or wire was expensive.

Networks didn't allow programs to be recorded for later play because of poor audio quality. Thus, big stars like Bing Crosby were forced to perform two shows a night in order to air the same program in different time zones. The Crosby Research Foundation sought patents that improved magnetic tape-recording techniques.

By the early 1950s, American companies were using plastic-based magnetic tape to produce audio recordings that were practical, affordable, and of high quality. Finally, performers could be taped and later aired in different time zones (Sterling & Kittross, 2002, p. 274).

FROM PROGRAMS TO FORMATS   With the popularity of television, network radio programs began to drop off dramatically, especially after the 1953–1954 season. The radio audience was watching TV instead of listening to the radio, especially at night, and advertisers followed the audience. As a result, the radio networks stopped producing radio programs or adapted them for television. As many of the popular radio network shows went to television, radio attempted to fill the void. Soap operas stayed on the radio until 1960 but then left for TV, leaving a large part of the day for local radio stations to fill (Willey, 1961).

The stations filled that time with music, which was often prerecorded. A blend of music, referred to as **middle of the road**, or **MOR**, was played by many stations. Others migrated toward musical genres and used record sales as a guide for selecting what to play. Creating programs for an all-music format was easy. And so, modern radio was born.

Beginning in the early 1950s, radio station formats went through many changes. MOR stations looked for ways to differentiate themselves from the other stations that played a mixture of musical styles. Top 40 formats featuring rock 'n' roll music became an important force in radio because they connected with baby-boomers, who were teens at the time. Whereas stations in the 1930s and 1940s had a mixture of programs— drama, comedy, music, quiz, variety—after the arrival of television, stations had to pick a musical format (e.g., rock 'n' roll, country, or MOR) or a talk format (e.g., news or religious). Eventually, many subcategories evolved within the formats. For example, rock 'n' roll stations produced offshoots like classic rock, alternative rock, pop, and contemporary. Over the years, radio changed from a medium of *programs* to a medium of *formats.*

Although news was often included for a few minutes each hour, most of the radio hour was filled with recorded or taped music. The announcer, now known as a **disc jockey (DJ)**, announced the titles of the songs, told jokes, and gave information about concerts and other events. The only content left for the station to produce was the commercials.

RADIO PRODUCTION AND DISTRIBUTION   A basic radio production system involved equipment that either picked up sounds, such as microphones, or reproduced previously recorded sounds, such as phonograph records and magnetic recordings. After the sounds were collected or played back, the signal then travelled to an **audio console** or **audio board.**

The audio board performed a number of functions. It modified the sound by increasing or decreasing the volume, changing the frequency, removing parts of the sound, mixing or combining the sound with other sounds, and then sending it to a storage device (i.e., magnetic audio tape) or the station transmitter. The radio station transmitter combined the audio signal with an electromagnetic wave signal, which was then sent to the transmitting antenna. The combined signal was emitted from the transmitting antenna in the form of invisible electromagnetic waves on the frequency assigned to the station.

> **ZOOM IN**   10.2
>
> Go to the Companion Website for this book, www.ablongman.com/medoffkaye1e, for a diagram of radio production.

Television

Operation

Television adopted the network radio model for business and operations and became immediately successful. Many network radio programs made a smooth transition to television, solving at least part of the question of what to show audiences. The television networks delivered entertainment shows the same way that radio did: through stations interconnected by AT&T wires. The networks provided the programming, and the stations merely broadcast it.

Television stations didn't get all of their programs from the networks, however. To fill nonnetwork times, stations either produced their own programs or found program sources. Television programming was more complicated and expensive to produce than radio programming. For instance, it required more rehearsal time, which involved more people and more equipment.

> **ZOOM IN**   10.3
>
> • Go to this link about early television studio dance and music production done in studio: www.richsamuels.com/nbcmm/garroway/boomballet.html.
>
> Download and view Segment 1 for the introduction by Dave Garroway, a television host on an early version of the *Today* show.
>
> Download and view Segment 2 for the performance.
>
> • See how makeup was used in early television by watching the newsreel at www.farnovision.com/media/newsreel.html.
>
> • Go to Mark Harmon's Thinking Visually website: http://excellent.comm.utk.edu/~mdharmon/visual.

Production

Television production in the 1940s and 1950s was quite a bit different than it is now. Cameras were huge, expensive, and limited in terms of technology. Since the early broadcasts were all in black and white, little consideration was given to color. Clothing or objects in the colors of pink and blue often appeared as identical tones of gray on a black-and-white screen, and colors like brown, purple, and even dark green yielded the same shade of dark gray. Moreover, in order to ensure that performers' facial features would be apparent onscreen, white face makeup and black lipstick were used.

Shooting outside the studio meant taking a heavy studio camera into the field and supplying it with power from an electrical outlet. (Keep in mind that cameras were not battery operated and portable until the late 1970s.) These factors limited the types of programs that could be offered live on television to those that justified the huge outlay of equipment, personnel, and vehicles. On-location shooting was thus limited to sporting events, concerts, big parades,

In the early days, a television studio camera often required more than one person to operate it.

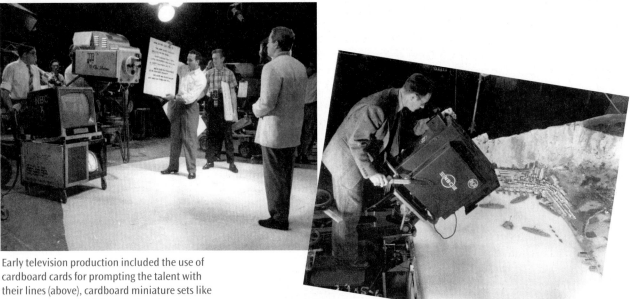

Early television production included the use of cardboard cards for prompting the talent with their lines (above), cardboard miniature sets like this harbor scene (right), and other simple devices like a drum showing program credits (below).

and special events like political party conventions, which were scheduled far ahead of their broadcast dates.

ZOOM IN   10.4
Go to www.ablongman.com/medoffkaye1e, the Companion Website for this text, to find out more about television studios.

Lighting equipment was also heavy, and the bulbs were very powerful. They had to be strong in order to generate enough light for the old cameras to reproduce pictures. Given this, the lights generated quite a bit of heat, often raising the temperature of a small set to an uncomfortable level.

Visual effects were primitive in these early days. Miniature sets made of cardboard were common. Titles were drawn or printed on cards and then placed in front of the camera.

REHEARSAL TIME   The production of a television drama or comedy required the actors to know their lines. This had not been the case in radio, where actors could perform their lines with a script in hand. As such, television, especially in its early days, was

A rehearsal for a 1950s broadcast television program.

more like live theatre, requiring quite a bit of rehearsing for actors to learn their lines as well as their movements.

A rehearsal required everything that was needed for the final taping: lighting, props/scenery, cameras, camera operators, engineers and other personnel, and studio space. Also, since one program would be rehearsing while another program was being aired, the station needed to have at least two studios. For this reason, the typical broadcast week included out-of-studio productions, such as sporting events (e.g., boxing, baseball), as well as in-studio productions.

PERSONNEL Operating a television station before 1950 required many more people than were needed to operate a radio station. Moreover, television personnel had to perform a variety of tasks, many of which were different from those in radio. In particular, the visual element of television created the need for makeup, hairstyling, and costumes plus a wide range of sets and props. The inset on page 224 shows the many departments and jobs needed to run a large television station, produce programs, and generate revenue in the 1950s. Their modern-day equivalents are identified, as well. Note the similarities between the items on these lists and the items you might find on a list of the personnel needed for a theatre production.

Cable

Cable television was a small business from 1948 until the early 1970s. Most early ventures were operated by a handful of owners in a small town. Large cities had not yet been wired for cable because plenty of free broadcast television signals were available. Early cable company owners took on many roles and often supervised many overlapping departments, including engineering, sales, and business.

FYI

Television Station Departments and Job Titles: 1950s versus Now

1950s JOBS		MODERN-DAY JOBS
Department	**Personnel**	General manager
Executive Offices	Station manager	Sales manager
	Sales manager	• Sales associates
	Program manager	News director
	Engineering	• Executive producers
Program Production	Writers	• Producers
	Directors	• Writers
Engineering	Engineers	• Editors
	Operating maintenance	• Graphics designers
Sales and Service	Salespersons	• Assignment editors
Scenic	Designers	• Photographers
	Artists	• Reporters/Anchors
Carpentry	Carpenters	• Sports
Property Shop	Property workers	Director of engineering
Electrical	Electricians	• Managers
Visual and Sound Effects	Effects specialists	• Maintenance engineers
		• Operating engineers
		• Building maintenance engineer/Carpenter
Paint Shop	Artists	Program development manager
	Painters	• Producers
Wardrobe	Costumers	• Directors
Control Room	Operating engineers	• Editors
Studio	Operating crew	• Promotions editors/Photographers
	Actors	Programming director
Dressing Rooms	Make-up artists	Traffic director
	Hairdressers	Marketing/Community relations director
Film Studio	Projectionist	• Station promoters
	Operating engineer	IT administrator (computer network/telephone people)
	Librarian	Human resource director
Master Control	Operating engineers	Accounting director
Transmitter	Operating engineers	• Payroll coordinator
	Maintenance engineers	• Business manager
		Interactive director
		• Website designers/editors

Source: Information about the 1950s jobs based on Hutchinson, 1950.

Operation

A cable company rarely had reason to produce programs because it simply offered existing shows to subscribers. The cable company's main function was therefore engineering: gathering television signals and packaging them for transmission to subscribers via the cable wires. The engineering department received television signals from both local and distant stations and sent them to the cable **head end**, where the signals were put on channels to send to the audience. Most cable systems had 12 or fewer channels, and the television signals they gathered were placed on the 12 VHF channels (numbered 2 through 13), regardless of what channel each signal had originally been broadcast on.

Eventually, as cable technology improved, those systems that carried more than 12 channels provided converters to their subscribers, allowing them to receive more than the 12 channels allowed on their television set's VHF tuner. The cable input was connected to the set-top converter, and another cable was connected to the television set. The subscriber merely tuned the television to channel 3 or 4 and then used the set-top box to select channels.

An early set-top cable converter box.

SALES AND MARKETING   The task of the sales and marketing department of a cable company was straightforward during the small-system era: It sold subscriptions for the basic (and only) array of channels it offered. The system didn't insert its own locally sold commercials, and it didn't have premium channels or pay-per-view programs to offer. And since only one cable system was franchised in a market, it didn't compete with other cable systems in its market. Its source of revenue came from subscriptions.

DISTRIBUTION   Once the various television signals were sent to the head end and placed on channels, all of the channel signals were sent out through a system of shielded coaxial wire (i.e., a conductor with a metal sheath around a common axis or center). The system for distributing the signals to subscribers resembled a tree with a trunk and branches. Coaxial cable was used (and still is) because it could carry many

Cable Distribution to Homes in a City

Signals are received by satellite, microwave, and broadcast antennas and combined at the *head end*. From the head end, the signal is sent through a system of wires that have amplifiers (i.e., the round symbols in the drawing) to boost the signal strength and continue the signal to houses connected to cable (i.e., the square symbols).

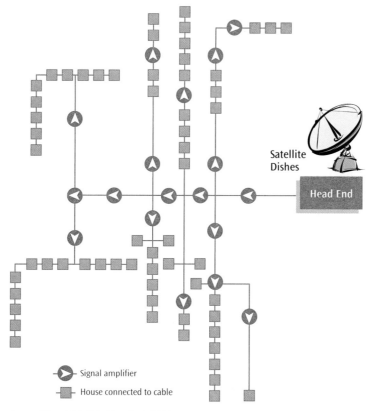

Source: "How Cable Television Works," 2004.

signals at once and reduced interference better than regular wire. Nonetheless, the television signals lost strength after traveling a distance on the wire, so amplifiers were used at regular distances to enhance the signals and make sure they were strong enough for television tuners to detect.

As the cable business became lucrative, it drew the attention of large media companies. They began buying up smaller cable systems in the 1970s, a trend that was later accelerated by the change brought on by satellite technology. In order to meet the demands of subscribers, cable systems had to become satellite capable. Home Box Office (HBO) became very popular in the late 1970s, and all cable systems were pressured to carry it. Larger companies, especially those that owned other businesses, often had the capital required for the upgrade to satellite.

Larger companies also had an advantage in acquiring franchises. Small cable companies could not afford to bid on large-city franchises because the cost to build such a system was too high. Therefore, the larger franchises made deals with the bigger companies, who could raise the large amount of money needed for financing. Ultimately, many small systems had to sell out because they could not afford to upgrade the systems they owned or expand to larger, more profitable markets. Since the 1970s, most small systems have been acquired by large multiple system operators (MSOs).

 **SEE IT NOW**

Radio

Structure of a Typical Station

From the early 1950s until the mid 1990s, the radio audience grew along with revenues. The number of stations increased dramatically, and most stations were able to show a profit and stay in business. Although the audience had shifted from AM to FM, most stations had a management structure that stood the test of time and worked well both in the small, independently owned stations and the stations that belonged to corporate groups.

Dramatic changes occurred in the mid 1990s as a result of the Telecommunications Act of 1996. Trends toward ownership consolidation and convergence in both radio and television changed how a station was organized and operated, and consolidating station jobs among group personnel became quite common.

Before 1996, a radio station often had a full array of managers and workers in each of its departments. But after 1996, some of the managers working for radio station groups performed managerial tasks for more than one station. This was especially common after an acquisition. For example, suppose a group like Clear Channel acquires four stations in a market. Before the acquisition, each of those four stations might have had its own program director. After the acquisition, the group will select one *regional* or *market program director,* who will be charged with making program decisions for all four stations. This trend also extends to other departments at the station. In sales, the four sales directors might be replaced by one sales director and one assistant director to manage sales for all four stations. It is also common practice for salespeople to sell for more than one station and possibly all stations in a group. Although selling for more than one station presents some obvious problems, like competition among stations within the same group, these issues are small when compared to the value of reducing expenses by decreasing personnel.

Typical Structure of a Small Radio Station

This flowchart and the one below show the departments usually found in radio stations, small and large. To see more organizational flowcharts, go to the Companion Website for this text: **www.ablongman.com/medoffkaye1e.**

Typical Structure of a Large Radio Station

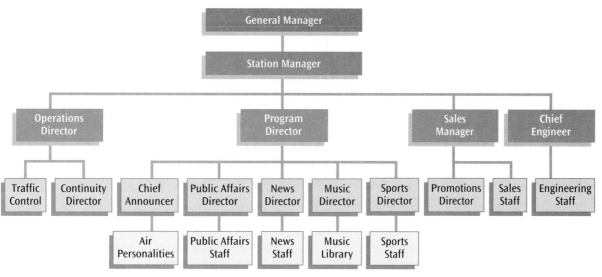

Source: Sherman, 1995.

In some cases, groups save money by combining the studios of several stations into one facility. Operating one large facility with several studios and on-air control rooms is often less expensive than operating several fully equipped studios at different locations. Namely, consolidation reduces overhead costs like bookkeeping, billing, subscriptions, professional membership fees, and insurance.

MANAGEMENT   Today, the **general manager** of a radio station is the top executive and responsible for all station activities. He or she supervises the station's activities and financial health. In many cases, the general manager supervises more than one station; typically, the same general manager is in charge of the AM and FM operations owned by the same company.

The **station manager** oversees one station and often answers to the general manager. Overall, the station manager has three important roles: to make the station function efficiently, to provide the maximum return to the owners or shareholders, and to adequately serve the commitments of the station's license. He or she is involved in day-to-day operations of the station and supervises all department managers. As such, the station manager selects the key people who will manage and operate the station and is in charge of hiring and firing station personnel. This means that the station manager must be familiar with the various labor unions active in broadcasting (Quaal & Brown, 1976). The station manager also must be knowledgeable about legal issues that may affect the station. Knowledge of FCC rules and regulations, as well as knowledge of local, state, and federal laws that impact the station and its operation, is crucial.

SALES   The sales department is responsible primarily for generating the revenue needed to keep the station in business. The sales staff is in contact with the business community, selling advertising to local, regional, and national businesses. The **sales manager** hires and trains the sales staff and sets sales goals. In larger stations, the sales manager's position is often split into two positions: *local sales manager* and *national (or regional) sales manager.*

Sometimes, the sales department is responsible for scheduling commercials as well as selling them. Most sales departments also have a **traffic manager** and staff to help with scheduling commercials and other program elements. In larger stations, one or more people also help with research and ratings, sometimes even conducting audience surveys to help the sales effort.

PROGRAMMING   The **program director (PD)** is responsible for everything that goes out over the air. He or she usually works closely with a **music director,** if the station has a music format, and a **news director,** if the station produces its own newscasts. Next down in the chain of command is a **chief announcer,** who supervises all the disc jockeys, newscasters, and other announcers. The PD often supervises a **director of production,** who in turn supervises the creation of commercials, promotions, and other prerecorded messages.

A Wired Newsroom

In a *wired newsroom,* many people can access news information for editing and scriptwriting. The news information is sent from a wire receiver to a wire server. The files are then sent through a router to a file server and to a news director or producer. Other producers or writers can access the information from the file server at workstations in the newsroom. After the information is edited and put into script form, it can be sent directly to the prompters on the cameras in the news studio. The newscaster reads the story from the script in front of the camera.

Source: Based on drawing from www.eznews.com/tour/tech.php.

The PD has always been responsible for music selection and scheduling. In addition, in many stations, the news operation is part of the programming department, especially stations that are almost all music with some news. Stations with a large news component, such as those that are news-talk or sports, often have a separate news department.

A Converged Newsroom

Consolidation has led to changes in how the news is created and distributed. In some companies that own multiple outlets, the news operations of several stations are combined into one operation with several distribution paths. For instance, in Phoenix, Arizona, Gannett owns KPNX-TV, the *Arizona Republic,* and a website, azcentral.com. Stories that might ordinarily be covered by three separate news operations can be covered by one operation and distributed by three. Gannett has a multimedia team of three reporters and a photographer that put together stories for its television station, newspaper, and website. The team interacts with the producers and managing editor at the television station to decide which stories will work best on which medium. Stories that air on television are often streamed on the website. While the newspaper side often focuses on longer stories with more context, the television side goes for shorter stories with more of a human element, which can be told in one to two minutes. One reporter may have stories on all three media. *Arizona Republic* reporter Brahm Resnik does a column for the morning daily paper, reports on KPNX from 5:00 to 7:00 A.M., and also has a column on azcentral.com.

For more about converged newsrooms, go to www.poynterextra.org/convergence/catalog.htm.

Reporter Brahm Resnik writes stories for a local newspaper column, reports them on a morning news show, and also presents them on an accompanying website.

The news director is responsible for writing, scheduling, and delivering newscasts throughout the day. If the station has a syndication service or a network that supplies some or all of the news, then the news director is in charge of the contractual agreements with those businesses. In addition, the news director is responsible for the entire staff, which may include the following:

- *News producers* who put together news stories and news programs
- *Reporters* who actually go out of the studio and gather news stories
- *Newscasters* who deliver the news to the audience in front of the camera or microphone
- *Specialized news personnel,* like play-by-play and color announcers for sports events
- *Weather specialists and meteorologists,* who are educated in meteorology and deliver the current weather and forecasts
- *Special reporters* who work as business analysts, environmental reporters, and so on

ENGINEERING/OPERATIONS   The station personnel responsible for the operation, care, and installation of technical broadcast equipment work in the engineering/operations department. In some stations, this department is split into an engineering department, which maintains and installs the transmitter and all technical equipment, and an operations department, which runs the equipment and makes sure that there is appropriate workflow from one area of the station to another. **Workflow** refers to a process like making sure that the tape (or disk or file) of a new commercial gets to where it needs to be in order to be aired at the right time.

The person in charge of the engineering area is the **chief engineer.** He or she hires people to install and maintain the equipment and also makes recommendations to the station manager or general manager about new technologies and equipment needed by the station. Knowledge about computers and computer networks has become much more important recently because all broadcast stations now rely heavily on computer technology for daily operation.

PROMOTION   Before the introduction of television, the need for radio promotion was less than it is now. Radio was unique and drew an audience as soon as radio equipment became available. It was the only electronic medium before World War II, and the audience could only choose from those stations they could receive in their homes. Until the late 1940s, the audience didn't have television, cable, satellite, or the Internet to divert its attention.

To be sure, that's all changed. Radio, like all electronic media, must promote itself to maintain an audience and stay financially viable. Today, the traditional goals for promoting a modern-day radio station are as follow:

1. *Audience acquisition:* To give listeners a reason to sample the station
2. *Audience maintenance:* To give listeners a reason to continue to listen to the station
3. *Audience recycling:* To give listeners a reason to return to the station (**Vertical recycling** gets the audience to return later in the day, and **horizontal recycling** gets the audience to return at the same **daypart**, or time period, later in the week.)
4. *Sales promotion:* To give advertisers a reason to buy advertising on the station
5. *Morale building:* To generate and maintain the station staff's energy and self-motivation

Radio promotion managers use two general methods for achieving their goals: **on-air promotion,** or using the station itself, and **external media,** or using other media, such as newspapers, to promote the station (Eastman & Klein, 1991). On-air promotion, the most common type of broadcast promotion, originally aired in unsold commercial **availabilities** during the day. In other words, a time slot, or availability, that had not already been sold by the sales department was used by the promotion department to promote the station. This practice changed in the 1970s, when promotional announcements became a scheduled entity that had purposeful placement and repetition. On-air promotions often plug other dayparts or programs along with giveaways, contests, and special events that involve the station.

External promotion utilizes all media other than the station itself. Radio stations often have **trade-out agreements**—in which media time or space is exchanged, rather than money—with television stations, local newspapers, and other media to promote the radio station's programming and personalities.

Promotion has become an integral part of the marketing strategy for broadcast radio stations. Building an audience for programs or formats in a competitive environment requires a careful and energetic plan, and the promotion must reach the potential audience with enough lead time to allow the audience to see the show. In addition, the promotion needs to be interesting enough to catch the attention of the intended audience.

Promotions are expected to generate ratings, revenue, and goodwill (i.e., to enhance the image of the station). These goals have to be accomplished while making sure that the promotional materials are in good taste, congruent with the overall station image, and realistic and factual enough not to create false expectations in the minds of the audience or advertisers.

ZOOM IN   10.5

For examples of internal and external station promotion for radio, go to the text's Companion Website: www.ablongman.com/medoffkaye1e.

CAREER TRACKS

Jason Moore-Greenke Promotions Director, Adult Contemporary Radio Station

● **What is your job? What do you do?**
Promotion director for a mainstream AC station in Portland, Oregon. I work synergistically with the sales and programming departments to increase ratings and revenue through station events, contests, and Web content. Other duties include supervising a part-time promotions staff and implementing the overall marketing of the station.

● **How long have you been doing this job?**
2½ years.

● **What was your first job in electronic media?**
A promotions assistant at Sports Radio 950 KJR-AM in Seattle, Washington.

● **What led you to the job?**
I interned, actively participated in my university radio station, and worked my way up from a part-time promotions assistant and board operator in a small market after graduating with a B.S. degree in electronic media.

● **What advice would you have for students who might want a job like yours?**
Earn a degree and be well rounded. Gain as much experience as you possibly can in every department as a student, intern, volunteer, or part-time employee. Do anything you can to get your foot in the door, and always be willing to learn more and work hard.

When did DVDs become available in the United States?

Television
Structure of a Typical Station

Operating a television station involves many different organizational schemes. Each group or station in a group might have a slightly different organization, but the departments discussed in the following sections are the ones that are most common to television stations today.

MANAGEMENT   The general management of a television station is performed by a person who is responsible for all its departments. The title of this person varies by company and depends on whether the person is responsible for one station or more than one. If more than one station is involved, the title of the person in charge is either **regional vice president** or **general manager.** The manager of a single station is usually called the **station manager.**

Typical Structure of a Television Station
This flowchart shows the departments usually found in a television station.

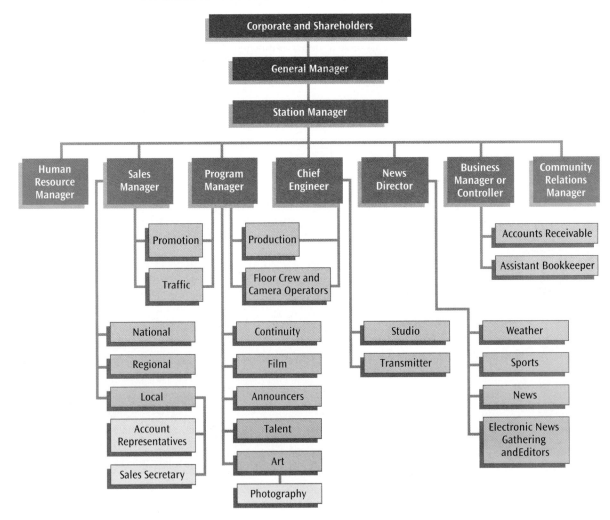

Both a general manager and a station manager have assistants and staff to help with management of the station. Their duties include planning for the future and setting goals, evaluating employee performance, hiring and firing, leading and motivating, and representing the station to the public and business community.

BUSINESS/FINANCE   The business or finance department is the place where money flows both in and out of the station. While the sales department makes the sales, the business department takes care of billing accounts receivable, such as payments that advertisers owe the station, and then collecting the money. When the station purchases equipment, like microphones, the business department is usually consulted first to see if the station can afford it. The business department also produces reports required by the government or by general management to determine the station's financial performance.

The head of the business department is known by a number of titles, such as **business manager, chief financial officer (CFO),** or **controller.** Other personnel are accountants and bookkeepers, who record transactions and debit or credit the transactions to the appropriate station accounts.

PROGRAMMING   The programming department in a television station deals primarily with program acquisition and scheduling, rather than program production. Since most television stations are either network owned and operated or network affiliates, they get most of their programs from the networks. The program director must fill the remaining airtime, which is usually accomplished by obtaining programming that's already been produced from an outside source, like a syndicator. Stations use outside sources for programming primarily because the expense of producing local television entertainment shows is very high and requires time, people, equipment, and often studio space. However, some programs, such as local public affairs and news-related shows, are usually produced and are almost always done inhouse.

NEWS   Most television stations produce a local news program. Local news is very profitable and brings an audience to the station for other programming. Given this, local television news department often have large staffs and receive strong support from general management. Most stations air newscasts at several times during the day, requiring many hours of news gathering and production, both in the studio and in the field.

The **news director (ND)** is responsible for all newscasts and personnel in the department. In addition to the ND and staff, there are producers of newscasts and news stories, as well as writers, story and script editors, assignment editors, video photographers, reporters, and anchors. Most stations also have several weathercasters and several sportscasters.

ENGINEERING   The engineering department has the responsibility of installing and maintaining all broadcast equipment used by the station, which includes not only the audio and video production equipment but the signal transmitting equipment, as well. Engineers are often split into several categories: **maintenance engineers,** who keep production equipment working; **operating engineers,** who keep the station on the air; **building/maintenance engineers,** who take care of the facility; and **information technology engineers,** who deal with computers and telephone networking.

Since the late 1990s, television engineering departments have been preoccupied with the enormous task of changing the station's signal from analog to digital. To do so involves switching transmitters and frequencies along with much of the production and signal-routing equipment in the station.

CAREER TRACKS

Jennifer Burgess   Television Anchor/Reporter

• **What is your job? What do you do?**

My job description is "anchor/reporter." However, the appropriate question would be, "What *isn't* my job?" At my station, I write the stories for and produce the morning newscast. I also put together the weather forecast for the day, and then I anchor both: news and weather. I also report during the day, after the morning show is over. My day-side responsibilities include turning one, sometimes two packages, helping produce for the 6:00 P.M. show, and writing a brief paragraph about the story I've covered during the day for an afternoon radio report. My day starts at 2:45 A.M., when my alarm clock goes off. I'm in at work by 4:15 A.M., and I never know exactly when I'll be done for the day—but 10 or 12 hours is not unusual.

• **How long have you been doing this job?**

I've been anchoring and reporting for nearly two years.

• **What was your first job in electronic media?**

Actually, my first job was at my university's student TV operation as a weather anchor and reporter. That was

great! My first professional job was actually as a production assistant and fill-in reporter. I guess you have to get your foot in somewhere.

• **What led you to the job?**

I knew I had to put some time in, and I really wanted to anchor. I figured I would set a timeline of one year. If I wasn't anchoring at my station in one year, then I would move on and try to get an entry-level anchor job somewhere else.

• **What advice would you have for students who might want a job like yours?**

Definitely get an internship at a large station. This business is all about contacts, street smarts, and hard work. Make contacts and keep them organized. Keep in touch with those contacts on a regular basis. Don't be afraid to be original yet professional, driven yet humble, and be prepared to be broke. Then, remember: There will be a payoff someday. And don't forget to help others out along the way, as well.

CAREER TRACKS

Doug Drew   Executive Director, News Division, 602 Communications

• **What is your job? What do you do?**

Executive director, News Division, 602 Communications. Conduct training for television stations and networks in reporting, producing, writing.

• **How long have you been doing this job?**

Six years.

• **What was your first job in electronic media?**

I was a reporter for the NBC affiliate in Flagstaff, Arizona.

• **What led you to the job?**

I spent four years as a reporter for the television station at Ohio University, where I went to school. OU allows students to produce and present a half-hour newscast each night. A few of the students hold paid positions, and I was fortunate enough to obtain

one of them. In addition, while I was at Ohio University, I also worked for the Associated Press Broadcast Division. With the opportunities to work at the television station and with AP while in school, in addition to my classwork in the radio-television program, I was more than ready to enter the real world of broadcast news.

• **What advice would you have for students who might want a job like yours?**

Get involved ASAP as an intern, or work in a broadcast newsroom while still in school. The hands-on experience is invaluable. When applying for jobs, employers will look beyond your education to see what experience you have.

SALES   Television sales departments are similar to radio sales departments in that they are divided by national and regional/local categories. However, television stations often have more salespeople, more assistants, and more people involved in audience research than radio stations. And because of television's larger audience, television advertising is more expensive and generates more dollars for the station than radio advertising.

The sales department usually has a **general sales manager,** a **national sales manager,** and a **local sales manager.** It also will have account executives, who sell spots; a traffic manager, who schedules commercials; and researchers, who interpret and prepare audience ratings information for use in sales.

COMMUNITY RELATIONS AND PROMOTIONS   A television station often has a community relations department that promotes the station and participates in community events. Another title for this department is *marketing,* as this department markets the station's product (i.e., its programs and personalities) to the audience.

The promotions department has developed an increasingly important role since the 1970s due to industry changes—primarily, the decreasing dominance of the networks, the rise in importance of local news, and the need to establish station identity among the numerous channels available from cable and satellite. The heavy competition for viewers (and of course, advertisers) has created a promotions effort in stations that is based on consumer research, competitive positioning, long-range strategizing, and targeting specific audience segments.

ZOOM IN   10.6
To view examples of television promotion, go to the Companion Website for this text: **www.ablongman.com/medoffkaye1e.**

CAREER TRACKS

Mavel Vidrio   News Promotions Director

• What is your job? What do you do?

I am the news promotions director at KLFY-TV. I create promotions to make the station look good on air and "teases" to promote the news.

• How long have you been doing this job?

I have been at this position for about four months. Before that, I was the commercial production director, responsible for creating commercials for clients of the station. Previously, I was a production assistant for the evening newscasts.

• What was your first job in electronic media?

My first job was a photojournalist at KSWT, a CBS-affiliate station in Yuma, Arizona. Well, that was my title, but I did a heck of a lot more than that. I was not only the photographer but also an editor and production assistant. My day would begin at 8:00 A.M. and would end at 11:00 P.M. and then start all over again the next day. It was a tiring but rewarding job because I gained so much experience there.

• What led you to the job?

I had no idea what I wanted to do with the rest of my life as of my junior year in high school. That changed when I took a television production course offered for the first time at the school. I took classes in college that would help me learn what I needed to know about production.

• What advice would you have for students who might want a job like yours?

My advice is to be patient and hard working in all you do because it reflects who you are. Internships are the way to go while in school. The more experience you can get, the better it is for you once you graduate and are out in the workforce. You have to adjust often and learn new things all the time. I'd also recommend learning good communication skills. The harder you work, the faster you can obtain your goals.

The average person watches how many hours of television a week?

HUMAN RESOURCES   A human resources department is found in larger stations that have large staffs. This department locates new employees through advertising and other search strategies and then provides orientation to them by explaining the benefits and services available. The human resources department also conducts exit interviews and sometimes offers placement help to employees that are leaving the station.

PRODUCTION   Television production personnel can be found in a variety of departments in the station. For example, those who operate television production equipment often work in the programming department but sometimes in the engineering department. Since much of what production personnel produce is commercials, the sales director may be in charge of this type of production. In a station that produces some of its own programs, production personnel may be found in the program development division of the programming department. *Station promotional announcements (SPAs)* are produced by production personnel, but staff members who shoot news video on location, known as *news photographers,* are usually part of the news department.

Studio versus Field Production

When a station produces its own television program, it originates either in the studio or outside the studio in the field.

STUDIO TELEVISION   Numerous programs are produced in television studios: at the network level, news, interview, talk, game, and quiz shows, along with dramas (mostly soap operas). Local news shows are almost always shown live from the local station's studio. Most other programs are stored on video tape and broadcast at a later time.

A television studio is a large, open space designed to control several aspects of the environment. The lighting and sound, for instance, are under complete control of the television crew and manipulated to fit the production. The television studio also is a temperature-controlled environment, which allows performers to be comfortable under the hot lights. The studio is soundproof, as well; that is, no noise from the outside world can be heard inside it. (Obviously, having a fire engine drive down the street outside the studio would be quite a distraction if the siren could be heard in the middle of a romantic scene in a soap opera.) The studio is wired so that microphones can be connected to a variety of places, often on each of the four walls of the studio.

Television studios are windowless to prevent unwanted light from hitting a scene. Lighting is always supplied by special video lights, most of which are attached to a system of pipes, called the **lighting grid**, that is attached to the ceiling. The lights are controlled from a centralized **lighting board** that allows a member of the lighting crew to connect numerous lights and control their intensities for use in a production.

The cameras in a studio are mounted on large, heavy, roll-around devices called **pedestals.** Using a pedestal, the camera operator can make smooth and easy camera movements in any direction. The pictures from the cameras are fed through camera cables to a small room near the studio called the **control room.** Inside the control room, the camera cables are connected to a **camera control unit** (CCU), which a crew member uses to control the color and brightness of each camera.

The video signal travels to a device called a **switcher,** which is similar to the audio board that processes the audio signal. The video signal sent to the switcher can be changed in many ways and combined with the signals from other cameras, video tape, or other video storage devices.

Character generators are like sophisticated word processors. They can add titles to pictures to create a credit **roll** at the end of a program, showing the names of the people who made the program, or a **crawl** across the bottom of the screen, as in the case of a

Typical Television Studio Floorplan

Here is the floorplan of a television studio. A news set is in the upper-left corner. The numbers along the dotted lines indicate the locations of lights. The connections for cameras, audio, telephone, and power are shown along the perimeter of the drawing. For a photo of a typical studio, go to www.ablongman.com/medoffkaye1e, the Companion Website for this text.

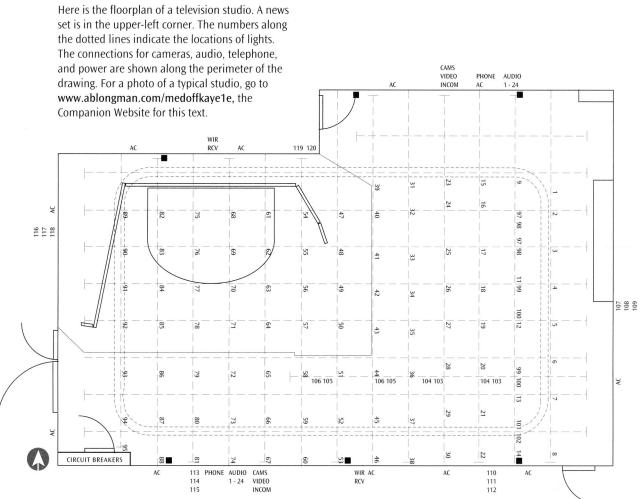

Source: NAU Television Services.

severe weather watch or special bulletin. **Special effects generators (SEGs)** can make a multitude of creative changes to the video, such as slow motion, color variations, or a strobe effect.

The switcher also produces the changes between cameras or video sources that keep the program moving. The change can be a **dissolve**, in which one shot slowly changes to another; a **fade**, or a slow change from black to a picture or from a picture to black; a **cut**, or an instantaneous change from one camera to another; or a **wipe**, as when one video image pushes another off the screen.

After leaving the switcher, the video signal goes to one or more **monitors** to allow the **director**, the person in charge of the actual production, to see what each camera sees, what pictures are available via other sources (e.g., video tape or special effects generators), and which picture is actually going on the air. The director can make changes as the production is happening. For example, he or she might suggest that one of the camera operators get a **close-up (CU)** shot, instead of a **wide shot (WS)**. He or she also might tell the **technical director (TD)**, the person who runs the switcher, to change from one camera to another to get a **medium shot (MS)**, perhaps of the host of the program.

ZOOM IN 10.7

Go to www.ablongman.com/medoffkaye1e, the text's Companion Website, to see examples of transitions (cuts, fades, dissolves, wipes) and the different kinds of television shots (close-up, zoom-in, and so on).

What appeared in every episode of Seinfeld?

Changes of shots are accomplished by using a set of commands that tell the technical director which video picture to use next. The director might tell the TD "Dissolve to camera 2," which means that the TD should use a dissolve transition from the current or video source to camera 2. The TD will push the appropriate button or move the appropriate lever on the switcher to accomplish the change requested by the director.

After leaving the switcher, the video signal is either stored on some type of storage device, like a video tape machine or DVD, or sent directly to the transmitter for broadcasting. In some productions, like when ESPN is covering a sports event, the signal is sent to a satellite uplink so the program can be transmitted by satellite to the cable system.

PORTABLE OR FIELD TELEVISION   After battery-powered cameras became available for news and general production in the late 1970s, news stories and entertainment programs could be shot outside the studio. Field production added a sense of realism to television that was missing in the earlier days of studio television. Instead of constructing a set for each scene or program, a portable video crew could go to a location appropriate for the scene or program.

In addition, portable video has allowed news photographers to shoot breaking news and have it aired almost immediately at the station in a process known as *ENG,* or *electronic news gathering.* Stations regularly use field crews to do live shots during their newscasts, which are sent to the stations via microwave. Portable video equipment also allow **videographers** to go to an advertiser's place of business and shoot live action, instead of using still pictures inside a store, restaurant, or car dealership. After the video is shot, the tape is edited by a **video tape editor**, who prepares it for airing.

Cable and Satellite Systems

There are about 9,900 cable systems in the United States, each of which has an agreement to operate within a given geographical area. The majority of these systems are owned by large national and multinational MSOs. The individual cable systems operate under the provisions of a franchise agreement with a local municipality (i.e., town or city).

Due to the nature of the equipment, cable systems must have many local employees to provide service for the head end, for wiring and amplifiers, and for customer "drops," or the wires that enter people's homes. Unlike group-owned radio stations,

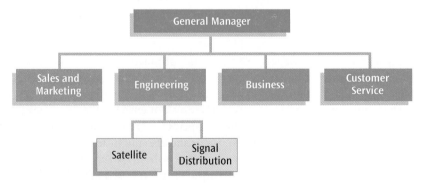

Typical Structure of a Cable System

A local cable system has four main departments under the
supervision of a general manager, as shown in this flowchart.

Typical Structure of a Satellite Distribution Company

This flowchart shows how a satellite distribution company is organized.

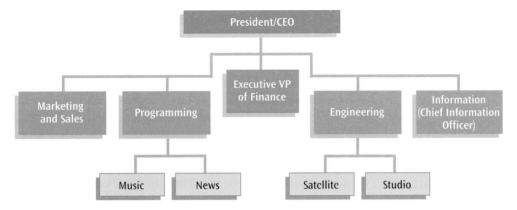

which can operate with fewer employees because of automation and voice tracking, cable systems don't make staff reductions because they are owned by MSOs. For example, a subscription to a broadband service involves a cable modem installation, a service that requires local personnel who have computer technology knowledge and experience and who can physically install the equipment.

The satellite industry relies on an organization or structure similar to that of broadcasting. It has senior management, such as a chief executive officer (CEO), at the top of the organization and an executive vice president and chief financial officer just below. This layer of management has four additional areas of responsibility, assigned to these departments: marketing and sales, programming, engineering, and information.

As is the case with large broadcast stations, numerous layers of subcategories are contained in each department or division. For example, in the programming department, a satellite radio station will have separate subdivisions for music, news, and sports. Engineering might have a satellite uplink subdivision and a studio subdivision. In satellite radio, both providers (XM and Sirius) program their own music. Some news and sports channels are provided by other services like CNN, ESPN, and National Public Radio.

Since most of the revenue for both satellite radio and satellite television comes from subscriptions, most of the promotional and sales activity deals with marketing to individual subscribers. In broadcasting, sales efforts are aimed at advertisers.

SEE IT LATER

Production and Distribution

As the electronic media make the change from analog to digital, some aspects of the industry are changing dramatically. In fact, the process of producing audio and video for the electronic media has been changing rapidly since the mid 1990s. High-quality audio and video production that in the past could only have been produced by expensive equipment that was manufactured for that purpose is now being produced by less expensive equipment that can do a variety of tasks with remarkable quality.

ZOOM IN   10.8

Camcorders may soon be constructed without the need for video tape. A camcorder with a built-in DVD-RAM recorder has been available for several years, and other nontape camcorders will likely follow.

For more information about camcorders, including camcorders without video tape, go to the Companion Website for this text: www.ablongman.com/medoffkaye1e.

Nonlinear Video Editing Procedure **FYI**

Video projects that are edited on a nonlinear editor start out as a collection of "raw," or unedited, video clips that are transferred or imported from a camcorder or video storage medium (e.g., a DVD, CD-ROM, or video tape) to the digital editor. This process is known as *digitizing*. The unedited video, or "clips," are assembled in an area, or "bin," for unedited video and labeled for easy identification. Each clip is viewed and can be trimmed to a specific length to exclude unwanted shots or frames. The clips are then assembled (similar to a cut-and-paste procedure) to construct a project of clips. Transitions and special effects are applied to the assembled video clips, and titles are added, as needed. The project is then previewed and re-edited, as necessary. The clips, transitions, effects, and titles are then combined and *rendered*, allowing the editor to make a complete file of all the video elements that have been put together. The final product is then transferred or exported to a medium (e.g., video tape or DVD) for distribution and exhibition.

For example, digital camcorders that cost less than $2,000 are now available in mini-DV format and capable of producing images better than most professional camcorders did only a few years ago. DVD-RAM camcorders are available, as well, which can record directly to a digital disk. This type of digital camcorder promises excellent quality, low cost, and small size, plus the medium (i.e., a disk) has no moving parts, as does a video cassette. The industry is moving away from video tape because it is bulky, prone to mechanical failure, and degrades with age and temperature extremes. Camcorders with built-in DVD recorders and digital storage devices, similar to the removable "jump" or card storage devices, may become commonplace in the near future.

Video editing is perhaps the area that has seen the greatest change in the past 10 years. Two types of editing systems are in use: linear and nonlinear editing systems. A **linear editing system** has two video tape recorders, or VTRs: the player or source and the recorder or editor. A device called a *controller* operates the two decks. The recording is made using video from the source that is recorded on the editor. The tape must be physically moved to find the correct location to select scenes for edits. News editors use linear editing to piece together the sequential events of a news story. Linear editors generally perform only simple edits (known as "*cuts only*").

A **digital**, or **nonlinear**, **editing system** is computer based and allows random access to any video scene that has been encoded into the editor. A digital system is set up similarly to the "My Documents" folder on a hard drive. All files are equally accessible. This random access process allows the editor to find desired shots or scenes almost instantaneously, without having to spend time fast forwarding or rewinding a video tape. Nonlinear editors can also perform many special effects and transitions.

Another aspect of nonlinear editing is that it allows more experimentation. In linear editing, the editor can put together a sequence of scenes on a tape, and once it's been completed, he or she can only add shots or scenes to the end of the program. If one or more shots must be added in the middle of the program, it must be rerecorded. With a nonlinear editor, on the other hand, shots or scenes can be added or removed anywhere in the program, and the computer adjusts the program length automatically. In sum, think of linear versus nonlinear editing in terms of typing versus word processing. When typing, you can only make changes that fit on the page or else you have to retype the entire project from the point of the change to the end. When word processing, the length of the document varies whenever changes are made.

As such, nonlinear editing allows editors and producers to experiment with creative styles and endings. In fact, without adding much time to the editing process, one program can be edited to include several different endings to show to a client or pilot audience. Commercials can also be edited into several variations for testing. Nonlinear editing gives producers and editors

Today, video editing is most commonly done using a computer and specialized software.

more creative flexibility. This flexibility also facilitates **repurposing**, or adapting programming material for different uses. For example, a 90-second story shown on CNN can be re-edited down to a 30-second version and shown on *CNN Headline News*.

In the future, video and audio editing will be performed on computers with editing software. Stand-alone hardware, like linear editors, will become rare, even though they may still be used in some news operations. Eventually, audio and video editing will be accomplished by inexpensive laptops and will be accessible to both consumers and media professionals.

Broadcast Media

Unless the FCC reverses its 25-year pattern of deregulating the electronic media, we can expect to see the trend toward consolidation continuing in the future. This will have several effects.

As corporate-owned broadcast groups get larger, they strive to become more efficient and more profitable. Consolidated stations can be cheaper to operate, as well. For example, as a group increases the number of classic rock stations that it owns, it can afford to produce high-quality programming in one place and send it to all of its stations. Or if a group owns 20 stations and 6 of them are of the classic rock format, buying programming for all 6 can be accomplished with one "classic rock package" buy. A group buy like this is also attractive to the program supplier, who can sell 6 markets with one sale. Buying programming for many stations gives group owners buying power, which translates into a lower cost per station, as a group will get a volume discount. Such economic leverage gives group owners a strong advantage over owners that buy programming for only one station.

Consolidation also streamlines sales operations. Fewer salespersons are needed as stations consolidate. One salesperson sells time for all the group-owned stations in the market or those with a similar format or audience demographic profile. Having fewer salespersons cuts down on training costs, travel costs, and costs in processing contracts and production. And when a commercial spot is produced at one location and sent electronically via a broadband connection to many stations, it saves time and the costs of duplication, shipping, and handling.

The broadcast networks may have to change their long-time tradition of having a schedule that begins in September and runs fabout 26 new episodes of successful prime-time shows each year. The networks have shown reruns right after the national "sweeps" periods in November, February, May, and August, giving other channels the opportunity to counter-program by starting new shows during these periods. The broadcast networks may have to change their timing if they want to keep their audience share.

The networks are moving toward more interactivity, a trend that is expected to continue. Jay Leno encourages viewers who enjoy the "Headlines" segment of his show to go to the NBC website to see more of them. Similarly, PBS gives more in-depth information online about what viewers see onscreen. In its *Antiques Roadshow*, one of the antiques experts may make a comment about not refinishing an antique chair, and a message will pop up at the bottom of the screen, suggesting that interested viewers should go to the website to learn why.

Digital broadcast television has the potential to change the way we watch television. For example, it will make it possible for one station to send several programs at once to the audience. In other words,

ZOOM IN   10.9
Go to the Companion Website, www.ablongman.com/medoffkaye1e, to see how digital television can allow more than one program to be sent at the same time and how it can allow high-definition television.

the local NBC affiliate might show *Dateline NBC* from the NBC network, but the audience will also be able to get several other programs from the station by simply adjusting their tuners—say, MSNBC, CNBC, and even a pay-per-view movie at the same time. Broadcast stations will have the capability to become multichannel video program distributors.

Cable Television

Cable companies are continuing to take advantage of the opportunities afforded to them as a result of the Telecommunications Act of 1996. Many MSOs have entered the business of telephony and data services and are investigating the possibilities of video on demand (VOD). These moves are not only in response to a desire to expand their revenue streams but also a reaction to the inroads made by competition and uncertainty about the future. Telephone companies and public utilities are also entering the field of wired delivery of telecommunications. Some cities have built their own broadband systems with fiber optic cable for the purpose of competing with cable companies. Direct broadcast satellite (DBS) television services have continued to add subscribers, some of whom were cable subscribers. Even broadcast television, with its upcoming change to digital, will have the capacity to offer multichannel programming and subscription services. The Internet, which has not yet been able to deliver full-screen, full-motion video in a practical way, may compete with cable in program delivery, if video compression and bandwidth improve.

Technology will result in an inevitable merger of services like telephone, cable, broadcast, and data. The cable industry is in a particularly strong position to offer some or all of these services because it already has a strong subscription base. Although the telephone companies are trying to expand their revenue streams by providing entertainment and data services, the cable companies have already had many years of experience at doing so. In the near future, cable will likely lose subscriptions because of competition, mostly from satellite television providers. The goal for cable is to be a one-stop provider of telephony, cable television, interactive video, video on demand, home shopping, online/Internet access, gaming, telemedicine, and tele-education (Janowiak, Sheth, & Saghafi, 1998).

Cable telephony may present the best future service for cable companies. The telephone business generates over $200 billion per year, while the cable business does less than $50 billion. Those cable companies that can move into this bigger market while providing entertainment and Internet access will be the most profitable. In the future, cable companies and telephone companies will likely combine to provide these comprehensive services. The future will be less cable and more broadband distribution of services.

In order to compete, cable television will have to provide more interactive programming. If this occurs, cable systems will need employees educated in high technology and an audience sophisticated enough to use it.

Satellite Delivery

The satellite industry—including radio, television, and cable— enjoys the advantage that satellite signals cover huge geographic areas. In fact, two satellites in geostationary orbit can

Women in the Industry

Despite years of pressure from the FCC to increase the number of women and minorities in positions of power in electronic media, research shows that there "continues to be a dearth of women in the executive suites and corporate boardrooms of entertainment companies" (Romano, 2002). In fact, women account for less than 15 percent of the top executive jobs at the 10 major entertainment companies (e.g., AOL Time-Warner, Disney, and Viacom). Women do, however, have an increasing presence as featured speakers at media and telecommunications conferences. One area that has shown an increase in women executives is news, where 30 percent of the executives of the national news outlets in broadcast and cable today are women.

cover the entire contiguous 48 states. Unlike cable and its ability to provide two-way communication through an infrastructure already in place, satellites are restricted in the two-way arena: that is, consumers cannot send or uplink from their homes or offices.

Although satellite may become the mass distribution system of choice in the future, it may not be able to provide what consumers want most: a one-stop telecommunications provider. Satellite delivery will most likely continue to operate as it has for the past 10 years, as a multichannel provider of entertainment and information that competes directly with cable for subscribers.

Summary

Beginning in the 1920s, radio was a dominant force, grabbing the attention of millions of Americans. Radio developed the business model of a medium that's supported by advertising dollars. Programming was mostly live and involved music performances. The radio industry also spawned the national networks, which rose to power in the late 1920s and have maintained that power ever since.

Television inherited the business model and network structure developed by radio and soon took its prime-time audience and programming, as well. By the early 1950s, television dominated electronic media, and radio, primarily AM, had to look for another programming formula. The networks had to adjust to the complicated task of producing television; as studios became larger, rehearsal time increased, expensive and bulky equipment was purchased, and additional personnel were hired and trained. The demand for television signals in rural areas gave birth to the cable television industry.

Radio responded to the decrease in audience listenership by moving away from live programs to programs featuring recorded music. Records were played on the air by disc jockeys, who spoke directly to the audience in an informal, conversational way. Radio changed from a medium of programs to a medium of formats.

Radio and television production have not changed much over the years. Program formats are similar, and production techniques have changed gradually with technology. The signal flow in both audio production and television production is much the same today as it has been for the past 50 years. The most significant change in production has occurred with the introduction of digital equipment. Compared to its analog counterpart, digital equipment produces a better-quality product and gives production personnel more flexibility to experiment.

Distribution patterns have changed over the past 50 years. Although radio transmission is much the same as it was in the 1920s, television distribution has changed greatly. Instead of receiving their programs directly over the air from broadcasters, about 80 percent of all the television audience receives television programs from either a cable system or a satellite television provider.

Satellite radio has also begun to sign up subscribers. Satellite radio is a subscription service that provides many channels of radio, some of which are commercial free. This service takes the format concept that radio adopted in the early 1950s and provides many variations of programming through one service.

The Telecommunications Act of 1996 has accelerated the consolidation of electronic media since its passage. Increasingly, more stations and media properties are owned by a smaller number of owners. Convergence in both technology and business is an ongoing phenomenon. Cross-ownership of media encourages the owners of one medium to use both its technology and content in another medium. Vertical integration within large media companies allows them to provide their own programming,

Excluding the Super Bowls, Olympic coverage, and episodes of the epic miniseries Roots, *what was the most-watched television show?*

whether through inhouse production or syndication units. Consolidation helps companies reduce operating costs by allowing one manager to run several stations at once, thereby lowering salary expenses.

In the future, consolidation and convergence can be expected to continue. The television industry may consolidate more if the FCC is allowed to raise the 35 percent cap on television station ownership. Technology may change the role that the cable and telephone companies play. As consumers move toward the use of broadband connections at work and at home, the cable and telephone companies may become one-stop telecommunications providers of entertainment, Internet access, and personal communication services.

The final episode of *M*A*S*H*, which aired in February 1983.

Corporate, Educational, and Institutional Media

 SEE IT NOW   **SEE IT LATER**

Corporate Media

Users of Corporate Media

Applications of Corporate Media

Production of Corporate Media

Program Distribution

Program Evaluation

In this chapter, you'll learn about:

- Different applications of corporate media production
- The difference between broadcast and nonbroadcast media
- The users and uses of corporate media
- The steps involved in corporate video production

Generally, when people talk about the media, they are referring to the electronic mass media of entertainment and information, including networks like NBC, local broadcast television stations, and cable channels like ESPN, CNN, and HBO. They also understand how these businesses make money. For instance, NBC and its local affiliates make money primarily by selling advertising to businesses that want to reach audiences. ESPN and CNN make money by selling commercials to advertisers and charging cable systems for carrying their channels. HBO and other premium channels make money primarily by charging a monthly premium to subscribers for their service.

These networks, stations, and subscription services employ many professionals who use their skills and talents in media production to produce programming for the entertainment and information industry. What most people don't realize, however, is that these media professionals represent only a portion of all the people who produce media. Many more media producers work in corporations, medical facilities, schools, government, and other organizations. In fact, a study commissioned in 2000 by *AV Video Multimedia Producer* magazine found that there were at least 10,000 companies and organizations that produced electronic media for uses other than entertainment and news.[1]

SEE IT NOW

Corporate Media

The programming produced for the mass electronic media of broadcasting, cable, and satellite delivery services is created to attract large audiences. In contrast, **corporate media** programs are designed for very specific audiences: say, salespeople within a corporation, students taking an engineering class on television via microwave delivery, or a satellite video conference for regional vice presidents of a large equipment company. Media programs like these are produced daily across the United States for purposes other than entertainment and news.

Media use for business is common. Motorola, Ford, IBM, and Sears are all examples of large corporations that produce media projects for international distribution. These projects are produced for their employees, customers, and other specific audiences.[2] Likewise, the government, organizations and associations, schools and colleges, medical and health care facilities, and religious groups all use corporate media.

Of these uses, almost all are considered **nonbroadcast**—that is, the final product is not shown over a broadcast station or network to a large general audience. The terms *nonbroadcast video, corporate video, corporate media,* and *industrial video* all refer to media programs created for specific audiences with goals other than entertainment. In this book, the term *corporate media* is used in a generic way to apply to all nonbroadcast media production.

These applications of media production are often overlooked because they lack the glamour and notoriety associated with entertainment and news media. Students who study electronic media typically aspire to work on *The Tonight Show,* to be an anchor for KNBC-TV in Los Angeles, or to produce a successful sitcom like *Friends.* Rarely do they dream of producing a six-minute demonstration on the installation of a new wiring harness in a Ford Taurus or an internal public relations program about the latest merchandising news from Wal-Mart. Yet more programs are produced by and for organizations than are broadcast to the general public (Smith, Wright, & Ostroff, 1998).

Students who are studying electronic media and learning basic media production skills may consider working in the less glamorous environment of corporate media, rather than in broadcast media. For many years, broadcasters have enjoyed having huge numbers of job applicants knock on their doors immediately after graduating from college. Graduates often go directly to broadcast stations or networks for their first jobs. What they find, though, are long lines of people looking for the same job. Because the broadcast stations have their pick of applicants, they can hire people at low salaries and minimal benefits. Essentially, broadcasting is an employer's market (Bolduc & Medoff, 1990).

Corporate media production, on the other hand, is not as popular as broadcasting and broadcast programs. New graduates don't usually give much thought to who wrote or performed the production tasks on a 12-minute demonstration video tape for a new farm tractor

ZOOM IN   11.1

To find out more about jobs in corporate media, go to **monsterjobs.com**. Enter "video producer" and look at the list of jobs that comes up. You will notice that most of the listings are for nonbroadcast jobs at places like the Houston Independent School District (educational), the Longaberger Co. (makes woven baskets), Morris Cerullo World Evangelism (religious), and The Scooter Store (maker of scooters and power wheelchairs). Sometimes, broadcasters like ABC do post listings, but those jobs are small in number compared to nonbroadcast jobs.

attachment. But companies like John Deere need people who are good at producing this type of work. In fact, many corporate media managers look for employees from among the ranks of current broadcast station workers.

The difference between the jobs available in broadcast versus corporate media is that corporate media often encompasses a wider range of skills and applications than broadcast media. Corporate media jobs include print and multimedia graphic designers, writers, editors, website designers, CD-ROM and DVD authoring, and both still and video photography. In corporate media, employees get to do a lot of different jobs, while in broadcasting, they often do the same job over and over.

Corporate Media's Business Model

Corporate media uses an entirely different business model than commercial media. In the corporate model, the client hires an inhouse or an outside independent production house to produce media for a specific purpose.

INHOUSE MEDIA UNITS   A company will have an **inhouse media unit** for two primary reasons: to save money (the inhouse unit will charge its own company less) and to maintain control over deadlines and personnel. In the early and mid 1980s, it was common for organizations to have their own media departments and equipment. But starting in the late 1980s, several factors changed, resulting in a trend that continues today: Most corporate media projects are produced outside the company, or **outsourced**, by professionals in independent production houses or by **freelance**, or contract, personnel.

One of the factors behind this trend was that inhouse media departments were expensive to support on a year-round basis. Salaried employees are paid regardless of whether they are busy and productive, and many companies simply couldn't justify paying annual salaries. In addition, corporate media became more sophisticated and required better equipment and better special effects to achieve the professional quality sought by media professionals. Technology was also changing rapidly, such that equipment often became obsolete in a short time. As a result of all these factors, many companies stopped supporting fully staffed inhouse media units. Instead, they kept just a few media professionals on salary to make sure the media work produced by outside sources was appropriate and of high quality.

Despite this trend toward outsourcing, many inhouse media production units still do exist because of the benefits they bring. Inhouse media personnel know their corporations or organizations better than outside services, which means their work is usually more knowledgeable about the subject matter and the corporate culture. Inhouse units often have their own personnel and some equipment but on occasion go outside for additional production personnel, talent, equipment, and services like postproduction and duplication.

Chargeback System   An inhouse unit must justify its existence regardless of the number of people it employs or the amount of equipment it owns. Whenever a project is produced inhouse, it must be paid for—at least on paper. One way an inhouse media unit gets money for its productions is by charging the division of the company that ordered the project. For example, suppose the public relations department of a large computer manufacturer wants to have a video to send out to local elementary schools about buying new computers. The production unit will create a budget for the project and submit it to the public relations department. If the public relations department approves the budget, work will proceed. After the video has been produced, the production unit will send the public relations department a bill for the work, and they will pay it with a transfer of funds or a check to the media department. This process of charging the requesting unit is called a **chargeback** system. It allows the production unit to get paid directly for its work and emphasizes the fact that even inhouse media production costs money.

Annual or Direct Budget Method   The **annual** or **direct budget** method can also support a media unit. In this method, the inhouse production unit receives a fixed amount of dollars each year or budget period. During that period, the unit is expected to produce media projects for other units in the organization. The annual budget might be based on a total of 10 media projects per year or 100 minutes of media projects produced in a year's time. Projects that go beyond that number will require either a chargeback or a supplementary budget. If less than 10 projects or 100 minutes are produced, the production unit might be required to give back some of its budget.

ZOOM IN   11.2
To link to the VAS Communications website, go to www.ablongman.com/medoffkaye1e, the Companion Website for this text.

Some inhouse media units contribute to the profitability of their companies by doing work for other organizations and charging them for their services. Usually, this type of work is taken on only after the home company's needs have all been met. Also, the unit will often charge outside clients more for its work than it would charge units within its own company.

INDEPENDENT PRODUCTION HOUSES   As noted earlier, the use of **independent production houses** to produce work for the corporate media industry started to take hold in the early 1980s, when media equipment became affordable and the demand for

CAREER TRACKS

Chris Wooley   Managing Producer, Media Production Agency

- **What is your job? What do you do?**
  I am the managing producer of VAS Communications (www.vascommunications.com), a media production agency serving primarily a biomedical clientele. My tasks vary from producer, director, writer, and account exec for clients.

- **How long have you been doing this job?**
  Since 1985.

- **What was your first job in electronic media?**
  First nonpaying job—seventh-grade instructional channel at my junior high school in Phoenix. First partially paying job—internship with current employer during junior year of college at Northern Arizona University. First professional job—producer in America West Airlines PR department.

- **What led you to the job?**
  I decided during my internship that this was the field I truly wanted to pursue. I appreciate the rush of others viewing your creation and having them learn from it or be entertained and wowed by it. What got me my first job at America West was a connection I made during my internship. It's really a small world in our market.

- **What advice would you have for students who might want a job like yours?**
  Internships provide, in most cases, the basic experience required to demonstrate you want to be a player in the field. They also provide firsthand connections. Work cheap, swallow your pride, and be willing to work hard for little pay until you establish yourself.

The Sony U-Matic video cassette, which came out in 1971.

corporate media grew. Independent producers flourished in the late 1980s, as corporations and organizations started to send out **bypass work,** or projects that had formerly been done by inhouse units.

Independent production houses often have expertise in numerous aspects of media production and make money by working for a variety of clients. They may specialize in videography (shooting video), editing, and writing as well as creating new media, such as DVD authoring and streaming media on the Internet. Because independent production houses offer a wide scope of specialties and expertise, they can provide ample career opportunities for college students with media production skills.

ZOOM IN   11.3

Go to the Companion Website, **www.ablongman. com/medoffkaye1e,** to link to Business Video Solutions, Inc., an independent corporate media production house. Or go directly to the company's site: **www.bvsinc.us/htm/success. htm.** View examples of their video work by clicking on one of the "Success Stories." Then click on the icon to view the video with either Quicktime or Windows Media Player.

Functions of Corporate Media

In the early 1980s, a corporation used video to show that it was on the cutting edge of technology. Since then (and especially during times of recession), however, corporate media has undergone strong scrutiny to test its efficiency and effectiveness. Unlike entertainment programs, which measure success in audience size or advertising sales, most corporate work must show that it contributes to increased revenue (and eventually profits), decreased expenditures, or other company goals that cannot be achieved in another less expensive way. For instance, a DVD produced to promote a product or service will be considered successful if it leads to an increase in sales.

Unlike broadcast media, corporate media is not transmitted from television stations; instead, it is exhibited in a variety of places. For example, a kiosk in a large hotel might show a video of local restaurants to help guests make dining decisions. Another common location for corporate media is the point of purchase. Department stores often have small monitors that play video tapes continuously to attract shoppers as they walk by. Products that are commonly shown on this type of media range from cosmetics to cleaning materials and vacuum cleaners.

Corporate media can also add value to a product. A computer peripheral like a scanner or webcam might advertise that it comes with a video that shows in detail how to install it and use it. Providing the video might make the product seem more attractive than competing products and encourage consumers to buy it. Providing a video or DVD is part of a trend to replace passive marketing techniques with a more interactive style, using moving pictures and images that have been customized to retailers and their customers (Greer, 2001).

Corporate media can also be used to directly decrease expenses. Reaching employees at branch locations can be costly, especially when the message that needs to be shared requires more than just a telephone conversation. Say, for instance, that the employer is going to change health plans and needs each employee to select a new plan from a list of alternatives. Sending a top executive out to every branch to talk to every employee will likely be time consuming and costly. Producing a media program that explains the new health benefit options might save the company many dollars in travel and executive time and effort. In addition, a good media presentation ensures that accurate information is repeated to all employees, thus reducing error as well as saving time and money.

Corporate media is also used to indirectly reduce expenses. Media programs can be used to help train new employees and to teach others to be more productive. Such programs can also be used to teach safety, to reduce downtime and absenteeism, and simply to boost morale and improve team work.

Users of Corporate Media

Nonbroadcast media programs are almost always designed for a very selective audience, such as students, salespeople, buyers of a new product, or employees. **Nonbroadcast media users** include business and industry, education, government agencies, medicine and health care, and organizations and professional associations. For these programs, the budgets and audiences are smaller and the goals are usually very specific (e.g., to inform salespeople in the company about a new product line).

Business and Industry

While shopping at Wal-Mart, you may hear what sounds like a radio station playing over the store's loudspeakers. It isn't broadcast radio; it's Wal-Mart radio. Similarly, if you go into the lunchroom at Motorola, you will probably see a television set showing a program about Motorola. Many businesses use such media to reach their customers and their employees through noncommercial means.

Education

The educational use of electronic media began before World War I with radio station WHA at the University of Wisconsin. Programming grew slowly and included 16mm film, filmstrips, and various audio recording formats; then, in the 1980s, video cassette production equipment became affordable (DiZazzo, 2000). Also in the 1980s, the technology to send two-way, real-time media to remote sites became accessible to most educational institutions. Live television was distributed via microwave signals through a service known as the **Instructional Television Fixed Service (ITFS)**, which beamed coursework to students at locations equipped to receive the special television signals.

This delivery of educational material is often referred to as **educational narrowcasting** because it targets a small, select audience. The general use of electronic media for delivering educational programs is referred to as **distance learning** and has provided career opportunities for many students of electronic media.

In addition to distribution via microwave transmission, educational institutions also use cable television (i.e., for one-way media but two-way audio via telephone). Cable provides an inexpensive way to reach students who are unable to physically come to the classroom. It also allows students to take a class that's so popular that all the classroom seats have been filled.

College courses are now being distributed over the Internet, as well. Courses designed for the Web may be streamed, which allows real-time viewing of class lectures, or files may be made available for downloading and viewing at any time. Some classes also provide lecture materials in text form. Web-based classes allow students to view lectures, take tests, and ask questions (via e-mail) at whatever time is convenient for them. Participating in class-based listservs and discussion groups can help students feel connected even if they do not physically attend the class.

In addition to bringing classes to students, educational institutions use corporate media to train personnel, create promotional

ZOOM IN   11.4
Business and corporations have been using media for many years to communicate both internally and externally. Go to the Companion Website for this text, www.ablongman.com/medoffkaye1e, to link to these corporate video examples: Sybase, Mack trucks, and Jet Airways.

- www.sybase.com/detail/1,6904,1019176,00.html has many viewable video and animation clips to show what Sybase is all about and how it has helped other companies. Note that there are files in Flash, .avi, and .wmv and also some .exe files to start small programs.

- www.macktrucks.com/default.aspx?pageid=439 tells all about Mack trucks and the company that produces them.

- www.rfmd.com/OTM%C2%AE%20Strategy.asp gives information about RF Microdevices.

- Do a search using Google or a similar search engine by typing in "Corporate Video." See what you can find out about business and industry use of corporate media to inform various audiences.

ZOOM IN   11.5
Go to the Companion Website, www.ablongman.com/medoffkaye1e, for examples of distance learning.

The government, which has been using film for instructional and other nonentertainment purposes since World War I.

announcements, document special events, archive research or grant work, and produce documentaries. Schools with sports programs use media in many ways to improve individual athlete as well as team performance.

Government

Government agencies at all levels use corporate media to help conduct their business. For instance, many local governments televise their meetings on cable TV for constituents to watch. Although this use of corporate media is not necessarily exciting, it serves a very practical function.

Police and fire departments are especially heavy users of media for such ongoing functions as training, surveillance, and documentation of crime or fire scenes. Police cars that make traffic stops often have a video camera aimed at the vehicle that is being stopped. A media record is created of the traffic stop and the behavior of the person involved. Fire departments often train their personnel by video taping practice fires and analyzing how the firefighters handled them.

> **ZOOM IN**   11.6
> See how a government agency, the U.S. Food and Drug Administration, uses its website and video conferences to distribute information. Go to **www.fda.gov/ora/training/Satellite/satmain.htm**.

Medicine and Health Care

Professionals in the fields of medicine and health care are commonly kept up to date about new techniques and products through corporate media. Video taping of surgeries is now commonplace, which means doctors can see and train for almost any kind of surgical procedure, including those that were formerly viewable only through the lens of a surgical microscope. Continuing education and various medical procedures are also streamed from the Web and available by satellite and CD-ROM or DVD. Patients can be educated about their illnesses and familiarized with treatment options and expected results through corporate media, as well.

Organizations and Professional Associations

Labor unions and other large organizations, like the Broadcast Education Association, use electronic media to communicate with their members and inform them about the benefits of belonging to the organization.

> **ZOOM IN**   11.7
> Go to the text's Companion Website, **www.ablongman.com/medoffkaye1e**, to link to the Broadcast Education Association to view a video about the organization and how it benefits its members.

Applications of Corporate Media

Corporate media can be applied in a variety of ways, such as education and training, product demonstration and sales, motivation, and both internal and external communication.

Education and Training

The use of corporate media for education and training comprises the majority of applications. In addition to the educational applications mentioned already, the use

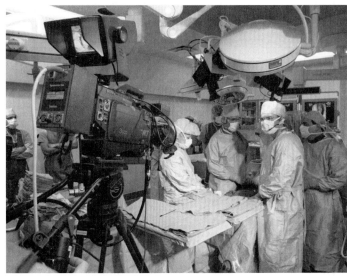

Video is shot in the operating room and then used to educate doctors about new surgical procedures.

of corporate media for training is quite extensive. Teaching safety procedures, new manufacturing processes, sales techniques, and equipment operation are typical training applications (Cartwright, 1990; Gayeski, 1991; Richardson, 1992).

Product Demonstrations and Sales

Product demonstrations are also typical corporate media projects and can be used in a variety of situations. A video can demonstrate the many ways a product can be used, which might be difficult to show in the store. Moreover, the video can replace a trained salesperson yet ensure that each interested customer will receive the same smooth sales pitch.

Videos for sales purposes are shown to or just given to consumers who visit a store or kiosk that sells the product. A sales video can be very helpful when the product or service is new to the marketplace, is highly technical, or represents a new concept and thus warrants a longer and more careful explanation than can be produced using some other approach.

Motivation

Motivational videos are used to provide the information and incentive that salespeople and other employees need to help them achieve corporate or personal goals.

ZOOM IN   11.8

Go to the Companion Website, www.ablongman.com/medoffkaye1e, to view streamed video or link to websites with examples of demonstration, sales, and motivation videos.

Internal Communication

Corporate media is most commonly used to distribute information among the employees of a large firm. The *size* of the company is an important factor here. While small companies can distribute information to employees by simply posting a bulletin in the employees' break room or lounge, larger companies cannot rely on this easy method to reach everyone. In fact, some companies are so large that distributing information via video tape isn't quick enough or even economical. Large, international firms, like Motorola, distribute information to employees around the world via satellite. Internal public relations media can be used to inform employees of new policies that may affect them—for example, health benefits, an office relocation, a change in the profit-sharing plan, a change in the top level of managers, a new drug policy, changes in paydays because of holiday office closings, and other topics that inform or prevent the spread of inaccurate information.

ZOOM IN   11.9

To view streamed video or link to websites with examples of corporate news shows and other internal communication, go to the Companion Website for this text: www.ablongman.com/medoffkaye1e.

Information such as this is also sometimes relayed in the form of an employee news show. This popular format follows the style of news delivery typical of a local television newscast, except that the "news" is all about the company, its employees, and other relevant topics. Negative news about the company is kept to a minimum, and the "news team" does not conduct investigative reporting about the company, unless the information will reflect positively on it.

External Communication

When a company or organization wants to communicate to the public, it can use corporate media to do so. For instance, a hotel might send a video or DVD describing its convention facilities to a large organization that routinely holds conventions in other

The Media Communications Association (MCA), formerly the International Television Association (ITVA).

cities. Sometimes, companies and organizations try to get their message out to the public through indirect methods. Rather than have a salesperson or other company representative play a tape for potential customers, a tape might be produced in the form of a news story, similar to one that would appear on the local television news.

In some cases, the story is actually placed in a television newscast. If the station feels that the story is timely, credible, and not simply a promotion for the company or product discussed, then it might air the story in a news or information show. These **video news releases**, when used in broadcast television, lend credibility as well as exposure to the product, service, or company.

ZOOM IN   11.10
- Go to the Companion Website, www. ablongman.com/medoffkaye1e, to view streamed video or link to websites with examples of video news releases and other external communication.
- Go to www.state.gov/r/pa/obs/vid for more examples of video news releases.

Program Types and Styles

Since corporate media needs only to attract the attention of its designated audience to fulfill its objectives, almost any form of media can be used to accomplish this goal. Simple narration is used most often because of the ease of production and low cost. Nonetheless, many other more entertaining formats are used, as well, such as dramatic style, sitcom style, news show style, docudrama, variety, or even quiz show style. The goal is to get the attention of the audience and then keep it long enough for the information to be delivered.

Production of Corporate Media

Producing a program for corporate media differs from that for broadcast entertainment in terms of where and how the program originates. Entertainment program production usually begins with an independent producer, who "pitches" an idea for a program to network or cable channel executives. The idea that has the best chance of being watched by a large audience is the one that will be chosen. Corporate media projects, on the other hand, are produced at the request of a client, who has a particular communication problem to solve. For example, a warehouse supervisor may realize that in the last 12 months, over 100 employee workdays have been missed because of injuries resulting from employees hurting their backs while lifting boxes in the warehouse. He or she may propose creating a video that demonstrates the proper way to lift heavy boxes. A corporate media manager/producer will consider the request and then determine if the problem can be solved effectively and efficiently by the use of electronic media. (Obviously, a problem that will be best solved with a print brochure should not be produced as electronic media.) The production process is initiated when the client seeks media services from an inhouse media department or goes outside the company to get help from an independent production house.

The actual production process for corporate media resembles that for entertainment. Both have similar stages during which similar tasks are performed. That process is described next in this chapter.

A takeoff on the game show *The Weakest Link* is used to educate doctors.

As with production for entertainment purposes, a corporate media project is produced in three stages: preproduction, production, and postproduction.

Preproduction

The production process begins once a corporate media manager or producer has decided that a client's problem can be resolved with a media project. The discussion then turns to issues relevant to production, such as goals or objectives, costs, and a timeframe for delivery of the finished product.

Stating the goals or objectives is key at this point because accomplishing them (e.g., learning the proper way to lift heavy objects) is the reason the media project is being produced. With professional corporate media, viewers are expected to learn, to change their attitude, to change their behavior, or some combination of these effects. Also, the results should be testable so as to measure whether or not the goals or objectives have been achieved.

Knowing the audience helps the corporate media producer create a program that will keep the audience's attention and get the intended message across. Knowing the audience also helps the media producer choose the appropriate terminology, style, and pacing. Knowing this information also helps the producer select a location or setting, a narrator or performer, and a level of sophistication for the presentation.

The next step is research by the producer or writer to ensure that the content of the project is both accurate and appropriate. A good project requires *fluency* in both the language used and the visuals shown. Such fluency can be achieved in several ways:

- By conducting interviews with knowledgeable individuals, such as content experts from the corporation requesting the media
- By reading published material and conducting Internet searches about the subject
- By viewing information that has been previously produced either for the client or about the client

After the research has been completed, the concept and program style are determined. The project might only require a simple narrated demonstration to achieve its stated goals. If the audience and the budget are somewhat large, then the project might take a more entertaining format to gain attention. The **treatment** is an encapsulation of the setting, characters, points of view, and information that will be presented in the media project. It should clearly explain the goals or objectives, the strategies that will be used to reach them, and the content of the project.

After the treatment has been written and approved by the client, the facts, figures, and visual ideas are organized to form an **outline** for the project. At the outline stage, it is easy to reorganize the ideas to meet the goals of the project. Submitting the outline to the client to make sure that the topics are presented in proper order can save quite a bit of script rewriting later on.

Next, a **storyboard** is created; it is a visual outline that shows the look of the project. The storyboard usually shows how the first shot of each scene in the project will appear. Each scene is shown in order of its presentation. Special pads of paper with blank TV screen outlines are available for storyboard making. Producers also sometimes use snapshots (especially given the common use of digital cameras) or clip art (stock drawings that can be purchased) to represent shots from scenes.

ZOOM IN   11.11

To view or link to websites with examples of storyboards, go to the Companion Website for this text: www.ablongman.com/medoffkaye1e.

Telecommuting, where people can work from their homes or anywhere else.

At this point in the creative process, it is time to write the full **script.** The scriptwriter must visualize the information from the outline and the storyboard and expand on it. If the outline is thought of as the skeleton, the scriptwriting process adds flesh to the bones. The script guides the production process, ensuring that the final product turns out as the client envisioned it.

The next step of the process involves selecting and assembling the production crew. The producer selects a crew consisting of the following:

- The **director** is the person who will take the written script and translate it into a visual reality. He or she is in charge of the crew for the actual production, or **shoot.**
- The **videographer** operates the video camera. In a studio project, the director can see what each camera is shooting and ask for adjustments in the shots as well as choose between cameras. In the field, the director relies more on the videographer to get the necessary shots because he or she doesn't always have a view of each shot as it's being recorded.
- The **audio engineer,** or sound person, is responsible for recording the sounds. This includes placing the microphones, making sure that the recording levels are appropriate for the project, and arranging for other sounds or sound effects.
- If the budget permits, additional people called **grips** are added to the crew to perform important functions like setting up media lights, holding microphones, setting props in place, and moving all of the equipment in and out of the location.
- The performers, or **talent,** for a media project are often actors and other people who are used to being in front of a microphone or camera. They usually don't work full time for the company producing the media, unlike the producer, director, and other crew members. Professional performers often belong to unions like the **Screen Actors Guild (SAG)** and the **American Federation of Television and Radio Artists (AFTRA).**

With a production team in place, the next step involves **scouting** the location or setting for the project. A good location has these qualities:

- allows the crew to move equipment in and out
- provides electrical power, if needed
- allows the crew to control lighting and sound, if needed
- prevents traffic, either vehicle or pedestrian, from interfering
- provides security for equipment and personnel
- provides protection from bad weather, if needed

In addition to location scouting, scheduling of all personnel and equipment is also accomplished during preproduction.

Production

Production is the phase of the process when the project is actually recorded. If the project is being shot in a television studio, most of the variables that can affect the production can be easily controlled. But location shooting requires a vigilant producer, director, and crew to maintain control over lighting, sound, traffic, and other variables that can cause problems. With proper preparation and a skilled crew, the project is **acquired,** or recorded, and ready for the final production stage of the process: postproduction.

Postproduction

Postproduction is generally synonymous with *editing* because all of the media and audio materials must be combined to create the desired media project. The **editor** takes the media and audio and carefully combines the best shots into a meaningful whole during postproduction.

The **raw footage**, or tape shot during production, is often shot out of sequence and in multiple **takes**. Takes are repetitions of the same shot or scene from different angles or using slightly different styles. The director and the video editor will select the desired version from an **offline edit,** which is a lower-quality version of the tape that's edited on inexpensive equipment. The offline edit version gives the producer an inexpensive and sometimes rough version of the project to show the client or to review later.

Once the offline version has been approved, the **online edit** is done using higher-quality equipment. Online editing equipment is sometimes very expensive, which means the producer may go to a **postproduction house** that rents out equipment (and sometimes an editor). The prices of equipment and software for computer-based online editors are dropping, however, so producers often have direct access to their own editors.

Program Distribution

Prior to the 1970s, when video cassettes and inexpensive cameras and editing systems became available, corporate *media* was really corporate *film.* Training and educational films have been produced for corporate employees and military personnel since the early part of the twentieth century. However, compared to video, film had a few drawbacks for this application (DiZazzo, 2000; Medoff & Tanquary, 2002).

Films were slower to produce, for instance, because they required shooting, developing, and then editing and reassembling for copying and distribution. Each copy of a film was thus expensive. Showing films also could be problematic. Film projectors were never as available or as easy to use as VCRs and DVD players are today. Given these issues, film showings were limited and a large number of people needed to attend a single showing. The audience was therefore required to be at a specific place at a specific time to view the film.

Corporate media today allows the audience to view in large numbers, in small groups, or even individually. Just as important, video tape and disk-based (CD-ROM or DVD) media allow parts of a program to be rewound and viewed repeatedly until the information has been understood and retained. Disk-based programs and the Internet permit interaction, as well, so the viewer can make sure that he or she comprehends one segment before going on to others. In addition, the use of a computer can allow tailoring the program to the user's level of need and provide him or her with feedback.

Since the early 1980s, corporate media productions have most often been distributed on video tape. But in recent years, they have been distributed increasingly on CD-ROM, DVD, the Internet, **local area networks**, known as **LANs** (for company employees within a building), and an **Intranet** (a private or corporate network accessible to employees in different locations). Live media productions are routinely distributed via satellite, although some are still distributed via microwave.

VHS video tape is still common, but other tape formats, like **SVHS** and **mini-DV**, are technically superior and have much better **resolution**, or picture sharpness. These newer formats are used for acquisition (the shooting of raw footage) for many media projects because they retain higher quality throughout the production process.

A current trend in the distribution of corporate media is to make copies available on CD-ROM or DVD. The interactive capability of these disk formats makes them suitable for instructional media. In addition, many computers today have the capability to **burn,** or record, files onto a disk easily and reliably. Disks are less expensive and less bulky than video tape, have no moving parts to break, and are easy to distribute via mail or another delivery service.

The Internet has opened up the possibility of distributing information to an entire corporation without incurring duplication fees. Information can be placed on a company website, and all employees connected to the LAN can visit the site and view the information. However, there are some technological problems. The main problem is **bandwidth.** Unlike audio information, which can be compressed into a small file that is easy to **stream** or **download,** video information is difficult to **compress,** or reduce to a manageable size. Video files are huge compared to audio files, causing the playback of video on a website to be choppy and less sharp than is the case with either a video tape or disk format. Moreover, video on the Web is usually not shown on the full screen; in fact, one-quarter screen or smaller is common. Projects that don't require high-quality video or a lot of detail are best suited for distribution on the Web. As compression software gets better and Internet connections get faster, the use of the Web for corporate media will increase.

The distribution method of choice for instantaneous feedback is **teleconferencing** or **media conferencing.** Other methods may be inexpensive and easy to use, but none of them provide high-quality, two-way video. Corporations often conduct high-level managerial meetings using teleconferencing in order to save travel expenses and time among participants. Educational institutions use teleconferencing for distance learning.

Several channels can be used to distribute two-way video. One is via satellite. Using this channel, each participant has a camera and microphone that are connected to a transmitter, which sends the signal up to a satellite that re-sends the signal down to receivers at the other participants' sites. Microwave signals and telephone lines are also capable of supporting teleconferencing, each with slightly different advantages and disadvantages. Teleconferencing can be conducted over the Internet, as well, with the use of specially equipped computers and appropriate software; however, the quality of the signal is lower than when using other methods because of bandwidth problems.

Program Evaluation

Program evaluation should be included in the overall production process. Thus, after the media project has been completed and shown to its audience, it should be evaluated. Since a corporate media project is produced to resolve a problem, the best time to measure the project's success is *after* the audience has viewed it. Usually, the audience will be affected in one or more of the following ways:

1. *Cognitive change:* The audience gains knowledge.
2. *Attitudinal change:* The audience changes its opinion or forms an opinion about something.
3. *Behavior change:* The audience changes its behavior after viewing the project.

Whether the audience *likes* the program isn't nearly as important as whether the program has achieved its goals or objectives. Again, the program was created to resolve a problem.

Also, corporate media often has a bottom-line goal. In other words, the client often has a project produced to make money or to save money, directly or indirectly. For example, if the employees in a warehouse learn how to lift heavy boxes with fewer injuries by watching a training video, the company will eventually save money because of fewer injuries, less absenteeism, lower insurance premiums, and so on. Although these effects may be difficult to measure in a direct way, most managers can see the bottom-line benefits.

Evaluation of a corporate media project can be made easier and more effective if questions like the following are addressed:

- Did production of this project eliminate the need for personal travel? Were travel dollars and personnel time saved by using the media?
- Did production of this project save money by eliminating the need for an expensive training session?
- Did distributing the project through electronic media versus other methods of distributing information save time?
- Did the project encourage more people to pay attention to the message than would have resulted from using other means of distribution?
- Were more people reached with the project than would have been using other means of distribution?
- What did the media project cost compared to what another means of distribution would have cost?

Obviously, answering these types of questions will lend insight into the value of a corporate media project.

Another approach is to look at the types of audience changes that are possible and then to test for these changes. For example, cognitive changes can be measured with before-and-after tests about the subject of the project. If an attitude change is desired from viewing a media project, audience members' attitudes should be measured both before and after viewing. Behavioral changes are more difficult to measure. In the case of the employees at the warehouse doing heavy lifting, direct observation of the lifting technique used by the employees after viewing the project would give a strong indication of its effectiveness.

 ## SEE IT LATER

Corporate electronic media exist because they can solve communication problems using both visual and auditory messages. As long as the need exists to communicate with employees, customers, or segments of the public, corporate media will exist to satisfy these needs.

As mentioned earlier, one clear trend in the use of corporate electronic media is outsourcing to independent production houses and freelance professionals. Doing so keeps corporate media costs low by limiting the number of full-time, inhouse employees. Many companies continue to hire people who can write and produce, but they often staff the crew with freelancers and hire independent production houses to provide space and equipment.

Another trend in corporate media is digitization. Since digital messages can take many forms, we can expect to see convergence continue in the corporate media world. All media will speak and understand one format: *digital*. As stated by the president of an independent media production house, "Digital media is the only package for different flavors of content" (Van Deusen & Faccone, 2001). Through *desktop editing*, a form of desktop publishing, a very small media department can create a large amount of electronic media messages with less cost and in less time than was previously possible with analog. As equipment and processes become increasingly digitized, media forms will converge. One person working at a powerful computer workstation will easily be able to edit video footage into a high-quality video tape or DVD or prepare the tape for streaming on a website.

Perhaps the area most likely to change is the distribution of corporate media. A company that can stream media from a website can, for instance, avoid the cost of making numerous copies of a video cassette and shipping them to employees at other branches or around the world. Since every employee with a computer and an Internet (or company Intranet) connection can access the website, video cassette machines, DVD players, and monitors will not be necessary.

The digital convergence of media is leading corporate media to a future where creating high-quality media will be easier and will require fewer people than before. In addition, more distribution methods will be available, making communication to the appropriate audience faster, easier, and less expensive.

Summary

Corporate media programs are used in many businesses and organizations throughout the United States. Unlike the broadcasting and cable delivery systems, which present mass media entertainment and information programs to a general audience, corporate media are produced for specific audiences and with specific goals in mind—namely, to increase revenue, decrease expenses, or satisfy a client. Users of corporate media include educators, government agencies, the medical and health professions, organizations and professional associations, and companies in many industries.

Corporate media programs are produced for education and training, product demonstrations and sales, motivation, and both internal and external communication. The process of producing corporate media is client oriented. Once the client's goals or objectives have been established, the program is created according to the preproduction, production, and postproduction steps. Corporate media projects may be produced inhouse by a media department within the company or outsourced to an independent production house that produces media for a number of different clients. Corporate media projects are distributed in many ways, including video cassette (usually VHS), CD-ROM and DVD, satellite, and recently, the Web.

Corporate media must be evaluated to determine the effects it has on its audience: cognitive effects, attitudinal or emotional effects, and behavioral effects. Unlike commercial media programs, the effectiveness of corporate media is also measured by comparing the results to the goals of the project.

One of the changes in corporate electronic media that can be expected in the future is a conversion to digital format. This change will present many opportunities. Digital equipment is smaller, lighter, and better than earlier analog equipment. Editing and other functions can take place on a computer that requires fewer operators, less costs, less space, and less maintenance yet provides better quality and easier distribution. In the future, distribution will likely involve more use of DVD and the Web and less use of video cassette, CD-ROM, and satellite distribution.

Notes

1. *AV Video Multimedia Producer* magazine commissioned a company named Scenic Wonders to conduct research on the corporate media industry in 2000. Since then, a slow economy has likely caused the closing of some inhouse media departments. Despite the downturn, media production is still considered a growth industry (Van Deusen & Faccone, 2001).

2. Other specific audiences would include news organizations. For instance, a corporation might have a video news release prepared to announce the launch of a new product. If the product is deemed newsworthy enough, the release might be shown by a television station (or news operation like CNN) during a newscast.

Corporate video costs about $1,000 to $5,000 per minute, and network entertainment video costs about $40,000 to $50,000 per minute.

Regulation, Legal Issues, and Ethics

CHAPTER 12

SEE IT THEN

The Beginnings of Regulation

The Basis for Regulatory Power

Overview of Regulation

Other Legal Concerns

SEE IT NOW

The Telecommunications Act of 1996

The FCC Today

Other Regulatory Influences

The FCC and Indecency, Obscenity, and Violence

The FTC and Advertising

SEE IT LATER

FCC Concerns

Other Legal Issues

Ethical Issues

In this chapter, you'll learn about:

- The philosophical basis for electronic media regulation in the United States
- The government agencies that create and enforce laws to regulate electronic media
- The legislation that has shaped electronic media
- The ethical issues in electronic media

Beginning with the First Amendment to the U.S. Constitution, which provides for freedom of speech and freedom of the press, and continuing with the passage of numerous regulations over the years, the federal government has sought to control the growth and development of electronic media. Believing that the airwaves are owned by the people, the government believes it has the right and the duty to protect that resource.

As you'll see in this chapter, regulation of electronic media has, in many ways, paralleled the history of the United States. In the early 1900s, such events as the sinking of the *Titanic* and American involvement in World War I brought about legal efforts by the government to protect its citizens via the media. In the 1920s and 1930s, agencies such as the Federal Communications Commission (FCC) were created to assume part of the regulatory role and to address such issues as technology, licensing, and ownership. The trend toward deregulation, which began in the late 1970s and gained momentum with passage of the Telecommunications Act of 1996, has continued into this new century, raising concerns among many in the industry about the effects of so few companies owning so many media providers.

The electronic media industry has faced numerous legal issues since broadcasting began, including the rights to free speech and privacy, accusations of libel and slander, concerns over obscenity and indecency, questions of programming content, and providing for copyright protection and taxation. Ethical issues have been raised, as well, such as paying for interviews, re-creating news events, and citing unnamed sources.

Although many of these topics have been touched on in other chapters, they will be considered in this chapter in the context of their legal and ethical significance. Students preparing for careers in electronic media will find this discussion both informative in terms of how this industry has evolved to its current place and insightful in terms of considering what the future might hold.

SEE IT THEN

The Beginnings of Regulation

The First Amendment to the Constitution states that "Congress shall make no law respecting an establishment of religion, or prohibiting the free exercise thereof; or abridging the freedom of speech, or of the press; or the right of the people peaceably to assemble, and to petition the Government for a redress of grievances." This provision goes along with the notion that in a democracy, people need access to information in order to make good decisions.

In fact, the argument that a free flow of information is vital to citizens' ability to make good decisions actually goes back further than the writing of the Constitution. In his 1644 book *Areopagitica,* English writer and poet John Milton expressed strong sentiment against any form of censorship. According to Milton, people should be exposed to a wide variety of opinions and ideas so they can apply reason and select the very best ideas. Even bad ideas and inaccurate information should be available because they present opinions and materials worth considering. Milton stated, "Let [Truth] and Falsehood grapple; who ever knew Truth put to the worse in a free and open encounter?" This concept, known as the **self-righting principle**, states that society can make adjustments and put itself on the right path if its citizens have many ideas and opinions from which to choose.

Closely related to Milton's self-righting principle is the concept of a **marketplace of ideas.** This term refers to a society in which ideas appear uncensored for consideration by the public, just as goods are presented in a marketplace. In the marketplace of ideas, people sample from the various sources of information and opinions, and because people are both rational and inherently good, they eventually find the truth. These concepts underlie the First Amendment to the U.S. Constitution.

The founders of this country, who put the First Amendment into law in 1786, certainly could not have envisioned the amazing technological innovations in mass media that have occurred since that time. Since the electronic media are technologically more complex than the print media, it should not be surprising that the federal government has always taken an interest in preventing interference problems stemming from stations using the airwaves to transmit their signals. The government also has shown interest in using electronic media for national security and in preventing commercial interests from monopolizing electronic media in order to prevent competition and avoid serving the public.

Poet and writer John Milton.

The Basis for Regulatory Power

Congress, as the law-making body of the U.S. government, has the right to regulate broadcasting because the airwaves belong to the people. Unlike newspaper companies, which can print and distribute newspapers wherever and whenever they like to as many people as they can, broadcasters must use the **electromagnetic spectrum** to transmit their information.

The important point to remember about the electromagnetic spectrum is that certain portions of it are used to transmit certain types of signals. Only a small portion of the spectrum is usable for broadcasting. The government considers it a scarce resource, much like it might consider water a scarce resource in some areas of the country. Use of the electromagnetic spectrum is therefore subject to regulation by the federal government on behalf of the people. The government wants to prevent monopolistic use and squandering of the electromagnetic spectrum, in particular. Hence, the government stepped in early on to regulate broadcasting and its use of the spectrum.

Overview of Regulation

The Early 1900s

In the very early days of radio, before regulation, the federal government quickly noticed that the medium could be used for humanitarian purposes. For instance, information about natural disasters and hazardous conditions for ships at sea could be transmitted

---

The *Titanic* Disaster

The Wireless Ship Act of 1910 mandated that ships at sea carrying 50 or more passengers had to have a radio capable of transmitting 100 miles or more and a trained operator. Unfortunately, this wasn't enough to help avoid disaster when the *Titanic* sank in April of 1912. Obviously, one operator can't be on duty 24 hours per day.

The *Titanic* began sinking just before 11:00 P.M. and finally went down at 2:00 A.M. Although the *Carpathia* did hear and respond to the radio distress calls sent out by the *Titanic*, it was 58 miles away. Other ships that were closer didn't have their radios operating at that late hour, which certainly cost many lives.

After the *Titanic* disaster, Congress amended the Wireless Ship Act of 1910 in order to require two trained radio operators, an auxiliary power supply, and the ability of the radio operator to communicate with the bridge of the ship. Also, the act was extended to include not only ships at sea but also those in the Great Lakes.

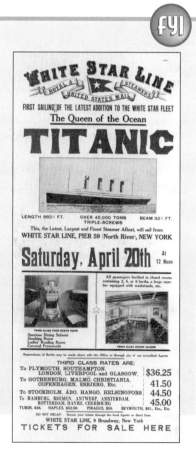

An advertisement for the first sailing of the British luxury passenger liner *Titanic*, which sank on the first leg of the voyage and never even made it to New York.

using radio broadcasting. The government also noticed that some broadcasting companies involved during the formative years of radio had shown monopolistic behavior. One such company was British Marconi, which had a policy to communicate only with the facilities that it owned. Numerous scandals also emerged among radio companies, such as patent fights and stock scandals (Sterling & Kittross, 2002, p. 41).

Congressional oversight of the budding broadcast industry began with passage of the Wireless Ship Act of 1910, which required all ships carrying 50 or more people to have onboard a wireless radio capable of transmitting and receiving signals over a distance of at least 100 miles. The radio had to be operated by a skilled operator and capable of communicating with the shore and other ships, regardless of the brand of radio equipment used. Following the sinking of the *Titanic* in April 1912, the act was amended to require that at least two trained operators be onboard and that the power supply for the radio had to be independent of the ship's main power plant. However, soon after the passing of this regulation came a new impetus for regulating radio.

The Radio Act of 1912 more carefully spelled out public policy regarding radio transmissions and standards of operation and in effect set down a few ground rules for radio. It also mandated that stations must be licensed by the U.S. Secretary of Commerce and that government stations had priority over airwaves that were beginning to become crowded with ship-to-shore service, hobbyists and experimenters, and the military. In addition, messages that were sent over the radio were to be private, reinforcing the notion of one-to-one communication. This law stood as the most important regulation affecting radio from 1912 until 1927.

World War I: 1917–1918

Radio operators had long understood that the U.S. government would take over radio transmissions if the country went to war. World War I had already started in Europe, and the United States was expected to be eventually drawn into the fray. At the beginning of the war in 1917, most private experimentation with radio stopped and amateur radio operators halted their transmissions, as well. The U.S. Navy took over operations of all commercial radio enterprises on April 7 and began recruiting amateur radio operators and experimenters to provide the military with people who were knowledgeable and experienced in radio. But as the war ended and recruits became civilians again, the navy realized that it lacked the experience and expertise to maintain its control over the radio industry.

After the war, the federal government was in the position to keep control of radio. Many people believed the government should do just that, considering the vicious competition between telephone and telegraph companies, the monopolistic leanings of radio companies, and examples in Europe of government control. Nonetheless, experimenters, hobbyists, and commercial radio companies like AT&T and Marconi pressured Congress and President Woodrow Wilson to return radio to the citizens and private industry. And so on July 11, 1919, the president acquiesced, and the military takeover of radio ended eight months later on March 1, 1920.

The Radio Act of 1927

The Radio Act of 1912 was adequate for regulating point-to-point radio as it existed from 1912 to about 1922. But when radio went beyond point-to-point communication and also provided point-to-multipoint communication, or broadcasting, this early legislation was no longer adequate to regulate commercial radio. The enormous problems regarding radio reception and interference (see Chapter 2) led the broadcast industry to ask the government for help. Congress responded to this request and other issues by establishing some basic guidelines for broadcasting in this country.

On February 23, 1927, President Calvin Coolidge signed the Radio Act of 1927 into law. This new law took control of radio from the Secretary of Commerce and gave it to the newly created **Federal Radio Commission (FRC)**. This agency was to have licensing authority over radio stations for one year, after which the responsibility would revert to the Secretary of Commerce. The FRC was comprised of five members, each representing one of the five geographical areas of the country, and each member was appointed to a six-year term.

In addition, the act addressed the equality of transmission facilities and issues of reception and service. The concept that the public owned the airwaves was made very clear, but the act stated that individuals and corporate entities could be licensed to operate stations. Criteria for ownership also were established because the number of applicants competing for frequencies exceeded the number of frequencies available on the electromagnetic spectrum. The statement reflecting these criteria—"**public interest, convenience, and necessity**"—set the tone for case law in subsequent legal disputes over who controlled radio and why. The government, through the FRC, was granting permission for operators to own radio stations. Moreover, those operators were responsible for their stations and would be allowed to operate freely as long as their service to the public was deemed adequate. In addition, it was made clear that government censorship of radio was not allowed.

The Communications Act of 1934

In 1933, President Franklin D. Roosevelt established a committee to study the nine different government agencies involved in public, private, and government radio, and by the end of that year, the committee had recommended that one agency should regulate all radio and related services. The result of that recommendation and subsequent bills sponsored in Congress was the Communications Act of 1934.

By 1934, the importance of broadcasting had become very clear both to the federal government and to the population in general. Although the Radio Act of 1927 had helped to organize and regulate radio, there were still some problems that Congress felt it needed to address. As just noted, several government agencies—including the Interstate Commerce Commission, the Federal Radio Commission, and the Department of Commerce—were regulating various aspects of electronic communication, but they were not working closely together. Congress had attempted to make the FRC a permanent agency but had not been able to do so.

The Communications Act of 1934 incorporated most of the Radio Act of 1927 and made several changes. Namely, the FRC was replaced by the **Federal Communications Commission (FCC)**, which was to have seven commissioners. Each commissioner would be appointed by the President of the United States and would serve a seven-year term. No more than four members could be from any one political party. The FCC was also authorized to regulate common carriers, such as telephone and telegraph.

The FCC set about tackling the problem of substandard programming in radio, which ranged from fortune telling and

Inappropriate Programming

These 14 topics are examples of programming deemed inappropriate in 1939 by the FCC. Obviously, topics such as numbers 8 and 11 are no longer considered inappropriate but rather are expected in many types of stations. The last two topics gave a glimmer of things to come in the form of the fairness doctrine.

1. Defamation
2. Religious intolerance
3. Fortune telling
4. Favorable references to hard liquor
5. Obscenity
6. Depictions of torture
7. Excessive suspense in children's programs
8. Excessive playing of recorded music to fill airtime
9. Obvious solicitation of funds
10. Lengthy and frequent advertisements
11. Interruption of artistic programs by advertising
12. False advertising
13. Presenting only one side of a controversy
14. Refusal to give equal coverage to two sides in a controversial argument

Source: Based on Sterling & Kittross, 2002.

excessive advertising to issues of obscenity and religious intolerance. And while it could not censor, it had the right to evaluate stations' policies and programs to make sure they were operating in the public interest. Between 1934 and 1941, the FCC examined many stations, but only two licenses were revoked and only eight others were not renewed. Perhaps more important, the FCC made radio stations aware that it was listening. A letter of inquiry from the FCC, often referred to as a "raised eyebrow" letter, would usually get the station's attention and initiate action to correct problems.

Advertising

The FCC has historically been concerned with broadcast advertising, especially in children's programs. However, in 1938, the Wheeler Lea Act designated that the **Federal Trade Commission (FTC)** should take over most of the responsibility for the regulation of advertising and gave it the power to find and stop deceptive advertising in any medium.

ZOOM IN   12.1

Learn more about the FTC at the agency's website: **www.ftc.gov**. In particular, click on "Formal Actions, Opinions & Activities" to read about some companies that have been subject to FTC action.

The Communications Act of 1934 also stated that there must be a recognizable difference between commercials and program content. That is, a station is required to disclose the source of any content it broadcasts for which it receives any type of payment. Further, the **sponsor identification rule** (Section 317 of the act) protects listeners from commercial messages coming from unidentified sponsors by requiring broadcasters to reveal sponsors' identities.

Chain Broadcasting

In 1938, the FCC decided to investigate network broadcasting (also known as *chain broadcasting*) to see whether controls were needed to prevent monopolistic behavior. In May 1941, *The Report on Chain Broadcasting* was released, containing the following regulations for networks:

- Limited network affiliation contracts to two years, rather than five years
- Prevented networks from making exclusive contracts with affiliates (which allowed stations with network affiliations to accept programs from other networks)
- Prevented networks from demanding large blocks of time from affiliates
- Allowed affiliates to reject some network programming (if they felt it was not in the public interest)
- Prevented networks from controlling advertising rates for nonnetwork programs
- Prevented stations from affiliating with a network that owned more than one network

These rules affected broadcasting in general and the networks in particular for many years. One of the direct results was that NBC was forced to divest one of its two networks, the NBC Blue network, which later became the ABC network.

Ownership

The FCC also created a rule that prohibited a licensee from owning two stations in the same service (e.g., AM or FM) in the same market. This rule came to be known as the **duopoly rule.** Also at this time, the FCC began to deal with the issue of **cross-ownership**, or where both a newspaper and a radio station or a radio station and a television station in the same market are owned by a single entity.

The Communications Act of 1934 simplified government regulation of electronic media in the United States. But because it was enacted before the introduction of technologies like television, cable, satellite, and microwave transmissions, the act required numerous additions and revisions over the next 60 years. Regardless, it remains as the single most important piece of legislation in terms of how it shaped the development of broadcasting and its related delivery systems.

Political Programming

The Communications Act of 1934 included a section devoted to regulating political programming. **Section 315** stated that any radio station that allowed a candidate for an elected office to use the station's time for political purposes had to allow all bona fide candidates for the same office an equal opportunity for airtime. News and public affairs programs were excluded from this provision. The term *equal opportunity* did not necessarily mean *equal time,* however. Rather, it meant that opposing candidates must have the opportunity to buy an equal amount of time.

Sixty days before an election, candidates could purchase time at the lowest unit rate available to any station advertiser. For example, if one candidate bought 25 60-second announcements in prime time, then all the other candidates also must be given the opportunity to buy 25 60-second announcements in prime time. Section 312(a)(7) stated that stations had to make a reasonable amount of time available to candidates for federal office.

Although Section 315 was adequate for regulating political speech on early radio, in later years, television made the rules difficult to enforce. Problems arose when candidates running for office appeared on regularly scheduled entertainment shows. For instance, when Ronald Reagan and Arnold Schwarzenegger ran for elected office, their movies, though not at all political, could not be shown on local stations without involving complications with Section 315 (Gentile, 2003).

When movies featuring actors-turned-politicians like Ronald Reagan and Arnold Schwarzenegger were shown during political campaigns, broadcasters raised concerns about Section 315 and providing equal television time for political candidates.

Although both broadcasters and the FCC were familiar with the phrase "public interest, convenience, and necessity," opinions differed as to what it meant in practical terms. Additionally, many broadcasters had questions about the FCC's authority to enforce this vague standard for programming. In 1946, the FCC attempted to clear the air somewhat by issuing a report known as the ***Blue Book*** (because it had a blue cover), which discussed its philosophy of broadcast programming. The report dealt with four types of radio programming that were of interest to the FCC in relationship to the phrase "public interest, convenience, and necessity": (1) sustaining programs (not sponsored), (2) local live shows, (3) public issue discussions/programs, and (4) advertising. Although stations complained that the *Blue Book* was restrictive, the FCC contended that it merely explained policy as it related to programming.

The *Blue Book* was used as a benchmark for FCC policy over the next three decades, even despite changes in the industry with the advent of network television. Moreover, the *Blue Book* received generally favorable reviews from both the government and citizens' groups. One policy derived from the *Blue Book* that dealt with broadcasters' handling of controversial issues eventually led to implementation of the fairness doctrine in 1949 (Smith et al., 1998, pp. 54–55; Sterling & Kitross, 2002, p. 331).

The Freeze: 1948–1952

After World War II, the United States was once again ready to focus on new technologies for purposes other than warfare. In 1948, there were only 16 television stations in the country, but construction got underway in earnest in order to meet the strong demand from the potential audiences of viewers. The FCC was inundated with applications for new television licenses, especially in the large markets, where available channels were scarce because only the 12 channels in the VHF band were available for television. Other questions persisted, such as whether to add channels, how to avoid interference, whether to create educational television channels, and how to select a color television system.

In late September 1948, the FCC decided to put a six-month freeze on considering any new applications for television licenses. Owners whose applications had been approved before that time, however, were allowed to continue construction of their stations and to begin broadcasting. The FCC expected that it would take six months to settle the issues, but it actually took about 3½ years. *The Sixth Report and Order* was signed on April 15, 1952, officially ending what has become known as "the freeze." The issues addressed during the freeze were resolved as follows:

* *Additional channels.* The FCC decided to supplement the 12 VHF channels available for television (channel 1 had been assigned to point-to-point audio use) with channels in the UHF (ultra-high-frequency) band, which consisted of channels 14 through 83. The high end of the band, channels 70 through 83, were reserved for translator and other low-power transmission uses for the benefit of smaller communities.
* *Educational channels.* Two hundred forty-two channels were reserved for educational television, which was about 12 percent of the 2,053 channels allocated for television station use across the United States. Unlike the allocation set aside for FM noncommercial radio (i.e., 88.1 to 91.9 MHz), these channels were not located within one part of the TV band but rather spread throughout the UHF and VHF bands. While commercial entities opposed this generous allotment of channels to education on the grounds that it made commercial channels less available in many cities, the ruling was upheld.

- *Color television.* During the freeze, both RCA and CBS presented the FCC with color television systems for consideration. The CBS system was adopted in 1950 after much deliberation and political fighting. Little effort was put forth to launch color television broadcasting, however, and manufacturers showed little interest in the CBS system. Although slightly better in some ways than the RCA system, the CBS system was a mechanical system and incompatible with existing black-and-white sets. Neither the industry nor consumers embraced color television quickly. Few programs were broadcast in color, and color television sets were very expensive to purchase. In December 1953, the FCC changed its previous decision and decided to adopt RCA's color system. Regardless, the manufacturing industry's indifference to color broadcasting and the audience's lack of interest in buying expensive TV sets prevented color television from becoming widespread until 20 years later.

Other Legal Concerns

Defamation

Defamation is a false attack on a person's reputation. If a person suffers humiliation, ridicule, or loss of good name or becomes the target of hatred as a result of comments or programs in the media, he or she may claim defamation, or **libel**, after the negative comments are published or broadcast. *Slander* is spoken defamation. *Libel,* or written defamation, is considered more serious because print is more permanent than the spoken word.

The constitutional standard for defamation comes from the U.S. Supreme Court case *New York Times v. Sullivan* (1964), which considered the First Amendment and an individual's right to punish the media for making negative comments about him or her. In a defamation case, the burden of proof is on the person who alleges the defamation or libel. In other words, the person who is attacked must prove that the media source was in error or even negligent in publishing the story. The finding for the media in *New York Times v. Sullivan* made it more difficult for individuals to win libel suits. Defamation or libel can be defended against by the media when the defamatory statements are true; when charges are made after the statute of limitations has run out (i.e., two years in most states); when the comments have resulted from coverage of statements made by a government official or political candidate or a normally reliable source; or when the statements are known to be commentary.

Editorializing

In 1941, the FCC discouraged broadcast stations from **editorializing**, or giving opinions on issues, as the result of an attempt by the Mayflower Broadcasting Corporation to take over a frequency used by WAAB in Boston.[1] Hearings held in 1939 resulted in Mayflower's competing application to be denied. Most important, however, the FCC stated that "the broadcaster should not be an advocate." This statement of policy, which became known as the **Mayflower doctrine**, told broadcast stations that their function was to entertain and inform, not to give their opinions. Most stations seemed

The Changeover to Digital TV

The dilemma of a mandated technological change, as experienced by RCA with color television from 1953 on, is what broadcast television stations and television set manufacturers are experiencing in the early part of the twenty-first century. While the FCC has mandated a changeover to digital television broadcasting by 2006, not many stations are actually broadcasting a full schedule digitally, for several reasons. For one, making the changeover from analog to digital broadcasting is very expensive, and stations are struggling to finance the change. Digital sets are also very expensive, so consumers are unlikely to spend thousands of dollars to buy one. In addition, over two-thirds of the viewing audience receives their broadcast stations through a cable system that may not be digital ready.

In combination, these factors present the true dilemma facing broadcast television stations: Spend millions of dollars to convert to a digital system that most of the audience will not be able to receive.

Some new flat-screen television sets are thin enough to hang on a wall.

comfortable with this role, since editorializing often generated bad feelings from listeners, politicians, and businesspeople who held opposing viewpoints.

Eight years later, with new commissioners in power, the FCC recommended the exact opposite: that stations *should* express opinions about controversial issues, as long as they provided an opportunity for the other side of the issue to be presented. This view was stated "In the Matter of Editorializing by Broadcast Licensees" (13 FCC 1246, 1949), also known as the *Cornell petition*.

This reversal in policy exemplifies the difficulty that broadcasters have faced for years in dealing with the rule-making body that governs them. The FCC, as a quasi-political body, changes policy with the change in the political orientation of the U.S. President and with changes in the commissioners of the organization.

The Fairness Doctrine

It was at this point, in 1949, that the **fairness doctrine** was born. Not only did this doctrine allow stations to editorialize, but it also expected them to provide programming that dealt with controversial issues and required them to provide reasonable opportunities for the presentation of opposing viewpoints. Note that this meant that a station had the responsibility to provide the opportunity for rebuttal but not necessarily equal time. In other words, a station that aired a 30-minute program that expressed one viewpoint did not have to provide the opposing viewpoint with 30 minutes of airtime, just an opportunity to express that viewpoint.

The FCC's intent was to reach an overall balance when dealing with controversial issues. Also, the FCC felt that the right for the public to know about controversial issues was more important than the right of a station to express its own opinion and exclude others. Using the scarcity of the airwaves as a basis for the decision, the **Red Lion standard** (*Red Lion v. FCC*, 1969) upheld the fairness doctrine and the FCC's right to "reasonably" regulate broadcasting. As a result, stations had to provide programming that dealt with controversial public issues as well as a reasonable opportunity for other points of view (Gillmor, Barron, Simon, & Terry, 1996; Smith et al., 1998).[2]

Industry Scandals

Disc jockey Alan Freed was called to appear before a congressional investigation committee and eventually lost his job for refusing to swear that he didn't accept payola.

A number of scandals and frauds have also left their mark on the electronic media industry. In the late 1950s, television quiz shows were found to be rigged. Producers of one show, under pressure from advertisers to get high ratings, decided in advance which contestants would win and coached them accordingly. This cheating prompted FCC action to ban this type of fraud.

Another fraud investigated by the FCC in the late 1950s was **payola,** or accepting bribes in exchange for the airing of music. When record companies saw the influence that getting their new music on radio stations had on sales, they offered gifts and money to disc jockeys who would play their music. A congressional investigation of this practice led to legislation preventing commercial bribery of this type.

A related type of bribery occurred when products and services were given free mentions on the air, not as part of regular commercials. This practice, known as **plugola,** not only angered Congress and the FCC but also station managers, who realized that this practice benefited the person giving the "plug" but not their own advertising revenue.

The result of all these scandals was a 1959 amendment to the Communications Act of 1934, prohibiting fraudulent quiz shows and the practices of payola and plugola.

Deregulation

After some 40 years of maintaining control over broadcasting and other electronic media, the FCC began to reverse itself in the late 1970s, when it came under pressure from two congressional groups. Liberal legislators maintained that the FCC needed to keep strict regulatory control over broadcasting because the phrase "public interest, convenience, and necessity" mandated doing so. Conservatives, on the other hand, felt that FCC regulation came at a high cost and that the marketplace of the media, with stations and other suppliers vying for audience attention, should be allowed to guide station behavior, not the government.

The conservatives and their marketplace concept won out, and in 1981, after many years of complaining about increased workloads and costs to comply with government regulations, the radio industry was somewhat deregulated by the FCC. As a result, radio stations were required to do less regarding the public interest aspects of programming. The television industry received some deregulation relief in 1984.

With these changes, stations were no longer required to complete the long and sometimes costly process of *community ascertainment*, in which they conducted interviews to learn about local civic issues. (Many stations still do this, however.) The form necessary for stations to submit for renewal of their license was considerably simplified and became known as the "postcard renewal form."

Perhaps most notable among the deregulatory actions was the one to eliminate the fairness doctrine. This action began in the early 1980s, but the FCC didn't vote to stop enforcing the doctrine until August 1987. The spirit of deregulation stems from both the First Amendment and the marketplace concept. Broadcasters wanted the same freedom from regulation that newspapers enjoyed and felt that programming should be determined by the marketplace (the audience), not bureaucrats.

In sum, the FCC agreed to some extent with broadcasters and legislators about the marketplace concept but perhaps took the notion further than was expected. Looking to the newspaper industry, which had no barriers to entry, the FCC sought to reduce the barriers for entry into the broadcast and electronic media businesses. The result was the addition of more stations and thus more competition from alternative delivery systems like cable, satellite, and multipoint multichannel delivery systems (MMDSs).

In the late 1980s, the push for broadcast deregulation slowed considerably, as Congress decided that the FCC had moved beyond what it had intended. Congress also decided it should play "a more direct role in the policy sandbox" (Sterling & Kittross, 2002, p. 560).

ZOOM IN 12.2

Go to www.fcc.gov/Forms/Form303-S/303s.pdf to download the form needed by a broadcast station to renew its license. Although deregulation has produced the "postcard renewal form," this site yields a 38-page file. If you scroll through it, though, you will find that it is a generic form for all types of broadcast station renewals: AM, FM, and TV. Also, much of the file contains instructions about how to fill out the form.

The Public Broadcasting Act of 1967

In the early 1960s, the FCC developed an interest in regulating more for the benefit of the public than for the benefit of commercial stations. One of the results of this change in interest was passage of the Educational Television Facilities Act of 1962, which helped fund the noncommercial stations. Then, just five years later, the distinguished Carnegie Commission on Educational Television concluded that a new and appropriately financed and directed television system was required for the United States. Specifically, the commission believed that a more prominent and effective system was needed to fulfill the country's needs (Sterling & Kittross, 2002, p. 425). Later that year, Congress passed the Public Broadcasting Act of 1967, which created the **Corporation for Public Broadcasting (CPB)** for the purpose of funding educational programs. The CPB then formed the **Public Broadcasting Service (PBS)** to distribute television programming and serve the function of a network. In 1970, **National Public Radio (NPR)** was established to serve as the radio program producer and distributor.

 **SEE IT NOW**

The Telecommunications Act of 1996

After decades of attempts and at least one full year of political negotiating and compromise, Congress passed the Telecommunications Act of 1996 by an overwhelming majority vote. This act, which was signed into law on February 8, 1996, and became effective immediately, was the first comprehensive rewrite of the Communications Act of 1934 and changed some aspects of electronic media dramatically. It had provisions in five major areas: telephone service, telecommunications equipment manufacturing, cable television, radio and television broadcasting, and obscenity and violence in programming.

TELEPHONE SERVICE   The 1996 act overruled state restrictions on competition in providing local and long-distance service. This made the regional Bell Telephone operating companies (also known as "Baby Bells" and RBOCs, pronounced "ree-boks") free to provide long-distance service outside their regions and required them to remove barriers to competition inside their regions. New **universal service rules** guaranteed that rural and low-income users would be subsidized and that equal access to long-distance carriers ("1 +" dialing) would be maintained.

TELECOMMUNICATIONS EQUIPMENT MANUFACTURING   The RBOCs were allowed to manufacture telephone equipment. The FCC was to enforce nondiscrimination requirements and restrictions on joint manufacturing ventures, and it was to monitor the setting of technical standards and accessibility of equipment and service to people with disabilities.

CABLE TELEVISION   The Telecommunications Act of 1996 relaxed the rules set down in the 1992 Cable Act, essentially removing rate restrictions on all cable services except basic service. In addition, telephone companies were permitted to offer cable television services and to carry video programming. Other provisions were that cable companies in small communities were to receive immediate rate deregulation, that cable systems had to scramble sexually explicit adult programming, and that cable set-top converters could be sold in retail stores (instead of being available only as rental units from the cable companies).

RADIO AND TELEVISION BROADCASTING   The 1996 act relaxed media concentration rules for television by allowing any one company to own stations that could reach 35 percent of the nation's television households, an increase from the previous limit of 25 percent. The major broadcast television networks (ABC, CBS, NBC, and FOX) were allowed to own cable systems but not other major networks (excluding the smaller networks: WB, UPN, and PAX).

A rule stating that a company could own up to seven AM, seven FM, and seven television stations.

All limits on radio station ownership were also repealed, but some restrictions remained on the number of local stations a company could own in any one market. In markets with 45 or more stations, one company could own 8 stations but no more than 5 in either AM or FM. In markets with 30 to 44 stations, a company could own 7 or less with only 4 in any one service. In markets with 15 to 29 stations, one company could own only 6 stations (4 in any or either service). In a market with less than 15 stations, only 5 could be owned by one company—3 maximum in either AM or FM and only 50 percent or less of the total number of stations in that market. In addition, the U.S. Department of Justice's Antitrust Division was assigned to look closely at large transactions to prevent any group that already had 50 percent of the local radio advertising revenue or was about to obtain 70 percent of the local advertising revenue in any one market from acquiring more stations in that market.

The 1996 act also made available additional frequencies for television stations for uses such as high-definition television, but the stations might have to return spectrum space or pay auction fees. Finally, all new television sets were required to have a **V-chip** installed to allow parents to block violent and sexually explicit programs from reaching children.

ZOOM IN 12.3

The Telecommunications Act of 1996 was the most significant legislation for electronic media since the Communications Act of 1934. To read the 1996 act, go to the FCC's website: www.fcc.gov/telecom.html.

The FCC Today

Although the FCC originally had seven commissioners, that number was reduced to five in 1982 as part of federal cost cutting. The president nominates the commissioners, and the Senate must approve them. Only three can come from any one political party. The FCC now has six bureaus or divisions, each with a specific area of administration: the Enforcement Bureau, the Wireless Telecommunications Bureau, the Media Bureau, the Consumer and Governmental Affairs Bureau, the International Bureau, and the Wireline Competition Bureau.

Licensing

One of the most important and newsworthy functions of the FCC has been and continues to be the licensing of broadcast stations, including the process of renewing licenses and overseeing the transfer of licenses when stations are sold. Obtaining a new broadcast license is a daunting process that requires time, money, and energy. Consulting engineers and communications attorneys are often needed to complete the necessary paperwork and to respond to questions and challenges by other entities competing for the same license.

Rule Making and Enforcement

In addition to the existing rules that have come from congressional legislation, the FCC can create rules for electronic media. In order to do so, the agency must announce its intent to create a new rule and then publish a draft of the new rule. After publishing the proposed rule, the FCC must wait for comments from both audiences and professionals in electronic media. Only after these comments have been considered can the FCC create the rule.

Through its Office of Strategic Planning and Policy Analysis, the FCC also attempts to review the overall past economic performance of the electronic media and to make projections for the future of the industry. After gathering this information, the FCC often asks media owners for input on how it can create rules or policies to help support the future success of the broadcast medium.

The Enforcement Bureau of the FCC has the responsibility of making sure that broadcasting and other electronic media follow the rules. As mentioned earlier in this chapter, if the FCC finds that a rule has been broken, it usually sends a letter of reprimand to alert the station of the violation. Doing so usually gets the attention of the station and leads to correction of the problem. If the letter does not get the desired response, the next action is usually a **cease-and-desist order** (i.e., stop or be penalized) and perhaps a fine (often referred to as a **forfeiture**), which may range from $25,000 to as much as $250,000 for each violation. Other actions that can be taken include a short-term renewal (i.e., six months to two years instead of eight years), or, in the case of repeated violations and a failure to correct problems, a nonrenewal or a revocation of the station's license. Although these drastic actions are rare, they do occur.

Organizational Flowchart of the FCC

Commissioners

Office of Inspector General

Office of Engineering and Technology
- Electromagnetic Compatibility Division
- Laboratory Division
- Network Technology Division
- Policy and Rules Division
- Administrative Staff

Office of General Counsel
- Administrative Law Division
- Litigation Division

Office of Managing Director
- Human Resources Management
- Information Technology Center
- Financial Operations
- Administrative Operations
- Performance Evaluation and Records Management
- Secretary

Office of Media Relations
- Media Services Staff
- Internet Services Staff

Office of Administrative Law Judges

Office of Strategic Planning and Policy Analysis

Office of Communications Business Opportunities

Office of Workplace Diversity

Office of Legislative Affairs

Wireline Competition Bureau
- Administration and Management Office
- Competition Policy Division
- Pricing Policy Division
- Telecommunications Access Policy Division
- Industry Analysis and Technology Division

Enforcement Bureau
- Office of Management and Resources
- Office of Homeland Security
- Telecommunications Consumers Division
- Spectrum Enforcement Division
- Market Disputes Resolution Division
- Investigations and Hearings Division
- Regional and Field Offices

Wireless Telecommunications Bureau
- Management and Resources Staff
- Auctions and Spectrum Access Division
- Spectrum Management Resource and Technologies Division
- Public Safety and Critical Infrastructure Division
- Mobility Division
- Broadband Division

Media Bureau
- Management and Resources Staff
- Office of Communication and Industry Information
- Policy Division
- Industry Analysis Division
- Engineering Division
- Office of Broadcast License Policy
- Audio Division
- Video Division

Consumer and Governmental Affairs Bureau
- Administration and Management Office
- Office of Information Resources Management
- Information Access and Privacy Office
- Consumer Inquiries and Complaints Division
- Reference Information Center
- Disability Rights Office
- Consumer Affairs and Outreach Division
- Office of Intergovernmental Affairs

International Bureau
- Administration and Management Office
- Policy Division
- Satellite Division
- Strategic Analysis and Negotiations Division

Source: Based on www.fcc.gov/fccorgchart.html.

Other Regulatory Influences

In addition to the U.S. Congress, which creates laws, and the FCC, which creates and enforces rules, other groups in the United States influence how the electronic media are regulated.

THE MARKETPLACE As mentioned earlier, since the 1980s, Congress has been inclined to let the marketplace decide what it wants and needs from electronic media, rather than continually create laws on behalf of the public. For example, rather than mandate programming to stations that are not serving all segments of the audience, the government allows existing stations to reformat programming and new stations to enter the marketplace to serve the unmet needs of certain audiences. This is especially true in radio. If a market lacks a station to reach the mature population with appropriate programming, a new station will eventually enter the market to do so or an existing station that has not been successful with one programming format will switch to another format to reach the unserved market. Obviously, the logic is that it is simply good business to serve the marketplace.

LOCAL GOVERNMENT Many of the laws that regulate electronic media don't come from the federal government but rather a state or local government. For example, laws against defamation, fraudulent advertising, and certain kinds of contests and promotions, as well as shield laws that protect the anonymity of a journalist's sources, are all made at the state and local levels. In particular, city and county laws and rules affect cable systems, which are franchised by cities and counties.

CITIZENS' GROUPS Citizens have often formed groups to exert pressure on the electronic media. Issues such as children's programming and violence in the media have sparked enthusiastic groups to send letters to stations and networks, advertisers, and Congress and the FCC, expressing their discontent. If well organized and sufficiently large, these groups can influence the opinion of legislators, who make laws for the electronic media. Citizens' groups can also persuade advertisers to avoid buying spots in programs that may be offensive because of gratuitous sex or violence.

LOBBYISTS *Lobbyists* are people who represent special interests and try to inform and influence legislators and decision makers. They are often lawyers, former legislators, industry leaders, and even former FCC commissioners. Trade organizations like the National Association of Broadcasters (NAB) and the National Cable Television Association (NCTA) often hire lobbyists to try to persuade legislators to embrace the organization's point of view on a major issue or some pending policy or legislation.

THE WHITE HOUSE Since the president appoints commissioners to the FCC, he obviously influence how the FCC conducts business. Although Congress must approve the president's nominations, once the names have been formally announced, the necessary confirmation is usually forthcoming.

In addition, the president also has influence through the **National Telecommunication Information Administration (NTIA).** As an agency of the U.S. Department of Commerce, the NTIA is the executive branch's principal voice on domestic and international telecommunications and information technology issues. It works to spur innovation, encourage competition, create jobs, and provide consumers with more choices and better-quality telecommunications products and services at lower prices. The NTIA also exerts influence on the president, the Congress, and the FCC.

THE COURTS   While the courts don't create rules or laws, they do decide on their legality and how they are interpreted. This means that if an electronic media company disagrees with an FCC ruling, it can appeal that ruling to the courts. Most such cases are heard by the U.S. Court of Appeals for the District of Columbia. A decision by this court can be appealed to the U.S. Supreme Court. In some cases, the courts can decide whether or not the FCC even has jurisdiction over the issue in question.

The FCC and Indecency, Obscenity, and Violence

Indecency

In late 1973, comedian George Carlin's expletive-filled monologue "Filthy Words," which repeated seven words too "dirty" ever to say on the airwaves, was broadcast in the middle of the day on a New York radio station owned by the Pacifica Foundation. The ensuing public outcry spurred the FCC to bar the broadcast of words that are **indecent**, or "language that describes, in terms patently offensive as measured by contemporary community standards for the broadcast medium, sexual or excretory activities or organs (*FCC v. Pacifica Foundation*, 1978).

ZOOM IN   12.4
The issues concerning obscenity and indecency are not always easy to understand and will probably change over time, as our society and culture change. Find out exactly what the FCC has to say about this type of material by going to www.fcc.gov/cgb/consumerfacts/obscene.html.

After years of challenges, including a ruling by an appeals court that found that the FCC was practicing censorship, the FCC ruling against Pacifica was upheld and the definition of indecency was affirmed by the U.S. Supreme Court in 1978. The FCC deems that children are less likely to be in the audience between 10:00 P.M. and 6:00 A.M. Therefore, *indecent* content not intended for children may be broadcast without penalty during this "safe harbor" time period, but *obscene* material cannot be broadcast at any time.

Inappropriate Programming Content

Certain kinds of expression (i.e., parts of programming) are not protected by the First Amendment and are prohibited in the electronic media. One such type of material is **obscenity**. In the 1973 case of *Miller v. California,* the U.S. Supreme Court held that obscenity could be determined by using these criteria:

- Whether the average person, applying contemporary community standards, would find that the work, taken as a whole, appeals to the prurient interest, and
- Whether the work depicts or describes, in a patently offensive way, sexual conduct specifically defined by the applicable state law, and
- Whether the work taken as a whole, lacks serious literary, artistic, political, or scientific value. (Gillmor et al., 1996, p. 144)

Clearly, these standards are somewhat vague and require some subjective judgment of a work to be made. Because individuals' views of these criteria differ, producers of electronic media are usually careful in creating materials for public exhibition.

Many people think that **pornography** is not protected by the First Amendment, but in fact, it is protected unless a court rules that it is obscene. This distinction is difficult to make and thus one that broadcasters have almost always avoided. Given this, commercial television broadcasters do not show pornography. Subscription services—like cable companies, DBS, MMDS, and the Internet—do show material that is considered pornographic but generally not obscene.

Michael Powell, son of Colin Powell.

Obscenity and Violence

Title V of the Telecommunications Act of 1996, also known as the **Communications Decency Act (CDA)**, was intended to protect citizens and especially children from obscene programming, with particular attention to material available on the Internet. Specifically, the act aimed at preventing pornography from being easily available to children and provided punishments for offenders that included fines of up to $250,000 and possible prison sentences.

At first glance, the CDA seemed reasonable enough, but it drew immediate criticism from civil libertarians and free-speech proponents. Critics felt that the term *indecent* was too vague and would therefore make compliance and enforcement nearly impossible in the vastness of the Internet. In the case of *Reno v. ACLU* (1997), the U.S. Supreme Court ruled the CDA unconstitutional because of vagueness. In this case, the Court addressed the notion of free speech on the Internet by stating, "In the absence of evidence to the contrary, we presume that governmental regulation of the content of speech is more likely to interfere with the free exchange of ideas than to encourage it" (Stevens, 1997).

Another provision of this section mandated that a television rating code be established to give interested individuals (i.e., parents) an indication of the amount of violence, sex, and offensive language contained in a program. Age- and content-based ratings for television programs can be seen in the upper-lefthand corner of the television screen at the beginning of each program and after some commercial breaks.

The FTC and Advertising

Deceptive Advertising

The FTC promotes and supports a free marketplace by ensuring that advertising is not untruthful, misleading, or deceptive. The FTC uses the following three criteria to determine whether advertising is deceptive:

> There must be a representation, omission, or practice that is likely to mislead the consumer.
>
> The act or practice must be examined from the perspective of a consumer acting reasonably in the circumstances.
>
> The representation, omission, or practice must be a material one. ("FTC Policy Statement," 1983)

The FTC issues sanctions against advertisers found guilty of deceptive advertising. Complaints are most commonly settled by requiring the advertiser to sign a **consent decree**, agreeing to stop misleading advertising practices. An advertiser who breaches the decree may be fined up to $10,000 a day until the deceptive advertising stops. If an advertiser refuses to sign a consent decree, the FTC has the authority to take the matter further by issuing a cease-and-desist order, demanding an end to the deceptive advertising. In this situation, the case would be brought before an administrative law judge, who could impose penalties or overturn the case.

If a cease-and-desist order is upheld, the FTC can require the advertiser to run corrective advertising to make up for the previously misleading ad. In 1972, for example, ITT Continental Baking was ordered to run corrective advertising because it had claimed its Profile bread to be beneficial to people watching their caloric intake. In fact, though, Profile bread had about the same calories per ounce as other breads on the market. In another case, Ocean Spray was forced to run corrective advertising after claiming that its cranberry juice cocktail beverage had more "food energy" than other fruit juices. The corrective advertising made clear that the extra food energy came from calories, not protein or vitamins. In 1978, the makers of Listerine mouthwash were required to run corrective ads to state that Listerine did not prevent colds or sore throats, as had been claimed in earlier advertising.

The effectiveness of corrective advertising was disputed by both the business community and the Reagan and Bush (the first Bush) administrations. Given this, the FTC has mostly discontinued using corrective ads as punishment for deceptive advertising (Smith, Wright, & Ostroff, 1998, pp. 281–282).

Nonetheless, the FTC continues to monitor misleading advertising. It recently settled a case with Snorenz, the manufacturer and promoter of an antisnoring mouth spray, for making unsubstantiated product claims. As part of the settlement, the FTC required all future Snorenz promotions to include two disclaimers: to encourage purchasers to see a doctor or sleep specialist and to list the common symptoms of sleep apnea ("Waking Up," 2001).

Infomercials

The FTC dropped the provision banning infomercials from radio in 1981 and from television in 1984. Generally, commercials that are over two minutes in length and that cross program content with product endorsement are considered **infomercials.** Many advertisers cleverly disguise their infomercials to look like informative programs, when they're really just selling products. Viewers often think they're watching programs when they're actually watching product promotions. Infomercials promoting everything from exercise equipment to get-rich-quick schemes can be found on television, especially late at night and in the early weekend hours. However, because children may have particular difficulty in distinguishing programs from commercials, the FTC has upheld the ban on infomercials aimed at children.

Controversial Products

In 1971, Congress banned cigarette ads from radio and television and later extended the ban to include all tobacco-related products. There had been a decades-old self-imposed ban on the broadcasting of hard-liquor commercials, but in 1996, the Distilled Spirits Council, an industry trade group, announced it was reversing the ban. In effect, this left the decision of whether to accept commercials for hard liquor up to the radio and television stations. Seagram's was one of the first advertisers to make its way to the airwaves, and other brands of hard liquor have followed, though somewhat timidly.

Spam Increases

There has been a dramatic increase in the amount of spam that has traveled through the Internet over the last few years.

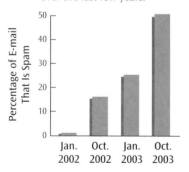

Source: "Do Not Spam" List, 2003.

Spam

Every day, the FTC receives about 40,000 complaints about Internet spam, and through the agency's encouragement, users have forwarded about 12 million pieces of spam (Lee, 2002). These millions of complaints have resulted in proposed legislation to combat this persistent nuisance, but so far, federal legislators have been unable to stop these cyber intruders and the FTC does not have regulatory power over e-mail. About half of the states have passed some type of spam-related law, ranging from Delaware's outright banning, to banning spam with false return addresses, to requiring "remove me" links, to demanding subject alerts on sex-related spam. Some states that do not have laws like these have sued spammers using laws on deceptive advertising.

Although many Internet service providers (ISPs) offer spam blockers, or special software that deletes spam, spammers have all kinds of ways to circumvent the system, including using ordinary subject lines like "From Betty" and "Returned message." Organizations such as the Coalition Against Unsolicited Commercial E-mail and spam. abuse.net are fighting for legislation that will protect the online community from unwanted e-mail. ChooseYourMail heads up the Spam Recycling Center, where consumers can forward their spam e-mails; the center then forwards the messages to the FTC (Freeman, 1999).

In December 2003, Congress passed the **Controlling the Assault of Non-Solicited Pornography and Marketing Act**, or **Can-Spam**. This act was written to eliminate the most offensive tactics used by spammers, including forging e-mail headers and sending pornographic materials. E-mail marketers are now required to have a functioning return address or a link to a website that can accept a request to be deleted from the e-mailing list. Although this is a good start toward protecting e-mail users, it does not necessarily protect against spam that originates in other countries.

> **ZOOM IN**   12.5
> Contact these spam-fighting organizations and websites for more information:
> - Coalition Against Unsolicited Commercial E-mail (CAUCE): www.cauce.org
> - spam.abuse.net: http://spam.abuse.net
> - Choose Your Mail: www.chooseyourmail.com/spamindex.cfm

SEE IT LATER

In early 2001, a new administration came to power along with the George W. Bush presidency. That new administration selected an FCC chairperson, and new commissioners were nominated and approved by Congress. Since the new administration was Republican and more conservative than the previous Democratic administration of President Bill Clinton, changes in FCC policies regarding broadcasting and electronic media were expected. The areas of digital conversion for broadcast television, spectrum availability, ownership (especially the television station ownership cap), program availability for multichannel services, and even how the First Amendment applies to broadcasting have all been reviewed by the Bush-appointed FCC commissioners over the past several years.

FCC Concerns

Digital Conversion

In 1996, the FCC appointed a task force to continue study of the mandated conversion to digital broadcasting by all television stations, which is scheduled to occur in 2006. Station owners are very much concerned that this expensive transition will be met with consumer indifference and technical difficulties with the cable companies that will deliver the digital signal to audience. In 2004, very few TV households had digital television sets.[3] In addition, not all cable companies were capable of both receiving and delivering a digital signal to subscribers.

Broadcasters also feel that unless it's required that all new television sets must have a digital-ready tuner, the audience for digital television signals will be too small to justify the eventual "give back" of the analog frequencies. The understanding is that by 2006, when stations are required to give back their analog frequencies (VHF channels 2 through 13 and UHF channels 4 through 83), 85 percent of the audience must be able to receive digital television broadcasts. If this audience criterion isn't met, then Congress will have to reassess its requirements for the frequency give back.

Congress is very interested in the broadcast stations' returning their analog frequencies to the government because these frequencies are highly sought after by newer wireless services. The frequencies will most likely be awarded by auction, which would obviously bring many dollars to the federal government.

Ownership

The FCC is mandated to review its rules every two years. In 2003, the FCC reviewed whether television groups can own stations that can reach more than 35 percent of the television households in the United States. Station ownership is a major issue. Some television groups would like to increase the number of stations they own, as radio groups have done. Relaxing the 35 percent cap rule for television ownership could bring changes such as the existing major networks buying many more stations and turning the television industry into an **oligopoly,** or one that is tightly controlled by a few companies and has little competition.

In June 2003, the FCC commissioners voted to raise the existing television ownership cap to 45 percent of the national audience, opening the door to more consolidation in the broadcast industry. Upon receiving a strong response against further consolidation, this FCC rule change was halted by the courts. This remains a hotly contested issue, however, and there will be serious debate in the marketplace about the need for more diversity in the television industry.

Another controversial issue is the ownership of programs by networks, which resulted from the elimination of the **financial/syndication rules (fin/syn)** in 1996. Previously, prime-time programming came from independent producers, who had majority ownership in their programs. Now, the major networks own most programs, such that they have control over how long the shows stay in prime time and then syndication after their prime-time runs are over. Since the major networks also own cable channels, they can make special deals for so-called inhouse showings on cable. These cable showings lower the value of a program for the syndication market. In sum, independent producers have diminished control and are being squeezed out of program production.

Cable Delivery

In 2002, the FCC extended until 2007 the rule requiring multichannel delivery system owners (e.g., cable and satellite television) who own or provide programming for their own services to make that programming available to the rest of the multichannel industry at a reasonable price. Without this rule, a company with large interests in broadcast and cable television could avoid making CNN and MTV programming available to the direct broadcast satellite (DBS) industry. Without access to a full array of programming, satellite services cannot compete with cable.

The multichannel programming access rule will stay intact until 2007, thus helping to support access to all programs by all multichannel services. If the rule is lifted after 2007, then the business of multichannel delivery will change significantly.

Another issue affecting cable delivery is voice over the Internet protocol (VOIP), which might have tremendous income potential for cable if the government and courts can decide whether it should fall within Internet regulation or telephone regulation. Whereas the telephone industry is heavily regulated, the Internet industry is lightly regulated, making VOIP a technology with huge profit potential for cable.

The First Amendment

The FCC has repeatedly insisted that it isn't interested in programming content and has no plans to dictate programming to the industry. Specifically, the FCC doesn't intend to require more children's or public affairs programming. However, there continues to be government interest in curtailing indecency in radio and violence and sex on television. Viewers who are outraged by what they deem to be objectionable content continue to pressure legislators to curb such programming.

Interest in indecent content surged after the 2004 Super Bowl half-time show, which featured Janet Jackson's partially exposed breast, Kid Rock wearing the American flag as a poncho, questionable lyrics and crotch grabbing by hip-hop artists, and a closing act that featured feathers and a Native American theme that was deemed offensive by many viewers. The FCC and CBS were immediately flooded with phone calls, letters, and e-mails from viewers who were fed up with such indecent displays, especially on a program watched by so many young viewers. Network executives were forced to explain their programming standards in special congressional hearings prompted by the post–Super Bowl uproar. The incident spurred the FCC to impose harsher fines on stations that air indecent programming.

In 2004, both the U.S. Senate and the House of Representatives passed bills that dramatically increased the fines levied against broadcasters for airing indecent material. The Senate version of the bill increased the maximum fine from $27,500 to $275,000. The House version increased the maximum FCC fine to $500,000 and provided for license revocation proceedings after three violations.

Other Legal Issues

A number of legal issues concern both electronic media professionals and audiences. Traditionally, the electronic media and especially broadcasting have received special treatment under the law because of the nature of these media. This treatment has not necessarily meant better or more privileged treatment by the government or the courts but rather different treatment.

The print media, because of their ease of entry into the marketplace and the fact that they don't use spectrum space, don't require a license to begin business. Moreover, the print media enjoy the full protection of the First Amendment (see earlier in this chapter). The print media are not overseen by a regulatory agency that's expected to control the technological and business aspects.

On the other hand, broadcasting and the other electronic media receive only partial protection from the First Amendment and have the FCC regulating most aspects of their technology as well as some of their business practices. This portion of the chapter looks at the legal issues faced by the electronic media, including free speech, privacy, libel and slander, copyright, and taxation.

Free Speech

The right to say what you want, when you want to, is expected and often taken for granted by people who live in the United States. The First Amendment guarantees the right to free speech; however, this right isn't always extended to the electronic media. The **scarcity theory**, born in the early days of radio, contends that because broadcasting uses parts of the electromagnetic spectrum and because the space is limited, Congress retains the right to protect it on behalf of the people. Also, because broadcasting is pervasive, Congress has always tried to protect children from being exposed to inappropriate materials. Regardless, both Congress and the FCC have conceded that it is nearly impossible to prevent children from being exposed to such materials over the airwaves.

The congressional right to regulate broadcasting was upheld in the U.S. Supreme Court in 1969 in *Red Lion v. FCC*. In this case, the Court held that Congress had the right to regulate the airwaves because of the scarcity principle. In addition, the Court upheld the fairness doctrine, discussed earlier, which required stations to make available opportunities for on-air rebuttal time to individuals with competing points of view. As mentioned already, the FCC eventually abandoned the fairness doctrine in the late 1980s because of the government's general deregulatory climate and the perception that many electronic media options were available at the time (in other words, a "lack of scarcity"). Another issue that encouraged the FCC to drop the fairness doctrine was the difficulty it encountered in trying to enforce it.

The downfall of the fairness doctrine has been something of a mixed victory for free-speech proponents. On the one hand, Congress can no longer force broadcasters to tell both sides of a story or force stations to find a spokesperson to give an opposing viewpoint to station commentary. On the other hand, audience members' opposing viewpoints will simply not be heard over the air, unless stations are somehow motivated to provide time for them.

Subscription-based electronic media are treated differently by the FCC on the issue of free speech. Specifically, services such as MMDS, DBS, and cable all enjoy more First Amendment protection than the broadcast media. The reason behind this is the fact that broadcasting is free and available to all, but subscription-based services are available only to those individuals who choose them and pay to have them. Thus, subscribers have control over what they watch.

The Internet also has the full protection of the First Amendment. Since almost anyone can publish on the Net (just as almost anyone can supposedly publish a newspaper or magazine), Congress and the FCC have essentially allowed Internet content to be unregulated. However, Congress has tried to regulate some kinds of content for some kinds of audiences. As noted earlier, the Telecommunications Act of 1996 originally included the Communications Decency Act (CDA), which attempted to limit the use of indecent material on the Net.

Privacy

The right to privacy, an ongoing concern for people in the United States, refers not only to the privacy of behavior behind closed doors but also to the right to privacy of personal information—namely, information about how people spend their money and their time. Generally, people don't want personal information like their phone numbers, addresses, credit card numbers, and medical information released without their consent.

Privacy is particularly relevant in the context of the Internet. **Cookies** are placed on users' computers when they visit certain websites, allowing companies to track the surfing behaviors of the individuals who visit their sites. What's more, because the Internet is used more and more for commerce between individuals, such as eBay auction transactions, as well as between individuals and commercial entities, there is strong concern that private information about individuals may be given to third parties. Of course, the focus of that concern is that private information like credit card numbers that are intentionally given to one person or company will be used surreptitiously by someone else.

Some groups have endorsed the notion that individuals should be able to protect their communication through the use of **encryption technology**, which scrambles information and makes it unintelligible to third parties. While this seems like a simple enough way to guarantee privacy, the U.S. government has restricted the availability of powerful encryption programs. In fact, the government believes that it should have access to personal data and that encryption technology hinders its information-gathering efforts.

Another privacy issue is the use of an individual's image without his or her permission. Celebrities and public officials relinquish much of their right to privacy when they gain popularity or become elected to public office. Private citizens are entitled to more protection, however. Recently, videos of individuals in partying mode have been marketed widely with great success (e.g., *Girls Gone Wild*). The individuals shown in the videos don't receive profits, raising the issue of whether they granted permission for use of their images. Thus far, the courts have held that individuals give up some of their right to privacy when they are in public places. The wide availability of video cameras has made many people aware of the fact that their public behavior may become everyone else's entertainment.

Libel and Slander

Although the First Amendment protects journalists to enable them to pursue the truth, there are some safeguards in place to protect people who have been publicly wronged by the media. As mentioned earlier in this chapter, the terms *libel* and *slander* are applied to information or programming that defames a person, resulting in harm such as loss of income or character as well as ridicule, hatred, shunning, or avoidance. Again, when defamatory work appears in print it is referred to as *libel,* and when it appears in electronic media, it is *slander.*

The terms *libel* and *slander* are sometimes interchangeable, and a person can be both libeled and slandered in the same program. For instance, if a script is written and published at the website of a broadcaster, it is libel. If the broadcaster also airs the script, it becomes slander, as well. Three criteria are applied to determine if material is libelous or slanderous: Was the material published? Does the material defame a person (or persons)? and Was the person identified clearly? If the material meets all three criteria, then the person mentioned may have been libeled and/or slandered and he or she may take legal action against the publisher of the material.

Copyright

Copyright law originated in Article I, Section 8(8) of the U.S. Constitution, which allowed authors rights to use their "writings and discoveries" for their own benefit. Copyright law has since been revisited and revised, and it has been upheld in the courts, generally protecting the creators of original works from their unauthorized use.

Specifically, someone who creates an original work can receive copyright protection for his or her lifetime plus 70 years for work created after January 1978 and 95 years for work created before that time. For example, a song written in 1985 and copyrighted by the composer will receive copyright protection until 70 years after the songwriter dies. If anyone wants to use the words or music to that song, he or she must obtain permission (generally in writing) from the songwriter or an agency designated to grant permission on the songwriter's behalf. Usually, the user of the material pays a fee to the creator for the privilege of using it.

Sometimes, authors and others allow a **licensing agency** to collect usage fees for them. In the case of musicians who create original music, certain organizations will negotiate and collect fees from others who wish to use their music. In the United States, there are two music-licensing agencies that perform this function. The **American Society of Composers, Authors, and Publishers (ASCAP)** was started in 1914, and **Broadcast Music, Inc. (BMI)** was started in 1940. BMI was formed during the height of network radio popularity to compete with ASCAP and be more friendly to the radio stations and networks.

These organizations negotiate **blanket fees** with users like broadcasters and production companies. A blanket fee is determined by using a formula to calculate the yearly amount a station will be charged to use all of the music licensed by the organization. That amount is based on factors such as the percentage of that organization's music the station plays per week, the size of the station's market, and the station's overall revenue. Large stations in large markets pay more than small stations in small markets.

If a copyright expires, then anyone can use the material without asking permission or paying a fee. Once a copyright has expired or if a work was never copyrighted, the material is considered to be in the **public domain.** Advertisers, performers, and writers like to use material that's in the public domain in their projects because no permission or payment is necessary. Public domain material is particularly attractive to those producing low-budget projects.

Educators and others can use copyrighted material without getting permission or paying a fee if their use of the material is noncommercial and limited. This allowance falls under Section 107 of the 1976 Copyright Act and is referred to as **fair use.** Using copyrighted material in this way must be carefully done, however, to be legal. To determine fair use, four issues should be considered: (1) the purpose or use of the material, (2) the characteristics of the original work, (3) the amount of the original work used, and (4) the possible impact that the use might have on the market for the original work (Demac, 1993; Kaye & Medoff, 2001). An example of fair use would be when a professor shows his or her class a short clip of a scene from a network television program. This material can be shown once within a short period of time after its original airing and then should be erased.

Beginning in the late 1990s, online file sharing of copyrighted music became a serious problem for the music industry. Internet users could go to various sites, such as Napster, and download music by copying files from other users who had connected to the site. The music industry claimed that it lost substantial revenue because so many people were getting music online instead of buying CDs. Despite the threat of legal action, individual users have continued to download music and even feature-length movies without paying for them. The music and movie industries are pursuing copyright violators. Regardless, music and movie downloading will likely continue to be a major issue as more and more people get broadband connections to the Internet, making file sharing quick and relatively easy.

> ## ZOOM IN   12.6
> Get both sides of the story about file sharing. First, go to **www.RIAA.com** to learn the point of view of a music-licensing agency. Then, go to **www.eff.com** to hear from an organization that does not consider online file sharing a crime.

The **Recording Industry Association of America (RIAA)** is the trade organization that represents the people and companies that produce 90 percent of the recorded music in this country. It aggressively attempts to identify people who share files containing copyrighted music, and when it does, it often prosecutes them for copyright violation (Enders, 2003). In late 2003, the RIAA filed hundreds of lawsuits against individual music file sharers (Veiga, 2003).

The **Digital Millennium Copyright Act (DMCA),** passed in 1998, was designed to protect creative works in this digital era. It prohibits the manufacture and distribution of devices or procedures that are designed to violate copyright law in the digital environment. In addition, this law requires ISPs to identify their customers who violate copyright law by using file-sharing services, and the RIAA uses this information to take action against these people.

Webcasters interested in playing copyrighted music can work with **SoundExchange**, an organization that represents record labels in a way similar to how ASCAP represents composers, authors, and publishers for music licensing. SoundExhange was originally a division of the RIAA that was formed to collect royalties resulting from the DMCA. It was spun off and became an independent nonprofit organization in late 2003.

Taxation

Taxation is generally not an issue for broadcasters and other electronic media with the exception of the Internet. The Internet and the World Wide Web hold the promise of generating enormous commerce in the future—perhaps as much as $218 billion by 2007, according to research projections ("E-Commerce: The Road Ahead," 2002). And with these new sales come tax revenues.

Many government entities with various types of tax jurisdiction are eyeing Internet commerce with the notion of collecting substantial sums of money. The issue is not only taxation of Internet commerce but rather multiple taxation on Internet commerce. For example, suppose someone in Arizona uses Virginia-based America Online to buy a car from a dealer in New Mexico and then has the car shipped to the buyer's daughter, who is going to college in Texas. Could any or all of the states involved charge tax on the transaction?

Currently, the answer is no, but there is considerable pressure to change the tax laws that govern online commerce. The Internet Tax Freedom Act, signed into law on October 21, 1998, placed a moratorium on Internet taxes until October 21, 2001. (That date was later extended to November 2003.) The temporary nature of this law reflected the fact that many tax jurisdictions were anxious to revisit the issue and that the volatile nature of the Internet and its commercial enterprises had many wondering about the Internet's future role in commerce.

The federal government's stance on Internet taxation has been to allow the market to dictate policy and to allow the Internet to develop more before placing restrictions on it (Piller, 1997). In late 2003, the House of Representatives passed HR 49, the Internet Tax Non-Discrimination Act, which permanently bans Internet-only taxes (Cox, 2003).

Ethical Issues

The regulation of electronic media gives broadcast stations and other electronic media entities guidance in terms of how to operate. For instance, the FCC provides rules that cover technical issues, ownership issues, hiring practices, and programming content. These rules provide standards by which to judge the actions of media entities. For example, broadcast stations may not conduct lotteries (although stations may accept advertising for government-run lotteries), operate with more power than their license permits, or refuse to sell advertising to a political candidate if his or her opponent has already purchased advertising on that station.

These rules are easy to find and generally easy to follow. And when they are violated, the FCC can issue punishment in the form of a fine or even a nonrenewal of a station's license. But what about issues that are not mentioned in the rules? Are there rules

In 1995, an FM radio station typically sold for just over $2 million. What was the price in 2000?

that state whether a news department should cover a particular story? Should a station salesperson sell advertising to a client who will not possibly be helped by the advertising? Should a disc jockey play a song performed by his friend's band and tout it as the number-one hit in the region, even if it's not?

These are not legal issues—that is, they may not have any legal consequences. But they are questions of right and wrong, or **ethical issues.** *Ethics* are the set of moral principles or values that guide people's behavior. Given that, behavior can be viewed as a series of choices between good and bad alternatives. In a situation in which there are no specific legal guidelines, people often rely on their ethics to help them make decisions.

Ethical Guidelines

Organizations such as professional associations often create formal ethical codes or guidelines for their members. These guidelines are provided to help individuals in the group make good decisions and to enhance the reputation of the group in general. Sometimes referred to as **applied ethics,** such guidelines can give group members specific information about what is considered acceptable or ethical behavior. When a group publishes a code of ethics, it is endorsed by the membership as a whole.

In electronic media, an example of an ethical code is the one from the Radio and Television News Directors Association (RTNDA). Issued to all members of the organization, this code recommends how electronic media news personnel should behave. The National Association of Broadcasters (NAB) established a code of ethics in 1929 for radio and another one for television in 1952. Both cover issues in programming and advertising and have been amended over time to keep pace with changes in the business and society.

ZOOM IN   12.7

Review the code of ethics of the Radio and Television News Directors Association (RTNDA) at either of these websites: www.missouri.edu/jourvs/rtcodes.html or www.rtnda.org/ethics/coe.shtml.

In general, ethical codes seem like good resources for personnel. Station managers, advertising salespeople, and programmers would all seem to benefit from having a standard set of ethical guidelines to help them make everyday decisions in the workplace. However, in the case of the NAB guidelines, some members of the organization felt that the guidelines were too restrictive and did not translate well in providing guidance in specific situations. Specifically, the NAB code created some concern among members who felt that its standard of limiting advertising minutes per hour of programming hampered their ability to make money for the station. In fact, this advertising limitation led to an antitrust suit that alleged that limiting advertising minutes per hour was forcing higher advertising prices and violated antitrust laws. As a result of this litigation and other complaints, the NAB revoked its code of ethics in 1983.

Another issue regarding ethical guidelines is that what is considered *ethical* can depend on whose perspective is being followed. This puts ethics more in the category of *art* than *science.* Resolutions of ethical dilemmas are not exact but rather ongoing and continually evolving, just as standards in society continually change with the times. Moreover, individuals will differ as to what constitutes ethical behavior at any given point in time. Only when there is widespread agreement about what is ethical does that principle become a law in society.

Ethical Dilemmas

News operations work through ethical dilemmas on a regular basis. Sometimes, broadcast stations that produce local news are pressured by people either to cover or not cover a certain story. For example, suppose an advertising client of a local broadcast TV station is opening a brand-new store in the mall and insists that the grand opening is a newsworthy event that should be covered by several reporters and a videographer. Generally, broadcast stations don't consider this type of event "hard news" and would choose not to cover it. But what if the client insists, saying that if the station doesn't cover the grand opening on the news, he or she will withdraw all advertising from the station?

PAYING FOR INTERVIEWS   Most reputable broadcast and electronic media news operations in the United States will not pay people for their interviews. Some will pay, however, if it gets them an exclusive interview or one that could not have been set up through any other means. The shows that practice so-called **checkbook journalism** are not typical network "hard news" shows but rather shows that leans toward a tabloid style of news, like *Extra, Inside Hollywood, A Current Affair,* and *Entertainment Tonight.*

> **ZOOM IN**   12.8
> Although professional broadcast journalists often shun the practice of checkbook journalism, an attempt to make it illegal was struck down as being unconstitutional. For more information about this case, which was tried in California shortly after the O. J. Simpson trial, go to www.courttv.com/legaldocs/rights/checkbook.html.

RE-CREATING NEWS EVENTS   In November 1992, *Dateline NBC,* a prime-time news magazine, produced a story on General Motors (GM) trucks and their tendency to explode into flames upon impact. The producers of the story tried to show how a pickup truck would ignite when hit by another vehicle but could not re-create it successfully. So to save the story and create some exciting video footage, the producers hired someone to place a small incendiary device inside the GM truck and then trigger it when the truck was struck.

The plan worked perfectly, and the resulting video was dramatic. However, the furor that resulted when GM found out what NBC had done was also dramatic. Realizing that it had stretched the truth in its story, NBC decided to publicly apologize in a *Dateline NBC* program. NBC also gave almost $2 million to GM, and the pending lawsuit was dropped. In addition, the president of NBC's news division was fired, as were others associated with the story, and the network's reputation was considerably damaged. Obviously, re-creating an event without indicating that it's a re-creation is a breach of ethics.

USING UNNAMED SOURCES   Using unnamed or anonymous sources is another practice that could be considered unethical and that could undermine the credibility of a news program or journalist. The problem with these types of sources is that their validity usually cannot be checked using external sources. In other words, the audience cannot verify the information and facts contained in the story.

In a highly unethical incident, an NBC news producer rigged the collision test of a General Motors pickup truck to show it exploding.

PLAYING DIRTY TRICKS   Broadcasting is a highly competitive industry, to the extent that the audience is measured continuously—for instance, in markets that have overnight audience ratings that show a station's performance from the night before. Given this level of competition, broadcasters may do everything they can to gain an edge in the ratings. And when they run out of traditional tactics, they will on occasion resort to untraditional tactics.

The programming department of a station may be so interested in the future programming of another station that it will resort to any means of finding out what that station is doing. Besides hiring away programming personnel from a competitor, stations have actually paid people to go through the garbage of another station to look for discarded internal memos, drafts of contracts, old research, and other bits of information that might give insight into what the competition is doing.

Competition among local newscasts is often quite intense, which sometimes prompts news operations to look for any opportunity to gain an advantage. In a market in which an attractive young woman anchored the number-one news show, the number-two station tried to find her a good job in another market. In fact, the competing station made tapes of the female anchor off the air and, without her knowledge, mailed them to stations in distant markets that were looking for a new anchorperson.

Where do we draw the line between aggressive competitive behavior and unethical behavior? It's hard, since many issues in electronic media fall in the "gray area" between what is and is not appropriate. Consider three more examples:

ZOOM IN 12.9

Go to the Companion Website for this text, www.ablongman.com/medoffkaye1e, for more examples of ethical issues and dilemmas facing professionals in the electronic media.

- A salesperson from a radio station has sold airtime to a local restaurant, whose manager wants to see if advertising will bring in new customers for the "two for the price of one" special. The restaurant is running ads on the station only for the one day, and it has not placed ads for the special on or in other media. Obviously, the salesperson wants the advertising to prove successful and feels pressure to get a large crowd out to the restaurant. One option is to call his or her friends and relatives and tell them to go to the restaurant that night, mentioning that they heard the ad on the radio. Another option is for the salesperson to add bonus spots for the restaurant to that day's commercial announcements but not tell the client. Both options involve questionable ethics on the part of the salesperson.

- The musical director of a college radio station has the responsibility for calling record companies to request CDs for airplay but knows that some companies will not provide free service to small stations, especially college stations. The director is under a great deal of pressure to get new music for the station. Should he or she simply avoid mentioning to the record companies that the station is a college station in order to get the free records?

- During a sweeps month, a television station has a contest to win $50 in free gas during a time when gas prices have jumped significantly. Viewers can win if they know a secret code word that will be given during a newscast. The station has its news anchors deliver numerous teases, and reporters do live shots in front of gas pumps during the newscast. In a one-hour newscast, the station devotes 10 minutes to contest information and talk. Is this information worthy of being in the newscast, or is it strictly promotional?

In addition to professional ethics, there are also personal ethical issues that involve electronic media, especially Internet usage. Here's another example to think about:

- Since Napster gained popularity in 1999, college students and others have enjoyed the ability to download songs from the Internet without having to pay for them. When this is done, however, the songwriters, copyright holders, performers, and record companies that produced the songs are not paid for their work. Given this, should individuals continue to download music for free?

Summary

The basis for regulation of the electronic media in the United States began with the First Amendment, which guaranteed that Congress "shall make no law" that alters freedom of speech or freedom of the press. Another historic guiding principle for regulation has been the notion of a marketplace of ideas. When all ideas are presented in a free and open marketplace, people will find the truth.

Congress regulates broadcasting because it uses the electromagnetic spectrum, a scarce resource, in order to conduct business. The government believes that the spectrum is owned by the citizens, and therefore, it has the right to protect it.

The regulation of radio began in 1910 with a law that required all ships carrying 50 or more people to carry a wireless radio capable of transmitting and receiving signals over 100 miles. The sinking of the *Titanic* led Congress to pass the Radio Act of 1912, setting down rules for the operation of radio transmitters and naming the U.S. Secretary of Commerce as the authority for radio. During World War I, the government took control of all high-powered radio stations to support the war effort and to maintain security. The Radio Act of 1927 was needed when radio changed from a point-to-point medium to a one-to-many or broadcast medium. The Federal Radio Commission established the criteria that broadcasting needed to operate in the "public interest, convenience, and necessity."

The Communications Act of 1934 established the Federal Communications Commission (FCC) to regulate the media. The FCC is concerned with many aspects of electronic media, including technology, licensing, and ownership. In addition, it has, over the years, been concerned with station editorializing and fairness concerning controversial issues. The FCC regulates broadcasting, cable, satellites, cell phones, and other services that require wireless or wired transmission of both entertainment and information.

Beginning in the late 1970s, the FCC began to deregulate the electronic media. Ownership rules were relaxed, as were the requirements for station license renewal. This trend continued with the passage of the Telecommunications Act of 1996. Again, ownership rules were changed, allowing telephone companies to buy cable systems and increasing the number of stations that could be owned by group owners.

In addition to Congress and the FCC, other groups also affect the regulation of electronic media, including the marketplace, local government, citizens' groups, the White House, the courts, and lobbyists. Each group has its own method of exerting regulatory pressure on electronic media.

Future issues include digital conversion of the television industry, which will affect not only broadcasting but cable and satellite delivery, as well. In addition, the maximum number of stations that a group can own will likely be considered in years to come.

The electronic media industry has faced numerous legal issues since broadcasting began. The issues of concern today include free speech, privacy, libel and slander, obscenity and indecency, inappropriate programming content, copyright, and taxation. Ethical issues have also been of concern, such as paying for interviews, re-creating news events, citing unnamed sources, and playing dirty tricks. Because ethical issues are not necessarily legal issues, there is no set of hard-and-fast rules to follow. Instead, media organizations sometimes create ethical codes or guidelines for their members to follow.

How long did it take Congress to approve the rewrite of the Communications Act of 1934?

Notes

1. The Mayflower Broadcasting Company contended that WAAB had endorsed political candidates and editorialized about controversial issues, thus violating its obligation to serve the public interest. The FCC denied Mayflower's attempt to take over WAAB's license for other reasons, but it did reaffirm that broadcasters should not editorialize.

2. One standard of government regulation of the media is known as the *Tornillo standard,* based on *Miami Herald Publishing Co. v. Tornillo* (1974). This case involved a newspaper that refused to carry a political candidate's reply to newspaper coverage that attacked him. The ruling was based on the First Amendment approach to the nonregulation of media. The implication was that if a newspaper is forced to allow politicians (or others subject to criticism) to refute negative stories about them, it will impede the newspaper's right to a free press.

3. Sales of digital television sets are projected to increase steeply over the next few years. The Consumer Electronics Association predicts sales of about 5 million sets in 2004, 8 million in 2005, and over 10 million in 2006. The total number of TV households in the United States in 2004 was over 108 million. Updates on these projections can be found at www.cea.org.

Influences and Effects of the Mass Media

CHAPTER 13

SEE IT THEN

Strong Effects
Limited Effects
Moderate Effects
Powerful Effects

SEE IT NOW

Research on the Mass Media
Effects of Mediated Violence
Effects of Offensive Song Lyrics
Effects of Video Games
Effects of the Internet
Agenda Setting
Uses of and Gratifications from
the Mass Media

SEE IT LATER

Media Violence
New Communication Technologies
Children's Nutrition

In this chapter, you'll learn about:

- How electronic media affect us
- The different approaches that are used to study media
- How the study of electronic media effects has changed over time
- The implications of media effects for U.S. society

It seems that whenever we turn on the television, we're subjected to an act of violence, some expression of profanity, or even a sexual word or image. Although we may not mind or even notice onscreen sex and violence, there's great concern about their effects on us—individually, socially, and culturally. Parents and legislators are especially concerned about the effects of violent content on children and young adults.

In fact, television content is blamed for many social ills, such as violent behavior, increased crime rates, a lower literacy level, and the breakdown of the family. But at the same time, television plays a very important and positive role in our lives. Television programs are socializing agents that teach us how to behave, show us what's right and wrong, expose us to other cultures and ideas, enforce social norms, and increase our knowledge about life in general.

Contemporary concerns about mediated messages are not limited to television but extend to the Internet and to song lyrics. The Internet is blamed for exposing children and young adults to unsavory material, and many claim that the very act of using the Internet for long periods of time may lead to social isolation.

Radio stations get heat for playing songs with racy, violent, and antisocial lyrics, as parents are afraid that their children will do whatever these songs suggest. Others, however, doubt whether media has such a strong influence. Dick Cavett, long-time humorist and talk show host, once commented, "There's so much comedy on television. Does that cause comedy in the streets?"

While television and other media can have positive effects, it seems as though most of the attention is focused on the negative effects. There's much debate concerning the degree to which the media influence our behaviors, values, and attitudes. Some critics claim that mediated content is very harmful and has a strong influence on us, especially children. Others claim that while television may have a mild influence, our existing values and attitudes filter out the negative images and words. For example, if a young woman sees an unethical act on television but has a strong sense of right and wrong, she won't be influenced to mimic what she sees on television.

The debate about the effects of media content is complex because *humans* are complex. There are no simple answers to the many questions concerning how mediated content affects us. This chapter begins with a historical look at concerns about mediated messages and the development of theories that help explain the connection between mediated messages and human behaviors and attitudes. The chapter next provides an overview of how the media and media influences are studied. Contemporary issues concerning violence on television and the effects of viewing such material are examined next. The chapter ends with a look at the implications of the effects of mediated content and the implementation of rating systems, V-chips, and other tools that screen offensive content.

SEE IT THEN

Strong Effects

Although we often think that concern about the influences of the mass media is a twentieth-century phenomenon, it had its origins in the era of the printing press. Religious and government organizations have attempted to suppress printed works that they deem ideologically contrary since the advent of the printing press. The rise of the penny press in the 1800s, which sizzled with sensationalized accounts of criminal activity, sexual exploits, scandals, and domestic problems, prompted community outcry about the negative social effects of reading such scintillating material. In the 1920s, parents protested violent content in motion pictures, and in the 1930s and 1940s, they focused on comic book violence.

In addition to religion and government, social elites have long been interested in suppressing the written word and keeping new ideas from the masses because knowledge is power and they have wanted to keep the power among themselves. With increased literacy and access to mass-produced writings came an even greater need to keep information out of the hands of the general public and to silence opposition.

The years between the end of World War I and the onset of the Great Depression were times of rebuilding and growth in the United States. People were migrating from their rural homes into the industrialized cities, leaving behind a network of friends and family and old ways of life, in which traditions, behaviors, and attitudes were passed along from one generation to the next and individuals were integral parts of their social circles. Moving to the city disconnected individuals from these ties and left them to assimilate into a new culture. Without family and friends to depend on, many city newcomers turned to newspapers, magazines, and books to learn about new ways of life and to keep up with current events. The mass media became a large and influential part of their lives.

Later, concerns about content extended to the social consequences of exposure to indecent, violent, and sexually explicit materials. Underlying these concerns was the strong belief that the mass media were all powerful and that a gullible public could be easily manipulated.

Scientists and others sought to explain the social and cultural changes brought on by migration to the cities, industrialization, and increased dependence on the media. They tied behavioral, attitudinal, and cognitive changes to the media and later developed theories to help explain how certain aspects of the media affect our lives.

As people migrated to the cities, newspapers took on a greater role in socializing them and keeping them informed.

A **theory** is basically an explanation of observed phenomena. Although researchers offer varying definitions of this term, one simple explanation states, in part, "Theories are stories about how and why events occur. " Another definition claims, "Theories are sets of statements asserting relationships among classes of variables" (c.f. Baran & Davis, 2000, p. 30). Mass communication theories are explanations, or stories, of the relationship between the media and the audience and how this relationship influences or affects audience members' everyday lives.

Magic Bullet Theory

In the 1920s, the United States was still struggling with the effects of World War I and rebuilding its economic and social structures. The newspaper was people's main source of information, but radio was beginning to build an audience.

Along with these new information and entertainment providers came the fear that the media could take over people's minds and control the way they thought and behaved. Given this, many thought of the media as a "magic bullet" or "hypodermic needle" that could penetrate people's bodies and minds and cause them to all react the same way to a mediated message. This concept of an all-powerful media was a widely held belief and was very frightening to people. These fears weren't unfounded when we consider the successful propaganda campaigns waged during World War I, the newness of the mass media, and the move to the cities that left many people without close social networks.

Propaganda and Persuasion Theories

During World War I, propaganda was used successfully to spread hatred across nations, to concoct lies to justify the war, and to mobilize armies. Although propaganda was used more intensely in Europe, it quickly spread to the United States. Starting in the 1920s, Americans followed Adolf Hitler's rise to power, which was aided by his domination over radio and carefully crafted propaganda campaigns. During this time, there was also a broad range of social movements in the United States. Radio was an especially powerful tool for spreading propaganda and persuasive messages.

ZOOM IN   13.1
Examples of World War I and World War II propaganda can be found at these sites:

- German Propaganda Archive (speeches, posters, writings)   www.calvin.edu/academic/cas/gpa
- Snapshots of the Past—World War I and II posters www.snapshotsofthepast.com
- Propaganda Postcards   www.ww1-propaganda-cards. com

A Nazi party election poster, urging German workers to vote for Adolf Hitler.

Definitions of **propaganda** vary slightly and often overlap with definitions of **persuasion**, but psychologist Harold Brown has distinguished between the two concepts. According to Brown, propaganda and persuasive techniques are the same but their outcomes differ. *Propaganda* is "when someone judges that the action which is the goal of the persuasive effort will be advantageous to the persuader but not in the best interests of the persuadee," whereas *persuasion* is when the goal is perceived to have greater benefits to the receiver than to the source of the message (Severin & Tankard, 1992, p. 91).

Limited Effects

Imagine that it's the night before Halloween in 1938. You live in a rural farmhouse in New Jersey. You don't have a telephone or a television, your nearest neighbor is half a mile away, and you depend on your radio to link you to outside world. The radio airwaves are filled with news about Hitler's rise to power in Germany, and rumors abound that outsiders are infiltrating the United States to initiate the fall of democracy. It's a scary world.

You settle in after dinner and tune your radio to the *Mercury Star Theater* program. You hear that tonight's program is a re-creation of H. G. Wells's *The War of the Worlds*. But if you weren't listening carefully or had tuned in a little late, you'd think the program was playing dance music. In that case, what would you do when the dance music was interrupted with a "news report" that a spaceship had landed in New Jersey and that we were at war with Mars? Would you have tuned to another radio station? Many radio receivers in those days could only pick up one or two stations. You wouldn't have had a television to turn on or a telephone to call your friends. Even people with telephones couldn't call out because the phone lines were jammed. Would you have just laughed off the reports, or would you have panicked?

When radio was still a relatively new medium, many listeners relied on it as their primary news source and believed what they heard. So when a "news report" broke into the dance music, many listeners believed that Martians were indeed invading the earth. Mass panic ensued. People jumped in their cars and headed somewhere, anywhere. They hid in closets and under beds. Some even thought of committing suicide. Many people, however, realized the broadcast was merely a rendition of *The War of the Worlds*. They listened with bemusement and thought the program was quite clever and entertaining.

Considering what we know today about the magic bullet theory, we should be able to conclude that everyone who heard *The War of the Worlds* broadcast panicked. According to the theory, the members of an audience have the same reaction to a mediated message. So why is it that some listeners went out of their minds with fear while others enjoyed the show? That's the question that researchers wanted to answer. Researchers at Princeton University took the lead, and in the years following the 1938 broadcast, many studies explored this question. Basically, scientists found that people's reactions to the show were influenced by many factors, such as education, religious beliefs, socioeconomic status, political beliefs, whether listeners tuned to the broadcast at the beginning of the program or sometime during the show, where listeners were during the broadcast (that is, rural home, city apartment), and whether they were alone or with others when listening.

Research about *The War of the Worlds* panic and other studies showed that the media are not as all powerful as once thought. Audience members did not all react in the same way to the same mediated stimulus because other factors in their lives filtered the message, such that they interpreted it in their own ways. The findings from this line of research led to the **limited-effects perspective**, which states that media have the power to influence people's beliefs, attitudes, and behaviors but that the influence is not as strong as once thought. Moreover, the media are not just evil political instruments but can have positive effects, as well. The fact that the media's influence is limited by personal characteristics, group membership, and existing values and attitudes makes us less vulnerable and not easily manipulated by what we see and hear.

Several other perspectives came out of limited-effects research. After conducting a series of studies, researchers Paul Lazersfeld and Elihu Katz discovered that rather than media directly influencing the audience, messages were being filtered through a **two-step flow** process. According to the two-step flow theory, messages flow from the media to **opinion leaders** and then to **opinion followers**. The process starts with **gatekeepers**, such as news producers, newspaper editors, and others who filter media messages. They pass the messages on to opinion leaders, or influential members of a community, who then pass on the messages to opinion followers, or the people the gatekeepers and opinion leaders are trying to influence. For example, suppose a neighborhood group opposes building a new road through their community. Rather than just send their antiroad messages to the mass public, they will be more effective if they persuade a smaller number of influential homeowners (opinion leaders) that the road will harm the neighborhood and then have that smaller group influence the larger group of neighbors (opinion followers) to rally against the road. The two-step flow theory supports limited effects by demonstrating that opinion leaders are often more influential than the media (Baran & Davis, 2000; Bryant & Thompson, 2002).

An alien spacecraft opens fire in a scene from the 1953 movie *The War of the Worlds*.

Further support for the limited-effects perspective emerged with the discovery of **selective processes.** Baran and Davis (2000) explain selective processes as "defense mechanisms that we routinely use to protect ourselves (and our egos) from information that would threaten us. Others argue that they are merely routinized procedures for coping with the enormous quantity of sensory information constantly bombarding us" (p. 139).

There are three basic ways that selective processes operate:

1. *Selective exposure* is the tendency to expose ourselves to media messages that we already agree with and that are consistent with our own values and beliefs.
2. *Selective perception* is the tendency to change the meaning of a message in our own mind so it's consistent with our existing attitudes and beliefs.
3. *Selective retention* is the tendency to remember those messages that have the most meaning to us.

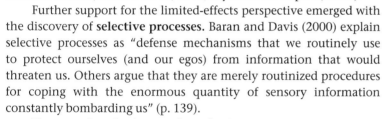

ZOOM IN 13.2

- To learn more about *The War of the Worlds*, visit these sites:

  www.museumofhoaxes.com/war_worlds.html

  www.war-ofthe-worlds.co.uk

- Also read original newspaper accounts of *The War of the Worlds* panic at this site:

  www.war-of-the-worlds.org/Radio/Original.shtml

- To listen to the entire 1938 broadcast, go to this site:

  www.craigwilliams.co.uk/waroftheworlds/intro.htm

- Here is the site of *The War of the Worlds* discussion board:

  http://history1900s.about.com/library/weekly/aa072701a.htm

Selective processes support limited effects by explaining how we filter out mediated messages so they don't affect us directly. Rather, we choose what messages to expose ourselves to and then screen and alter the meanings of those messages so they're consistent with our current attitudes and beliefs. Long-lasting effects are further limited because we remember only the messages that had meaning to us in the first place.

Moderate Effects

The 1960s, and especially the late 1960s, were marked with social unrest and instability. Many major cities were besieged by riots and protests, which all too often ended in violence. With these events, concerns arose about the effects of watching newscasts that aired footage of riots and other violent situations. Could the viewing public, and children in particular, discern between fictionalized violent content and violent news content?

On the one hand, the media claimed that there was no relationship between viewing violence and increased aggression; in other words, the media claimed they had a limited effect on the viewing public. Yet on the other hand, the media claimed to their advertisers that they could indeed persuade the public to purchase certain products; in other words, the media had a strong effect on viewers. The limited-effects perspective was questioned in light of this inconsistency, and new research indicated that media effects were likely not as limited as previously believed (Baran & Davis, 2000).

Police tangled with demonstrators at the 1968 Democratic National Convention, one of many violent incidents during that year.

In the early 1960s, Stanford University psychologist Albert Bandura began studying the effects of filmed violence on children. For example, in one variation of Bandura's so-called Bobo doll experiments, children watched a short film of other children playing with Bobo dolls. (A Bobo doll is an air-filled, plastic doll that's weighted at the bottom, so when it's punched, it bounces down and then comes back up.) One group of children was shown a film of kids punching and kicking their Bobo dolls and yelling angry, nonsensical words while doing so. A second group of children was shown a film of children playing nicely with their Bobo dolls. After viewing one of the films, each child was given his or her own Bobo doll to play with. As it turns out, the children who viewed the film of the kids playing nicely with their dolls were also gentle with their own dolls,

---

Violence in the 1960s

Although the decade began peacefully, many factors contributed to violence in American society that sent shock waves throughout the country and the government. Namely, the civil rights movement raised awareness about perceptions of inequality, President John F. Kennedy was assassinated in 1963, and civil unrest and even civil disobedience resulted from U.S. involvement in the Vietnam War. Riots in urban areas of New Jersey and California and demonstrations in many states also led to violence. The Reverend Dr. Martin Luther King, Jr., a civil rights advocate and leader, and Senator Robert F. Kennedy, a presidential candidate and brother of the late president, were both assassinated in 1968.

Congress became concerned about violence in society and what caused it. The media, and especially violent television programs, became a target of blame for contributing to social violence. Newscasts on television also delivered stark images of the realities of the war in Vietnam, causing Americans to rethink their attitude about the war. Near the end of the decade, Congress decided to gather scientific information about the causes of violence in society. The U.S. Surgeon General supported numerous studies that investigated the relationship between violence in the media and violence in society.

Numerous books have been written about the 1960s and the struggles that U.S. society experienced, including Bloom and Breines (2002), Horne (1995), and Isserman and Kazin (2000).

but the children who watched the Bobo dolls being subjected to violent play also kicked and punched their dolls and spouted nonsensical words while doing so (Bryant & Thompson, 2002).

Bandura and other researchers demonstrated that children and adults learn from observation and **model** their own behavior after it, whether what they see is in real life or in films or on television. Further, the media teach people how to behave in certain situations, how to solve problems and cope in certain situations, and in general present a wide range of options upon which to model their own behavior, thus lending support for a stronger influence.

ZOOM IN   13.3

To learn more about Albert Bandura and his work, visit these sites:

- www.ship.edu/~cgboeree/bandura.html
- www.colostate.edu/Depts/Speech/rccs/theory32.htm
- http://fates.cns.muskingum.edu/~psych/psycweb/history/bandura.htm

Powerful Effects

While the debate about media effects continued, studies were commissioned to specifically test the amount of influence that television content (especially violence) had on viewers, particularly children and young adults. In 1969, the U.S. Surgeon General's Scientific Advisory Committee on Television and Social Behavior was created to conduct research on television's influence on children's behavior. After two years of extensive study, the committee concluded that there was enough evidence to suggest a strong link between viewing televised violence and performing antisocial behavior and that the link was not limited only to children who were predisposed to aggressive behavior.

In one study, children imitated film-mediated aggression by beating up Bobo dolls.

The report stirred up much controversy. One on side, parents, medical associations, social groups, teachers, and mental health specialists called for restrictions on televised violence. On the other side, the television industry pointed to research on limited and moderate effects and lobbied hard against any new Federal Communications Commission (FCC) regulations regarding programs for children. The industry finally bowed to pressure and agreed to limit the extent of violence in *children's programs* and to times when children would be less likely to watch. Television programs in general, however, continued to contain violence, and so, the struggle to limit such content continued (Baran & Davis, 2000).

More evidence supporting the **powerful-effects perspective** came to light in the 1980s, when several major violence studies concluded that viewing violence is strongly related to aggressive behavior. Additionally, *The Great American Values Test* demonstrated that television could influence beliefs and values. This half-hour television program was actually a research project, in which viewers first assessed their own values and then the program pointed out inconsistencies to get viewers to question their values and change their minds. The amazing thing is that it worked. A half-hour program was influential enough to change viewers' attitudes and values. Even more important, researchers found that those viewers who were more dependent on television were more likely to change their attitudes. *The Great American Values Test* and other similar research lent further credence to the idea that the media do indeed have a powerful influence on the viewing public (Severin & Tankard, 1992).

In this chapter, the perspectives on effect size are neatly delineated, but this has been done to simplify a very complex issue. While there has been a dominant perspective at any given time (such as limited effects, powerful effects, and so on), research findings have not always been consistent. Within each era of thought, numerous studies have demonstrated different outcomes.

The powerful-effects perspective dominates today, but it is very different from the magic bullet theory of yesterday. Enough is known about the influence of the mass media to know that not all people respond in the same way to the same message. The powerful-effects model is much more complex than that. In addition, it's been realized that the circumstances must be right for certain effects to occur. Most young viewers today have grown up watching an enormous amount of violent television, yet they are not all aggressive and violent, as would be suggested by the magic bullet theory. Rather, some viewers may be influenced and may become more aggressive than others under some circumstances.

SEE IT NOW

Research on the Mass Media

The discussion up to this point has made it clear that determining how good or bad media content is and how it may or may not influence you is not a simple matter. To date, about 3,500 research studies have been conducted that look just at the effects of mediated violence (Potter, 2003). These studies are not conducted casually but follow strict procedures and methods. Researchers today employ several methods for learning about how people use the mass media and how the mass media influences people socially and culturally.

Survey Research

Gathering information about the media audience involves a systematic method of observation that results in data that can be measured, quantified (or counted), tested, and verified. **Survey research** is one of the oldest research techniques and perhaps the most frequently used method of measuring the electronic media audience. Surveys are used to explain and describe human behaviors, attitudes, beliefs, and opinions. Survey research usually entails some sort of questionnaire or observation. Individuals may be asked questions about what they think about the new season's television program line-up, what programs they watch, and how often they watch. Survey research is designed to be as objective and unbiased as possible. No attempt is made to manipulate behaviors, opinions, or attitudes but rather to record them as accurately as possible.

Content Analysis

Content analysis is a research method used to study the content of television programs, song lyrics, and other mediated messages. For example, content analysis reveals the number of times indecent language is used on television, the number of times violence is promoted in song lyrics, and the number of times a story about the war on Iraq is mentioned as the lead story on network news programs. Although content analysis doesn't tell about media effects or audience use of media, it does tell about the content to which television viewers and radio listeners are exposed.

Laboratory Experiments

Experimental methods allow researchers to isolate certain factors they want to study. **Laboratory experiments** usually involve a *test group,* which is exposed to the variable under study, and a *control group,* which is not exposed to the variable. For example, researchers may be interested in knowing whether viewers with digital cable service change channels more often than those with expanded analog cable service. In a laboratory setting, individuals in the control group would watch expanded basic cable and those in the test group would watch digital cable. The number of times the viewers in each test group changed channels would be compared, and researchers would then know whether having digital cable service led to more channel switching.

The biggest drawback to laboratory experiments is that people may not behave or react in a lab as they do in real life. For instance, people at home may switch channels less often than in a lab, where perhaps factors such as boredom and knowing they're part of an experiment might change their behavior.

Researchers are interested in how and why viewers watch television.

Field Experiments

The purpose of a **field experiment** is to study people in their natural environment, instead of in an artificial laboratory setting. Researchers using this method may not have as much control over outside factors, but the tradeoff is that they get to observe people as they behave in real-life situations. Again, it may be more valuable to observe viewers switching channels in their own homes, where they're more likely to behave as they normally do, than in a lab, where they may behave differently. Then again, knowing someone is observing your behavior may cause you to behave differently.

Effects of Mediated Violence

Despite the numerous studies that have examined the effects of mediated violence, a consensus about the power of those effects is still lacking. The question now turns from the strength of media effects to the media effects themselves. Generally, media content influences the way we behave, the way we think, and the way we react emotionally.

What happens when viewers repeatedly see characters being killed? What happens when young adults see onscreen nudity? What happens when children hear others on television yelling profanities? People react differently to such content, and just how they're affected depends on many factors. Sometimes, the effects are long lasting and sometimes they're fleeting. Sometimes, they are more intense than at other times, depending on social, psychological, and situational factors. After watching a violent show with a friend, you could feel fine but your friend might be too hyped up to sleep.

We all like to think that we're immune from the influences of the mass media, and we have probably all heard someone say something like "I watched a lot of TV when I was growing up, and I'm not a murderer, so it didn't hurt me." This **third-person effect**, in which individuals claim that they're not as susceptible to mediated messages as others, often leads to an emphasis on other people's viewing habits, rather than on one's own. But researchers have shown through years of research that there are some commonalities in the ways we react to various mediated content.

One of the most comprehensive television violence studies was a joint effort by researchers at the University of California, Santa Barbara, and three other universities in the late 1990s. Here are some of the major findings from the National Television Violence Study (Federman, 1998):

> **fyi**
>
> **Media's Contribution to Violence**
>
> When Americans were asked if various media contribute to crime in the United States:
>
> • 92 percent said television contributes to crime.
> • 82 percent said video games contribute to crime.
> • 91 percent said local television news contributes to crime.
>
> *Source:* Potter, 2003.

Finding: Six out of ten programs contain violence.
Consequence: Viewers are overexposed to mediated aggression and violence.

Finding: Television violence is still glamorized. Seven out of ten violent acts go unpunished.
Consequence: Unpunished violence is more likely to be imitated by viewers.

Finding: Four out of ten violent acts are initiated by characters who are attractive role models.
Consequence: Viewers are more likely to imitate characters they judge as being attractive.

Finding: Four out of ten violent scenes include humor.
Consequence: Humor trivializes the violence and thus contributes to desensitization.

Finding: About half of all violent scenes show pain or harm to the victim.
Consequence: Showing pain and suffering reduces the chance that viewers will learn aggression from media violence.

Finding: Fewer than 5 percent of violent programs feature an antiviolence message.
Consequence: Viewers aren't exposed to alternatives to violence or shown nonviolent ways to solve problems.

Behavioral Effects

We learn how to behave by watching what other people do and then following those examples. The same principle applies to how the media affect us. We take behavioral cues from the media and apply them to our own lives. For instance, media content such as song lyrics and television violence can influence the way we behave, whether positively or negatively. The following types of behavioral effects have been documented.

ZOOM IN 13.4

For more information about media violence, read "The Eleven Myths of Media Violence," by W. James Potter (2003—see References). Also try the following sites:

- American Academy of Pediatrics   www.aap.org/advocacy/childhealthmonth/media.htm
- ACT Against Violence   www.actagainstviolence.org/mediaviolence

IMITATION   There is particular concern that people may imitate what they see on television or hear in songs. With imitation, viewers may reproduce the same behavior they witnessed or heard. In a well-publicized lawsuit, a parent claimed that her 5-year-old son set fire to a house after witnessing the cartoon characters Beavis and Butthead commit the same act. Although there has been much publicity about cases like this, in which children have engaged in extreme behavior that they have imitated from television, these cases are rare. It's also very difficult to say whether a viewer directly imitated what he or she saw or already had a predisposition to violent behavior and aggressive actions and merely used television as an excuse (Baran & Davis, 2000).

IDENTIFICATION   It could be that viewers, especially children and young adults, identify with television characters in a broader sense. Young viewers may want to be like their favorite characters and so take on the same characteristics without really imitating their behaviors. Children may wear T-shirts, for instance, with the pictures or names of their favorite television personalities or characters or even walk or talk the same as their idols, but they will not usually imitate taboo behaviors.

INHIBITION/DISINHIBITION   Punishment and reward influence the likelihood of individuals' modeling and imitating mediated behavior. When negative or aggressive behavior is punished, the likelihood that viewers will behave in a similar manner decreases because their level of inhibition increases. That is, viewing a character being punished or dealing with another type of negative feedback creates an *inhibitory effect* in viewers. They don't want to experience the same punishment and so will likely refrain from engaging in the same negative behavior. On the other hand, positive reinforcement creates a *disinhibitory effect*. When a negative action is rewarded, inhibition decreases and so the likelihood of repeating the bad behavior increases. That's why many people are imploring the media to stop glamorizing violence and to show the perpetrators living with the real consequences of their actions. Disinhibition also occurs when an authority figure directs a person to behave badly, therefore *displacing responsibility* from the perpetrator ("He told me to do it").

AROUSAL   Viewing televised violence also arouses people's emotions. If a viewer is feeling somewhat aggressive or stressed and then watches a violent program, he or she may become more stimulated and his or her initial aggressiveness or stress may intensify and lead to aggressive or violent behavior. Some coaches believe that showing aggressive sports films to a team shortly before a game heightens the players' levels of arousal and makes it more likely that they'll play harder.

CATHARSIS   Although most evidence supports the contention that viewing aggression leads to increased arousal, there is some support for the opposite perspective: that viewing violence leads to *catharsis*, or the release of aggressive feelings. Catharsis supporters contend that viewing violence satisfies people's own violent or aggressive urges and that watching others act out feelings of anger relieves our own aggressive feelings. Either way, people may behave more passively after watching onscreen violence. Although some empirical evidence points to a catharsis effect (Feshbach, 1961; Feshbach & Singer, 1971), the validity of this notion is largely based on tradition, rather than scientific observation and testing (Baran & Davis, 2000).

DESENSITIZATION   Viewing certain types of content may also lead to desensitization, or the dulling of natural responses due to repeated exposure. For example, the more acts of violence or the more sexual behaviors we see on television, the less effect they have on us. When car alarms were still a novelty, everyone would stop and look around and wonder if a vehicle was being broken into when they heard one go off. Now when an alarm shrieks, most people don't pay any attention, such that car alarms have just become a nuisance. Similarly, through repeated exposure, we've become desensitized to television images, as well. And just as our reactions to car alarms have become dulled, so, too, have our reactions to real-life situations. When we're desensitized to television violence, we're less likely in real life to help someone in trouble or call the police or to feel aroused or upset when we witness violence.

FOUR-FACTOR SYNDROME   Studies have found a link between viewing pornography and criminal sexual behavior (Malamuth & Donnerstein, 1984; Marshall, 1989), which has led researchers to suggest a model about the major effects of viewing pornography. After considering the findings of numerous studies, Cline (1994) put forth the major effects, known as the *four-factor syndrome,* which consist of addiction, escalation, desensitization, and the tendency to act out or imitate mediated sexual acts. The syndrome is sequential; that is, the effects occur in this sequence over time. *Addiction* to pornography may develop after repeated exposure to the material. *Escalation* occurs next when the viewers want more and stronger stimuli. Viewers become *desensitized* to pornography (and even antisocial or illegal behavior) and thus tend to believe the pornographic behavior is acceptable. Finally, viewers tend to *imitate* the pornographic behavior. Individuals exhibited the four-factor syndrome despite the legal or social consequences of behaving in the deviant or sexually unacceptable manners shown in the pornographic material.

Affective and Emotional Effects

When viewers see a character being mutilated, shot, thrown over a cliff, stabbed, beat up, run over by a train, mangled in a car crash, or harmed or killed in another horrendous way, they can't help but react emotionally. Viewers also react emotionally to positive images, such as characters getting married, performing acts of kindness, showing physical affection, and so on.

Everyone experiences some sort of emotional reaction to a mediated image, even if that reaction has become blunted due to overexposure. But it's the negative images that we focus most of our attention on. Most Americans were glued to their television sets as they watched the horrors of September 11, 2001, unfold. Viewing the intense violence of the day increased levels of posttraumatic stress symptoms and anxiety, especially among heavy television viewers. About 18 percent of viewers who watch more than 12 hours of television per day reported increased distress levels after 9/11, compared to 7.5 percent of those who watch television less than 4 hours per day (Kalb, 2002). These findings are further evidence of how viewing violence and other horrors affects our emotions—and often for a long period of time.

Cognitive Effects

Viewing television also affects how and what we think about the world around us. The images we see on television influence our perceptions of real life and other people. Televised portrayals of minorities, women, families, and relationships all influence our social and cultural attitudes.

At first, the studies regarding these groups focused on measuring the *number* of programs that women and minorities appeared in. But recently, the concern has been more with how these groups are *portrayed* and the mediated *effects* they have on viewers. Through their portrayals of women, minorities, gays, and others, the mass media teach and reinforce societal norms and values. This socialization process continues throughout our lives but is especially powerful when we're young. Even though not all stereotypical depictions are negative, they are nonetheless harmful because they objectify, depersonalize, and even deny individuality (Enteman, 1996). In addition, television and the other mass media may provide the dominant or perhaps the only view of certain groups in society (Perse, 2001).

CULTIVATION   Gerbner and associates (1976, 1978) have spent many years examining how television cultivates our world view. In particular, they have conducted **content analyses,** which examine television content and compare it to real life and viewers' perceptions of actual life. Once programming content has been analyzed, comparisons can be made between real life and what is shown on television.

Baran and Davis (2000) offer the following questions for you to use in assessing your own perceptions of the actual world:

1. What percentage of all working males in the United States are employed in some aspect of law enforcement?

   In the real world: 1 percent
   On television: 12 percent

2. What are your chances of being involved in an act of violence in any given week?

   In the real world: 0.41 percent (less than half of 1 percent)
   On television: 64 percent of all characters encounter violence

3. What percentage of all U.S. crimes are violent crimes (murder, rape, robbery, and assault)?

   In the real world: 10 percent
   On television: 77 percent

Were your answers closer to the "real world" or to the "on television" answers? Many viewers say that because much of what they see on television is fictional, it really doesn't influence their perceptions because they know what they're seeing isn't real. However, research does indeed show that our cognitive perceptions are shaped by television. Moreover, the influence is especially strong on viewers who watch television more than the average number of hours. Heavy television viewers' estimations of real-life violence and crime levels are more closely in accord with those portrayed on television. For example, compared to light viewers of violent television, heavy viewers are more likely to fear being a victim of violent crime, to exaggerate their chance of being victimized, and to go out of their way to secure their homes and buy guns for protection (Gerbner et al., 1978). In sum, heavy viewers believe the world is a scarier place than it really is.

In what 2002 made-for-cable-television movie was the F-word spewed 15 times in the first 15 minutes?

There are also concerns that cultivation may lead viewers to accept violent acts as a normal part of life and to think of violence as an acceptable way to solve conflicts. Television cultivates a **mean-world syndrome,** in which viewers think that the world is a mean and scary place to live and alter their behaviors accordingly, all based on television's warped depiction of real life (Baran & Davis, 2000; Bryant & Thompson, 2002; Dominick, 1996; Gerbner & Gross, 1976; Gerbner et al., 1978; Massey & Baran, 2001; Severin & Tankard, 1992; Signorelli, 1990).

It's especially difficult to dismiss violence and not believe that the world's a scary place when the news media blow crime coverage way out of proportion. For instance, the national homicide rate decreased 33 percent between 1990 and 1998, yet television coverage of murders increased 473 percent (Comarow, 2001). In 2002, it seemed that whenever you turned on the television, there was another child abduction story or a report on how to protect children from what seems to be a spike in kidnappings. But in reality, the number of child abductions has actually decreased since the 1980s. Furthermore, of the 50 million school-age children in the United States, about 200 are abducted by strangers each year and 50 of these are murdered. Some 3,400 children die in car accidents and 5,000 are killed by firearms, but these deaths receive little media coverage (Livingston, 2002).

Effects on Children

As stated earlier, children and young adults may be particularly susceptible to mediated words and images, both positive and negative. Programs like *Sesame Street,* which are educational and nonviolent, can help children learn positive social behaviors, enhance their imaginative powers, and even develop problem-solving skills. Studies conducted over the years have shown that children who watched *Sesame Street* when they were young later demonstrated higher academic achievement and better reading skills than children who did not watch the program. This effect was shown among children who were in grade school and even when they reached high school (Anderson, Huston, et al., 1998b; Zill, 2001).

Conversely, negative images, especially depictions of violence, can cause children short- and long-term harm. Since children watch television on average more than three hours per day, there is no doubt that it influences their perceptions of the world, their attitudes toward society, and their behaviors. For instance, children may become anxious around strangers and be afraid to go out, or they may develop long-term, debilitating social problems. As it is, between two-thirds and three-quarters of children ages 6 to 11 feel intense anxiety about violence, guns, and death (Steyer, 2002).

Studies that have examined children and their reactions to frightening content have shown that their reactions differ by age. Very young children are frightened by scary characters and situations, while older children are more affected by threats of either realistic or abstract stimuli, not just scary images by themselves (Cantor, 1998).

Effects of Offensive Song Lyrics

Ten years after the hoopla surrounding comedian George Carlin's 1973 expletive-filled radio monologue, which repeated seven words too "dirty" ever to say on the airwaves, attention was focused on the indecent words found within song lyrics. After being offended by the lyrics in the Prince song "Darling Nikki," Tipper Gore, wife of then-Senator Al Gore, founded Parents Music Resource Center (PMRC) to protect children

Comedian George Carlin became well known for a monologue that featured seven "dirty" words.

A Season on the Brink, which was based on the life of college basketball coach Bobby Knight.

Both Jello Biafra, singer for the punk rock group Dead Kennedys, and the group 2 Live Crew were charged with producing "material harmful to minors," but both sets of charges were later dropped.

and young adults from the influences of indecent and violent lyrics. This group believed that young people would do what the songs lyrics suggested and would be inclined to accept deviant behavior as normal.

Hearings before the Senate Commerce Committee in 1985 led to the record industry voluntarily putting parental advisory stickers on record albums and CDs that contained "profanity, violence or sexually explicit lyrics, including topics of fornication, sado-masochism, incest, homosexuality, bestiality and necrophilia" (Cockburn, 2000). Rockers such as Joey Ramone and Frank Zappa, who called Tipper Gore a "cultural terrorist" (DeCurtis, 1992; Sutton et al., 2000), strongly objected to the warning labels and accused PMRC of censoring artistic expression. Eventually, charges were filed against Jello Biafra (lead singer of the Dead Kennedys) for producing "material harmful to minors" (Cockburn, 2000) and against 2 Live Crew for their album *Nasty As They Wanna Be,* on which the F-word was used 226 times. Although the album was found to be obscene in the state of Florida, federal charges against 2 Live Crew were dropped, as were the charges against Jello Biafra (Black, 2000; Mathews, 1990).

PMRC is not as active as it used to be and is now viewed as too "middle-of-the-road" (Gowen, 1993) for conservative groups such as the American Family Association, which continues to press for government censorship of objectionable song lyrics. During Senate Commerce Committee hearings in 2000, PMRC called for more specific warnings on stickers. For example, "Christina Aguilera might get a warning for mild sexual content, while one from bad-boy rapper Eminem should get the ultimate warning" (Oppelaar, 2000, p. 126). However, a Federal Trade Commission (FTC) report showed that 74 percent of parents are satisfied with the current voluntary sticker system (Oppelaar, 2000). Although the controversy continues, it seems unlikely that additional warnings or censorship will be initiated in the near future.

Effects of Video Games

During the year 2000, about 49 million people in the United States played some type of online computer game (Barnes, 2002). In this country, revenues from computer and video games are greater than movie receipts (Barnes, 2002), and 9 out of 10 households with children have rented or owned a video or computer game (Quittner, 1999). Further, the average American spends 75 hours per year playing video games—more than double the time spent in 1997—and 70 percent of college students play video games "at least occasionally" (Lewis, 2003). Online and video computer games have indeed proliferated and become an everyday part of life for many people of all ages ("TV, Video Games," 2001).

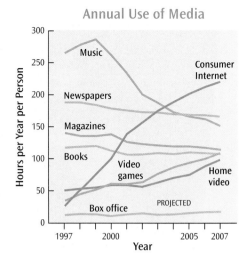

Annual Use of Media

Source: Lewis, 2003.

As video games have become more popular, there has been growing concern about the social effects, especially increased aggression, that stem from playing such games. Studies suggest that video games may be more influential than television, for several reasons: (1) they're more interactive, which increases involvement; (2) a large percentage of games involve violence as the main activity and players are encouraged to "kill" and injure as many of the "enemy" as possible to win; and (3) the games' portability makes them somewhat of a companion, as they can be played most anywhere (McDonald & Kim, 2001).

People play online and video games for all types of reasons: to enjoy thrills, to relieve stress, to escape, for something to do, to make online friends, and so forth. But is playing such games just an innocent pastime? Some people contend that video games have become the newest scapegoat for all of society's ills, yet evidence has shown that playing video games leads to increased aggression and increased perception of aggressiveness in others (Bushman & Anderson, 2002). Children may be particularly susceptible to the effects of video games. As stated by McDonald and Kim (2001), "Children identify quite closely with electronic characters of all sorts, and . . . these identifications may have important implications for their emotional well-being as well as for the development of their personality" (p. 241).

Playing video games may also be addictive. Playing violent video games stimulates psychoneurological receptors that give the player a "high," producing symptoms similar to those induced by drugs and other pleasurable activities. High levels of body and brain involvement also lead to the production of dopamine, a neurotransmitter "that some believe is the master molecule of addiction" (Quittner, 1999).

Some feel that playing video games may be addictive, given the high levels of body and brain involvement.

ZOOM IN   13.5

To learn more about the relationship between video games and aggression, enter "video games" + "aggression" as a search term in **Yahoo.com**.

Effects of the Internet

Studies have shown that people are spending slightly less time with traditional media and more time online (BBDO, 1996; "Internet Eats into TV Time," 1996; Kaye & Johnson, 2003; Scarborough Research, 2001). In fact, some people are actually spending *too* much time on the Web. They have become so used to being online that other activities, like socializing with friends and studying for college, have suffered. Internet addiction is a topic of concern for many who find themselves addicted to online games, newsgroups, e-mail, file sharing, and simply surfing. College students, who enjoy freedom from parental supervision and unlimited access to the Internet through broadband connections in college campus dorms, are at particular risk for Internet addiction. They sometimes find that the stress of school, work, and social situations leads them to seek a safer, less demanding environment on the Internet. There, they can escape from real-life problems and socialize with new and perhaps anonymous chat room friends (Young, 2003).

Health professionals have been interested in dealing with online addiction for some years now. The Center for Online Addiction, founded in 1995, is a private, nonprofit behavioral health care firm whose goal is to help people with problems related to online activities that tend to consume an unhealthy proportion of their time. The center provides a number of services, including educational materials, counseling through e-mail, chat rooms for online addicts, and telephone counseling (Center for Online Addiction, 2004).

College students are at particular risk for Internet addiction.

ZOOM IN 13.6

To learn more about online addiction and its treatment, go to www.netaddiction.com

Are you addicted to the Internet? Take these tests to find out:

- www.netaddiction.com/resources/internet_addiction_ test.htm
- www.findingstone.com/services/tests/_onlineaddiction test.htm

Agenda Setting

Agenda setting refers to the mass media's power to influence the importance of certain news issues as perceived by the audience. In other words, an agenda of what people are supposed to think about is set when the news media select which stories to air. Agenda setting is a function of the *gatekeeping* process that news media practice daily. Because of the time and space constraints of radio and television, news producers select (or gatekeep) stories and events to cover and then present on the air. These stories and events become increasingly important to the audience with repetition and consistency across various media. When an event is the lead story on the broadcast and cable networks' news segments, people believe it to be of utmost importance, when, in fact, other events may be more noteworthy but for various reasons be largely ignored. If the media don't air a story, people don't think it's important.

For the last 20 years, agenda setting has been studied in the context of media effects. A *cumulative effects model* of agenda setting looks at the repetition of certain messages and themes in the media. After viewers repeatedly see and hear about events and topics in the newspaper headlines or on the evening television newscast, they begin to believe that these are the important issues in society. The cumulative effects model assumes that these effects are observable only after repeated exposure.

How much television does the average person view in a week?

Agenda setting can be thought of as the ability of the news media to focus our attention and concerns on certain issues. Newscasts are often criticized for focusing attention on, say, a murder trial in order to move attention away from a politically heated issue, such as the national debt or high unemployment rate. In this sense, the news media do not tell us what to think but rather what to think about (Baran & Davis, 2000; Bryant & Thompson, 2002; Cohen, 1963).

Agenda setting has recently moved to the forefront as the FCC has attempted to loosen restrictions on media ownership and consolidation. Basically, media conglomerates such as News Corp.—which already owns the FOX News Channel, Twentieth Century Fox television and film studios, the *New York Post,* and other media properties—are hoping to own even more media outlets. Broadcast ownership groups would be able to buy more stations in a single market and also be allowed to enjoy cross-ownership (in which newspapers and television and radio stations can be owned by the same corporation), if the FCC gets its way. The FCC gave in to public opinion in 2003 by agreeing not to increase ownership limits ("FCC Eases Media Ownership Rules," 2003). Nonetheless, some media corporations and members of the FCC continue to press for relaxed ownership rules ("Media Ownership," 2004).

ZOOM IN   13.7
Link to more information about agenda setting at these sites:

- www.wfu.edu/~louden/Political%20Communication/ Bibs/AGENDA.html
- www.agendasetting.com/agenda/theory.asp

As the number of separately owned news outlets continues to decrease because of aggressive consolidation, there will be fewer individual "voices" (or media owners). All of the news to all of the outlets will be fed from one common source. Consumer advocates, civil rights groups, religious groups, small broadcasters, writers, and concerned citizens fear that instead of getting several different perspectives about a certain issue, we'll get one perspective—likely that of the corporate owners. An increase in agenda setting is also likely to occur, as media conglomerates' interests will be served through their news outlets. They can give prominence and positive "spin" to issues that may help them (such as tax breaks) and squelch stories that may hurt them (such as recalls on products that the media corporation is financially tied to).

Uses of and Gratifications from the Mass Media

So far, this chapter has examined the ways in which the media, especially television, influence their audiences—or as some would say, how the media *use* their audiences. This chapter will now turn its attention to how audiences use the media. The **uses and gratifications approach** examines how audiences use the media and the gratifications derived from this use. This perspective is based on the premise that people have certain needs and desires that are fulfilled by their media choices, either through use of the medium itself or through exposure to specific content (Canary & Spitzberg, 1993; Kaye & Johnson, 2004; Lin, 1993; Palmgreen, Wenner, & Rosengren, 1985; Perse & Ferguson, 1992; Rubin & Bantz, 1989; Walker & Bellamy, 1989; Walker, Bellamy, & Truadt, 1993).

The uses and gratifications model is used to answer such media use questions as these: Why do some people prefer listening to television news than reading the newspaper? Under what conditions is an individual more likely to watch a sitcom rather than a violent police drama? What satisfactions are derived from watching soap operas? The model is based on these assumptions: (1) The audience actively and freely chooses media and content; (2) individuals select media and content with specific purposes in mind; (3) using the media and exposure to content fulfills many gratifications; and

(4) media and content choice are influenced by needs, values, and other personal and social factors (Rosengren, Wenner, & Palmgreen, 1985).

The more a particular medium or content gratifies audience members' needs, the more likely audience members are to continue using that medium or depend on that content. For example, if a viewer's need for feeling smart is fulfilled by a particular game show, he or she will probably continue watching that show. Audiences watch particular shows, listen to particular music, and even select specific websites for many reasons, such as to escape, to pass time, to unwind, to relax, to feel less lonely, and to learn about new things.

Sometimes, it's not just the content that's gratifying but rather the medium itself. The act of watching television, regardless of what's on, may be relaxing, or the act of surfing the Internet, regardless of the sites you're accessing, may gratify the need to feel like you're doing something productive or becoming informed. Think of the number of times that you've flopped down on the sofa, grabbed the remote, turned on the television, and just laid there, surfing the channels. You didn't care too much about what was on, but somehow, just being in front of the television felt good.

We watch television in two primary ways: instrumentally and ritualistically (Rubin, 1984). **Instrumental viewing** tends to be goal oriented and content based; viewers watch television with a certain type of program in mind. Conversely, **ritualistic viewing** is less goal oriented and more habitual in nature; viewers watch television for the act of watching, without regard to program content. Research has suggested that perhaps television-viewing behavior shouldn't be thought of as either instrumental or ritualistic but as falling along a continuum. In other words, in one viewing session, we may watch somewhat instrumentally and somewhat ritualistically, moving between these two extremes (Lee & Lee, 1995, p. 12).

ZOOM IN   13.8

- Next time you watch television, think of why you turned on the set and why you chose the particular program you're watching.

- Think of the last time you watched television. Did you watch ritualistically or did you turn on the television to watch a particular program?

The uses and gratifications approach is important to understanding how audiences use the mass media and their reasons for doing so. The theory connects media use to the audience's psychological needs and attitudes toward the media, and it also explains how personal factors influence media use. Additionally, the uses and gratifications model tracks how new communication technologies change media use habits and how social and cultural changes influence content selection.

SEE IT LATER

In today's world, television is the central focus of many people's lives. The remainder of this chapter will therefore discuss the implications of media effects and how television content is shaping our future.

Media Violence

Concerns about media violence and its effects on viewers, especially young adults and children, continues to generate heated debate among families, parents, educators, activists, the media industry, and legislators. While everyone is out to protect his or her own interests, there is a general consensus that viewing too much violent or objectionable content may, under some circumstances, have serious social and personal consequences. Thus, the argument centers on what, if anything, should be done to curb violent images.

On the one hand, many believe that objectionable content should not be curtailed because of the possibility of its causing negative effects or because some viewers are offended by it. Many strongly believe that it's the parents' responsibility to monitor what their children watch on television, what music they listen to and buy, and what Internet sites they visit. Moreover, if viewers are offended by certain content, they should stop watching, listening to, or using it. In other words, viewers are responsible for their own exposure to offensive content. On the other hand, many believe that the media are responsible for the content they air and should curb violent and negative images for the good of society as a whole.

It's difficult to sift through all the arguments, especially when parents are leaning on legislators to clean up television yet taking their kids to see decidedly violent and sexual movies. Given these and other contradictory behaviors, it's understandable why the television industry is reluctant to voluntarily censor its content but instead rallies hard against further regulations on violent, sexual, and verbal content.

When we look at the time children spend watching television versus interacting with their parents, a disturbing trend emerges. In the mid 1960s, American children spent an average of 30 hours a week with their parents, whereas now, they spend an average of 17 hours with their parents. Not only has the amount of parent/child time decreased, but the typical child today spends an average of 40 hours per week in front of the television or using the computer, radio, or other electronic media. Additionally, the average preschooler watches over 20 hours of television and videos per week. Most children have witnessed about 8,000 killings before the age of 12 and 200,000 acts of violence before the age of 18 (Lavers, 2002; Steyer, 2002). Furthermore, by the time a child graduates from high school, he or she will have spent about 33,000 hours watching television as compared to about 13,000 hours in school (Steyer, 2002). It's hard to make the argument that media doesn't influence children and young adults when so much of their lives are media centered.

By the time a child graduates from high school, he or she will have spent about 33,000 hours watching television, or about 2.5 times as many hours as spent in school.

In an attempt to appease concerned parents, legislators, and others who rallied to clean up the airwaves, Congress passed the Telecommunications Act of 1996. It mandated that all television sets with screens larger than 13 inches be equipped with V-chips or other means of blocking objectionable content. To further protect children from violent and sexual images, the 1996 law required the FCC to adopt a program ratings system, which was implemented in 1997.

Ratings critics fear that violence and sexual content may actually increase, as producers can now justify such content because viewers will be warned and given the opportunity to avoid such programming, if they desire. Research has shown that mediated violence and objectionable content have indeed increased since 1998. The Parents Television Council, a conservative group dedicated to increasing wholesome family fare, reported that in the 2000–2001 television season, violence increased 70 percent. Additionally, the study found that incidents of profane language, which are considered verbal aggression, were up 78 percent to 2.6 instances per hour (Lavers, 2002; Littleton, 2001). A more recent study examining the use of objectionable language found that programs aired by the seven broadcast networks in 2001 contained 7.2 incidents of foul language per hour and that the earliest hour of prime-time programming contained just as many offensive words as the latest hour (Kaye & Sapolsky, 2004).

Some broadcasters do not comply with the content ratings system and object to its use. One executive producer expressed the fear that content ratings will jeopardize the success of certain programs. He pointed to *ER* as containing violence due to the nature of its being an emergency medical program but qualified that the violence isn't of the same type as on other programs (Pember, 2001). Critics also contend that viewers don't really pay attention to the content ratings, so there's no reason to use them. Even parents don't seem to use the ratings system. Two years after the system was introduced, only about 50 percent of parents used it as a way to control their children's viewing, only about 10 percent even knew how their children's favorite shows were rated, and almost 20 percent had never even heard of the ratings system ("Half of All Parents," 1998; Schneider, 1997; Steyer, 2002). Still other viewers claim that the ratings system is inadequate and doesn't accurately reflect program content. If it did, they believe it would be used more often.

V-chips were also supposed to prevent viewers from accessing violent and objectionable content. Yet in 2001, four years after the 1997 V-chip requirement, only about 40 percent of all parents had V-chip-equipped televisions and just 7 percent even used the device (Steyer, 2002). Despite the fact that the ratings system and V-chips are generally ignored, more means of blocking objectionable content are available in the marketplace. ProtecTV and other similar devices mute over 400 offensive words and phrases from television programs and edit profanities out of closed-captioned scripts (Poovey, 2002).

Conservative viewers, parents, and policymakers have aligned themselves with FCC member Kevin Martin, who has raised concerns to the FCC about objectionable programming and proposed designating one hour each evening as a family viewing hour of wholesome programming. Martin has also asked television networks to voluntarily cut back on violent, sexual, and offensive programs. The industry has countered that V-chips, language-muting devices, and a content- and age-based ratings system all protect children from objectionable content. Furthermore, the industry has argued that the protections are already in place and that it's up to parents to use them effectively (McConnell, 2003).

Children and Media Exposure

Among children under the age of 2:

- About 25 percent have a television in their bedroom.
- About 66 percent use a computer, television, or DVD in an average day.

Among children under the age of 6:

- The average number of hours spent with a computer, television, or DVD is about 2 hours per day.
- The average amount of time spent reading or being read to is about 40 minutes per day.

Source: Hopkinson, 2003.

New Communication Technologies

New communication technologies have given rise to new uses of media. Activities such as remote channel changing, taping programs, fast-forwarding through commercials, and watching videos all employ new media technologies that have altered existing television-viewing patterns (Kaye & Johnson, 2004; Lin, 1993; Perse & Ferguson, 1992; Rubin & Bantz, 1989; Walker & Bellamy, 1989; Walker, Bellamy, & Truadt, 1993). Satellite radio is sure to change existing radio-listening habits, just as satellite television has altered how people select programs when offered hundreds of channels instead of 60 or so.

The Internet has already changed and will continue to change people's uses of traditionally delivered media, such as radio and television. For example, one study of politically interested Internet users found that in the year 2000, news magazines appeared to take the hardest hit from the Internet, as these users relied more on online political news and information. The study also found that between 1996 and 2000, politically interested Internet users significantly decreased their time with radio, especially those who had come to rely on the Web and bulletin boards/electronic-mailing lists as their primary sources of political information (Kaye & Johnson, 2003).

Children's Nutrition

Also of great social concern is that children's eating habits may be influenced by watching television and by watching commercials, in particular. Studies have found that the percentage of body fat and incidence of obesity are highest among children who watch four or more hours of television a day and lowest among those who watch an hour or less a day (Andersen, Crespo et al, 1998a; Crespo et al., 2001). What's more, the incidence of obesity increases the more hours children spend watching television (Dennison, Erb, & Jenkins, 2002; Dietz & Gortmaker, 1985). An earlier study found that children who are heavy television viewers tend to eat more snacks between meals than light television viewers (Clancy-Hepburn, Hickey, & Nevill, 1974).

Even though parents are the strongest influence on children's eating habits, commercials help set food preferences. With the number of overweight children doubling from 1980 to 2002, there's no denying that the United States is witnessing an epidemic of obese children. Today, almost one in seven children between the ages of 6 and 19 is

Among children, the incidence of obesity increases with the amount of time they spend watching television.

considered severely overweight, which is three times the rate of obesity in the 1960s (Dietz, 1990; Irvine, 2002). Hospital costs for treating obese children have tripled since just the early 1980s.

Blame is being placed on the food industry for making sugar- and fat-laden foods and on the advertising industry for making such foods attractive to children. Each year, the average child sees 10,000 food advertisements, 95 percent of which are for fast foods, sugary cereals, soft drinks, and candy. In all, $12 billion is spent on advertising to children each year. McDonald's alone spends over $1 billion on advertising. In stark contrast, the National Cancer Institute has only $1 million a year to promote the healthy eating of fruits and vegetables. Likewise, the federal government's entire budget for promoting nutritional education is one-fifth of what Altoids spends annually on advertising its mints (Ryan, 2002).

Calls have gone out to curb the growing epidemic of overweight and otherwise unhealthy children by limiting or even banning junk food advertising during children's programming and on child-oriented websites. Proponents of food advertising regulations claim that junk food advertising is a public health issue, just like the consumption of tobacco products, and that unhealthy foods should be banned from the airwaves, just as tobacco products are.

The abundance of junk food advertising has parents, activists, and other concerned entities urging their legislators to battle it out with the food and advertising industries. Sweden and Norway already have bans on junk food advertising, and Great Britain may be the next country to follow suit.

Summary

Various perspectives are offered to explain the effects of media content on people individually, socially, and culturally. Those perspectives include the strong-effects model and magic bullet theory; the limited-effects model and the research that stemmed from the broadcast of *The War of the Worlds;* the moderate-effects model; and the powerful-effects model, which takes many factors into consideration when examining media influence.

Viewing media violence may affect people behaviorally, emotionally, and cognitively. Viewers, especially children, may imitate aggressive behaviors, identify with unsavory characters, become anxious and fearful, and become desensitized to violence in real life. Repeated exposure to mediated violence breaks down social barriers and may influence antisocial behaviors.

The media, especially television, socializes and shapes people's attitudes, values, and beliefs about the world around them. Program content and commercials both strongly influence the way we think about ourselves and others, as well as sex, food, tobacco, and other life concerns. The Internet also strongly influences our behavior, especially socially. Further, some individuals are addicted to watching television and using the Internet, and as a consequence, they forget about the world and fail to meet responsibilities.

The television and Internet industries, parents, psychologists, educators, legislators, activists, and other interested parties are struggling with the many social and cultural issues surrounding the media and its use and content. In this struggle, rights to freedom of speech go head to head with the desire to protect viewers from objectionable content. Arguments include whether viewers need protection and what negative effects mediated content may have. Some worry that our fascination with television and the Internet is turning us into media junkies, who live in darkened rooms, transfixed to our screens.

These concerns will not likely be settled in the near future and, in fact, are more likely to grow as television screens get larger and more involving and our dependence on computers and the Internet deepens.

New Technologies, New Lifestyles

CHAPTER 14

SEE IT NOW AND SEE IT LATER

Messaging Systems

Computers

Music

Television

Cameras

Home Networking

A Wireless World

In this chapter, you'll learn about:

- The newer electronic media communication devices and how they affect your lifestyle
- New communication devices that affect how we communicate with others
- The ways these new devices are increasing our ability to use computers
- How new electronic media devices are helping us to become media creators as well as media consumers

Up to now, this book has focused on the uses of electronic media for communicating to the mass audience. You've learned about the origins of radio and the subsequent development of broadcast and cable television. You've read about how the Internet was created and how new communication technologies, such as satellite television and radio, have emerged. You've also found out how media systems and corporations operate and how programming is created and distributed. Finally, you've learned about the social and cultural changes brought about by the electronic media. All this information so far has been presented on a macro level and from a media perspective. But now, the book is going to turn its attention to how new communication technologies affect your life on a personal level. The older broadcast media were used primarily to communicate to a mass audience, but today, newer electronic devices and technologies allow for the personalization of messages.

Think of this chapter as a guide to personal communication devices, such as cell phones and personal digital assistants—what they are, how they work, and how you can incorporate them into your everyday life. But in addition to providing simple descriptions of these new gadgets, this chapter discusses the cultural implications they have and how they affect your personal lifestyle.

The current and future uses of new communication technologies and devices are so completely intertwined that rather than separate this chapter into the three major sections found in previous chapters—See It Then, See It Now, See It Later—current trends are tied in with forecasts.

 ## SEE IT NOW AND SEE IT LATER

Messaging Systems

Cell Phones

In an episode of the popular sitcom *Friends*, Ross was getting married (again), this time to Emily in England. As his friend Joey was about to walk down the aisle with Emily's mother, her cell phone started to ring. She answered it and handed the phone to Joey. Much to Ross's annoyance, Joey not only took the call but also held up the phone throughout the ceremony, so a friend back in the States could listen.

Although this incident was just a funny scene in a television sitcom, many people today could tell a similar tale. Stories about cell phones ringing during speeches given by the president and the Queen of England pervade the media. In fact, in response to these increasing interruptions, George W. Bush banned cell phones from his staff meetings. Clearly, no event or location is sacred: Cell phones can be heard ringing during funerals, in theaters, during concerts, and in classrooms. And of course, the common practice of using a cell phone while driving brings up safety issues, as well.

Opinions vary regarding proper cell phone behavior. Some people say that public cell phone use is often annoying, intrusive, and irritating, while others view such use as acceptable and even the norm. Is the frenzy of cell phone use a passing trend, a technological step forward, or a new style of communicating that's become a permanent part of our culture?

Cell phones have had a huge impact on us, socially and culturally. In some respects, we've become tethered to our friends and family, as cell phones are often used for purposes of surveillance. Some people are so connected that they have to let

ZITS/by Jerry Scott and Jim Borgman

someone know where they are every second of the day. Moreover, their families and friends come to expect this of them and may become alarmed if the ongoing messages stop. In some ways, cell phones make us feel less lonely because we're in constant contact with others. And because of the low cost of making a cell call, we often call just to alleviate loneliness or boredom, not necessarily because we have anything interesting to say.

There was a time when answering machines gave people a new way to project their self-image and impress others with a clever outgoing message. Many people thought of their answering machine as a barometer of popularity and couldn't wait to get home and see how many messages were waiting. Whether they filtered their calls, conducted business, increased their independence from landline phones, or built their self-esteem, people quickly came to depend on answering machines. Like answering machines, cell phones make us feel popular, important, and needed. Consider that at one time, getting a cell phone call would result in others giving you admiring glances.

How times have changed! Cell phones are now often a source of annoyance, especially when used in public places. Think of how many times you've been in the grocery store and heard someone who's called home to ask, "Honey, do you want Twinkies or Ding Dongs?" It almost seems that cell phones have taken away our ability to make even the most mundane decisions on our own.

Despite the trivial uses of cell phones, for most people, the advantages far outweigh the disadvantages. Cells phones help us keep in touch on important matters and give us comfort when physically isolated. What's more, they are convenient and easy to use and, in many cases, less costly than making long-distance calls over traditional lines. They can also be credited with saving lives in emergencies.

College students rely on cell phones more than ever. In the past, college students had to share a landline phone among roommates. Now, each student can have a personal line. Cell phones also can be used as alarm clocks and personal memo makers. (Just call your own number and leave a message for yourself.) Many cell phones have games, a large variety of ring tones, and even the capability to take and send pictures—plus, they take better messages than roommates.

The advent of cellular technology has also changed the nature of telephone communication. Whereas telephones were once used primarily for personal communication, cellular service now includes commercial communication. Advertisements, stock quotes, headline news, and other such messages can be sent directly to cell phones.

For many people, this is an overload of information. We're bombarded with commercial messages, pelted with sound bites, and bored to death with the tedious details of our friends' and families' lives. Every ring of the cell phone means more information. At some point, people begin to question how much information they really need and to wonder when keeping in touch crosses the line to being under surveillance.

Personal Digital Assistants

A *personal digital assistant (PDA)* is a handy little device that frees you from the burden of lugging around a three-ring daily organizer complete with an address book, a calendar, a to-do list, and pages of reminders and other notes. All that and more fits onto one small, palm-sized electronic device.

PDAs are actually tiny computers that retrieve, store, and send information to other PDAs and computers. Apple's Newton was the first PDA-type organizing and messaging computer. Introduced in 1993, Newton was an immediate hit; sales soared to

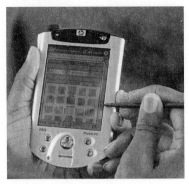

A stylus is used to select functions on a PDA, or personal digital assistant.

50,000 units in the first 10 weeks the product was on the market. But users quickly became disillusioned with Newton's poor handwriting recognition, complexity of use, size, and expense (Freudenrich, 2002; MacNeill, 1993).

The Palm Pilot debuted in 1996 and promised to be a lightweight, small, easy-to-use organizer with enough memory to store thousands of addresses and notes. Its simple interface caught on with the public, and now the name *Palm* is almost synonymous with *PDA*, even though several other manufacturers also make PDAs (including Compaq and Hewlett Packard). When you hear people talking about their Palm, you know they mean their PDA.

Whether you need a PDA depends on your lifestyle. You can use a PDA to record your appointments and special events, to store contact information (addresses, phone numbers, e-mail, birthdays), to remind you of homework assignments and projects, and to keep track of your expenses. Rather than lug a laptop computer around, some students attach a miniature keyboard to their PDA and take notes during class. And in some cases, classmates can send notes and other information via infrared beams back and forth between their PDAs (Freudenrich, 2002).

With some PDAs, you can send and retrieve e-mail, play games, receive news and other information from the Internet, download music, store photos and movies, get driving directions, and create and download word-processing files. As handy as this may be, there is, once again, the issue of feeling overwhelmed by an excess of information. Critics question the need for having such immediate and often trivial information at our fingertips and are also concerned about people's overreliance on these devices (at the expense of their own memories). Like cell phones, PDAs are often ego boosters because they present an image of being busy and important. PDA owners reap the benefits of the device's practical utility, while at the same time gratifying the personal need for recognition and status (Freudenrich, 2002).

Multifunctional Devices

A cell phone is a cell phone is a cell phone. Right? Wrong! Some cell phones are multifunctional and go beyond simply acting as a telephone and an answering machine. Instead of juggling both a cell phone and a PDA, many consumers are opting for an all-in-one device. Several manufacturers boast new models that are fully functional PDAs and cell phones.

You can even turn your cell phone into a camera. Some manufacturers offer camera-equipped phones that let you snap photos and whisk them off to friends and family via e-mail. Imagine studying abroad and sending a photo of yourself standing in front of the Eiffel Tower to your friends and family back home. About 30 million people around the world are taking pictures with their cell phones, and about 120 million are expected to follow suit by 2005 ("World Wide Camera Phones," 2003).

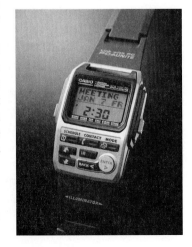

Yet another new device is the combo cell phone/wristwatch. Although it's perhaps a bit awkward to use, it is otherwise convenient, and you'll be sure to turn some heads with this handy tool. But like most new communication devices, six months after you spend your hard-earned money to buy it, it will have become obsolete and be replaced with a better, less expensive model.

A Casio PIM (personal information management) wearable data viewer, also known as a "smart watch."

Staying on the topic of watches, in early 2003, Microsoft introduced *smart personal object technology (SPOT)* software that's powered by tiny but powerful microchips. Several watchmakers are manufacturing SPOT-enabled watches, which owners can configure to receive news, sports, weather, traffic, stocks, and other information from a Microsoft website. The information is beamed to the watch's liquid crystal display screen. Users can also send messages with these watches (Krane, 2003).

More than just fancy gadgets, these multipurpose cell phones, PDAs, and watches serve the purpose of keeping us constantly connected to information sources and to other people. As their functional utility increases, the personal gratification we receive from them also increases. These devices become more than just tools for telling time or keeping a schedule. Rather, they keep us involved in the world. Our own personal sphere widens as we let in more and more information, which has led some people to wonder just how much we can absorb before reaching an emotional and psychological limit.

Third Generation

You'll probably come across the term *G3* more frequently in the years to come. G3 stands for "third generation" wireless service. The first generation was comprised of early analog cell phones and services. The second generation provided digitized phones and services. The third generation promises more efficient delivery and multimedia capabilities. In fact, the third generation hasn't even been born yet, but we're beyond the second generation into what's known as *G2.5*.

Source: Brass, 2002.

Telephones and the Internet

Plain old telephone service (POTS) is suffering from the growing competition of cell phone monthly services, which are increasingly more affordable and often include unlimited long-distance calling and other cost-saving benefits. Dealing yet another blow to standard landline phone services is **Internet telephony**, which is a way to make long-distance phone calls over the Internet (Baig, 2002a).

Also known as *voice over Internet protocol (VOIP)* and *IP telephony,* Internet telephony doesn't cost as much as a call using POTS because it uses a packet-switching system, similar to the Internet. Packet switching is much more efficient than the POTS circuit-switching system, in which the circuit is open and dedicated to the call. With packet switching, the connection is kept open just long enough to send bits of data (a packet) back and forth between the caller and the receiver; this means the connection time is minimized and there's less load on the computer. In the transmission space taken up by one POTS call, three or four Internet calls can be made. Basically, Internet telephony digitizes your voice and compresses it so it will flow as a series of packets through the Internet's limited bandwidth (Tanaka, 2001; "What Is Telephony?" 2002).

There are several ways to make a VOIP call:

- *Computer to computer.* This is probably the easiest type to hook up, and long-distance calls are free. In most cases, all you need is an Internet connection, special software (e.g., MSN Explorer), plus speakers and a microphone. All you pay for is your regular monthly Internet service provider (ISP) or cable modem fee. Several companies offer low-cost software for VOIP calls.
- *Computer to telephone.* If you want to call someone's telephone from your computer, you'll need to sign on with a provider. That company will typically give you the software for free but will charge a per-minute rate for your calls.
- *Telephone to computer.* With a special calling card or calling number, you can make a call to a computer, but only as long as the receiver is using the same vendor's software as the caller.
- *Telephone to telephone.* Using this system, you make a call from your telephone, which is connected to an adapter that digitizes your voice. It then sends your voice through your modem to your ISP or Internet telephony provider's network, which converts the signal back to analog and sends it on to the receiver's telephone (Tyson, 2002a).

This may all sound way too complicated to be worth saving a few pennies, but for many, VOIP calls have become a great alternative to POTS and cell phones. In 2001, people across the globe spent 9 trillion minutes talking on the telephone. Of all those minutes, 10.9 billion were spent on Internet-based calls in 2000, but that figure almost tripled in 2001. By 2005, an estimated 774 billion minutes will be spent conversing over the Internet ("Small Talk," 2001).

ZOOM IN   14.1
Go to the Companion Website for this text to learn more about Internet phone calls: www.ablongman.com/medoffkaye1e.

Computers

Wearable Computers

Just when you think you've seen it all, you meet a woman walking down the street wearing what looks like a headband with an eyepatch. But as you get closer, you realize she has a computer strapped to her head.

The wearable computer is not a new concept, but except for some industry use, it really hasn't hit the consumer market until now. Xybernaut's Poma (or *personal optical mobile assistant*) is a go-anywhere computer. The 2002 model included a 10.9-ounce, pocket-sized processor with 32 megabytes of memory and a Windows CE operating system, plus a wireless modem for an Internet or e-mail connection.

ZOOM IN   14.2
Check out Poma at www.vrealities.com/poma.html.

The Poma's processor is wired to a hand-operated optical pointing device (or a keyboard, for when you're sitting at a sidewalk café) that controls the onscreen cursor. An onscreen keyboard function lets you point to letters using your optical pointing device. The screen, or display, is an adjustable 2.8-ounce, 1-inch square that hangs in front of your eye from the headband. You can wear it on either your left or right eye, depending on which one is dominant. Even though the screen is so small, the effect is similar to looking at a 13-inch computer screen from two feet away.

Poma is limited in some of its operations, and without a keyboard, it's unlikely that you'll use this device to write term papers. But it is sure easier to travel with than a laptop, and it could be really convenient for quick Internet research or digital music playback. Although some may consider Poma and other wearable computers nothing more than expensive toys, they may soon be surprised. In a few years, these devices could become just as commonplace and necessary as your wristwatch. According to one forecast, by the year 2007, 6 out of 10 people ages 15 to 50 will don some sort of portable communication device for at least six hours a day (Baig, 2002b).

Music

Private Audio

Remember when you thought wireless headphones were the coolest invention around? Now, we have **private audio**, which makes

IBM's wearable PC is a full-fledged portable computer.

headphones, wireless or wired, obsolete. Why put a contraption on your head when you can have audio signals directed solely to you?

The *hypersonic sound system (HSS)* can take an audio signal from any source (television, stereo, CD, or computer), convert it to ultrasonic frequency, and direct it to any target up to 100 yards away. Normal speakers use vibrating parts that move air to form the sound waves that scatter around a room. But HSS converts these scattered audible waves into ultrasonic waves (which humans can't hear) and then processes them through the HSS system into audible ultrasonic signals that can be directed to any target.

HSS has many practical applications. It would sure make dorm life much better; one roommate could watch television while the other blasted the stereo, and neither would hear what the other heard. Likewise, a car full of passengers could all listen to their own music, or a nightclub could have several dance floors, each playing a different type of music and none interfering with the others (Reno & Croal, 2002).

Although HSS and other similar systems hold promise for directional audio, they still have technical shortcomings. Furthermore, high cost will likely keep this technology out of the consumer market for a number of years.

> **ZOOM IN**   14.3
> Go to the Companion Website for this text to see how HSS works: www.ablongman.com/medoffkaye1e.

File Sharing

The music industry has blamed a three-year decline in CD sales on file swapping and CD burning. And with tens of millions of music lovers sharing their favorite tunes free of charge, the industry is scrambling for ways to thwart these activities. Lawsuits are one solution to the problem, but perhaps a better answer is the use of so-called *smart CDs.*

Advances in copy protection technology have led to smart CDs, which curb the ability to use file-sharing services but still allow limited copying and sharing of music. For example, on one type of smart CD, each song is written twice: once for playback on a CD player and once as a media file for computer playback. Music lovers can "burn" each song three times per computer and e-mail it to a limited number of friends, who can listen to each song up to 10 times. Songs are locked so they can't be played and distributed through file-sharing networks (Veiga, 2003).

Music industry executives and music lovers both see the smart CD as a compromise that still serves their own needs. Music files can be shared, yet the industry maintains some control over their distribution. Personal use and copyright protections are both respected, as well (Veiga, 2003).

Smart CDs provide one legal option for sharing music among friends.

Television

Watching television is no longer a matter of turning the channel selector back and forth among three or four networks. Instead, it has turned into the art of selecting what you want to watch and when from among hundreds of broadcast, cable, and satellite-delivered channels, all available 24/7. Even more decisions are involved: Should you get rid of your VCR and buy a DVD player instead? What are the benefits of buying a digital video recorder, and how do you work one? Should you give up your cable service if favor of DBS?

Given all this, many people complain that watching television isn't as easy as it used to be. Even so, they must admit to the benefits of television watching today. We have many more viewing choices and much better visual and audio quality. We can also record programs to watch at a later time, so we're free from the constraints of a program schedule.

The cutting-edge changes in television viewing today come from digital video discs (DVDs) and digital video recorders (DVRs).

Digital Video Discs

When you look at the number of people you know who have DVD players, it's hard to recall that this technology only hit the consumer market in 1997. DVDs have almost taken over video cassette recorders (VCRs) in this relatively short amount of time. In 2001, DVD sales jumped 25 percent to about 14.1 million players (Arthur, 2002), almost more than the 14.9 million VCRs sold in the same year (Klopfenstein, 2002). Furthermore, DVD sales are expected to grow to about 20 million by 2005 (Emling, 2002a). DVDs have truly taken the consumer market by storm and are one of the fastest-growing consumer electronics products ever invented (Suciu, 2003; Thomaselli, 2003).

DVD has definite advantages over VHS. DVD video and audio quality is much higher than on VHS tapes, and DVDs last much longer than the 15- to 25-year VHS tape lifespan. Although a DVD player is still a bit more expensive than a VCR, prices continue to drop. The big advantage to holding onto your VCR is the ability to tape your favorite shows. Some DVD *recorders* have entered the market, but they're still priced a bit higher than most consumers can afford. Also, the recording process can be a bit complicated, and this is compounded by the lack of industry standards and incompatible formats.

Not everyone can afford a DVD player, but relying on their old VCR could put them at a disadvantage. Some major movie rental and retail chains have drastically scaled back the number of VHS titles they offer in favor of DVDs, especially since 2002, when DVD sales and rentals overtook those of VHS tapes (Thomaselli, 2003). VCR owners also worry that switching to DVD will leave their VHS tapes to collect dust. In fact, VHS tapes can be transferred to DVD via a professional service or with a do-it-yourself kit. Using a kit, you can store your VHS images on your computer hard drive. Some kits even let you edit the content or add your own special effects before writing to the DVD (Rothman, 2002).

A Phillips digital television recording device.

Digital Video Recorders

In Chapter 6 on programming, DVRs were discussed from an industry perspective. In this chapter, we'll take another look at DVRs but from a consumer perspective. Specifically, this section will explain how DVRs work, how they boost your television viewing, and what advantages and disadvantages this system has.

The three major DVR manufacturers and products are TiVo, Microsoft Ultimate TV, and SonicBlue ReplayTV. A DVR is a set-top box (actually, a computer) that attaches to your television and to a broadband cable or digital subscriber line (DSL) connection. (A phone line connection won't work with most newer models.) In addition to the purchase price, using a DVR requires an additional monthly subscription fee.

What you get with a DVR is a high-quality recording system that can hold from 40 to 320 hours of programming, depending on the system. You simply program the DVR to record your favorite programs (sometimes, even two at a time) and then play back each show whenever you want to watch it. To date, the most-replayed moment in TiVo history is Janet Jackson's infamous "wardrobe malfunction" during the 2004 Super Bowl halftime telecast. An estimated 400,000 viewers

TiVo Subscribers

- 95 percent say it's easier to use TiVo than a VCR.
- 90 percent channel surf less than before they subscribed.
- 80 percent watch recorded prime-time programs at other times of the day and on weekends.
- 50 percent watch up to 2 hours' more television each day.
- 40 percent would rather give up their cell phone than their TiVo.

Source: Stone, 2002.

recorded and then replayed the stunt two or more times (Stone, 2004).

Better yet, with a DVR, you can actually pause and re-play a show even as it's being broadcast. You can also tape one show while playing back another. DVRs include point-and-click program guides, as well.

DVRs are catching heat from the television networks over what may be their most popular features: skipping commercials and sending recorded programs over the In-ternet. Whereas a VCR records commercials but leaves it up to the consumer whether to watch them, a DVR can be set to exclude commercials all together (Croal, 2001). As you can imagine, this does not set well with the television networks, since commercials are vital to their industry. TBS and other networks want to charge DVR users an annual fee of about $250 to enjoy the pleasure of ad-free television (Baig, 2001; Flynn, 2001).

The television industry is also upset at the thought of DVR users sending recorded programs over the Internet. Let's say you're the only one of your friends that sub-scribes to HBO, but you all love *The Sopranos*. You can be the hero by recording each episode and sending it to your non–HBO subscribing friends. The networks claim that sending recorded programs infringes on their copyright and that program swapping is no different than file swap-ping, which has been declared music piracy. In reality, it's unlikely that many users are going to bother sending programs, especially since it takes so long to do so. A stan-dard half-hour program can take up to 8 hours to send, and if recorded in a high-quality format, up to 24 hours (Baig, 2001).

The use of DVRs is changing our lifestyle and especially how we watch television. Instead of channel surfing, viewers can determine their own program lineup and watch recorded shows in any order they wish (Baig, 2001). This feature offers great potential for controlling children's television-viewing habits. Parents can record only those pro-grams they wish their children to see and limit children's viewing only to recorded shows. Instead of bringing up a new generation of channel surfers, today's parents may be rearing children who "think that TV means you sit down and see a list of stuff that's been recorded for you" (McGinn, 2002). DVRs also influence more instrumental view-ing habits, as viewers can select a program to watch and turn off the television when they're finished.

Introduced in 1998, the DVR has been slow to catch on with the general consumer market. Industry analysts blame the high cost, and others say that the DVR's complex image has kept people at bay. Many viewers still want television viewing to be relatively effortless. They just want to turn it on and push some buttons. Nevertheless, industry analysts project that by 2010, about half the nation's households will own a DVR (Stone, 2002).

There's also a chance that DVRs will be distributed through local cable systems in the future, like digital cable boxes are today. Instead of purchasing your own DVR, you'll rent one from your cable operator, who will decide which features (such as commercial skipping) to include.

Combatting DVR Ad Skipping

How do U.S. advertisers plan to combat consumers' DVR ad skipping?

- Program sponsorship: 63 percent
- Product placement: 49 percent
- Ad placement within DVR menus: 40 percent
- Interactive ads: 35 percent
- Ads in video-on-demand programs: 30 percent
- Program guide ads: 26 percent

Source: Elkin, 2002a.

DVR Projections

- Current penetration: 3.8 percent of U.S. households
- Projected penetration by 2007:   20 percent of U.S. households
- Percentage of programming that's viewed as time shifted in DVR households: 70 percent
- Percentage of advertising that's fast-forwarded through in DVR households: 55 percent
- Percentage of advertising that's fast-forwarded through in all U.S. households: 11 percent
- Projected television advertising revenue lost by 2007:   11 percent
- Projected dollar amount of TV ad revenue lost by 2007: $5.5 billion

Source: Curry, 2003; Kim, 2003.

ZOOM IN   14.4

Learn more about DVRs by visiting these sites:

- www.digitalnetworksna.com/replaytv/default.asp
- www.tivo.com
- www.ultimatetv.com

New Ways to Watch Television

With the coming of digital television delivery, television sets are taking on new shapes and forms. New flat-panel and LCD (liquid crystal display) displays and front-projection sets turn the average living room into a home theater. These sets are so thin and lightweight that they can fit in all kinds of new places; some displays can be hung on the wall.

Selecting from among these televisions of the future comes down to what's important to you: size, viewing angles, flexibility, and price. One thing to keep in mind, whether looking at a plasma or LCD TV, is that some brands are sold as *monitors,* which means you'll need to select a separate tuner and speakers. A front-projection set beams images onto a screen, similar to an old film projector. Again, a tuner and speakers are not included, and most models require a darkened room for viewing (Croal, 2002b).

The information in the FYI box on the next page reflects technology and prices in 2003. Keep in mind that improvements happen quickly and prices are likely to fall dramatically over the next few years.

ANOTHER NEW WAY TO WATCH TELEVISION   When a 52-inch television screen just isn't big enough or when solitary viewing just isn't any fun, head to your local movie theater for showings of programs that used to be delivered only through television. Regal Entertainment Group, the nation's largest theater operator, is extending its offerings to include live sporting events, rock concerts, documentaries, and other types of programs.

New types of televisions include flat-panel or plasma (above), liquid crystal display (LCD) (lower-right), and front-projection models (upper-right).

San Francisco, with 257 locations.

Comparison of Plasma, LCD, and Front-Projection Television

FEATURE	PLASMA	LCD	FRONT-PROJECTION
Screen size	32 to 63 inches	10 to 40 inches	Variable but large
Viewing angle	OK from almost any angle	Dims at side angle	Some distortion at side angle
Flexibility	Cannot be used with a PC	Can be used with a PC	Cannot be used with a PC
Aspect ratio	Mostly 16:9	16:9 or 4:3	16:9 or 4:3
Price	$3,000 to $30,000	$700 to $11,000	$2,500 to $45,000

Source: "The Big Picture," 2003.

Because this is different from showing films and videotapes, Regal has invested $70 million for the technology to beam compressed files by satellite or disk delivery to digital projectors at about 4,900 movie theater screens nationwide. So if you can't buy tickets to the hottest summer concert or the big football rivalry, head to your local Regal cinema. As one happy customer says, "It's not like watching a game on TV at all, because the sound is so incredible . . . and the screen is so damn big" (Setoodeh, 2003, p. 23).

Cameras

Webcams

E-mail and instant messaging have made keeping in contact with friends and family much easier than it used to be. But add a webcam and you have the ability not only to type to your friends but also to see them as they see you. A *webcam* is a simple, low-cost device that transmits live images between computers. Webcam software connects to the camera and grabs a frame from it periodically. Whereas the regular video that we see on television runs at 30 frames per second, webcam software grabs fewer frames because 30 frames per second requires lots of bandwidth. For example, a webcam on a university campus that shows a mostly static scene might be set to capture a still image from the camera once every 5 or 10 seconds.

When people use a webcam for instant messaging, the software might be set to capture 5 to 15 frames per second. At 5 frames per second, the movement is choppy and lags behind the real action. At 15 frames per second and above, the action looks pretty good. The problem is that the more frames per second, the more bandwidth required. Although the quality of most webcams is not very good, adding some lighting and making sure the focus is right will usually yield a pretty good picture.

The simplicity of a webcam setup has encouraged many people to put images on their homepages. Although many are mundane—showing people at work or play or displaying an image of the family goldfish—some people have used webcams for money-making opportunities. Webcams are also great devices for communicating with family members in the service or with a boyfriend or girlfriend studying abroad. You can mug for the camera and send all kinds of goofy images back and forth. A webcam can help ease the loneliness in these situations by visually connecting people.

The Internet abounds with live webcam sites that promise looks at college coeds, lonely housewives, pets, a live colony of ants, and

ZOOM IN 14.5

Watch an ant colony and the inside of a refrigerator at these sites, respectively:

- www.antcam.com
- www.beerlovercam.com

Internet users can connect using webcams.

just about anything or anybody you can imagine. One guy even has a webcam inside his beer refrigerator. You don't have to be a famous rock star with a reality program to be live on the screen. With a webcam setup, you can let the world into your life.

Critics contend that webcams appeal to people who are voyeuristic and that except for parents and a few close friends, most people really don't care about peeking into the boring lives of others. However, webcams also have more serious uses. For example, they are used for Internet conferences, as public relations tools (such as a city or university campus streaming live webcam images for potential visitors), and for correspondence-type courses. Some radio station websites entertain users by focusing webcams on their disc jockeys at work.

ZOOM IN   14.6

Check out these webcam links:

- Radio station   www.kcrw.com/cam/cam-a.html and www.kcrw.com/cam/cam-b.html
- WebCam World   www.webcamworld.com
- EarthCam   www.earthcam.com/usa/louisiana/neworleans/bourbonstreet

ZOOM IN   14.7

Go to the text's Companion Website to see how webcams work: www.ablongman.com/medoffkaye1e.

Digital Cameras

A digital camera is a camera that captures single, still images for the same uses as a regular film-type still camera. Digital cameras range from models with a very low price, low resolution, and only a few features to pricier models with more features that may deliver photographic quality as good as that found with expensive film cameras. However, expert photographers will probably argue that the quality of a digital camera doesn't come close to that of a 35 mm camera (Croal, 2001).

One allure of digital photography is instant gratification. After you snap a picture, you can instantly view it on the camera's LCD screen. Not only do you get the satisfaction of seeing the shot right away, but if you don't like it, you can delete it and take another picture. Digital photography eliminates the heartbreak that comes upon seeing an out-of-focus picture of Buckingham Palace or some place where you can't easily return. The same goes for important events, such as first birthdays and family reunions.

Once you download an image to a computer or upload it to the Web, you can edit it for quality and size. Moreover, you can easily change the contrast, brightness, colors, size, or just about anything else. Then you can print the image out on a color photo-quality printer. Basically, with a digital camera, you're not only the photographer but

ZOOM IN   14.8

See how digital cameras work at the Companion Website for this text: www.ablongman.com/medoffkaye1e.

also the developer and the editor. You can also send digital pictures instantly via e-mail, post them on a website, or save them on a disk or CD for viewing on a home video monitor or television.

Although film cameras continue to be popular, digital *camcorders* can now be found in 4 out of 10 U.S. households (Consumer Electronics Association, 2003). One of the best parts of owning a digital camera is that you don't have to lug around stacks of heavy photo albums. You can store your collection on a computer hard drive or on CDs.

Home Networking

There was a time when one television per household was enough to satisfy people's viewing needs. As the price of the average television set decreased, the number of channels available increased, and family members got tired of fighting over what to watch, television sets started popping up all over the house—in the bedroom, in the kitchen, and even in the bathroom.

In some ways, we are also on the verge of becoming multicomputer households. Families are getting tired of fighting over who gets to use the computer. Mom wants to work on finances, Dad wants to surf the Web, one child wants to check e-mail, and one wants to play online games. Who wins? Many households have resolved this dilemma by buying several home computers. This multicomputer arrangement works fine until it comes to sharing Internet access. Who gets to connect to the Internet?

Home networking may be the answer here. In 2001, PC networks could be found in about 6 million online households, and by 2005, this number is projected to increase to about 23 million, or one-third of Internet-connected homes (Emling, 2002b).

ZOOM IN   14.9
Go to **www.ablongman.com/medoffkaye1e,** the Companion Website for this text, to see how a networked home works.

If you have one phone line and one cable line running into your home but have two or more computers, you'll probably want to set up an inhome network. This allows more than just sharing Internet access. With an inhome network, you can share a printer, share files, and play multiple-user games. There are several ways to set up a home network. You can wire your house with data cable, connect through your phone line, or run Ethernet cable across the house from one computer to another (Croal & Jaffe, 2002).

Simple home networking isn't enough to meet most people's growing demands. For instance, an inhome dial-up Internet connection just can't compete with the high-speed services available. It's not just a matter of speed; it's a matter of quality, too. Newer game consoles, like PlayStation2 and Xbox, and new entertainment systems will deliver digital music, recorded television shows, and streaming video within the next few years to network-connected televisions. These systems will all rely on a high-speed connection to deliver the highest-quality experience. Cable and DSL modem connections, also known as **broadband Internet services**, are the new gateways to the Internet:

- **Cable.** Cable companies provide television channels via fiber optic cable/coaxial cable connection or just through coaxial cable, and they can deliver Internet access over the same connection. The large bandwidth is the key to the speed of delivery. A cable modem connection can many carry more bits of data than a dial-up modem and thus deliver the Internet 100 times faster (Franklin, 2002b).
- **DSL.** DSL is a very high-speed connection that uses telephone lines. Voice conversation only uses a part of the bandwidth that's available on copper telephone wires. DSL uses the extra bandwidth for Internet delivery. In other words, you can connect to the Internet and talk on the telephone at the same time using a DSL line (Franklin, 2002a).

Whether you use a cable or DSL service, it will cost you about twice as much as a standard dial-up service. Even so, the monthly cost hasn't kept users away from broadband. In 2001–2002, about one in five home Internet users paid for high-speed access, with about 10 percent to 13 percent selecting cable and 7 percent selecting DSL (Berquist, 2002; Elkin, 2002b). By 2003, broadband use had increased to about 28 percent of U.S. homes, which still left about seven out of ten homes with dial-up Internet service ("Broadband Use Increases," 2003).

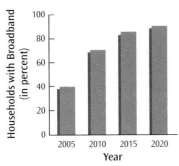

Broadband–U.S. Household Penetration Forecast

Source: "Residential Broadband Forecasts," 2002.

With home networking and broadband access, family members and roommates can all have high-speed, private access to the Internet. Unlike the community atmosphere that goes with television viewing, Internet use is largely a private activity. Only on rare occasions do people gather to use the Internet. Critics charge that home networking and broadband service make Internet access so convenient that individuals prefer to retreat to their private corners, rather than associate with others. And so while the utility of home networking and broadband is beneficial, it could lead to increased social isolation and less conversation among household members.

A Wireless World

To encourage settlement of the American West in the mid 1800s, prominent newspaper editor Horace Greeley urged, "Go west, young man, go west." If he were alive today, he would probably exhort us to venture into an even newer territory with "Go wireless, young man, go wireless."

Wired home networking may work for many households, but it can be difficult to figure out and people get tired of tripping over all those cables and wires. The household of the future will toss out those old wired connections in favor of wireless ones.

Wireless fidelity, more commonly known as **WiFi**, unleashes us from the miles of spaghetti-like cables and wires that hold us hostage to wall space and points of access. Do you want to surf the Internet while sitting in your backyard? You can. Do you and your roommate want to use the Internet at the same time from your own computers? No problem.

WiFi became accessible to consumers when Apple introduced its AirPort Base Station in 1999 (Levy & Stone, 2002). Since then, several companies have come out with wireless routers that let you receive wireless signals via any Mac or PC that has a wireless card. Once you have added the wireless card, you can simply plug your Internet connection into your wireless router, which then beams cyberdata to your computer.

WiFi is about more than just being able to network your home computers. It makes it possible to pick up Internet signals from almost anywhere. You can't see them and you can't feel them, but in many cafés, coffeehouses, airports, universities, and other public places, Internet signals are bouncing off the walls and through the walls—like cordless phone wireless signals that travel from room to room. Wireless signals also often spill as far as 1,500 feet into outdoor spaces (Levy, 2001). Like a cell phone, WiFi operates as a kind of radio. The WiFi standard, officially known as 802.11, finds its home on a part of the radio frequency (2.4 gigahertz) that's designated for microwaves and cordless phones; it's low powered and unregulated by the FCC (Johnston, 2002; Levy & Stone, 2002).

WiFi is also about more than getting on the Internet. Forget about the mess of cords strung across and under your desk. Thanks to Bluetooth's short-range wireless technology, your computer, printer, peripheral, and mobile devices can all communicate wirelessly (Croal, 2002a).

Wireless isn't perfect. Some of its disadvantages include the expense of purchasing an access point (a wireless router-type of device) and the expense and hassle of installing a wireless card into your PC. In addition, the speed of data transmission may fluctuate, and WiFi can interfere with cordless phones and satellite radio; wireless signals are also sometimes blocked by walls and other solid objects. The best wireless signal is obtained in a large, unobstructed space, like an airport terminal or a large office, that has few ceiling-to-floor walls. Despite these issues, once wireless has been set up, it's quick and easy to use and compatible with most computers and hand-held devices (Rocks, 2002; Tyson, 2002a).

Wireless capability is positioned to change the way we use our computers and otherwise function in our everyday lives. With a hand-held or pocket PC, you'll be able to download the latest news while taking a walk, check your e-mail while ordering lunch, and collect research for your homework assignment while working out in the campus gym. Many universities are already *wireless ready,* which means their students can take their laptops deep into the library stacks, to the student union, or anywhere on campus to surf the Internet. Cerritos, California, was one of the first cities to install wireless transmitters throughout its area, making it the largest "hotspot" in the nation. All Cerritos residents, businesses, and employees have high-speed wireless access from any place in town, whether at a café, at home, or in a city park ("Southern CA Town," 2003). As other cities become wireless, we'll have Internet service available at our fingertips 24/7.

> ⌖ **ZOOM IN**   14.10
> Go to the Companion Website for this text to see how wireless technology works: www.ablongman.com/medoffkaye1e.

Summary

Throughout this book, you have learned how broadcasting had to evolve to survive increased competition from new communication technologies and changing audience needs. Although it's doubtful that broadcasting, as we know it, will ever become obsolete, it may have to carve out its own niche to remain competitive in the modern world of personal communication devices. Industry analysts insist that people will continue to turn to broadcast radio and television to fulfill their entertainment and information needs, but it could be that the needs served in the future will be very different than those served today. In all likelihood, broadcasting will remain an important source of information and entertainment that appeals to the masses, but it will yield to newer communication technologies for the delivery of personalized news and services.

New communication technologies are creating a world in which the mass media are becoming more personal. Users determine which types of news stories they want to receive, what types of information are relevant to their lives, and when and where they want to be exposed to information. Commercial messages are tailored to personal characteristics and lifestyles. The electronic media will still reach the masses, but they'll reach people on a more personal level.

Enter the **grid.** Imagine riding in a car that's automatically steering you to your destination while also scanning your stock portfolio in 3-D, transmitting your vital statistics to your physician as part of your annual exam, knowing that your mechanic is monitoring your car's performance for engine trouble, and keeping an eye on your favorite television program. Also, you're wearing an ensemble that was coordinated by microchips embedded in your body.

More advanced than any current technology, the grid is a "linkage of many servers into a single system in which complex computing tasks are broken down and parceled out among the various machines" (Foroohar, 2002, p. 34J). It's sort of a super supercomputer. The grid acts as a "universal translator between previously incompatible computer systems. They can also turn information into visual representation of, or solution to, a problem" (Foroohar, 2002, p. 34J).

Actor Tom Cruise tries to escape the grid in the movie *The Minority Report.*

Big businesses are clearing the way for the grid, which they consider to be one of the most advantageous and time- and money-saving inventions of the last 200 years. By embedding microchips in inanimate objects (and even in humans), companies can link to each other, to consumers, to governments, and to other institutions. The director of grid computing for Sun Microsystems claims, "The nineteenth century was about the steam engine, and the twentieth century was about the combustion engine. I believe the twenty-first century will be about grid engines" (Foroohar, 2002, p. 34L).

The grid has the potential of creating a real-life version of *The Minority Report,* in which the hero, played by Tom Cruise, is flooded with personalized ads and followed at every move. He reaches his breaking point and discovers that the only way to escape the grid is to have a black-market eyeball transplant. Privacy advocates fear that such intrusion could become a reality as soon as 2012. Others claim, however, that consumers will always have the ability to disable smart chips and to control the information collected about and transmitted to them.

References

CHAPTER 1

Bangemann, M., & Oreja, M. (1997). Green paper on the convergence of the telecommunications, media and information technology sectors, and the implications for regulation towards an information society approach. Available online: http://europa.eu.ent/ISPO/convergencegp/greenp.html.

Bonchek, M. (1997). *From broadcast to netcast: The Internet and the flow of political information.* Doctoral dissertation, Harvard University, Cambridge, MA. Available online: www.esri.salford.ac.uk/ESRCResearchproject/papers/bonch97.pdf [Retrieved June 30, 2004].

Chester, J., & Larson, G. (2002, January 7). Something old, something new. *The Nation.* Available online: www.thenation.com/docPrint.mhtml?i=20020107&s=chester.

Corporation for Public Broadcasting. (2003). Time spent with media. Available online: www.cpb.org.

Dizard, W. (2000). *Old media, new media.* New York: Longman.

How many online? (2001). *NUA Surveys.* Available online: www.nua.ie/surveys [Retrieved January 14, 2002].

Kaye, B. K., & Johnson, T. J. (2003). From here to obscurity: The Internet and media substitution theory. *Journal of the American Society for Information Science and Technology, 54*(3), 260–273.

Kaye, B., & Medoff, N. (2001). *The World Wide Web: A mass communication perspective.* Mountain View, CA: Mayfield.

Markus, M. (1987). Toward a "critical mass" theory of interactive media: Universal access, interdependence and diffusion. *Communication Research, 14*(5), 491–511.

Medoff, N., Tanquary, T., & Helford, P. (1994). *Creating TV projects.* White Plains, NY: Knowledge Industry.

National Cable Television Association. (2003). Industry overview. Available online: www.ncta.com.

National Telecommunication Information Agency. (1999). Falling through the Net: Defining the digital divide. Available online: www.ntia.doc.gov/ntiahome/digitaldivide.

Neufeld, E. (1997, May 5). Where are the audiences going? *MediaWeek, 7*(18), S22–S29.

Nielsen Media Research. (2003). Data based on NTI people meter sample. Available online: www.tvb.org/rcentral/mediatrendstrack/tv/timespent.asp.

Pavlik, J. (1996). *New media technologies.* Boston: Allyn & Bacon.

Potter, W. (1998). *Media literacy.* Thousand Oaks, CA: Sage.

Pruitt, S. (2002, September 25). Online piracy blamed for drop in CD sales. *PCWorld.com.* Available online: www.pcworld.com/news/article/0,aid,86326,00.asp.

Roper Starch. (1997). America's watching: Public attitudes toward television. Available online: www.fcc.gov/Bureaus/Mass_Media/Notices/1999/fcc99353.pdf.

Schramm, W. (1988). *The story of human communication: Cavepainting to microchip.* New York: HarperCollins.

Schramm, W. (1954). *The process and effects of mass communication.* Urbana, IL: University of Illinois Press.

Shane, E. (1999). *Selling electronic media.* Boston: Focal Press.

Shannon, C., & Weaver, W. (1949). *The mathematical theory of mass communication.* Urbana, IL: University of Illinois Press.

Silverblatt, A. (1995). *Media literacy.* Westport, CT: Praeger.

Sterling, C., & Kittross, J. (2002). *Stay tuned: A history of American broadcasting.* Mahwah, NJ: Erlbaum.

Straubhaar, J., & LaRose, R. (2004). *Media now.* 4th ed. Belmont, CA: Wadsworth.

Walker, J., & Ferguson, D. (1998). *The broadcast television industry.* Boston: Allyn & Bacon.

Why Internet advertising? (1997, May 5). *MediaWeek, 7*(18), S8–S13.

CHAPTER 2

Banning, W. (1946). *Commercial broadcasting pioneer: WEAF experiment, 1922–1926.* Cambridge, MA: Harvard University Press.

Benjamin, L. (1993, Summer). In search of the "radio music box" memo. *Journal of Broadcasting and Electronic Media,* 325–335.

Broadcasters start digital radio service. (2003, June 17). *USA Today.* Available online: www.usatoday.com/tech/news/2003-06-17-digital-radio_x.htm [Retrieved July 1, 2003].

Clinton: "Internet in every hut." (2000). *Reuters Wired News.* Available online: www.wired.com/news/print/0,1294,34065,00.html [Retrieved July 15, 2002].

Clinton unveils plan for "next generation of Internet." (1996). CNN. Available online: www.cnn.com/US/9610/10/clinton.internet [Retrieved July 15, 2002].

Goodman, M., & Gring, M. (2003). The radio act of 1927: Progressive ideology, epistemology, and praxis. In M. Hilmes (Ed.), *Connections: A broadcast history reader* (pp. 19–39). Belmont, CA: Wadsworth.

Gordon McLendon and KLIF. (2002). *Encyclopædia Britannica.* Available online: www.britannica.com/eb/article?eu= 130611 [Retrieved December 6, 2003].

Gross, L. (2003). *Telecommunications: Radio, television, and movies in the digital age.* New York: McGraw-Hill.

Hilliard, R., & Keith, M. (2001). *The broadcast century and beyond.* 3rd ed. Boston: Focal Press.

Lessing, L. (1956). *Man of high fidelity: Edwin Howard Armstrong.* Philadelphia: Lippincott.

Lewis, T. (1991). *Empire of the air: The men who made radio.* New York: HarperCollins.

Public interest, convenience, and necessity. (1929, November). *Radio News.* Available online: www.antiqueradios.com/frc.shtml.

Settel, I. (1960). *A pictorial history of radio.* New York: Citadel Press.

Sterling, C., & Kittross, J. (2002). *Stay tuned: A history of American broadcasting.* Mahwah, NJ: Erlbaum.

Whitmore, S. (2004, January 23). Satellite radio static. *Forbes. com.* Available online: www.forbes.com/columnists/2004/01/23/0123Whitmore.html.

CHAPTER 3

Auletta, K. (1991). *Three blind mice: How the TV networks lost their way.* New York: Random House.

Bellamy, R., & Walker, J. (1996). *Television and the remote control: Grazing on a vast wasteland.* New York: Guilford Press.

Faulk, J. (1964). *Fear on trial.* New York: Simon & Schuster.

Federal Communications Commission (FCC). (1998, November). Digital television consumer information. Available online: www.fcc.gov/Bureaus/Engineering_Technology/Factsheets/dtv9811.html [Retrieved April 15, 2003].

Foley, K. (1979). *The political blacklist in the broadcast industry: The decade of the 1950s.* New York: Arno.

Gillmor, D. (2004, January 11). Putting ads in the hands of the public. *San Jose Mercury News.* Available online: www.siliconvalley.com/mld/siliconvalley/business/columnists/dan_gillmor/7684606.htm [Retrieved January 20, 2004].

Greppi, M. (2001, November 19). NBC, Young and Granite roll the dice. *Electronic Media.* Available online: www.craini2i.com/em/archive.mv?count=3&story= em178785427096220069 [Retrieved December 8, 2001].

Halberstam, D. (1993). *The fifties.* New York: Ballantine Books.

Hendrik, G. (1987). *The selected letters of Mark Van Doren.* London, LA: Louisiana State University Press.

Higgins, J. (2004, January 5). The shape of things to come: TiVo's got a gun. *Broadcasting & Cable,* p. 33.

Hilliard, R., & Keith, M. (2001). *The broadcast century and beyond: A biography of American broadcasting.* Boston: Allyn & Bacon.

Home video index. (2004). New York: Nielsen Media Research.

Hutchinson, T. (1950). *Here is television: Your window to the world.* New York: Hastings House.

Jessell, H. (2002, August 5). Sink or swim: With a set-top box of their own, TV broadcasters can take their place in the digital future. *Broadcasting & Cable,* pp. 14–16.

Labaton, S. (2003, September 4). U.S. Court blocks plan to ease rule on media owners. *New York Times.* Available online: www.nytimes.com/2003/09/04/business/media/04FCC.html?hp=&pagewanted=print&position= [Retrieved October 8, 2003].

Maynard, J. (2004, February 4). TV-on-DVD popularity a threat to networks. *Arizona Republic,* p. D1.

Mitchell, C. (1970). *Cavalcade of broadcasting.* Chicago: Follett Books.

Ritchie, M. (1994). *Please stand by: A prehistory of television.* Woodstock, NY: Overlook Press.

Romano, A. (2004, January 5). The shape of things to come: Keeping up with the nerds. *Broadcasting & Cable,* p. 32.

Schatzkin, P. (2003). *The boy who invented television.* Burtonsville, MD: Team Com Books.

Schwartz, E. (2000, September/October). Who really invented television? *Technology Review.* Available online: www.technologyreview.com/articles/Schwartz0900.asp.

Smith, F., Wright, J., & Ostroff, D. (1998). *Perspectives on radio and television.* 4th ed. Mahwah, NJ: Erlbaum.

Sterling, C., & Kittross, J. (2002). *Stay tuned: A history of American broadcasting.* Mahwah, NJ: Erlbaum.

Vaughn, R. (1972). *Only victims: A study of show business blacklisting.* New York: Putnam.

Walker, J., & Ferguson, D. (1998). *The broadcast television industry.* Boston: Allyn & Bacon.

CHAPTER 4

Browning, L. (2003, November 23). New rules may set off a cellphone scramble. *New York Times.* Available online: www.nytimes.com/2003/11/23/business/yourmoney/23cell.html [Retrieved December 10, 2003].

Carroll, R. (2003, August 5). Hanging it up. *Redding Searchlight,* pp. C-8, C7

Chicago v. FCC. (1999). Available online: www.techlawjournal.com/broadband/1991209.htm [Retrieved April 5, 2002].

Chin, F. (1978). *Cable television: A comprehensive bibliography.* New York: IFI/Plenum.

Clarke, A. (1945, October). Extra-terrestrial relays. *Wireless World,* pp. 305–308.

Consumers Union. (2002). Abusing consumers and impeding competition: The state of cable television industry, 2002. Available online: www.commondreams.org/news2002/0724-10.htm [Retrieved September 10, 2002].

Creno, G. (2002, July 24). Teen buyers fuel boom in cellular accessories. *Arizona Republic,* p. D1.

Davis, L. (1998). *The billionaire shell game: How cable baron John Malone and assorted corporate tycoons invented a future nobody wanted.* New York: Doubleday.

Federal Communications Commission (FCC). (1980). Cable television exclusivity rules and inquiry into the economic relationship between broadcasting and cable television. 79 FCC 2d 663.

Federal Communications Commission (FCC). (1976). Report and index in docket 20487. 57 FCC 2d 625.

Federal Communications Commission (FCC). (1972). Cable television report and order. 36 FCC 2d 143.

Graham, J. (2002, March 12). Video on demand lifts off. *Arizona Republic,* p. D3.

Greenville, SC, tops in U.S. cell phones-study. (2002, October 4). *Wireless Review.* Available online: www.wirelessreview.com/microsites/newsarticle.asp?mode=print&newsarticleid=2639899&releaseid=&srid=11393&magazineid=9&siteid=3.

Hahn, D., & Dudley, P. (2002, May). The disconnect between law and policy analysis: A case study of drivers and cell phones. Available online: http://aiebrookings.pjdoland.com/amin/pdffiles/working_02_07.pdf.

Hazlett, T. (1989). Wiring the constitution for cable. *Regulation: The Cato Review of business and government.* Available online: www.cato.org/pubs/regulation/regv12n1/reg12n1-hazlett.html.

HBO v. FCC. (1977). 567 F. 2d 9.

Head, S., Spann, T., & McGregor, M. (2001). *Broadcasting in America: A survey of electronic media.* Boston: Houghton Mifflin.

Higgins, J. (2003, August 25). DBS customers happier than cable users. *Broadcasting & Cable,* p. 3.

Internet radio coming to a car near you. (2003, May 19). *Dayton Business Journal.* Available online: http://dayton.bizjournals.com/dayton/stories/2003/05/19/daily1.html [Retrieved July 1, 2003].

Kageyama, Y. (2003, July 10). Cellphones with cameras creating trouble. *Arizona Republic,* p. A18.

Kanellos, M. (2003, May 19). Start-up aims to improve WiFi calls. C/NET News.Com. Available online: http://news.com.com/2100-1037-1006547.html.

Massey, K., & Baran, S. (2001). *Introduction to telecommunications: Converging technologies.* Mountain View, CA: Mayfield.

National Cable and Telecommunications Association (NCTA). (2004). Television and cable households: 1983–2003. Available online: www.ncta.com/Docs/PageContent.cfm.pageID=304 [Retrieved July 1, 2004].

Number of VOD users to reach 17 million. (2002, June 18). *NUA Internet Surveys.* Available online: www.nua.ie/surveys/index.cgi?f=VS&art_id=905358030&rel=true.

Parsons, P. (1996). Two tales of a city. *Journal of Broadcasting and Electronic Media, 40*(3), 354–365.

Parsons, P., & Frieden, R. (1998). *The cable and satellite television industries.* Boston: Allyn & Bacon.

Phillips, M. (1972). *CATV: A history of community antenna television.* Evanston, IL: Northwestern University Press.

Sidener, J. (2002, February 2). Census finds technology gains across age groups. *USA Today.* Available online: www.usatoday.com/tech/news/2002/02/04/tech-census.htm [Retrieved May 5, 2002].

Somayaji, C. (2003, November 28). Satellite TV lures cable clients. *Rocky Mountain News.* Available online: www.rockymountainnews.com/drmn/business/article/0,1299,DRMN_4_2462881,00.html

Sterling, C., & Kittross, J. (2002). *Stay tuned: A history of American broadcasting.* Mahwah, NJ: Erlbaum.

Television antennas for apartments. (1947, May). *Electronics,* p. 96.

Throw away your set-top box. (2003, September 10). *Wired News.* Available online: www.wired.com/news/technology/0,1282,60377,00.html?tw=wn_story_related [Retrieved September 12, 2003].

Veronis, Suhler, & Stevenson Media Merchant Bank. (2003). Communication industry forecast, 2003. Available online: www.vss.com [Retrieved February 4, 2004].

Yutkin, J. (2002, May). Interview with Don Anderson. Available online: http://cablecenter.org/library/collections/oral_history_detail.cfm?SelectedHistory=198 [Retrieved July 8, 2002].

CHAPTER 5

Almost three-quarters in U.S. online. (2001). *NUA Surveys.* Available online: www.nua.ie/surveys [Retrieved January 14, 2002].

American Internet user survey. (1997). Emerging Technologies Research Group. Available online: http://etrg.findsvp.com/Internet/findf.html [Retrieved January 7, 1998].

Amis, D. (2002, September 21). Weblogs: Online navel gazing? *NetFreedom.* Available online: www.netfreedom.org.

AudioNet. (1997, February 4). What is AudioNet? Available online: www.audionet.com/about.

Berkman, R. I. (1994). *Find it online.* New York: McGraw-Hill.

Berniker, M. (1995, October 30). RealAudio software boosts live sound, music onto the Web. *Broadcasting & Cable,* p. 67.

Bimber, B. (1996). The Internet and political transformation. Available online: www.sscuf.usb.edu/~survey/poltran2.htm.

Blood, R. (2001). Weblogs: A history and perspective. *Inkblotsmag.com.* Available online: www.inksblotsmag.com/features/essays/Weblogs.php.

Bollier, D. (1989). How Americans watch TV: A nation of grazers. *Channels Magazine* [Special Report], pp. 41–52.

Bonchek, M. S. (1997). *From broadcast to netcast: The Internet and the flow of political information.* Doctoral dissertation, Harvard University, Cambridge, MA. Available online: www.esri.salford.ac.uk/ESRCResearchproject/papers/bonch97.pdf.

Bowman, L. M. (2002, September 5). Death knell sounded for Web radio? CNETNews. Available online: www.cnet.com.

Broadcasting & Cable Yearbook 2002–2003. (2002). Newton, MA: Reed Elsevier.

Bromley, R. V., & Bowles, D. (1995). The impact of Internet use on traditional news media. *Newspaper Research Journal, 16*(2), 14–27.

By the numbers. (2004, April 26). *E-week,* p. 18.

Cai, X. (2002, August). *Are computers and traditional media functionally equivalent?* Paper presented at the annual meeting of the Association for Education in Journalism and Mass Communication, Miami, FL.

Callaghan, D., & Gibson, S. (2001, November 5). E-biz alternatives. *E-week,* pp. 11, 14.

Changing online population. (2000). *Pew American and Internet Life.* Available online: www.pewinternet.org/reports.

Clear Channel returning to Net streaming. (2001, June 18). *Industry Standard.* Available online: www.thestandard.com/article

Cohen, W. (2000, March 6). Napster is rocking the music industry: The popular Web site as powerful enemies. *U.S. News & World Report, 128*(9), 41.

Cole, J. I. (2001). *The UCLA Internet report 2001: Surveying the digital future.* Available online: www.ccp.ucla.edu.

Cortese, A. (1997, February 24). A way out of the Web maze. *Business Week,* pp. 95–101.

Croal, N. (2003, March 17). This can't be legal. *Newsweek,* p. 61.

Daily Internet activities. (2003). *Pew Internet and American Life.* Available online: www.pewinternet.org/reports/index.asp.

Dizard, W., Jr. (2000). *Old media, new media.* New York: Longman.

Eager, B. (1994). *Using the World Wide Web.* Indianapolis, IN: Que Corporation.

Emling, S. (2002a, July 21). Sound machines. *Atlanta Journal-Constitution,* pp. Q1, Q4.

Emling, S. (2002b, June 9). Upstarts send AOL a message. *Atlanta Journal-Constitution,* pp. E1, E4.

Ferguson, D. A., & Perse, E. M. (1993). Media and audience influences on channel repertoire. *Journal of Broadcasting and Electronic Media, 37*(1), 31–47

First U.S. Web page made its debut 10 years ago. (2001, December 13). *Knoxville News-Sentinel,* p. C1.

Foley, M. J. (2003, June 16). Microsoft blog policy coming down the pike? Microsoft Watch. Available online: www.microsoft-watch.com/article2/0,4248,1128705,00.asp.

Foust, J. (2002). The Internet and the World Wide Web. In A. E. Grant and J. H. Meadows (Eds.), *Communication technology update* (pp. 165–174). Boston: Focal Press.

Fowler, G. A. (2002, November 18). The best way . . . Find a blog. *Wall Street Journal,* p. R8.

Frauenfelder M., & Kelly, K. (2000, Winter). Blogging. *Whole Earth,* pp. 52–54.

Freese, D. D. (2002). New media, new power. Tech Central Station. Available online: http://techcentralstation.com/1051.

Getting serious online. (2002). Pew Research Center. Available online: www.pewinternet.org/reports.

Greenspan, R. (2003, July 24). Blogging by the numbers. Click Z Network. Available online: www.clickz.com/big_picture/applications/article.php/2238831.

GVU's tenth WWW user survey. (1998). Georgia Institute of Technology, Graphic and Visualization and Usability Center. Available online: www.cc.gatech.edu/gvu/user_surveys/survey-1998-10.

Hafner, K. (2001, December 6). The 30-year path of e-mail. *New York Times.* Available online: www.nytimes.com.

Half a billion online. (2001, October 1). *NUA Surveys.* Available online: www.nua.ie/surveys [Retrieved January 14, 2002].

Half of all college students prepared to surf Internet. (1999, July 8). Click Z Network. Available online: www.clickz.com.

Hall, S. (2003, August 27). Soap uses online vote to choose cast. *Marketing Wonk.* Available online: www.marketingwonk.com/archives/categories/media_convergence.

Hamilton, A. (2003, April 7). Best of Warblogs. *Time,* p. 91.

Haring, B. (1997, August 11). Web sites strive to brand their names into users' minds. *USA Today,* p. 4D.

Heeter, C. (1985). Program selection with abundance of choice. *Human Communication Research, 12*(1), 126–152.

Heeter, C., D'Allessio, D., Greenberg, B., & McVoy, S. D. (1988). Cableviewing behaviors: An electronic assessment. In C. Heeter and B. Greenberg (Eds.), *Cableviewing* (pp. 51–63). Norwood, NJ: Ablex.

Hicks, M. (2004, August 17). AOL releases Netscape browser update. *E-week.* Available online: www.eweek.com/article2/0%2C1759%2C1637042%C00.asp.

Ho, D. (2002, June 21). Royalites set for Web songs. *Tennessean,* p. 1E, 4E.

Homes with Net access watch less TV. (1998). ZDNet. Available online: www.zdnet.com/zdnn/stories.

How many online? (2002). *NUA Surveys.* Available online: www.nua.com/surveys.

Husted, B. (2002, January 20). And the beat goes on. *Atlanta Journal-Constitution,* pp. P1, P4.

IM users increasing in U.S. (2001, November 19). *NUA Surveys.* Available online: www.nua.ie/surveys [Retrieved January 14, 2002].

Internet and American life. (2000). Pew Research Center. Available online: www.pewinternet.org. [Retrieved January 14, 2002].

Internet eats into TV time. (1996, January 12). *St. Louis Post Dispatch*, pp. 6C, 8C.

Internet history. (1996). Silverlink LLC. Available online: www.olympic.net/poke/IIP/history.html.

Internet news audience goes ordinary: Online newcomers more middle-brow, less work oriented. (1999). Pew Research Center. Available online: www.people-press.org/tech98mor.htm [Retrieved January 14, 2002].

Internet penetration demographics. (2004, April 19). *E-week*, p. 18.

Irvine, M. (2002, September 16). Eighty-six percent of all collegians jump on Net to study, stay in touch. *Knoxville News-Sentinel*, p. A3.

Jesdanun, A. (2001, October 14). In online logs, Web authors personalize attacks, retaliation. *Florida Times-Union*. Available online: www.Jacksonville.com/tu-online/stories/101401/bus_7528493.html.

Johnson, T. J., & Kaye, B. K. (in press). Wag the blog: How reliance on traditional media and the Internet influence credibility of weblogs among blog users. *Journalism and Mass Communication Quarterly.*

Johnson, T. J., & Kaye, B. K. (2002). Webelievabilty: A path model examining how convenience and reliance on the Web predict online credibility. *Journalism and Mass Communication Quarterly, 79*(3), 619–642.

Judge cues Napster's death music. (2002, September 3). *Wired News*. Available online: www.wirednews.com.

Kaye, B. K. (1998). Uses and gratifications of the World Wide Web: From couch potato to web potato. *New Jersey Journal of Communication, 6*(1), 21–40.

Kaye, B. K., & Johnson, T. J. (2004). Blog day afternoon: Weblogs as a source of information about the war on Iraq. In R. D. Berenger (Ed.), *Global media go to war* (pp. 293–303). Spokane, WA: Marquette.

Kaye, B. K. & Johnson, T. J. (2003). From here to obscurity: The Internet and media substitution theory. *Journal of the American Society for Information Science and Technology, 54*(3), 260–273.

Kaye, B. K., & Johnson, T. J. (2002). Online and in the know: Uses and gratifications of the Web for political information. *Journal of Broadcasting and Electronic Media, 46*(1), 54–71.

Kaye, B. K., & Medoff, N. J. (2001). *The World Wide Web: A mass communication perspective*. Mountain View, CA: Mayfield.

Keefe, B. (2002, May 5). RealNetworks aims to be cable TV for the Web. *Atlanta Journal-Constitution*, p. E3.

Kiplinger monitor. (2003, October). *Kiplinger's*, p. 24.

Kolata, G. (2001, October 31). Veiled messages of terrorist may lurk in cyberspace. *New York Times*. Available online: www.nytimes.com/2001/10/30/science/physical/30STEG.html.

Kreschbaumer, K. (2003, January 20). Dotcom scores with TV Web sites. *Broadcasting & Cable*, pp. 1, 69.

Kreschbaumer, K. (2002, September 2). Making Internet radio local. *Broadcasting & Cable*, p. 28.

Krigel, B. L. (1999, May 11). The Grateful Dead for MP3—With limits. CNET. Available online: http://news.com.com/2100-1023-225691.html.

Krol, C. (1997, September 29). Internet promos bolster networks' fall programs. *Advertising Age*, p. 40.

Krol, E. (1995). *The whole Internet*. Sebastopol, CA: O'Reilly & Associates.

Kurtz, H. (2002, July 31). How Weblogs keep the media honest. *Washington Post*. Available online: www.washingtonpost.com.

Let's make a deal. (2001, March 5). *Newsweek*, p. 63.

Levy, S. (2003a, March 29). Blogger's delight. MSNBC. Available online: www.msnbc.com.

Levy, S. (2003b, September 22). Courthouse rock? *Newsweek*, p. 52.

Levy, S. (2002a, July 15). Labels to Net radio: Die now. *Newsweek*, p. 51.

Levy, S. (2002b, August 26). Living in the blog-osphere. *Newsweek*, pp. 42–45.

Levy, S. (2002c, May 20). Will the blogs kill old media? *Newsweek*, p. 52.

Levy, S. (1995, February 27). TechnoMania. *Newsweek*, pp. 25–29.

Liedtke, M. (2000, September 26). Grateful Dead isn't laid back when it comes to fighting music pirates. Canoe.com. Available online: http://canoe.ca/JamMusicArtistsG/gratefuldead.html.

Lin, C. A. (2001). Audience attributes, media supplementation, and likely online service adoption. *Mass Communication and Society, 4*, 19–38.

Listserv. (2003). *Webopedia*. Available online: www.webopedia.com/TERM/L/Listserv.html.

Majority of U.S. college students on Net. (2002, October 7). *NUA Surveys*. Available online: www.nua.com/surveys/index

Mandese, J. (1995, March 13) Snags aside, nets enamored of 'net. *Advertising Age*, p. S20.

Marc Andreessen, co-founder of Netscape. (1997). Jones Telecommunications and Multimedia Encyclopedia Homepage. Available online: www.digitalcentury.com/encyclo/update/andreess.htm [Retrieved January 21, 1998].

Markus, M. L. (1990). Toward a "critical mass" theory of interactive media. In J. Fulk & C. Steinfield (Eds.), *Organizations and communication technology* (pp. 194–218). Newbury Park, CA: Sage.

Millard, E. (2003, May 7). The bottom line of the new browser wars. *E-commerce Times*. Available online: www.ecommercetimes.com/perl/story/21450.html.

Miller, S. C. (2002, September 5). For the obsolete-TV owner, a smart PC screen may serve. *New York Times*. Available online: www.nytimes.com/2002/09/05/technology.

More fun than TV? (2002, May 13). *Newsweek*, p. 40P.

Most Net users won't pay for music. (2001, October, 2). *NUA Surveys*. Available online: www.nua.ie/surveys [Retrieved January 14, 2002].

Napster previews new service. (2002, January 10). *New York Times*. Available online: www.nytimes.com/aponline/technology/AP-Napster.html.

Net and TV are not mutually exclusive. (2001, December 17). *NUA Surveys*. Available online: www.nua.ie/surveys [Retrieved January 5, 2002].

Neufeld, E. (1997, May 5). Where are audiences going? *MediaWeek, 7*(18), S22–S29.

Nie, N., & Ebring, L. (2000). Study offers early look at how home Internet is changing daily life. Available online: www.stanford.edu/dept/news/pr/00/000216internet.html.

Noack, D. R. (1996, June). Radio, radio: Radio stations are blooming on the Internet as the Net becomes a radio medium. *Internet World*. Available online: www.webweek.com.

Outing, S. (2002, July 18). Weblogs: Put them to work in your newsroom. PoynterOnline. Available online: www.pointer.org.

Palser, B. (2002). Journalistic blogging. *American Journalism Review, 24*(6), 58.

Pavlik, J. V. (1996). *New media technology: Cultural and commercial perspectives*. Boston: Allyn & Bacon.

Perse, E. M., & Dunn, D. G. (1998). The utility of home computers and media use: Implications of multimedia and connectivity. *Journal of Broadcasting and Electronic Media, 42*, 435–456.

Petrozzello, D. (1995, September 11). Radio + listeners: A match made on the Internet. *Broadcasting & Cable*, p. 34.

Progressive Networks launches RealAudio Player Plus. (1996, August 18). RealAudio. Available online: www.realaudio.com/prognet/pr/playerplus.html.

Quittner, J. (1995, May 1). Radio free cyberspace. *Time*, p. 91.

Radio fans tuning online. (2001, April 9). *NUA Surveys*. Available online: www.nua.ie/surveys [Retrieved January 14, 2002].

Radio stations shut down Internet audio. (2001, April 22). *Valdosta Daily Times*, p. 8A.

Rafter, M. (1996a, October 30). Progressive Networks wants to drown out all other Web sounds. *St. Louis Post Dispatch*, p. 5C.

Rafter, M. (1996b, January 24). RealAudio fulfills Web's online sound promise. *St. Louis Post Dispatch*, p. 13B.

Reader demographics. (2002, June 25). Available online: www.andrewsullivan.com.

Reynolds, G. (2002, January 9). A technological reformation. Tech Central Station. Available online: www.techcentralstation.com/1051.

Richtel, M. (2002, September 3). Napster says it is likely to be liquidated. *New York Times*. Available online: www.nytimes.com.

Richtel, M. (2001, November, 29). Free music is expected to surpass Napster. *New York Times*. Available online: www.nytimes.com/2001/11/29/technology/29MUSI.html [Retrieved November 29, 2001].

Roberts, J. L. (2003, October 13). Pay 2 play. *Newsweek*, pp. 47–48.

Rosenberg, S. (2002). Much ado about blogging. *Salon*. Available online: www.salon.com/tech/col/rose/2002/05/10/blogs.

Rubin, A. M. (1984). Ritualized and instrumental television viewing. *Journal of Communication, 34*(3), 67–77.

Rupley, S. (1996). TV shows could be the next wave in Web content. *PC Magazine*. Available online: www.pcmgn.com/search/1502/pcm00017.htm.

Schwartz, J. (2001, October 29). Page by page history of the Web. *New York Times*. Available online: www.nytimes.com/2001/10/29/technology/ebusiness.

Segailer, S. [Executive producer]. (1999). *Nerds 2.0.1: A brief history of the Internet* [Television broadcast]. Public Broadcasting Service.

Seipp, C. (2002). Online uprising. *American Journalism Review, 24*(5), 42.

Self, C. (2003, September 22). Admitted copyright offenders avoid suits. *Daily Beacon*, p. 1.

Shane, E. (1999). *Selling electronic media*. Boston: Focal Press.

Shaw, R. (1998, March 16). Bandwidth, ads make Web TV-like. *Electronic Media*, p. 18.

Shifting Internet population recasts the digital divide debate. (2003, April 16). Pew Internet and American Life. Available online: www.pewinternet.org/releases.

Silence, M. (2003, October 3). Limbaugh's faux pas is Web hit. *Knoxville News-Sentinel*, p. A22.

Spors, K. K. (2003, October 26). Musicians get little from 99-cent songs. *Knoxville News-Sentinel* [*Wall Street Journal* Supplement], p. WSJ3.

Stellin, S. (2001, November 1). Web addresses sprout new suffixes, needed or not. *New York Times*. Available online: www.nytimes.com/2001/11/01/technology/circuits.

Stempel, G., III, Hargrove, T., & Bernt, J. P. (2000). Relation of growth of use of the Internet to changes in media use from 1995 to 1999. *Journalism and Mass Communication Quarterly, 77*, 71–79.

Stone, B. (2004, January 12). OK with pay for play. *Newsweek*, p. 10.

Students would pay for Napster. (2001, April 11). *NUA Surveys*. Available online: www.nua.ie/surveys [Retrieved January 14, 2002].

Taylor, C. (1997, July 5). Net use adds to decline in TV use; Radio stable. *Billboard*, p. 85.

Taylor, C. (1996a, November 11). Tube watchers, unite. *MediaWeek*, pp. 9–10.

Taylor, C. (1996b, September 23). Zapping onto the Internet. *MediaWeek*, p. 32.

TCP/IP green thumb: Effective implementation of TCP/IP networks. (1998). *LAN Magazine, 8*(6), 139.

36 billion e-mails per day by 2005. (2001, September 24). *NUA Surveys*. Available online: http://www.nua.ie/surveys [2002, January 14].

TV v. Net: Not a zero-sum game. (1998). *Wired*. Available online: www.wirednews.com.

TV watching down as Net use rises. (2001, May 14). Scarborough Research. Available online: www.nua.ie.

Weblogs offer forum for attack reactions. (2001, October 12). *USA Today*. Available online: www.usatoday.com/tech/news/2001/10/12/web-logs.htm.

What's your daily dose? (1997, November 18). *PC Magazine*, p. 9.

Why Internet advertising.? (1997, May 5). *MediaWeek*, pp. S8–S13.

Wolcott, J. (2002, May). Blog nation. *Business 2.0* Available online: www.business2.com/articles/mag.

Yahoo! Dictionary Online. (1997). Available online: www.zdnet.com/yil/content.

Yousefzadeh, P. (2003, February 7). Weasel words. Tech Central Station. Available online: www.techcentralstation.com.

Yu, S. (2003). Televised dog show to feature online polling. Poynter Online Journalism. Available online: www.onlinejournalism.com/ojc/topics/index.php?tID=35.

CHAPTER 6

About *Meet the Press*. (2003). MSNBC. Available online: www.msnbc.com/news/102219.asp.

Ahmed, S. (2001). History of radio programming. Available online: http://web.bryant.edu/~history/h364proj/fall_01/ahmed/Other_radio_programs.htm.

Albiniak, P. (2003, May 12). More Oprah crowds out successors. *Broadcasting & Cable*, p. 43.

Albiniak, P., & Bednarski, P. J. (2004, January 26). Happier days at NATPE. *Broadcasting & Cable*, p. 24.

American Family. (2002). PBS.com. Available online: www.pbs.org/lanceloud/american.

Amos 'n' Andy Show. (2003). Museum of Broadcast Communications. Available online: www.museum.tv/archives/etv/A/htmlA/amosnandy/amosnandy.htm.

Atkins, L. (2003, October 3). Finally, liberal radio. *Philadelphia Inquirer*. Available online: www.philly.com/mld/inquirer/news/editorial/6919581.htm.

Bird, J. B. (2003). *Roots*. Museum of Broadcast Communications. Available online: www.museum.tv/archives/etv/R/htmlR/roots/roots.htm.

Broadcasting & Cable Yearbook 2002–2003. (2002). Newton, MA: Reed Elsevier.

Brooks, T., & Marsh, E. (1979). *The complete directory to prime time network TV shows*. New York: Ballantine Books.

Butler, J. G. (2001). *Television: Critical methods and applications*. Cincinnati: Thomson Learning.

Campbell, R. (2000). *Media and culture*. Boston: St. Martin's Press.

Captain Kangaroo. (2003). The Fifties Web. Available online: www.fiftiesweb.com/tv/captain-kangaroo.htm.

CBS buckles under *Reagans* pressure. Tough times for telepics. (2003, November 10). *TelevisionWeek*, p. 10.

Dizard, W., Jr. (2000). *Old media, new media*. New York: Longman.

Dominick, J. R. (1999). *The dynamics of mass communication*. New York: McGraw-Hill.

Eastman, S. T., & Ferguson, D. A. (2002). *Broadcast/Cable/Web programming*. 6th ed. Belmont, CA: Wadsworth.

Falwell says *Teletubbies* character is gay. (1998, February 10). Holland Sentinel Archives. Available online: www.hollandsentinel.com/stories/021099/new_teletubbies.html.

Famous weekly shows. (1994–2002). Old Time Radio. Available online: www.old-time.com/weekly.

Golden years. (1994–2002). Old Time Radio. Available online: www.old-time.com/golden_age/index.html.

Gomery, D. (2003). Movies on television. Museum of Broadcast Communications. Available online: www.museum.tv/archives/etv/M/htmlM/moviewsontel/moviesontel.htm.

Gordon D., & Sigesmund, B. J. (2003, August 11). Queen for a day. *Newsweek*, pp. 50, 52.

Grant, A. E., & Meadows, J. H. (2002). *Communication technology update*. Boston: Focal Press.

Gross, L. S. (2003). *Telecommunications*. Boston: McGraw-Hill.

Gundersen, E. (2002, November 22). Uncovering the real Osbournes. *USA Today*, p. E1.

GVU's tenth WWW user survey. (1998). Georgia Institute of Technology, Graphic and Visualization and Usability Center. Available online: www.cc.gatech.edu/gvu/user_surveys/survey-1998-10.

Harmon, A. (2002, May 23). Digital video recorders give advertisers pause. *New York Times*. Available online: www.nytimes.com/2002/o5/23/technology.

Head, S. W., Sterling, C. H., & Schofield, L. B. (1994). *Broadcasting in America*. Boston: Houghton Mifflin.

Hilliard, R., & Keith, M. (2001). *The broadcast century and beyond*. 3rd ed. Boston: Focal Press.

How NPR works. (2003). National Public Radio. Available online: www.npr.org/about/nprworks.html.

Ingram, B. (2003). *Captain Kangaroo*. TV Party. Available online: www.tvparty.com/lostterrytoons.html.

Java, J. (1985). *Cult TV.* New York: St. Martin's Press.

Jenkins, D. (2002, December 19). From Ozzie to Ozzy. About.com. Available online: http://classictv.about.com/library/weekly/aa121902a.htm.

Johnson, P. (2002). Fox News enjoys new view—From the top. *USA Today,* pp. 1A–2A.

Johnson, T. J., & Kaye, B. K. (2002). Webelievabilty: A path model examining how convenience and reliance on the Web predict online credibility. *Journalism and Mass Communication Quarterly, 79*(3), 619–642.

Kaye, B. K. & Johnson, T. J. (2003). From here to obscurity: The Internet and media substitution theory. *Journal of the American Society for Information Science and Technology, 54*(3), 260–273.

Kaye, B. K., & Johnson, T. J. (2002). *Gone with the Web: Media substitution theory and traditional media in an online world.* Paper presented at the annual meeting of the Broadcast Education Association, Las Vegas, NV.

Klein, S. (2000). It's a myth that Internet journalism is less accurate. Available online: www.content-exchange.com

Lafayette, J. (2003, November 10). *Reagans* pressure shifts to Showtime. *TelevisionWeek,* pp. 1, 38.

Massey, K. B., & Baran, S. J. (1996). *Television criticism.* Dubuque, IA: Kendall/Hunt.

Masterpieces and milestones. (1999, November 1). *Variety,* p. 84.

McGinn, D. (2002, November 11). Guilt free TV. *Newsweek,* pp. 53–59.

Mershan, P. W. (2003, February 28). *Amos 'n' Andy* spurred controversy, and many collectibles. *News Journal.* Available online: www.mansfieldnewsjournal.com/news/stories/20030228/localnews/1078705.html.

NATPE 2000 conference directory. (2000). Santa Monica, CA: National Association of Television Program Executives.

NPR's growth during the last 30 years. (2003). National Public Radio. Available online: www.npr.org/about/growth.html.

Over and history. (2002). National Association of Television Program Executives. Available online: www.natpe.org/about.

Parsons, P. R., & Frieden, R. M. (1998). *The cable and satellite television industries.* Boston: Allyn & Bacon.

Pew Research Center. (2000). Internet sapping broadcast news audience: Investors now go online for quotes, advice. Available online: www.people press.org/media00rpt.htm.

Peyser, M. (2002, November 25). Return to Ozz. *Newsweek,* pp. 80–81.

Peyser, M., & Smith, S. M. (2003, May 26). Idol worship. *Newsweek,* pp. 53–58.

Peyton Place. (2002). Available online: http://members.aol.com/AlisnRod.

Premiere Radio Networks. (2002). Available online: www.premrad.com.

Public Broadcasting Service: An overview. (2002). Public Broadcasting Service. Available online: www.pbs.org/insidepbs/facts/faq1.html.

Public television audience. (2002). Public Broadcasting Service. Available online: www.pbs.org/insidepbs/facts/faq3.html.

Rautiolla-Williams, S. (2003). *The Howdy Doody Show.* Museum of Broadcast Communications. Available online: www.museum.tv/archives/etv/H/htmlH/howdydoodys/howdydoodys.htm.

ReplayTV 4000. (2002). ReplayTV. Available online: www.replaytv.com/video/replaytv/replaytv_4000_features.asp.

Rimmer, T., & Weaver, D. (1987, Spring). Different questions, different answers? Media use and media credibility. *Journalism Quarterly, 64,* 28–36, 44.

Roper, B. W. (1977). *Changing public attitudes toward television and other mass media, 1959–1976.* New York: Television Information Office.

Ryan, L. (2003, November 10). Tough times for telepics. *TelevisionWeek,* pp. 1, 38.

Schlosser, J. (2002a, January 28). Is it check-out time at NATPE? *Broadcasting & Cable.* Available online: www.tvinsite.com/broadcastingcable.

Schlosser, J. (2002b, March 4). Organization outlines initiatives to bring studios back to show. *Broadcasting & Cable.* Available online: www.tvinsite.com/broadcastingcable.

SIQSS. (2000). Study offers early look at home Internet is changing daily life. Available online: www.stanford.edu/dept/news/pr/00/000216internet.html.

Sterling, C., & Kittross, J. (2002). *Stay tuned: A history of American broadcasting.* Mahwah, NJ: Erlbaum.

Top 20 cable networks. (2003). National Cable and Telecommunications Association. Available online: www.ncta.com.

Top 25 shows. (2002, May 13). *Broadcasting & Cable,* p. 19.

TV first. (2003). Cabletelevision Advertising Bureau. Available online: www.cabletvadbureau.com.

UCLA report finds Internet surpasses television. (2000). Available online: www.uclanews.ucla.edu.

Walker, J. R., & Ferguson, D. A. (1998). *The broadcast television industry.* Boston: Allyn & Bacon.

What Is TiVo? (2002). TiVo. Available online: www.tivo.com/experience/index.asp?frames=no.

What Is Ultimate TV? (2002). Ultimate TV. Available online: www.ultimatetv.com/whatis.asp.

Williams, P. (2003, August 10). The Osbournes vs. The Nelsons: Has that much changed in 50 years? About.com. Available online: http://classicrock.about.com/library/misc/blozzie_ozzy.htm.

CHAPTER 7

Ackman, D. (2003, January 24). Super Super Bowl ads. *Forbes.* Available online: www.forbes.com/2003/01/24/cx_da_0124topads.html.

Advertising patterns in prime time findings. (1999). Phase One Communications. Available online: www.phaseone.net/pages/PTFindings.html [Retrieved June 16, 2001].

Begun, B. (2002, December 23). Music: How much do you like it? *Newsweek,* p. 9.

Bulkeley, W. M. (1999, November 22). We're watching you. *Wall St. Journal,* pp. R32, R46.

Bulova story, The. (2003). Bulova Watch Company. Available online: www.asksales.com/Bulova/Bulova.htm.

Campbell, R. (2000). *Media and culture.* Boston: St. Martin's Press.

Center for Media Education. (1997). *Children and television.* Available online: www.cme.org./children/kids_tv/c_and_t.html.

Chen, A. (2002, August 19). How to slam spam. *E-week,* pp. 34–35.

Collette, L. (2002). Cable television. In A. E. Grant & J. H. Meadows (Eds.), *Communication technology update* (pp. 49–60). Boston: Focal Press.

Cuneo, A. (2002, October 7). Simultaneous media use rife, new study finds. *Advertising Age,* pp. 3, 40.

Dominick, J. R. (1999). *The dynamics of mass communication.* 6th ed. Boston: McGraw-Hill.

Dominick, J. R., Sherman, B. L., & Copeland, G. A. (1996). *Broadcasting cable and beyond.* 3rd ed. New York: McGraw-Hill.

Dorey, E., & MacLellan, A. (2003). *Spread the word—Encourage viral marketing.* DDA Computer Consultants, Ltd. Available online: www.dda.ns.ca/resource/articles/spreadtheword.html.

E-Commerce: The road ahead. (2002, September 30). *Newsweek,* p. 38V

Elkin, T. (2003a, September 8). Making the most of broadband. *Advertising Age,* p. 86.

Elkin, T. (2003b, September 22). Spam: Annoying but effective. *Advertising Age,* p. 40.

Emergence of advertising in America. (2000). John W. Hartman Center for Sales, Advertising and Marketing History, Duke University. Available online: http://scriptorium.lib.duke.edu/eaa/timeline.html [Retrieved June 4, 2001].

Fact book: A handy guide to the advertising business. (2002, September 9). *Advertising Age* [Supplement].

Fitzgerald, K. (2002, June 10). Eager sponsors raise the ante. *Advertising Age,* p. 18.

Freeman, L. (1999, September 27). E-mail industry battle cry: Ban the spam. *Advertising Age,* p. 70.

FTC action: Hillary Clinton calls on Congress to re-empower agency. (2000, October 9). *Advertising Age,* pp. 58, 60.

Giles, M. (1998, October 18). Fighting spammers frustrating for now. *Atlanta Journal-Constitution,* pp. H1, H4.

Gladwell, M. (2003). Alternative marketing vehicles: The future of marketing to one. *Consumer Insight.* Available online: www.acnielsen.com/download/pdp/pubs.

Godes D., & Mayzlin, D. (2002). *Using online communication to study word of mouth communication.* Social Science Research Network. Available online: http://papers.ssrn.com.

Goetzl, D. (2002, February 14). TV clutter study: Problem escalates. *Advertising Age.* Available online: www.adage.com.

Gross, L. S. (1997). *Telecommunications: An introduction to electronic media.* 6th ed. Madison, WI: Brown & Benchmark.

Grumann, C. (1996, February 21). Soap operas invade the Internet. *St. Louis Post Dispatch,* p. 3E.

Head, S. W., Spann, T., & McGregor, M. A. (2001). *Broadcasting in America.* 9th ed. Boston: Houghton Mifflin.

Herlihy, G. (1999, September 26). Deliver me from spam. *Atlanta Journal-Constitution,* p. P1.

History. (2004). Agency.com. Available online: www.agency.com/our-company/history.

Introduction to electronic retailing. (2001). Frederiksen Group. Available online: www.fredgroup.com/ftvu_er101.html [Retrieved June 16, 2001].

Jockeys can wear ads in Derby. (2004, April 29). *CNN Money.* Available online: www.cnn.money.com.

Kaye, B. K., & Medoff, N. J. (2001a). *Just a click away.* Boston: Allyn & Bacon.

Kaye, B. K., & Medoff, N. J. (2001b). *The World Wide Web: A mass communication perspective.* Mountain View, CA: Mayfield.

Khermouch, G., & Green J. (2001, July 30). Buzz marketing. *Business Week.* Available online: www.businessweek.com/print/magazine/content/01_31/b3743001.htm.

Kindel, S. (1999, Fall). Brand champion. *Critical Mass,* pp. 56–58.

Kranhold, K. (1999, November 24). Banner ads are driving Web purchases. *Wall Street Journal,* p. B9.

Linnett, R. (2003, September 15). *Friends* tops TV price chart. *Broadcasting & Cable,* pp. 1, 46.

Love it or hate it. (2001, September, 25). *Pittsburgh Post-Gazette,* p. E-3.

Massey, K., & Baran, S. J. (2001). *Introduction to telecommunications.* Mountain View, CA: Mayfield.

Massey, K., & Baran, S. J. (1996). *Television criticism.* Dubuque, IA: Kendall/Hunt.

McGinn, D. (2001, August 27). Maxed out! *Newsweek,* pp. 34–40.

Media trends track. (2003). Television Bureau of Advertising. Available online: www.tvb.org/rcentral/mediatrendstrack/gdpvolume/gdp.asp?c=gdp1.

Neff, J. (2003, August 25). Spam research reveals disgust with pop-up ads. *Broadcasting & Cable,* pp. 1, 21.

O'Guinn, T. C., Allen, C. T., & Semenik, R. J. (2000). *Advertising.* Toronto, Canada: South-Western.

Orlik, P. B. (1998). *Broadcast/Cable copywriting.* Boston: Allyn & Bacon.

Pogue, D. (2002, June 27). Puncturing Web ads before they pop up. *New York Times.* Available online: www.nytimes.com/2002/06/27/technology/circuits.

Riedman, P. (2003, September 22). Looking beyond Beyonce. *Advertising Age,* p. 34.

Ritchie, M. (1994). *Please stand by.* Woodstock, NY: Overlook Press.

Russell, J. T., & Lane, W. R. (1999). *Kleppner's advertising procedure.* Upper Saddle River, NJ: Prentice Hall.

Shane, E. (1999). *Selling electronic media.* Boston: Focal Press.

Singer, D.G, Singer, J. L., & Zuckerman, D. (1997). *The parent's guide: Use TV to your child's advantage.* Available online: http://npin.org/pnews/1997/pnew697/pnew697e.html.

Sivulka, J. (1998). *Soap, sex and cigarettes.* Belmont, CA: Wadsworth.

Smith, L. (2003). Commercials steal the spotlight. Available online: www.amherst.k12.oh.us/steele/news/record/record.php?articleID=262.

Stern, L. (2003, May 12). Using your head. *Newsweek,* p. E2.

Stone, B. (2002, October 24). Those annoying ads that won't go away. *Newsweek,* pp. 38J, 38L.

Stone, B., & Lin, J. (2002, August 19). Spamming the world. *Newsweek,* pp. 42–44.

Stone, B., & Weil, D. (2003, December 8). Soaking in spam. *Newsweek.* Available online: www.newsweek.com.

Super Bowl costs. (2004, March 8). *Fact Pack* [Supplement to *Advertising Age*].

Tedeschi, B. (1998, December 8). Marketing by e-mail: Sales tool or spam? *New York Times.* Available online: www.nytimes.com/search [Retrieved February 19, 1999].

Top 10 advertisers in 12 measured media. (2003, June 23). *Advertising Age* [Special Report], p. S-24.

Top 25 shows in ad pricing. (2004, March 8). *Advertising Age* [Special Report], p. S-4.

Trends in television. (2000). Television Advertising Bureau. Available online: http://tvb.org/rcentral/mediatrendstrack/tv/tv.asp?c=timespent.

TV first, A. (2003). Cabletelevision Advertising Bureau. Available online: www.cabletvadbureau.com.

U.S. ad spending totals by media. (2004, March 8). *Fact Pack* [Supplement to *Advertising Age*].

Vanden Bergh, B. G., & Katz, H. (1999). *Advertising principles.* Lincolnwood, IL: NTC Business Books.

White, T. H. (2001). *United States early radio history.* Available online: www.ipass.net/~whitetho/part2.htm [Retrieved June 4, 2001].

Winner of the most industry awards in 1999. (1999). Ogilvy Interactive. Available online: www.ogilvy.com/o_interactive/who_frameset.asp.

CHAPTER 8

AC Nielsen Entertainment partners with CBS for real-time audience research [Press release] (2001, April 18). Nielsen Media Research. Available online: www.acnielsen.com/news/corp/2001/20010418.htm.

Ad supported cable surpasses all 7 broadcast networks by 7.5 share points. (2003, March 11). Cable Television Advertising Bureau. Available online: www.cabletvadbureau.com/03pressreleases/030311.htm.

Albiniak, P. (2003, February 10). Cold weather, hot ratings. *Broadcasting & Cable,* p. 13.

Albiniak, P. (2003, March 3). In reality, it was the weirdest sweeps ever. *Broadcasting & Cable,* p. 20.

Anna's not so big now. (2003, March 10). *Broadcasting & Cable,* p. 6.

Arbitron radio market report reference guide (2002). Arbitron. Available online: www.arbitron.com/downloads/purplebook.pdf [Retrieved February 28, 2002].

Beville, H. M., Jr. (1988). *Audience ratings.* Hillsdale, NJ: Erlbaum.

Big pipe cable rankings. (2001). Available online: www.cablefax.com/cfax/rankings/archives/index.html.

Boyce, R. (1998, February 2). Exploding the Web CPM myth. *Online Media Strategies for Advertising* [Supplement to *Advertising Age*], p. A16.

BroadcastWatch. (2001, November 5). *Broadcasting & Cable,* p. 24.

DeMoraes, L. (2004, May 8). *Friends* finale hoopla snags 52 million fans. *Washington Post,* pp. C1, C7.

DiPasquale, C. B. (2002, October 8). Nielsen to test outdoor ratings system. *Advertising Age.* Available online: www.adage.com/news.cms?NewsId=36254#.

Dreze, X., & Zufryden, F. (1998). Is Internet advertising ready for prime time? *Journal of Advertising Research, 38*(3), 7–18.

Eastman, S. T., & Fegruson, D. E. (2002). *Broadcast/Cable/Web programming.* Belmont, CA: Wadsworth

Flannagan, M. (2002, May 12). Local TV will pay big bucks for Nielsens. *Knoxville News-Sentinel,* pp. A1, A13.

Friedman, W., & Fine, J. (2003, August 18). Media sellers pay the price for blackout. *Advertising Age,* pp. 1, 31.

Goodale, G. (2003, November 19). The man who's tuned out. *Arizona Daily Sun,* pp. C1, C3.

Greppi, M. (2003, December 1). ABC network's five-act play. *TelevisionWeek.* Available online: www.tvweek.com/topstorys/120103abcnet.html.

Hall, R. W. (1991). *Media math*. Lincolnwood, IL: NTC Business Books.

Hansell, S. (2001, July 23). Pop-up ads pose a measurement puzzle. *New York Times*, pp. C1, C5.

Hutheesing, N. (1996, May 20). An online gamble. *Forbes*, p. 288.

Improving their swing. (1998, February 2). *Online Media Strategies for Advertising* [Supplement to *Advertising Age*], p. A45.

Jenny Jones' days are numbered. (2003, February 10). *Broadcasting & Cable*, p. 13.

Kaye B. K., & Medoff, N. J. (2001). *The World Wide Web: A mass communication perspective*. Mountain View, CA: Mayfield.

Market survey schedule and population rankings. (2004). Arbitron. Avaliable online: www.arbitron.com/radio_stations/home.htm.

Morrow, T. (2002, May 14). Knox stations replacing Nielsen system. *Knoxville News-Sentinel*, p. D1.

Nielsen to test electronic ratings service for outdoor advertising [Press release]. (2002, October 8). Nielsen Media Research. Available online: www.nielsenmedia.com/newsreleases/2002/Nielsen_Outdoor.htm.

Pursell, C. (2003, October 13). *Sharon* holds on to solid ratings. *TelevisionWeek*, pp. 1, 32.

Ryan, L. (2003, November 17). Sweeps declines for all but CBS. *TelevisionWeek*, p. 3.

Schumann, D. W., & Thorsen, E. (1999). *Advertising and the World Wide Web*. Mahwah, NJ: Erlbaum.

SeePoint kiosks get Vegas visitors in touch with new CBS programming [Press release]. (2001, May 1). SeePoint. Available online: www.seepoint.com/PressRelease.asp?PressReleaseID=3.

Shane, E. (1999). *Selling electronic media*. Boston: Focal Press.

Shaw, R. (1998, March 2). At least there are no Web sweeps (yet). *Electronic Media*, p. 17.

Snyder, H., & Rosenbaum, H. (1996). Advertising on the World Wide Web: Issues and policies for not-for-profit organization. *Proceedings of the American Association for Information Science, 33*, 186–191.

Top new shows. (2003, October 6). *TelevisionWeek*, p. 1.

Top 10 cable networks. (2003, November 10). *TelevisionWeek*, p. 34.

Voight, J. (1996, December). Beyond the banner. *Wired*, p. 196.

Vonder Haar, S. (1999, June 14). Web retailing goes Madison Avenue route. *Inter@ctive Week*, p. 18.

Walmsley, D. (1999, March 29). Online ad auctions offer sites more than bargains. *Advertising Age*, p. 43.

Warren, C. (1999, Fall). Tools of the trade. *Critical Mass*, p. 22.

Weakest Link, Other Half are out. (2003, March 17). *Broadcasting & Cable*, p. 11.

Webster, J. G., & Lichty, L. W. (1991). *Ratings analysis*. Hillsdale, NJ: Erlbaum.

Webster, J. G., Phalen, P. F., & Lichty, L. W. (2000). *Ratings analysis*. Hillsdale: Lawrence Erlbaum.

What's new for the portable People Meter. (2001). Arbitron. Available online: www.arbitron.com/portable_people_meters/home.htm.

Who we are and what we do. (2002). Nielsen Media Research. Available online: www.nielsenmedia.com/who_we_are.html.

Zipern, A. (2002, January 15). Effort to measure online ad campaigns. *New York Times*. Available online: www.nytimes.com/2002/01/15/business/media/15ADCO.html.

CHAPTER 9

Alabarran, A. (2002). *Media economics*. 2nd ed. Ames, IA: Iowa State Press.

Future is bright for powerline broadband, The [Press release]. (2004, July 14). FCC. Available online: www.fcc.gov [Retrieved July 29, 2004].

Greenspan, R. (2003, Sept. 5). Home is where the network is. *Cyberatlas*. Available online: http://cyberatlas.internet.com/big_picture/applications/article/0,,1301_3073431,00.html [Retrieved July, 2004].

Greppi, M. (2001, November 19). NBC, Young and Granite roll the dice. *Electronic Media*. Available online: www.craini2i.com/em/archive.mv?count=3&story=em178785427096220069 [Retrieved February, 2004].

Higgins, J. (2004, January 5). Cable cash flow flows. *Broadcasting & Cable*. Available online: www.broadcastingcable.com/archives.

Jessell, H. (2004, January 5). Dotcom redux. *Broadcasting & Cable*. Available online: www.broadcastingcable.com/archives.

Kerschbaumer, K., & Higgins, J. (2004, January 12). Utah's uncable surprise. *Broadcasting & Cable*. Available online: www.broadcastingcable.com/index.asp=articlePrint&articleID=CA374134 [Retrieved February 25, 2004].

Kuchinskas, S. (2003). Research firm says Wi-Fi will go bye-bye. internetnews.com. Available online: www.internetnews.com/wireless/print.php/2233951.

Lind, R., & Medoff, N., (1999). Radio stations and the World Wide Web. *Journal of Radio Studies, 6*(2), 203–221.

Naftalin, C. (2001). Strike two: FCC's EEO rules repealed for the second time in three years. *Telecommunications Law Update, 3*, 1. Available online: www.hklaw.com/content//newsletters/telecom/3telecom01.pdf [Retrieved February, 2004].

NBC v. United States. (1943). 319 U.S. 190.

Ownership limits split stations and networks. (1998, July 27). *Television Digest*, p. 16.

Parsons, P., & Frieden, R. (1998). *The cable and satellite television industries*. Boston: Allyn & Bacon.

Romano, A. (2002, December 20). Cable's big piece of the pie: In 2002, it had larger share of audience than broadcast networks. *Broadcasting and Cable*, p. 37.

Smith, F., Wright, J., & Ostroff, D. (1998). *Perspectives on radio and television*. 4th ed. Mahwah, NJ: Erlbaum.

Sterling, C., & Kittross, J. (2002). *Stay tuned: A history of American broadcasting*. Mahwah, NJ: Erlbaum.

Thorsberg, F. (2001, April 20). Web radio goes silent in legal crossfire. *PC World*. Available online: www.itworld.com/Tech/2427/PCW010420aid47983/pfindex.html [Retrieved March 2002].

Trick, R. (2003, May). Powell: Newspapers to "fare well' in cross-ownership decision. *Presstime*, p. 8.

Veronis, Suhler, & Stevenson Media Merchant Bank. (2003). Communication industry forecast, 2003. Available online: www.vss.com [Retrieved February 4, 2004].

Walker, J., & Ferguson, D. (1998). *The broadcast television industry*. Boston: Allyn & Bacon.

CHAPTER 10

Dick, S. (2001). Satellites. In E. Thomas & B. Carpenter (Eds.), *Mass media in 2025*. Westport, CT: Greenwood Press.

Eastman, S., & Klein, R. (1991). *Promotion and marketing for broadcasting and cable*. 2nd ed. Prospect Heights, IL: Waveland Press.

Gross, L. (2003). *Telecommunications*. 8th ed. Boston: McGraw-Hill.

Head, S., Sterling, C., & Schofield, L. (1994). *Broadcasting in America*. Boston: Houghton Mifflin.

Hilliard, R., & Keith, M. (2001). *The broadcast century and beyond*, 3rd. ed., Boston: Focal Press.

How cable television works. (2004). Howstuffworks.com. Available online: http://entertainment.howstufffworks.com/cable-tv1.htm [Retrieved February 26, 2004].

Hutchinson, T. (1950). *Here is television*. New York: Hastings House.

Janowiak, G., Sheth, J., & Saghafi, M. (1998). Communications in the next millennium. *Telecommunications, 3*, 47–54.

Kaye, B., & Medoff, N. (2001) *The world wide web: A mass communication perspective*. Mountain View, CA: Mayfield.

Parsons, R., & Frieden, R. (1998). *The cable and satellite television industries*. Boston: Allyn & Bacon.

Quaal, W., & Brown, J. (1976). *Broadcast management*. New York: Hastings House.

Romano, A. (2002, September 2). "Dearth of women" in top spots. *Broadcasting & Cable*, p. 9.

Settel, I. (1960). *A pictorial history of radio*. New York: Citadel Press

Sherman, B. (1995). *Telecommunications management*. New York: McGraw-Hill.

Sterling, C., & Kittross, J. (2002). *Stay tuned: A history of American broadcasting*. Mahwah, NJ: Erlbaum.

Thottam, G. (2001). Cable. In E. Thomas & B. Carpenter (Eds.), *Mass media in 2025*. Westport, CT: Greenwood Press.

Turner, E., & Briggs, P. (2001). Radio. In E. Thomas & B. Carpenter (Eds.), *Mass media in 2025*. Westport, CT: Greenwood Press.

Willey, G. (1961). End of an era: The daytime radio serial. *Journal of Broadcasting, 5*, 97–115.

CHAPTER 11

Bolduc, W., & Medoff, N. (1990, Fall). Preparation for entry level jobs in media production: A survey of broadcast television and professional media production managers. *Feedback*.

Cartwright, S. (1990). *Secrets of successful media training: The training with media casebook*. Belmont, CA: Wadsworth.

DiZazzo, R. (2000). *Corporate media production*. Boston: Focal Press.

Gayeski, D. (1991). *Corporate and instructional media*. 2nd ed. Englewood Cliffs, NJ: Prentice-Hall.

Greer, D. (2001, June 1). Window shopping. *VideoSystems*.

Medoff, N., & Tanquary, T. (2002). *Portable vedia: ENG and EFP*. Boston: Focal Press.

Richardson, A. (1992). *Corporate and organizational video*. New York: McGraw-Hill.

Smith, L., Wright, J., & Ostroff, D. (1998). *Perspectives on radio and television*. 4th ed. Mahwah, NJ: Erlbaum.

Van Deusen, R., & Faccone, A. (2001). *Dynamic media in transition*. White Plains, NY: Knowledge Industry.

CHAPTER 12

Cox, C. (2003). House passes Cox bill to permanently ban Internet taxes. Available online: http://cox.house.gov/html/release.cfm?id=696 [Retrieved August 22, 2004].

Demac, D. (1993). Is any use "fair" in a digital world? Media Studies Center, Freedom Forum. Available online: www.mediastudies.org/CTR/Pulbications/demac/dd.html [Retrieved December 2000].

"Do not spam" list near final approval. (2003, November 23). *Arizona Republic*, p. 81.

E-commerce: The road ahead. (2002, September 30). *Newsweek*, p. 38.

Enders, S. (2003, June 25). Stop or we sue says the RIAA. TechTV. Available online: www.techtv.com/news/news/story/0%2C24195%2C3463091%2C00.html [Retrieved July 14, 2003].

Freeman, L. (1999, September 27). E-mail industry battle cry: Ban the spam. *Advertising Age*, p. 70.

FTC policy statement on deception. (1983). Available online: www.ftc.gov/bcp/policystmt/ad-decept.htm [Retrieved August 12, 2004].

Gentile, G. (2003, August 13). Schwarzenegger films to trigger equal time rule. *Laredo Morning Times*, p. 10A.

Gillmor, D., Barron, J., Simon, T., & Terry, H. (1996). *Fundamentals of mass communication law*. Minneapolis: West.

Kaye, B., & Medoff, N. (2001). *The world wide web: A mass communication perspective*. Mountain View, CA: Mayfield.

Lee, J. S. (2002, June 27). Spam: An escalating attack of the clones. *New York Times*. Available online: www.nytimes.com/2002/06/27/technology/circuits/27SPAM.html?pagewanted= [Retrieved July 18, 2002].

Miami Herald Publishing Co. v. Tornillo. (1974). 418 U.S. 241, 94 S.Ct. 2831.

New York Times v. Sullivan. (1964). 376 U.S. 254.

Piller, C. (1997, May). Net regulation: How much is enough? *PC World*, p. 60.

Reno v. ACLU. (1997). 117 S.Ct. 2329, 138L.Ed.

Smith, L., Wright, J., & Ostroff, D. (1998). *Perspectives on radio and television: Telecommunication in the United States*. 4th ed. Mahwah, NJ: Erlbaum.

Sterling, C., & Kittross, J. (2002). *Stay tuned: A history of American broadcasting*. Mahwah, NJ: Erlbaum.

Stevens, J. (1997). *Reno v. ACLU*. Available online: http://supct.law.cornell.edu/supct/html/96-511.zs.html [Retrieved August 22, 2004].

Veiga, A. (2003, July 24). Tech war over file swapping. CBSNews.com. Available online: www.cbsnews.com/stories/2003/09/02/tech/main571144.shtml [Retrieved August 22, 2004].

Waking up to anti-snoring claims. (March, 2001). FTC consumer feature. Available online: www.ftc.gov/bcp/conline/features/snore.htm [Retrieved August 22, 2004].

CHAPTER 13

Andersen, R. E., Crespo, C. J., Bartlett, S. J., Cheskin, L. J., & Pratt, M. (1998a). Relationship of physical activity and television watching with body weight and level of fatness among children. *Journal of the American Medical Association, 279*, 938–942.

Anderson, D. N., Huston, A. C., Wright, J. C., & Collins, P.A. (1998b). *Sesame Street* and educational television for children. In R. G. Noll & M. E. Price (Eds.), *A communications cornucopia: Markle Foundation essays on information policy*. Washington, DC: Brookings Institution.

Baran, S. J., & Davis, D. K. (2000). *Mass communication theory*. 2nd ed. Belmont, CA: Wadsworth.

Barnes, B. (2002, March 5). Play time: Online games are booming: And the growth isn't coming for kids. *Wall Street Journal*, p. R6.

BBDO. (1996, August). Survey on WWW browsing. Techsetter hotline. Available online: www.techsetter.com/bbdo/surv/lastsurv/lastsurv.aug96.html.

Black, G. D. (2000). Bleep! Censoring rock and rap music. *Journalism History, 26*(2), 83–84.

Bloom, A., & Brines, W. (Eds). (2002). *Takin' it to the streets*. New York: Oxford University Press.

Bryant, J., & Thompson, S. (2002). *Fundamentals of media effects*. Boston: McGraw-Hill.

Bushman, B. J., & Anderson, C. A. (2002). Violent video games and hostile expectations: A test of the general aggression model. *Personality and Social Psychology Bulletin, 28*(12), 1679–1686.

Canary, D. J., & Spitzberg, B. H. (1993). Loneliness and media gratifications. *Communication Research, 20*(6), 800–821.

Cantor, J. (1998). *"Mommy, I'm scared": How TV and movies frighten children and what we can do to protect them*. San Diego: Harcourt Brace.

Case, T. (2002, June 3). Going to extremes. *Mediaweek*, p. 18.

Center for On-Line and Internet Addiction. (2004). Homepage. Available online: http://netaddiction.com/services/history.htm.

Clancey, M. (1994). The television audience examined. *Journal of Advertising Research, 34*(4), Special Insert.

Clancy-Hepburn, K., Hickey, A., & Nevill, G. (1974). Children's behavior responses to food advertisements. *Journal of Nutrition Education, 6*(3), 93–96.

Cline, V. B. (1994) Pornography effects: Empirical and clinical evidence. In D. Zillmann, J. Bryant, & A. Huston (Eds.), *Media, children, and the family: Social scientific, psychodynamic, and clinical perspectives*. Hillsdale, NJ: Erlbaum.

Cockburn, A. (2000, October 2). The Gore's cultural wars. *The Nation*, p. 10.

Cohen, B. C. (1963). *The press and foreign policy*. Princeton, NJ: Princeton University Press.

Comarow, A. (2001, April 23). Scary news, soothing numbers. *U.S. News & World Report*, p. 74.

Crespo, C. J., Smit, E., Troiano, R. P., Bartlett, S. J., Macera, C. A., & Anderson, R. E. (2001). Television watching, energy intake, and obesity in U.S. children. *Archives of Pediatric and Adolescent Medicine, 155*, 360–365.

DeCurtis, A. (1992, September 3). Tipper: Dems send wrong message. *Rolling Stone*, p. 17.

Dennison, B. A., Erb, T. A., & Jenkins, P. L. (2002). Television viewing and television in bedroom associated with overweight risk among low-income preschool children. *Pediatrics, 109*, 1028–1035.

Dietz, W. H. (1990). You are what you eat—What you eat is what you are. *Journal of Adolescent Health Care, 11*, 76–81.

Dietz, W. H., & Gortmaker, S. L. (1985). Do we fatten our children at the television set? Obesity and television viewing in children and adolescents. *Pediatrics, 75*, 807–812.

Dominick, J. R. (1996). *The dynamics of mass communication*. Boston: McGraw-Hill.

Duffy, T. (1992, July 25). The spotlight turns to freedom in the arts. *Billboard*, pp. 1, 70.

Enteman, W. (1996). Stereotyping, prejudice, and discrimination. In P. W. Lester (Ed.), *Images that injure: Pictural stereotypes in the media* (pp. 10–14). Westport, CT: Praeger.

FCC eases media ownership rules. (2003, June 2). *Arizona Republic*. Available online: www.azcentral.com/arizonarepublic.

Federman, J. (1998). *National television violence study, Vol. 3: Executive summary.* Center for Communication and Social Policy—University of California, Santa Barbara. Available online: www.ccsp.ucsb.edu/execsum.pdf.

Feshbach, S. (1961). The stimulating versus cathartic effects of a vicarious aggressive activity. *Journal of Abnormal Psychology, 63,* 381–385.

Feshbach, S., & Singer, R. (1971). *Television and aggression: An experimental field study.* San Francisco: Jossey-Bass.

Gerbner G., & Gross, L. (1976). Living with television: The violence profile. *Journal of Communication, 26,* 173–199.

Gerbner G., Gross, L., Jackson-Beeck, M., Jeffries-Fox, S., & Signorielli, N. (1978). Cultural indicators: Violence profile no. 9. *Journal of Communication, 27,* 171–180.

Gowen, A. (1993, April 15). Tipper Gore quits PMRC. *Rolling Stone,* p. 20.

Half of U.S. parents are using TV ratings. (1998, June 14). *St. Louis Post Dispatch,* p. D4.

Hopkinson, N. (2003, October 29). For media-savvy tots, TV and DVD compete with ABCs. *Washington Post.* Available online: www.washingtonpost.com.

Horne, G. (1995). *Fire this time: The Watts uprising and the 1960s.* Charlottesville, VA: University of Virginia Press.

Internet eats into TV time. (1996, January 12). *St. Louis Post Dispatch,* p. 6C.

Irvine, M. (2002, August 25). The heaviest generation. *Knoxville News-Sentinel,* p. A13.

Isserman, M., & Kazin, M. (2000). *America divided: The civil war of the 1960s.* 2nd ed. New York: Oxford University Press.

Kalb, C. (2002, August 19). How are we doing? *Newsweek,* p. 53.

Kaye, B. K., & Johnson, T. J. (2004). A Web for all reasons: Uses and gratifications of Internet resources for political information. *Telematics and Informatics, 21*(3), 197–223.

Kaye, B. K., & Johnson, T. J. (2003). From here to obscurity: The Internet and media substitution theory. *Journal of the American Society for Information Science and Technology, 54*(3), 260–273.

Kaye, B. K., & Sapolsky, B. S. (2004). Watch your mouth! An analysis of profanity uttered by children on prime time television. *Mass Communication and Society, 74*(4).

Lavers, D. (May 13, 2002). The verdict on media violence: It's ugly and getting uglier. *Washington Post,* pp. 28–29.

Lee, B., & Lee, R. S. (1995). How and why people watch TV: Implications for the future of interactive television. *Journal of Advertising Research, 35*(6), 9–18.

Lewis, P. (2003, September 2). The biggest game in town. *Fortune,* pp. 132–142.

Lin, C. A. (1993). Adolescent viewing and gratifications in a new media environment. *Mass Comm Review, 20*(1&2), 39–50.

Littleton, C. (2001, August 1). Watchdogs rap TV offenders. *Hollywood Reporter,* p. 63.

Livingston, G. (2002, July 28). Sense and nonsense in the child abduction scares. *San Francisco Chronicle,* p. D6.

Lowery, S. A., & DeFleur, M. L. (1995). *Milestones in mass communication research.* New York: Longman.

Malamuth, N. M., & Donnerstein, E. (1984). *Pornography and sexual aggression.* Orlando, FL: Academic Press.

Marshall, W. L. (1989). Pornography and sex offenders. In D. Zillmann & J. Bryant (Eds.), *Pornography: Research advances and policy considerations.* Hillsdale, NJ: Erlbaum.

Massey, K., & Baran, S. J. (2001). *Introduction to mass communication.* Mountain View, CA: Mayfield.

Mathews, T. (1990, July 2). Fine are or foul? *Newsweek,* pp. 46–52.

McConnell, B. (2003, January 27). FCC's Martin wants more family-friendly fare. *Broadcasting & Cable,* p. 26.

McDonald, D. G., & Kim, H. (2001) When I die, I feel small: Electronic game characters and the social self. *Journal of Broadcasting and Electronic Media, 45*(2), 241–258.

McQuail, D. (2000). *Mass communication theory.* 4th ed. London, England: Sage.

Media ownership and deregulation. (2004). Journalism.org. Available online: www.journalism.org/resources/research/reports/ownership/deregulation2.asp.

Oppelaar, J. (2000, September 18). Music business rates the ratings. *Variety,* p. 126.

Palmgreen, P., Wenner, L. A., & Rosengren, K. E. (1985). Uses and gratifications research: The past ten years. In K. E. Rosengren, L. A. Wenner, & P. Palmgreen (Eds.), *Media gratifications research* (pp. 11–37). Beverly Hills, CA: Sage.

Pember, D. (2001). *Mass media law.* Boston: McGraw-Hill.

Perse, E. M. (2001). Media effects and society. Mahwah, NJ: Erlbaum.

Perse, E. M., & Ferguson, D. A. (1992). *Gratifications of newer television technologies.* Paper presented at the annual convention of the Speech Communication Association, Chicago, IL.

Poovey, B. (2002, April 15). Device lets viewers bleep at home. *Knoxville News-Sentinel,* p. C3.

Potter, W. J. (2003). *The eleven myths of media violence.* Thousand Oaks, CA: Sage.

Quittner, J. (1999, May 10). Are video games really so bad? *Time,* pp. 50–59.

Rosengren, K. E., Wenner, L. E., & Palmgreen P. (1985). *Media gratifications research.* Beverly Hills, CA: Sage.

Rubin, A. M. (1984). Ritualized versus instrumental viewing. *Journal of Communication, 34,* 67–77.

Rubin, A. M., & Bantz, C. R. (1989). Uses and gratifications of videocassette recorders. In J. L. Salvaggio & J. Bryant (Eds.), *Media use in the information age: Emerging patterns of adoption and consumer use* (pp. 181–195). Hillsdale, NJ: Erlbaum.

Ryan, J. (2002, May 30). Children now facing adult health issues. *Knoxville News-Sentinel,* p. B4.

Scarborough Research. (2001, May 14). TV watching down as Net use rises. Available online: www.nua.com/surveys.

Schneider, M. (1997, February 10). Kids ignore ratings. *Electronic Media,* p. 1.

Severin, W. J., & Tankard, J. W., Jr. (1992). *Communication theories: Origins, methods, and uses in the mass media.* 3rd ed. New York: Longman.

Signorielli, N. (1990). Television's mean and dangerous world: A continuation of the cultural indicators perspective. In N. Signorielli & M. Morgan (Eds.), *Cultivation analysis* (pp. 85–106). Thousand Oaks, CA: Sage.

Steyer, J. P. (2002). *The other parent.* New York: Atria.

Sutton, L., Neill, M., Hamm, L., & Morse, E. (2000, January 17). On the record for Zappa. *People Weekly,* p. 19.

Television and obesity among children. (2002). National Institute on Media and the Family. Available online: www.mediaandthefamily.org/facts/facts_tvandobchild.shtml.

TV, video games and the Internet: How much is too much for kids? (2001, June/July). *Health News,* p. 9.

Walker, J. R., & Bellamy, R. V. (1989). *The gratifications of grazing: Why flippers flip.* Paper presented at the annual meeting of the Speech Communication Association, San Francisco, CA.

Walker, J. R., Bellamy, R. V., & Truadt, P. J. (1993). Gratifications derived from remote control devices: A survey of adult RCD use. In J. R. Walker & R. V. Bellamy (Eds.) *The remote control in the new age of television* (pp. 103–112). Westport, CT: Praeger.

Young, K. (2003). What is Internet addiction? TechTV.com. Available online: www.techtv.com/callforhelp/features/story/0,24330,3322433,00.html.

Zill, N. (2001). "Does *Sesame Street* enhance school readiness?" Evidence from a national survey of children. In S. M. Fisch & R. T. Truglio (Eds.), *"G" is for "growing": Thirty years of research on children and* Sesame Street (pp. 115–130). Mahwah, NJ: Erlbaum

CHAPTER 14

Arthur, D. (2002, August 2). DVD format taking over the home video market. *Redding Searchlight,* p. D1.

Baig, E. (2002a, May 1). Price is right for using the Net for phone calls. *USA Today,* p. 6D.

Baig, E. (2002b, April 3). This "wearable computer" fits like a glove. *USA Today,* p. 6D.

Baig, E. (2001, December 26). ReplayTV has fans, lawyers salivating. *USA Today,* p. 2D.

Berquist, L. (2002). Broadband networks. In A. E. Grant & J. H. Meadows (Eds.), *Communication technology update.* Boston: Focal Press.

Big picture, The. (2003, March). *Consumer Reports,* pp. 10–23.

Brass, L. (2002, February 10). Data transmission likely to be next cell phone stage. *Knoxville News-Sentinel,* pp. D1, D8.

Broadband use increases. (2003, April 22). *Sacramento Business Journal.* Available online: http://sacramento.bizjournals.com/sacramento/stories/2003/04/21/daily19.html.

Brown, D. (2002). Communication technology timeline. In A. E. Grant & J. H. Meadows (Eds.), *Communication technology update.* Boston: Focal Press.

Caller I.D. (2002, April 15). *Advertising Age,* p. S2.

Cellular Telecommunication and Internet Association. (2002). Glossary. Available online: www.wow-com.com/consumer/faq.

Consumer Electronics Association. (2003). Digital camcorders. Available online: www.ce.org/publications/books_references/digital_america/digital_imaging/digital_camcorders.asp.

Croal, N. (2002a, October 28). The other wireless. *Newsweek,* p. 53.

Croal, N. (2002b, September 16). TV thin is definitely in. *Newsweek,* p. 63.

Croal, N. (2001, December 10). This time it's personal. *Newsweek,* pp. 68–71.

Croal, N., & Jaffe, B. R. (2002). Networking made easy. *Newsweek,* p. 55.

Curry, S. R. (2003, September 1). PVR threat growing. *TelevisionWeek,* p. 10.

Elkin, T. (2002a, November 4). Getting viewers to opt in, not tune out. *Advertising Age,* pp. 10, 12.

Elkin, T. (2002b, April 8). Pipe dreams. *Advertising Age,* pp. 12–15.

Emling, S. (2002a, July 7). DVD soon will occupy top position in family room. *Atlanta Journal-Constitution,* pp. Q1, Q2.

Emling, S. (2002b, July 21). Sound machines. *Atlanta Journal-Constitution.* pp. Q1, Q4.

Flynn, L. (2001, November 5). Networks see threat in new video recorder. *New York Times.* Available online: Available: www.nytimes.com/2001/11/05/technology/circuits.

Foroohar, R. (2002, September 16). A new way to compute. *Newsweek,* pp. 34J–34O.

Franklin, C. (2002a). Howstuffworks.com. Available online: www.howstuffworks.com/dsl1.htm.

Franklin, C. (2002b). Howstuffworks.com. Available online: http://www.howstuffworks.com/cable-modem3.htm.

Freudenrich, C. C. (2002). How personal digital assistants (PDAs) work. Howstuffworks.com. Available online: www.howstuffworks.com/pda.htm.

Johnston, S. J. (2002, March 11). Entering the "W" zone. *InfoWorld,* pp. 1, 44.

It's history. (2003, March 17). *Newsweek*, p. 14.

Kim, H. (2003, September 29). PVRs to hit 20% by '07. *Advertising Age*, p. 6.

Klopfenstein, B. (2002). Home video technology. In A. E. Grant & J. H. Meadows (Eds.), *Communication technology update*. Boston: Focal Press.

Krane, J. (2003, January 9). Microsoft's Gates touts consumer gadgets. Excite.com. Available online: http://apnews. excite.com/article/20030109/D7OER2Q00.html.

Levy, S. (2001, December 10). Living in a wireless world. *Newsweek*, pp. 57–58.

Levy, S., & Stone, B. (2002, June 10). The WiFi wave. *Newsweek*, pp. 38–40.

MacNeill, D. (1993, December 15). Newton notes. *Mac Monthly*. Available online: www.pencomputing.com/ Newton/NewtonNotes3.html.

McGinn, D. (2002, December 16). Tending tots with TiVo. *Newsweek*, p. 9.

Reno, J., & Croal, N. (2002, August 5). Hearing is believing. *Newsweek*, pp. 44–45.

Residential broadband forecasts. (2002). Technology Futures, Inc. Available online: www.tccsmd.org/TskFrc/ householdbroadband.pdf.

Rocks, D. (2002, February 11). Wireless networking: Misery awaits you. *Business Week*, pp. 82–83.

Rothman, W. (2002, September 5). Burning your own DVDs. *New York Times*. Available online: www.nytimes.com/2002/09/05/technology/circuits.

Setoodeh, R. (2003, August 25). Really big screen TV. *U.S.News & World Report*, p. 23.

Small talk. (2001, September 17). *Newsweek*, p. 72.

Southern CA town to create city-wide Wi-fi "hot spot." (2003, December 4). *Radio and Internet Newsletter*. Available online: www.kurthanson.com/archive/news/120403/ index.asp.

Stone, B. (2004, February 16). TiVo's big moment. *Newsweek*, p. 43.

Stone, B. (2002, July 29). The war for your TV. *Newsweek*, pp. 46–47.

Suciu, P. (2003, March 10). I want my DVD player. *Newsweek*, p. 26.

Tanaka, J. (2001, September 17). PC, Phone home! *Newsweek*, pp. 71–72.

Thomaselli, R. (2003, September 1). The next DTC: DVD explodes. *Advertising Age*, pp. 1, 22.

Tyson, J. (2002a). How IP telephony works. Howstuffworks. com. Available online: www.howstuffworks.com/ip-telephony.htm.

Tyson, J. (2002b). How wireless networking works. Howstuffworks.com. Available online: www. howstuffworks.com/wireless-network.htm.

Veiga, A. (2003, September 22). "Smart" CDs aim to halt file-sharing. *Knoxville News-Sentinel*, pp. C1, C2.

What is telephony? (2002). About.com. Available online: http://netconference.about.com/library/weekly/ aa032100a.htm.

World wide camera phones. (2003, September 15). *E-week*, p. 22.

Index

ABC (American Broadcasting Company)
    affiliates of, 47
    cable television and, 71
    origins of, 39, 47, 202, 203, 266
    ownership of, 202, 203, 207
    as radio network, 39, 47, 202, 203
    as television network, 47, 203
ACT. *See* Action for Children's Television
Action for Children's Television (ACT), 51
Ad auctions (and online advertising), 193
Addictive behaviors (and electronic media), 306, 307
ADI. *See* Area of dominant influence
Adjacencies (in television advertising), 154
Advanced Research Projects Agency (ARPAnet), 84
Adventures of Ozzie and Harriet, The, 124
Advertiser-supported services, 150
Advertising, 141–170
    agencies for, 145, 146, 148, 164–165
    audience and, 151, 152–153, 154, 156, 157, 158, 159, 162–164, 173, 184–185, 187–188, 192. *See also* Audience analysis
    brand image/loyalty and, 151–152
    buying and selling of, 188–194, 228, 230–231, 235
    on cable television, 65, 133, 149, 150, 157–159, 191–192
    campaigns for, 165–166
    children and, 168, 278, 312–313
    commercial model and, 5
    consumers' views on, 163, 169, 184–185
    control over, 146, 148, 200
    cost of, 143–145, 146–147, 151–152, 153, 154, 155, 156, 157, 158, 160, 163, 167, 168, 171, 173, 187–188, 189–191, 193, 235
    culture and, 152, 167, 168
    deceptive practices in, 168, 277–279
    definition of, 142
    economy and, 141, 152
    ethical issues in, 186, 286–287, 288
    evolution of electronic media and, 9
    exchanges of, 193–194
    on Internet, 94, 97–98, 99, 152, 159–164, 178–179, 187, 192–194, 278–279
    lengths of commercials, 149, 152, 154
    marketing and, 142. *See also* Marketing
    in newspapers, 5, 33, 143
    origins of, 141, 142–150
    prevalence of, 141, 151, 152, 167, 168
    promotion and, 142. *See also* Promotion
    purposes of, 141, 142, 151, 152, 167, 202, 278

    on radio, 27, 33, 48, 94, 109, 143–147, 152–154, 155, 188–191, 197–198, 228, 230–231 27, 33, 48, 94, 109, 143–147, 152–154, 155, 188–191, 197–198, 228, 230–231
    regulation of, 149, 167, 168, 266, 277–279
    on satellite television, 195
    sponsorship and, 145–149, 200, 266
    stereotypes promoted by, 168
    on television, 5, 48, 49, 52, 53, 97, 146–150, 152, 154–157, 188–191, 195–196, 197–198, 235
    trend following/setting and, 152
    types of, 145–150, 152–153, 155, 158, 159–161, 178
    viewing behaviors and, 157, 159, 195–196, 323
Advertising agencies, 145, 146, 148, 164–165
Advertising campaigns, 165–166
Advertising exchanges, 193–194
Advertorials (ads on Internet), 160–161
Affiliate stations, 47–48, 52–53, 55–56, 131, 132, 137, 201, 202–203, 204, 207, 208–209. *See also* Network system, in television
AFTRA. *See* American Federation of Television and Radio Artists
Agency.com, 165
Agenda setting, 307–308
Air shifts, 34
Alcoholic beverages (and advertising), 278
All-Channel Receiver Act (1962), 45–46
All-news stations, 112. *See also* News programming
AM radio, 34–35, 36, 111–112. *See also* Radio
Amateur radio operators, 23, 25, 26, 31, 33, 87, 107, 264
America's Funniest Home Videos, 123, 125
American Broadcasting Company. *See* ABC
American Family, An, 123
American Federation of Television and Radio Artists (AFTRA), 94, 212, 255
American Marconi, 24, 25. *See also* Marconi Company
American Research Bureau (ARB), 172, 173. *See also* Arbitron
American Society of Composers, Authors, and Publishers (ASCAP), 28, 212, 284
American Telephone & Telegraph (AT&T), 25, 29, 30, 70, 80, 199, 264
Amos 'n' Andy, 109
Amplitude modulation (AM), 34. *See also* AM radio

Analog signals/media, 10, 37, 78, 280
Andreesen, Mark, 84
Annual budget method, 248
Answering machines, 70, 317
Anthologies (on television), 49, 116. *See also* Dramatic programming
Anti-leapfrogging rule, 64
Applied ethics, 286
AQH. *See* Average quarter hour
ARB. *See* American Research Bureau; Arbitron
Arbitron, 172, 173–174, 178, 182, 184, 194, 195
Area of dominant influence (ADI), 173
Armstrong, Edwin H., 27, 35–36
ARPAnet. *See* Advanced Research Projects Agency
Arousal (as media effect), 301
ASCAP. *See* American Society of Composers, Authors, and Publishers
Aspect ratio, 56
Asynchronous media, 6
AT&T. *See* American Telephone & Telegraph
Audience analysis, 171–196
    advertising and, 151, 152–153, 154, 156, 157, 158, 159, 162–164, 173, 184–185, 187–188, 192
    for cable television, 184
    challenges in, 175, 176–177, 178–179, 192
    consumer profiling and, 184–187, 282–283
    for corporate media, 254
    effects of mass media and, 299–300
    information produced by, 179–182
    for Internet, 178–179, 185, 187, 282–283
    methods of, 164, 172–173, 173–179
    origins of, 172–173
    programming and, 195, 199
    purposes of, 171, 173, 184–187, 194, 230
    for radio, 171, 172–177, 182, 186, 194, 230
    regulation of, 179
    reports of, 182–184
    for satellite television, 195
    technology of, 171–172, 172–173, 194–195
    for television, 171, 173–177, 183–184, 186–187, 194–195, 202
    viewing behaviors and, 195–196, 299–300
Audience flow, 136
Audimeters, 172
Audio console/board, 220–221
Audio production. *See* Radio, production of

Audion tubes, 21, 108
Automobiles
   Internet connections in, 38
   radios in, 31, 36, 176
   satellite delivery in, 37, 74, 75, 79
   telephones in, 70
Average quarter hour (AQH), 181–182
Ayer, Francis, 143

Baird, John Logie, 42
Ball, Lucille, 118
Bandura, Albert, 296
Bandwidth, 9, 36, 38–39, 80, 257
Banner ads, 159, 160, 187, 192
Bartering (in advertising), 191
Basic cable, 150. See also Cable television
Behavioral effects (of electronic media), 7,
   301–302
Bell, Alexander Graham, 3, 19, 199
Bell Telephone/Bell Labs, 70, 76, 272
Berners-Lee, Tim, 84
Biltmore agreement, 32
Blacklisting, 49–50
Blocking (and program scheduling), 136
Blogs/Blogging, 14, 83, 86, 102–104
Blue Book, 268
Blue network (of NBC), 29, 31, 32, 39, 47,
   108, 202, 203, 266. See also National
   Broadcasting Company
"Blue Sky" period (of cable television
   development), 67
BMI. See Broadcast Music, Inc.
Bobo doll experiment, 296–297
Boston Newsletter, 143
Brand image/loyalty, 151–152
Bridging (and program scheduling), 136
British Marconi, 25, 264. See also Marconi
   Company
Broadband Internet service, 327
Broadcast Education Association, 251
Broadcast Music, Inc. (BMI), 212, 284
Broadcast star model, 200–202
Broadcasting/Broadcast networks. See also
   Networks/Network systems
   cable television and, 64, 65–66, 71, 97,
      100, 133, 137, 157–158, 208
   consolidation and, 241. See also
      Consolidation
   corporate media vs., 246, 249, 250
   definition of, 24
   dominance of, 61, 133, 202, 207, 265
   Internet and, 94, 100, 101
   at local level, 39, 52–53, 57, 126
   models of, 97, 200
   origins of, 5, 264
   ownership of, 202–210, 213–214, 272.
      See also Ownership
   of political issues, 26, 28, 31, 267–268,
      269–270
   of radio, 21, 23, 24, 25–26, 27, 28, 38, 94,
      143–145, 202–203, 204–207, 209–210,
      213. See also Radio
   regulation of, 43, 57, 264, 264–265, 266,
      269, 281, 282
   scheduling of, 241
   of television, 41, 42, 43, 51, 97, 101, 126,
      133–134, 154, 202–210. See also
      Television

Brown, Harold, 294
Browsers, 84, 86, 91, 97. See also Internet;
   World Wide Web
Budget method, 248
Bulova (watch company), 147
Burgess, Jennifer, 234
Bush, George, W., 279
Business plans. See Models
Business/finance (as element of station
   operation), 223
Business/industry (use of corporate media),
   250, 252–253
Buzz marketing, 161

Cable Act of 1992, 272
Cable Communications Policy Act of 1984,
   68
Cable News Network. See CNN
Cable penetration, 70
Cable television, 62–68, 70–73
   advertising on, 65, 133, 149, 150,
      157–159, 191–192
   audience analysis and, 184
   broadcast television and, 64, 65–66, 71,
      97, 100, 133, 137, 157–158, 208
   competition for/with, 66–67, 74, 150,
      158, 184, 195
   consolidation and, 68, 72, 73, 210, 212,
      214, 226
   copyright issues and, 65–66
   delivery services for, 64–65, 68, 75
   digital technology and, 70, 71, 78, 242,
      279
   franchising of, 66–67, 68
   integration of, 72–73
   Internet and, 78–79, 91, 191,
      327–328
   localism and, 158
   microwave delivery of, 75
   models of, 63, 67, 97, 200
   music provided by, 37
   network system and, 41, 149
   operation of, 224–226, 238–239
   origins of, 41, 45, 46, 52, 61, 62–64, 88,
      217, 223
   ownership of, 66–67, 68, 72–73,
      210–211, 212, 214, 226
   patents for, 64
   political issues in, 66–67
   prevalence of, 53, 54, 65, 66, 70, 78, 150,
      191, 214–215, 238, 242
   programming of, 63, 64, 65–66, 71–72,
      75, 127, 133, 135, 224–225, 280
   ratings/shares of, 184
   regulation of, 62, 64–65, 66, 68, 71, 72,
      238, 242, 272, 280, 281
   satellite delivery of, 64–65, 68, 74, 226,
      242–243
   specialization of, 135, 150, 158
   subscriptions for, 65, 68, 71, 133, 135,
      150, 157, 200, 225
   technology of, 63–64, 66, 67, 71–72, 75,
      78, 224–225, 238–239, 242
Cable Television Consumer Protection Act
   of 1992, 71
Caching (of computer files), 192
Call sign rule, 27
Camcorders, 240, 326

Cameras
   as personal electronic media, 325–326
   for television production, 221–222,
      236–238, 240
Can-Spam. See Controlling the Assault of
   Non-Solicited Pornography and
   Marketing Act
Capital Cities Communications, 55, 203
Careers
   availability of, 15, 245–247
   competition for, 15
   in corporate media, 245–247, 258
   ethical issues and, 286–288
   in news programming, 228–230, 233,
      236
   preparation for, 197, 246–247
   in radio, 218, 223, 224, 226–231
   regulation and, 206, 262
   in television, 223, 224, 232–238
   types of, 201, 218, 246–247. See also
      specific media/types
Carlin, George, 276, 304
Carnegie Commission on Educational
   Television (CET), 51, 271–272
Carriage rules, 64
Cars
   Internet connections in, 38
   radios in, 31, 36, 176
   satellite delivery in, 37, 74, 75, 79
   telephones in, 70
Catharsis (as media effect), 301–302
Cathode ray tube, 42
CATV. See Community antenna television
CBS (Columbia Broadcast System)
   advertising and, 146
   affiliate stations of, 47, 48, 207
   audience analysis by, 186
   color television and, 46–47, 269
   news programming by, 32
   origins of, 30–31
   ownership of, 55, 207–208
   political issues and, 120
   as radio network, 30–31, 146, 202
   as television network, 47, 48, 55
CDA. See Communications Decency Act
Cease-and-desist order, 206, 274, 277–278
Cell phones, 13–14, 70, 76, 79, 80, 316–317,
   318–319. See also Telephones
Center for Online Addiction, 307
Cerf, Vinton, 84
CET. See Carnegie Commission on
   Educational Television
Chain broadcasting, 28, 266–267
Chargeback system, 247–248
Chat rooms, 13, 85–86
Checkbook journalism, 287
Chief engineer (of radio station), 230. See
   also Engineering/Operations
Children's programming
   advertising and, 168, 278, 312–313
   nutrition and, 312–313
   objectionable content in, 273, 276, 277,
      281, 282, 291–202, 296–298, 304,
      309–311, 323
   regulation of, 298
   on television, 119, 128–129, 273, 276,
      273, 276, 277, 281, 282, 291–202,
      296–298, 304, 309–311, 323

violence in, 291, 296–298, 301–302, 304, 306, 309–311
Churn (as subscriber turnover), 159
Clark, Jim, 84
"Clean Slate Amnesty" program, 96
Clear Channel Communications, 12, 37, 74
Clearance (airtime from local stations), 48
Click-throughs (and online advertising), 192
Clinton, Bill, 279
Clio Awards, 166
CNN (Cable News Network), 9, 41, 54, 56, 65, 97, 99, 126, 127, 135
Codes of ethics, 286. *See also* Ethical issues
Cognitive effects (of electronic media), 7, 303–304
College radio stations, 23, 30, 87–88, 113, 250
Color television, 41, 46–47, 269
Columbia Broadcast System. *See* CBS
Columbia Phonograph Broadcast System (CPBS), 31
Comcast Cable Communications, 72, 133
Comedic programming
    on radio, 109, 276
    on television, 53, 118, 122, 181
Commercial model, 5, 12
Commercialism, 12
Commission on the Causes and Effects of Violence (1968), 51
Communication, 2–5, 17
Communications Act of 1934, 45, 68, 265–266, 267, 271, 272
Communications Decency Act (CDA), 277, 282
Communism, 49–50, 118
Community antenna television (CATV), 45, 63
Community ascertainment, 271
Community relations (as element of station operation), 235. *See also* Promotion
Compression (of signals/files), 10, 70, 71, 80, 257
Computers, 318–319, 320, 327–328. *See also* Internet; World Wide Web
ComScore Media Metrix, 178
Conrad, Frank, 23, 24, 25
Consent decree, 277
Consolidation
    agenda setting and, 308
    broadcasting and, 241
    cable television and, 68, 72, 73, 210, 212, 214, 226
    definition of, 12
    effects of, 209
    radio and, 38, 57, 213, 214, 226
    regulation of, 12, 38, 54, 209–211, 241, 308
    telecommunications companies and, 80
    television and, 41, 54, 56, 57, 58, 209–210
Consumers
    on advertising, 163, 169, 184–185. *See also* Audience analysis
    analysis of, 184–187
    media literacy and, 15
    profiling of, 184–187, 282–283

Construction permits (CPs) (for broadcast stations), 205
Content analysis, 299, 303
Controlling the Assault of Non-Solicited Pornography and Marketing Act (Can-Spam), 279
Convergence
    corporate media and, 259
    definition of, 8, 10, 11
    digital technology and, 10
    Internet and, 8, 9, 10–11, 37–38
    radio and, 37–38, 226
    regulation and, 10, 53
    television and, 53, 54, 57
    voice/data networks and, 80
Cookies (and online profiling), 187, 282–283
Coolidge, Calvin, 265
Cooperative advertising, 191, 194
Copyright Act of 1976, 66, 284
Copyright issues, 283–285
    cable television and, 65–66
    downloading and, 14, 95–96, 284–285
    legal provisions, 283–284
    music programming and, 9, 11, 28, 93–94, 95–96, 212, 284–285
Copyright Royalty Tribunal, 66
Cornell petition, 270
Corporate media, 246–260
    applications of, 250–253
    audience analysis for, 254
    broadcasting vs., 246, 249, 250
    careers in, 245–247, 258
    convergence and, 259
    cost of, 247–248, 249
    definition of, 246
    digital technology and, 259
    distribution of, 250–251, 256–257, 259
    evaluation of, 257–258
    Internet and, 250–251, 256–257
    model of, 247–249
    origins of, 249
    production of, 253–256, 258–259
    programming of, 253
    purposes of, 246, 249–250, 257–258
    technology of, 256–257
    users of, 250–253
Corporation for Public Broadcasting (CPB), 51–52, 113, 128, 272
Corrective advertising, 278. *See also* Advertising
Cost per point (CPP), 188
Cost per thousand (CPM), 188, 193
Cost per transaction (CPT), 193
Counterattack, 49
Counterprogramming, 137
CPs. *See* Construction permits
CPB. *See* Corporation for Public Broadcasting
CPBS. *See* Columbia Phonograph Broadcast System
CPM. *See* Cost per thousand
CPP. *See* Cost per point
CPT. *See* Cost per transaction
Creative boutiques (as advertising agencies), 164
Credit card purchases, 77
Cronkite, Walter, 32

Crossley, Archibald M., 172–173
Cross-ownership, 12, 53, 54, 57, 58, 68, 208, 212, 266. *See also* Consolidation
Culture, 315–330
    advertising and, 152, 167, 168
    electronic media and, 7, 14, 15. *See also specific media*
    Internet and, 8, 83, 90
    media literacy and, 13, 15
    newspapers and, 11, 126
    personal electronic media and, 70, 315–316. *See also specific media*
    radio and, 5, 7, 31, 33, 34
    rock 'n' roll and, 110
    telephone and, 70, 316–317, 318–319
    television and, 7, 41, 45–46, 50–51
Cumulative persons (cume), 182
Cume ratings/shares, 182
Cyber advertising agencies, 165. *See also* Internet, advertising on
Cybercasting, 87, 94. *See also* Online radio

Data transfer, 77, 80, 85, 86
Day, Benjamin, 3–5
Dayparts (in radio programming), 188–189, 230
DBS. *See* Direct broadcast satellite
De Forest, Lee, 21, 23, 24, 108
Deceptive advertising, 168, 277–279. *See also* Advertising
Defamation, 269
Desensitization (as media effect), 302
Designated market areas (DMAs), 173, 175
Desktop production. *See also* Production
    corporate media and, 259
    Internet and, 211
    origins of, 13
    radio and, 37
    technology of, 13, 37
    television and, 240–241
Diaries (used in audience analysis), 172, 173–175, 177
Digital cameras, 326
Digital Millennium Copyright Act (DMCA), 284–285
Digital technology
    cable television and, 70, 71, 78, 242, 279
    convergence and, 10
    conversion to, 10, 46, 47, 56–57, 58–59, 71, 78, 195, 214, 233, 239–241, 242, 259, 279–280
    corporate media and, 259
    definition of, 10
    radio and, 10, 37, 38–39. *See also* Satellite radio
    regulation of, 10, 57, 78, 279–280
    television and, 10, 46, 47, 56–57, 58–59, 71, 78, 195, 214, 233, 241–242, 279–280
    viewing behavior and, 241–242
Digital video decoders/discs (DVDs), 58, 322
Digital video recorders (DVRs), 58, 79, 138–139, 322–323
Digitization, 10. *See also* Digital technology
Dille, John, 209
Diode tube, 21

Direct broadcast satellite (DBS), 73–74, 79, 242, 280, 282. *See also* Satellite television
Direct budget method, 248
Director (of television production), 237–237, 255. *See also* News director; Program director
DirecTV, 56, 74, 79
DISH Network, 56, 74, 79
Disinhibition (as media effect), 301
Disk jockeys (DJs)
    origins of, 23, 34, 110, 220
    programming and, 34, 114–115, 220
    scandals involving, 34, 114–115, 270–271
    technology and, 37, 38, 69
Disney Studio/Disney Company, 32, 207
Display (as characteristic of mass media), 6
Distance (as characteristic of mass media), 6
Distilled Spirits Council, 278
Distribution
    of cable television programming, 225–226
    as characteristic of mass media, 6
    of corporate media, 250–251, 256–257, 259
    of educational programming, 250–251
    of radio programming, 220–221
    of television programming, 239
DJs. *See* Disk jockeys
DMAs. *See* Designated market areas
DNS. *See* Domain name system
Domain name system (DNS), 89
Downloading
    bandwidth and, 9
    copyright issues and, 14, 95–96, 284–285
    definition of, 8
    of movie files, 14
    of music files, 9, 13, 14, 94, 95–96, 284–285
    speed of, 9, 87, 94
    of video information, 257
Dr. Phil, 125, 131,173
Dramatic programming
    on radio, 108–109
    on television, 49, 116, 121–122
Drew, Doug, 234
DSL service, 328–329
DTV (digital television), 10, 46, 47, 56–57
Du Mont, Allen, 203
Du Mont network, 47, 55, 203
Duopoly rule, 53, 266
DVDs. *See* Digital video decoders
DVRs. *See* Digital video recorders

E-mail, 13, 84–85, 86
EchoStar/DISH Network, 56, 74, 79
Ed Sullivan Show, The, 116
Editing. *See also* Production
    of audio, 13
    of video, 13, 238, 240–241, 256, 259
    technology of, 13, 238, 256, 259
Editorializing (by broadcasting stations), 269–270
Educational narrowcasting, 250
Educational programming
    corporate media and, 250, 251–252
    distribution of, 250–251

on radio, 113
    regulation of, 268, 271–272
    on television, 51–52, 268
Educational Television Facilities Act of 1962, 271
EEO. *See* Employee Equal Opportunity
Electrical scanning, 42
Electrical telegraphy, 18–19. *See also* Telegraph
Electrical telephony, 19. *See also* Telephone
Electrical transcriptions (ETs), 220
Electromagnetic spectrum, 263, 281–282
Electromagnetic theory, 20
Electronic mail. *See* E-mail
Electronic mailing lists, 85, 86
Electronic media. *See also* Mass media
    business of, 197, 245–246. *See also* Operation; Ownership
    careers in. *See* Careers
    consumers of, 15, 184–187
    costs of, 12
    culture and, 7, 14, 15. *See* Culture
    definition of, 5
    effects of, 7, 15, 51, 53. *See also* Mass media, effects of
    evolution of, 9–10, 11, 15, 61
    marketing via, 152. *See also* Advertising; Marketing
    mass media vs., 5
    models of, 5, 6, 19, 61, 76. *See also* Models
    origins of, 2–6
    personal nature of. *See* Personal electronic media
    prevalence of, 1–2, 7, 15
    profits of, 12
    purposes of, 1, 7, 12, 245–246
    regulation of. *See* Regulation
    study of, 15
    trends in, 10–12, 13–14
    types of. *See* specific media
Electronic news gathering (ENG), 54
Electronic television, 42–43. *See also* Television
Electronic transcriptions, 68–69
Emotional effects (of electronic media), 7, 302
Employee Equal Opportunity (EEO), 206
Encyrption technology, 283
ENG. *See* Electronic news gathering
Engineering/Operations. *See also* Operation
    of corporate media, 255
    of radio station, 218, 230
    of television station, 233
ESPN, 54, 65, 127
ETs. *See* Electrical transcriptions
Ethical issues, 285–288
    in advertising, 168, 286–287, 288
    in cell phone use, 80
    competition and, 287–288
    downloading, 14
    for media professionals, 286–288
    in news programming, 287
    statements of, 286–287
European Laboratory of Particle Physics, 84
External/internal communication (and use of corporate media), 250, 252–253
Extramercials (as Internet ads), 160

Fabacher, Trey, 190
Fairness doctrine, 268, 270, 271, 282
Family hour (on television), 53
Fanning, Shawn, 95
Farnsworth, Philo T., 42
Faulk, John Henry, 50
Fax machines, 70
FBI. *See* Federal Bureau of Investigation
FCC. *See* Federal Communications Commission
FCC vs. Pacifica Foundation, 276
Federal Bureau of Investigation (FBI), 49
Federal Communications Commission (FCC), 273–274
    cable television and, 62, 64–65, 66, 68, 71, 72, 238, 242, 272, 280, 281
    cell phones and, 70, 76, 80
    consolidation and, 209–210, 241, 308
    construction permits and, 205
    digital conversion and, 10, 57, 78, 279–280
    discipline by, 205–206
    FM broadcasting and, 36, 111–112
    leadership of, 213, 215, 273, 279, 311
    licensing freeze by, 41, 44–48, 62, 268–269. *See* Licenses/Licensing
    localism and, 39, 52–53, 57, 202
    operation of, 273–274
    origins of, 261, 265–266
    ownership and, 12, 53, 54, 57, 202, 204–205, 208, 212, 266, 272–273, 280, 308
    payola scandal and, 34, 270–271
    plugola scandal and, 270–271
    programming and, 205, 265–266, 272, 273, 276–277, 281–282
    purposes of, 30, 202, 285
    radio operations and, 218
    satellite delivery and, 39
    telephone and, 272
    television broadcasting and, 43, 57, 269
    television programming and, 51, 52–53, 129–130, 298
    television technology and, 45–47
Federal Radio Commission (FRC), 30, 218, 265
Federal Trade Commission (FTC)
    consumer profiling and, 187
    deceptive advertising and, 168, 277–279
    origins of, 266
    music programming and, 304–306
    purposes of, 266
Feedback (in communication models), 3, 4
Fessenden, Reginald, 21, 23
Fiber optic network, 80
Field experiments, 299
Field television, 238
File sharing, 9, 11, 95–96, 284–285, 321. *See also* Music programming
Fin/syn. *See* Financial interest and syndicate rule
Financial interest and syndicate rule (Fin/syn), 53, 129–130, 280
First Amendment, 261, 262, 276, 279, 281, 283
First-run syndicated programs, 131, 137. *See also* Syndicated programming

Fixed buys, 189–190
Flat-panel televisions, 324, 325
Fleming, John, 21
Fleming valve, 21
Floaters (ads on Internet), 160
FM radio, 35–36, 38, 111–112
Focus groups, 186
Four-factor syndrome (as media effect), 302
FOX network
    affiliate stations of, 204, 207
    cable television and, 71, 201
    Internet and, 102
    origins of, 54, 55, 56, 133, 203–204, 207
    ownership of, 12, 55, 74, 308
    programming of, 55, 58, 102, 127, 130,
        201, 203–204, 208–209, 308
    ratings of, 180
    revenues of, 55, 203
    syndication by, 201
Franchising (of cable television), 66–67, 68
Franklin, Benjamin, 143
FRC. See Federal Radio Commission
Free speech, 261, 262, 281–282
Freed, Alan, 110
Frequency discounts (in advertising), 190
Frequency modulation (FM), 35–36
Front-projection televisions, 324, 325
FTC. See Federal Trade Commission
Full-service advertising agencies, 164

Game shows, 117–118, 122, 124–125, 137,
    175
Gannett (company), 58
Gatekeepers (of news programming), 127,
    295, 307
GE. See General Electric
General Electric (GE), 25, 29, 42, 55, 203
General management
    of radio station, 218, 227–228
    of television station, 232–233
Global positioning satellite (GPS), 195
Gore, Tipper, 304–305
Government (use of corporate media), 251
Government subsidy/ownership model,
    199
GPS. See Global positioning satellite
Grandfathering (and cross-ownership), 12
Grateful Dead, 96
Graylisting, 50
Great American Values Test, 298
Gross rating points (GRPs), 188
GRPs. See Gross rating points
Gulf War, 55
Gutenberg, Johannes, 3, 143

Hammocking (and program scheduling),
    136
Harding, Warren G., 26
HBO (Home Box Office), 41, 52, 54, 65, 68,
    72, 127, 128, 133, 135, 150, 226
HDTV. See High-definition television
Head end, 66, 72, 73, 75, 224
Head-to-head programming, 137
Health care (use of corporate media), 251
Herrold, Charles D. "Doc," 23, 24, 25
Hertz (as unit of radio frequency), 20
Hertz, Heinrich, 20

Hieroglyphics, 2–3
High-definition television (HDTV), 56, 57
Hitler, Adolf, 293
Home Box Office. See HBO
Home networking, 327
Hooks (and music programming), 186
Hooper, C. E., 172–173
Hoover, Herbert, 27, 144–145
Hot clocks, 114, 115
Households using television (HUT), 181
HSS. See Hypersonic sound system
Human resources (as element of station
    operation), 236
HUT. See Households using television
HTML. See Hypertext markup language
Hypersonic sound system (HSS), 321
Hypertext, 91
Hypertext markup language (HTML), 91, 92

I Love Lucy, 118, 131
IBM, 166
IBOC. See In band, on channel
IBS. See Internet Broadcast Systems
Iconoscopes, 42
Identification (as media effect), 301
IE. See Internet Explorer
IM. See Instant messaging
Image advertising, 149
Imitation (as media effect), 301
In band, on channel (IBOC), 10, 38
Indecency (in programming), 272, 272,
    276, 277
Independent production houses, 129, 129,
    130, 248–249, 258, 280
Independent stations, 47, 64, 202
Industrial Revolution, 18, 143
Infinity Broadcasting, 37, 114
Infomercials, 160–161, 200, 278
Information overload, 167, 317
Information programming. See News
    programming
Inhibition (as media effect), 301
Inhouse media units, 247
Instant messaging (IM), 13, 86, 104–105
Instructional Television Fixed Service
    (ITFS), 250
Instrumental viewing, 98, 309
Interactive advertising agencies, 165
Interconnect buys (and cable television
    advertising), 158, 191–192
Internal/external communication (and use
    of corporate media), 250, 252–253
International Radio Telegraph Company, 26
Internet, 83–106. See also World Wide Web
    access to, 38, 81, 89, 215, 242, 327–328
    advertising on, 94, 97–98, 99, 152,
        159–164, 178–179, 187, 192–194,
        278–279
    audience analysis for, 178–179, 185, 187,
        282–283
    broadcasting and, 94, 100, 101
    cable television and, 78–79, 91, 191,
        327–328
    content on, 91–93, 215, 277, 279
    convergence and, 8, 9, 10–11, 37–38
    corporate media and, 250–251, 256–257
    culture and, 8, 83, 90

    definition of, 5–6, 8, 84
    delivery systems for, 78–79, 80–81
    domain names on, 90
    educational programming and, 250, 256
    effects of, 307
    music programming on, 212
    navigation of, 91, 97. See also Browsers
    networks and, 97–98, 99
    news programming on, 93, 99–100, 101,
        102–104, 127
    operation of, 88–90
    origins of, 83
    ownership and, 211
    prevalence of, 6, 8, 83, 90
    radio and, 9, 37–38, 87–88, 93–94, 100,
        105, 138, 211–212
    regulation of, 211, 278–279, 282,
        282–283
    resources of, 84–86. See also E-mail
    spam on, 161–162, 278–279
    taxation and, 285
    technology of, 87, 88–90, 94, 97, 215
    telephone service and, 81, 91, 319–320
    television and, 5, 9, 88, 97–101, 138
    users of, 90, 94, 98, 192–193, 312
    viewing behaviors and, 98, 192–193, 312
Internet Broadcasting Systems (IBS), 99
Internet Explorer (IE), 84, 91
Internet protocol (IP), 89
Internet service providers (ISPs), 13, 78–79,
    91, 160, 279
Internet Tax Freedom Act, 285
Internet Tax Non-Discrimination Act, 285
Interstitials (as Internet ads), 160
Intranet, 256
IP. See Internet protocol. See also
    Transmission control protocol
ISPs. See Internet service providers
ITFS. See Instructional Television Fixed
    Service

JCET. See Joint Committee on Educational
    Television
Joint Committee on Educational Television
    (JCET), 51
Joint sales agreement (JSA), 207
JSA. See Joint sales agreement
Jupiter Media Matrix, 178

Kennedy, John F., 50, 296
Kennedy, Robert, 50, 296
Kentucky Horse Racing Authority, 167
Kinescopes, 42, 48
King World Productions, 131, 132
King, Martin Luther, Jr., 50, 296
Korean War, 49
Kraft Television Theater, 49, 116, 146, 200

Laboratory experiments, 299
LANs. See Local area networks
LCD televisions, 324, 325
Leading in (and program scheduling), 136
Leading out (and program scheduling), 136
Legal issues, 269–272, 281–285. See also
    Regulation
    appeals of rulings, 276
    cell phone use, 80

Legal issues *(continued)*
    copyright, 9, 11, 14, 28, 65–66, 93–94,
        95–96, 212, 283–285
    downloading, 14, 95–96
    free speech, 261, 262, 281–282
    online radio, 212
    patents, 20, 21, 25, 35–36, 42, 64
    privacy, 262, 282–283
    scandals, 34, 114–115, 117–118, 148,
        270–271
Levin, Gerald, 65
Libel, 269, 283
Licenses/Licensing
    awarding of, 205, 273
    competition for, 205, 273
    FCC freeze on, 41, 44–48, 62, 268–269
    programming and, 107
    of radio stations, 23–24, 26, 27, 28, 30,
        107, 202
    renewal of, 207, 266, 271, 274
    requirements of, 30, 273
    revocation of, 205–206, 207, 266, 274
    of television stations, 41, 43, 44–48, 62,
        202
Licensing agencies/fees (for music
        programming), 9, 93–94, 212, 284
Lighting (for television production), 222,
        236
Limited-effects perspective, 294–295. *See
        also* Mass media, effects of
Linear editing system, 240–241
Linear model (of communication), 4
Liquid crystal display televisions. *See* LCD
        televisions
Listservs, 85
Live journals, 14
Live production
    of radio programming, 219
    of television programming, 48, 147–148
Live remotes, 219
LMA. *See* Local marketing agreement
Lobbying/Lobbyists, 275
Local access channels, 136
Local area networks (LANs), 256, 257
Local marketing agreement (LMA), 207
Local origination channels, 65, 135–136
Lodge, Oliver, 20
Low-power FM (LPFM), 38
LPFM. *See* Low-power FM
Lucky Strike Hit Parade, The, 145–146

Made-for-television movies, 120, 127,
        128
Magazine style (of television advertising),
        147. *See also* Spot advertising
Magic bullet theory, 293
Major League Baseball, 167
Make-goods (in advertising), 190
Management. *See also* Operation
    of radio station, 218, 227–228
    of television station, 232–233
Marconi, Guglielmo, 5, 20–21
Marconi Company, 24, 25, 204, 264
Marketing. *See also* Advertising
    approaches to, 152, 161
    definition of, 142
    as element of station operation, 225, 228

Marketplace of ideas (concept of
        information/opinions), 262, 271, 277
Martin, Kevin, 311
Mass communication, 3, 4
Mass media, 6–7
    agenda setting by, 307–308
    characteristics of, 6, 8–9
    comparison of, 8–9
    competition among, 9–10
    definition of, 3, 8
    effects of, 291–298, 300–307, 308–309
    electronic media vs., 5. *See also* Electronic
        media
    evolution of, 9–10
    origins of, 3–5
    penetration and, 8, 70
    research on, 293, 294, 298–299
    types of. *See specific types*
    uses of, 308–309
    World Wide Web vs., 8–10. *See also* World
        Wide Web
Master antenna system, 63
Mathematical model (of communication),
        4
Maxwell, James Clerk, 20
Mayflower doctrine, 269–270
MBS. *See* Mutual Broadcasting System
McCarthy, Joseph, 50, 118
McGraw, Phil, 125, 131
"Mean world" syndrome, 304
Mechanical scanning, 42
Media conferencing, 257
Media literacy, 13, 15
Media-buying services, 164–165
Medicine (use of corporate media), 251
Meet the Press, 126
Messaging systems, 316–318
Meters/Metering devices (for audience
        measurement), 175–176, 177
Metro survey areas (MSAs), 174
Microwave delivery, 61, 75
Middle of the road (MOR) (music
        programming), 220
Miller vs. California, 276
Milton, John, 262
Miniseries (on television), 120, 121, 127,
        128
MMDSs. *See* Multichannel multipoint
        distribution systems
Models, 198–216. *See also specific models*
    of broadcasting, 97, 200
    of cable television, 63, 67, 97, 200
    of communication, 3–5. *See also specific
        models*
    of corporate media, 247–249
    definition of, 3
    of electronic media, 5, 6, 19, 61, 76
    of network system, 201–203, 217, 221
    origins of, 198
    of radio, 19, 25, 27, 31, 145, 198–200,
        217
    of satellite radio, 200
    of satellite television, 200
    of television, 97, 198–202, 208–209, 217,
        221
Moderate-effects perspective, 296–297. *See
        also* Mass media, effects of

Montuori, John, 177
Moore-Greenke, Jason, 231
MOR. *See* Middle of the road
Morse code, 18–19, 20, 21, 23
Morse, Samuel F. B., 3, 5, 18
Mosaic, 84, 91
Motivational training (and corporate
        media), 252
Movies (on television), 120–121, 127–128
Mozilla, 91
MP3 technology, 95, 212
MSAs. *See* Metro survey areas
MSNBC, 71, 102, 127, 133
MSOs. *See* Multiple system operators
MTV, 41, 54, 65
Multichannel multipoint distribution
        systems (MMDSs), 73, 75, 215, 282
Multichannel video program distributors
        (MVPDs), 64
Multiple system operators (MSOs), 71, 72,
        210–211, 214, 226. *See also*
        Consolidation
Multiplexing (of digital signals), 71
Murdoch, Rupert, 55, 203
Murphy, Reggie, 185
Murrow, Edward R., 32, 50, 118
Music box memo, 24. *See also* Sarnoff,
        David
Music programming
    audience analysis and, 185, 186
    cable television and, 37
    copyright and, 9, 11, 28, 93–94, 95–96,
        212, 284–285
    disk jockeys and, 34, 114–115, 220
    early broadcasts of, 21, 23, 26, 28
    file sharing and, 9, 11, 95–96, 284–285,
        321
    Internet and, 212
    licensing fees for, 9, 93–94, 212, 284
    localism and, 110
    objectionable content in, 304–306
    paying for, 114, 270
    personal electronic media and, 95,
        320–321
    on radio, 7, 34, 36, 37, 38–39, 69, 93,
        108, 109–111, 212, 219, 220, 270,
        304–306
    rating systems for, 305–306
    recording of, 220
    regulation of, 304–306
    on television, 41, 116–117
    on websites, 93–94
Must-carry rule, 64
Mutual Broadcasting System (MBS), 31
MVPDs. *See* Multichannel video program
        distributors

NAB. *See* National Association of
        Broadcasters
Napster, 95–96, 284
Narrative programming (on television),
        121–122. *See also* Dramatic
        programming; Serial dramas;
        Situation comedies
Narrowcasting, 24, 97, 250
National Association of Broadcasters (NAB),
        28, 53, 112, 275, 286

National Association of Television Program
Executives (NATPE), 137–138
National Broadcasting Company. *See* NBC
National Cable Television Association
(NCTA), 275
National Educational Television (NET), 51
National Football League, 208–209
National Public Radio (NPR), 113, 128, 272
National Science Foundation, 84
National Telecommunication Information
Administration (NTIA), 275
National Television System Committee
(NTSC), 43, 46
National Television Violence Study, 300
NATPE. *See* National Association of
Television Program Executives
NBC (National Broadcasting Company)
affiliates of, 47, 48
cable television and, 71
competition for, 30–31
origins of, 29
ownership of, 55
as radio network, 29, 35, 202, 266
as television network, 47, 48, 55
NCTA. *See* National Cable Television
Association
Near video on demand (NVOD), 72, 135
NET. *See* National Educational Television
Netscape Navigator, 84, 91
Network affiliates, 201, 202–203. *See also*
Affiliate stations
Network compensation model, 201–202,
208–209
Network owned and operated stations (O &
Os), 201
Networks/Network systems. *See also*
Broadcasting/Broadcast networks
advertising and, 150, 152, 153, 154, 155,
158
cable television and, 67, 149
competition for/among, 30–31, 52–53,
54, 55, 56, 58, 67, 97–98, 130, 132,
136, 149, 150, 158, 184, 195, 207
definition of, 28, 201
dominance of, 5, 34, 47, 52, 54, 97, 133,
202, 207
Internet and, 97–98, 99
models of, 201–203, 217, 221
origins of, 217
ownership and, 55, 201, 202–210, 213,
272–273, 280. *See also* Ownership
programming by, 114, 118, 126, 129,
132, 133–134, 214
of radio, 5, 28, 29, 30–31, 34–35, 47, 114,
152, 153, 176, 202, 217
regulation of, 48, 266, 272–273. *See also*
Regulation
of television, 5, 41, 47–48, 52, 53, 54,
55–56, 58, 64, 67, 97, 99, 118, 126,
129, 130, 132, 133–134, 136, 149, 150,
176, 201, 202–203, 217, 280
Net World Communications, 204
New York Sun, 3–5
New York Times v., Sullivan, 269
News Corporation, 12, 55, 74, 213, 308
News director, 228, 229, 233. *See also* News
programming

News programming
agenda setting in, 307–308
on cable television, 127. *See also* CNN
careers in, 228–230, 233, 236
control over, 127
corporate media and, 253
credibility of, 287
criticism of, 127
effects of, 307–308
as element of station operation,
228–230, 233
effects of, 295
ethical issues in, 287
on Internet, 93, 99–100, 101, 102–104,
127
prominent figures in, 32, 126–127
purposes of, 307–308
on radio, 32, 111–112, 228–230
technology and, 54
on television, 54, 118, 126, 233, 236,
287–288
types of, 126–127
News/talk format, 112. *See also* News
programming
Newsgroups, 85, 86
Newspaper/radio war, 32
Newspapers
advertising in, 5, 33, 143
culture and, 11, 126
effects of, 293
online versions of, 11, 98–99
models of, 5
origins of, 3–5, 143
political issues and, 28
radio and, 22–23, 31, 32, 108
television and, 43, 126
Newton (as personal digital assistant),
317–318
NHI. *See* Nielsen home video index
Nielsen, A. C., 172–173. *See also* Nielsen
Media Research
Nielsen home video index (NHI), 184
Nielsen Media Research. *See also* Audience
analysis
methods used by, 158, 173–174, 175,
176, 178, 184, 186, 187, 195
origins of, 172–173
reports by, 182–184
Nielsen NetRatings, 178
Nielsen station index (NSI), 182–184
Nielsen television index (NTI), 182–184
Nipkow, Paul, 42
Nixon, Richard, 50, 52
Noble, Edward J., 202
Noncommercial media, 51–52, 128–129,
113, 246, 271. *See also* Corporate
media
Nonduplication rules, 64
Nonlinear editing system, 240–241
Nonnarative programming (on television),
121, 122–128. *See also* Game shows;
Movies; News programming
NPR. *See* National Public Radio
NSI. *See* Nielsen station index
NTI. *See* Nielsen television index
NTIA. *See* National Telecommunication
Information Administration

NTSC. *See* National Television System
Committee
Nutrition (and children's programming),
312–313
NVOD. *See* Near video on demand

O & Os. *See* Network owned and operated
stations
Obesity (and children's programming),
312–313
Obscenity (in programming), 272, 276, 277
Off-net programs. *See* Off-network
syndicated programs
Off-network syndicated programs, 131,
137. *See also* Syndicated programming
Oligopoly, 72, 280
One-to-many model (of communication),
3, 5, 76
One-to-one model (of communication), 3,
5, 70, 76
Online audio, 138. *See also* Online radio
Online journals, 14
Online polling, 100–101, 125
Online radio, 9, 37–38, 87–88, 93–94, 100,
105, 138, 211–212. *See also* Radio
Online video, 5, 9, 88, 97–101, 138. *See also*
Television
Operation. *See also* Ownership; Production
of cable television station/system,
224–226, 238–239
of Internet services, 88–90
of radio station, 218, 226–231
of satellite system, 239
of television station, 221, 232–238
Opinion leaders/followers, 295
Oprah Winfrey Show, The, 131, 132, 137, 173
Osbournes, The, 123, 124
Outsourcing, 165, 247, 258
Owner groups, 209–211. *See also* Ownership
Ownership, 202–210. *See also*
Licenses/Licensing
of broadcast stations, 202–210, 213–214,
272
of cable television stations, 66–67, 68,
72–73, 210–211, 212, 214, 226
consolidation of. *See* Consolidation
costs of, 205, 206
by groups, 209–210, 22
of Internet services, 211
of/by networks, 55, 201, 202–210, 213,
272–273, 280
operation vs., 207. *See also* Operation
qualifications of, 204–205
of radio stations, 12, 37, 38, 57, 202–203,
204–207, 209–210, 213, 214, 226,
266–267, 272–273
regulation of, 12, 53, 54, 57, 202,
204–205, 208, 212, 266, 272–273, 280,
308
of television stations, 43, 53, 54, 56, 57,
137–138, 202–210, 272–273, 280
trends in. *See* Consolidation;
Convergence
Ozzie and Harriet, The Adventures of, 124

Pagers, 76
Paley, William S., 30–31, 146

Palm Pilot (as personal digital assistant), 318
Parabolic antennas, 75
Paradigm breakers, 6
Parents Music Resource Center (PMRC), 304–305
Parents Television Council, 311
Parsons, L. E., 63–64
Participation advertising, 147–149
Participations (in television advertising), 154
Patents
    for cable television, 64
    for radio, 20, 21, 25, 35–36
    for television, 42
Pattiz, Norm, 69
PAX network, 56, 133, 184, 207
Paxson, Bud, 56, 207
Pay cable, 65, 66, 150. See also Cable television
Pay-per-view channels, 135. See also Cable television
Payola scandal, 34, 114–115, 270–271
PBS. See Public Broadcasting Service
PDAs. See Personal digital assistants
Pearl Harbor, 33
Penny press newspapers, 3–5
People meters, 175–176, 194
People using radio (PUR), 181
People using television (PUT), 181
Per-set tax model, 199
Personal digital assistants (PDAs), 79, 317–318
Personal electronic media, 315–330
    culture and, 70, 315–316. See also Culture
    music programming and, 95, 320–321
    origins of, 7, 70
    program scheduling and, 138, 139
    types of. See specific types
    World Wide Web and, 97
Personal optical mobile assistant (Poma), 320
Persuasion (and mass media), 293–294
Petition to deny renewal (of license), 207
Phone numbers, 80
Photographers, 236, 238. See also Cameras
Pictographs, 3
Pilots (as samples of television programs), 129
Pitching (ideas for programs), 129, 253
Playlists, 34, 38, 115
Plugola scandal, 34, 270–271
PMRC. See Parents Music Resource Center
Pods (in television advertising), 154
Point-to-multipoint model (of communication), 61, 68
Point-to-point model (of communication), 19, 31, 61, 70, 79
Political issues
    broadcasting of, 26, 28, 267–268, 269–270
    cable television and, 66–67
    news programming and, 112
    newspapers and, 28
    radio and, 26, 28, 31, 112
    regulation and, 267–268, 275, 279
    television and, 52, 116, 120

Poma. See Personal optical mobile assistant
Pop-under ads, 160, 178
Pop-up ads, 159–160, 178
Popoff, Alexander, 20
Pornography (in programming), 272, 276, 320
Portable people meters (PPMs), 194–195
Portable television, 238
Powell, Michael, 213, 215
Powerful-effects perspective, 297–298. See also Mass media, effects of
PPMs. See Portable people meters
Preece, William, 20
Preempting (of programming), 55
Premiere Radio Networks, 114
Premium channels, 135
Prime-time access rule (PTAR), 52–53
Prime-time programming, 131, 133–134
Printing press, 3, 143
Privacy (right to), 262, 282–283
Private audio, 320–321
Private cable, 74. See also Cable television; Satellite television
Producers (of programming), 201
Product demonstrations, 147–148, 252
Product placement (in advertising), 154–155, 194
Production (of programming). See also Distribution; Operation; Ownership; Programming
    for corporate media, 253–256, 258–259
    cost of, 114
    as element of station operation, 228–229, 236
    for radio, 114, 217–218, 219–221, 228
    sources of, 129–132, 201, 241
    for television, 217–218, 221–223, 233, 236–238
Production companies, 129, 132
Professional organizations (use of corporate media), 251
Program directors, 115, 219, 228–229
Program wheels, 114, 115
Programming, 107–140
    advertising and, 146, 148, 200
    audience analysis and, 195, 199
    of cable television, 63, 64, 65–66, 71–72, 75, 127, 133, 135, 224–225, 280
    of corporate media, 253
    delivery of, 137–138
    as element of station operation, 224–225, 228–229, 233
    licensing and, 107
    by networks, 114, 118, 126, 129, 132, 133–134, 214
    objectionable content in, 272, 273, 276–277, 281, 282, 291–292, 293, 296, 297–298, 300–307, 309–313
    paying for, 114, 132–133
    production of. See Production
    of radio, 7, 28, 32, 34–35, 36, 38–39, 47, 48, 57, 68–69, 88, 93–94, 107, 108–115, 139, 145–146, 175, 188–189, 217, 219–221, 228–229
    recording of, 52, 54, 58, 79, 138–139, 322–323

regulation of, 205, 265–266, 272, 273, 276–277, 281–282
    of satellite radio, 75, 114, 138, 239
    of satellite television, 74, 79, 280
    scheduling of, 114–115, 136–137, 195–196, 241
    sources of, 113–114, 129, 137–138, 201, 219, 221, 233, 239, 253
    technology and, 138
    of television, 5, 44, 46, 47, 48, 49, 50, 51–53, 54, 55, 79, 88, 97, 98–99, 100–101, 115–139, 146–147, 175, 176, 186–187, 195–196, 214, 221, 224–225, 233
    types of. See specific types
Promotion. See also Advertising
    definition of, 142
    as element of station operation, 155, 230–231, 235
    in radio, 155, 230–231
    in television, 155, 235, 236
Propaganda, 293–294
PSAs. See Public service announcements
Psychographics, 162–163
PTAR. See Prime-time access rule
Public access programs, 65
Public affairs programs, 126
Public and Broadcasting—A Procedural Manual, The, 206
Public Broadcasting Act of 1967, 51, 271–272
Public Broadcasting Service (PBS), 51–52, 128–129, 130, 133, 272
Public files (of broadcast stations), 206
"Public interest, convenience, and necessity," 30, 265, 268
Public service announcements (PSAs), 155
Public television, 51–52, 128–129, 130, 133, 272
Puffery (as exaggeration in advertising), 168
PUR. See People using radio
Push technologies (and online advertising), 192
PUT. See People using television

Quiz shows, 117–118, 148, 270

Radio, 17–40, 108–115
    advertising on, 27, 33, 48, 94, 109, 143–147, 152–154, 155, 188–191, 197–198, 228, 230–231
    AM vs. FM, 34–36
    amateur operators/hobbyists of, 23, 25, 26, 31, 33, 87, 107, 264
    audience analysis for, 171, 172–177, 182, 186, 194, 230
    broadcasting of, 21, 23, 24, 25–26, 27, 28, 38, 94, 143–145, 202–203, 204–207, 209–210, 213
    cable television and, 37
    careers in, 218, 223, 224, 226–231
    consolidation and, 38, 57, 213, 214, 226
    convergence and, 37–38, 226
    culture and, 5, 7, 31, 33, 34
    digital technology and, 10, 37, 38–39. See also Satellite radio
    distribution of, 220–221

effects of, 293–295
formats of, 5, 28, 34, 35, 36, 37, 68, 110, 111, 220
Internet and, 9, 37–38, 87–88, 93–94, 100, 105, 138, 211–212
licensing of, 23–24, 26, 27, 28, 30, 107, 202
localism of, 38, 57, 110, 153, 191
as mass medium, 23–27
models of, 19, 25, 27, 31, 145, 198–200, 217
music on. *See* Music programming
network system of, 5, 28, 29, 30–31, 34–35, 47, 114, 152, 153, 176, 202, 217
newspapers and, 22–23, 31, 32, 108
objectionable content on, 272, 273, 276–277, 281, 282
operation of radio station, 218, 226–231
origins of, 5, 17, 18–23, 87, 107
ownership of, 12, 37, 38, 57, 202–203, 204–207, 209–210, 213, 214, 226, 266–267, 272–273
patents for, 20, 21, 25, 35–36
political issues and, 26, 28, 31, 112
prevalence of, 5, 8, 25–30, 36, 94, 109, 214, 217, 220
production in, 114, 217–218, 219–221, 228
programming by, 7, 28, 32, 34–35, 36, 38–39, 47, 48, 57, 68–69, 88, 93–94, 107, 108–115, 139, 145–146, 175, 188–189, 217, 219-221, 228–229. *See also* Programming
purposes of, 24, 27, 32, 263–264
ratings/shares of, 179–180, 181, 182
regulation of, 18, 21, 23–24, 25, 26, 27, 28, 29, 30, 33, 36, 38, 39, 93–94, 199, 218, 263–265, 267, 271, 272–273, 304–306
revenues earned by, 27, 33, 38, 39
satellite delivery of. *See also* Satellite radio
scheduling of, 34
sponsorship in, 145–146, 200
technology of, 7, 20–21, 23, 24, 25, 26–27, 28, 29, 31, 36, 37, 87, 88, 94, 108, 109, 219
television and, 5, 7, 37, 38, 43, 47, 48, 88, 109, 115, 220, 223
websites of, 93–94, 101
Radio Act of 1912, 23, 264
Radio Act of 1927, 30, 264–265
Radio and Television News Directors Association (RTNDA), 286
Radio Corporation of America (RCA)
color television and, 46–47, 269
ownership of, 203
radio and, 25, 29, 30, 35, 203
television and, 42, 55, 203
Radio diaries, 173–174
Radio markets reports, 182
Radio telegraphy, 5
Radio waves, 20–21
"Raised eyebrow" letter, 205–206, 266, 274
Rather, Dan, 32, 126

Rating codes/systems
for music programming, 305–306
for television programming, 277, 310–311
Ratings (and audience analysis), 179–181, 182–184. *See also* Audience analysis
RCA. *See* Radio Corporation of America
Reagans, The (miniseries), 120
RealAudio/RealNetworks, 87, 97
Real-time audio, 87. *See also* Online radio
Reality shows, 123–125
Recording Industry Association of America (RIAA), 9, 96, 212, 284, 285
Red Channels, 49–50
Red Lion v. FCC, 270, 280
Red Lion standard, 270
Red network (of NBC), 29, 31, 108. *See also* National Broadcasting Company
Regulation, 261–290
of advertising, 149, 167, 168, 266, 277–279
agencies of, 30, 261, 275. *See also* Federal Communications Commission; Federal Radio Commission; Federal Trade Commission
of audience analysis, 179
of broadcasting, 264, 264–265, 266, 281, 282
of cable television, 62, 64–65, 66, 68, 71, 72, 238, 242, 272, 280, 281
consolidation and, 12, 38, 54, 209–211
convergence and, 10, 53
of digital technology, 10, 57, 78, 279–280
of employment practices, 206, 262
evolution of electronic media and, 10, 12, 261–262
influences on, 275–276
of Internet, 211, 278–279, 282, 282–283
licenses/licensing and. *See* Licenses/Licensing
local level of, 275
of music programming, 304–306
of networks, 48, 266, 272–273
of online music providers, 93–94
origins of, 262
of ownership, 12, 53, 54, 57, 202, 204–205, 208, 212, 266, 272–273, 280, 308
philosophies behind, 18, 29, 30, 53, 54, 57, 64, 66, 214, 241, 261, 262, 268, 271, 272, 275, 285
political issues and, 267–268, 275, 279
of programming, 205, 265–266, 272, 273, 276–277, 281–282
of radio, 18, 21, 23–24, 25, 26, 27, 28, 29, 30, 33, 36, 38, 39, 93–94, 199, 218, 263–265, 267, 271, 272–273, 304–306
of satellite radio, 39
of satellite television, 39, 66, 73, 74, 280, 282
of television, 41, 43, 44–47, 48, 51–53, 54, 56, 57, 129–130, 267, 271, 272–273, 298
Rehearsing (and television production), 222–223
Renfroe, Jay, 130
Reno v. ACLU, 277

Rent-a-citizen practice, 67
Repetition (and program scheduling), 137
Report on Chain Broadcasting, The, 202, 266
Repurposing (of programming), 241
Reynolds, Glenn, 103
RIAA. *See* Recording Industry Association of America
Rich-media banner ads, 159
Ritualistic viewing, 98, 309
Rock 'n' roll, 7, 110–111. *See also* Music programming
Roosevelt, Franklin D., 33, 43, 118, 265
ROS. *See* Run of schedule
Rotation (of songs on playlist), 115
Routers (and Internet access), 89
RTNDA. *See* Radio and Television News Directors Association
Rule of sevens, 54, 209
Rule of twelves, 209
Run of schedule (ROS) (in advertising), 190

SAG. *See* Screen Actors Guild
Sales
corporate media and, 252
as element of station operation, 225, 228, 235, 241. *See also* Advertising
Sales managers, 235
Samples (in audience analysis), 176
Sarnoff, David, 22–23, 24, 35, 42, 46, 199
Satellite Home Viewers Act (SHVA) (1999), 74
Satellite master antenna television (SMATV), 73
Satellite radio
models of, 200
operation of, 239
origins of, 10, 68–69
prevalence of, 79, 242–243
programming of, 75, 114, 138, 239
providers of, 10, 37, 74–75, 79
regulation of, 39
subscriptions for, 37–38, 74, 79, 200, 239
technology of, 73, 74, 242–243
Satellite television
advertising on, 195
audience analysis and, 195
cable television and, 64–65, 68, 73, 74, 226, 242–243
models of, 200
music provided by, 37
network system and, 97
operation of, 239
origins of, 52, 53, 61, 66, 88
prevalence of, 208, 214–215, 242–243
programming of, 74, 79, 280
providers of, 56, 74, 79
recording of, 79, 139
regulation of, 39, 66, 73, 74, 280, 282
subscriptions for, 37, 74, 200, 239
technology of, 37, 56, 68, 73–74, 208, 242–243
Satellites (types of), 73, 242–243
Scarcity theory, 281–282
Schramm mass communication model, 4
Schramm/Osgood communication model, 4

Scientific Advisory Committee on Television and Social Behavior, 296, 297–298
Scouting locations, 255
Screen Actors Guild (SAG), 255
Scripts (for corporate media), 254
SDTV. *See* Standard definition television
Seamless programming, 136
Search for extraterrestrial intelligence (SETI), 3
Selective processes, 295
Self-right principle, 262
Senate Commerce Committee (and objectionable music programming), 305
Serial dramas, 108–109, 121–122. *See also* Dramatic programming
Servers (and Internet access), 89
Set meters, 175
Set-top boxes
    cable television and, 272
    digital conversion and, 10, 57, 58–59, 71
SETI. *See* Search for extraterrestrial intelligence
Shannon/Weaver communication model, 4
Shapp, Milton, 64
Shared antenna system, 63
Shares (and audience analysis), 179–181. *See also* Audience analysis
Ships/Shipping, 19, 22–23, 24
Showtime, 54, 65
SHVA. *See* Satellite Home Viewers Act
Simulcasting, 34
Sirius Satellite Radio, 10, 37, 74, 79, 239
Situation comedies (sitcoms)
    social awareness programming and, 53
    on television, 53, 118, 122, 181
Sixth Report and Order, The, 45, 268
Size-based pricing (and online advertising), 193
Skyscrapers (as ads on Internet), 160
Slander, 283
Smart CDs, 321
Smart personal object technology (SPOT), 319
"Smart" watches, 318–319
SMATV. *See* Satellite master antenna television
Soap operas, 108–109, 121–122, 220. *See also* Dramatic programming
Social unrest/awareness (and television programming), 41, 50–51, 53, 125–126
Sony, 32
SoundExchange, 285
Spam (as Internet advertising), 161–162, 278–279
Special effects (for television production), 222, 237
Spiderman, 167
Sponsorship, 145–149, 200, 266
Sports programming, 119–120
Sports/news format, 112. *See also* News programming; Sports programming
SPOT. *See* Smart personal object technology

Spot advertising, 147–149, 200
Spots (as commercials), 149
Standard definition television (SDTV), 56, 57
Station compensation, 48
Station manager, 232–233. *See also* Management; Operation
Station promotions, 155, 230–231, 236. *See also* Promotion
Steganography, 105
Stereo broadcasting, 36
Stereotypes (and advertising), 168
Stewart, Bill, 111
Storage (as characteristic of mass media), 6–7
Storyboards (for corporate media), 254
Storz, Todd, 111
Streaming technology, 87. *See also* Online radio
Stripping (and program scheduling), 137
Stubblefield, Nathan, 21
Studio television, 221–222, 236–238. *See also* Production, of television
Stunting (and program scheduling), 137
Subscription model, 200
Super Bowl advertising, 156
Supergroups (of station owners), 209
Superheterodyne receiver, 27
Superstations, 9, 64–65, 72
Superstitials (as Internet ads), 160
Survey research, 299
"Sweeps" periods, 175, 241
Switcher (for video signal), 236, 237
Synchronous media, 6
Syndicated exclusivity rules, 64, 66
Syndicated programming, 53, 64, 69, 114, 130, 131–133, 137–138, 155, 201, 212

Takano, Kent, 134
Talk shows, 125–126, 137, 173
Target advertising, 150
Target audience, 151, 188. *See also* Audience analysis
Tarlton, Bob, 64
Taxation (of Internet transactions), 285
TCP. *See* Transmission control protocol
Telecommunications Act of 1996, 10, 12, 37, 56, 57, 202, 209, 212, 226, 261, 272–273, 277, 282, 310
Teleconferencing, 257
Telegraph model, 199
Telegraph, 3, 5, 17, 18–19, 199
Telephone
    audience analysis and, 172
    cable television and, 242
    culture and, 70, 316–317, 318–319
    Internet and, 81, 91, 319–320. *See also* Internet
    invention of, 3, 5, 19, 20–21, 70, 199
    providers of, 81, 91, 242
    regulation of, 272
    technology based on, 70, 76, 316–317, 318–319. *See also* Cell phones; Pagers
Telephone coincidental method, 172
Telephone model, 199

Telephone recall system, 172
Television, 41–60, 115–139
    advertising on, 5, 48, 49, 52, 53, 97, 146–150, 152, 154–157, 188–191, 195–196, 197–198, 235
    affiliate stations, 47–48, 52–53, 55–56, 131, 132, 137, 201, 202–203, 204, 207, 208–209
    audience analysis for, 171, 173–177, 183–184, 186–187, 194–195, 202
    broadcasting of, 41, 42, 43, 51, 97, 101, 126, 133–134, 154, 202–210
    careers in, 223, 224, 232–238
    color systems for, 46–47
    consolidation and, 41, 54, 56, 57, 58, 209–210
    convergence and, 53, 54, 57
    culture and, 7, 41, 45–46, 50–51
    delivery systems of, 5, 9, 41, 58, 51, 75, 88, 97–101. *See also* Broadcasting, of television; Cable television; Microwave delivery; Satellite television
    digital conversion of, 10, 46, 47, 56–57, 58–59, 71, 78, 195, 214, 233, 239–241, 242, 259, 279–280
    independent stations, 47
    Internet and, 5, 9, 88, 97–101, 138
    licensing of, 41, 43, 44–48, 62, 202
    localism and, 57, 126, 155, 191
    models of, 97, 198–202, 208–209, 217, 221
    music programming on, 41
    network system of, 5, 41, 47–48, 52, 53, 54, 55–56, 58, 64, 67, 97, 99, 118, 126, 129, 130, 132, 133–134, 136, 149, 150, 176, 201, 202–203, 217, 280
    newspapers and, 43, 126
    objectionable content on, 272, 273, 276–277, 281, 282, 291–292, 293, 296, 297–298, 300–307, 309–313
    operation of station, 221, 232–238
    origins of, 5, 7, 41, 42–43, 88, 97, 115
    ownership of, 43, 53, 54, 56, 57, 137–138, 202–210, 272–273, 280
    patents for, 42
    political issues and, 52, 116, 120
    prevalence of, 5, 8, 43, 88, 146, 268
    production in, 217–218, 221–223, 233, 236–238
    programming of, 5, 44, 46, 47, 48, 49, 50, 51–53, 54, 55, 79, 88, 97, 98–99, 100–101, 115–139, 146–147, 175, 176, 186–187, 195–196, 214, 221, 224–225, 233. *See also* Programming
    purposes of, 50
    radio and, 5, 7, 37, 38, 43, 47, 48, 88, 109, 115, 220, 223
    ratings/shares of, 179–181, 182–184
    recording of programming of, 52, 54, 58, 79, 138–139, 322–323
    regulation of, 41, 43, 44–47, 48, 51–53, 54, 56, 57, 129–130, 267, 271, 272–273, 298
    revenues of, 53, 55, 58, 214
    sponsorship in, 146–147, 148, 149

technology of, 5, 7, 10, 41, 42, 43, 45–47, 48, 53, 54, 56–57, 58, 97, 101, 214, 221–223, 233, 239–241, 268, 322–325
viewing behaviors and, 98–99, 100, 136–137, 157, 159, 195–196, 241–242, 299–300, 309, 310, 312, 321
violence on, 50–51, 53, 272, 277, 281, 291, 292, 309–310
websites of, 97–99, 101
Television cameras, 221–222, 236–238
Television City Research Center, 186
Television diaries, 175
Television quotient data (TVQs), 187
Tentpoling (and program scheduling), 136
Terrorism, 85, 102, 105, 138, 152
Texaco Star Theater, 146–147
Text messaging, 14, 58. *See also* Cell phones
Theory (definition of), 293. *See also* Models
Third-person effect, 300
Thomas, Lowell, 32
Time (as characteristic of mass media), 6
Time/Time Warner, 65, 72
Time shifting, 52
Titanic, 21–23, 24, 261, 263, 264
TiVo, 58, 138, 322
TLD. *See* Top-level domain
Tobacco industry (and advertising), 149, 278
Toll broadcasting model, 27, 145, 199–200
Top 40 (radio format), 34, 35, 69, 111
Top-level domain (TLD), 89
Total survey areas (TSAs), 174
Trade-out agreements (in advertising), 191, 231
Training (and use of corporate media), 250–252
Translators (for transmitting television signals), 62
Transmission control protocol (TCP), 89
Treatment (as description of program), 129, 254
Triode tubes, 21
TSAs. *See* Total survey areas
Turner, Ted, 9, 64, 126
TVQs. *See* Television quotient data
Twenty-One, 117–118
Two-step flow process, 295

UBI. *See* United Independent Broadcasters
UFH. *See* Ultra-high frequency band
Ultra-high frequency band (UHF), 41, 45–46, 47, 268
Underwriting (of noncommercial radio stations), 113
Uniform resource locators (URLs), 97, 98
United Fruit, 25
United Independent Broadcasters (UBI), 30
United Paramount Network. *See* UPN
United Paramount Theaters, 47, 203
Universal service rules, 272
Uploading (of material online), 8
UPN (United Paramount Network), 56, 133, 184, 207
URLs. *See* Uniform resource locators

U.S. Surgeon General, 296, 297–298
USA Today, 11, 185
Uses and gratifications approach (to mass media), 308–309

V-banners. *See* Video banner ads
V-chips, 273, 310, 311
Van Doren, Charles, 117–118
Variety shows, 116–117
VCRs. *See* Video cassette recorders
Vertical integration, 72
Very-high frequency band (VHF), 41, 45–46, 48, 268
VHF. *See* Very-high frequency band
Viacom, 207–208, 209
Victor Phonograph Company, 30
Video banner ads (v-banners), 160
Video cassette recorders (VCRs), 52, 54, 208
Video editing, 13, 238, 240–241, 256
Video games, 306
Video logs, 104
Video news releases, 253
Video on demand (VOD), 72, 80, 214, 242
Video production. *See also* Production, of television
    by amateurs, 123, 125
    editing and, 13, 238, 240–241
    news programming and, 54
    technology of, 13, 54, 238
Videographers, 238, 249, 255
Vidro, Mavel, 235
Vietnam War, 41, 50, 296
Viewing behaviors
    advertising and, 157, 159, 195–196, 323
    audience analysis and, 195–196, 299–300
    digital technology and, 241–242
    effects of mass media and, 299–300
    for Internet, 98, 192–193, 312
    for television, 98–99, 100, 136–137, 157, 159, 195–196, 241–242, 299–300, 309, 310, 312, 321
Violence (in programming), 50–51, 53, 272, 277, 281, 291, 292, 296–298, 300–304, 309–314
Viral marketing, 161
Visual effects (for television production), 222, 237
Vlogs, 104
VOD. *See* Video on demand
Voice over Internet protocol (VOIP), 81, 280, 319–320
Voice tracking, 37
VOIP. *See* Voice over Internet protocol
Voluntary audience contribution model, 199

Walson, John, 63
War of the Worlds, The, 33, 294–295
Watches, 318–319
WB Television Network, 56, 133, 184, 207
Wearable computers, 320
Weaver, Pat, 147, 148
Webcams, 325–326

Webcasting, 9. *See also* Internet; Online radio
Weblogs, 14, 83, 86, 102–104
Webmercials, 160
Websites. *See also* Internet; World Wide Web
    advertising on, 160–161, 162–163, 166, 178–179, 187, 192–194
    audience analysis and, 178–179, 187, 192
    music programming on, 93–94
    navigation of, 84, 86, 97
    of news organizations, 93, 101
    prevalence of, 86
    of radio stations, 93–94, 101
    of television networks, 99, 101
    of television programs, 98–99
    of television stations, 97–98, 101
Welles, Orson, 33
Wells, H. G., 294–295
Western Union, 19
Westinghouse, 23, 25, 26, 27, 29, 42, 207
Westwood One, 69, 114, 203
Wheeler Lea Act, 266
WiFi. *See* Wireless fidelity
Wilson, Woodrow, 264
Winfrey, Oprah, 125, 131, 132, 137
Wire services, 32
Wireless cable, 75. *See also* Cable television
Wireless fidelity (WiFi), 81, 215, 328–329
Wireless Ship Act of 1910, 23, 263, 264
Wireless transmission, 20–23, 75, 81, 263, 264
Wooley, Chris, 248
World War I, 23, 25, 26, 199, 204, 250, 261, 264, 293, 293
World War II
    radio and, 32, 33, 36, 202
    television and, 7, 41, 43, 44, 47, 48, 49, 146, 268
World Wide Web. *See also* Internet
    advertising on, 94, 97–98, 99
    characteristics of, 8–10
    content on, 9–10, 91–93, 98–99, 104
    culture and, 86
    definition of, 8, 84, 86
    navigation of, 91, 97. *See also* Browsers
    news programming on, 93, 99–100
    origins of, 8, 84
    political issues in, 102–104
    regulation of, 95
    technology of, 8–9, 97, 101
    television and, 88, 100
    traditional media vs., 8–10. *See also* Mass media
    viewing behaviors and, 98, 100

XM Satellite Radio, 10, 37, 74, 79, 239

Yield management, 189
Young, Owen, 25

Zipping/Zapping (and television commercials), 157, 159
Zworykin, Vladimir K., 42

This constitutes a continuation of the copyright page.